Ladina Social Activism in Guatemala City / 1871–1954

Patricia Harms

LADINA
SOCIAL ACTIVISM
IN GUATEMALA CITY
1871–1954

University of New Mexico Press / Albuquerque

© 2020 by University of New Mexico Press
All rights reserved. Published 2020
Printed in the United States of America
First Paperback Edition, 2022

ISBN 978-0-8263-6145-5 (cloth)
ISBN 978-0-8263-6387-9 (paper)
ISBN 978-0-8263-6146-2 (e-book)

Library of Congress Control Number: 2020933519

Cover illustration: Revolutionary crowds. *El Imparcial*, October 22, 1944.
Designed by Mindy Basinger Hill
Composed in 10/14 point Minion Pro.

para las mujeres guatemaltecas

Contents

List of Illustrations   ix
Acknowledgments   xi

Introduction / Because Everyone Has Forgotten / *1*
One / Writing Women into History, 1871–1930 / *22*
Two / Dictating Feminisms: Women and Gender in Ubico's
   Guatemala, 1930–1944 / *69*
Three / A Small Payment for a Large Debt: Maternal Feminism,
   Revolutionary Mothers, and the Social Revolution, 1944–1950 / *106*
Four / We Are Already Citizens: Suffrage, Gender, the Catholic Church,
   and Revolutionary Politics, 1944–1950 / *143*
Five / Even a Grain of Sand: Urban Ladinas, the Cold War, and the
   First Inter-American Congress of Women, Guatemala City, 1947 / *185*
Six / Living in the World We Imagined: The Alianza Femenina Guatemalteca,
   Socialist Feminism, and the Cold War, 1950–1954 / *215*
Seven / God Doesn't Like the Revolution: The Archbishop,
   the Market Women, and the Gender of Economy, 1944–1954 / *258*
Epilogue / The Return to Silence / *289*

Appendix A / Naming the Nameless / *299*
Appendix B / Guatemalan Female Jobs Profile, 1920–1950 / *314*
Appendix C / School Attendance, 1950 / *316*
Appendix D / Number of Teachers, 1950 / *317*
Notes / *319*
Bibliography / *375*
Index / *397*

Illustrations

Tables

Table 1.1 / National Literacy Rates in 1920 / *57*
Table 1.2 / Occupational Profile for Women / *65*
Table 2.1 / National Literacy Rates in 1940 / *86*
Table 2.2 / Literacy Rates for Guatemala City, Chimaltenango, and Sacatepéquez in 1940 / *86*
Table 3.1 / Infant Mortality and Deaths at Birth, 1947–1951 / *128*
Table 3.2 / Guatemalan Women's Professional Profile / *133*
Table 4.1 / National Literacy Rates, 1950 / *165*
Table 4.2 / Eligible Women Voters in the Municipality of Guatemala, 1950 / *165*
Table 4.3 / Registered Voters, 1947–1953 / *177*
Table 4.4 / Population Growth and Voter Turnout in Elections, 1944–1958 / *179*
Table 6.1 / Prices on Primary Commodities, 1940–1952 / *251*

Figures

Figure 1.1 / Rosa Rodríguez López / *54*
Figure 2.1 / Luz Valle / *83*
Figures 2.2a, 2.2b / Advertisements for *Nosotras* / *87*
Figure 2.3 / *Nosotras*, May 1933 / *89*
Figure 3.1 / Aída Sándoval, Hilda Balaños, and Julieta Castro de Rólz Bennett / *111*
Figure 3.2 / María Chinchilla Recinos / *113*
Figure 3.3 / Revolutionary crowds / *117*
Figure 4.1 / "Window to the People" / *157*
Figure 6.1 / The Urrutia family / *225*

Acknowledgments

A variety of funding sources contributed to the completion of this work. Research trips to Guatemala and archives in the United States were funded by the Center for Latin American Studies, the Graduate and Professional Students Associations, and the History Department's Social Justice Award at Arizona State University. A dissertation fellowship from the Division of Graduate Studies provided funding for a year of writing. At Brandon University, two research grants from the Brandon University Research Committee provided critical funding for the final stages of research. I also extend a thank you to the staff at the Archivo General de Centro América in Guatemala City, the Library of Congress in Washington, DC, and the Benson Latin American Collection at the University of Texas at Austin. None of this work would have been possible without their dedication to the preservation of historical documents and support of researchers.

As with all such projects, this book stands on the work and intellectual contributions of many other scholars, intellectuals, and activists. My academic career has been influenced by many mentors, and it gives me pleasure to thank them here. Drs. Alan Neely, Mark Taylor, and David Carrasco provided critical insights into Latin American history during my years at Princeton Theological Seminary. At Arizona State University, I am grateful to the faculty and graduate students for their friendship and academic generosity. In particular I want to thank Drs. Susan Gray, the deeply missed Rachel Fuchs, Lynn Stoner, Andrew Barnes, and Robert Trennert for their unfailing support and encouragement. A special thank you to Dr. Noel Stowe. Your kindness and generosity will never be forgotten. Joel Satterlee, Eric Meringer, Shawn England, Karin Enloe, Jeffrey Shepherd, Francine Valcour, Matt Makley, and Ute Chamberlain were important companions during graduate school years. A special thank you to my dissertation committee, upon which this book is based. Dr. Cindy Forster of Scripps College, your commitment to Guatemala and justice sets the highest standard for academics and activists alike. Drs. Gayle Gullett and Ed Escobar, your passion for teaching, guidance, and wisdom as my teaching mentors have remained with me during the first years of my own career. A special thank you to Dr. Edith Couturier for your generous hospitality on multiple visits to the Library of Congress and to Kathy and Don Moreau in Austin. As this project matured, the work of Guatemalan scholars David Carey, Jim Handy, J. T. Way, Gabriela Torres, Deborah Levenson, Karla Koll, Mario Higuerros, Hector Castan, Ana Cofiño, and Ana Silvia Monzón has been critical to my intellectual development and understanding of Guatemala. A special thank you to Jorge Nallim and the Reading Group for the Study of Power and Resistance in Latin America, where I presented several sections of this work. A word of thanks to all those at the Seminario Anabautista Latinoamericana in Guatemala City. I am thankful to Clark Whitehorn and Sonia Dickey and the University of New Mexico Press for their support of this work, and to the anonymous readers for their questions and insightful comments. A special thank you to my editor, Norman Ware, whose meticulous reading of this work enriched its quality.

This work on women in Guatemala City is also indebted to the rich historiography of Latin American women's history. I wish to thank Eugenia Rodríguez Sáenz, Anne McClintock, Ana Cofiño, and Ana Silvia Monzón, who have pioneered women's histories in Central America. Margaret Power and Donna Guy have provided intellectual and moral support that has enriched this project. Finally, there are no words to express my gratitude to my dissertation adviser and pioneer of the field, Asunción Lavrin, who has continuously reminded me that all women and all their stories matter. Latin American women and particularly Central American women continue to be understudied, and your breadth of wisdom and curiosity inform every element of this work. Your continued friendship is a treasure beyond compare.

This work would not have been possible without the support of my family. My parents, Jacob and Margaret Harms, provided moral and physical support, caring for my children while I was on various research trips. My sister Josephine Schulz, her husband Bruce, and brother Wendell Harms provided welcome respite when research and family trips brought me back to Winnipeg. My children Berrigan and Wilhelm have lived with this project their entire lives. Your interest in the lives of women who lived in another time is a testament to your love and kindness, as this work often took me away from time with you. Thank you for reminding me of what is really important in life. Finally, how do I thank my partner, Craig Miller, who provided endless physical, psychological, and financial support through graduate school and the first years in the academy? Your passion for justice is matched by your kindness and patience, which permeates my life and this work. Thank you!

Introduction

BECAUSE EVERYONE HAS FORGOTTEN

A general uneasiness lay over the crowd of women as they walked down Sexta Avenida in Guatemala City.[1] They were marching in the annual parade made mandatory by dictator Jorge Ubico to celebrate their teaching profession and the nation's educational system. Dressed entirely in black, this somber group of several hundred women was anything but celebratory as they moved silently arm in arm through the empty street. Over the prior several months, public life in the capital city had become increasingly tense as mounting opposition to Ubico's presidency emerged from both the university and the middle-class ladino population. As they reached the corner of Seventeenth Street, soldiers on horseback rushed out upon the marchers, indiscriminately shooting into the columns of women.[2] Several young women went down as the rest ran in panic. One woman, María Chinchilla Recinos, was shot with her mother standing by her side. As she hovered over the body of her slain daughter, María's mother looked up at the soldier and pleaded with him to kill her as well. Four other women were injured in the shooting, including Aída Sándoval, Hilda Balaños, Esperanza Barrientos, and Julieta Castro de Rólz Bennett, in an event that shocked the capital city (see fig. 3.1).[3] The military blocked ambulances and medical aid for the injured women, many of whom were members of the Catholic Teacher's Association, the Asociación de Maestras Católicas de Guatemala.[4] It was Sunday, June 25, 1944, and middle-class teachers had been gunned down in the streets. The Guatemalan revolution had begun, and women had died for a nation that did not consider them to be citizens.

Julia Urrutia and her mother, Ester de Urrutia, were among the hundreds of women at the June 25 march. Just twenty years old, Julia witnessed the murder of María Chinchilla Recinos and the agony of her mother. For the next four months until the decisive overthrow of Ubico on October 22, 1944, Julia and Ester threw themselves into the burgeoning revolutionary movement, founding new political parties and participating in the emergent suffrage movement. Although Ubico resigned from his office on July 1 in response to intense citywide protests following the murder of Chinchilla Recinos, he left a puppet administration composed of a triumvirate of generals.[5] The promised elections never materialized, and by September the capital city was in sociopolitical limbo. On October 1, assassins directly linked to Ubico's administration murdered the outspoken anti-Ubico newspaper editor of *El Imparcial*, Alejandro Córdova. Outrage at this political murder erupted throughout the city, and thousands attended his public funeral. As a representative of the female affiliate of the Renovación Nacional, one of the newly formed pro-revolutionary political parties, Ester de Urrutia spoke at his funeral of Córdova's courage and the senselessness of his death.

By October, the capital city was becoming increasingly mutinous, and during the night of October 20 a revolt from within the Guatemalan army broke out, soon joined by students, teachers, workers, and residents, that unified the capital's population across class and ethnic lines. Like many other *capitaliños*, Ester de Urrutia opened up her home to families fleeing the fighting and even to defecting soldiers, many of whom were hungry and terrified. Against their mother's wishes, Julia and her brother Edmundo left the house and witnessed the battle between Ubico loyalists and revolutionary forces, many of whom were civilians anxious for political change.[6] Julia's fourteen-year-old brother Oscar left to join the revolutionaries from their home close to the center of historic Zone One.[7] Just two days later, on October 22, the revolutionaries defeated the remnants of the military loyal to Ubico, and a new political era dawned for Guatemala.

For the next ten years, Julia Urrutia and Ester de Urrutia participated in a wide array of sociopolitical activities designed to improve the lives of all Guatemalans. Both women actively campaigned for suffrage during the months leading up to the new constitution of March 1945, with Julia speaking publicly in at least one of the national rallies. As an educator, Julia felt a special affiliation with the first revolutionary president Juan José Arévalo's educational reforms and volunteered to build and teach in the experimental rural community of Poptún in northern Guatemala.[8] Following the presidential election of Jacobo Árbenz in 1951, Ester increased her activism, joining and eventually becoming secretary general of the Alianza Femenina Guatemalteca, a pro-revolutionary women's association designed to address the systemic inequality of both ladinas and indigenous women. As the Árbenz administration introduced political and economic reforms designed for Guatemala's most disenfranchised citizens, Ester de Urrutia kept pace, calling for fundamental structural changes specifically for rural and indigenous women. She attended several international conferences, representing Guatemalan women in transnational dialogues regarding poverty, working-class women, world peace, and race relations. Ester also led the Alianza in their challenge to Guatemala's middle and upper classes by highlighting the economic and physical abuse of domestic workers.

In the chaotic months following the overthrow of Jacobo Árbenz in June 1954, the Urrutia family sought refuge in the Argentine embassy and then exile in Argentina. Ester and her husband, Manuel Urrutia, returned several years later, and until her death in 1963 Ester remained committed to the social and political ideals established during the revolution. Through the repressive decades of the 1960s–1980s, the Urrutia family continued to struggle for social change. Reminiscent of her grandmother's struggle for social justice, Ester de Urrutia's granddaughter, Maritza Urrutia, joined the revolutionary group the Guerrilla Army of the Poor (EGP) during the 1980s. On July 23, 1992, Maritza was kidnapped and held at a secret prison known as La Isla, within the military police headquarters compound. Her captivity and release is well documented in Dan Saxon's *To Save Her Life*. Maritza's aunt, Julia Urrutia, continues to work in the field of education, adamantly believing that access to education and to reproductive options remain critical challenges for Guatemalan feminists and women in general.

I first met Julia Urrutia in the summer of 2004. Given her name by Guatemalan historian Ana Silvia Monzón, I called Julia. At the age of eighty-three, her voice was warm and youthful, and her response to my request for an interview was "como no," why not? When I arrived at the Urrutia home, she came to the gate to unlock it. As she worked the lock, I asked her the one question on my mind: "Why did you agree to meet with me? I am a complete stranger, and yet you are welcoming me into your home." As the gate opened, she turned to me with eyes filled with tears and said, "because everyone has forgotten us."

Gender, Race, and Nation

Julia Urrutia's frank response to my question, "because everyone has forgotten," reflects the pain experienced by her family and thousands of other Guatemalans in the aftermath of the Guatemalan revolution (1944–1954). However, her response also speaks to the broader absence of ladinas from the historical record, who have been essentially erased by the dual machinations of a dictatorial Guatemalan state aligned with embedded hierarchical sociopolitical structures. Since the ascendancy of Liberalism in 1871, the authoritarian nature of the Guatemalan state has consistently relied upon the political tools of terror and silence to rule with impunity. A series of dictators, including Justo Rufino Barrios (1873–1885), Manuel Estrada Cabrera (1898–1920), and Jorge Ubico (1931–1944), severely limited democratic practices, and few outside of the tiny circle of economic and political elites could influence the state, excluding the vast majority of the Guatemalan population. This political transformation envisioned by the Liberal state, which political leaders referred to as "modernization," was an inherently masculine project, dominated by an ideology of "order and progress," a perspective emphasized within the historical narratives of the era. Although ladinas actively engaged the state in a variety of sociopolitical associations during the revolutionary decade such as education, health care, and legal status, their actions were interpreted as apolitical and therefore not significant for the nation writ large. When high-profile, politically affiliated groups like the Alianza Femenina Guatemalteca assumed an overtly political stance, they were relegated to the historical margins as pawns of a communist agenda or as mere "female associations" of national political parties, and little effort has gone into understanding their ideals, which frequently conflicted with those of their male counterparts. The subsequent historiography by all pro- and antirevolutionary men has uniformly ignored or dismissed ladina contributions.

A series of devastating political military dictatorships and a civil war following the overthrow of Jacobo Árbenz in 1954 have garnered most academic attention in recent decades. Initiated by disaffected supporters of the 1944–1954 revolution, the thirty-six-year conflict had cataclysmic results for millions of Guatemalans. Urban ladinos and ladinas were the initial targets of this violence as the state attempted to neutralize the power of labor unions, university organizations, and human rights associations. The highland indigenous communities, however, became the victims of genocidal levels of violence during the early 1980s. Since the publication of the groundbreaking *I, Rigoberta Menchú: An Indian Woman in Guatemala* in 1983, academics and activists alike have chronicled this devastating period known as *la violencia*, creating a sophisticated body of work, much of it from an anthropological and ethnohistorical perspective.[9]

The state of the archives reflects Guatemala's disruptive twentieth-century sociopolitical history. Following the June 1954 overthrow of democratically elected President Árbenz, thousands of Guatemalans like the Urrutia family went into exile. However, in the process of protecting themselves against the anticommunist backlash, they destroyed personal records related to their work during the 1944–1954 era. In addition, the US State Department gathered a wide array of documents related to any active groups organized by urban ladinas in an attempt to indict the Árbenz administration of communist sympathies. In the ensuing political and social chaos, thousands of primary sources were brought to the United States, many of which are currently held in the Library of Congress in an archive known as the Guatemalan Documents. Consequently, Guatemalans have little access to their own historical records, further obscuring the pre-1954 era. Valiant Guatemalan scholars such as Marta Elena Casaús Arzú, Ana Silvia Monzón, Ana Lorena Carrillo Padilla, and Ana Cofiño are working to bridge this profound gap, and this study is highly indebted to their work.

The very identity of "ladina" has been another critical factor in obscuring the activism of urban women. Ethnicity is an important signifier of opportunity and social status in Guatemala, a country deeply divided by race and class. Most observers agree that the terms "ladino" and "ladina" are cultural rather than biological constructions whose meaning has been affected by economic, political, and social factors over the past two hundred years. Anthropologist Carol A. Smith notes that the use of the term "ladino" remains unique in Guatemala, having been replaced by "mestizo" in the rest of Central America by the early twentieth century. She notes that what distinguishes "ladina" from "indigenous" is based upon "a changing system of social classification, based on ideologies of race, class, language, and culture," created during the emergence of the coffee economy in the western highlands.[10] Guatemalan scholar Arturo Taracena Arriola expands on this by noting that, following the Liberal ascent to power after 1871 and the expansion of the coffee economy, the state solidified ethnic identity due to its need for indigenous labor, which was forcibly elicited under the *mandamiento*.[11] In so doing, the Liberal state contributed to a rhetorical formation of a strict binary between indigenous people and ladinos. This constructed divide has been further solidified by marked class differences, creating a series of binaries including urban/rural, elite/poor, and indigenous/ladino, none of which is particularly enlightening for ladina history.

During the period under study, more than half of Guatemala's population identified as indigenous Maya, speaking more than twenty-one separate languages and maintaining cultural practices distinct from the European Hispanic roots of the ladino and ladina population. A majority of scholarship on Guatemala has focused on the coercive and frequently brutal nature of both the colonial and the modern state toward Maya indigenous communities. As Cecilia Menjívar notes, the "concentration on the indigenous Maya has resulted in a lopsided production of knowledge" evidenced by an impressive body of work.[12] There has been, however, little study on ladinos and ladinas, who constitute the other half of the population.[13] In contrast to the extensive analysis of the social, economic, political, and gender implications of the histories between the Guatemalan state and indigenous peoples, the political and social roles of ladinos and ladinas have not been well examined, and even less is understood regarding their relationship to the state.[14]

In its simplest form, to be ladina or ladino is to be Spanish speaking, not to identify with a specific indigenous language or community, and not to wear indigenous clothing known as *traje*.[15] The implications of the term, however, are far more complex and fluid, as evidenced by an inability of both scholars and Guatemalans themselves to arrive at a definition. Diane Nelson goes so far as to suggest that the term cannot withstand analysis at all and "decomposes under the pressure of analysis into myriad terms that mark class, distinction, color, and history."[16] As Claudia Dary Fuentes notes, this definition is characterized by what ladino and ladina are not rather than by what they are, creating the misperception of a "homogenous group forgotten by anthropologists and historians."[17] Menjívar's definitions are helpful for this study, as she identifies ladino and ladina as a place in between the elite Spanish-speaking state and the indigenous communities.[18] While the elite discriminate against the ladino, the latter in turn discriminate against indigenous groups, thereby belonging to neither group and representing both nationals and foreigners within their own country.[19] For a majority of the period under examination here, ladinas did not benefit from the state, and therefore this binary that aligns them with it does not disclose their lived reality. As Nelson asserts: "Casual references to a 'ladino state' ignore the enormous costs borne by the majority of ladinos who are not represented there."[20] This "place in between" characterizes much of the ladina experience in which they enjoyed some limited mobility and developed symbiotic relationships with the state when beneficial. This study reveals that ladinas occupied a multiplicity of sociopolitical positions that found them aligned with the state to advocate for inclusion, such as regarding the educational system, while at other times in opposition to it in order to advocate for legal and civil reforms. At times, ladinas joined political movements designed to overthrow the state. Therefore, identifying the location ladinas occupied is essential and can only be successful if it eschews the binary between the indigenous and the state.

The majority of evidence left by urban ladinas is silent on the question of ethnic identity, an absence for which several explanations are possible. Their literature consistently references other Guatemalan women through economic indicators such as whether they are working-class women, domestic workers, market women, or simply the poor, rather than through specific ethnic identities. Most of their writings express deep concern for women in poverty, or for mothers struggling to raise their children. Within all the material surveyed for this project, ladina writers described other women as indigenous only three times, an indication of the country's deep class and racial divisions. It is also likely that the cultural marker of ethnic identity was so ubiquitous with poverty and low social standing that class indicators played a more critical role in their sociopolitical imaginations. For some urban ladinas, the lives and social conditions of indigenous women no doubt elicited little concern.[21] Journalist Luz Valle publicly discussed indigenous women more than any other writer, raising concerns over their economic vulnerability and lack of access to education, chastising her peers for their poor treatment of domestic servants and market women. While no conclusions should be drawn from these brief examples, there appears to have been a thread of consciousness among urban intellectuals influenced by J. Fernando Juárez Muñoz and the Generación del 1898.[22]

An Answer for Julia Urrutia

This study is a response to Julia Urrutia's indictment of the historical record and begins the recovery of ladina histories in Guatemala City between 1871 and 1954. More specifically, it tracks the emergence of their associations designed to address sociopolitical issues during a series of Liberal dictatorships in which all manner of activity was severely curtailed. Although it was subsumed by limited political and social spaces, an examination of ladina activism reveals a well-connected community with a cohesive woman-centered consciousness. While it is tempting to interpret all pre-1944 activities as instigators of the revolution, sources clearly establish that the rhetorical and theoretical groundwork for maternal feminism was developed during the years leading up to the revolution. As the first full-length monograph on urban ladinas in Guatemala City prior to the 1970s, this book follows a chronological narrative identifying those women involved in a wide range of political and social associations designed to address their sociopolitical status as women. This emphasis on women's history goes against current trends that focus on gender analysis, an approach that historian Sandra McGee Deutsch notes "is not a compensatory exercise. Without basic knowledge of women's familial, political, professional, and associational roles, it is difficult to write gender history, or indeed any kind of history."[23] This study begins to outline the primary trajectory of ladina history in Guatemala City, which is why as many individual names as possible have been recorded within the narrative. When the number of names interrupts the overall narrative, they have been recorded in the endnotes and in appendix A. While many of the women noted in this book deserve biographies of their own, that is not possible within the scope of this project.

The histories uncovered here have been shaped by reoccurring political dictatorships that flourished between 1870 and 1944. The brief expansions of social and political opportunities followed by intense and sometimes violent contractions played an influential role in shaping urban women's movements. Much of their story remains hidden in the shadows of dictatorial censorship, only emerging for brief periods in which they maintained a frenetic pace in order to accomplish their goals. These ruptures in movements and the need for continuous negotiation with a series of repressive political systems resulted in a fragmented feminist or woman-centered ideology. Three significant transitional *aperturas*, or openings, between periods of repression provided the sociopolitical space in which women could act: the rise of Liberalism beginning in 1871, the moderate period of reform following the 1920 revolution, and then finally the 1944 revolution, which created a singular era of political democracy in Guatemalan history. Jane Jaquette suggests that these periods of transition from military dictatorship to democratic government are not politics as usual. Rather, they offer new opportunities that reflect a general willingness to rethink the basis of social consensus.[24] This study clearly establishes that these political moments offered women the space in which to act upon their ideals, disrupting existing notions of gender to mobilize, even if just temporarily. These fleeting opportunities, in which women seized the moment to exert their own authority to affect civil and political change, shine through the historical record. Within a consistently oppressive political milieu, these aperturas always closed again under the next military regime.

In a political landscape characterized by dictatorships, it is not simply the spaces between authoritarian regimes that defined Guatemalan feminism and women's activities, but the dictatorships themselves. Building on Joan Wallach Scott's assertion that gender is one of the recurrent references by which political power has been conceived, legitimated, and criticized, this work begins with the premise that the Guatemalan Liberal state was constructed and remained dependent upon clearly established notions of ethnicity, class, and gender.[25] This has been well documented by a variety of Latin American scholars as a pattern throughout the region.[26] Gender analysis of Guatemalan dictatorships suggests that while dictators believed men to be either political allies or enemies, and thereby severely curtailed their movements, the same dictators believed women to be politically neutral. This specific gender structure identified women as essentially apolitical actors, thereby allowing them to write and even publicly organize during the most repressive political periods. Therefore, literature and journals became the avenue through which ladinas processed their sociopolitical ideas, revealing how they navigated strictly patriarchal and politically repressive parameters. Not all dictators were alike, however, and this study follows the women's work through three distinct periods of oppression. Few studies on Latin American women have explored gender under dictatorships.[27]

While the overall goal here is to write urban ladinas back into Guatemalan history, the subsequent gender analysis of their story fundamentally alters current interpretations of the modern Guatemalan state. Although scholars have uniformly concluded that the urban ladino and ladina community benefited the most from the revolutionary decade of 1944–1954, ladinas soon realized that they were not the equal recipients of its benefits. While they participated in the overthrow of Jorge Ubico and the democratization of society, they were not invited to share in its democratic bounty. Consequently, ladinas engaged in a second revolutionary struggle, one alongside of and frequently in opposition to that of their male counterparts, whose gender ideals did not include women in the practice of political power and social influence.

This work is indebted to a small but growing body of work on urban Guatemalan women, and to contemporary ladinas who pioneered the first histories of urban ladinas. Guatemalan historians Marta Elena Casaús Arzú and Ana Silvia Monzón have produced several critical studies on the intellectual and revolutionary circles that were active during the first half of the twentieth century. A piece on the Sociedad Gabriela Mistral during the 1920s by Casaús Arzú locates the first self-identified feminist movement in the intellectual circles of the period, identifies the various members of the Generación del 20, and elucidates the role of journalist Luz Valle within this movement.[28] In 2002, Monzón identified some of the most prominent women during the revolutionary decade, identifying the relationships and professional linkages between women's associations.[29] Ladinas frequently aligned themselves with working-class women, using their journals to highlight their labor, educational, and legal struggles, and this book is influenced by several studies on working-class ladina and indigenous women in and around Guatemala City. Norma Stoltz Chinchilla's 1977 "Industrialization, Monopoly Capitalism, and Women's Work in Guatemala," and Lorena Carrillo Padilla's

Luchas de las guatemaltecas del siglo XX, provide theoretical models regarding women and industrialization, arguing that working-class women retained their historical influence within the artisan sector due to Guatemala's relative lack of industrialization. The extent of their social influence can be seen in the 1920 revolution and the narrowly lost bid for suffrage.[30]

This study begins to bridge the histories of women in Guatemala City early in the twentieth century with contemporary women's movements. Three recent works have highlighted various aspects of ladinas' lived experiences from the 1980s through the first two decades of the twenty-first century. Norma Stoltz Chinchilla and Ana Lorena Carrillo focus on the role of revolutionary and civil organizations in which rural and urban, ladina and indigenous women began to work together. Their work surveys an array of women's movements and the creation of the first interethnic organizations, which they call a "transcendent break in Guatemalan women's history."[31] They have begun the complex process of analyzing the ways in which both indigenous women and ladinas in rural and urban spaces have navigated the violence of recent decades, creating women's movements and feminist circles that include both indigenous women and ladinas. Susan Berger's 2006 *Guatemaltecas* also focuses on recent women's associations, analyzing the relationship between globalization and neoliberal democratization. As women have attempted to work with the state, Berger concludes that this has drawn Guatemalan women away from their protest position. Within this process, however, women continue to define their own feminist ideals within localized contexts. Cecilia Menjívar's *Enduring Violence: Ladina Women's Lives in Guatemala* moves the spotlight from institutional violence to the intimate experience of social violence and poverty in the daily lives of ladinas in eastern Guatemala.[32] This pivotal monograph sheds new light on the lived experiences of violence and socioeconomic inequalities that constitute life for the vast majority of Guatemalan women.

This study is also indebted to David Carey's *I Ask for Justice*, a valuable critical addition to the historiography of Guatemalan women. Utilizing court records, Carey sensitively analyzes Maya women's use of the justice system to determine how they negotiated for themselves. Although Carey focuses on the experiences of Kaqchikel Maya women, his findings as to how they navigated a seemingly impenetrable system to defend their rights parallel and support this study. Although ladinas in Guatemala City enjoyed benefits specific to their class and ethnicity far beyond those in Carey's study, all of these women lived under the same Liberal patriarchal state. Therefore, his gendered analysis of the state provides critical theoretical background for this work.

Ladina Feminisms

Building on these studies, the foundational inquiry for this work has been a deceptively simple question: Where were the women? The answer has been a decisive one. The evidence is incontrovertible that, following the rise of Liberalism in 1871, women participated or attempted to participate in every aspect of sociopolitical life in Guatemala City, maintaining a feminist consciousness even during the most difficult of political circumstances. The existence of Guatemalan feminism prior to 1954, however, has been shrouded in silence, a silence so pronounced that Chicana historian Vicki Ruiz has concluded that it was relegated to "self-expression and creativity rather than political action."[33] Ruiz's hypothesis is confirmed by this study, which has identified poetry, literature, and journalism as the roots of feminist ideology within the urban ladina community. Grounded in a Liberal authoritarian political context, proto-feminists utilized its ideology to point out the state's failings both for women in a most general sense and for poor and indigenous women in particular. The early ladina movements mirrored the lack of political diversity in the Guatemalan state during the late nineteenth and early twentieth centuries, a characteristic that distinguishes them from other Latin American feminisms, which aligned themselves with a variety of political ideologies including liberal and conservative, Marxist and Catholic. As Christine Ehrick emphasizes, although feminism is an international movement, it is fundamentally shaped by local and national realities.[34] With little political diversity possible, Guatemalan feminisms remained fundamentally uniform and Liberal oriented in nature until 1944.[35]

Given the politically complex nature of the Guatemalan state, the question arises as to whether feminism can exist within such a context. Several theorists offer ideological solutions helpful to the Guatemalan context. Patricia Mohammed identifies feminism as the embodiment of "two simultaneous processes: a consciousness of the subordinate position in which women are viewed in society; and the actions which those who regard themselves as feminist take to redefine this unequal position."[36] Although Guatemalan women could seldom act on their ideals, employing Mohammed's theory, ladinas clearly articulated an awareness of their sociopolitical inequality. Temma Kaplan further differentiates the element of consciousness, distinguishing female from feminist. Kaplan identifies the first as a "recognition of what a particular class, culture, and historical period expect from women[,] [which] creates a sense of rights and obligations that provides motivation for action."[37] Implementing theories from both Mohammed and Kaplan, the ladinas in this study can be identified as having a feminist consciousness, expressing a clear awareness of their gendered sociopolitical context in their journals. During the political apertures, they acted upon a highly developed feminist consciousness to form feminist- and woman-centered associations to effect change.

Determining how ladinas with this feminist consciousness precisely navigated their complex political landscape broadens our notions of feminism and feminist activism. From its inception, the Guatemalan Liberal national project was conceived of, or imagined if you will, as a masculine endeavor. This is not unusual, as Cynthia Enloe points out, since nationalisms are typically sprung from masculinized memory, masculinized humiliations, and masculinized hopes, and here again Guatemala is no exception.[38] Taking into account Deniz Kandiyoti's perspective that women "strategize within a set of concrete constraints that reveal and define the blueprint of what [Kandiyoti] term[s] the patriarchal bargain of any given society, which may exhibit variations according to class, caste and ethnicity," the actions of Guatemalan ladinas become clearer.[39] Eager to participate in Liberalism's new ideology focused on progress and modernization, urban ladinas challenged its patriarchal constructs and postulated new visions that included all Guatemalans, at times even the poorest and most marginalized in their society. With few political options at their disposal, the ladinas in Guatemala City employed a complex set of negotiations with the Guatemalan state in which they contested, challenged, and expanded the boundaries of patriarchal restrictions.[40] They explored and challenged the nature of the Liberal state, published histories and contributions of women, created and sustained both educational and social reform institutions, and at times even reflected upon their own privilege in a national context of extreme poverty and marginalization. Examining the intellectual contributions of these women reveals another version of Guatemalan nationalism, one born out of an alternative worldview emerging simultaneously alongside the masculinized Liberal project.[41] Although their ideals were marginalized to the point that they could only imagine a place for themselves, their sociopolitical imaginings do not emerge from a static and disempowered position. Rather, their imaginings were active and engaged with contemporary reality, bearing the potential to become socially and politically disruptive.

This potential was realized by the advent of the Guatemalan revolution, an era of such significance for urban ladinas that it is difficult to overemphasize its impact. The ten years of social democracy provided them with the opportunity to transform ideology into social action, and hundreds of women like Julia and

Ester de Urrutia moved from a world of imagination to one of action. Forming political parties and civil associations, they advocated for health care and education, changes in the civil code, and suffrage, which was granted to literate women in 1945. Their political ideology remained relatively unified during the first several years of the revolution, and journalist Luz Valle celebrated all efforts to participate in public life no matter their political affiliation. The most visible activists institutionally identified with the nutrition and daycare centers, a maternalism that had dominated ladina circles since the 1880s.[42] Although these efforts were frequently dismissed as apolitical, the associations created to address economic and social inequality were in fact highly political, injecting the revolutionary state into the daily lives of thousands of women and children. The opportunity to develop latent political ideas during the decade of democracy also revealed the political diversity in the urban ladina community. During the second revolutionary administration of Jacobo Árbenz (1951–1954), another form of feminism emerged with the Alianza Femenina Guatemalteca. Merging the dominant maternal feminism with an overtly political agenda, the Alianza employed gender, class, and ethnic analysis to critique Guatemalan society from a socialist perspective, challenging the very foundations of Guatemala's social, economic, and political system.

Although the enfranchisement of literate women in 1945 represented a significant achievement, it was only one of many sociopolitical ideals held within the urban ladina community. Consequently, during the ten years of democracy, a wide variety of reform movements and political activism emerged, reflecting genuine political diversity in Guatemala City. The existing hypotheses assume that feminist activity dwindled in the aftermath of suffrage, but a closer analysis demonstrates that the achievement of suffrage marked the beginning of intense political engagement. As ladina political activity establishes, the ability to exercise their political rights as citizens also attracted previously apolitical actors such as antifeminists and antirevolutionary women of all social classes. As will be discussed in the last chapter of this book, their presence played a pivotal role in the eventual resignation of democratically elected President Árbenz. Therefore, this study demonstrates the need for further examination of women's political activism beyond the granting of suffrage, and the development of new activist patterns for Latin American historiography.

This study is indebted to the extensive scholarship on the Guatemalan revolution. Early historiography focused primarily on revolutionary political factors and particularly the influence of US foreign policy.[43] The intellectual shift to place Guatemalans at the center of scholarly analysis has contributed new social histories that have begun to document the revolutionary experiences of many more Guatemalans.[44] While the 1944–1954 decade is believed to be an era of revolutionary social and political change led by middle-class urban ladinos, influential historians such as Jim Handy, Cindy Forster, and Greg Grandin expose the fragility of this assumption by describing a country deeply influenced by race and class.[45] As Forster argues: "Among the most difficult obstacles to revolutionary transformation was the exclusion of that majority by many Ladino revolutionaries."[46] This study extends their analysis and interpretations to argue that the revolution ignored another majority within the population. Rural and urban, ladina and indigenous women were uniformly dismissed as potential revolutionary actors, an attitude that Forster aptly concludes came back to haunt the revolutionary state.[47] Integrating the presence and activities of ladinas in Guatemala City builds upon the existing historiography, disrupting the highly masculinized story of the revolution's emergence and successes, and reveals a more complex set of social and political dynamics.[48]

Elaborating on Forster's conclusion that women were largely ignored as political actors directly addresses another long-standing historiographic conversation. In light of the revolution's brief but remarkable success, analysts have long grappled with its downfall in 1954. Here again, Handy, Forster, and Grandin point to a variety of possible factors including the inability or unwillingness of the country's leadership to fully incorporate the majority rural indigenous population in a meaningful way. This work affirms how women's participation was largely ignored by revolutionary leaders, particularly in their failure to include illiterate women through suffrage (roughly 70 percent of ladinas and 96 percent of indigenous women). In contrast, the Catholic hierarchy and the revolutionary opposition identified the potential political power of newly enfranchised female voters and the social power of demonstrations. They recruited urban women of all social classes, creating a symbolically powerful antirevolutionary movement that aligned with broader global Cold War affiliations. As a result, this work contributes to a small but growing body of scholarship that focuses on right-wing women who actively sought to remove progressive politicians from office, such as Margaret Power's *Right-Wing Women in Chile*, Sandra McGee Deutsch's *Las Derechas*, and Victoria González and Karen Kampwirth's *Radical Women in Latin America*.[49]

The integration of urban ladinas into analyses of the Cold War expands and complicates the relationship between the Guatemalan revolution and the US State

Department. Despite the moderate tenor of the Arévalo administration, by 1947 the State Department had become increasingly hostile over Guatemala's refusal to sign the Inter-American Treaty of Reciprocal Assistance, or Rio Pact.[50] In the midst of growing tensions between the two countries, Guatemalan women hosted an interhemispheric gathering in August 1947 called the First Inter-American Congress of Women. Female delegates from across the Americas discussed a broad range of topics, frequently contradicting the State Department's positions on international politics, women's equality, and particularly economic reforms. The Guatemalan delegates to the congress came under international criticism before and after the event for their suspected "communist sympathies." The role played by Guatemalan delegates and by the congress in general supports recent assertions that "the most important aspects of the Cold War were neither military nor strategic, nor Europe-centered, but connected to political and social development in the Third World."[51] Gender analysis of the 1947 congress, a burgeoning Cold War narrative, and urban ladinas contribute to another understudied element of Cold War historiography, namely the role of Latin American women.

Ladinas in the Capital

The geographic focus for this book is La Nueva Guatemala de la Asunción, or Guatemala City, the economic and administrative capital of the country. Guatemala City became the capital of the colonial audiencia in 1775, following an earthquake that destroyed the old capital of Antigua. In 1821, the city became the focal point of independence from Spain and served as the capital of the United Provinces of Central America for a brief period. Located in the south-central part of the country in the Valle de la Ermita, it became the largest city in Central America.

The modernization so desired by the Liberals following their rise to power in 1871 helped develop Guatemala City into a dynamic economic and literary center. Normal schools for both men and women were established here, and the city operated as a literary hub where a wide variety of journals and newspapers were published and distributed across the isthmus, giving the city the highest literacy rate in Guatemala.[52] The Liberal quest for modernization attracted business entrepreneurs from across the Western Hemisphere, particularly following the introduction of transportation and communication technologies by Manuel Estrada Cabrera. While desiring modernization and integration into the North Atlantic capitalist system, the nineteenth-century Liberal state did not seek to industrialize Guatemala as did other Latin American nations, and rather became dependent upon coffee as the primary agricultural product.[53] This created a reinvigoration and expansion of precapitalist forms of labor control and exploitation, in the words of historian David McCreery.[54] In turn, this led to socioeconomic instability in rural areas, producing a flood of migrants into Guatemala City. Here, women found stable if poorly paid employment opportunities, and the city emerged as an iconic space where opportunity and repression, modernization and elements of colonialism, coexisted, though often uneasily.[55] Consequently, while the political and economic transformation of Guatemala City was conceived as a highly masculinized and modern project, the capital city itself became a rather feminine space, numerically dominated by women seeking social and economic opportunities.[56]

Modernization offered intriguing and contradictory possibilities for all women, ladina and indigenous, middle and working class. Middle-class ladinas, who represent the majority of educators and writers in this study, occupied historic Zone One, the core of nineteenth- and early twentieth-century Guatemala City. Here, they lived and worked, surrounded by the poorer barrios in which working-class women were employed in a variety of occupations in the formal and informal economy. Poor ladina and indigenous women, already active in family agriculture, domestic labor, and community markets, dominated a number of artisan-based industries including pottery, ceramics, bakeries, textiles, and the production of alcohol upon their arrival in Guatemala City. They also retained a monopoly in the tobacco industry.[57] Although data for the period is not definitive, McCreery estimates that close to one-third of all women in Guatemala City labored as domestics and in cottage industries.

By the end of the nineteenth century, the capital had become a highly stratified city, its success dependent upon economic inequality. As Catherine Komisaruk notes, the presence of poorly paid migrant women provided for the essential daily needs of the middle and upper classes. By freeing ladinas from household chores, "servant women thereby made possible the work of the growing ladino labor force in an array of industries and government functions."[58] Domestic help became a ubiquitous element in the middle-class ladina household. Living on the furthest margins of opportunity and social acceptability, these women occupied spaces outside of Guatemala City itself, traveling daily into its center to work in the homes and markets scattered throughout the capital. In a system based upon unpaid or poorly paid labor designed to benefit the few, education and health-care opportunities remained elusive for the working class. Children were needed to support the household income, and few were able to take advantage of education. With little or no access to health care, childbirth and child-rearing remained perilous activities for poor women, who more often than not were also the economic heads of their households. Liberal-era society became economically dependent upon enforced labor drafts and the labor of poor women, and yet these women remained metaphorically and practically invisible to the ruling elite and urban middle classes.

Despite its incontrovertible role as a dynamic national and Central American center, Guatemala City has only recently enjoyed scholarly attention. A welcome group of studies have emerged documenting the contemporary crisis created by unprecedented levels of social violence and economic instability since the signing of the 1996 peace accords. As this instability continues to unfold in devastating ripples throughout the city's sociopolitical infrastructure, a series of thoughtful social histories shed new light on individual lives ranging from religious practitioners to street children, gangs, and labor unions.[59] Two particular studies that highlight the contradictions inherent in the Liberal quest for modernity provide significant insight for this study on ladinas. J. T. Way's *The Mayan in the Mall* tracks both the lived experiences of indigenous and poor people in the capital city as well as their place in the imaginations of the state and ladino intellectual circles. Highlighting the numerous contradictions inherent in contemporary Guatemala City, Way argues for coherence within the chaos, the natural by-product of the Liberal modernization project. The second newly minted study on modernity and Guatemala City is Michael Kirkpatrick's "Optics and the Culture of Modernity in Guatemala City since the Liberal Reforms." In this brilliant study, Kirkpatrick tracks the culture of modernity devised by Liberal reformers who succeeded in creating the aesthetics of modernity if not the economic foundation necessary to realize it. His particular insight of *cultura de esperar*—the culture of waiting, hoping, and expecting—aligns particularly well with ladina experiences of imagining identified in the present study. Ladinas in Guatemala City identified with the Liberal modern project, eagerly believing that they were its intended targets. However, their rapid marginalization from its potential benefits relegated their ideas and activism to a site of imagining rather than reality. This study draws upon Kirkpatrick's analysis of the Liberal state and Guatemala City, both of which remain understudied fields in Guatemala.

Chapter Descriptions

The women whose stories are recovered in this work left compelling evidence of their ideals and visions. These documents, however, have survived only sporadically, and in order to re-create elements of ladina history in Guatemala City, I have depended upon a wide range of primary sources including national newspapers representative of both radical and conservative political ideologies, periodicals published by women, Catholic papers and pastoral letters, records of the Jefatura Política in Guatemala City, labor journals, political party records, papers of the Women's International League for Peace and Freedom, national census data, and US State Department records. A loose collection of broadsides and street literature held in the Library of Congress, the University of Texas at Austin, and the Archivo General de Centro América in Guatemala City provide invaluable information. Although this project is not interdisciplinary, it utilizes interdisciplinary secondary sources on Latin American women as a methodological necessity. Therefore, theories on women from political science, anthropology, and religious studies along with historical accounts have been incorporated into the analysis. A number of oral testimonies from Guatemalan women and men who were eyewitnesses to historical events throughout the 1930s, 1940s, and 1950s have also been integrated into this study. Their stories provide the most compelling element of this exciting and complex historical period. By integrating their living memories into documentary evidence, a more nuanced and sophisticated analysis is possible.

An examination of urban women in Guatemala City between 1871 and 1954 establishes that their activities in fact place them firmly within a wide range of debates contemporary to their period. Often considered to be outside the mainstream women's movements, Guatemalan women, as confirmed by this study, were not only aware of these broader conversations but integrated these ideas into their own ideologies. Frequently politically repressed and isolated from their transnational peers, these women nevertheless engaged with international philosophies regarding society and gender within their own context. As a result, this work addresses and engages with larger Latin American historiographies on feminism, suffrage, social reform, child welfare movements, the Cold War, revolutionary movements, education, and politics. While the following chapters address a wide range of subjects, what ties them together is the focus on ladinas in Guatemala City. The final chapter on the antirevolutionary movement integrates the activities of poor and working-class women. These historical actors made up a small network that engaged with one another until 1954 despite holding a variety of sociopolitical ideals, and each chapter that follows introduces new dimensions of their activism.

The first chapter focuses on the rise of a proto-feminist consciousness between 1871 and 1930. Evidence of feminism during this era can be found primarily in the literary contributions of ladina educators and prominent literary figures centered in the capital, Guatemala City, rather than in formal organizations and political activity. Writing women back into history during the 1880s, sisters Vicenta Laparra de la Cerda and Jesús Laparra published two journals for women. *La Voz de la Mujer* and *El Ideal* exposed the fragility of the Liberal government's quest for modernization and in some cases its very fallacy by challenging the state to follow through on its promises of "order and progress." Although neither the legal nor the civil status of women was affected by the work of the Laparra sisters, they actively refuted the notion of Guatemalan women as weak, unintelligent, and untrustworthy. Perhaps, most significantly, the Laparras created an ideological and literary legacy for another generation of women who resurfaced during the 1920s. The brief period of reform that emerged following the 1920 revolution gave women the opportunity to organize around issues of gender equality, health care, education, and labor regulations. A small group of middle-class and elite writers and poets formed Guatemala's first feminist organization, the Sociedad Gabriela Mistral. In essence, their work wrote women back into history.

Although publishing during the Jorge Ubico dictatorship (1931–1944) was a dangerous business, Luz Valle and Gloria Menéndez Mina launched two journals, *Nosotras* and *Azul*, exclusively for women. In order to manage their public profile, Valle and Menéndez Mina were required to walk a fine line between presenting their own ideas while remaining within the tight parameters established by an oppressive regime. Chapter 2 explores the nature of the feminism they projected and its impact on the circle of literary women and educators for whom the journals were published, providing the intellectual preparation necessary for the revolutionary decade that followed.

In contrast to the previous seventy years, the decade between 1944 and 1954 stands alone as an era of political and social freedom in Guatemala. During this revolutionary period, women participated as active agents in the process of nation building and contributed to the variety of visions put forth for a new country. Women moved from the fringes of society and politics to take center stage, actively shaping the character of the revolution. Political and social organizations emerged designed to address women's suffrage, staggering illiteracy rates, rural poverty, and class and racial inequality. Chapter 3 identifies women's participation in the military engagements of June and October 1944 and examines the rise of the institutionalization of a maternal feminism. Particular attention is paid to the feminist ideals introduced by Elisa Martínez de Arévalo, the wife of president Juan José Arévalo.

Chapter 4 focuses on the campaign for suffrage that unified the urban ladina community. Granted suffrage in 1945, literate women immediately created female affiliations with existing political parties representative of an array of ideologies. While their numbers remained small, women's voting power was significant, as evidenced by the attention garnered during both municipal and national political campaigns. The archbishop of Guatemala became an active participant in the electoral process in order to conscript thousands of literate women to elect antirevolutionary candidates, despite direct constitutional directives that forbade political interference by a religious body. Historians such as Susanne Jonas and Cindy Forster have suggested that one of the revolution's failings was its negligence of this new voting block, and this chapter explores the critical juncture between women's political affiliations and the nature of political campaigns in order to ascertain the validity of this heretofore untested hypothesis.[60] Chapter 4 refers to broadsides and the Hojas Sueltas along with political campaign ads in the national newspapers.[61]

The First Inter-American Congress of Women is the subject of chapter 5. Attended by representatives from nineteen nations across the Americas, the 1947 congress represents a significant watershed for Guatemalan women's movements, transnational organizing, and the birth of the Cold War. For Guatemalans, the presence of politically and socially conscious women from across the continent provided important moral support during a period of nation building. In Guatemala City, these women created an inter-American mandate that drew its ideologies from the 1945 Chapultepec resolutions and directly confronted the militarization advocated by the Rio Pact written during the same month of August in Brazil. These resolutions directly confronted US hemispheric hegemony and drew a firestorm of national and international criticism, creating a schism within an otherwise unified Guatemalan women's movement.

In November 1950, political power passed peacefully from one president to another for the first time in Guatemalan history.[62] Jacobo Árbenz came to power with more than 60 percent of the vote. Embracing the maternalism of the Arévalo feminists, the women of the Alianza Femenina Guatemalteca expanded the boundaries of women's political activity. Chapter 6 explores the Alianza's gender analysis, directly confronting the revolution's unwillingness to incorporate women in a meaningful way. Discontented with the results, they crossed both race and class lines to align themselves with poor and indigenous women. The women of the Alianza stood alone in their analysis, revealing how the very foundations upon which the modern state was created simultaneously privileged men and disenfranchised women. Their role in the final days of the revolution contributes to a growing body of work that emphasizes the significance of internal factors to the revolution's demise.

The seventh and final chapter focuses on the relationship between the Catholic Church, Archbishop Mariano Rossell y Arellano, and the urban women who supported his antirevolutionary movement. Opposition to the revolution emerged from many sectors of Guatemala City, including from some of the very women who had helped to overthrow Jorge Ubico in 1944 and who represented a broader transnational transition from an antifascist to an anticommunist political position by the 1950s. However, the most public and successful leader of the opposition was the Catholic archbishop Rossell y Arellano, who, despite his initial approval of the revolutionary government, soon became one of the leading opponents of the enacted social reforms, particularly agrarian reform. Under his tacit approval, innumerable demonstrations and protests contributed to the destabilization of Guatemalan society, undermining the revolution during its critical and fragile transition. This chapter will explore how women who had participated in the revolution in 1944 also became critical instruments of its demise in 1954.

One

WRITING WOMEN INTO HISTORY, 1871–1930

> A woman is a very unhappy creature. Study the female existence, from birth to the grave, and you will be convinced that we are not lying.
> —*Vicenta Laparra de la Cerda*, La Voz de la Mujer, *August 22, 1885*

> As we can see, women are still chained by ignorance: her emancipation is necessary, and feminism will provide awareness and understanding of the true value of life.
> —*Rosa Rodríguez López*, El Imparcial, *November 21, 1925*

> If the nineteenth century was the human rights of men,
> then the twentieth century will be the regaining of rights for women.
> —*José de Prado*, El Imparcial, *December 25, 1926*

The embryo of Guatemalan feminism emerged within a rapidly shifting political landscape. As the triumphant ideology following decades of struggle with Conservative forces, Liberalism offered women the rhetorical possibility for inclusion, citizenship, and education while simultaneously reinforcing patriarchal privilege. This hypocrisy was not lost on the pioneers of feminism, and they employed a variety of strategies both to argue for political inclusion and to point out Liberalism's contradictions. The effectiveness of their ideas, however, was severely limited by a generalized political repression, with the state tolerating little political diversity. Although at times it appeared that these women existed in a state of suspended intellectual animation, writing out their political and civil resistance merely to one another, they nevertheless created a cohesive communal identity bound by a clear feminine and even feminist consciousness.

Following its rise to power in 1871, the Liberal state modernized the country, transforming Guatemala's economic, social, and political realms. The foundation for this national renovation was the escalation of coffee production, and, to that end, coastal ports, the rail lines, and communication systems were all designed to facilitate coffee exports and the import of goods from the North Atlantic industrial nations such as the United States, Great Britain, and France. Modernization also brought new social ideas regarding women, gender, and education, which the country's leaders were far less eager to embrace. Therefore, women, the working class, and indigenous communities were not integrated into the national project as equal partners but marginalized as objects to be used by modernization as labor, whether it be in coffee fincas, markets, or homes. Urban ladinas identified this contradiction in their journals, creating social and political spaces in which they proclaimed their unequal legal and social status.[1] Their gender and class analysis was incorporated into the burgeoning education system, creating a generational legacy. Despite intense challenges, by the 1920s small groups of women had successfully initiated campaigns on women's legal and social rights, some groups openly identifying themselves as feminist. Therefore, while Liberal male reformers were actively reconfiguring Guatemala's sociopolitical and economic landscape, a small group of ladinas was also reimagining all aspects of Guatemalan society that acknowledged and celebrated their contributions.

Dictatorial regimes dominated the political era between 1871 and 1930, which required these women to develop unique strategies to speak and act on their own behalf. Although they took full advantage of the political transitions between dictatorships, most of their intellectual development occurred during periods of repression and even terror under political dictatorships. The first decades of Liberal rule offered one such transitional period as the political elite solidified its power to create a stable nation-state. Although issues of national inclusion were not resolved during the late nineteenth century, the Liberals created rhetorical opportunities, however muted.[2] Following the overthrow of Manuel Estrada Cabrera in 1920, another aperture formed, allowing a broad range of political and social ideals to flourish. Urban ladinas took advantage of this freedom to enact social reforms in child care, education, and working-class labor. While these political transitions offered women the possibility for change, they became agents of change on their own terms through educational and social reforms. Consequently, although the presidencies of General José María Orellana (1921–1926) and Lázaro Chacón González (1926–1930) brought back more repressive political regimes, the nature of Guatemalan political society had fundamentally shifted and offered city residents the opportunity to engage socially and politically on an unprecedented scale.[3]

Several types of movements emerged during this sixty-year gestational period, at times forming temporary cross-class associations. The first urban movement formed around the sisters Vicenta and Jesús Laparra, whose journals for women *La Voz de la Mujer* and *El Ideal* exposed the contradictions inherent in Guatemalan Liberalism. While the literary women and educators attracted to their message were unable to act politically, they directed their reform efforts at the education system. During the 1920s, another literary group, the Sociedad Gabriela Mistral, expanded upon these nascent ideas, adopting an overtly feminist perspective on education and civic equality while avoiding a direct campaign for suffrage. The efforts of working-class women surfaced with the Partido Unionista movement, an eclectic group who successfully overthrew dictator Estrada Cabrera and held power for eighteen months during 1920 and 1921. Although they left little evidence of their ideas, they drew upon their labor networks to argue for their rights as citizens through male union colleagues, narrowly losing a bid for women's suffrage in 1920–1921. The Sociedad Protectora del Niño, a child-care center in Guatemala City, became the most concrete social reform movement of the era, created through a network of associations and individuals, shortly after the overthrow of Estrada Cabrera. Unlike their peers across Latin America, these organizations did not perpetuate a variety of political ideologies or feminist ideals. Constrained by political circumstances, their efforts were winnowed down to the most essential elements of women's equality, namely education, civil and legal status, and, sporadically, working-class women's rights. The question of reproductive rights is absent from any of these movements, and, with only modest industrialization in Guatemala at the time, no broad-based initiatives around working women's health, labor rights, or child welfare emerged. Except for a brief period around the 1920 revolution, urban ladinas rarely bridged the deep chasms of ethnicity and class to create associations with indigenous women.

The scholarship available for the period under investigation here analyzes the political, economic, and labor policies of the era, focusing on the coercive laws imposed upon indigenous communities to ensure the production of coffee.[4] A few biographies and fictionalized parodies offer glimpses into the long dictatorship of Estrada Cabrera (1898–1920), such as Miguel Ángel Asturias's novel *El Señor Presidente*.[5] Gender analysis through the lens of literary women, teachers, and journalists, however, reveals this to be a highly dynamic era despite their muted activism. Viewing Guatemala City as a highly feminized space exposes the politically astute women who created and supported emergent civil institutions. Although their destiny was frequently affected by dictatorial political whims, these pioneers of ladina activism provide a more complex portrait of the early

Liberal period in Guatemala City, underscoring the accomplishments of and challenges faced by all urban women.

The Liberal State, Gender, and the Catholic Church

During the late nineteenth century, liberalism became the organizing principle for the newly triumphant oligarchic elite, an ideology that touched off a series of reforms transforming almost all aspects of social, political, and economic life. Throwing off the last Conservative president, Vicente Cerna, in 1871, the Liberal presidencies of Miguel García Granados (1871–1873) and Justo Rufino Barrios (1873–1885) initiated an era known as La Reforma. Envisioning an aristocratic, modern republic based upon Enlightenment liberties and a diversified economy, the group of elite coffee planters who formed the core of the Liberal Party became infatuated with all aspects of progress, including technology, community, and transportation.[6] Although rhetorically directed at all Guatemalans, these reforms were designed to benefit the elite. To support such an enterprise, the Liberals developed a strong state that actively intervened in the economy and society to facilitate and promote export production. To make this possible, the triumphant coffee elites needed cheap land and labor as well as access to overseas markets. Consequently, they developed a series of institutions designed to bring Guatemala's diverse population under state control such as a modern police force, an expanded prison system, a recodification of civil law, and a uniform system of public administration. Aligned with the state, coffee planters designed a series of laws to coerce indigenous communities into providing cyclic periods of labor, known as the *mandamiento*. Enforced in 1877, it allowed the governor of each department to grant planters' requests for agricultural labor drafts from the indigenous communities not unlike the repartimientos of the eighteenth century. Consequently, Guatemala entered the modern global capitalist system as a supplier of raw materials and a buyer of manufactured goods, without undergoing industrialization.

Liberals governed through the authority of wealthy elite males, whose presumption of social superiority entrenched their political privilege as a natural right. A highly masculinized project, the Liberal state created a legal apparatus designed to bolster patriarchy and class hierarchy. Political scientist Nikki Craske argues that relations of power are either supported or undermined by gender relations.[7] The two pieces of legislation Liberals enacted during this formative period clarified women's subordinate position amid a myriad of far-reaching reforms. First, the

1879 constitution solidified the foundation of a strictly patriarchal and hierarchical society, determining that only literate men over twenty-one years of age were eligible for citizenship and political participation. While this law maintained the historical exclusion of women and illiterate men, Guatemalan Liberals created a critical caveat. As historian Wade Kit points out, under this constitution illiterate men including indigenous men were eligible to vote, but not in secret like their literate counterparts. This proviso had two critical and contradictory results. First, it provided Liberals with a functioning democracy, albeit a potentially coercive and limited one, establishing literacy as a critical component for citizenship.[8] Second, in imbuing indigenous illiterate men with political personality, they established a hierarchy of citizenship, placing illiterate men above literate women. Ladinas seized upon this codified discrepancy to advocate for their political rights over the following decades. This tension, however, remained unresolved right through the 1944–1954 revolutionary decade in practice if not in theory because male politicians continued to see illiterate and indigenous men as more natural political allies than ladinas or indigenous women.

The second and far more invasive reform reaffirmed the colonial civil familial structure known as Patria Potestad. Approved under president Barrios in 1877, Patria Potestad guaranteed men full authority and control over their families, including wives and daughters. Article 46 of the civil code decreed that women had no legal identity outside of marriage and could not speak for themselves without the written authority of their husbands.[9] Laws protecting women's right to inherit family property established during the colonial era were also removed, further reinforcing their subordination to patriarchal authority. In contrast to Guatemalan Conservatives, who worked with the Catholic Church to preserve the nation's social order, "Liberals envisioned individual families controlled by powerful patriarchs as the cornerstone of their new societies. In short, the male-headed household was foundational to state building."[10] The patriarchal family symbolized the Liberal nation in which God, emblemized through the state, represented the nation's father while patriotism served as a gender counterpart providing a mother's affection. The home was envisioned as a microcosm of the state where women remained subordinate to the head of house, whether husband or father, just as the household remained subordinate and bound to the grand state father through the feminine patriotism of love. The happiness of this great family depended upon the four virtues of love, obedience, respect, and work.[11] Consequently, in Guatemala, the Liberal state emerged as a racially hierarchical and gendered entity, creating an intricate network of oppression for women whose severity was mitigated or amplified by class position and ethnicity.

In contrast to their Conservative predecessors, Liberals perceived the Catholic Church and its traditional values to contradict the burgeoning political ideology of "order and progress." Therefore, the Barrios government initiated a series of laws known as *desamortización* or disentailment designed to weaken the church's political and economic influence.[12] Progress was implemented through a systematic body of reforms designed to radically diminish the political and economic power of the Catholic Church through the expulsion of religious orders, the abolition of the tithe, and state confiscation of all church property; the funds generated were used to create the Guatemalan National Bank. Avowed adversaries throughout the Liberal era, the interests of the Catholic Church and the state intersected at only one point, namely in the political, legal, and social subordination of women. Following the Vatican's lead, the Guatemalan church maintained strict ideas regarding national gender roles. Decrying all forms of feminism and female emancipation, particularly laws supporting divorce, secular marriage, and salaried work, the church mandated that the only proper social position for women remained within the home. These Catholic gender precepts were codified in the Liberal state's constitution and the civil code.[13]

The tight ideological collusion between patriarchal and religious gender precepts undergirded a suffocating position for women within an unyielding political and social network of laws and cultural norms. Urban ladinas from the middle and upper class were almost completely excluded from all forms of employment and higher education. This reality compounded the isolating effects of the sociolegal system, and with few options of resistance available, urban ladinas resorted to the creation of literature and poetry to express their dissatisfaction. Caveats existed within this repressive system, however, depending on one's particular socioeconomic status. As historians Catherine Komisaruk and David Carey point out, poor and working-class women more often than not lived outside the reality of these interlocking repressive laws. Communities and families understood and valued the economic contributions of these women even if the formal state did not; Komisaruk asserts that poor and working-class women were not bound by elite notions of honor.[14] Carey's critical study on gender and the legal system supports this lived reality, and while state laws kept all women subordinated, women of the lower classes used the system to their own benefit, working in and occupying the public sphere regardless of civil laws and gender mores.[15]

This perfect collusion over gender norms was marred by the legalization of divorce in 1894, and Guatemala remains a peculiar exception in Latin America in this regard. In a legal conversation that lasted from 1883 until 1894 when divorce became law, politicians weighed the pros and cons of divorce and the modern state. Eager to enhance the facade of modernity, divorce was accepted even though it defied Catholic ideology and law.[16] The law was clearly designed to benefit men over women, who enjoyed few civil protections or economic opportunities. Employment for women was virtually nonexistent outside of the underpaid and usually informal labor of the working class. Urban ladinas of the middle and upper class were barred from the formal economy (with the exception of teaching), severely limiting their ability to live economically independent lives. Consequently, divorce was an option few women sought.[17]

Few men publicly refuted these dominant gender norms, although there are indications that some ladinos shared the ideals expressed in *La Voz de la Mujer* and *El Ideal*. In 1896, law student Rodolfo G. Rivas presented a legal argument for women's civil and political equality. Appealing to the state's desire to appear modern, Rivas reminded leaders of the growing movement to acknowledge women's civil equality among their northern industrialized neighbors and trading partners.[18] He noted that in Guatemala women were considered to be merely vessels of reproduction, identified politically and socially only in their role as mothers. Rivas argued that the intellectual, physical, and moral virtues possessed by women were precisely the civic qualities that Liberalism demanded of its citizens, and he condemned their complete legal exclusion within marriage. Had not women proven their positive influence in the home and society? he pondered. Although he was not optimistic that they might gain any political rights, he argued that until Guatemalan women were granted the most basic civil rights, there could be no hope of them gaining political rights.[19] Employing the Liberal mantra that, as mothers, women were the first educators of future Guatemalan citizens, Rivas wondered aloud whether there could be anything more beautiful than women working alongside men, adorned with all the rights and obligations afforded to them. In an argument that would be used repeatedly by legal reformers until 1945, Rivas also pointed out that the ambiguity of the word *los* in constitutional wording opened the possibility for its inclusion of all Guatemalans, including women.

The First Voices: Vicenta Laparra de la Cerda and Jesús Laparra

Women in Guatemala City identified several key spaces within this multifaceted web of overlapping legal and civil codes in which to effectively act. The coercive elements designed to enhance state control were supplemented by genuine social changes designed to elicit at least a modicum of popular support from the masses.[20] The rhetoric of citizenship and education within broad-based economic and scientific reforms offered the possibility of some real inclusion.[21] Liberalism's new emphasis on education offered a new employment opportunity for young women, especially those from the working class. The banishment of religious orders had left what little social welfare programs there had been in disarray, and to fill these vital social gaps, middle-class women joined some of the elite to create new Catholic charity associations to support orphanages and education centers. For urban ladinas, these education and social reform opportunities offered the only avenue for social mobility and self-awareness, as they transformed their role as teachers and mothers into a powerful analytical tool. Identifying the gap between reality and Liberal rhetoric, a small group of urban ladinas built the foundations of the first Guatemalan feminist ideas.

Two of the most critical voices who influenced the formation of early Guatemalan feminism rose from a humble rural family, a social and geographic background that shaped their feminist consciousness. Unlike a majority of early Latin American feminists, Vicenta and Jesús Laparra were not born in a large urban center, nor were they of elite or even middle-class origins. Rather, the sisters rose to their stature as literary and educational leaders through their intellectual talents. Although the Laparra sisters became the undisputed leaders of Guatemala City's women's movement, their values were established by earlier life experiences reflected in their concern for the working poor, Catholic labor unions, prisoners, and particularly poor and indigenous women. While social mobility was severely limited during the nineteenth century, their personal journey from rural obscurity to national literary stature demonstrates that it was indeed possible. The sociopolitical trajectory of the Laparra sisters would become a pattern replicated by thousands of young female educators across Guatemala during the late nineteenth and early twentieth centuries.[22]

Vicenta and Jesús Laparra were born in the mountain city of Quetzaltenango, roughly one hundred kilometers northwest of Guatemala City.[23] An important political center during the preconquest period for both the Mam and K'iche' Maya, it remained an indigenous city during the nineteenth century with more than half of its small population composed of K'iche' Maya. The Laparra sisters' parents, Nicolás Laparra and Desideria Reyes, were a humble, working-class family, a social position that clearly influenced their daughters' later concerns for poor and indigenous women.[24] Jesús was the eldest sister, born on October 14,

1820, while Vicenta arrived eleven years later on April 5, 1831. Their mother died in 1836 when Vicenta was five years old, a pivotal event that shaped both their personal lives and their literary careers. As Vicenta would recall in later years, "My sad childhood was washed by a flood of tears; my youth passed in groans; like a faded flower without fragrance that is crushed into oblivion."[25] Their family troubles were compounded by the political volatility characteristic of Guatemala's nineteenth century. When Conservative General Rafael Carrera invaded Quetzaltenango in 1840, Nicolás fled with his children—Jesús, Vicenta, and their sister, Josefa—to Comitán de las Flores, Mexico. There, Jesús founded a school for girls, where Vicenta received her early education. Although it is unclear how their father was impacted by the political upheavals of the 1840s, the Laparra family eventually returned to Guatemala sometime after 1850.[26]

Following their return, the sisters pursued divergent professional careers. While Jesús Laparra remained in Guatemala, Vicenta married military officer César de la Cerda Medinacelli in 1853, moving first to Santa Ana, El Salvador, and then to San José, Costa Rica.[27] While it is not clear why they moved, it is likely related to political conflicts affecting Laparra's military husband.[28] Taking full advantage of the international contacts she nurtured, Vicenta carved out a teaching career unusual for the time, running a school for girls in Santa Ana and then becoming the director of the Colegio Nacional de Señoritas in San José. While in Costa Rica, two of their young children, Cayetano and Angela, died, and they returned to Santa Ana in 1863 in an attempt to escape their enormous grief, moving back to Guatemala City permanently the following year. Vicenta's troubles did not end, however; following the birth of her last child, Salvador, in 1866, she suffered a postpartum paralysis that afflicted her for the next ten years.[29]

Using poetry and literature as a creative outlet for their pain and loss, Vicenta and Jesús emerged as the country's first literary leaders and female journalists. While Vicenta Laparra has received more national recognition, it was her sister who broke through significant gender barriers first. While Vicenta was living in El Salvador, Jesús Laparra collaborated with thirty-six other women to publish a book of poetry, *Ensayos poéticos*, in 1854. Just a year before the publication of the sisters' groundbreaking journal, *La Voz de la Mujer*, Jesús published her second book, *Ensueños de la mente*, in 1884, in which she explored the impact of the deaths of their mother, Desideria, and Vicenta's children. Never marrying, Jesús remained a prolific poet, often expressing her intense affection for her sister Vicenta, and for her nieces and nephews. In one example, Jesús reflects on Vicenta's personal difficulties: "Beautiful reminder of my beloved mother, I cradled you in my arms back in your childhood. To see you surrounded by sorrows now, my poor heart goes to pieces! Your life is a cup of bitterness. Days without fragrance and light. Ever more misfortune adding to the heavy cross you bear."[30] Just months before the publication of the Laparras' second journal, *El Ideal*, Vicenta's beloved sister Jesús died in January 1887, leaving her to carry on alone.[31]

Vicenta Laparra de la Cerda rapidly surpassed her sister's literary accomplishments as an educator, poet, and dramatist. She is credited with more than thirty works, including novels, dramas, comedies, and a variety of poetry and prose. She worked and published throughout most of her adult life, only slowing down just a few years before her death. She is credited with founding Guatemala's national theater, and her drama *El ángel caído* appeared on stage at the Teatro Nacional de Guatemala on July 18, 1885, just two months before the publication of *La Voz de la Mujer*. Following the dissolution of the journals *La Voz de la Mujer* and *El Ideal*, Vicenta published another journal for the city's educators, *La Escuela Normal*, during the 1890s. This publication reunited her with *El Ideal* colleague Rafaela del Águila. In her final years, Vicenta wrote three more novels, the last one appearing on August 15, 1897. An accomplished Guatemalan writer and one of the country's first feminists, she died of a heart condition on January 29, 1905, at the age of seventy-four.[32]

The work of Jesús and Vicenta Laparra definitively establishes Guatemala City as a literary center during the nineteenth century. Their books are the first publications for and by women in Guatemala and some of the earliest literary works in Latin America, joining the ranks of Peruvian Flora Tristan and Brazilian Nísia Floresta Brasileira.[33] These pioneers not only carved out literary space for subsequent women writers but also thwarted patriarchal assumptions of female ignorance even as the Liberal state was restricting women's socioeconomic roles. While some literary scholars have suggested that women who write for other women participate in their own professional segregation, Erin Finzer in fact argues that this practice creates a community of female readers, who in turn validate and facilitate a growing number of women writers. While Finzer comes to this conclusion with respect to Guatemalan writers during the 1930s, it holds true for the pioneers of Guatemala's literary movement during the mid-nineteenth century.[34] However, it is not only the time period in which they wrote but the nature of the literature itself that is groundbreaking. Much of their writing reflects the frailties of life during the nineteenth century, not only their personal tragedies but the social and political limitations imposed upon them by the state. Consequently, the publication of poetry books and journals by the Laparras and their literary circle reflects the collective sociopolitical marginalization of women and arguably represents the prototype of the twentieth-century genre of *testimonio*.[35]

La Voz de la Mujer and *El Ideal*

Guatemala's first journals for and by women, *La Voz de la Mujer* and *El Ideal*, emerged during the sociopolitical transformations sweeping through Guatemala City. Vicenta Laparra de la Cerda and Jesús Laparra drew upon the nascent intellectual community to create the city's first female social space in which to write and think. The women's movement that created and was then sustained by these pioneering journals actively engaged in contemporary social and political debates, including on the legal and civil status of women. While the Laparra sisters ostensibly wrote for other, like-minded women, their gendered critique of the state apparatus in fact directly challenged the authority and effectiveness of the government. While they framed their position within a Liberal ideology, supporting ideas of modernization, progress, and nation building to reform a backward and economically stagnant nation, the Laparra sisters argued for inclusion within the Liberal project. As a result, they successfully created an ideological platform for a proto-feminist community based on a shared concern for the rights of women, gaining a reputation among other journalists across the isthmus.[36] Joined by dozens of other newspapers and journals during the 1880s, these writers starkly revealed the disparity between political ideology and reality, their work ever mindful of the complex nature of the Liberal project.[37]

The two rather modest journals *La Voz de la Mujer* and *El Ideal* reflected the broader cultural dynamism sweeping Guatemala City. In the limited political world of the late nineteenth century, writing provided the best if not the only intellectual outlet for women (and men, for that matter) interested in reform of any kind. Liberalism's burgeoning rhetoric of modernization helped to initiate a vibrant groundswell of social and political ideas, which found expression in a rapidly expanding journalistic world across the isthmus, writers all eager to weigh in on their transforming world. In fact, as historian Michael Kirkpatrick points out, the very term "modernism" may have been coined in Guatemala's capital, a city and region traditionally perceived to exist only on the margins of culture and progress.[38] The sale of four hundred copies of *El Ideal* in its first week of publication is evidence of this intellectual vitality.[39] Both *La Voz de la Mujer* and *El Ideal* drew their readers from the growing normal school population, socially conscious elite women, labor unions, and Catholic social reform societies, creating fragile new alliances among previously distinct groups of women and men. Such alliances were extremely difficult to maintain in Guatemala's stratified social structure, and these journals were responsible for creating the first tenuous threads for a cross-class movement that would ultimately flourish during the late Estrada Cabrera era, culminating in the Partido Unionista in 1919.[40]

The first women's journal in Guatemala (and in Central America), *La Voz de la Mujer* was launched on August 22, 1885. Never more than four pages in length, only five issues were published, four between August 22 and September 12 and a fifth on November 14. While Vicenta and Jesús were its sole editors, publishing the small journal was a communal effort, and Javier Valenzuela assisted in *La Voz*'s production at La Aurora Press.[41] The sisters' second journal, *El Ideal*, began publication a few months after Jesús's death in 1887, and it ran weekly from December 10, 1887, until April 28, 1888, averaging six to eight pages in length. Without her sister now, Vicenta gathered an editorial board composed of J. Adelaida Chavéz, Isabel M. de Castellanos, and Carmen P. de Silva. In addition, Celinda D. Darmes, Rafaela del Águila, and Sara María G. S. de Morena provided freelance contributions. Felipe Silva, Carmen's husband, provided assistance in the publication of *El Ideal* without compensation.[42]

These pioneers of journalism were part of a larger sociopolitical milieu in which they were vulnerable to the political whims of dictatorial political leaders unwilling to entertain real dialogue over critical social issues. Consequently, although *La Voz de la Mujer* claimed to be politically neutral, President Manuel Lisandro Barillas (1885–1892) accurately understood its message to be a direct challenge to his presidency. After only five issues, Barillas banned its publication, despite an outcry of support from other Guatemalan journals such as *El Pensamiento Católico, El Republicano, La Voz de Centro-América, La Carídad,* and *Loca*.[43] In fact, *La Voz de la Mujer* was just one among many victims of the publication prohibition issued by the state in late 1885. Although discouraged, Laparra de la Cerda attempted to avoid political opposition with her second journal, *El Ideal*, by placing it under the protection of doña Encarnación Robles de Barillas, president of the Catholic charity La Sociedad de Caridád and the wife of President Barillas, who had repressed the Laparras' first publishing effort.[44] The extended run of *El Ideal* allowed Laparra de la Cerda to explore themes introduced in *La Voz* more thoroughly, specifically the exclusion of women from education. Despite Laparra de la Cerda's efforts to protect this second journal, it too was barraged by opposition and finally forced into silence. As she noted in her last editorial on April 28, 1888, despite its termination, the journalists' work had opened up a path for all Central American writers, shadows of the possibilities that already existed for their southern and northern sisters and brothers.[45] Sadly, Laparra de la Cerda concluded, their own definitions of "woman" were incompatible with those upheld by the national government.

Although the journals claimed to be apolitical, the Laparra sisters in fact addressed a wide range of political issues. Their interpretations of the rights of women, the nature and social influence of motherhood, and the compatibility of Catholicism with a Liberal political milieu directly confronted the modernization project. The inaugural editorials of both journals positioned the Laparra sisters and their colleagues vis-à-vis two of the most contentious political issues of their day: the political inclusion of all Guatemalans within the new Liberal state and the role of Catholicism. The two editorials attempted to sidestep their political message by falling back on the dominant gendered perception of women in the political arena. "What does the weak sex know of the founding of a nation, and diplomacy amid government representatives?"[46] Notwithstanding this disclaimer, the first edition of La Voz immediately challenged a recent political speech by none other than the Guatemalan president. Following a violent incident at a local penitentiary, Barillas justified his use of brute force against the prisoners by stating that these Guatemalans understood only the law of the stick and the gag.[47] Laparra de la Cerda urged Guatemala's new leader to work for the glory and motherhood of their nation without compromising the dignity of its citizens. While she condemned the crimes committed by the prisoners, she reminded the president of the larger Liberal goals of progress and civilization, which affected the destiny of all Guatemalans. Laparra de la Cerda's confrontation with Guatemala's president was significant and frankly radical within her social and political context.

However, Laparra de la Cerda's particular use of gendered language for political purposes distinguishes her as one of Latin America's pioneer feminists. In a mantra utilized by women across Latin America, she employs the notion of woman as the moral gauge for Guatemalan politics. On behalf of all Guatemalan mothers, Laparra de la Cerda asked President Barillas to cast aside oppression and uphold the dignity of all men, who were their sons, husbands, and fathers. Aligning herself with the poor and indigenous populations, her employment of the social identity of "mother" became a valuable instrument in the ideological development of political motherhood.[48] In one particular situation, she criticized President Barillas's political authority explicitly in the names of wives and mothers, using motherhood as a primary identity and clearly distancing her remarks from her identity as a woman. This particular defense has been noted by David Carey, who examines how Guatemalan women within the judicial system frequently utilized their identity as mothers to advocate for leniency or sympathy. While claiming higher moral ground demonstrated Laparra de la Cerda's understanding of the contemporary currents of early Latin American feminism, at other times she claimed the right to speak not as a morally superior woman but as a patriotic mother, patriotism being the second "mother" of all Guatemalans.[49] "Believe us sir, *La Voz de la Mujer* will always speak the language of truth, because we are driven by the good impulse of patriotism, which is the second mother of your children."[50] Laparra de la Cerda manipulated motherhood in times of crisis or political danger across class and ethnic lines in Guatemala.[51]

Laparra de la Cerda directly challenged the state using Liberal notions of family as the foundation of any modern society and skillfully separated the identity of mother from that of woman. "A woman with the sacred titles of both wife and mother ought to also have rights and liberties. . . . [A] woman should not be a robot doing what her husband tells her."[52] In other words, motherhood was not an inherent gender identity. Employing the Liberal emphasis on individualism, she encouraged the Liberal state and Guatemalan society to incorporate the reverence reserved for motherhood into the broader notion of womanhood. Just as mothers were revered, so too must women be honored. Even while Laparra de la Cerda couched her arguments in the contemporary language of nineteenth-century Liberal ideology, she questioned legislation designed to establish social and political hierarchical order. She pointed out to the political establishment that they were jeopardizing the future of Guatemala by confining women to the singular role of mother. Squelching the rights of mothers and women, the bearers of future generations, hurt future political goals as well. Her epistemological interpretation, a tactic she employed in all of her confrontations with the state, separated the biological role from an essentialized feminine identity. Consequently, she could argue that the state must respect individual women who could potentially become mothers as much as it claimed to respect mothers. Laparra de la Cerda's attitude was hardly the response expected from the "weaker sex" ignorant of matters of state and diplomacy.

While Liberal notions of motherhood credited them as the foundation of society, women did not have legal or civil status, and Laparra de la Cerda exposed this contradiction in her journals. She asked, if women were the foundation of Guatemalan society, why were they treated as invisible by men? On the one hand, she noted, men treated women with veneration and placed them on pedestals. Then, they "smilingly decree that women are not people," clearly referring to both the 1879 constitution and the 1877 civil code, which eroded women's rights in the home.[53] In frustration, she asked: "Are we not the same species as you?"[54] While her challenge to the existing patriarchal structure is striking, it is the raw emotion in her words that is particularly impressive. "We turn our cries to the heavens imploring: but sir, in what time do we live? In the nineteenth century, you tell us?"[55] Laparra expressed the pain Guatemala's social structure and gender notions inflicted on those marginalized within it.

The use of motherhood as a political tool for Latin American feminists has historically been highly effective. As Francesca Miller notes, the belief in women's different mission lies at the heart of feminist movements in Latin America and differentiates them from the predominant forms of feminism in North America and Europe. Rather than reject their socially defined role as mothers and as wives, feminists frequently acted to protest laws that threatened this role.[56] This became an effective avenue by which women moved from their home into formal employment such as teaching, transforming motherhood from an inert force into a dynamic one. Motherhood was essential to the social body and demanded care and sustenance; it had the capacity in feminists' view to generate much good for the motherland.[57] Even though engaged in political and economic matters, when women did so in the name of motherhood on behalf of their children and the well-being of their families, patriarchal society more often tolerated their actions. In her dissection of mother from woman when it served her political purposes, Laparra de la Cerda countered prevalent nineteenth-century feminist thought. She utilized motherhood in a politicized sense to argue against abuse, tyranny, and violence, without placing all women in this position. Consequently, her ideas are antecedents of contemporary feminisms that emerged later in the twentieth century, which challenge motherhood as an essentialized identity.[58]

In a similarly contradictory manner, *La Voz*'s first editorial also claimed that the journal would not discuss matters of faith, because Guatemala was already a Catholic country and the journal's female readers did not need further religious instruction. Laparra de la Cerda noted that *La Voz* was designed to defend the morality and dignity of Catholic women, and would only discuss issues of significance for women. Immediately following the editorial in the pages of the journal was an article by Jesús Laparra entitled "La luz en el desierto" (A light in the desert).[59] Here, she elaborated upon the role of women as a source of positive social influence and linked this ability to the Catholic faith, which functioned as an oasis in the midst of life's difficulties.[60] In an age of Liberal onslaught against the Catholic Church, *La Voz* reminded its readers that Catholicism was alive and well, and served a social purpose by challenging poverty and homelessness. Addressing the deep-seated fear the Guatemalan patriarchal secular leadership had of feminist activity motivated by religion, *La Voz* assured the patriarchy that Catholic women had no ulterior motives other than to serve Guatemalan interests. "No sirs, we neither want emancipation nor to place ourselves in a land of tyranny because this is incompatible with the natural sweetness of women."[61] Furthermore, politicians held to the belief that women's religious affiliation with Catholicism placed them naturally in opposition to the Liberal agenda. Laparra de la Cerda asserted, however, that the Liberal notion of Catholicism as incompatible with its political agenda was a direct insult to women.[62] Here, she assured Liberal leaders that Catholic women would not oppose their quest for "order and progress." To achieve modernity, Guatemalan politicians believed that the country's citizens must be freed from all archaic religious influences, and yet here a group of women insisted that they could be both Catholic and civic minded. In doing so, the Laparra sisters once again challenged the authority of a secular Liberal state and its unwillingness to address the social ills of its citizenry. Although willing to participate in Guatemala's modernization project, they argued that Catholicism had a role in the new world of order and progress. The Laparra sisters were not alone in their efforts, and Catholic women continued to challenge the government during the 1890s on matters of policy and education.[63] This would remain a common theme in Guatemala City women's movements, again highlighted in 1945 when Gloria Menéndez Mina argued that Catholicism was not a valid argument against women's suffrage.

These writers used Liberal ideas to argue for their own inclusion, establishing that women had both the right and the skills necessary to act as citizens. Although the Laparra sisters were acutely aware that Liberal rhetoric held little promise of sociopolitical inclusion for women, it remained their only avenue in that direction. The identification of women's rights in the Liberal language of modernization created a theoretical foundation for urban ladinas that continued well into the mid-1950s, with the exception of the socialist democratic model employed by women of the Alianza Femenina Guatemalteca during the Árbenz presidency. Alongside their petitions for inclusion in the national project, however, the women of *La Voz de la Mujer* and *El Ideal* also critiqued the state for its reach, which extended into their homes through civil codes that buttressed a pervasive patriarchal milieu. For Laparra de la Cerda, the home represented the central and primary locus of inequality, which began the first time a baby girl opened her eyes. According to Laparra de la Cerda, fathers in particular were dismayed by the birth of daughters, since only sons carried on the family name. Once born, a daughter witnessed the sadness in her parents' faces. From the moment of birth, a woman's life was marked by unhappiness as she entered a world dominated by men.[64] The patriarchy legally supported within the home extended into society and culture, access to education, and finally women's legal status, representing four roots of social inequality. Laparra de la Cerda's identification of women's inequality challenged the very foundation upon which the Liberal state had been constructed, whose laws restructured Guatemala as a heterosexual patriarchal family.

Despite their claims to the contrary, Laparra de la Cerda and her colleagues engaged directly with the political state, prompting the question of what exactly they understood politics to be, and the role of women in this new Liberal landscape. The 1879 constitution declared women incapable of citizenship due to their perceived physical and intellectual shortcomings, thereby excluding them from any meaningful political participation.[65] The legal reality established by the Liberal state, however, did not stop Vicenta Laparra from directly addressing political issues, believing that women had something to contribute. The writers in *El Ideal* claimed that politics was not a subject for women because it was simply too dangerous, a conclusion likely reached after the publication of *La Voz de la Mujer* was terminated, and they protected the new publication by claiming that it was a literary organ by and for educated women and writers.[66] The arguments in both *La Voz* and *El Ideal* represent a sophisticated and nuanced debate on the social and political rights of Guatemalan women reflective of the structure identified by scholar Hilda Sabato. Here, Sabato pays particular attention to the tension between rhetoric and reality in nineteenth-century Liberal states, identifying the spaces in which historically marginalized political actors such as urban ladinas in Guatemala City could potentially act. She notes that within Liberal modernization women were generally excluded from the core of public life and relegated to the private realm. However, as the network of institutions originating in civil society expanded in urban centers, their interaction with the formal state and political realm produced a space of mediation, a "public sphere."[67] Through their work in their own associations and newspapers, women could gain a visible public presence. While this type of public activity is distinct from the traditional concept of the public sphere as customarily inhabited by men, Sabato argues that this expanded definition "allowed scholars to depict and name a set of institutions and practices that originated in civil society but, at the same time, operated in relation to the political realm, to the state."[68] Although the writers of *La Voz de la Mujer* and *El Ideal* may not have been aware of the public sphere they were creating (although it is highly possible that they were), the Liberal state certainly understood its challenge to their political sovereignty and moved quickly to silence their efforts.

Sabato's identification of the relationship between civil associations and their political implications is particularly evident in both Vicenta's and Jesús's concern over the poverty manifested daily on the streets of Guatemala City.[69] As Vicenta stated quite simply, one only had to look out one's window to see the poor. Liberalism's modest attempts at modernization created an urban demand for female labor beyond the home. Here, unskilled laborers found a precarious existence primarily within the informal labor market and small, low-skilled industries.[70] Even as women's rights were reduced, women were simultaneously being drawn into the labor market, albeit a small one; and poor and working-class women were required to work both within and outside of the home.[71] Separated from extended family networks and frequently abandoned by partners or husbands, poor women were particularly socially and economically vulnerable in the urban areas. In the city, life was a daily struggle, and working-class women bore the brunt of this system.[72] Although it would not become part of a global feminist language until a hundred years later, Laparra de la Cerda highlighted the concept of the "double workday syndrome" as a pivotal social malady afflicting women, and she warned the political elites not to forget the weak, the poor, and disabled in their search for economic and social progress.[73]

The legacy of *La Voz de la Mujer* in the ladina community extended far beyond what its brevity might suggest. Despite their inability to enact any legal or civil change, the journal's contributors created the first public discourse over the rights of women and the state in the capital city.[74] In their multiple roles as writers, journalists, and teachers, the Laparra sisters and their colleagues influenced an entire generation of educators and students, establishing the principle feminist rhetoric utilized by urban ladinas through the mid-twentieth century. While these early attempts failed to facilitate concrete change, the writers of these journals framed a critical argument for future political and social activity, and others continued their struggle in the subsequent decades.

Educating and Educated Ladinas

Education quickly became the singular avenue for Guatemalan women to improve their intellectual and social status, a possibility exemplified by Vicenta and Jesús Laparra. Although the Liberal state had established education as a central pillar in its broader modernizing project, it was far less prepared for the generations of educated women its policies created. Young women from across the country entered the normal schools established in the largest urban centers, facilitating an unprecedented social shift of women from rural, working-class, and artisan families into an emergent, urban, educated middle class.[75] The relatively autonomous space of urban centers allowed for freedom of consciousness as educators and students alike sought to define the social needs of Guatemalans, and women in particular. Consequently for ladinas, there was no more important issue than education, and their intense efforts and direct involvement in the education system created a cadre of activists.[76] Although this early movement did not succeed in making legal changes, the foundation of the urban ladina movement of the twentieth century can be traced to the circle of educators who coalesced around the Laparra sisters and *El Ideal*.

During the nineteenth century, women's accessibility to education depended upon the fortunes and designs of the two primary political parties, the Liberals and the Conservatives. Although frequently subsumed within larger debates over the nature of a modern Guatemalan state, education nevertheless became one of the central pawns in their ideological struggle. Until 1871, the pendulum of education swung between a drive to create a broad-based public system, or to leave it in the hands of the Catholic Church. While the debate over education was heated, the reality was that with few exceptions education remained available only to the elite.[77] With the definitive rise of Liberalism after 1871, women's fortunes shifted, because in their attempt to re-create the modernization and progress of industrialized nations, Guatemalan politicians deemed the education of women to be necessary for a modern society. The writers of *El Ideal* capitalized on the prevailing gender norms that accepted teaching as a natural extension of motherhood, focusing most of their attention on education. Linking Liberal success to women's access to education, the women of *El Ideal* affirmed the home as the nation's foundation: "If women as mothers are the heart and soul of the nation, then they must be educated.... How fortunate for the spouse and children when they have a wonderful mother and wife, who is intelligent and educated, to be the teacher of the home."[78] However, writers Carmen P. de Silva and Rafaela del

Águila extended the metaphor, arguing that educated women in the home were capable of teaching morality and patriotism because the "home is indispensable for the association of ideas, the equilibrium of the soul, and the community of ideas."[79] The cornerstone of Liberal reform lay within the education of young women in preparation for motherhood, and Vicente Laparra de la Cerda and her colleagues readily adapted this ideal to suit their own agenda, which included increased access to education for all young women.

Education standards in Guatemala were far below those of the North Atlantic regions, and so President Barrios passed several laws to improve the methods of education and increase the number of schools. The 1875 Ley Orgánica de Instrucción Pública Primaria mandated a new school curriculum that included algebra, geometry, physics, mechanics, natural history, physiology and hygiene, geography, Central American history and geography, office methods, and business, offered specifically for boys.[80] According to the law, these courses were also available to female students, with additional courses in needlework, domestic economics, and skills "specific to their gender." In reality, however, schools offered girls only the most elementary education focusing primarily on domestic and manual skills. Further amendments to the Ley Orgánica de Instrucción Pública in 1879 and 1882 were designed to implement education reforms more rapidly.[81] However contradictory, incomplete, and self-serving these education reforms under the Liberal reform remained, they were of some consequence for Guatemalan women.[82]

The increase in the sheer number of schools enabled more children to attend. For example, in 1874, 183 schools for girls existed with a total of 6,312 students. This represented an increase from 1866, for when available data reports only 8,074 students in the entire country, both male and female. By 1874, a total of 20,528 attended school, and by 1887, 49,351 students attended primary school, with approximately 1,500 enrolled in secondary and normal schools, and the university. By 1901, there were 429 elementary girls' schools.[83] While this represents a substantial increase, in a country of approximately two million people, the simple fact remained that only a fraction of eligible children attended school, male or female.[84]

With the Liberal desamortización, a majority of Guatemala's teachers had left the country, and the state now moved to establish teaching centers to fill the gaps left by Catholic personnel. The first normal school for men was established in 1875, and just four years later, the Instituto Normal de Señoritas, Belén, was opened for women teachers.[85] A direct descendant of the defunct convent school Colegio de Belén established in the 1860s under the Bethlemite Order, the Instituto Normal de Señoritas, Belén, had been transformed first into the Colegio Nacional de Niñas (September 15, 1875) before becoming the country's first teacher training center for women.[86] On June 28, 1888, a second normal school, the Escuela Normal de Señoritas, was founded to assist in the training of more teachers, and the two schools were unified in 1899.[87] The impact of this new social institution was evident when teaching was listed as a profession for the first time in the 1893 census.[88] The true impact of the normal school, however, would become clear in the following decades as the Instituto Normal de Señoritas, Belén, emerged as the pivotal center for ladina activism in Guatemala City, a tradition that continues to the present day.

The patriarchy's deep ambivalence and even fear regarding the social implications of educated women was identified quickly by the writers of both *La Voz de la Mujer* and *El Ideal*.[89] Warning Guatemalan politicians that the Liberal project would fail if women were not integrated as essential elements of family and society, Laparra de la Cerda and her colleagues maintained a steady diatribe in support of education. In order for Liberals to achieve their national goals, the writers believed that men needed to "respect the beliefs and rights of mothers, giving them liberty in order to practice good, and granting guarantees, so that women can struggle to uplift their children under the double mantle of virtue and maternal love to make them heroes of the *patria*."[90] Assuming that the mothers of a new scientific and progressive nation must be well educated, where, asked *El Ideal*, were the schools? Where was this new progress for women? The authors insisted that women were willing to work hard to create a new patriotism but needed the training in order to accomplish this task.[91]

Although Guatemala is traditionally perceived to be a backwater of Latin American culture and education, an examination of the country's educational system reveals that normal schools in fact developed on par with and even earlier than in some larger Latin American nations. Francesca Miller developed an early template describing three broad phases discernable in the rise of women in education across Latin America, which remains useful.[92] The first arose around the general idea of educating girls and women, while the second debated the precise nature of this education. The third and final phase entailed the establishment of educational institutions that admitted women. The development of women's education in Guatemala follows a similar pattern, but an examination of the lives of Jesús and Vicenta Laparra suggests a caveat to Miller's model. The Laparra sisters initiated many of these educational ideas, and they themselves achieved an unusual level of education for the mid- to late nineteenth century; their literary skills granted them exceptional national status as poets and writers. In turn, the Laparra sisters educated other young women in national institutions as well as in their own schools. Jesús founded her own school while in exile in Mexico with her family, and Vicenta created her own school for girls in Guatemala City in January 1888. Their colleague Rafaela del Águila became the director of the Instituto Normal de Señoritas, Belén, on June 28, 1888, and participated in the first pedagogical congress held in Guatemala in 1881.[93] The critical element in their story is that they themselves established the schools that demonstrated the possibility and social significance of education for women. These first educators and feminists were in fact not just the beneficiaries of the vibrant sociopolitical trends identified by historians as critical to the rise of Latin American feminism, but also their creators. While this particular example might be interpreted as exceptional, the creators of *La Voz de la Mujer* and *El Ideal* played an integral role in the establishment and acceptance of women's educational institutions by the Liberal state. In turn, along with women across the hemisphere, they facilitated an emergent awareness of the gendered nature of political and social inequity.

The role of the Laparra sisters and their cohorts in this educational transformation demonstrates the direct correlation between normal schools, educated women, and the rise of female activism first identified by historians Steven Palmer and Gladys Rojas Chaves in Costa Rica.[94] While the women clearly benefited from the Liberal emphasis on an educated citizenry with the establishment of schools and training centers for teachers, they also moved into the vacuum left by the Catholic personnel exiled from Guatemala, creating education centers made necessary by this paucity of personnel. The Laparra sisters definitively demonstrate the depth of women's participation in the transformation of the educational system, a historic process as revolutionary as any for Guatemalan women. Ultimately, while urban ladinas participated in the new educational opportunities now spreading across Latin America, the dictatorial nature of Liberal governments until 1944 stymied the dynamism evident in the early formation of the Guatemalan educational system, muting the critical foundations of urban Guatemalan feminism.

The Estrada Cabrera Era (1898–1920) and the 1920 Revolution

Vicenta Laparra de la Cerda lived to see the beginning of what would become the longest dictatorship in Central American history. Characterized by cruelty and political repression, Manuel Estrada Cabrera maintained order through his alliance with the military, even assassinating members of his own legislature when it suited his political needs. However, Estrada Cabrera did not comply with the standard caudillo rules that dictated alliances with powerful associates. Rather, he chose to isolate himself politically through complicity with the United Fruit Company (UFCo), a US company that established a presence in Guatemala in 1899. The UFCo had established a virtual monopoly over rail transportation in Guatemala by 1912 through the renamed International Railways of Central America, and the company benefited from generous tax exemptions and outright land gifts.[95] To maintain social order, Estrada Cabrera discouraged intellectual expression during a period marked by extreme self-censorship, compelled by threat of terror. As David Carey succinctly concludes: "Even as he used any means possible to prevent social unrest, Estrada Cabrera obscured such national shortcomings as penury, illiteracy, and racism."[96] The impact of these contradictory policies on the residents of Guatemala City can be seen in the virtual silence of intellectual and political dissent. The strategies that urban ladinas developed to cope with Estrada Cabrera's seemingly impenetrable stranglehold only exacerbated this archival silence, leaving little evidence of their ideas or activities. Contemporaries of the Laparra sisters lowered their public profile, retreating to home meetings and informal associations, a strategy employed by other urban residents anxious to retain their intellectual autonomy, including members of working-class unions, where women played a significant role. In the safety of these gatherings in individual homes or coffeehouses known as *tertulias*, intellectual and political ideas could be openly discussed. Women wrote literature to convey political dissension and to maintain a literary and increasingly feminist consciousness. While their numbers remained modest, they sustained an identifiable community exchanging a range of sociopolitical ideas even as the dictatorship muted any public expression of them. Therefore, although only tenuous threads and anecdotal evidence remain of their autonomous networks, additional clues can be found in the diverse membership of the Partido Unionista and their successful overthrow of the dictator in 1920.[97]

Estrada Cabrera's concern for Guatemala's international reputation, rather than for his fellow Guatemalans, dominated his internal policies, offering several social spaces in which activists could organize. For Estrada Cabrera, Guatemala's international reputation with its North Atlantic trading partners as a modern and progressive nation was at stake. To that end, the president postured himself as a defender of two socioeconomic elements, namely the educational system and a productive working class. Estrada Cabrera demonstrated his alliance with these institutions through social services and several pieces of legislation, including the Ley Protectora de Obreros (Protection Law for Workers).[98] Under his mother's tutelage, Estrada Cabrera established a birthing center for working-class women and their children in 1913.[99] The Asilo de Maternidad Joaquina, named for the mother Manuel Estrada Cabrera adored, was the only birthing center available in Guatemala for pregnant working women.[100] In a further attempt to support urban workers, Estrada Cabrera established kindergartens and night schools for adults. The president also addressed the poor quality of education, sending the principal of the women's normal school to Cuba for training. And although the organization would later be criticized as an instrument of US foreign involvement, Guatemala participated in the creation of the Central American Institute of Pedagogy in 1907, designed to establish a uniform educational pedagogy across the isthmus.[101] However, alongside these urgent reforms, Estrada Cabrera chose appearance over substance, establishing a series of monuments to Minerva, the Roman goddess of education. These imposing and bizarre stone exhibitions were scattered throughout Guatemalan urban centers, while elaborate annual festivals showcased students and teachers in military-style parades. As the president poured precious state funds into these superficial overtures to education, teachers went without pay for months at a time, the state treasury unable to pay its educators.

As the beneficiaries of these contradictory reforms, the urban working class and educated ladinas responded with deliberate strategies to navigate the complex political terrain. The 1891 papal encyclical *Rerum Novarum*, designed to thwart the populist appeal of Marxism, had galvanized Catholic workers' associations throughout Guatemala City. Mutual aid societies in artisan communities were the first to form, and by 1920, forty separate societies and associations existed in the capital city. Although a transition to industrialization commonly results in a loss of influence for women in artisan communities, as Norma Stoltz Chinchilla demonstrates, such a transition did not occur in Guatemala, and urban working-class women maintained an active institutional role within their own unions and labor circles.[102] As a result, working-class women retained their historical base within the artisan economic sector, the extent of whose influence would become clear following the 1920 revolution.

The organized working class aligned itself ideologically with the established network of educators that had coalesced around the Laparra sisters. Catholic workers' journals addressed working-class activist concerns and published articles by the ladina literary community including Vicenta Laparra de la Cerda, whose work appeared frequently in *La Semana Católica* during the late 1890s, encouraging their activism. By the 1910s, despite the self-censorship practiced by so many during the Estrada Cabrera era, working-class journals such as *El Grito* openly discussed politics, Catholicism, and even feminism. When Peruvian Haydée González assumed *El Grito*'s directorship in 1916, she escalated its social critiques to include gender analysis of early twentieth-century urban life. Reminiscent of Laparra de la Cerda, González emphasized the socioeconomic struggles of working-class women both in the home and in society, publishing articles on such topics as domestic violence and the rights of women. Encouraging her readership to establish the intellectual connection between social justice and structural gendered disadvantages, González carefully raised the question of suffrage in several editions. Given that the issue of suffrage emerged immediately following the 1920 revolution, it is clear that *El Grito* was publicly reflecting a broader conversation taking place among a cross section of Guatemala City residents. In her journal, González highlighted the contributions of many educators, including the celebrated principal of the Instituto Normal de Señoritas, Belén, Natalia Górriz de Morales.[103] Careful to publicize the accomplishments of Estrada Cabrera's presidency, the publication simultaneously cultivated the literary careers of many women, including Isaura de Menéndez Mina, mother of Gloria Menéndez Mina, who would become the editor of the women's journal *Azul* during the 1940s. Following Haydée González's unexpected death at a very young age, *El Grito* was carried on into the 1920s with a revised title, *El Grito del Pueblo*.[104]

Given the restrictive political environment, both the working-class associations and urban ladinas adopted a political strategy designed to ostensibly support the president. Muting whatever misgivings they might have had, these activists formed political associations that allowed them to function in the political sphere. Working-class activists formed political clubs in 1904, 1910, and 1916 designed to support Estrada Cabrera's presidential bids despite the fact that they were democratic charades. However contradictory his policies on education might have been, ladina educators declared their support for his 1916 campaign. A proclamation supporting the president's third term was signed by hundreds of urban women, including Luz Valle, a young journalist who would eventually publish during a later dictatorship under Jorge Ubico (1931–1944). As Valle discovered during the Estrada Cabrera regime, even the modest spaces offered under dictatorships were of some consequence (see chapter 2). This tacit support won them limited favor as educators and allowed them to successfully navigate a seemingly impenetrable political system.[105]

Estrada Cabrera's incompetent response to the devastating earthquakes of December 1917 and January 1918, as well as the 1918 influenza epidemic, strengthened an opposition movement coalescing among an eclectic array of social groups. Workers, labor associations, educators, and the Catholic elite, including Bishop José Piñol y Batres, all voices represented in journals such as *El Grito*, threw their support behind this emergent movement. Officially formed on December 25, 1919, the Partido Unionista, led by Silverio Ortiz, consisted of thirty-one prominent citizens and eighteen representatives of the city's organized laborers, including tailors, carpenters, barbers, clerks, bakers, blacksmiths, masons, and railroad workers.[106] Popular political support for the Partido Unionista came from the artisan circles in which working-class women were a significant presence, as evidenced by the broad-based democratic demands including universal suffrage.[107] Created under a banner of Central American unity and proclaiming "Dios, Unión, Libertad," the Unionists came to office representing the diverse interests of the working class, the Catholic Church, university students, laborers, and urban ladinas. During the street protests that were an influential aspect of revolutionary protest against Estrada Cabrera, dozens of women were injured or killed.[108] Eventually alienating even his own handpicked legislative assembly, Estrada Cabrera was declared legally insane on April 8, 1920, and the Partido Unionista placed their own candidate, Carlos Herrera, into office.[109]

The 1920 revolution ushered in a decade of intellectual and social dynamism, as the sociopolitical ideals born in the tertulias and journals were extended into the public sphere. Reminiscent of the political transition during the 1880s, a publishing frenzy ensued during the early 1920s. Several influential twentieth-century newspapers such as *El Imparcial* and *Nuestro Diario*, as well as smaller journals such as *Vida* and *Studium*, began publication during this period of relative intellectual freedom, unleashing a wide variety of intellectual, educational, and social reform ideals.[110] Many of these initiatives were characterized by a series of false starts, reflecting the embryonic stage of this rapid sociopolitical transformation. Ultimately, as Wade Kit notes, "unable to create a political consensus, reactionary military and oligarchical forces forestalled the movement toward reform and reconstituted the coffee planter–military compact."[111] Although political space narrowed following Herrera's overthrow in 1921, neither the José María Orellano nor Lázaro Chacón González presidencies were able to reestablish full sociopolitical control to silence these ideals.

James Scott identifies a revolution as an "interregnum," a place "between the moment when a previous regime disintegrates and the moment when a new regime is firmly in place . . . a political terrain that has rarely been examined closely."[112] This is particularly true of the 1920 revolution in Guatemala, which has not enjoyed much historical scrutiny. From the perspective of urban ladina history, the eighteen-month window of the Herrera presidency represents a pivotal period that had repercussions for the remainder of the twentieth century. The elements of social justice and democratic ideals present in the public discourse during these months provide evidence of the cross-class collaboration furtively developed in the shadows of the Estrada Cabrera regime, as public debate immediately emerged over political rights for women and illiterate men. In this less restrictive political milieu, the urban community eagerly applied emergent intellectual ideas regarding education, health care, and race to their sociopolitical context, organizing for improved labor rights, the creation of a Guatemalan Red Cross, and a society for the protection of children.

During their brief time in power, the first and possibly the most radical of reforms introduced by the Partido Unionista occurred just weeks after the overthrow of Estrada Cabrera. Declaring full democracy to be a central tenet in their political platform, the Partido Unionista introduced suffrage for women and disenfranchised men in the National Assembly on May 14, 1920. The ensuing political debate pitted traditional notions of women against the reality of their actions during the revolution.[113] To support their argument for women's suffrage, politicians used women's involvement during the recent revolution as evidence of their political acuity. On March 11, 1920, more than ten thousand men, women, and children risked their lives in a series of political demonstrations against the Estrada Cabrera regime, during which dozens of women were injured or killed.[114] During this unprecedented public debate on women's political rights, those in opposition, such as Pablo Rabasso Ferrer (a congressional deputy from Mazatenango), declared women too inept and ignorant to be able to vote. The Unionista response remained consistent. "This man has eyes, but he does not see. Have not the women of Guatemala helped to bring down the dictatorship of Estrada Cabrera? Yet, the vote is withheld from them."[115] The Unionista position no doubt articulated the fear fueling the resistance to women's political participation.

> If the women of Mazatenango vote, we can have total confidence that other more equitable men, more just men will represent the coffee and cocoa growers with the same ability as Ferrer since women who participate in the social and

political development of the country have the same intelligence and aptitude as the men.[116]

Despite its defeat, legislators continued to press for full suffrage, reflecting some level of consensus over citizenship for women.[117] In 1921, lawyer Adolfo Moreno raised the issue again, arguing that excluding women from citizenship violated Guatemala's constitutional premises. The core of his argument lay in the ambiguity of the 1879 constitution, which gave "literate Guatemalans" over the age of eighteen the right to vote. Moreno, a representative from the district of Izabal, argued that constitutional Articles 5 and 8 had been interpreted exclusively as a male right because of the use of the word "los," which signified the male gender. Echoing Rodolfo Rivas's 1896 argument, Moreno challenged the existing wording of the constitution because it did not specify men, and therefore it must include women. In 1879, legislator Rafael Montufár had argued that, due to deficiencies in their physical and intellectual makeup, women were incapable of performing political functions, as had been demonstrated by the disappointing experiences in those countries where the ballot had been given to them.[118] This argument held little weight, given that women were not allowed to vote in any nation in 1879 and just a few by 1920.[119] Moreno deftly averted the historical argument by pointing to the readiness of women to suffer and die for their nation during the 1920 revolution as proof of their political acuity. A commission entrusted with constitutional reforms in early January 1921 once again broached the question of suffrage. In an extraordinarily close vote of eight to seven, suffrage for women and disenfranchised men lost by one vote, and Guatemala narrowly missed becoming the first country in the hemisphere to allow full democratic participation, since Canada and the United States had only incomplete democracies at that time.[120]

Signaling their affiliation with the new administration, the Association of University Students also held public debates over the sociopolitical rights of women. In contrast to the opposition among members of the Generación del 20, the students reflected a growing transnational acceptance of the political rights of women. Before a group of his peers, Augusto Nero Barrios M. not only argued that women had political rights but suggested that they should be able to hold office.[121] He extended his analysis to women's broader social rights and their civil disenfranchisement. Barrios reminded his audience that Article 46 of the Guatemalan civil code decreed women to have no legal identity outside of marriage, comparing their status to that of slaves. How was the civil code anything else, he asked, given that women were unable to speak for themselves, or engage in a contract or waive an existing one without the written authority of their husband?[122] Aligning himself with the dominant Liberal ideal that marriage should be a civil agreement, Barrios argued that marriage represented the subjugation of women.

Despite the ultimate defeat of suffrage, several significant issues emerged from this unprecedented debate on citizenship. First, the call for suffrage came from the working class and labor unions and not from a feminist movement, as was common elsewhere in Latin America. During the brief Herrera presidency, organized labor continued to press for female suffrage, indicating the extent of influence women held within working-class associations. Second, the suffrage movement did not distinguish between literate and illiterate women, thereby reflecting democratic ideals on par with those of Costa Rica and Canada.[123] The close vote and the sustained effort for suffrage suggest that it might indeed have come to pass if the Herrera administration had not been overthrown just eighteen months later, and offer a curious historical exception to broader patterns within the Latin American suffrage movement. This debate revealed both the growing interest in making a legal case for the acceptance of broader notions of citizenship and women's suffrage, along with the grammatical subterfuge of the word "los" to give the constitution a presumption of male dominance. In a similar reformist fashion, the Partido Unionista declared that it would not return to the charade of earlier voting practices for indigenous men, who could not vote in secret. In fact, the wording from the constitutional vote in early 1921 only expressed concern over women's lack of political experience and not over their organic civic ability or political acuity.[124] This peculiarity within the continent-wide suffrage story was achieved through an intellectual collusion among ladina educators, writers, and the working class in Guatemala City. With roots in the pre–Estrada Cabrera era and developed surreptitiously during his dictatorship, suffrage surfaced in the political platform of the Partido Unionista.

Once Herrera was overthrown in December 1921, the emergence of a women's-rights discourse from within the working class in Guatemala City did not translate into a discernable feminist organization.[125] Although labor organizers continued to work for women's equality in other aspects of Guatemalan life, they no longer had the political power to bring about legislative change. However, the ideals surrounding women's sociopolitical status had permeated the urban working-class consciousness, and just a few years later, on November 24, 1925, more than 150 female coffee pickers (*escogedoras*) mounted a strike against a powerful German planter, Federico Gerlach, at La Moderna coffee plantation on the edge of Guatemala City. Following a protracted labor struggle during which many of these women lost their jobs, a comprehensive labor law was passed on April 30, 1926, with provisions that were remarkably similar to the strikers' earlier demands.[126] The workday and workweek were limited to eight hours and forty-eight hours, respectively, and nursing mothers were permitted fifteen minutes every three hours to feed their children. Furthermore, women were guaranteed one-half of their salary during the four weeks prior to and five weeks following birth (as paid maternity leave), and they could not be fired during that period of time. In support of the striking women, *El Imparcial* ran a series of three articles titled "El problema femenista" during November 1926, declaring that the working woman was the foundation of the happiness of the home, society, and nation. The articles expressed concern over the number of hours a majority of women worked and openly supported those labor unions that assisted women. The editor's conclusion that the hostility men exhibited toward women workers should be understood as the men's problem and not the women's reflected a fundamental shift in the debate on working women. Despite its limited impact on national politics and gender roles, a sense of justice for working women (at least those involved in the unions and social reform movements) pervaded the decade.[127] It is ironic that Central America's first labor strike was executed by indigenous female coffee pickers. Historically ignored by the state for its economic contributions, coffee picking did not appear on the 1921 census as an occupation, highlighting again the state's blindness toward indigenous women in Guatemalan society.[128]

The proponents for women's rights shifted back from their working-class base to the literary circles of the upper middle class and the intellectual elite, and Guatemala's first overtly feminist organization emerged from within the ranks of this elite. Dubbed the Generación del 20 by writer Miguel Ángel Asturias, this loosely affiliated group of ladino and ladina intellectuals became the most influential reformers of the 1920s in Guatemala City, representing a vast social network bound to one another by strong academic, professional, political, and social ties. Sustained through tertulias, unionist clubs, Masonic lodges, and *teosofía* (theosophical) societies, personal and public regeneration permeated their reform ideals.[129] The intellectual and spiritual ideology of teosofía was fundamental to their vision. Its core values lay in its inherent sense of retributive justice or karma, which had the power to restore the balance of nature and enable individuals to create justice internally and externally.[130] This particular ideology held great attraction for Guatemalans whose individual intellectual and physical freedoms were frequently repressed. Consequently, teosofía remained popular here well beyond the time it had run its course in other Latin American countries. Long denied the ability to hold public discourse on social ills of the day, daily papers and journals were inundated by an explosion of ideas influenced by these philosophies for the next decade.

Creating a feminist counterpoint to the male-dominated Generación del 20, literary women formed the Sociedad Gabriela Mistral (SGM). Feeling a deep affinity with Chilean writer and feminist Gabriela Mistral's ideals on teosofía (she joined a theosophist lodge in 1911), the group named themselves after this best-known Latin American woman of the time.[131] Their self-ascribed mentor held similar views on working women and motherhood in particular, and this circle embraced her 1923 publication *Lecturas para mujeres*.[132] Her belief in a socially unified American hemisphere and a concern for indigenous peoples resonated with the ideas of the SGM for Guatemala, who were also active in a variety of groups focused on the unification of Central America during the first half of the twentieth century. Mistral visited Guatemala in 1931, where she received an honorary degree and gave a speech entitled "On the Unity of Culture" regarding the importance of the university and educational pedagogy in shaping culture throughout the Americas.

The SGM was founded by outspoken and charismatic Rosa Rodríguez López. While many of her ideas echoed those of the Laparra sisters, Rodríguez López's familial origins could not have been more dissimilar. Surrounded by wealth and privilege as children of a powerful coffee grower, Rosa and her sister Graciela Rodríguez López received an education available only to the Guatemalan elite.[133] Her tenure in the Convent of the Holy Names in Oakland, California, turned Rodríguez López off of Catholicism; the SGM in fact frequently accused women of the same social class of religious fanaticism and hypocrisy. Upon her return to Guatemala, Rodríguez López turned her considerable intellect into poetry and activism, publishing extensively in the Generación del 20 journal *Vida*. Moving to Mexico City in 1926, she eventually immigrated to the United States, where she became an influential leader in the Chicano labor movement before having her legal status in the United States revoked.[134] Rodríguez López returned briefly in 1949 to work with the influential teaching union the Sindicato de Trabajadores de la Educación de Guatemala, but moved once again to Mexico following the overthrow of Jacobo Árbenz in 1954.

The SGM's inaugural meeting took place on November 2, 1925, at the Rodríguez López home. The founding members came from the well-educated and very small urban ladina circle, including well-known poet Martha Josefina Herrera, Clara Rubio de Escalar, María de Michel, Magda Mabarak, and Luz Valle, the latter then working for *El Imparcial* (Valle's contributions to Guatemala's women's movements will be further discussed in chapters 2 and 3).[135] Rosa Rodríguez López assumed the presidency, while Matilda Rivera Cabeza served as vice president and Elisa Mencos R. acted as secretary. The feminism espoused by the Sociedad Gabriela Mistral was deeply influenced by theosophical ideas and remained relatively conservative and maternalistic in nature, although somewhat expansive in ideals regarding ethnicity and racism, economic disparity, and the political repression of women.[136] Indicative of the influence of teosofía, the women of the SGM directed the core of their feminism inward in order to instruct, educate, and purify the thoughts of women and overcome notions of personal inferiority.[137] Abolishing a sense of inferiority represented the necessary first step to reaching a higher plane of spirituality, which would in turn translate into concrete political and social changes. To that end, education became the primary emphasis within their feminism. Reviving the modest proposals put forth by the Laparra sisters a generation earlier in *El Ideal*, Rodríguez López advocated for accessible education for all Guatemalans, which would in turn elevate all women and restore their civic and legal rights.[138] She wrote in *Vida*: "Women continue to be attached to ignorance; their emancipation is necessary. Feminism will make women become conscious by obtaining an adequate education, and they will be prepared for a much more ambitious future."[139] In contrast to some of their working-class peers of the 1920s, the group never advocated for women's suffrage, believing that women were not ready to participate politically due to a lack of self-awareness and education. Rodríguez López was, however, of the opinion that Guatemalan women would eventually find their way to politics.[140]

One of the critical distinctions between the women of the SGM and the Laparra sisters lay in the social position each of these generations occupied. Although the SGM reflected a deep concern for working-class and poor women, the women themselves represented the upper middle class and the elite of Guatemalan society, and most of their social critique was directed toward their own social class. Unlike the vast majority of Guatemalan women, these elite women had access to education and benefited directly from Guatemala's inequitable class structure, a privilege they frequently acknowledged. Expressing frustration over her peers' reticence to take advantage of their educational opportunities, Rodríguez López criticized even her own mother, whom she once described as "a peacock, who never emerged from her boudoir until eleven o'clock in the morning."[141] Colleague

FIGURE 1.1 Rosa Rodríguez López. *Studium*, 1921.

and writer Martha Josefina Herrera noted ironically that nowhere was the need for education more evident than within Guatemala's elite circles: "Although women might be able to dance beautifully, move within elite social circles, and be polite, they neither read nor study."[142] For too long, she claimed, women had been raised to consider ignorance a virtue and had been discouraged from earning even an elementary education. "Nice" women raised "nice" children, but how did this help bring civilization to the nation? She concluded that women without a moral or civic conscience produced mediocre children. In a culture where motherhood represented the apex of a woman's life, the SGM exposed the privilege of the elite class to delegate even this most sacred task to others. Rosa Rodríguez López minced no words in her accusation that elite women did not even do their job as mothers, "abandoning [their children] to the stupid servant for a life of frivolity or laziness."[143] Rodríguez López's harsh statement about servants reflected her evolving feminism and perspective on class, ethnicity, and gender.[144] While she would sacrifice everything for the labor rights of the working class in the United States during the 1930s and 1940s, at this young age, her ideals were still in a formative stage, challenged by the interactions of class and ethnicity. The feminist position of women in the SGM during the 1920s did not include the cadre of uneducated indigenous domestic workers responsible for raising the children of the middle and upper classes. However, as their continued work and writing demonstrate, the class and gendered critiques of some within the SGM evolved to include ethnicity, the first hints of which would appear in the journal *Nosotras*, published by Luz Valle during the 1930s.

Despite the relative modesty of the Sociedad's calls for reform, backlash to their feminism came swiftly from within their own intellectual circle, where male members remained firmly entrenched in traditional patriarchal mores.

Dr. José Epaminondas Quintana held a great deal of influence in the capital city as a physician, and he supported many of the social reform groups such as the Sociedad Protectora del Niño, holding medical seminars for women on health and child care. However, he maintained that education for women must remain within the bounds of a maternal philosophy: "Women represent the receptacle for men's seed and they must not lose their femininity or their piety, tenderness, and impulsiveness."[145] Rodríguez López and her colleagues anticipated this narrow, classic argument, assuring their male peers that they had no intention of destroying the family.[146] Quintana's insistence that women existed for men's biological imperative was dogma that remained fundamentally undisturbed by these nascent feminist movements and reflected the dominant ideology of the middle and educated urban classes. This opposition from their own social circles would continue to be one of the greatest obstacles for urban ladinas throughout the next several decades.

While the majority of the Sociedad Gabriela Mistral's feminism remained within the realm of idealism, the short-lived organization left a practical legacy that would fundamentally alter the women's movement for the next several decades. Concerned with the intellectual poverty of their peers, they created a library, run by Dolores Ramírez Fontecha, designed to provide women with a wide range of literary and philosophical works. This modest endeavor immediately came under criticism, and the women had to justify the library's creation by employing the popular Liberal sentiment that educated women resulted in educated children. Access to books would allow women to bring both their hearts and their intelligence to the role of motherhood. The SGM also started a weekend school for women in the office of the national paper *El Imparcial* through their connection Luz Valle. The Escuela de Artes y Oficios Femeniles was designed to provide young women with a practical business education, the new cutting edge in Guatemala.[147] Their primary contribution, however, was their involvement in the successful campaign that opened up the Universidad de San Carlos de Guatemala to women. This singular achievement shifted the subsequent trajectory of the urban ladina movement because women such as Graciela Quan Valenzuela were now able to receive law degrees at the university, Quan Valenzuela ultimately shaping the successful argument for suffrage. Following this remarkable success, the Sociedad Gabriela Mistral faded from public view with the departure of Rosa Rodríguez López for Mexico City in early 1926. Several of the founding members, including Luz Valle, maintained the organization's ideals through Valle's journal, which emerged just a few years later.[148]

The last attempt to create a sustained debate on women's suffrage during the 1920s took place during the same year that Rosa Rodríguez López left Guatemala. Suffragists from the working class and remnants of the Sociedad Gabriela Mistral continued to press for gender reforms in education and labor. On the whole, the suffragists argued that women were not indifferent to political events, because politics penetrated the home and the workplace.[149] In late November 1926, an organization calling itself the Liga Nacional once again openly argued for women's suffrage, joining a chorus of voices emerging from the pages of the national papers.[150] Although the idea surfaced briefly, it had gained enough strength by the end of the year for José de Prado to ask whether feminism had arrived in Guatemala.[151] These ideas were quickly subsumed by the emergence of the Jorge Ubico regime, and Prado's question would not be publicly answered until 1944.

Access to education had represented one of the core concerns for urban ladinas, and through the Generación del 20 they participated in the regeneration of educational reform. The reality of Estrada Cabrera's empty rhetoric was evident through the generalized lack of access to education, low attendance, and dearth of qualified teachers that characterized the Guatemalan educational system. In fact, teaching was not listed as an occupation in national censuses throughout the Estrada Cabrera dictatorship. In 1921, Guatemala had only 1,134 female teachers in the entire country, 356 of whom worked in the municipality of Guatemala City. Of this number, only 445 held normal school degrees, a mere 15 percent of the teaching population. In other words, out of a total of just over 3,000 teachers, more than 2,652 teachers, male and female, were appointed to their positions without even minimum qualifications.[152] With a national illiteracy rate of almost 87 percent (a very slight improvement over the 1893 statistic of 88.63 percent), it is hardly surprising that only 41,162 students were registered in schools nationwide. The urban areas boasted a slightly more positive rate of literacy. In the central zone, in three of the larger urban areas (Guatemala City, Chimaltenango, and Sacatepéquez), literacy for women was 32 percent, an improvement over the national average of 12 percent (out of a total of 149,550 women over the age of seven, 47,612 were literate; see table 1.1).[153] Only 2,133 students attended all other national education institutions in the country, including secondary schools, normal schools, special schools, and professional centers.[154] Consequently, reforms focused on increasing the number of schools, along with centers available for teacher training.

The populist educational ideals of Mexican educator José Vasconcelos coincided well with the predilection for teosofía among ladinos and ladinas, and intellectual reformers integrated these two diverse influences to address Guatemala's multifaceted educational crisis. A Central American Teachers' Conference held in 1920 in Guatemala City set the stage for reforms adopted by the governments of Herrera, Orellana, and Chacón.[155] Several initiatives also enrolled poor and working-class women in literacy courses through innovative programs and night schools. Founded by the Federation of University Students in Guatemala City in April 1923, the Universidad Popular was designed to combat illiteracy, disseminate the principles of science for practical purposes, improve the social education of individuals, and teach the principles of sanitation, hygiene, and personal health. Although Ubico closed the university in 1932, its ideals remained alive, and it reopened in October 1944.[156] In order to improve pedagogical methods, a contest was held in the capital city to send teachers to study overseas; future revolutionary president Juan José Arévalo was among the three successful candidates sent to Argentina.[157] Although modest, education reforms during the 1920s created substantial improvements in the actual number of additional schools along with an increase in the number of children attending school. In 1927 (the last statistics available for the decade), the minister of public education reported that 103,859 children were enrolled in primary school, with 80,997 in attendance.[158] Despite continued high truancy rates, the numbers clearly indicate a significant shift. In centers of higher education, 3,729 students were reported to be enrolled in secondary, normal, and special schools. Altogether, this totaled 107,588 students, with 84,118 in actual attendance.[159] The absence of reporting on university attendance is explained by the fact the Universidad de San Carlos de Guatemala was only reopened on January 15, 1928.[160]

The second aspect of educational reform focused on the nature of education and how it should be delivered to children. The prevailing sentiment that the classroom represented merely the extension of the home remained entrenched within the state and society, which facilitated the continuation of women teachers. The few references to this subject in the available sources focused not on

TABLE 1.1 National Literacy Rates in 1920[1]

	LITERATE	ILLITERATE	TOTAL	% LITERATE OVER 7
Women	95,677	709,737	805,414	11.9
Men	112,732	666,081	778,813	14.5

1. Dirección General de Estadística, *Censo de la República de Guatemala, 1921*, 71. These calculations are for Guatemalans over the age of seven years.

whether women should receive an education, but rather for what purpose and in what manner it should be imparted.[161] There was a generalized consensus on the benefits of educating women among those Guatemalans who addressed the issue. Even those skeptics who were hesitant about the integration of women into the university saw the danger of denying them access to education, believing this to be the underlying cause of the rise of feminism.[162] For these opponents, education became an instrument against the rise of a Guatemalan feminist movement. The editor of *El Imparcial*, however, argued that the difficult realities created for women by spousal abandonment or death necessitated increased access to education. Educated single mothers who could financially support themselves were beneficial not only to their own family but to society at large.[163] For many educational leaders, significant fear remained over the exact nature of education for women, a fear that would be assuaged by Jorge Ubico's expansive reentrenchment of traditional gender norms in the education system during the 1930s. The tension between these two perspectives remained fundamentally unresolved until the mid-twentieth century.

The growing intellectual shift to integrate teosofía with the secularization of education promoted by leaders such as Vasconcelos in the urban teaching core was reflected in a column written by María Teresa Llardén de Molina in *El Imparcial*.[164] Although the column ran for only a few months, Llardén de Molina represented those Guatemalan teachers who believed in a separation of education from the religious influences of Catholicism, creating a pedagogy influenced by scientific rather than religious principles.[165] Llardén de Molina was a passionate advocate for education, believing that, next to food, it represented the principal necessity of life.[166] Her column explored such diverse topics as children and the movies, new methods of instruction (including alternative settings such as the outdoors), and a variety of historical subjects.[167] She was the first educator to promote a bachelor's degree program, and to that end, she founded a preparatory school, the Escuela Preparatoria, in 1918.[168] Her school took in students from seven to nineteen years of age. Llardén de Molina did not, however, live to see the first group of students graduate, dying in 1924. Her daughters took over the leadership of the school, first Elisa Molina Llardén de Farner, and then Clara Molina Llardén in 1927.[169] Reminiscent of Vicenta Laparra de la Cerda, María Teresa Llardén de Molina took advantage of a vacuum in the education system to initiate change on her own terms. While the paucity of quality educational institutions can be interpreted as symptomatic of government neglect, the situation also created an opportunity for enterprising urban ladinas to initiate their own centers. Women such as Llardén de Molina seized the opportunity presented by the great chasm in education and in so doing broke through significant barriers for women. Years later, on the twenty-fifth anniversary of her directorship of the school, daughter Clara Molina Llardén attributed both her own personal success and the school's success to the vision of her mother, María Teresa Llardén de Molina.[170]

The ladina reformers who shared Llardén de Molina's educational perspective faced several challenges to educational reform. First, the removal of education from within the bounds of religion created fear over the possible loss of morality among the nation's young people. Articulating the fears of many men and women, J. F. Juárez Muñoz expressed concern over the lack of moral instruction in the current curriculum.[171] He linked contemporary reforms in education with such "social ills" as the rise in divorce rates. The perception that the secularizing influences in the educational system represented a moral danger to children remained throughout the 1920s, although it did not dominate the national dialogue.[172] A second major concern was the issue of coeducation. Education remained segregated by gender during this period, but under the proposed reforms, children were to be placed together. Those unhappy with coeducational schools believed that the dignity of women could only be maintained by gender separation.[173]

The educational reforms undertaken during the 1920s concretized the ideals of the Liberal modernizing state and essentially removed the teaching core from the auspices of Catholicism. Improving access to education for the working class demonstrated a continued alliance between intellectual ladinos and ladinas, an element that would prove to be significant throughout the Ubico dictatorship and the revolution. Despite the imperfect nature of the reforms, the number of teachers in Guatemala increased dramatically, creating a professional and educated path for urban ladinas. Teachers such as María Teresa Llardén de Molina established women as public figures with some social authority, a trend that would only increase in the following decades. Although it represents a pivotal era for the fomentation of intellectual ideas among the urban ladina community, when the 1920s are examined from a gendered perspective, the reforms are modest at best. While the increase of funding for education and a new emphasis on basic health care benefited all women, the modest increase in literacy rates from 1920 to 1940 reveals only limited success in education reform. Even the Sociedad Gabriela Mistral believed that the lack of educational opportunities made Guatemalan women unprepared for political participation. This period, however, allowed for the establishment of reform ideas, which was one of its most important contributions to Guatemalan society. As educators, women played a key role in the establishment of educational reforms, influenced the pedagogical models implemented, and in some cases created institutions based on their educational standards.

Until 1920, the paucity of resources directed at education paled in comparison with the utter neglect of health care and social welfare programs; Estrada Cabrera had not considered a healthy population to be a vital measurement of modernity. In contrast to other Latin American Liberal states that had embraced both education and social reform within their modernization projects, Guatemala had not. Consequently, seizing the sociopolitical openness of the Herrera government, members of the Generación del 20 initiated a wide array of social reforms. The ideological framework for these reforms was a complex intersection of genuine concern, class prejudice, and *puericultura*, a pervasive ideology throughout Latin America. In a manner reminiscent of their educational endeavors during the 1880s, urban ladinas now took it upon themselves to create the city's first social reform network.

The desamortización during the 1870s and 1880s had removed a majority of the Catholic sisters who had provided the only social safety nets in Guatemala City (the orphanage Hospicio Nacional Centro Educativo, discussed in chapter 7, was the one exception). Although health statistics are sketchy at best and fairly inaccurate for the period, social indicators such as infant mortality rates from later periods reveal a country bereft of health care.[174] Medical journals such as *Studium* carried anecdotal evidence regarding the grim implications of poverty in the capital city. In 1922, *Studium* noted that 15,000 women had died in childbirth or because of pregnancy complications, representing 1 out of every 150 pregnancies. Several studies carried out several decades later during the 1940s confirmed that more than 96 percent of children in Guatemala City never received health care due to the insufficient salaries of poor working women.[175] The lack of attention given to public health by the state is evidenced by the simple fact that there was no government agency for health until 1931, and health concerns fell under the jurisdiction of the Ministry of Government and Justice.

The primary impetus for social reforms came from the physicians, lawyers, and intellectuals in the Generación del 20, and they embraced *puericultura*, the dominant ideology influencing social reformers across Latin America. The puericultura movement in Latin America emphasized that the strength of a nation lay in the physical health of its families. This regeneration included the need to educate mothers in all aspects of child care, a revitalization of moral values, education, and the incorporation of the socially marginalized.[176] There is a critical caveat here, however. As Donna Guy points out, child welfare was championed through family reform and not through or for the empowerment of women.

> Male professionals viewed the family as a terrain that offered themselves and the state new worlds to shape and influence. They ignored the specific roles for mothers and treated the family as a unit based upon a sanitised poor child monitored by middle-class physicians. They considered private charities, and municipal and national governments as a source of money and power that would enable them to create the modern working-class family that would supply the future generation of citizens. If the state intervened early enough, they reasoned, levels of infant mortality would decline and, equally important, the family would serve as the socialising base of the Americas. Such a mission was so important that only men could undertake it.[177]

The particular gendered constructs within this ideology complemented the class and gendered norms of the dominant Guatemalan reformers, who embraced puericultura enthusiastically. The benefits of any efforts were undeniable, but when conducted within gendered and class-based constructs, they effectively alienated those with knowledge and ability such as local midwives and health practitioners and placed traditionally educated men at the helm, endowing them with both moral superiority and educational authority.

The center of this multifaceted initiative was the Sociedad Protectora del Niño (SPN), a project established and financially supported by a small group of urban ladinas. Established on October 31, 1920, the SPN was founded by three ladinas, María Herrera de Aschkel, Marta Escobar de Richardson, and Rosa de Mora, who created a network of orphanages, lunch programs, health-care centers, and other programs for poor women and their children.[178] Three primary centers worked together to provide health services, education, food, and shelter for Guatemala City's poorest children. The three centers were Casa de Palomo, directed by Enriqueta Haas; Casa de Candelaria, directed by Luz de León Cofiño; and Casa de Santuario, directed by Esmeralda B. García.[179] An annual bulletin, *El Niño*, reported on the activities and progress of the SPN. The female-centered initiative that created the SPN was mitigated by the highly masculinized realm of the medical community, which marginalized women's traditional authority in the home and family. In spite of the patriarchal tenor of the reform movement and more generally the capital city itself, these women initiated the largest social reform project in Guatemala at the time. The ability to practice leadership and to develop pedagogy regarding child care and family health attracted a network of women who remained somewhat independent of male authority. In so doing, the center became the laboratory in which the expansive social ideals and maternal feminisms of the revolutionary era were born.

In a world bereft of professional opportunities for women (see table 1.2), the opportunity for volunteerism evidenced by the SPN offered them a chance to exercise authority within a semiautonomous milieu to affect real change. Unlike many female reformers in other Latin American countries, these women were not medical professionals themselves but responded to the obvious needs of the poor as middle- and upper-class volunteers. Deemed to be an appropriate activity for women, caring for orphans and impoverished families facilitated the rise of urban ladinas in their struggle to support those caught living in the grip of intense poverty. Here again, Donna Guy notes that the perceived gender-appropriate nature of their work gave these women the social authority to act.[180] Although their efforts did not generate any shifts in gender norms, the institutions they established provided two decades of experience that would flourish during the revolutionary period, an era in which social welfare reformers assumed an unprecedented profile. While these modest social reforms emerged from a genuine concern, they also flew in the face of a state whose function was dependent upon a deeply hierarchical class structure. These modest efforts produced a new identity for the new reformers, and they formed a social network in which health-care concerns and contemporary social reform ideals could be discussed, if not always acted upon. With few exceptions, these same women emerged as the most visible feminists of the 1920s, or those with a feminist consciousness, which in turn also solidified the strong maternalistic vein in the Guatemalan feminism movement, shifting its identity away from the comprehensive idealism of women such as Rosa Rodríguez López and the Sociedad Gabriela Mistral.

The life of one of the SPN's founders, Rosa de Mora, is indicative of the potential of such volunteerism. As the spouse of well-known physician and active member of the Generación del 20 Federico Mora, Rosa de Mora would have been well aware of the health issues facing children, and she played a prominent role in the elite charity circles of Guatemala City. Along with her charity work, Mora was involved in a wide variety of social and political activities throughout the 1930s, 1940s, and 1950s. Rejecting the political feminism of the Alianza Femenina Guatemalteca, Mora represented a maternal feminism that most urban ladinas could endorse. Her reputation continued to grow throughout the revolutionary decade, and in the months following the overthrow of Jacobo Árbenz, Mora successfully ran for political office. In 1956, she became the first woman deputy in the Guatemalan Congress.

The SPN functioned as the educational and health-care nexus for a complex network of associations throughout the capital city. Its three founders worked closely with a variety of institutions to initiate public health programs for Guatemala's most disadvantaged. Physicians from the Rockefeller Foundation paid frequent visits to the Sociedad Protectora del Niño, providing medical advice and training on child care to its staff.[181] The SPN worked closely with male members of the Generación del 20, inviting the assistance of Drs. Federico Mora and Epaminondas Quintana, who lectured on maternal health care and hygiene for children.[182] The primary literary vehicles for health reform were the journals *Studium* and *Vida* and, to a lesser extent, the national press. During the first half of the 1920s, information on topics ranging from personal hygiene to venereal diseases to the benefits of exercise was distributed through the newspapers and student medical journals such as *Studium*, which was edited by Drs. Mora and Epaminondas Quintana.

The first Central American Child's Welfare Congress, held in Costa Rica in September 1921, offered the Guatemalan reformers the opportunity to learn some of the contemporary formal scientific principles around child welfare reform. The Costa Rica congress focused on four broad campaigns: the first was on childhood diseases, the second on the sanitation conditions of households, the third on nutritional needs, and the fourth on the general welfare of children.[183] The concerns of Guatemalan elite Catholic women's associations integrated the interrelated matters of health care and education into the contemporary educational pedagogy on mothers and children, or puericultura, forming an informal network throughout the 1920s.[184]

While concern for the health of women and children was apparent in the measures introduced during the 1920s, the mandates for change still came from male doctors and reformers from Guatemala and the United States. This particular characteristic of the health-care reform had important consequences for women. Reformers representing the Generación del 20 wrote extensively on health care for working-class and poor women and children, resulting in campaigns for vaccinations and basic hygiene practices. For example, the Lázaro Chacón presidency approved an act regulating the practice of the medical profession on March 26, 1928.[185] Only midwives who had received their training and accreditation from the one medical facility in Guatemala were legally allowed to practice.[186] In order to monitor the situation more carefully, doctors created a guide for expectant mothers and urged them to register the births of their children.[187] The restriction placed on the exercise of midwifery had a particular consequence for poor and working-class women, effectively marginalizing traditional forms of knowledge. As Donna Guy notes, all over Latin America, midwives and female family members or friends delivered far more babies than trained male physicians. "By submitting themselves to male professionals, women would be bypassing traditional forms of information regarding pregnancy and depending directly on the doctor."[188] This particular group associated with the SPN bought into this elite view, while the later social reformers under Arévalo would challenge these traditional forms of authority to include class.[189]

As a reforming ideology, puericultura permeated Guatemala City's education and social reform community. Based on the notion that educating women in child care benefited the entire nation, the reform community encouraged puericultura to permeate the broader urban educational landscape. Through innovative programs such as literacy programs and night schools, they disseminated puericultura to the poor and working-class women of Guatemala City. Founded by the Federation of University Students in April 1923, the Popular University combated illiteracy, disseminated the principles of science for practical purposes, improved the social education of individuals, and taught the principles of sanitation, hygiene, and personal health. A section for women was established, offering elementary and advanced courses in both academic and commercial subjects, including physical education, hygiene, and the care of children. By the end of its first year, the university had graduated a class of twenty women in infant care.[190] Along with a dental school and a school of nursing, the School of Medicine and Surgery of the University of San Carlos opened a school for midwives offering three-year courses.[191] The school for midwives focused on the educational principles of puericultura, attempting to reach into indigenous communities on the margins of the city and into the rural areas.

To disseminate this information, several conferences were held during the 1920s. Working with the Sociedad Gabriela Mistral, Dr. Epaminondas Quintana held a conference on puericultura in 1926. Believing that ignorance was the primary factor perpetuating Guatemala's numerous health problems, physicians and social reformers agreed that education was a necessity rather than a privilege. Of the many concerns related to poverty and family health Quintana raised, women's maternal health dominated the conversations. Quintana's curriculum stressed medical care and education before pregnancy to ensure healthy mothers and infants. He argued that both women and men should get medical certificates of health before marriage, an emphasis on both partners being unusual for the time. He cautioned women to have their children before the age of twenty-five, as this improved the chance of healthy newborns. Relatively conservative with regard to gender issues, Quintana urged women to treat their body as a temple, focusing on the beauty of platonic love rather than the realm of sexual love. Quintana also worked to enact legislation with regard to puericultura. He urged the Guatemalan government to enact labor laws to protect pregnant women and abandoned children. At a minimum, working women should be allowed three weeks off both before and after birth to rest and take care of their newborns.

TABLE 1.2 Occupational Profile for Women[1]

	% of Total Economic Output		% of Women Involved in Industry	Total Number of Women Involved in Industry	
	1893	1921	1921	1921	1940
Agriculture	67.78	68.32	0.07	2,597	7,169
Pottery	0.40	0.44	86	1,964	2,926*
Alcoholic beverages	8.00	0.06	52	295	59
Food	1.26	1.45	45	3,388	30,131[2]
Clothing	3.10	2.62	72	9,754	10,589*
Manufacturing	13.00	0.42	87	1,906	not listed
Cakes, pastry, and candy	12.00	0.1	88	447	included in food category in 1940
Domestic services	11.97	12.33	97	62,020	838,101[3]
Tobacco	1.30	0.5	99	2,621	1,165
Weaving	4.61	2.81	53	7,766	15,549*
Teaching				1,134	3,083*

*Notes an increase from the 1921 census.

1. Dirección General de Estadística, *Censo de la República de Guatemala, 1921*, 71. These calculations are for Guatemalans over the age of seven years.

2. The food, and cakes, pastry, and candy categories for 1921 are combined in the 1940 census.

3. The striking increase in the domestic service category for 1940 is explained by the inclusion of 753,591 housewives (in addition to 84,510 actual domestic workers) counted in the census, reflective of Ubico's self-attributed role as defender of female honor.

Despite a trend in intellectual circles to oppose US imperialism, the systemic lack of health-care resources required that social reformers align themselves with those who had the necessary resources. Founded on April 22, 1923, the women's auxiliary of the Red Cross of Guatemala was formed under the leadership of Anita R. Espinoza.[192] It, too, supported orphanages for homeless children and disseminated health-care information through lectures, films, printed matter, and personal visits to instruct parents on childhood diseases. The Red Cross played a major role in Guatemala's health care, as it reorganized and extended health institutions, a lepers' home, and a mental health facility. By the middle of the decade, it had also initiated a hygiene campaign, opened a tuberculosis ward in the Guatemala City general hospital, improved sanitary conditions and provided proper drainage for poor sectors of Guatemala City, and founded a children's home. In July 1926, the Red Cross and a young physicians' society divided Guatemala City into sections for the purpose of administering vaccinations. The government embraced these civil efforts, bringing both the Red Cross and the Sociedad Protectora del Niño under the administrative scrutiny of the Public Charity Department. For their efforts, both the SPN and the Red Cross received government funds, with the Red Cross receiving 15,000 quetzals monthly.[193]

Conclusion

The nature of Liberal modernization fundamentally shaped the roots of the Guatemalan women's movement, as they were brought into this national project through clearly demarcated social and political boundaries. A small group of urban ladinas identified the contradictions in modernization to create spaces in which to act upon their ideals. The first voices to emerge with a feminist consciousness helped to establish Guatemala City as a literary center where urban literate women wrote and published for one another as an expression of self-fulfillment and political resistance. In so doing, women such as Vicenta Laparra de la Cerda and Jesús Laparra created a feminist platform unique for their time period. Although Liberal modernization had been conceived of as a fundamentally masculine project, these women were not content with merely being recipients of its limited benefits, transforming it into a rhetorical foundation for ladina feminism.

Women reemerged in definable movements during the 1920s, as cross-class affiliations among women engaged in a wide variety of social and political activities, gaining an unprecedented national profile. Their active role in the demonstrations against Manuel Estrada Cabrera earned women the respect of many men in the Catholic political parties and labor unions. Their heroic efforts were rewarded with the legislative introduction of suffrage by political leaders of the triumphant Partido Unionista in both May 1920 and January 1921. Although women's unprecedented access to government channels through their spouses and female affiliates of the Partido Unionista was swiftly thwarted with the overthrow of Carlos Herrera in 1921, this singular historical moment afforded women and their allies the opportunity to promote suffrage for the first time.

The 1920s offered opportunities to organize and integrate new ideologies, and those in the upper class seized the opportunity to address the abysmal health and education conditions of the poorest Guatemalans. The precursor of the modern social reform movement, the Sociedad Protectora del Niño established the first permanent women's network based on social concern for poor children and mothers. This social charity formed the backbone of national health care for this sector of the Guatemalan population and brought women to the forefront of a national project. The founders of the SPN, Rosa de Mora, María Herrera de Aschkel, and Marta Escobar de Richardson, used their elite status to create a woman-centered association focused on the social concerns of the poor fused with notions of feminism and maternal social charity. As such, the SPN became the model for the orphanages and nutrition centers established in the 1940s and 1950s.

Guatemala's first feminist organization emerged by the mid-1920s to publicly challenge patriarchal ideas regarding women in education and the home. The ability to control one's own mind became of paramount importance for this generation of Guatemalan feminists, an understandable emphasis given their recent emergence from a twenty-two-year dictatorship. As a result, educational reform and access to it became a central mantra in their demands to the state and to society in general, demands that continue to the present day. While the Sociedad Gabriela Mistral was short lived, it was through this vehicle that women challenged gender norms in a sustained effort for the first time since the 1880s. Despite their modest calls for educational reform, the patriarchal backlash was a reminder of the challenges ahead.

The reform ideals that dominated the 1920s were abruptly ended in 1931 with the presidency of Jorge Ubico. For fourteen years Ubico ran Guatemala autocratically, overturning virtually all of the social reforms related to education and health care. No longer able to sustain a formal feminist network, women of the Sociedad Gabriela Mistral reverted to the tactics employed during the Estrada

Cabrera era, maintaining their ideas through literary societies and social interests, not perceived to be a threat by the Ubico administration. Dormant through fourteen years of dictatorship, the ideas nurtured by this small group of women represented the genesis of another, more radical time of reform just two decades later. Perhaps the most important contributions of these pioneers were those least tangible. These women succeeded in creating a literary community, albeit a small one, where none had previously existed. They publicly defined women as both intelligent and capable, and eager to participate in the modernization of society. Their most telling accomplishment may simply be, however, that they represented a vanguard of educated women who in turn educated an entire generation of young women through their schools, normal schools, and journals. In 1943, a teacher by the name of Encarnación Nufio Duarte celebrated a career that had spanned fifty years. In an interview with *El Imparcial*, Duarte named Rafaela del Águila, Vicenta Laparra de la Cerda's journalist colleague and friend, as an important influence in her teaching career.[194] Laparra de la Cerda's dream that her ideas would sustain women in future years indeed had come true.[195] In 1945, the Vicenta Laparra de la Cerda School would open in Guatemala City to honor her life, work, and memory.

DICTATING FEMINISMS
WOMEN AND GENDER IN UBICO'S GUATEMALA, 1930–1944

The spirit, the intellect, has no sex.
—*Luz Valle*, Nosotras, *February 1932*

Beyond the transcendental mission [motherhood] women play,
eminent women are working, studying, and sacrificing
for the benefit of humanity.
—*Luz Valle*, El Imparcial, *June 27, 1936*

Under the shadow of fear and silence for fourteen years,
Today we raise the banner of our patriotism, intact.
—*Gloria Menéndez Mina*, Azul, *June 1944*

Following a decade of moderate sociopolitical reforms in Guatemala City, Jorge Ubico's election to office in 1930 ushered in the harshest dictatorship in Guatemala's long history of dictatorial regimes. In the midst of a treacherous political milieu during which Ubico repressed all manner of intellectual autonomy and journalistic effort, two women in Guatemala City published journals specifically for the educated ladina. Despite Ubico's attempt to attain complete sociopolitical control and alienate Guatemalans through fear and ignorance, writers Luz Valle and Gloria Menéndez Mina successfully maintained a community of intellectuals, teachers, and social reformers in the capital and other urban areas across the country through their journals. Valle and Menéndez Mina walked a fine line between intellectual autonomy and boundaries created by Ubico's reconfiguration of Guatemalan society in order to carve out a space for sociopolitical resistance. In so doing, their journals *Nosotras* and *Azul* underscore the paradoxes present in Ubico's gendered socioeconomic policies. Just how successful they were became evident in the days leading up to and following the 1944 revolution, as the teaching community that had coalesced around their journals became one of the pivotal forces in the overthrow of Ubico in 1944.

Just how Luz Valle and Gloria Menéndez Mina were able to publish in an otherwise repressive state system is directly attributable to the nature of Ubico's gendered socioeconomic policies, established in the face of burgeoning global depression in the early 1930s. His gendered manipulation of Guatemala's social structure in fact represented a broader gendered discourse being shaped by new social politics across Latin America, as leaders sought to place men in the workplace and women in the home during the depression era.[1] In an effort to stem increasingly popular views of feminism among urban ladinas, Ubico incorporated and reframed feminist ideals into a national gendered model. To that end, new laws reinforced a national patriarchy, equally marginalizing all women under the law, regardless of ethnicity or class. He formalized the role of women in the home, rhetorically assuming the role as husband and father of the nation. The state appropriated the role of defender of women's honor, building on the overwhelming sentiment of Guatemalan men that women belonged in the home.

This particular gendered structure created some unexpected space within an otherwise repressive milieu. The reversal of the modest gains achieved during the 1920s drew women who might otherwise have been content with the status quo into a position of critique. Their marginalization from the formal labor market and any political participation facilitated the ability of many urban women to question their life conditions and historical invisibility as both social and political actors.[2] This growing gendered consciousness was facilitated primarily by two journals, *Nosotras* and *Azul*, published throughout the majority of the Ubico era. As editors, Luz Valle and Gloria Menéndez Mina positioned themselves against Ubico vis-à-vis two of the most critical social avenues available to urban ladinas, namely the educational system and the development of a modest, internalized, feminist self-consciousness. Expressed in albeit muted tones, these journals sustained a feminine and sometimes feminist culture, advocating for improved educational opportunities for girls and women, international cooperation in matters of global peace, and at times even the legal equality of women. Although the ideas expressed in the journals regarding women and feminism remained primarily within Ubico's gendered parameters, the writers successfully created a network of politically and socially minded women. Employing what Erin Finzer refers to as a "mask during the decades of repressive dictatorship in Guatemala,"[3] these writers became highly adept at writing and reading between the lines in order to comply with their restrictive political milieu. Just how critical these journals were in creating and maintaining a cohesive community dedicated to women's concerns became evident in the weeks and months following Ubico's resignation at the end of June 1944. While Valle and Menéndez Mina could not have foreseen the impact of their work, the journals effectively articulated and preserved ideals of the 1920s that reemerged in July 1944, determining the fundamental feminist trajectory of the revolutionary decade within the urban ladina community. Therefore, investigating their work offers a rare opportunity to understand how they successfully navigated through a political dictatorship, a historical period in Guatemala that has remained relatively ignored.

The Ubico era (1930–1944) remains understudied due in large part to a lack of primary sources.[4] Jorge Ubico's intellectual repression is evident by the profound lack of primary sources created by journalists, intellectuals, and even the literary community during his tenure. His repression of these communities has created an aversion among Guatemalan intellectuals to study his presidency. Semibiographical works by Carlos Samayoa Chinchilla and Rafael Arévalo Martínez illustrate this historiographic tendency. In a well-established pattern, these writers examine the health-care and educational policies, and the politics, of the 1920s and then catapult over the Ubico era to contextualize the reemergence of these policies as revolutionary ideals following his June resignation.[5] When the Ubico era is noted in historical studies, Guatemalans emphasize the political repression and social fear. The only two monographs to study this period date back to the 1970s, in which Joseph A. Pitti and Kenneth Grieb provide critical economic and political analysis in a semibiographical approach.[6]

Two recent studies on modernity in Guatemala City have broken the long historical silence on the capital, integrating the Ubico era in expansive analyses. As mentioned in the introduction, J. T. Way's recent study on globalization and development in Guatemala City as well as Michael D. Kirkpatrick's "Optics and the Culture of Modernity in Guatemala City since the Liberal Reforms" explore economic and intellectual developments over the *longue durée* of the Liberal state since its definitive rise to power in 1871.[7] Their social and political analysis provides critical background in which to contextualize the activities of urban ladinas during the 1930s.

Although studies focused on Guatemala City expose deep resistance to the Ubico regime, analysis from rural Guatemala suggests a more complex experience of the Ubico era. Cindy Forster and Greg Grandin offered the earliest analyses of the rural areas in *The Time of Freedom* and *The Blood of Guatemala*,

Dictating Feminisms 71

respectively.⁸ Although both historians focus on the brutal labor practices experienced by the rural population (which was and remains primarily indigenous), their analyses demonstrate a more complex relationship between Ubico and rural and indigenous communities. Julie Gibbings confirms this complexity, demonstrating how critical the political intimacy Ubico established with the Q'eqchi' Maya in the Alta Verapaz region was to the legitimization of his presidency in some rural areas.⁹

Analysis of Valle's and Menéndez Mina's work in Guatemala City both contradicts this rural experience with Ubico as well as offers a window into the urban ladina experience with the dictatorship. The network of women responsible for producing these journals, along with their readership, cannot be labeled as a coherent movement or identifiable group. Rather, they shared their ideas outside of the public sphere, and any opinions voiced publicly in the journals were subdued, as if speaking through gritted teeth. In spite of the muted tone of their voices in these journals, and also because of it, their defensive strategies become evident during a time when few other Guatemalans recorded their thoughts. As Deniz Kandiyoti proposes, analyzing how women strategically navigated patriarchy represents a new entry point for examining its particular structure in a particular time period.¹⁰ *Nosotras* and *Azul* are valuable primary documents created in a context of intense intellectual and political repression; they offer the rare ability to trace the intellectual ideas of these ladinas during a period of silence.¹¹ These journals offered a critical literary and intellectual space not only for women, but for men as well. Future revolutionary politicians Carlos Manuel Pellecer and Juan José Orozco Posadas published articles in *Azul*, as well as future Nobel laureate Miguel Ángel Asturias.

The journals also introduced a gendered perspective to this unstudied era that parallels recent work by historian David Carey.¹² Focusing on the legal experiences of Kaqchikel women and men, Carey's analysis of laws regulating sex and gender roles through the late nineteenth and first half of the twentieth centuries examines the ways in which the legal system and society were permeated by patriarchal notions. His close reading of court documents also demonstrates how rural women navigated this complex legal terrain, in turn finding ways to circumvent patriarchal constraints intended to control them. While Ubico's state utilized laws to control them, rural and indigenous women nevertheless engaged the system to advocate for themselves and their children. Carey's conclusions regarding the self-determination of Kaqchikel women resonate with actions taken by urban ladinas. They, too, engaged the state, assuming their right to education and legal equality as citizens. Consequently, this study joins Carey's in furthering our understanding of women's experiences during a time of political repression from a variety of geo-ethnic and class positions.

Depressing Gender in 1930s Guatemala

Jorge Ubico's ascent to the presidency in 1930 was facilitated by his deep Liberal roots. The godson of president Justo Rufino Barrios (1873–1885), Ubico's father Arturo had served as president of the National Assembly for sixteen years.[13] Educated at the military academy, Jorge Ubico held a variety of political posts including governor of Alta Verapaz and member of the legislative assembly in the state of Amatitlán; he was a presidential candidate in 1922 following the military coup against Carlos Herrera y Luna. Losing the presidency to José María Orellano, Ubico was posted to the Secretariat of War, where he dealt harshly with political unrest, killing hundreds of political opponents during Orellana's presidency.[14] When President Lázaro Chacón suffered a stroke in December 1930, a brief battle for political control between political factions ensued. Ubico emerged victorious, winning the presidency with 605,841 votes to his opponent's zero.

Jorge Ubico's election to the presidency shifted the trajectory of the modest social, political, and economic reforms established during the 1920s. In the political spaces created by the Herrera presidency, labor expectations had erupted along with a growing discourse of social justice and democratic principles. Now faced with falling coffee prices, Ubico had to mollify these increasingly urgent voices with the stark reality of the burgeoning global depression. To create a palpable facade of democracy and economic modernity for Guatemala's North Atlantic trading partners, Ubico artfully reconfigured the nascent social reforms to suit his political agenda, fusing concepts of modernity, democracy, and fascism. To offset the authoritarian elements of his rule, Ubico cultivated his particular brand of totalitarian nationalism by metaphorically configuring Guatemala as one family with himself as father, assuming the nickname "Tata" throughout his presidency. Tata, however, did not treat his children equally. He reaffirmed the historically close relationship of the state with Guatemala's economic elite class while adopting a paternalistic attitude toward the rural and indigenous communities. Because those communities had been traditionally ignored or abused by the state, Ubico's personal appearances throughout rural Guatemala endeared the dictator to many Guatemalans over the next decade. The urban intellectual ladino and ladina middle class, however, experienced

Dictating Feminisms 73

the Ubico era in a fundamentally different way. Although Ubico's strict economic policies created unprecedented economic growth for the urban middle class, their high social and political expectations carried over from the 1920s remained unfulfilled. Consequently, in order to avoid the potential political threat posed by this dissatisfied social sector, Ubico chose to alienate them both intellectually and politically.

Ubico's campaign promise to restabilize the economy following the stock market crash of October 1929 was made more difficult with the 1930 drop in coffee prices. Countries like Guatemala that were dependent upon one or two primary agricultural products became particularly vulnerable to global price fluctuations and generally fared poorly. Since coffee and bananas represented 90 percent of the country's exports, scholars have generally concluded that Guatemala along with the rest of Central America suffered a severe economic decline. Coffee prices fell dramatically from $0.22 to $0.08 cents from 1929 to 1931, and the value of Guatemala's exports dropped by 40 percent from 1928 to 1932.[15] However, as economist Victor Bulmer-Thomas argues, while the Guatemalan and El Salvadoran economies fluctuated intensely, the impact across Central America was less severe than has generally been believed. Ubico's alignment with Guatemala's economic elite and his strict laws against state and local corruption mitigated the severity of the depression.[16] In addition, Ubico reestablished Guatemala's international credit and cultivated stronger business ties with the United States. As a result, the Guatemalan economy fared better than that of many Latin American regions during the global depression.

This economic stability came at a high political price, however, as Ubico rapidly bolstered his control through the reconstitution of all social, economic, and political laws. He maintained strict intellectual control by personally censoring all news; journalists preserved a modicum of intellectual autonomy only by reporting on the mundane, even as labor unions were abolished and workers persecuted.[17] Ubico's political repression was particularly ferocious, and those politicians who refused to comply with his legal revisions faced persecution or exile.[18] When he changed the constitution to allow for his continuous reelection, many Guatemalans fled the country, printing attacks against Ubico from Costa Rica and Mexico. Consequently, Ubico was able to amalgamate his political influence into a single political party ruling without opposition, the Liberal Progressive Party. When a popular revolt erupted in neighboring El Salvador, Ubico's fear of communism erupted into paranoia. In response to events in El Salvador, he had dozens of Guatemalan labor leaders suspected of collusion jailed and tortured. In September 1934, Ubico uncovered an apparent conspiracy against his presidency and had almost twenty men summarily executed.[19] No one seemed immune from this violent repression, and it ultimately reached the middle- and upper-class ladina community. Ubico's forces murdered hundreds of suspected political opponents during his first years in office, while many others spent the decade in prison.[20] The husband of the well-known literary figure Magdalena Spínola was personally assassinated by the president. Although Ubico directed most of his repression at his male political opponents, women were not immune from arrest for political and labor organizing.[21]

These repressive sociopolitical policies created an ambivalent attitude among Guatemala City residents. Ubico's harsh legal policies resulted in a severe penal system that discouraged even petty crime. As a result, in Zone One (the historic center of the city), doors could be left unlocked, and neighbors walked the streets at night without fear; residents later recalled this time with fondness, even if they did not support Ubico's political regime. This sense of safety is particularly poignant in contrast to the current levels of violence that make Guatemala City one of the most dangerous cities in the Western Hemisphere.[22] These same harsh policies also resulted in increased sociopolitical repression for the urban middle class, marginalizing them from centers of power and limiting their ability to create a viable political opposition. The modest democratic spaces of the 1920s had fostered a small but increasingly influential cadre of teachers, journalists, lawyers, and physicians, and as their numbers grew throughout the 1930s alongside a relatively strong economy, these contradictions generated a tension that would steadily increase as the decade progressed.[23]

While he alienated the urban middle class and forged economic bonds with the elite, Ubico adopted a paternalistic approach toward the rural and indigenous population. Although Ubico militarized the government in order to extend his authority into the rural areas, replacing department governors with loyal military officers, he adopted a personal approach with rural Guatemalans. His personalized visits have been immortalized by journalist Federico Hernández de León, who accompanied him throughout his travels.[24] During these personal encounters, Ubico would dispense legal advice and immediate justice, a practice endearing him to many in rural areas who had experienced the Guatemalan state as abusive and neglectful in equal measures. Simultaneously, however, Ubico established vagrancy laws in 1933 that required rural indigenous men to provide two weeks of involuntary service per year or be exempted by a payment of one quetzal per week. The consequences of such policies are evident in the contradictory opinions rural and indigenous communities continue to express about the Ubico era.[25] J. T. Way summarizes the contradictory effects of Ubico's policies on rural and indigenous communities in this way:

> The Ubico state mobilized modernist discourses and fascist forms of corporate socio-political organization while promoting a racist lord and peon economy. In short, totalitarianism, the agro-economy, the exploitation of Mayan and mestizo workers, and imperialism, itself steeped in racist ideology, all became written upon the landscape and embedded in the Guatemalan culture of development.[26]

Therefore, while the macro view painted Guatemala as economically stable during the depression, a perspective supported by Ubico's inaccurate census data, its effects on the working class were far less positive. The rapid decrease in coffee prices had a devastating impact on the rural and agriculturally dependent economy. Government expenditures were sliced in half, and workers in the rural areas and particularly in the volatile agricultural sector saw their wages fall by as much as 50 percent, creating a flood of migrants to the urban centers in search of employment.

Although the majority of these migrants were working-class men in search of alternatives to coffee and banana plantation work, a new sector of workers emerged from among these economic refugees: namely, the middle- and even lower upper-class women who joined the flood of new urban migrants. This cadre of young women with rural sensitivities entered Guatemala City's normal schools to train as teachers, one of the few economic avenues available to them. As a result of this shift, between 1920 and 1940, the number of female teachers countrywide almost tripled, with more than 1,200 female teachers in Guatemala City alone (see table 1.2).[27] Although these numbers appear rather small, in a country bereft of professional women, thousands of newly educated teachers had a palpable impact on the capital city. It was these women who were galvanized by the journals published by Luz Valle and Gloria Menéndez Mina, eventually coalescing into a cohesive, identifiable movement. One of these urban newcomers was María Chinchilla Recinos, whose eventual assassination by Ubico's military forces would galvanize the capital city against the dictator in 1944.[28]

The experience of the Muralles family exemplifies the socioeconomic transition of the depression era. Following the drop in coffee prices, the Muralles family lost their small coffee plantation and moved to the capital city. The daughters, Elisa Muralles Soto, Mélida Muralles, and Morelia Muralles, who had grown up amid privilege, now attended the Instituto Normal de Señoritas,

Belén, becoming teachers in order to financially support their parents. Due to marriage restrictions on teachers, they remained single throughout the Ubico era and eventually became part of the growing anti-Ubico movement among ladina teachers in the capital city. They participated in the teachers' march on June 25, 1944, and witnessed the murder of Chinchilla Recinos. Elisa Muralles Soto (the only sister to marry once it was permissible to do so) became politically involved, campaigning for presidential candidate Juan José Arévalo and cofounding one of the most important revolutionary political parties, the Frente Popular Libertador. In 2004, well into their eighties, all three sisters continued to live together in their parents' home in historic Zone One, having retired from lifelong teaching careers but remaining active in their parish working on behalf of women of all social classes.

In the face of this shifting profile of Guatemala City's labor force, Ubico reconfigured gendered social norms, simultaneously reasserting the traditional familial imaginary, positioning himself as the patriarchal figurehead of father, and concretizing patriarchy in Guatemalan society. In his imaginary, women existed only as spouse and mother, and he formalized the role of housewife as an occupation into national law and census data (see table 3.2). To solidify this subordinate position, constitutional reforms explicitly denied women any possibility of citizenship. Along with the change in constitutional language from "los guatemaltecos" to "los hombres," or men, in 1935, the country's national law explicitly stated that women's only rightful function in society remained within the family as vessels of reproduction.[29] Ubico co-opted the 1920s intellectual views on puericultura and social health education, legalizing prenuptial hygiene exams.[30] He legislated the exclusion of married women from the formal labor market, constituting their social role in the home. To ensure the generational impact of these policies, Ubico mandated an educational curriculum based on domestic skills for female students. Drawing upon the moral support of like-minded Guatemalan women, Ubico frequently printed hundreds of names to publicly justify and validate the flagrantly undemocratic nature of his government.

The sector of urban teachers presented a problem in this stifling system intended to legalize the sociopolitical and economic marginalization of women. Economically independent and essential to the country's facade of democracy and modernity, women teachers were difficult to ignore and control. Therefore, Ubico understood that a different strategy was required with the cadre of newly educated young women emerging from Guatemala's normal schools. Consequently, he attempted to sow social fear over the presence of educated women.

Using his political party's newspaper, *El Liberal Progresista*, Ubico reminded Guatemalan men of the dire consequences of educated women. In one such article titled "When the Woman is the Man of the Home," he warned men that the inevitable outcome of any marriage that supported an educated and working woman was always divorce.[31] Of course, since divorce was legal, these words were designed to create only uncertainty and fear in order to maintain the gendered status quo Ubico so desired.

Using legislation as a weapon against women, Ubico enacted several laws clearly designed to control women at the most intimate level. Legalizing the social uncertainty created by educated female teachers, he forbade single teachers to marry. Only teachers already married could remain in their positions, narrowing the parameters of one of the few occupations open to women. He also extended his rigid control onto female teachers' very bodies. In 1941, the secretary of public education, J. Antonio Villacorta, announced that all female administrative staff, teachers, and school janitors were required to have hygiene exams.[32] These attacks on the education system were particularly threatening because this was both a highly feminized space and women's sole avenue for sociopolitical activism. Indicative of their determination, an entire generation of young women teachers remained single, and education became a central battleground of both repression and activism for a small but influential group of urban women.

This particular reconfiguration of repressive gender norms produced a complex and dangerous terrain for Guatemalan women. As mothers and wives, Guatemalan women were symbolically elevated as national symbols when Ubico consecrated domesticity into a formal profession, including it as such in the 1940 census data. For those women who were able to live within these established parameters, the social control and state protection offered by Ubico created a familial social space of some consequence. His metaphorical extension of himself as father or husband over all women provided some of the city's most vulnerable with legal avenues for social and economic protection. Women were encouraged to file petitions against their husbands or male partners for child support and alimony, as their abandonment reflected poorly on the patriarchal foundation of the nation. David Carey argues that Ubico's self-promotion to male protector of all women extended into the penal system and offered rural and indigenous women real moments of justice.[33] Simultaneously, however, the Ubico regime was exceptionally harsh on women whose actions fell outside of gender norms, including new laws that "heightened surveillance of pregnant women and criminalization of unchaperoned girls." This lack of legal protection "was reinforced by interlocking tiers of male relatives, employers, their husbands' employers, police, jailers, and rapacious authorities at every step in the system."[34] Consequently, women had little recourse in the face of domestic or sexual violence.

Ubico, however, only employed gendered imagery for rhetorical purposes, and neither he nor his political party integrated women into the political process as other right-wing movements in countries such as Chile and Brazil had done.[35] In her work on Brazil during the 1930s, Susan Besse argues that this type of social rigidity is essential to political control: "Maintaining social hierarchy required maintaining binary oppositions between classes and between sexes. Any attempt to dissolve either of these oppositions threatened the entire system of power."[36] Her analysis resonates with Ubico's rule of Guatemala, as a reassertion of women's social and economic subordination to men remained critical to Ubico's reconstitution of strict political control. Simply stated, his personal ideas about women and gender became state policy. His military dictatorship faced few challengers, and while he rhetorically employed the image of family and particularly women to uphold his political grip, Ubico did not integrate the political or moral support of women into his administration. In her analysis of Chilean women during the Pinochet dictatorship (1973–1990), Marcela Ríos Tobar identifies the possibility for activism within this particular type of gendered space. "This inequality, and the ideological exaltation of a subservient role for women in society, had the contradictory effect of legitimizing women's intervention in the public sphere.... In so doing, the [Pinochet] regime excluded and repressed the ways in which men had participated in politics and opened the door for women's political intervention."[37] Ríos Tobar argues that the repressive nature of dictatorship facilitated Chilean women's ability to question their life conditions and their historical social position, and her hypothesis holds true for Guatemalan women during the Ubico era. In this particular location, urban ladinas carved out space in which to write, work, and even oppose elements of the Ubico regime, both shaping and being shaped by Ubico's political stranglehold. Within this highly gendered political repression, women were perceived to be politically neutral, neither ally nor enemy, and it is this particular position that offered Guatemalan women a space unavailable to men.

Nosotras and *Azul*

The literary world of Guatemala City had always been a highly masculinized space, a world in which ladino men of the middle and upper classes had the power to control ideas and influence culture.[38] To offset this intellectual monopoly, literary urban ladinas had formed alternative autonomous spaces such as their small journals and tertulias, writing and sharing their work with one another, since the late nineteenth century. Within the relative safety of these feminized spaces, the tertulias sustained both feminist and political ideas distinct from those of their male peers, and the 1930s journalists Luz Valle and Gloria Menéndez Mina became the direct beneficiaries of this distinct intellectual circle. Menéndez Mina's mother, Isaura de Menéndez Mina (a respected writer and social commentator during the early twentieth century), had been active in the Catholic labor movement during the 1910s and was a frequent contributor to the working-class Catholic paper *El Grito*.[39]

The sociopolitical reforms of the 1920s facilitated new intellectual opportunities, and the journalistic career of Luz Valle illustrates the value of these modest changes. She began publishing poetry in the newspaper *Diario de Centro América* and the medical student journal *Studium* in 1923.[40] By 1924, she had joined *El Imparcial* as a staff member and regular contributor, writing a page entitled *La Pagina del Hogar* (Home Page).[41] Valle's work with *El Imparcial* throughout the 1920s no doubt helped her to establish the journal *Nosotras* in 1932.[42] Gloria Menéndez Mina had less formal literary experience when she began publication of *Azul* in 1939, and there can be little doubt that her mother's respected writing career facilitated Menéndez Mina's own journalistic endeavors. She began writing in the late 1920s, and her work appeared sporadically in national papers, including *El Imparcial* throughout the 1930s.

The defunct Sociedad Gabriela Mistral was reconfigured by a group that included Luz Valle and Gloria Menéndez Mina into the Sociedad Vitalista de Guatemala in 1929.[43] The Vitalist Movement embodied a diffuse group of ideas that included a concern for the advancement of the human condition. Dissatisfied with capitalist and socialist ideologies, the movement's founder, Alberto Masferrer, advocated for a third way "in a modernized version of Catholic corporate humanism."[44] Recognizing those who had benefited least from Liberal reforms, Masferrer's notion of the basic rights of life included adequate nutrition, clothing and shelter, potable water, and access to employment, education, and health care. These ideas coalesced well with teosofía's spiritual and intellectual rejuvenation currently advocated by the urban ladina women's movement, thereby extending its influence. Within this amorphous ideology, self-realization took precedence, fundamentally shaping the urban ladina community's ideas regarding feminism and education.[45] With its emphasis on internal transformations as much as external ones, the Vitalist Movement became an ideal tool of resistance during the Ubico regime.

The tenacity of these historical literary circles was realized with the creation of the journals *Nosotras* and *Azul* during the 1930s. Employing the strategies of self-realization and tactical political support over the decades, Luz Valle and Gloria Menéndez Mina now identified and adapted to the gendered parameters of Ubico's regime to become the informal leaders of an informal women's movement. Dependent upon the institutional protection of established newspapers and Ubico supporters, both women were able to establish publishing careers during a time of intellectual repression. As Erin Finzer argues, the work of Central American female poets has been historically dismissed by the male-dominated intellectual and political realm as feminine and inconsequential. So, just as the tertulias protected political resisters during the Estrada Cabrera dictatorship, now these two journals provided protection for the ladina literary community. "In this context of tyranny, in which people knew how to 'read' what could not be said in print," poems and other fictional writing in *Nosotras* and *Azul* could be interpreted for what Guatemalans could not explicitly say.[46] Both women maintained their intellectual networks in a variety of ways, and there is sporadic evidence to suggest that they may have met clandestinely with women from across Central America. They disseminated this information, publishing what they could in their journals and spreading more politically sensitive ideas through their informal networks in Guatemala City.

The question that arises from using these journals as historical sources during a period of political repression is how to determine the authenticity of the ideas presented. However, what makes both *Nosotras* and *Azul* so valuable as historical sources is that both editors continued to publish following the overthrow of Ubico and throughout the Guatemalan revolution. In the triumphant weeks that followed Ubico's resignation, *Azul* erupted with political and social commentary articulating the general euphoria of urban residents. Both Valle and Menéndez Mina provided critical leadership in a variety of women's movements during the ten years of revolutionary reform that followed (they will appear repeatedly in the following chapters). Both women joined the Comité Pro-Ciudadanía (Pro-Suffrage Committee), an association that achieved women's suffrage in March 1945. Menéndez Mina used her influence to further advance the cause of inter-American solidarity, going to the Women's National Press Club in Washington, DC, to stir interest for the creation of a Pan American society.[47] She then became a leading advocate for the First Inter-American Congress of Women in

1947. Following its success, Menéndez Mina continued her work to reestablish the Inter-American Commission of Women.[48] Her national influence would be confirmed when Guatemala's first lady, Elisa Martínez de Arévalo, appointed Menéndez Mina as her personal secretary.

Luz Valle did not assume as prominent a role, but she promoted women's legal and civic rights throughout the revolutionary decade through her editorials. Her series of articles following the October 1944 revolution represented nothing less than the magna carta of a new women's movement (see chapter 3). She continued to be an informal spokesperson for the maternal feminist movements during the Arévalo administration and maintained an active journalistic career, writing editorials for *El Imparcial* throughout the "ten years of spring." Given the overwhelming evidence their work provides, it is clear that both Valle and Menéndez Mina subverted their own ideals to conform to Ubico's political expectations. Their specific identity as journalists and poets also served to protect them within a hostile political environment. When it became safe to publish their true sociopolitical ideas following Ubico's resignation in June 1944, Valle, Menéndez Mina, and many other contributors did just that, confirming Finzer's supposition.

Luz Valle became the first journalist since the Laparra sisters to publish specifically for a female audience, producing the first edition of *Nosotras* in 1932.[49] In what appears to be a Guatemalan literary tradition, Valle was joined by her sister Amália, who acted as staff administrator at *Nosotras*. Luz Valle could not have picked a more challenging year to begin publication, due to the political changes sweeping the isthmus. Several populist leaders were assassinated, allowing a series of depression-era dictators to emerge. In Nicaragua, revolutionary leader Augusto Nicolás Calderón de Sandino was murdered by General Anastasio Somoza García. In El Salvador, Farabundo Martí's failed communist uprising was brutally suppressed by the dictator General Maximiliano Hernández Martínez with the murder of an estimated thirty-two thousand El Salvadoran peasants. La Matanza (the massacre) would have a particularly significant impact on the social consciousness of future Guatemalan first lady María Vilanova de Árbenz, due to her father's complicity in the event, a transformation that ultimately led her to the Alianza Femenina Guatemalteca. Fueled by his paranoia of communism, Ubico responded to these regional events with the swift and violent repression of Guatemala's Communist Party and organized workers.[50]

Gloria Menéndez Mina's journal *Azul* emerged at another pivotal historical moment, appearing in November 1939 during the first months of World War II. *Azul: Revista del Hogar* continued until 1949 with sporadic interruptions neces-

FIGURE 2.1 Luz Valle. *Nosotras*, 1932.

sitated by financial constraints. While *Nosotras* addressed concerns related to an informal but cohesive community of educators, the topics addressed in *Azul* focused on the violence and social crises surrounding the early years of World War II. Using the platform created by *Azul*, writers analyzed global events through the lens of a traditional Latin American feminist belief that women occupied a higher moral ground from which to critique politics and society in general. Menéndez Mina frequently addressed questions regarding violence and the impact of war in her journal. Following the tradition established by both the Laparra and Rodríguez López sisters, Gloria was joined by her brother Rubén Menéndez Mina, who worked with subscriptions. Rosa Rodríguez López's sister Graciela de Mata Amado joined Gloria in her efforts working as a reporter. Gloria's editorial partner, Aurea Hernández de León, was the daughter of newspaper editor (*Nuestro Diario*) Federico Hernández de León.[51] Although Aurea left *Azul* after four years in April 1943, the journal had matured sufficiently for Gloria Menéndez Mina to continue on as sole editor.[52] Hernández de León's long publishing experience no doubt provided the women with experience and opportunity, but his presence also presented an increased threat to their autonomy. As a personal friend of Jorge Ubico, Federico Hernández de León frequently accompanied the president on tours of the countryside.[53] While this relationship may have protected Menéndez Mina, it also placed her directly under Ubico's scrutiny. High social status had not protected other Guatemalans, and there is no doubt that Menéndez Mina played a delicate game of political negotiation while publishing *Azul*.[54] Despite her ambiguous position, Menéndez Mina was invited to meet with the visiting Peruvian ambassador and his wife in in 1941, providing Ubico with a public model of a professional and yet feminine Guatemalan woman.

Although the community of literate and educated ladinas remained relatively small throughout the Ubico years, as editors of women's journals, both Valle and Menéndez Mina created a vital space for this burgeoning intellectual community.

Dictating Feminisms 83

The rhetoric of modernization and patriotism became the most effective strategies to maintain a modicum of neutrality as they walked the fine line between self-determination and authoritarian rule. As an intellectual position they could authentically embrace as well as subvert for their own needs, patriotism had been a defensive strategy employed by all feminists since the Laparra sisters. Using a complex fusion of Catholicism, elements of teosofía, puericultura, and maternalism, both editors emphasized notions of patriotism by devoting a great deal of space in their journals to Guatemala's geography, rich cultural heritage (including that of the indigenous Maya), and Catholic faith. Luz Valle in particular highlighted rural, agrarian scenes, including photos of indigenous communities and especially of indigenous women. Although both editors employed Ubico's rhetoric of fatherland and patriotic loyalty, they simultaneously reframed it, cultivating a sense of belonging for their readers that symbolized both love of country and love of self.

Patriotism and service to others was a powerful core in Latin American feminism for which Valle and Menendez Mina could openly advocate. Within this patriotic mantra, Valle and Menéndez Mina called on their readers to care for their fellow Guatemalans through social reforms and education. As historian Asunción Lavrin points out: "There was in feminism . . . a powerful and positive message of service to society that not even its enemies could dismiss."[55] In 1940, Menéndez Mina claimed that citizenship was more than patriotism, that it was also a love of service for humanity and a consciousness of one's existence.[56] It was precisely this aspect of their feminism that made it difficult for Ubico to pinpoint these qualities as political opposition. After all, it was precisely middle- and upper-class Catholic women with whom Ubico surrounded himself to create a facade of national support.[57] With few exceptions, neither journal directly challenged the government to include women through either civil or legal equality, allowing for their survival within a hostile political terrain.

Just as patriotism proved to be an effective strategy through which to articulate their particular brand of feminism, the journalists found invoking the Liberal rhetoric of modernization equally successful. Since the nineteenth century, Liberal leaders had attempted to modernize Guatemala through the mantra of order and progress. Invoking these ideas of modernization so dear to Ubico, Valle argued that women's rights did not represent a contradiction to it but rather were an inevitable outcome of modernization and progress. Echoing Rosa Rodríguez López's frustration, Valle insisted that ladinas were not merely frivolous and stupid, urging her readers to refute the dominant notions of women as weak and insecure.⁵⁸ Rather, women had proved themselves capable of engaging in a wide variety of intellectual and professional positions. For Valle, the incontrovertible proof could be found in women's participation in the sciences, the arts, and the political landscape. The problem for Valle was that she had firsthand evidence to support her argument because of Ubico's restrictions on education and employment. Therefore, in a rather remarkable shift of perspective, Valle showcased activities that demonstrated the intelligence and hard work of working-class Guatemalan women, even highlighting those who created small businesses and worked in the informal economy. In so doing, she contextualized her feminist ideals within a cross-class framework, spanning deeply entrenched barriers. Although it is not a consistent element of her feminist ideology, it is a trait that resurfaced consistently throughout her journalistic career.

It is precisely these types of publications that Erin Finzer argues enabled these ladina journalists and writers to assert their intellectual power into a masculinized urban milieu. By inserting their ideas in print media, "women began not only to produce, but also to disseminate, their newfound discursive power."⁵⁹ Further, because these women writers were participating in an exclusive, male-dominated world, they effectively broke down the power previously reserved only for men. Therefore, the ideas expressed here in poetry, short fiction, and photographic essays celebrating Guatemala's geography contributed to the ladina integration into the capital city's intellectual landscape. For these women, the intellectual ideas expressed in the journals became a gateway to the political sphere. The fact that both journals supported the writing careers of important male writers during a time of severe intellectual repression, including the Nobel Prize recipient for literature, Miguel Ángel Asturias Rosales, only strengthens Finzer's argument.

The number of literate urban Guatemalans had grown since the 1920s despite the fact that the education system had failed the vast majority of the country's population. From a national perspective, the national literacy rates for women between 1920 and 1940 had improved only slightly (see table 2.1), confirming historian Chester Lloyd Jones's conclusion that the printed page still held no message for a large majority of the population.⁶⁰ However, an examination of the urban literacy rates in the capital city and surrounding areas reveals a dramatic increase in literate women. The department of Guatemala, as well as the two surrounding departments of Chimaltenango and Sacatepéquez, reported a literacy rate of 54 percent in 1940 (See table 2.2). Since women represented more than half of Guatemala City's population (89,052 out of 166,456), the capital city and other urban centers offered the journals *Nosotras* and *Azul* a sizeable literate community.⁶¹

Dictating Feminisms 85

TABLE 2.1 National Literacy Rates in 1940[1]

	LITERATE	ILLITERATE	TOTAL	% LITERATE OVER AGE 7
Women	360,695	907,986	1,270,932	14.06
Men	523,855	769,311	1,295,312	20.41

1. Dirección General de Estadística, Quinto censo general de población, levantado el 7 de Abril de 1940, 312–13. These numbers exclude all children under the age of seven.

TABLE 2.2 Literacy Rates for Guatemala City, Chimaltenango, and Sacatepéquez in 1940[1]

	LITERATE	ILLITERATE	TOTAL	% LITERATE
Women	108,418	128,118	236,536	54
Men	127,130	99,597	226,727	43.9

1. Dirección General de Estadística, Quinto censo general de población, levantado el 7 de Abril de 1940, 312–13.

Of the two, *Nosotras* enjoyed a wider readership, in part perhaps because Valle directed her journal at two distinct and significant groups. Much of *Nosotras*'s content reflected the concerns and professional lives of the cadre of female teachers, a majority of whom lived and worked in the capital, and she actively sought their readership. The journal was also circulated in secondary schools and the influential normal school for women, the Instituto Normal de Señoritas, Belén. With a staff in eight departments throughout the country, the journal was distributed to teachers and smaller normal schools.[62] Valle, however, also wrote for urban middle-class and upper-class ladinas in general, publishing articles on Guatemalan geography, Catholicism, and interesting tidbits for home decorating along with literature and poetry. With the exception of teachers, urban ladinas were the only other literate women in Guatemala at this time.

Azul did not enjoy as wide a distribution as *Nosotras* and had a smaller centralized staff. However, Menéndez Mina's ideas were directed toward the same social groups, the teaching core and middle-class ladinas who would rise up against Ubico in 1944.[63]

FIGURES 2.2A AND 2.2B Advertisements for *Nosotras*, 1932.

Nosotras and *Azul*: "Feminism Is Not a Problem in Guatemala"

For urban ladinas, the journals *Nosotras* and *Azul* became the primary sites for the articulation and dissemination of the two feminist streams in existence (on a very limited level) by the urban ladina community during the 1930s and early 1940s. While the two streams frequently overlapped and were for all intents and purposes indistinguishable during the Ubico era, their differences would become clear during the revolutionary decade.

Walking a tightrope between intellectual autonomy and Ubico-era gender norms, the journals advocated feminist ideals that focused primarily on improved access to education and the development of an internalized feminist consciousness, two safe spaces available to Guatemalans during the Ubico regime. While superficially aimed at domestic concerns, both Valle and Menéndez Mina articulated the subverted intellectual ideas of the 1920s along with broader goals that in fact emerged into two distinct forms of feminisms that flourished during the 1944–1954 era.

Dictating Feminisms 87

These two versions of feminist consciousness (since they could not be called "movements" in any real sense during the Ubico era) emerged from aligned but distinct origins.⁶⁴ The source for both of these streams was the Sociedad Gabriela Mistral, where the first hint of these separate yet parallel nuances were articulated by Rosa Rodríguez López and Gloria Menéndez Mina's mother, Isaura de Menéndez Mina. While Rodríguez López focused on the legal inequality of women and their disenfranchisement from the education system, Isaura de Menéndez Mina centered her efforts on the intellectual and spiritual rejuvenation that feminism offered women.⁶⁵ Gloria Menéndez Mina's emphasis on the redemptive role of an ambiguous spirituality and Catholicism closely followed that of her mother, while Luz Valle echoed that of her SGM colleague. Rosa Rodríguez López had been far more willing to directly confront social and gender inequalities than other urban ladinas, and Valle channeled this attitude into her own publishing. Drawing upon intellectual ideals developed by the masculine intellectual circles of the Generación del 20, Valle refashioned them into a distinctly ladina perspective, arguing for the intellectual equality of women.

Valle's feminist ideals not only incorporated her gender analysis but included a clear class and ethnic component. Although she drew upon the ideas generated by her contemporaries, as historian Marta Elena Casaús Arzú notes, Valle's intellectual foundations were also deeply influenced by the intellectual currents of an earlier group known as the Generación del 1898.⁶⁶ This turn-of-the-century intellectual movement was dominated by J. Fernando Juárez Muñoz, whose conversion to teosofía shifted his views on race considerably. "He proposed that indigenous peoples be incorporated into a positive *nacionalidad* through full citizenship, one based on their own culture and identity, access to education and specific legislation that protected native rights to citizenship and to just work, health care, and education."⁶⁷ Fusing elements from the Generación del 1898 and Alberto Masferrer's Vitalist Movement, Valle produced gendered analysis on Guatemalan society fused with compassion and concern for social justice.⁶⁸ However, these concerns did not translate into direct political activism the way it would with groups such as the Alianza Femenina Guatemalteca during the 1950s.

Valle extended Masferrer's economic ideals into her class and ethnic analysis of the social reality of indigenous women, in a marked departure from her Generación del 20 peers. She frequently directed her readers' attention to Guatemala's rural indigenous women, emphasizing the beauty of their culture and the depth of their spiritual practices.⁶⁹ While on a superficial level these actions could be understood to parallel Ubico's efforts to promote tourism,

FIGURE 2.3 *Nosotras*, May 1933.

Valle's work reflected a multifaceted social analysis. Masferrer's insistence that all people had the right to education, adequate nutrition, and safe housing resonates throughout Valle's work. Witness to the poverty of market women in Guatemala City, she encouraged her middle- and upper-class peers to pay fair prices for their fruits and vegetables, urging them not to bargain market women down to a lower price. She challenged her readers not to add a half or even a quarter of a cent to their purses, but to pay a fair price so that the market women could feed their children. Extending the perception of lower-class women as mothers worthy of respect, Valle encouraged ladinas to treat their indigenous servants kindly, with warmth and even love.[70] She reminded her readers that when they treated their servants harshly, the servants' children were witnesses to this treatment. Moved by the poverty and abusive treatment experienced by indigenous women and children, Valle tempered her words for an audience reticent to hear such sentiments by drawing on the shared experience of motherhood to advocate for women perceived to be inferior by ladino society. Given the ubiquitous presence of indigenous domestics and the pervasive racism in urban ladina culture, Valle's statements are striking.

Luz Valle directed her words not just to her readership but toward a broader debate that was underway in early 1937. During the 1930s, influenced by European racialist eugenic theories, Guatemalan intellectuals held paternalistic views regarding the civilization of indigenous people. Believing in their inferiority and need for civilization or ladinization, Guatemalan intellectuals were incongruent with the rest of Latin America, and the fear of an indigenous uprising remained a constant concern in the ladino imagination.[71] This dominant racialized conversation was punctuated by a few voices who provided a counterargument. One of

Dictating Feminisms 89

these debates occurred in January 1937 between anthropologist Antonio Goubard Carrera and Ramón Aceña Durán. Influenced by Mexico's *indigenismo* policies, Goubaud Carrera (who became director of Guatemala's Instituto Indigenista Nacional in 1945) also drew his intellectual perspective from the Generación del 1898 and Alberto Masferrer.[72] Now, along with *El Imparcial* editor David Vela, Goubaud Carrera published a series of articles countering the dominant negative perception of indigenous people.[73] One can only imagine the reaction of Guatemala City residents to Goubaud Carrera's assertion that "the complex, coherent Indian mentality 'is the equal to ours.'"[74] This was the context in which Luz Valle cautioned her readers to respect the humanity of market women and domestic servants just weeks later. In insisting that the lives of indigenous women be taken into account, Valle positioned herself as a singular female voice within a highly masculinized intellectual movement.

Lacking the ability to practice their feminist ideas, these differences were of little consequence for urban ladinas, who fluidly integrated elements of both feminist streams, which together could be broadly defined as a Liberal pro-democratic maternalism that emphasized the legal and civil rights of women. These streams were unified in their strongly antifascist, pro-democratic political perspective. However, once urban ladinas were able to practice feminism within the highly politicized milieu of the revolutionary era, these differences became distinct and ultimately split the urban ladina community in August 1947 (see chapter 5). Luz Valle remained somewhat distinct from the Menéndez Mina group, as her emphasis on class and ethnic identity separated her from a majority of her urban ladina peers. In many ways, Valle's ideas represent a bridge between the overtly politically active women of the revolutionary decade and women represented by Menéndez Mina and *Azul*, who transitioned from an antifascist position to one of anticommunism as national politics began to increasingly address the class and ethnic divides sparked by socioeconomic inequality.

The journals articulated and sustained a feminine culture dominated by maternalistic concerns, ideals that had much in common with the gender norms established by the Ubico administration, which held women to be angels and defenders of the home and society. Ubico's ever growing repression within the educational system as well as against women themselves accelerated an awareness among the cadre of educators, intellectuals, journalists, and urban citizens of their marginalized social, economic, and political position. Both Valle and Menéndez Mina were aligned with the social reform movement and supported associations dedicated to poor women and children, such as the Sociedad de

San Vicente de Paul and the Sociedad Protectora del Niño (Society for the Protection of Children). Incorporating the central role of motherhood in their feminist ideology therefore kindled both a genuine identity, which they willingly embraced, as well as an effective strategy to subvert their true political intentions in Ubico's Guatemala. The extent to which this particular tactic was successful is evidenced by Jorge Ubico himself. In 1932, his government-sanctioned paper *El Liberal Progresista* spoke highly of Luz Valle, calling her journal *Nosotras* a noble literary endeavor. The paper claimed that while feminism had posed a problem in other parts of the Americas, "feminism was not a problem in Guatemala."[75] Therefore, while the journals supported Ubico's ideology and fostered his notions of gender among the middle-class educators who represented the bulk of their readership, Valle and Menéndez Mina generated a multifaceted consciousness that in turn facilitated a revolutionary movement that erupted once political freedom was possible.[76]

Like their peers across Latin America, both Luz Valle and Gloria Menéndez Mina grappled with notions of femininity and feminism, two core concepts that Lavrin has argued are critical to interpreting women's history in Latin America.[77] Femininity was understood as the qualities that constituted the very essence of being a woman, embodying both socially constructed characteristics as well as the biological functions of womanhood and motherhood.[78] Many women associated with these two journals were preoccupied with the effects of modernity on the feminine element of women, a characteristic that had offered them their sole foundation for activism in the past. Therefore, women like Valle and Menéndez Mina who championed for the changing of sociopolitical roles for women were constantly required to demonstrate that feminism would "neither damage gender relations nor the natural bonds established within the home by husband and wife or mothers and children," to both their supporters and detractors.[79]

Of the two journals, *Azul* spent considerably more time defending women's femininity, and Gloria Menéndez Mina identified the tension created by the emergent new working roles available to women. Menéndez Mina urged her readers to conserve femininity for the benefit of society, in order to educate and spiritually influence children, insisting that women could participate in a wide variety of intellectual and physical activities without losing their femininity.[80] "The new woman must constantly walk the line between lauding the role and work of women while also maintaining her femininity."[81] To assure her male readers, Menéndez Mina reiterated that feminism did not mean loss of femininity; if women appeared unfeminine, it was lost through their own actions and not due to any ideas.⁸² Two years later, Menéndez Mina issued another editorial on the role of women. "Little by little, slowly, women have made their way until they are almost equal to their male companions, without stopping first of all to be a woman, a full woman who without ignoring the supreme order of maternity, thinks, works and remains dignified through her tenacious efforts."⁸³ Menéndez Mina supported the political and social advances of women, but she never failed to remind her readers of the centrality of motherhood and its influence on society. Although she worked within narrow parameters, maternal feminism not only served as an effective strategy against Ubico but was an ideal she could sincerely embrace.

Limited as she was in her ability to comment on internal political circumstances, Menéndez Mina frequently used international events to express her feminist ideals. She commented on events surrounding World War II, and the profound social and political upheaval created by the conflict and the opportunities it offered. "In the midst of the destruction of war, where men do not come home and women have taken over the offices and workplaces of men no longer there, women continue to march relentlessly to the future."⁸⁴ Furthermore, she noted that when men returned from war, women must be there to greet them as women. Menéndez Mina consistently argued that, given the opportunity the war had afforded them, women were just as capable as men in their ability to work and exercise their intellect. Filling in the professional positions left vacant by men engaged in the war, women were demonstrating their morality and capabilities without losing their feminine nature. Representing a counterpoint to Valle's provocative feminism (by Guatemalan standards), Menéndez Mina endeavored to placate her readers with a more feminine version of feminism. However, she also emphasized the moral role women must play during times of war and conflict, again identifying another dominant element in Latin American feminism. In a world devastated by World War II, Menéndez Mina emphasized the morally superior nature of women that kept them out of the dirty realm of politics. The extent of her influence on matters of peace would become evident during the 1947 Inter-American Congress of Women and the Guatemalan association with the Women's International League for Peace and Freedom. Closely aligned with Catholicism, pacifism, and social service to the poor, Gloria Menéndez Mina linked her feminism indelibly with femininity, essentially addressing the deep-seated fear of many men and women regarding the feminist threat.

Although Luz Valle challenged a broad range of socioeconomic policies during the Ubico era, it was finally her views on marriage that drew the ire of Guatemala

City's patriarchs. In what was clearly intended to be a provocative position, she challenged both the purpose of marriage as well as women's role in it. Valle challenged married women to develop their characters through faith, love of family, and social activities in order to earn more than indifference from men.[85] She encouraged women to develop independence from their husbands and men in general, and she placed the responsibility on women to change their subordinate social status. To support her argument, Valle ran articles by men who confirmed that they wanted strong and intelligent marriage partners.[86] And she challenged unmarried women to think about the purpose of marriage itself. In a time when intelligent women had the ability to do anything they wanted to, she lashed out at frivolous girls who lived only to get married and urged them not to return to the humiliation of the harem, the chains of slavery, and the darkness of obscurity.[87] Married women represented the foundation of patriarchal society in Ubico's Guatemala, while single and thereby uncontrollable women threatened his authoritarian order.

The timing of Luz Valle's increasingly open feminist expressions was hardly coincidental. By the mid-1930s, Ubico was losing the ladino political support that had buoyed him through the first half of the decade, and in response had become increasingly authoritarian. Therefore, patriarchal social control became ever more critical to his authoritarian political success. As Valle continued to challenge patriarchal control, she drew swift retaliation from urban ladino patriarchs who, while dissatisfied with Ubico's political leadership, shared his views on gender norms. Her suggestion that marriage did not represent all women's sole ambition drew vitriol from other urban ladino professionals, and those eager to maintain the patriarchal status quo quickly responded to Valle's guidance on marriage. Two of the most adamant defenders of the status quo spoke vehemently against all like-minded ladinas and Luz Valle in particular. The subsequent debate over the role of women provides an enlightening perspective on the depth of patriarchy faced by these women. Between April and July 1937, Dr. Carlos Martínez Durán (physician) and Dr. Jorge Luis Arriola (psychiatrist) published their own series of articles called *La Mujer ante la Vida*, also in *El Imparcial*. Martínez Durán and Arriola outlined what they perceived to be women's physiological and intellectual limitations, in a direct response to Valle's claims of women's physical and intellectual equality. According to these two men, Guatemalan women should understand that the house is the world in miniature and that all the problems of race, religion, and society can be worked out in this microcosm. "When a women does not believe in the significance of her home in this way, both the marriage and the children are jeopardized."[88] In other words, if a woman wanted to create social change, she should do it at home.

Biological characteristics had long been used by both feminists and their detractors to debate the legal and civil rights of women. In a manner similar to that of many other Latin American feminists, Valle contended in all of her work that women were neither equal nor unequal, but rather distinct from men.[89] Likewise, her detractors utilized biological differences between men and women as supposed evidence to support their claims, arguing that women were incapable of participating in the same kinds of professions as men. Dr. Martínez Durán used the medical field as an example to support this argument. Women were not suitable to be physicians because they were unable to be either professional or discreet. Women did not possess a good memory and were therefore unable to retain the necessary information for a physician.[90] Martínez Durán used the fact that not a single Guatemalan woman had graduated from the medical school to substantiate his claims, although in the same breath he acknowledged the discrimination that faced any woman who entered medical school. Women were equally unsuited for work as musicians, as they were neither creative nor abstract. Despite all of these obstacles, he still encouraged women to strive to be as good as men and continue in the educational system. Given this array of psychological and intellectual deficiencies, Arriola concluded in his articles "Perfíl de la señorita bien" and "La tragedia de la señorita bien" that, despite their best efforts, the only good solution for the deficiencies of young women was marriage.[91]

Although broadly addressing all Guatemalan women, Carlos Martínez Durán directly attacked Luz Valle and her small circle of literary women. In one such article, "Actividades sociales e intelectuales de la mujer," he did not challenge the ability of women to write. Rather, Martínez Durán attacked Luz Valle as a woman. "We do not think that Guatemalan women lack the ideas or talent to write. . . . Take the example of Juana [a Guatemalan poet]. [She] as a symbol of womanhood knew how to write the perfect poem. Two of the best verses in her life were her husband and her children."[92] Unable to defend his position in any other way, Martínez Durán attacked Valle as an unmarried woman. As Temma Kaplan points out, "mothers and other women outside the control of men . . . disrupted patriarchal systems, and in risking the stability of their homes, schools and workplaces, confronted not only the government but also the men of their classes and ethnic groups."[93] The vitriol with which Valle's ideas were met certainly resonates with Kaplan's assertions.

Luz Valle was defended by colleague and friend Julia Meléndez de DeLeón, who responded to this series of attacks by calling their ideas a pessimistic view of feminine culture. An educator by profession, she echoed Valle, reiterating that women were neither inferior nor superior, but rather distinct from men.[94] Further, she argued that motherhood was not the only option for women but one of the many possibilities open to strong and intelligent women. In a manner reminiscent of Vicenta Laparra de la Cerda's plea, Meléndez de DeLeón asked men to believe that women wanted to work alongside them, helping to create a better future, both materially and spiritually.[95] She too encouraged younger ladinas to seek out professions such as nursing, teaching, and medicine as suitable outlets for any unfulfilled maternal instincts. In a final sarcastic and humorous comment, she dedicated a soliloquy to Dr. Carlos Fletes Sáenz, another outspoken opponent of women's equality, whose caustic rhetoric would resurface during the suffrage debate in 1944. In "No llores, mujer" (Do not cry, woman), Meléndez de DéLeon assured women that the salvation to all of their problems of depression and loneliness was simply motherhood.[96]

However, the true threat to Guatemala City's urban patriarchal control lay not in Luz Valle's words but in her articulation of the socioeconomic reality. Increasing economic pressures made women's economic contributions both unavoidable and necessary. However, their move into the formal economy threatened an entire sociopolitical system dependent upon women's unpaid labor and subservient social role. The rapid increase of women in the teaching profession challenged the existing structure where individual interests subverted the collective whole. However, Ubico's integration of a patriarchal structure into his national sociocontrol also impacted men as his self-elevation to the status of national "father" undermined the patriarchal power of urban ladinos. *El Imparcial* editor Alejandro Córdova published this public debate clearly believing that exposure and criticism of Luz Valle's ideas would benefit the patriarchal structure. A supporter of Ubico during the 1930s (Córdova was assassinated by Ubico in October 1944 for the anti-Ubico political position he had adopted by then), Córdova allowed Valle to write for months on feminist issues that were still considered radical for Guatemala. Although men were always considered to be a political threat by Ubico, they actively supported a deeply gendered system that privileged men over women. Luz Valle stopped writing her *El Imparcial* column following these verbal attacks and only renewed her affiliation with the newspaper following Córdova's assassination.

However careful both Valle and Menéndez Mina were to avoid attracting

Dictating Feminisms 95

Ubico's attention, his authoritarian rule considered feminists and women's associations suspect. Uprisings in El Salvador during the first months of 1934 touched off the regional repression of dissident political ideologues. In Guatemala, Ubico launched an anticommunist tirade, jailing and executing any perceived political opposition, including journalists. In response, Valle defended her journal: "We have neither disturbed the social order inciting the masses, nor lit the dangerous spark of feminism as a political organization."[97] She emphasized that *Nosotras* was designed only for the home and women and that its distinctly feminine quality came from its support of the female literary community. To prove her point, following this brief editorial, Valle wrote another one entitled "El hogar y la vida," an inane piece on the importance of the home for women. While it was not in Valle's usual style, it followed Ubico's ideals. Gloria Menéndez Mina also employed this successful tactic early in her journalistic endeavors. Menéndez Mina had very few confrontational articles on suffrage or equality.[98] However, following one such piece, she immediately retracted her position in another publication and defended Ubico's stance on the reduction of legal rights for Guatemalan women.[99] Menéndez Mina also found herself defending her work, reminding both her audience and the opposition that *Azul*'s goal was to advance a feminine culture based on motherhood.[100] "Since motherhood was an affirmation of femininity, the mother who performed other social tasks could not be accused of masculinization."[101] These seemingly transparent attempts to placate Ubico appear to have been successful.

Noticeably absent from the feminisms expressed in either of these journals are concerns related to reproductive rights and sexuality (sexual behavior was publicly addressed for the first time by women of the Alianza Femenina Guatemalteca during the 1950s). Although these women in Guatemala no doubt held concerns over legal and reproductive rights within the family, their silence is indicative of the social and political restraints of the world in which they lived and worked, which did not allow for public discussion on such matters. Their silence is an anomaly although not unusual for this particular time period. A few voices representing pioneering female physicians and organization leaders had raised the subject of sexuality during the late nineteenth and early twentieth centuries in the Southern Cone nations of Argentina, Uruguay, and Chile.[102] But, as Asunción Lavrin explains: "Women found it difficult to discuss sex education openly . . . because it . . . require[d] explanation of body functions and concrete references to venereal diseases and prostitution."[103] The solution to this discomfort lay in the topic of a single morality. Addressing the double standards of morality allowed reformers the opportunity to raise the topics of sex education, the abolition of regulated prostitution, and venereal disease without expressly discussing sex and body functions. Guatemala represented an exception here. The country did not have any female physicians, and leaders of social reform associations only raised concerns relating to puericultura and generalized health care. Any public discussion over prostitution remained the purview of newspaper editors.[104]

Educating Domesticity

Since an uneducated populace was vital to Jorge Ubico's successful socioeconomic control, the educational system became one of the key elements in his reconfiguration of Guatemalan society. However, because education was also a barometer by which the international community measured a country's level of modernity, Ubico used depression-era economics as an excuse for his neglect of education. Advocating for a reduction of national resources for education and setting limits on the number of students able to attend school, Ubico soon distinguished himself even from Estrada Cabrera's (1898–1920) harsh political system. Whereas Estrada Cabrera had benefited politically from a rhetorical facade that promoted education, Ubico and the elite class needed physical laborers. The intellectual devastation that resulted from his policies became evident even to his strongest allies, and by 1941 Ubico's official newspaper had to admit Guatemala's great intellectual void.[105]

Deeply suspicious of an educated populace, Ubico employed what Deborah Levenson refers to as "inverse hegemony."[106] Believing that communism was the inevitable outcome of education, Ubico restricted both educators as well as the entire education system. All education materials were censored, and Ubico blocked the entry of any books he believed to be subversive into Guatemala.[107] Teachers were not allowed to travel outside of the country, so that they would remain ignorant of any ideas he deemed inappropriate. Those who did travel for any reason were forced to do so under false pretenses. In order to cross the Guatemalan border to visit a family member living in southern Mexico during the 1930s, teacher and later cofounder of the Frente Popular Libertador Elisa Muralles Soto had to list her profession as "mother" rather than "teacher."[108] Teachers were required to spend a year in a rural school following completion of their normal school training in Guatemala City, a policy Kenneth Grieb argues effectively removed graduates from the capital city, ensuring that they would spend a period of isolation in Guatemala's remote rural areas, far from the centers of political power.[109] Utilizing his own official newspaper, Ubico issued a steady stream of support for his repressive educational policies.[110] Rather than use education to bring all Guatemalans into a "national" culture, as other Latin American states had done effectively, Ubico deepened the chasm between the presidency and its citizens, creating a state perceived to be both alien and dangerous by at least some of its citizens.

Under the guise of economic constraints, Ubico brought the Ministry of Education under military control. Faced with a global depression, the state established quotas in 1932 to limit the number of students who could enter secondary, normal, and specialized schools, declaring that it was not obligated to provide more than a primary level of education.[111] While only the primary schools were initially militarized, secondary institutions assumed a semimilitarized tenor. Ubico blocked the only avenue of education for working-class adults when he closed the Popular University in 1932. *Nosotras* contributor Malin D'Echevers was quick to speak out following its closure.[112] Although she acknowledged the official state explanation of inadequate funding during a period of economic difficulties, she reminded readers of the limitations of capitalism. True social reform emerged from a place of spirituality and not financial obligations, and D'Echevers urged the government to reconsider its decision.[113] Designed for poor, working adults, the university's closure essentially consigned many urban Guatemalans to a lifetime of ignorance and poverty.

The overt militarization of the nation's centers of higher education was precipitated in 1938 by a student revolt at the University of San Carlos in Guatemala City. In response, Ubico brought the universities and normal schools under his direct control in a further attempt to dilute the growing middle-class unrest. The new law required all students to participate in reserve training under regular army officers, and graduates were commissioned as lieutenants, not teachers.[114] This act effectively placed all teachers under the arm of the military, thereby stemming any political resistance from this social sector. The patriarchal nature of the military and the predominance of women in the teaching population would have made this particular law exceptionally intimidating for women. It is with particular irony then that Luz Valle would announce in October 1944 that an "army" of ladina educators was ready to serve the revolution (see chapter 3).

The statistics on student attendance and student-teacher ratios reveal the complexity of the situation facing educators. As the numbers indicate, the stark reality was simple. Guatemalan children did not attend school, but the reasons why are far more complicated. Statistics are not readily available for the Ubico era due to his administration's general disinterest in education. However, later findings reveal the extent of the problem. In 1953, the Alianza Femenina Guatemalteca noted that out of 381,075 rural children, only 55,649 were registered in school. The statistics were better in the urban centers, although out of 153,819 children, 80,297 were not attending classes.[115] In addition, the student-teacher ratios indicated that in the early years, teachers had classrooms with more than sixty children.[116] A census in 1950 reveals that roughly 90 percent of indigenous children did not attend school despite five years of revolutionary reforms.[117] David Carey's research in Kaqchikel communities indicates a deep distrust for an educational system that supported the assimilation of indigenous children into ladino culture, given that lessons were only offered in Spanish.[118] In addition, poverty played a key role, and children stayed home to support their families in either the informal economy or agricultural production. Those children who did attend school demonstrated signs of extreme poverty and malnutrition, as teachers reported in the journal *Nosotras*, and had trouble concentrating. The challenges faced by children in such a context were further exacerbated by the poor quality of many rural teachers, in particular where low salaries and remote locations failed to attract more qualified personnel.[119]

Despite its significance for nation building and social control, the role of education and teachers remains an understudied field in Guatemala and across Latin America. It is a curious historiographic silence in light of analysis by scholars such as Benedict Anderson, who has noted the significance of the classroom as a pivotal space in which the state can develop a unified sense of consciousness in its citizens, both culturally and politically, creating an "imaginary nation."[120] Historian Mary Kay Vaughan has used Anderson's analysis to argue that in Mexico, rural schools became arenas for cultural politics, pivotal to the long and relatively stable political rule of the fledgling Partido Nacional Revolucionario (PNR), which later became the Partido Revolucionario Institucional (PRI). "The school became the arena for intense, often violent negotiations over power, culture, knowledge and rights. In the process, rural communities carved out space for preserving local identities and culture, while the central state succeeded in nurturing an inclusive, multiethnic, populist nationalism based upon its state commitment to social justice and development."[121] Ubico inverted this ideology to align himself with other Latin American states; in a period of "massive market collapse and unprecedented state intervention . . . [Ubico] became convinced of the need and capacity to transform culture for purposes of integration, rule and development."[122] However, unlike Mexican leaders, Ubico did not have to contend or negotiate with a mobilized rural population. Unable to dismantle the educational system out of a need to maintain a modicum of modernity and progress, Ubico simply subverted the educational system to assert further sociopolitical control over all Guatemalans.

The classroom, particularly in the rural areas, was a transformative site for some educators, allowing them to develop an awareness of the deep class and ethnic divides in Guatemala, a unique sociopolitical perspective afforded few other Guatemalans. A majority of teachers were urban ladinos and ladinas sent to all corners of the country, bridging the historical divide between urban and rural, ladino and indigenous. The evidence of the country's social inequities and racial injustice was plainly visible in the malnourished bodies and on the exhausted faces of their young students in the classroom. Ubico's deliberate efforts to maintain social inequality by enacting vagrancy laws, crushing urban labor unions, and maintaining a mono-agricultural economy produced what many Guatemalan (and other) scholars refer to as feudal economic conditions. For many urban ladina educators, this reality combined with Masferrer's vital minimum ideology mitigated the generally racist attitudes prevalent in urban society. Consequently, their experiences as educators created a social consciousness and a site for activism unique to the generalized restrictive social milieu under the Ubico regime.

While many of their peers believed that indigenous children were incapable of learning due to their inherent ethnic inferiority, Valle and her contributors adamantly disagreed. Using their vantage point from the classroom to reveal the contradictions inherent in Ubico's educational policies and his depression-era economics, the teaching core argued that overwork and not ethnic identity lay at the heart of indigenous children's poor school attendance and results. Malin D'Echevers highlighted the intense poverty of school-age children and the dismal futures they faced without an education.[123] Although her article appears to address a dire social concern, it was also an attack on Ubico's educational policies, challenging the dictator's irrelevant policies in the face of stark and overwhelming poverty.[124] Juan José Orozco argued that the intellectual deficiencies the children manifested in the classroom were not organic but were rather a direct result of their poor nutritional status. The future revolutionary politician and supporter of ladina suffrage questioned how indigenous peoples could be Guatemala's economic backbone when, he noted, little was done to meet their physical needs.[125] Author and physical education instructor Raúl Lorenzana exposed the struggles of teaching children who arrived at school hungry and tired. Malnutrition and overwork took its toll on young bodies, which made educating them difficult. Lorenzana encouraged teachers to help the children by teaching them basic hygiene rules and how to mend their clothes. The cautionary words of Lorenzana and others regarding the deep psychological and physical scars created by poverty were yet another criticism of a state unwilling to integrate this reality into sociopolitical reform. In an era when the educational needs of all Guatemalans and particularly those of indigenous populations were neglected, Luz Valle challenged her ladina audience to improve their teaching for their indigenous students.[126]

Valle was quick to respond to the systemic educational changes, using her journal *Nosotras* to reach more than half of all Guatemala's teachers. In the first years of publication, Valle printed several direct attacks on Ubico's educational policies. In 1933, she openly contradicted Ubico's policies on education from the perspective of the teachers, identifying the intense challenges facing teachers and encouraging them not to give up hope. Dedicating an entire edition to the benefits of the teaching profession, Valle called on her readers to raise the standards of teaching and resist Ubico's low educational standards. Guatemala, she declared, needed teachers who taught with their hearts as well as their intellect. The country needed women who uncovered the ambition of their students and raised their own standards of excellence.[127] Despite the fact that her critiques were often presented in vague terms, Valle's views on Ubico's policies were clear. In the waning months of the dictatorship, Gloria Menéndez Mina also openly attacked the educational system. Pointing out that Guatemalan women were forced to contend with an educational system that only instructed them in tasks of the home, Menéndez Mina argued that women across the world had supported the world's economy as men engaged in battle during the two world wars.[128] She was careful, however, not to make any particular mention of those who made it so difficult for women to reach such achievements. Valle also directly raised questions over not only education policy but the support given to Ubico by the US State Department. The Generación del 20 ideology contained a strong anti-imperialistic vein, which in the case of Guatemala was directed at the United States. Here, too, Valle challenged education policies when she published an article from a recently published book, *El Maestro*. Written by Guatemalan Flavio Guillén, the book took exception with the dominance of the United States over Guatemalan educational pedagogy. Guillén stated that Guatemalans must work to educate their own citizens by creating an indigenous pedagogy and not through a foreign curriculum that did not suit their own context.[129]

Following Ubico's anticommunist campaign in 1934, Valle became more cautious in her political criticisms. Within this increasingly restrictive intellectual milieu, Guatemala's educational system became a key battleground during the 1930s for the urban ladina women's movement. Despite its systemic foibles, education remained one of the few forms of employment and paths of professional development for women, particularly those of the urban middle class, representing the lifeblood for social mobility, self-realization, and resistance to the state. Within this semiautonomous space, the journals *Nosotras* and *Azul* created an essential hub for female teachers in which they created alternative pedagogical models and resisted state assimilation. Luz Valle's insistence that women needed economic independence, and her open touting of their abilities, in *Nosotras* challenged the status quo and contradicted the authoritarian ideal that women must be controlled particularly during times of economic difficulty. Valle also effectively challenged the fallacies inherent within Ubico's gendered constructs. Contemporary patriarchal notions dictated that a woman's realm of influence and duty lay within the home. However, as Valle repeatedly pointed out, this educational model contradicted the reality created by the depression, which made women's paid labor critical for the survival of many families.

At issue here for Valle as well as for hundreds of other teachers were the national pedagogical models that Ubico had reconfigured in order to educate women and girls to fulfill their destiny. This policy essentially elevated education to one of the primary instruments of Ubico's reconfiguration of the gendered sociopolitical structure. José Vásquez's pedagogical text *La mujer en el hogar* (The Woman in the Home), published at the end of the 1920s under the auspices of the Ministry of Education, served as Ubico's ideological foundation for this national transformation. Encapsulating the fears of changing sociopolitical mores for women during the openness of the 1920s, Vásquez articulates the ideals of patriarchal ladino culture for mothers and wives. For Vásquez, education for women must be tempered by the reality of their existence. "In women, the vocational spirit is more vague or imprecise because it is dominated by the natural call to the mission of motherhood."[130] Some might remain single and need to work in factories, while others from the middle class had more opportunities to use their education. In light of this uncertain future, the best way for women to influence political life, he claimed, was to create sons who were well educated and ready to lead the nation. Based upon the notion that women educated to work outside of the home would become independent and therefore unhappy, education for girls and young women centered upon notions of domesticity.[131]

Contending that the destiny of women was only to feed and educate children (or boys more specifically), school curriculum taught that women did not have time to busy themselves with politics. Consequently, the curriculum as outlined by Vásquez focused on marriage, motherhood, physical education and physical attributes, morality, and labor. In short, the less women thought or spoke, the better it appeared to be for Vásquez.[132] Most poignantly, existing textbooks were revised to include arguments against women's suffrage.[133] Given that more than 60 percent of all teachers were women, the reality that women qualified to teach the rights and duties of citizenship were not allowed to exercise them has a peculiar piquancy. Although Valle was extremely cautious in her critique of the dominant pedagogy, its presence in her writing hints at the frustration experienced by many female teachers who were required to remain bound by the gendered bias of education. In an attempt to mitigate its worst detrimental impacts, Valle challenged home economics teachers to include science in their teaching to help cultivate thinking among their students. When women are scientifically intelligent, Valle argued, they create intelligent children who contribute to their country's economy.[134]

Despite the intense educational repression, two ladinas broke significant educational barriers during the early 1940s. It was with understandable pride that Gloria Menéndez Mina dedicated an entire issue of *Azul* to María Isabel Escobar, Guatemala's first female doctor, who also happened to be the niece of Dr. José Epaminondas Quintana, highlighted in chapter 1. Presented as the embodiment of the strong, emancipated, and intelligent woman, Escobar emerged as an informal, emotional mentor for all urban ladinas. In turn, Escobar penned her thanks to *Azul* for working daily against ignorance and incomprehension, claiming that all women could accomplish what she had achieved through hard work and perseverance.[135] In 1943, Graciela Quan Valenzuela became the first Guatemalan woman to earn a law degree. Her thesis proposed a legal argument for the suffrage of literate women, a document that created the theoretical foundation for the successful suffrage campaign in 1945 (see chapter 4); sections of the thesis were published in *Azul* following the overthrow of Jorge Ubico in 1944.

The cadre of urban educators who survived Ubico's restrictive educational policies that demoted women to mere vessels of reproductivity believed that they had earned the right to participate in the new state during the months following Ubico's overthrow. The maintenance of a cohesive community with pivotal intellectual opinions that diverged from those of the dictatorial state led them to believe that they had earned the right to take direct leadership. In 1945, the

Dictating Feminisms 103

minister of public education took an extended sabbatical, and Gloria Menéndez Mina campaigned for the elevation of educator María Albertina Gálvez to this influential position. Reflecting the intense simplicity of their position, Menéndez Mina argued that her posting represented a simple matter of justice for all Guatemalan women.[136] The posting of a male colleague to a leadership role in a profession dominated and sustained by women, however, set the stage for the remainder of the revolution. As the cadre of urban ladina educators were soon to realize, their successful efforts to resist and finally overthrow a dictatorship were not sufficient evidence in a patriarchal society.

Conclusion

Ubico's particular sociopolitical policies designed to strengthen his regime in concert with the global depression created a curious and contradictory space for women in the capital city. Urban ladinas developed gendered strategies to adeptly navigate this repressive political period using the journals *Nosotras* and *Azul* as instruments for their activism. Although literary women and educators had long been the foundational actors for the urban movement, it was never more evident than during the Ubico dictatorship. Constructed as a hierarchical and patriarchal institution of power, the Ubico state was a hostile entity to the world imagined by these women. Utilizing *Nosotras* and *Azul* as tools, Valle and Menéndez Mina facilitated a new class and gendered consciousness within the teaching community using their journals as instruments of state resistance. While their male colleagues were forced into silence and exile, Valle and Menéndez Mina nurtured ideas that flourished into real social and political institutions during the ten years of democracy that followed.

In their struggle for intellectual autonomy in Ubico's Guatemala, *Nosotras* and *Azul* maintained a feminist consciousness among a critical cadre of readers. What emerged was an informal women's movement that was fervently antifascist, pro-democratic, and fundamentally Liberal in nature, characteristics that would define urban ladinas in Guatemala City until the late twentieth century. The community surrounding these journals created a bridge between the 1920s and the revolutionary decade. It was from their ranks that political opposition grew against the regime of Jorge Ubico, and *Nosotras* and *Azul* became the instruments for such expression. They cultivated a community that held views that were distinct from those of the dictatorial regime, views that found freedom of expression and action during the following ten years of democracy. The imaginings of a minority in this urbanized world contained a broader vision that included indigenous children and women. Their vision of an imagined world that included women's education, concern for the poor, and a unique spiritual vision infused with both Catholicism and teosofía found a voice in the first months of the revolution. Luz Valle and Gloria Menéndez Mina along with hundreds of readers lived in a suspended animation, actively imagining a world in which they belonged. Through Herculean efforts amid an often dangerous political milieu, they established informal social networks through journals and associations distinct from both the state and, frequently, male peers. The ability to retain and nourish an independent identity made it possible for these women to survive the decade of patriarchal dictatorship. The extent to which they maintained this movement in a repressive context became evident in the days leading up to and following the revolution. Their leadership of the suffrage campaign immediately following Ubico's resignation in 1944 and the creation of several political parties critical to the revolutionary decade are testament to the tenacity and maturation of their feminist ideals, muted but not destroyed by dictatorial restraints.

Three

A SMALL PAYMENT FOR A LARGE DEBT
MATERNAL FEMINISM, REVOLUTIONARY MOTHERS, AND THE SOCIAL REVOLUTION, 1944–1950

Women of Guatemala—Let's form a common front to give children a promise of the future—a new concept of the homeland, making their duties and responsibilities known from the first dawn of life!
—*Gloria Menéndez Mina*, Azul, *June 1944*

The women's army is ready and waits for its orders.
—*Luz Valle*, El Imparcial, *December 13–14, 1944*

It is clear that the men of the October revolution saw the disasters of the dictatorship and rushed to remedy them: they legislated a modern Constitution, decentralized government power, returned its autonomy to municipalities, did what was necessary to do on the political side.
But for the child? And single women? And the Indian? And the malnourished? And the sick? And the unfortunate?
This aspect outside of the law was taken up by the women of the October revolution. In this they have been involved. In this they have insisted.
In this they have revealed the issues.
And in this they have triumphed.
—Diario de Centro América, *October 8, 1948*

Luz Valle and Gloria Menéndez Mina could scarcely have imagined the ways in which the sociopolitical ideals they had nurtured in *Nosotras* and *Azul* for more than a decade now erupted into the public sphere following the June uprisings. Demonstrating the intellectual influence of the two journals, the networks of educators and reformers associated with them moved immediately into the center of revolutionary activity. Vital to the overthrow of Jorge Ubico, present at every protest, at every pro-revolutionary march, in every labor union, in every school, in every business and marketplace, Guatemalan women quite simply participated in shaping the revolution's birth.[1] Believing that they had earned the right to participate fully in the revolutionary project, women eagerly extended their activism into the sociopolitical realm, influencing and creating social reform institutions as well as the education system. For urban ladinas, the decade of relative sociopolitical freedom and democratic reforms that followed stands alone in Guatemalan history.

The social reform movement created by urban ladinas emerged in the embryonic spasms of revolutionary optimism. One of the most successful projects undertaken by women in the capital city, the *comedores infantiles* and *guarderías infantiles* (nutrition and daycare centers) symbolized the revolution for Guatemala City's poorest and most vulnerable citizens. Extending a historical concern for the well-being of mothers and children into a new revolutionary feminism, social reformers, educators, and journalists joined forces with working-class women from the markets and small industries to establish a series of childcare and nutrition centers. Along with women involved in long-standing charity circles and first lady Elisa Martínez de Arévalo, those involved included poor women themselves, representing an unprecedented cross-class collaboration. While the project was not a traditional state initiative, civil associations such as this brought the revolution to the marginalized corners of the city. As scholar Hilda Sabato reminds us, associations like this offer a more inclusive democracy than what might otherwise be available to this particular sector of society. Therefore, while the comedores infantiles and guarderías infantiles were not perceived to be political in nature, Sabato's theory suggests that they carried political influence, forming a link between the ruler and the ruled.[2] As such, the women and their social reform movement represented a new political ideal for their nation, or, to use their word, a new *patria*.

While social reforms such as the comedores infantiles and guarderías infantiles brought the revolution closer to its democratic ideals, Guatemala City's entrenched gendered and racialized duality remained intact. As identified by the editor of *Diario de Centro América* in 1948, the revolutionary project continued to occupy what was essentially a masculine space in which the country's existing power structures remained dependent upon separate and unequal political and social spheres. While the political system underwent significant transformations following the revolution, Guatemalans continued to identify political concerns as the purview of men. Therefore, the social reform institutions and activism within the educational realm was perceived to be "outside of the public sphere" and therefore the domain of women despite the fact that their efforts altered the revolutionary trajectory to include social and political reforms otherwise unaddressed. While ladinas were praised for their efforts on behalf of children, the poor, and the sick, it was work perceived to be outside of the center of political significance. This rhetorical sociopolitical hierarchical structure also relegated indigenous concerns to the feminine sphere or a nonpolitical space, an issue that will be discussed in greater detail in chapter 4. The urban ladina struggle for sociopolitical equality therefore was potentially disruptive not only from a gendered perspective but from a class and ethnic one as well, which explains the often vitriolic backlash to their campaigns for equality.

The success of these social reform projects soon elevated them as symbols of the revolution's ideals, and elements of social welfare were incorporated into the formal state structure. While the institutionalization of the comedores infantiles and guarderías infantiles was arguably a success for women reformers, historian Paulo Drinot has pointed out the effects of just such a process in highly gendered societies. According to Drinot, the rhetorical shift from needs (associated with the private sphere and women's social activism) to rights (associated with the public sphere and male legislative action) has the effect of moving an initiative outside of women's purview. In his introduction to *The Great Depression in Latin America*, Drinot notes that this process was reproduced in several Latin American countries, which during the 1930s began to establish the foundations of social welfare systems: "In such processes, typically, social assistance and social protection initiatives pioneered in early years by women activists were either co-opted or sidelined by the new state institutions established to protect and 'improve' the population."[3] So, although women such as Rosa de Mora (founder of the Sociedad Protectora del Niño) had been responsible for the first pioneering social reform projects, the institutionalization of these efforts placed them back in the masculine domain.

The marginalization of women's revolutionary efforts reinforced the primacy of maternalism within their feminist ideals as one of the few acceptable avenues in which to facilitate social and political change. Although these women did not create an official feminist organization, a series of formal and informal associations designed to create social and legal reforms emerged with strong ties to the influential first lady, Elisa Martínez de Arévalo. A significant number of these women acted out of their religious beliefs, creating organizations to help the poor influenced by the work of San Vicente de Paul and the Sociedad

Protectora del Niño. Others acted out social reforms first conceived during the 1920s combining elements of puericultura and the spiritual practice of teosofía. While these ladinas represented a broad spectrum of political ideologies, they were drawn together in the first years by their desire to address the historically neglected social needs of their country.

As a result of this sociopolitical context, urban ladinas worked largely outside of male authority, effectively navigating the masculinized political system to develop autonomous institutions based on their hard-won experiences. Understanding their struggle within the broader patriarchal structure, these women insisted upon their independence from male oversight. It became evident that they had been correct in their caution when, before the end of the Arévalo administration, the state established the first school of social work in Guatemala and appointed only men as administrators and teachers to a classroom of women who had founded the country's social work movement. While revolutionary rhetoric offered all Guatemalans the possibility of participation, tension between rhetoric and reality revealed the limits of gender and class reforms. Despite efforts to challenge this system, revolutionary public discourse continued to honor this asymmetrical arrangement that largely marginalized women from any real practice of power.

The relationship between Latin American feminisms, social reform movements, and their positionality with the state has been extensively explored in recent literature.[4] In fact, the study of Latin American women's history is predated by histories of the family, and the historiography continues to be associated closely with motherhood.[5] In Guatemala City, the deep maternalism present among ladina feminists and activists created an amorphous and fluid relationship between the identities of "feminist" and "social reformer" that is perhaps unique in Latin America. A generalized lack of political and ideological freedom in Guatemala provided little opportunity to practice feminism or politics, resulting in little to no entrenched ideologies within the women's associations. Consequently, there was little distinction between the two identities throughout the Arévalo era as women flowed seemingly effortlessly from one organization to another, responding to the urgency of social needs rather than heeding to a strict ideological agenda. However, this social reform movement included more than traditional middle-class educators and feminists, and elite philanthropic members of Catholic charity networks who worked in separate organizations, as exemplified by the social reform movement in Argentina.[6] Rather, Guatemala City's social reform movement collaborated with the most disenfranchised women, those working in the marketplace, representing an unprecedented cross-class collaboration, an experience that stands in contrast to what was happening in other Latin American countries.

While the Guatemalan revolutionary decade has been studied extensively, the participation of women is absent from the scholarship and, in fact, largely forgotten. Therefore, fundamental questions as to the role women played in the revolution itself and the ensuing social reforms remain unaddressed. How well were they integrated in the revolutionary project? To what extent did these urban women benefit from revolutionary reforms? Incorporating Guatemalan women into the story of the revolution is more than simply adding their names to the historical record, although this, too, is a critical step in historical recovery. Gender analysis challenges the revolution's formative period by posing new questions and new problems. As a result, new watershed moments are recovered. In short, adding women to the ten years of spring fundamentally reframes the revolution, its goals, its accomplishments, and its shortcomings.

The Revolution of Gender or the Gender of Revolution?

The birth of the Guatemalan revolution has been traditionally pinpointed as the military uprising that took place during three days in October 1944, a highly masculinized, definitive overthrow of Jorge Ubico's government. For urban ladinas, however, the revolution and opportunities for sociopolitical reform began months earlier, in June 1944. Ubico's resignation on June 30 created a political power vacuum for the next four months, a transitional space in which sociopolitical gendered norms were disrupted and became potentially transformative. Jane Jaquette argues that the transition from dictatorship to democracy frequently allows a society to rethink the basis of social consensus, a transitional potential upon which urban ladinas seized.[7] This rupture after more than a decade of a dictatorial regime allowed ladinas the opportunity to publicly identify key reforms they had so long yearned to enact. Following the military revolution in October, patriarchal social and political power returned. Consequently, gender analysis of the revolution reveals that the months between April and October represent the most formative period of the revolutionary era for Guatemalan women.

The resignation of Jorge Ubico was the culmination of a growing escalation of political opposition to his presidency that had begun early in 1944. In January 1944, members of the *Nosotras* and *Azul* circles formed literary societies whose real intent was the creation of an opposition movement to Ubico (see chapter 4). By April and throughout May, university students, emboldened by the growing

FIGURE 3.1 Women injured by Jorge Ubico's military: Aída Sándoval, Hilda Balaños, and Julieta Castro de Rólz Bennett. *El Imparcial*, June 26, 1944.

lack of political support for Ubico, were publicly demonstrating, although their demands were largely confined to academic issues.[8] Their public assertiveness, however, represented a serious political challenge to Ubico's authority. By mid-June, ferment had spread to the teaching community, and teachers began to resist the mandatory military exercises. Women joined in the clandestine operations spreading across the city, surreptitiously using the perception of their political neutrality as women to pass messages around the escalating opposition movement.[9] The way in which Guatemalan women used established gender norms to participate in covert operations against Ubico's government would be repeated in Cuba just a few years later during the 1950s by women working against the Fulgencio Batista regime.[10] Ubico suspended constitutional guarantees on June 22, 1944, in response to these activities and increased military presence throughout the city, escalating the small but growing death toll. The day before the pivotal teachers' march, 311 prominent Guatemalans presented a petition calling for the reestablishment of the constitution to the presidential palace.

Although the anti-Ubico movement galvanized around her as the quintessential revolutionary symbol, María Chinchilla Recinos was not the only person killed on June 25 during the teachers' march. In fact, dozens of people had been injured or killed during popular demonstrations earlier in the day, some having been burned by phosphorus bombs.[11] Although the teachers' march had been prearranged, they used the opportunity to protest Ubico's earlier attacks on the demonstrators. Following a period of contemplation at the Church of San Francisco, the group of teachers, who included Julia and Ester de Urrutia as well as the Muralles sisters (Elisa Muralles Soto, Mélida, and Morelia), had walked only three blocks before being fired upon by Ubico's soldiers. The military blocked all medical aid to the injured, and many people, including Archbishop Mariano Rossell y Arellano, personally drove injured people to the hospital.

On June 26, the marchers and witnesses of Chinchilla Recinos's death petitioned President Ubico directly, calling for his resignation.

> As mothers and Guatemalan women representing all social sectors, we have witnessed the massacre of our children and ourselves. . . . The panic provoked by the murder of men, women, and children has removed what little remaining sympathy that you had and convinced us of your inability to govern the destiny of our country. For the good of Guatemala, we implore you to see the situation that has been created and to give up power without further bloodshed.[12]

Emboldened by the marchers, shopkeepers in Guatemala City kept their shops closed throughout the day despite Ubico's order to conduct business as usual.[13] Finally, on June 30, Jorge Ubico resigned and replaced himself with a triumvirate of generals. Having been denied the right to hold a funeral mass for her daughter by Ubico, María Chinchilla's mother immediately organized a large funeral on July 14. Fundraisers were held throughout July to help María's mother pay for the expenses. Hundreds of capital residents attended the service, and her grave became a pilgrimage site for Guatemalans from all social sectors.[14]

Despite the death of dozens of other capital residents during the month of June, it was the murder of María Chinchilla Recinos that captured Guatemala City's imagination and provided the anti-Ubico movement with a perfect revolutionary symbol. Young and attractive, Chinchilla Recinos's pleasant face and manicured hairstyle symbolized the quintessential ladina of the 1940s. As an educator, she fit comfortably into existing middle-class notions of womanhood. Ironically, she held no particular political views, participating in the June 25 march only for the sake of her mother, a factor that only served to compound her mother's grief. Despite the death of numerous other Guatemalans on that day, the murder of an apolitical, unarmed middle-class ladina violated all contemporary gender norms. Ubico's transgression of these entrenched gender ideals enabled both pro- and antirevolutionaries to use María Chinchilla as a symbol for their struggle for the next decade. Her membership in the Association of Catholic Teachers provided a group of Catholic women in February 1945 with the ideal symbol to petition the Arévalo government to overturn Article 17 of the constitution, which maintained the separation of church and state.[15] The feminist organization Alianza Femenina Guatemalteca also effectively used Chinchilla's martyrdom during the 1950s both to honor the past sacrifices of revolutionary women and to celebrate their future

FIGURE 3.2 María Chinchilla Recinos, martyr of the 1944 teachers' march. *El Imparcial*, June 25, 1944.

possibilities. As the threat of US invasion and overthrow of Jacobo Árbenz grew stronger in June 1954, the Alianza named their all-female military brigade after Chinchilla. Her martyrdom continued to be honored following the end of the revolution, confirming her symbolic political neutrality, and contemporary educators and feminist organizations continue to recognize her memory in the annual Teachers' Day celebrated every June twenty-fifth.

Unlike later female heroines of revolutionary movements, María Chinchilla Recinos did not create any kind of new ladina identity. The Guatemalan revolution did not produce the soldadera of the Mexican revolution, the fighting Cuban revolutionaries such as Vilma Espín, or the iconic image of the anonymous Nicaraguan woman holding a baby at her breast with a machine gun slung over her shoulder.[16] Chinchilla Recinos in fact stands in sharp contrast to other contemporary revolutionary women with the exception perhaps of the middle- and upper-class Cuban women who demonstrated against the Batista regime during the 1950s. However, just as with the image of the Nicaraguan nursing revolutionary female soldier, Chinchilla Recinos's image symbolized both the extent and the limitations of revolutionary womanhood in Guatemala.[17] Her distinctly apolitical stance did not challenge the political or the patriarchal structure and actually affirmed its existence, thereby creating a revolutionary symbol that both pro- and antirevolutionary sympathizers could embrace. Consequently, although both ladina and indigenous women made significant contributions throughout the revolutionary decade, only María Chinchilla Recinos is remembered. While armed struggles later in the twentieth century would disrupt traditional gender norms, if only incompletely (Cuba, 1959; Nicaragua, 1979; and El Salvador, 1970s and 1980s), Guatemala's 1944 revolution does not fit this pattern.[18]

The Guatemalan revolution was mercifully brief with comparatively small loss of life, historical particularities that became critical to the maintenance of traditional gender roles.[19] The resignation of Jorge Ubico at the end of June occurred without a sustained violent uprising, and the military coup d'etat that followed four months later in October lasted for only three days. The demonstrations and strikes mounted by university students and urban civilians were largely nonviolent and intended to express dissatisfaction with Ubico's policies rather than create a military confrontation. The three-day armed insurrection itself remained primarily a military affair, as middle-class officers staged an overthrow from October 20 to 22.[20] Although revolutionary efforts were supported by civilians throughout Guatemala City, the armed uprising did not require the participation of a large number of insurgents or civilians and provided little opportunity for women to act outside of their traditional gender roles.[21] Their participation in providing safe houses, emergency medical care, and food for the insurgents fell within accepted gender parameters, obscuring their contribution. Although a number of women participated in the armed conflict itself, their efforts have not been interpreted as critical to the revolution's ultimate success.

In fact, as a revolutionary symbol María Chinchilla Recinos emblemizes the gendered complexity of the revolutionary decade. Scholar Valentine Moghadam has identified two patterns related to the role of women that appear in revolutionary processes. The first pattern is democratic, modern, and egalitarian, one that holds the emancipation of women at its core. The second is a patriarchal model that stresses gender differences rather than equality, tying revolutionary reform to women within the family rather than as individuals.[22] The Guatemalan revolution does not fit comfortably within either pattern, essentially straddling the two models. On the one hand, Guatemala's revolutionary political goals and discourse were fundamentally democratic, revising antiquated notions of citizenship for all and employing a modern populist agenda. Maxine Molyneux has suggested that one of the litmus tests of a state is its ability to maintain the support of groups it claims to represent.[23] Although some political and intellectual leaders genuinely believed that these political ideals included women, a majority certainly did not. As the most significant legal reform, suffrage was granted only for literate women, disenfranchising almost all indigenous women and roughly 70 percent of ladinas, demonstrating that they were not the primary targets of revolutionary political reform. The paramount goal for both the Arévalo and Árbenz governments remained the political integration of rural men. As a result, women remained firmly entrenched in a familial identity within the revolutionary reforms, something a majority of women and men eagerly continued to embrace. The relationship between women and the revolutionary state was further complicated in Guatemala by deep class and ethnic divisions, affirming Molyneux's caution against the false assumption that all women hold the same goals or are affected in similar ways by particular laws.[24] Therefore, while revolutionary democratic rhetoric offered a theoretical sociopolitical space for women, the intransigent patriarchal milieu offered little hope for meaningful inclusion, and these two fundamental positions remained unresolved.[25]

In the weeks following Chinchilla's death, Guatemalans moved quickly to seize the social and political momentum created by Ubico's departure. After fourteen years of mundane reporting, newspapers now were filled with stories about social and political activities. Numerous political parties were formed within hours of Ubico's resignation (see chapter 4), and several urban ladinas made efforts to identify and bury every person killed by Ubico's forces during the June uprisings.[26] As July and then August waned, however, political uneasiness returned as the presidential elections promised by the triumvirate of generals who replaced Ubico in power never materialized. The media continued to press for further political reforms, and on October 1, 1944, *El Imparcial*'s editor, Alejandro Córdova, was assassinated, an act generally understood to have been ordered by Jorge Ubico. Once a supporter, by 1944 he had become an outspoken critic of Ubico's government. Ester de Urrutia, representing of one of the newly created political parties, the Renovación Nacional, spoke at Córdova's funeral. His death and funeral reenergized the pro-revolutionary movement in the capital, propelling both the military and the civilian opposition into an armed insurrection.

The military element of the October revolution is well documented and dominates the historiography of the revolutionary era.[27] On October 19, 1944, a small group of military officers, including Jacobo Árbenz and Francisco Javier Arana, attacked the National Palace. During the night, weapons were distributed to civilians. The following morning, the military struck at garrisons across the city, essentially removing the last resistance. By the afternoon of October 20, acting president Juan Federico Ponce Vaides surrendered and left the country. On October 24, Ubico requested asylum in the United States and left the country, taking with him the last vestiges of his dictatorship.[28]

There is more to this well-known narrative, however. Hundreds of workers joined the movement, which some argue turned the tide in favor of the revolution.[29] The main police barracks were held by groups of women, who "started tearing up the paving stones and chanting, 'Lynch them! Kill them!' and charging the building with kitchen knives.... Meanwhile some fifty women clamored for weapons but were held back, while dozens of others sent their teenage sons into

A Small Payment for a Large Debt 115

battle. Children manned the barricades."[30] Another group of indigenous women protected a stash of weapons for the revolutionary forces while shouting, "We are defending our nation."[31] Some women, such as Berta de Figueroa, fought directly on the front line, although she was an exception.[32] Other women put themselves directly into the line of fire by leaving their homes to volunteer their services at the hospital. When the hospitals were full, the women of the Catholic charity San Vicente de Paul took the injured into their homes during the night, many of whom were children.[33] Ester de Urrutia opened her home to frightened young soldiers, providing them with food and shelter. Although these tasks were directly related to the success of the October revolution, revolutionary leaders did not interpret the women's actions as essential to the revolution's triumph because they fell within traditional gendered divisions of labor.[34]

While it is not possible to quantify or qualify women's contributions to the revolution's success, their actions indicate the existence of a broad cross-class consciousness regarding the struggle in which they were engaged. Aware of these implications, Luz Valle moved immediately to rectify the revolutionary record through a series of articles published in *El Imparcial*.[35] In direct contrast to the male images and narratives dominating the media, Valle highlighted vivid examples of female heroism from both June and October, insisting that these actions demonstrated conclusively that women were just as capable of patriotism. "Without previous instruction, modern woman understood her mission, acting purely on instinct."[36] Valle's depictions of these heroic efforts, however, did not penetrate the urban revolutionary consciousness, and by the end of October the image of María Chinchilla Recinos's martyrdom had been seared into the revolutionary imaginary.

The Second Revolution: "A New *Patria*"

The intransigent patriarchal milieu solidified by the military and masculinized victory in October belied and obscured another revolution occurring simultaneously in Guatemala City. The euphoria ladinas experienced over Ubico's resignation at the end of June was quickly replaced by the sobering realization that their struggle for a place in this emergent new public arena had only just begun. Already organized in literary associations and educator networks, these women cofounded the most important political parties of the revolution within days. Embedded in the political platforms of these new parties were political and social ideals such as democracy, citizenship for all Guatemalans, educa-

FIGURE 3.3 Revolutionary crowds. *El Imparcial*, October 22, 1944.

tional reform, and social welfare, ideals that were advocated throughout both the Arévalo and the Árbenz presidencies. It quickly became apparent to these women, however, that a majority of their male colleagues had no interest in integrating women into their ranks and in fact immediately marginalized them from positions of political authority, a process further explored in chapter 4. Understanding that the state and its male leaders were unwilling to integrate them into formal political authority, these women chose to establish their own sphere of influence, exploiting the sociopolitical freedom of the new era. Rather than directly confronting male patriarchy in every project, they worked largely outside of institutional boundaries and formal male-dominated associations, defining their own reforms without the overt interference of men. They created a parallel reform movement distinct from the male revolutionary hierarchy, born of their own perceptions and lived experiences as teachers and social welfare volunteers. Receiving no formal response from the revolutionary leaders to Luz Valle's clarion declaration that "the women's army is ready and waits for its orders," the urban ladina community embarked upon a second and vastly more

A Small Payment for a Large Debt 117

challenging revolutionary process. The women in this second revolution would attempt to integrate themselves into every facet of Guatemalan society, with the hope of changing its gendered foundation.³⁷

Urban ladinas within the network of *Nosotras* and *Azul* readers, led by experienced journalists Luz Valle and Gloria Menéndez Mina, now publicly claimed their rights and obligations within the revolutionary project. Drawing upon the concepts of patriotism they had been developing among their readership, the two journalists now outlined their claims for public participation and citizenship. In the hours following Ubico's resignation, Menéndez Mina launched this call: "Women of Guatemala! Let's form a common front to give children a promise of the future—a new concept of the homeland, making their duties and responsibilities known from the first dawn of life!"³⁸ In a special editorial, "Épica gloriosa," Isaura de Menéndez Mina, Gloria's mother, emphasized the role of all Guatemalans in the armed insurrection, emphasizing the actions of young people and the cross-class participation.³⁹ Luz Valle extended the revolutionary patriotism that infused Gloria Menéndez Mina's rhetoric to include an overtly feminist agenda, claiming that Guatemalan women had always felt two great responsibilities, to the home and to the country, which she insisted was not contradictory. For women, the love of home was easily translated to a love of nation because women as mothers were concerned about the future of their children. Therefore, they were also equally capable of making clear political decisions in the best interests of their family. What had kept women ignorant of politics, Valle argued, was not their disinterest but the sociopolitical repression of the Ubico era and particularly the lack of news. "Show me women who do not understand politics and I'll show you a river of tears and an ocean of desolation."⁴⁰ Thankfully, she noted, the days were over when women understood politics but could not act on their knowledge. In this new era, they could now participate in the political process. In other words, women had always silently suffered the consequences of politics while being unable to effect any change within the political system. While Vicenta Laparra de la Cerda had deconstructed motherhood from the identity of woman in her defense of women's rights in the 1880s, Valle used the imagery of home and nation as relational concepts. Establishing maternalism as the indelible link between home and nation, Valle claimed a legitimate place for women in the revolution. Her feminist vision included all women, and she explicitly named the disabled, the working class, the forgotten single women, and domestic servants.⁴¹

Valle traced their preparedness for civic participation to the work of educators, crediting teachers, both past and present, with inciting the greatest social and political revolution. According to Valle, women were prepared for political participation thanks to the work of teachers who had educated generations of young women and men precisely for the possibility of this moment, when Guatemalans could participate in their own political affairs.[42] Thanks to these teachers, women believed themselves to be efficient, capable of self-denial, and filled with self-worth. Here at last, Luz Valle could finally articulate the internal feminist consciousness that she and Gloria Menéndez Mina had been cultivating through their journals.

In a manifesto that spanned weeks of editorials, Valle articulated a ladina feminism forged during previous decades though long dormant. Creating a platform that integrated both political and social rights, Valle's proposal essentially outlined the two dominant threads of urban feminism that would characterize the following decade. The first was evidenced by the social reform activities undertaken immediately following Ubico's resignation in June, while the second movement would be embodied and articulated by the Alianza Femenina Guatemalteca, who interpreted maternal feminism directly into a socialist political ideology (see chapter 6). For women so long silenced, this was no less than a clarion call to action. Effectively incorporating notions of maternal feminism with a new patria, Valle now offered a new revolutionary symbol for urban ladinas to emulate. Rejecting the passive image of Minerva as the historical symbol of wisdom and the arts associated with the teaching community during the Estrada Cabrera era, Valle inverted it to underscore their ideals. In a series of editorials, *Bajo el Arco de Diana: Nueva Era Femenina*, Valle chose Diana, the Roman goddess of hunting, childbirth, women, and action, to accurately symbolize their emergent ideals. Employing this action-oriented goddess as her guide, Valle insisted that women wanted to be incorporated in Guatemala's political life, using the example of the Unión Femenina Guatemalteca and their campaign for suffrage. Although they would not be successful until March 1945, the suffragists had been responsible for introducing the first sustained debate over citizenship in Guatemala City since 1920 (see chapter 4).

With this claim to citizenship, Valle noted, came increased responsibilities, including the need for women to work collectively for social reform, and she outlined their goals, fusing elements of accountability, citizenship, and intellectual pursuits.[43] She claimed that every woman had a role to play, that every home could be transformed into a school where all children learned to read and grow up in a dignified manner. Valle noted that only when the Guatemalan revolution implemented protective and humane laws to address illiteracy, the lack of social assistance, and the vulnerability of single women and children would the ladina community be satisfied. She highlighted domestic workers as a social class deserving of special attention. Having been concerned about the lives of poor and indigenous women and children, Valle now publicly speculated how the emergent feminist movements (presumably of the middle and upper classes) might work with Guatemalans of all social classes.

One of the central conundrums of the revolutionary era is the state's rejection of the energy and vision of the urban ladina community. Even as teachers and activists addressed some of the most urgent social and political challenges, ladinas were restricted from positions of any real power. While they engaged in social reforms and political activities that disrupted gender norms, a debate on gender roles remained conspicuously absent from the public realm. The extent of patriarchal anxiety was evidenced by writers such as Luz Valle, who soothed her reticent male audience with assurances that feminist ideals neither detracted from essential qualities of femininity nor replaced their need of men. Historian Cindy Forster's analysis of the revolution supports this perspective, noting a deep resistance to the incorporation of women at all levels, concluding that women remained largely unmobilized on the basis of gender. In fact, she argues that revolutionary men had more in common with their male counterrevolutionary opponents than with their female revolutionary colleagues, a fact borne out in the numerous biographies of the era.[44]

The marginalization of women as political subjects had serious ramifications for the revolution's long-term welfare. The parallel gender structure articulated in *Diario de Centro América* demonstrates the demarcation of the female sphere. Social reforms and the care of children, orphans, and the disabled were identified as female work, essentially affirming and solidifying the gendered binary of masculine and feminine spheres. Relegating their efforts to the social realm depoliticized ladinas, who were in fact critical to the revolution's success. The Catholic Church moved into this vacancy, leading the rhetoric regarding gender roles. Affirming women's traditional social position of wife and mother, church leaders nevertheless exploited the issue for their own political concerns. Theirs, however, was a defensive position, arguing that the church existed to protect women from changing gender norms. They called upon women to act on behalf of their "natural" roles as mothers and wives in order to preserve the traditional political order and deter fundamental change, an enterprise in which the antirevolutionary movement would become highly successful as the decade progressed.

Nowhere was this sociopolitical marginalization more evident than in the education system, a space historically dominated by urban ladinas. Having survived the teachers' march, ladina educators entered the revolutionary decade with a clear sense of social responsibility and high expectations for reform from the presidential educator Juan José Arévalo. As they had expected, the first democratically elected president immediately began to reverse Ubico-era policies, believing that the revolution's success lay in an educated populace. The revolutionary project established education as both a philosophical ideal and a concrete goal, institutionalized in Decree 20.[45] Analysts believed that literate men and women could be courted by both labor unions and political parties more quickly, and health campaigns could be propagated through inexpensive pamphlets. Education became inextricably linked to the revolution's success from the perspective of intellectual leaders because it allowed people to function as conscientious political and social citizens. Consequently, the state directed enormous resources to the expansion of educational programs and the training of teachers.

In the weeks following the October revolution, education became obligatory, free, and secular under the ruling junta.[46] The Arévalo government followed up with a comprehensive set of reforms, exerting a great deal of time and effort in determining the exact course of action necessary. The state's expenditure on education increased 800 percent, the number of rural schools grew by nearly 90 percent, and for the first time in history the government allocated more money to education than to the military.[47] These policies paid particular attention to rural and indigenous communities, particularly the issue of class size, the number of children who completed each grade, and how many children repeated grades. They highlighted how late some children started attending school, noting that some were repeating the second grade at the age of fifteen. In the capital city, a majority of girls started the first grade at the age of nine rather than the ideal age of seven.[48]

As with all other social indicators, education statistics revealed the neglect of previous administrations. The initial educational recommendations made by the newly minted minister of education, Carlos González Orellana, and the Arévalo administration were based upon the 1940 census data, which was revealed to be unreliable. Basing his conclusions on this old data, González Orellana noted that 64 percent of school-age children did not attend school, while another thirty-four thousand children only attended when not needed to economically support their families.[49] When the 1950 census was completed, the depth of the educational crisis was revealed, affirming that one administration of well-intentioned leaders simply had been unable to effect significant change. In fact, the 1950 census indicated a situation more critical than previously believed, revealing the discrepancies in access to education between the urban and rural settings, and between ladino and indigenous populations. The national average of school attendance was in fact only 12.1 percent, with more boys than girls attending school. While the national literary rate was 28.1 percent (see appendix C and table 3.2), rates were more optimistic for the urban population, with 65.3 percent for men and 52.9 percent for women.[50] The rural and indigenous populations had much lower percentages, with indigenous women at the bottom with a literacy rate of merely 4 percent. It also became clear to the Arévalo state that, given the lack of schools, as much as 90 percent of indigenous children did not attend school.[51]

> Opportunities for Indians to enter secondary school are rare since the majority of the rural schools teach only the first two grades. Teaching is in Spanish, with little or no attention paid to practical subjects [reading or writing]. It is no wonder that the Indian adults resist this type of schooling—only 1,711 rural students finished their course of study in 1947–1948, a year in which the attendance was put at 69,162. Attendance in the rural areas is generally irregular due to poor transportation, the disinterest of the Indian parents, and unenthusiastic teaching, conditioned partially by wages of Q30 per month, inadequate training, and poor teaching materials.[52]

In response to this national crisis, the Arévalo state issued a call for forty thousand to fifty thousand new teachers, and hundreds of young women enrolled in normal schools. By 1946, the primary normal school in Guatemala City, the Instituto Normal de Señoritas, Belén, was overflowing with more than eight hundred students who had responded to the higher wages, new work opportunities, and generalized revolutionary fervor over the importance of education. In fact, every normal school in the country became overwhelmed by the number of registered students, and as a result, a second normal school was established in Guatemala City on April 11, 1946. The Escuela Normal para Señoritas "Centro América" opened in a festive ceremony presided over by the minister of public education, Manuel Galich, and even though the building was in disrepair, the need for new teachers was so urgent that the administration opened it ahead of the necessary repairs.[53] Luz Valle's 1937 ally, educator, and leader in the struggle for suffrage Julia Meléndez de DeLeón became the school's director. She had expansive goals for the new schools, which included training teachers for rural schools, helping foster the theater arts, working with municipal authorities, engaging in national transformation, and encouraging communication between teachers in rural areas and local authorities.

The role of teachers during the revolution evolved into a complex sociopolitical manifestation of ideals in Guatemala City. The number of female teachers far outpaced the recruitment of male teachers, increasing by some 2,441, or approximately 44 percent, to a total of 5,524 (see appendix B).[54] The hundreds of new teachers became the representatives of the revolution, particularly for those sent into rural areas. Working daily with students, teachers were frequently the only government representatives small and isolated communities ever encountered. As a result, they became critical transmitters of government policies and programs, even used as reliable gatherers of information about communicable diseases.[55] They were used to monitor the health status of their students and became critical census takers for the important 1950 census, which scholars believe was the most accurate census in Guatemalan history up to that point. To their credit, these young women took whatever opportunities were available to them, and the revolutionary decade offered opportunities for higher education as they entered both the normal schools and the university in unprecedented numbers. Although the educational sphere in Guatemala had been highly feminized since the 1880s, once it had been identified as one of the revolution's core values, educational policy was placed firmly in the masculinized field of politics. Despite their experience and expertise (the number of female teachers had always been double that of men), women were restricted from assuming positions of influence or seniority, and few female educators were elevated to such status. Cindy Forster's conclusions support these findings, arguing that ladinas were only reluctantly integrated into the revolutionary project as educators and then largely barred from the practice of revolutionary equality: "It was an exclusion only rarely relaxed . . . and only a handful entered the ranks of politicians or senior officeholders."[56] Gloria Menéndez Mina highlighted this discrepancy in 1945 following the extended sabbatical of the minister of public education. Campaigning for long-time educator María Albertina Gálvez to this influential position, the journalist argued that her posting to the ministry was a simple matter of justice for all Guatemalan women.[57] Despite these efforts, no women served in this position throughout the revolutionary decade. After decades of advocacy in the face of dictatorships and limited resources, education was essentially removed from the historical purview of women.[58]

The challenges of working in male-dominated organizations became immediately apparent to social activists, a lesson they integrated into the social reform movement that began less than two months after the murder of María Chinchilla Recinos. Meeting at the Club Guatemala on August 19, a gathering of women sought to facilitate the creation of a development program for their city's poorest citizens. Identified as the "society of friends" by the editor of *El Imparcial*, they represented a diverse segment of urban society including teachers, the traditional elite, Catholic charity circles, and the founders of the Sociedad Protectora del Niño along with women from the newly minted revolutionary political parties.[59] Bound by a common social consciousness, their broad goals included many elements of puericultura initiated during the 1920s, such as the improvement of living conditions in the home, education in hygiene, the increased availability of health care, education for pregnant women, and guidance in the care of children. To paraphrase historian Susie Porter, the group created a social platform in which the maternalization of women's rights was intrinsically bound.[60] However, within this maternalized sphere they included an economic component, insisting that in order to successfully create long-term benefits, poor women also needed employment and an adequate salary. Although the group did not have much influence to make institutional economic changes to improve the lives of the urban poor, in connecting traditional maternal reforms with broader economic security, the "society of friends" introduced a new element to the existing social reform ideology in Guatemala City. Although a majority of urban ladinas remained reticent to address structural issues, this initial gathering demonstrated that they understood the deep inequalities of the Guatemalan context. However, precisely how to address this historical inequality would become one of the most divisive elements in the urban ladina community now that action was possible.

If the socioeconomic ideals introduced by the "society of friends" appeared ambitious in light of their inexperience, they were in fact modest in light of urban social statistics. Seventy years of Liberal governments designed to benefit the agricultural and political elite had resulted in a generalized lack of concern for the basic needs of the poor and working class. However, the ladina activists had little reliable data on which to base their efforts. The picture was so incomplete that Oscar Juárez y Aragón, the author of a 1943 study on birthrates and infant mortality, did not believe that he could make any definitive conclusions. What is clear, however, from the available data is that life for the vast majority of residents in Guatemala City was a precarious affair. The statistics Juárez y Aragón collected during the first six months of 1943 painted a bleak picture of life for many urban Guatemalans. Out of a total of 3,964 births in Guatemala City during that period, only 1,235 took place in a hospital. Although 803 infants were reported to have died within their first year of life, only 135 of them did so in a hospital. During the same six-month period, out of 7,928 children born countrywide, 1,606 of them died, giving Guatemala an infant mortality rate of 202/1,000, the highest in Latin America at that time.[61] Juárez y Aragón's dire conclusions were confirmed by government statistics retrieved from the Department of Social Assistance in 1949 that disclosed that of the 140,596 children born in Guatemala, only 6,801 received medical attention, leaving 135,795 with no health care, a full 96 percent.[62] Conclusions reached by the government's Instituto Guatemalteco de Seguridad Social (IGSS) confirmed these findings, revealing that 26,993 Guatemalan children up to the age of five died each year.[63] Scholar Leo Suslow corroborated these figures again in his 1954 study on the Guatemalan social security system, leading him to conclude that "there existed in Guatemala conditions of backwardness and social misery so pronounced that they make urgent and non-deferrable the adoption of measures conducive to lifting in a systematic and gradual form the level of living of our people."[64]

Luz Valle's assertions that women understood politics through its implications in the home were far more accurate than even she may have intended. For most women in Guatemala City, the home was the site where they were born, lived, gave birth, and usually died, with no access to adequate medical care for themselves or their children. The informal market economy offered no social protection, and so the home also became the place where children suffered from treatable diseases such as diarrhea and enteritis (3,647 reported cases among children), intestinal parasites (4,435), respiratory illness such as tuberculosis (4,623), malaria (2,654), and influenza (2,216), as reported in 1947 by *Nuestro Diario*.[65] For those children fortunate enough to survive, more than 75 percent remained malnourished. Juárez y Aragón's findings confirmed what advocates such as Malin D'Echevers, Juan José Orozco, and Raúl Lorenzana had been writing about in *Nosotras* since the early 1930s. These statistics had been evident in the faces of schoolchildren witnessed by educators, confirming what everyone in Guatemala already knew.[66] A majority of Guatemalans did not receive adequate medical care, and the country did not have enough doctors. According to the IGSS, established in 1946, the vast majority of the country's physicians worked in Guatemala City (75 percent of the total of 390), creating a ratio of 1 physician for every 695 inhabitants in the capital. In direct contrast, the ratio of doctors to the population outside of the capital was 1 for every 32,437 citizens.[67]

While this data served as the impetus for the establishment of the comedores infantíles and guarderías infantíles, it was another study in 1947 that confirmed the urgency to increase and expand the project. A study on maternal health by Moisés Ortega Ávila, conducted between January and June 1947, discovered that out of 3,372 births in the capital city during that six-month period, 287 women died of complications during or after childbirth. Out of a total population of 198,157, only 310 women sought medical attention during pregnancy every month, and many of these suffered from syphilis, anemia, and intestinal parasites.[68] Tuberculosis ranked as the most significant mortality factor for women between fifteen and fifty years of age, accounting for almost 29 percent, or eighty-one deaths, during that period. In response to these findings, a national campaign against tuberculosis was initiated. The startling results concluded that well over 90 percent of Guatemalan women did not have health care during pregnancy or the birth process.[69] Following his analysis, Ortega Ávila concluded that prenatal care was an urgent priority for Guatemala City, and he strongly advised that centers like those established by Elisa Martínez de Arévalo for children also be established for pregnant women.[70]

These stark statistics were embodied in the lives of thousands of women, men, and children without access to education, health care, or employment coexisting uneasily with the middle and upper classes in Guatemala City. Consequently, poor and working-class women used whatever means were at their disposal to advocate for themselves and their children, petitioning the court system to report spousal abandonment and spousal abuse, and requesting the return of property as well as child support. They pleaded with the Jefatura Política, the governor's office, for the department of Guatemala to intervene in cases of neighborhood violence, destruction of property, and even unsafe working conditions. Market women used their collective energies to promote safer work spaces and resist intrusions by the state that detracted from their meager earnings. Following the October revolution, the Jefatura Política received so many petitions for child support from women that the office initiated a general call for all men delinquent in their payments to come forward in the hope that this would alleviate the need to address the situation on a case-by-case basis. The gendered implications of this fragile existence became clear to the revolutionary leaders through a petition submitted in 1946. In a letter addressed to the governor, a woman outlined her crisis. Her spouse had been aligned with the pro-revolutionary forces and was killed in the October revolution. Now, as a single mother with five children, she could no longer feed all of them. She was now requesting assistance to place two of the youngest children in the city's orphanage, the Hospicio Nacional Centro Educativo, near the center of Zone One, where they would receive food and care (the Hospicio would play an important role in the antirevolutionary movement and will be further discussed in chapter 7).[71] Along with the obvious anguish inherent in such a petition, the woman's current situation revealed the precarious nature of life.

The Arévalo government addressed aspects of these alarming social indicators through the establishment of the 1947 Labor Code and the 1948 Social Security Act. The Labor Code addressed some of the inequities of women's labor and restricted the rights of employers to use child labor. Article 147 established that the work of women and children must be "especially suited to their age, physical condition, and moral and intellectual development."[72] Article 151 prohibited employers from differentiating between married and single women with respect to the work they were assigned, dismissing pregnant or lactating women, or forcing women to work excessively during the last trimester of pregnancy. Article 152 declared that all female workers had to be on maternity leave with pay thirty prior to delivery and forty-five days following birth. A new law created a Department of Maternity and Infancy under the auspices of the National Department of Hygiene. While these measures were critical new pieces of labor legislation for those in the formal labor market, which did include some women, the vast majority of at risk women and children did not participate in it, operating instead in the informal market and agricultural sectors. Consequently, neither of these two legislative reforms addressed the country's inherent social inequities as they related particularly to women. Nor did they solve the problem of poverty for economically vulnerable families who depended upon the labor of all family members in order to survive.

A deep gender bias remained at the heart of the Arévalo labor reforms, mitigating their impact on urban women. First, they were mostly effective within the formal labor sector, thereby sidestepping the majority of female workers who overwhelmingly worked in the informal economy. The competition for any open job, particularly unionized jobs, was fierce, and employers were hesitant to hire any women, even during the revolutionary decade. Second, the laws assumed men to be the primary wage earners, affirming their male privilege vis-à-vis all other workers and dependents. However, although statistics are not available, all evidence points to the reality that a significant percentage of poor and working-class women in Guatemala City functioned as head of household, contradicting the generally held view that women's income was secondary to the household. All of these factors point to the same conclusion Karin Rosemblatt reached in her work on Chile, namely that "political elites justified political and

TABLE 3.1 Infant Mortality and Deaths at Birth, 1947–1951[1]

YEAR	INFANT MORTALITY	DEATHS PER 1,000	DEATHS AT BIRTH	DEATHS PER 1,000
1947	14,736	109.9	4,156	30.1
1948	16,081	117.4	4,539	33.1
1949	14,304	101.7	4,309	30.6
1950	15,493	113.4	4,137	30.3
1951	14,031	92.7	4,524	29.9

1. Suslow, "Social Security in Guatemala," 33.

economic entitlements by acknowledging (male) workers' productive contributions to the nation and by linking the rights and responsibilities of workers to their role as family heads."[73] Therefore, the social reform movement addressed a critical socioeconomic space ignored by broader political and economic reforms, and its ideals found an ally in the likes of first lady Elisa Martínez de Arévalo, whose own political and social ideals coalesced powerfully with the dominant feminisms and social ideals of middle-class ladinas. Her familial origins as a working-class woman would influence the movement to incorporate this particular group into the foundations of the reform movement, changing the course of the revolutionary era for thousands of women and children.

Elisa Martínez de Arévalo: Political Maternalism

With the 1944 revolution, another parental style of leadership emerged in the form of Elisa Martínez de Arévalo, the wife of President Juan José Arévalo.[74] Jorge Ubico had used gender norms to justify his authoritarian rule, maintaining sociopolitical control as a benevolent father figure through personal presidential visits. Appearing randomly on his motorcycle throughout the country, Ubico would bestow justice or punishment at his discretion. These actions served to reduce crime and potential political resistance, instilling fear or loyalty depending upon the circumstance. In stark contrast to the self-appointed father of the nation, Martínez de Arévalo entered the public sphere with personal warmth, intelligence, and compassion. Eager to understand and support her adopted country, she went into the streets of Guatemala City to speak with women of all social classes. Concerned particularly with the pervasive poverty of working-class women, she went directly into the markets to discuss these issues with the city's most vulnerable population. Poor and working-class women now found an ally in the first lady, and she became known to city residents as simply doña Elisa, connoting the affection and intimacy she had established. With the arrival of Elisa Martínez de Arévalo, parental authority shifted from a harsh tyrannical father to a nurturing motherly presence.[75]

Latin American presidential wives have received little scholarly attention with the notable exception of Argentine first lady Eva Perón, whose assumption of political power alongside her husband has provoked extensive analysis and criticism.[76] In marked contrast to the stereotypical presidential wife who remained in the political shadows lending support to elite charity circles, Martínez de Arévalo along with her successor, María Vilanova de Árbenz, assumed public and political profiles. Despite her extensive work, however, Martínez de Arévalo has received practically no academic attention. Ironically, like Eva Perón, Elisa Martínez de Arévalo was Argentine, born in Tucumán, to a lower middle-class family. She met and married Juan José Arévalo while he was studying at the National University of Tucumán, in exile from the Ubico regime. A teacher by profession, she taught in Buenos Aires until September 1944, when the couple returned to Guatemala to pursue Arévalo's presidential bid. Drawn together by their shared social principles, once in office the couple used their political position to translate ideals into political action. Although Arévalo's rather vague notions of spiritual socialism have been criticized as the cause of his haphazard implementation of economic and social reforms, Martínez de Arévalo enacted concrete reforms designed to improve the lives of poor and working-class women and their children, earning her the affectionate nickname "mother of Guatemala's children."

Her normal school education and the social mobility it offered explain in part Martínez de Arévalo's unique social and political perspective. While scholars have identified education to be a key factor in the rise of Latin American feminism, less attention has been paid to the social mobility of these young women. The rise of normal school training for teachers drew rural women into urban centers across the region, bringing with them class consciousness and social sensitivity. The sociopolitical consequence of the upward mobility of this particular social sector has not been closely examined. However, the work of Martínez de Arévalo and other like-minded women she encountered in Guatemala City who were eager to create cross-class alliances suggests that further analysis would be fruitful. Drawing everyone into a single association, the first lady helped to create the largest project undertaken by the revolutionary social reformers, elements of which remain in operation to the present day.[77]

The allegiance developed among the middle and lower classes with doña Elisa, however, did not extend to the upper classes in the capital city. Despite their initial eagerness to work with Martínez de Arévalo, her insistence that poor women must be more than simply objects of social reform alienated many among the elite charity circles who preferred a traditional charity model over deeper social reform. Many simply refused to associate with the poor women whom Elisa invited into her home. The Central Intelligence Agency would later redirect the ensuing criticisms from these elite women onto Martínez de Arévalo, accusing her of mismanaging the children's lunch programs and daycare centers. These same critics reinterpreted her desire to work with poor women as evidence of her personal insecurity, of not wanting to be around more attractive women.[78] As doña Elisa quickly discovered, challenging Guatemala's hierarchical class structure earned a vitriolic response from many who had initially welcomed her.

Despite clear differences in their personal styles, the similarities between the social welfare projects they enacted beg a comparison between the two presidential wives, Argentines Eva Perón and Elisa Martínez de Arévalo. Scholars have argued that Perón's public concern for the poor emerged from her own experiences of social and economic marginalization. Although not as poor as Perón, Elisa Martínez's own humble origins clearly do not conform to the elite backgrounds common to presidential wives. Both women shared a deep concern for women and children, a preoccupation some believe arose out of their mutual childlessness.[79] Both women were jointly supportive of one another's work, with Martínez de Arévalo speaking highly of Eva Perón's work on several occasions. In turn, Perón maintained a relationship with those in charge of the Guatemalan daycare centers and lunch programs, sending financial assistance in support of the work.[80] Both projects were markedly maternalistic in nature, and both women worked closely with the lower classes, maintaining a highly personal style of leadership. However, that is where the similarities end.

Eva Perón's political ambitions played an integral role in her charity work. As Donna Guy notes, Perón performed her acts of charity with an eye for her own interests. "Throughout her life Eva remained the head of her own institution, thereby refusing to share the social status she accrued from performing welfare."[81] More altruistic than her Argentine counterpart, Elisa Martínez de Arévalo acted within a broader circle of reformers including the least visible in Guatemalan society, appointing others rather than herself to leadership positions. In addition, Martínez de Arévalo extended her idealism beyond social welfare to institutional reforms. In keeping with the broader goals of the "society of friends," her ideals included an economic element; she advocated the creation of jobs, which would help offset the desperate poverty in which so many women and children found themselves. While the work of comedores infantíles and guarderías infantíles shared much in common with Perón's foundation, Martínez de Arévalo's work in fact predates it by at least a year. Although the brevity of the revolutionary project allowed for the implementation of only modest systematic economic reforms, Martínez de Arévalo's economic development component within a broader social reform model set her ideas apart from those of Perón. While Perón was devastated by the sociopolitical slights by the elite, it appears to have mattered less to Martínez de Arévalo, whose work and political prestige were not dependent upon the traditional elite women's circles. The antagonism Martínez de Arévalo received, however, did contribute to the growing alienation of the revolutionary project by the Guatemalan elite and the United States, who drew parallels between Arévalo's modest socioeconomic reforms and communism.

The pro-revolutionary elite and emergent social reform movement warmly embraced Martínez de Arévalo's efforts. Under her leadership, the unprecedented social reforms offered a distinctly new sense of nationalism as the poor were directly integrated into the national revolutionary project. Drawing likeminded women together, she helped to create the second revolution in the face of patriarchal resistance. Essentially working outside of the political process, Martínez de Arévalo sought broad-based civil support for these activities. Just as her successor, María Vilanova de Árbenz, confronted the nation's patriarchal system through the work of the Alianza Femenina Guatemalteca, Martínez de Arévalo aligned herself with the city's poorest to confront the equally powerful and deeply rooted hierarchical class structures. In short, her leadership was essential to the achievements of Guatemala City's social reform movement. When Martínez de Arévalo returned to Guatemala for a visit in 1952, more than ten thousand women and children gathered at Olympic Stadium to honor her, indicative of her contributions. The activism of Martínez de Arévalo and her circle of social reformers represents a singular era in Guatemala.

A Small Payment for a Large Debt

The women who joined forces in August 1944 to address Guatemala's social needs were neither physicians nor politicians, as was common among other Latin American reformers. Historically disenfranchised from virtually every aspect of socioeconomic life with the exception of teaching, professional women were virtually nonexistent, and their economic profile remained remarkably similar to that of the 1880s (see table 3.2). Although a few gender barriers had been broken by the late 1940s, primarily by women working as lawyers and doctors, their numbers remained extremely low. The social reform movement provided an alternative model of power and authority, symbolizing the emergence of a maturing feminism within their ranks, one that forged social justice concerns for the poor with broader notions of puericultura, suffrage, and citizenship.

The comedores infantíles and guarderías infantíles represented the foundation for Guatemala's social reform and first child protection movement. The most successful project initiated by those in the second revolution, a network of child-care and nutrition centers was established throughout the country. In a marked departure from the Sociedad Protectora del Niño and the Catholic charity network, these centers embraced a new model of social reform. As a joint project among civilians, the intentions behind it extended beyond the customary charitable approach. Its goals envisioned a comprehensive approach to pervasive socioeconomic inequities precisely because its founders came from all social classes. When the first centers established in Guatemala City became instantly successful, many more were quickly created in cities around the country. These centers allowed children to remain close to their mothers during the day while providing them with a clean and safe place to play, rest, and eat. Not only did this project directly benefit more than ten thousand children by the end of the revolutionary period, but it was a unique and perhaps singular collaboration in Guatemalan history up until this point. The network of daycare and nutrition centers established the presence of the revolutionary government in the daily lives of the country's most vulnerable and directly influenced the creation of the country's first school of social work.[82]

Elisa Martínez de Arévalo brought a wealth of knowledge to Guatemala, as Argentina had been an influential leader in the creation of social reform programs and the child welfare movement since the turn of the twentieth century.[83] Originating in Buenos Aires in 1916, eight Pan American Child Congresses had been held throughout the Americas to promote and enact legislation on behalf of children.[84] Attempting to make up for lost time, Guatemalan social reformers eagerly engaged with this hemispheric trend that measured the well-being of mothers and children as barometers for national modernity, exerting a great deal of effort to enact similar reforms.[85] Drawing upon the examples of Argentina, Chile, and Mexico, Guatemala joined the Instituto Interamericano del Niño in 1946, sending politician Juan José Orozco to the United States to tour

TABLE 3.2 Guatemalan Women's Professional Profile

PROFESSION	1920[1]	1940[2]	1950[3]
Pharmacists	5	29	40
Schoolteachers	1,134	3,083	5,524
Lawyers/Notaries	0	6 (primarily notaries)	4
Doctors	0	8	10
Dentists	0	3	2
Nurses	0	260	276
Musicians/Teachers	1	27	69
Religious Workers/Nuns	43	108	137
Domestics	62,020	838,101[4] (84,510)	38,189[5]

1. Dirección General de Estadística, *Censo de la República de Guatemala, 1921*, 285–87.

2. Dirección General de Estadística, *Quinto censo general de población, levantado el 7 de Abril de 1940*, 867–69.

3. Dirección General de Estadística, *Censos de la República de Guatemala, 1950*, 219.

4. The skewed number in 1940 comes from Jorge Ubico counting all housewives as domestic workers.

5. The actual number was no doubt much larger.

boys' orphanages. Guatemala also sent delegates to the ninth Child Congress in Caracas, Venezuela, in 1948, a transnational meeting that both affirmed their ideals and provided models for the neophyte social reformers.[86] Their efforts to promote social reform in Guatemala continued after Arévalo's term in office with the new first lady, María Vilanova de Árbenz, and the Alianza Femenina Guatemalteca (see chapter 6).

Synergy for the initial project emerged from several sectors in Guatemala City that coalesced in the months following the October revolution. Having met in August 1944, the "society of friends" were eager to address the city's enormous social challenges, bringing with them some experience of social reform programs from the 1920s. Although somewhat limited in their experiences, they had the conviction that social reforms represented an integral rather than a subsidiary element of the emerging democracy. The second group critical to the ultimate outcome were the women working in Colón Market, one of nine public markets scattered throughout the city, who immediately understood the implications of the October revolution. Within days, they had organized to petition the new government for improved working conditions, and they came to the inaugural meetings with clear ideas for concrete reforms.[87] Unwilling to wait until her husband's inauguration and building upon the energy and vision emerging from sectors throughout the city, Elisa Martínez de Arévalo called an initial planning meeting at her home on February 20, 1945.[88] Several leaders from the female affiliates of the political parties, the Renovación Nacional and Frente Popular Libertador, attended, presenting the program for social development envisioned in August 1944. Following this initial consultation, Martínez de Arévalo visited some of the markets in Guatemala City, accompanied by the female affiliates of the Renovación Nacional, the following week. According to eyewitness accounts, Martínez de Arévalo spoke directly with these women, asking them specifically how the government might meet their needs. In a subsequent meeting held on April 5, 1945, Martínez de Arévalo invited women representing all social and political sectors to her home, believing that "who better understood the problems of the poor than poor women themselves."[89] A seven-hour meeting ensued in which women from newly minted political parties, students, teachers, and women from Guatemala City's markets discussed their ideas. As a result, a twofold plan was proposed. First, daycare centers near the markets and workplaces of working women would be established, followed by nutrition centers scattered throughout the city.

Several critical conclusions about how to proceed with this project emerged from these first meetings, findings that remained pivotal to the core nature of the project for the next decade. The group held a common belief that Guatemala's new democratic spirit honored political diversity within their ranks.[90] Therefore they made a conscious decision to include women of all political sectors. Furthermore, in keeping with this democratic fervor, the founders believed that their efforts should remain apolitical, not bound to any specific bias. Therefore, any recipients of the programs should not be dependent upon any political affiliation. Finally, the group believed that they should remain a female-centered organization, barring the involvement of men. As will be discussed in chapter 4, these women had already been marginalized in their own political parties and clearly had no desire to struggle against patriarchy in this project as well. Consequently, they created a project that offered an autonomous feminized space that empowered working poor women and children.

However, something else also emerged from this meeting that fundamentally altered the trajectory of the movement. Some of those from the elite social circles who had originally attended the August 1944 meetings and had eagerly embraced Martínez de Arévalo and her ideals, now withdrew their support from the project. Her insistence that working-class women must be included in the planning organization confronted Guatemala's deeply entrenched hierarchical structure, and they were unwilling to continue their collaboration. Consequently, the project moved forward as a cross-class initiative among middle- and working-class women without the traditional elite charity circles, symbolizing a new democratic era. While Martínez de Arévalo's insistence on the involvement of the poor in this project is an issue that cannot be overstated, their engagement in the program also guaranteed better chances of success. In a similar dining hall program established in 1941 in Mexico City, historian Nichole Sanders noted that many of the poor resisted participating in the new programs out of suspicion of the middle- and upper-class reformers' intentions.[91] The veracity of Martínez de Arévalo's approach became immediately evident with the success of the nutrition centers and daycare programs across the city. Within months, thousands of children were able to spend their days in a safe and clean environment, receiving medical care and adequate nutrition.

The significance of the unusual nature of this collaboration is further evidenced by the absence of the moralizing rhetoric that usually accompanied charitable activities. There can be little doubt that incorporating the presence and visions of the working class influenced the nature of the work. Quite simply, they were not helping other women; they were working alongside of them. The poor were not merely objects upon which to enact reforms but were integral to the reforms themselves. The particular nature of the movement also demonstrated a level of obligation felt by many of the middle-class reformers. A year into the project, Gloria Menéndez Mina noted that this work represented simply a small payment for an enormous debt.[92] However, the revolutionary era allowed the market women and the poor working class to demonstrate their keen awareness of the current sociopolitical climate. Experiencing a new degree of empowerment, these historically marginalized women now advocated for themselves whenever possible and, in so doing, were able to broaden the imagined "place for themselves" that had previously been only the privilege of the literate middle and upper classes.

This shared cross-class vision culminated in another innovation closely related to the nutrition centers. The guarderías infantíles were child-care centers created specifically to address the child-care needs of market women in Guatemala City—the nutritional, medical, and educational needs of their children.[93] Initially funded by the Guatemalan state, the first guardería was established in La Palmita, the second in Guarda Viejo, and the third next to Colón Market. So urgent was the need for safe child care that the first center in La Palmita was opened within months on September 3, 1945, while the second opened just two months later on November 20. The organizers were concerned over the quality of the building for the third daycare center, but they went ahead with the project using an existing dilapidated structure. They weighed the risks over the intense need of the market women, whose children were forced to accompany them to work, playing and napping on the open ground. In spite of the inadequacy of the facility, this center opened on March 20, 1946, and was available for eleven hours each day (open from 7:00 a.m. until 6:00 p.m.). Medical care was provided to the children, and women working at the center soon discovered that many of these children carried contagious and potentially life-threatening illnesses such as tuberculosis. To treat the ill and to protect the other children, a home in Antigua, La Aurora, specifically designated as a sanatorium for children ill with tuberculosis, opened on November 20, 1946, also providing vaccinations.[94] Within a year of their establishment, three new daycare centers served as the daytime home to thousands of urban children. Although the guarderías infantíles centers included small maternity wings, following Ortega Ávila's 1947 report outlining the health issues faced by pregnant women, the association constructed a maternity unit in October 1950, the first since the Asilo de Maternidad Joaquina established in 1911 by Estrada Cabrera.[95] The Primera Maternidad Cantonal was designed exclusively for the use of mothers without the economic means to access medical care.

The second aspect of the project included a series of nutrition centers, which were frequently established alongside the daycare centers.[96] Although the association overseeing the nutrition centers remained separate from the daycare centers, many of the same women were involved in both projects. In a separate meeting on April 1, 1945, representatives from all social sectors met again to establish a breakfast and lunch program. This meeting included future first lady María Vilanova de Árbenz, Clemencia Rubio de Herrarte, Matilde R. de Bianchi, and Gloria Menéndez Mina. Calling themselves the Asociación de Damas Pro-Comedores Infantíles, they organized to promote the Asociación Pro-Comedores Infantíles.[97] Indicative of the multiple roles played by many urban women, Mélida Montenegro de Méndez (a founder of one of the first revolutionary political parties, the Frente Popular Libertador) was appointed the first president, while Victoria Chajón Chúa worked as the secretary.[98] The first two comedores were established in La Palmita in October 1945 and La Parroquia in November 1945, serving breakfast to children from ages two to twelve years. Their popularity spread and others quickly followed, including Guarda Viejo in May 1946, Cantón Barillas and La Reformita in January 1947, El Gallito in September 1948 (the difficult lives of the poor in this barrio are memorialized in Cristóbal Monzón Lemus's work *Camino de adolescente: La vida de Ramón en el barrio "El Gallito"*), and Cantón Landivar in October 1948.⁹⁹ By the end of the Arévalo administration, nine nutrition centers had been established in Guatemala City, including Ex-Castillo San José in May 1946 and La Floresta. Nine more centers were established in other departments, including Jalapa in October 1950, Zacapa in February 1951, El Progreso in November 1946, Salamá in March 1951, Antigua in November 1946, Chimaltenango in February 1948, Sololá in June 1946, Totonicapán in June 1948, Quetzaltenango in June 1946, and Cobán in November 1951. In total, these centers daily fed more than ten thousand children. Although the Ministry of Social Assistance supported both the guarderías and the Asociación de Damas Pro-Comedores Infantíles, a majority of the money was raised by the women organizers themselves, and they maintained the institutional autonomy of the project.¹⁰⁰

These reform ideals had farther-reaching political implications than might otherwise be imagined. First, the overwhelming economic needs of a majority of Guatemalans made this humanitarian work essential to the broader revolutionary goals of transforming Guatemalan life. Second, the political transformation from dictatorship to democracy created a great deal of economic and social uncertainty for many Guatemalans of all classes, and these daycare and nutrition centers helped to stabilize an uncertain economic future for many of the capital city's poorest residents. Although the revolution reformed the political and legal system, a world dominated by men, this new group addressed the daily needs of poor Guatemalans who were, by and large, disenfranchised from revolutionary participation through illiteracy, poverty, and gender. That is, the social reformers brought revolutionary ideals into social spaces that had been untouched by the broad political and structural reforms. In essence, the reforms adhered to the two separate spheres of revolutionary activity, political and social, divided by gender. Finally, their actions revealed a new kind of Guatemalan woman, one who was both civically and politically conscious.¹⁰¹

Elisa Martínez de Arévalo worked feverishly until the very end of her husband's presidency, inaugurating a new maternity unit in Guatemala City in September 1950, with thirty-one beds along with extensive pre- and postnatal care, and a new children's hospital with 160 beds in Puerto Barrios on February 4, 1951.¹⁰² The demand for more beds was so high that plans were underway to expand further into the rural areas even as her term came to an end.

The success of the social reform movement caught the attention of formal state actors. By 1948, more than sixteen institutions with some element of social reform operated in Guatemala City, including some Catholic Church initiatives and the Sociedad Protectora del Niño. A unanimous decision to coordinate all of these efforts following a meeting in December of that year resulted in the formation of Guatemala's first school for social work.[103] The school was sponsored by the Guatemalan Institute of Social Security (Instituto Guatemalteco de Seguridad Social, or IGSS), which had been established in 1946. The IGSS was the first social security system "based upon the method of social budgeting in the Americas." Prior to its establishment, the only social insurance available in Guatemala was for the army and select groups of civil servants, and the new system was designed to offset the historical negligence of the government.[104] With the support of dozens of experienced social reformers, the IGSS invited Dr. Walter Pettit, a former dean of the New York School of Social Work, to consult on the project. Urban ladinas with decades of experience were integrated into the organizing committee, including Rosa de Mora, Carmen Rodríguez Beteta, María Isabel Escobar, Graciela Quan Valenzuela de Reina, Marta Escobar de Richardson, Mélida Montenegro de Méndez (president of the Asociación de Damas Pro-Comedores Infantíles), and Lily de Pullín (Sociedad Protectora del Niño).[105]

The ideological underpinnings of the school for social work rested upon two primary focuses. First, the school was designed to provide education and tools for those programs and personnel already established. To that end, it was created specifically for those already working, providing evening and weekend courses. Its second objective lay in providing those already working with a professional degree, to formalize the work that had been accomplished without any acknowledgment for decades. The school was subsequently established on January 21, 1949.[106] Among the first graduates of the social work program were Mélida Muralles, one of the three Muralles sisters who became teachers during the 1930s (her sister Elisa was one of the founding members of the Frente Popular Libertador) and Marta Escobar de Richardson, one of the three founders of the Sociedad Protectora del Niño.

The institutionalization of the social reform movement confirmed all the concerns of its original founders. While the steering committee integrated the wisdom accumulated by the ladina community, the instructors of this new school remained all male, dismissing the hard-earned decades of experience urban ladinas and the working class brought to the subject.[107] In light of these developments, the wisdom behind the original insistence that the comedores infantíles and guarderías infantíles must remain autonomous of men or male associations became ever more clear. While the ability of these centers to act autonomously of the patriarchal system had led directly to a formal recognition of their work, their formalization marginalized those who had initiated the work, as they lacked the formal credentials deemed necessary to hold positions of authority. The institutionalization of the ladina social reform movement is not unprecedented. Donna Guy identified a similar process in her work on Argentina, noting that by the 1940s women had been effectively removed as child welfare specialists throughout Latin America. Male professionals viewed the family as a terrain upon which to create a modern working-class family that would supply future generations of citizens and impose nationalist ideas. Subsequently, they ignored specific roles for mothers and treated the family as a unit based upon sanitized poor children monitored by middle-class physicians. "Such a mission was so important that only men could undertake it."[108] The absence of women in the first social work school supports Guy's premise that this remained a masculine project.

Christine Ehrick has identified similar patterns in her work on Uruguay, where beneficent and other social reform work raised women's profile while relegating them to second-class status vis-à-vis their male peers. She notes that it is this contradiction, whereby women were enlisted to uphold social hierarchies and accept their own subordinate status, that formed a paternalistic liberal feminism during the late nineteenth and early twentieth centuries.[109] Although the Uruguayan women were able to find a role within the political hierarchy, it was a diminished one. In a strikingly similar fashion, Guatemalan social reformers found themselves caught in the asymmetrical power dynamics created by patriarchal gender norms. While they actively struggled against this marginalizing process within the political sphere, they were less successful within the social realm. International visitors were routinely taken on tours of the comedores infantíles and guarderías infantíles, which quickly became showpieces of the Arévalo government.[110] Founder and director of the Universidad Femenina de México Adela Formosa de Obregón presented Elisa Martínez de Arévalo with the highest honor of distinction to acknowledge her work.[111]

The establishment of the daycare and nutrition centers challenged the traditional social role played by the Catholic Church and its elite charity circles. The Arévalo and Árbenz governments publicly criticized the church on several occasions for its unwillingness to address the root causes of poverty. Martínez de Arévalo and her supporters, many of whom were not of the elite social class, directly impugned these historical benevolent associations by presenting broad-based social reforms designed to alleviate poverty rather than just mask it. The archbishop, Mariano Rossell y Arellano, understood that it would not be politically wise to directly confront the construction of these new children's centers, and so he chose to create a new program of his own under church auspices. The church thus established two schools for indigenous children in the capital: in 1945, a boys' school, the Colegio Santiago, and in 1949, a girls' school.[112] In the face of Guatemala's stark social challenges, the establishment of new children's homes for the poor can certainly not be seen as a problem. However, when analyzed within the context of the church-sponsored antirevolutionary campaign against both the Arévalo and Árbenz administrations, it is clear that the conflict extended into the social care of children and poor families.

Conclusion

Few could have imagined the rapid course of events that would transform Guatemala's political landscape during 1944. The revolution introduced sweeping political reforms that represented populist socioeconomic ideals. In a nation whose political history has been characterized primarily by oppressive dictatorships, the simple freedom to express their ideas, to organize and demonstrate, and to advocate without fear of a violent response emerged as the defining factor for women of Guatemala City. By no means does my argument imply that race and class were irrelevant to the social construction of the revolutionary period. However, these factors were mitigated by the freedoms allowed and the concerns raised over basic fundamental human rights. Recent work by David Carey on Kaqchikel women notes a similar complexity that defies the boundaries of racism or class. He notes that "although Guatemala's economic, political, and social structures oppressed them as poor, as Maya, and as females, Kaqchikel women found ways to minimize their marginalization and at times to improve their status. They were neither powerless nor autonomous. Where other sources ignore or misrepresent them, their own historical narratives present women as protagonists."[113] This freedom was a far more significant element than the boundaries defined by race, class, or gender. Therefore, while legal and social patriarchy remained a formidable obstacle, this democratic period allowed these women an unprecedented ability to organize on their own terms. Even the most conservative women believed that they had been empowered to create their own history, or, as Josefina Maldonado Cifuentes stated in 1948, "women are writing the history of Guatemala in gold."[114] The world that many of these women had been dreaming about and imagining for decades had started to become a reality.

When Luz Valle's clarion call that the women's army was ready for its orders went unanswered, women created their own separate revolutionary sphere. In her work on revolutions and gender, Maxine Molyneux distinguishes between two types of women-centered interests: strategic gender interests and practical gender interests. Strategic gender interests are those that focus on women's subordinate position, often termed "feminist" for their level of gender consciousness.[115] The social reforms initiated by the "society of friends" fell within practical gender interests, the immediate response to severe social needs in Guatemala City. As revolutionary as political reforms, the second revolution also created an autonomous feminine space that addressed those concerns that had been marginalized from the center of revolutionary political reforms. Women's insistence that children, women, the poor, and the sick must be included in the revolutionary project fundamentally altered its trajectory. The subsequent social program designed to support the daily needs of thousands of urban residents was a marked departure from all previous social reforms, defying historical cleavages along class and ethnic lines, combining what Molyneux identifies as both strategic and practical gender interests.

The feminism of the urban community found expression in the social reform movement, engendering a maternalism that simultaneously expressed women's feminist ideals and aligned with broader revolutionary ideals. Descended directly from the social reform movements of the 1920s, the Arévalo feminists represented the educated and socially elite. Poised and ready to act, women such as Rosa de Mora, Gloria Menéndez Mina, Luz Valle, Mélida Montenegro de Méndez, and Angelina Acuña de Castañeda, to name just a few, worked diligently to alleviate the overwhelming health-care and education needs of Guatemala City's children and working poor. The comedores infantíles and guarderías infantíles improved the lives of Guatemala City's poorest residents through education, hygiene, health care, and child-care programs. As a result, the work of Elisa Martínez de Arévalo and the "society of friends" transformed the daily lives of thousands of working mothers and their children. However, there is a caveat to this picture. Inverting the typical social charity model, Martínez de Arévalo insisted that their efforts must include the vision and experience of the poor themselves. By engaging in the social reform projects, poor and working women influenced the nature of the Guatemalan revolution not merely by being acted upon but as actors in their own right, generating a revolutionary act in its own right. Although the founders of this social reform program also provided critical leadership in the legal struggle for suffrage and citizenship, the reforms initiated by the civil organization addressed needs arguably far more critical to the survival of many women and children than legal status. The energy expended on these programs attests to its social significance for all those involved. It was as revolutionary a space for those involved as was the national political sphere.

Four

WE ARE ALREADY CITIZENS
SUFFRAGE, GENDER, THE CATHOLIC CHURCH, AND REVOLUTIONARY POLITICS, 1944–1950

We are already citizens!
—*Gloria Menéndez Mina,* Nuestro Diario, *February 8, 1945*

Our vote . . . is a purely spontaneous expression of our capacity, of our morality, and of our patriotism.
—*Herminia Bermúdez Maldonado,* El Imparcial, *November 26, 1948*

Since our Constitution already authorizes the citizenship of women so that they can have the same rights as men, the beautiful idea of democracy can be seen as women deposit their vote in the ballot box for the first time.
—*Leopoldo Sierra Contreras,* Nuestro Diario, *September 1, 1948*

The June 25 march of teachers became one of the pivotal impulses for the October revolution and for the creation of the ladina political persona shaping and affirming subsequent gender norms for the next decade. The event itself unified city residents, who universally shared the moral outrage over Jorge Ubico's violation of gender norms against middle-class ladina educators. For those ladinas hoping for citizenship, the march became proof of their political acuity, and they threw themselves into the political arena, forming political parties and launching the campaign for suffrage. Members of newly formed revolutionary political parties competed with one another for power and influence within a traditionally exclusionary political structure, and the stakes for political power remained high for the next ten years. Newly enfranchised women struggled to establish themselves alongside their male revolutionary counterparts in a society deeply ambiguous about the public and political role of women. Despite women's tireless efforts, the entrenched gender norms did not fundamentally shift in a simmering landscape of unresolved tension between rhetoric and reality.

Women initiated the campaign for suffrage in this complex political terrain. Since women remained largely invisible both as political subjects and as citizens during the revolutionary era, the campaign for suffrage in Guatemala has been generally recognized as a by-product of the revolution's nod to modernity, subsumed by the historical attention given to the political role of illiterate and rural men whose votes brought Jacobo Árbenz to political office. The brief and ultimately successful campaign for suffrage, however, reveals a complex picture of activism and struggle against an intransigent patriarchal political system. Despite efforts to create an inclusive democracy, the revolution did not generate a fundamental shift of gender norms, and men continued to dominate all aspects of its sociopolitical power structure. Deeply rooted patriarchy and racism precluded suffrage for illiterate women who made up the rural, poor, and indigenous population, and without their sustained efforts the campaign that resulted in suffrage for literate women would have been unsuccessful. Although the small number of literate female voters did not gain much attention during the presidential races, the power of female voters became most evident in municipal elections. Literate women became eligible to vote in 1945, missing the first presidential election but participating in the 1950 presidential election[1] as well as three national municipal elections held in November 1948, 1950, and 1952.[2] Limited municipal elections also occurred in January 1946 and 1947, and they were closely scrutinized to determine both female and illiterate male participation in anticipation of the first national municipal vote in November 1948.[3]

The antirevolutionary movement identified the potential influence of the female voter and embraced the newly enfranchised ladina community. The anticommunist rhetoric warned of the revolution's dire consequences for the future of the home, motherhood, and the family. Endorsing strong Catholic values and affirming traditional notions of womanhood, conservative political parties simultaneously affirmed the traditional apolitical roles of women while actively courting women's votes. Consequently, urban middle-class women became pivotal voters against both the Arévalo and Árbenz governments and played a particularly significant role in municipal elections. Although these female voters abandoned traditional gender norms in order to participate in the political realm, they voted for political parties that endorsed the primary role of women as wives and mothers, thus maintaining their traditional social role. While the historiography has emphasized the beneficial relationship between Guatemala City residents and the revolutionary state, many urban ladinas who aligned themselves with the conservative politicians in fact viewed the Arévalo and Árbenz administrations as dangerous, as something to be opposed at all costs. Consequently, rather than supporting the revolutionary project, a majority of women in Guatemala City remained apolitical or actively participated against pro-revolutionary political parties. In so doing, these women confirmed revolutionary politicians' worst fears about enfranchising women voters.

Of all the elections during the revolutionary period, the highly contested 1948 municipal elections were a pivotal moment in the political participation of Guatemalan women. In response to the archbishop's call, thousands of women flocked to the voter registration stations. While their political presence was not tangible in the national presidential elections due to the sheer number of illiterate male voters, the influence of the female vote was most keenly felt in the municipal races in the capital city. Filling the gap left vacant by disinterested revolutionary political parties, the Catholic Church and conservative parties reached out to the newly enfranchised urban ladina voter. Consequently, while the Arévalo administration maintained its political mandate with broad-based national support from urban and rural illiterate men, the active female voter during the revolutionary period was a conservative, pro-clerical, middle-class, ladina resident of the capital city.

Although the historiography has expanded significantly since Francesca Miller first identified the profound absence of Latin American women's political history in 1991, far too little is known about Latin American women's political involvement in the post–World War II era. The historiography continues to focus on the years following the 1975 UN declaration of the Decade for Women. Therefore, significant gaps persist in our overall understanding of politically active women, particularly the implications of their campaigns for suffrage.[4] As a growing number of studies on Brazil, Peru, Argentina, Chile, and Mexico corroborate, in contrast to the pattern developed in European and US political activism (seen in the first and second wave feminist movements), Latin American women frequently escalated their political activities following suffrage. However, scholarship does not reflect this historical paradigm shift, and consequently, once suffrage was granted, little analysis exists as to how or even if women used the right to vote, and what the impact was on national politics.[5] An examination of politically active Guatemalan women confirms this pattern, demonstrating that they were dynamic political activists. In fact, their struggle offers a unique model of how women fought for and then employed their new political citizenship. For them, like for so many other Latin American feminists, suffrage did not represent an end goal of their ideals. Rather, it became a platform that launched thousands of women directly into a decade of intense sociopolitical activity. As such, the story in Guatemala reinforces the particularities of Latin America's suffrage movements and the political role of women during an understudied time period. Although many of the most politically active Guatemalan women were exiled after 1954, they continued their activism, and some, such as Alaíde Foppa Falla, emerged as internationally influential feminists. Therefore, tracking the political activity of Guatemalan women during the suffrage campaign and how they implemented their new political power addresses an element of Latin American women's history still relatively unknown.

Politics, Gender, and Suffrage: A New *Patria*

For ladinas, the Guatemalan revolution was born in the hours following the resignation of Jorge Ubico, as democratic and socially transformative ideals so long repressed emerged into the public sphere. A flurry of political organizing ensued as urban ladinas and ladinos organized the most critical political parties and associations of the revolutionary era in the early days of July 1944. Following the military attack on the teachers' peaceful demonstration, these women now believed themselves to be the rightful heirs of a new sociopolitical era, or, as Luz Valle termed it, a "new patria." Their struggle for political citizenship aligned neatly with the democratic rhetoric escalating from all political sectors in Guatemala City, a discourse that was so evidently in contrast to the exclusion of women. This idealism, however, directly confronted the historically entrenched marginalization of women that was enforced by the structural elements of class and ethnicity. Prevailing gender ideas dictated that women be conservative and reactionary to change, thereby making them natural antagonists to any revolutionary transformations.

The depth to which the revolutionary political sphere was both an imagined and a realistic masculinized realm is confirmed by the biographies of the era.[6] Consequently, those women who crossed into this historically privileged masculine space were continuously thwarted by presumptions of their inherently antipolitical nature, creating a hostile environment along the entire political spectrum. While the traditional revolutionary narratives focus primarily on the period following the triumphant revolution in October, for urban ladinas it was events between June and October that represent their pivotal revolutionary formation.

Evidence of the ensuing gendered struggle emerged immediately following Ubico's resignation. Several civil commissions were formed in response to this political rupture to meet with the military junta Ubico established to rule in his absence. The first comprised educated and literary ladinas including Elisa Hall de Asturias, Malin D'Echevers, Concha González Solis, and Carmen Estela Lima, along with male colleagues Luis Coronado Lira, Manuel Eduardo Rodríguez, and Gregorio Padilla. Although the generals were amenable to the meeting, when they learned that the commission included women, the meeting was cancelled on the premise that the junta was too busy.[7] Undeterred by this obvious patriarchal snub, following Ubico's June 30 resignation, urban ladinas continued their political activity with the formation of several of the most important political parties of the revolutionary decade. Established on July 2, 1944, the Renovación Nacional (RN) was organized by the urban teaching community.[8] As one of the thirteen women who signed the inaugural document formalizing the party, Elisa Muralles Soto (one of the three Muralles sisters mentioned in chapter 2) recalls her role in establishing a political party with pride, especially since the RN provided pivotal political support for presidential candidate Juan José Arévalo.[9] The other early influential revolutionary party, the Frente Popular Libertador (FPL), was established a few days later by university students, intellectuals, artists, workers, industrialists, and agriculturalists, many of whom were also women (fig. 4.1). Their political platform included suffrage for women, and they invited "anyone with honorable intentions and a civic consciousness" to join.[10] These two parties unified in late 1945 to form the Partido Acción Revolucionaria (PAR), and while they split eighteen months later, the PAR survived as a formative pro-revolutionary political party.[11]

Following the formation of the Renovación Nacional and Frente Popular Libertador in the first two weeks of July, the flurry of ladina political organizing diminished dramatically. In fact, in the midst of an array of frenetic social and political activities, women quite simply disappeared from the public discourse, a silence that continued into mid-August. Then, inexplicably, they reemerged on August 18 with the announcement that a new female affiliate of the Renovación Nacional had been formed under the leadership of Enriqueta López y López de Gómez. According to López y López de Gómez, the women had organized to create long-term change in civil society.[12] The use of the term "civil society" is striking here, given that these women had been instrumental in creating the official political party. Just days later, on August 23, the female affiliate of the FPL announced its formation with Elisa Hall de Asturias and Concha González Solis as president and vice president, respectively. Several among the FPL leadership had been intellectual leaders during the 1930s and would continue their political work during the 1950s through the Alianza Femenina Guatemalteca.[13] Well-known revolutionary-era politician Manuel Galich joined the women's meeting to support their organization. The two political affiliates unified ideologically over one presidential candidate, namely Juan José Arévalo, and the ladina teaching community campaigned fervently until his return from exile in Argentina to Guatemala City in September 1944.

No public accounting addresses this absence of ladina activism between early July and late August, but several realities point to possible explanations. First, many educated and professional ladinos who had been exiled, imprisoned, or silenced during the Ubico era returned en masse to Guatemala City following his June 30 resignation. Accounts of these returning exiles pervade the revolutionary biographies and public discourse of the era. One of the best-known political exiles, Clemente Marroquín Rojas, the editor of the newspaper *La Hora* and conservative politician, swam across a river separating Guatemala and Mexico and into a pivotal leadership role in the new revolutionary era. As the capital city hailed the triumphant return of these heroes into the masculinized political realm, ladinas were quickly marginalized from the organizations they had helped create. Although pro-revolutionary and pro-suffrage politicians hailed ladina activism as a significant political force, the highly gendered and stratified world of politics was not fundamentally reformed by Ubico's resignation (nor would it be by the October revolution). Within this entrenched structure, many male revolutionaries so long denied space in the political sphere could not even imagine sharing power with women, who were subsequently relegated to female affiliate parties. The message of just who was to be included in the revolution had become clear. Caught up in the maelstrom of revolutionary politics embedded within a patriarchal structure, a critical sector of politically active women was marginalized from meaningful political power even before the October revolution had occurred.

The particular way in which Guatemalan women were politically marginalized has broader Latin American parallels. In the aftermath of World War II, notions of democracy and broad-based political participation were sweeping the hemisphere. Although Latin American feminists had promoted the theoretical idea of women's suffrage primarily through inter-American congresses and associations for decades, they had remained unsuccessful until the 1930s and 1940s. After World War II, however women were increasingly recognized as a significant political force that directly confronted an entrenched patriarchal political system. Therefore, in order to retain women's growing political power, male politicians employed a strategy common throughout the region with the creation of female political affiliates. As Francesca Miller notes, this was a tactic that at once mobilized women on behalf of specific political parties while simultaneously marginalizing them from leadership and policy-making power.[14] This became a particularly effective strategy for novice Guatemalan politicians unwilling to share newly acquired political influence.

The silence between July and August also reflects the vast gulf in opinion in the capital city over the political implications of the June 25 teachers' march and the murder of María Chinchilla Recinos. While everyone shared in the moral outrage over Chinchilla Recinos's death, interpretations of its repercussions varied greatly among Guatemala City residents. The ladinas who participated in the march believed that the event demonstrated their civic commitment, bravery, and political capabilities, therefore establishing their right to citizenship. While there was an almost unanimous opinion that these women had acted bravely in the face of unprovoked violence, opinions varied on whether their actions necessarily translated into a right to citizenship. Therefore, although the event became a pivotal moment for the development of a civic and political consciousness among ladinas, a majority of Guatemala City residents did not share this particular interpretation.

Into this space of silence and political uncertainty during July and August, Jorge Ubico's sitting political party, the Partido Liberal Progresista, attempted to stall any possible women's movement and reassert patriarchal control. Concerned by the growing legitimacy of urban political activism, they urged women to return to the traditional gender roles where women reigned as "queen of the home" and "empress of the kitchen." Claiming that women had no right to raise themselves to the same level as men, the petition produced by members of the National Assembly cautioned capital city residents that women did not have the preparation necessary to participate in politics.[15] Reminiscent of Ubico's desire to legitimize his authoritarian rule, they published a petition signed by hundreds of Guatemalan women.[16] Eager to maintain a modicum of social control in the increasingly anxious months following Ubico's resignation, the political power structure capitalized on the gendered fear raised by the specter of hundreds of politically active women with the moral imperative of the June 25 march to engage in the political realm. As Lorraine Bayard de Volo notes in her work on the Sandinista revolution in Nicaragua, antirevolutionary forces used these discursive efforts in an attempt to redirect women's energies back into the home and away from the enthusiasm generated by revolutionary possibilities.[17]

A communique between the female affiliate of the Partido Acción Revolucionaria and its leadership two years later in 1946 offers another possible explanation for the silence of July and August 1944.[18] Chita Ordóñez de Balcárcel, the leader of the PAR's female affiliate, petitioned the male leadership for further support. In a two-page treatise, Ordóñez de Balcárcel highlighted women's contributions to both the party itself as well as the broader revolutionary project. She noted their role in the creation of the child-care and literacy centers for children and their mothers in and around Guatemala City in partnership with first lady Elisa Martínez de Arévalo. She also noted that they had increased the number of female affiliations for the PAR. However, she warned her male counterparts that women in the PAR were becoming increasingly frustrated over the lack of acknowledgment and financial support for their work. Deriding her male colleagues, she reminded them that the female affiliate had not even been given office space in which to work. While these women had been honored for their work in the social realm, Ordóñez de Balcárcel's letter reveals the resistance they experienced in the political realm. Not only do her words offer an explanation for the silence in the weeks following the formal organization of the political parties in July 1944, the letter offers a window into the dynamics of the revolutionary political parties and their female affiliates.[19] For ladinas eager to participate fully in revolutionary politics, there can be little doubt that they had two interrelated battles to fight. The first challenge was to reform the entrenched and inequitable sociopolitical structures, while the second was to reform the consciousness of a patriarchal society.

While their political efforts in early July were subsumed within the broader masculine revolutionary narratives, diminishing both their influence and their achievements, ladinas formed another association in early July, this one exclusively female. Created on July 3, 1944, alongside the first revolutionary political parties, the Unión Cívica Guatemalteca, the association for suffrage, emerged with a clear agenda. Founded by women of all political affiliations, the Unión Cívica Guatemalteca held broad democratic goals, including greater electoral participation, assurance of a fair democratic process, and, most importantly, suffrage for women. They joined both the PAR and the FPL in support of the Arévalo presidential candidacy.[20]

The women at the forefront of the suffrage movement emerged directly from the intellectual networks formed through *Nosotras* and *Azul*. In the waning years of Ubico's regime, teachers (some of whom became part of the suffrage campaign) had already formed associations designed to resist Ubico's intellectual repression, if not the presidency itself. In the early months of 1944, under the guise of intellectual and literary pursuits, two organizations in particular established the principals upon which all of their revolutionary efforts were founded. Drawing together some of Guatemala's most distinguished ladina writers around shared interests in poetry, literature, and the role of women in global peace movements, Malin D'Echevers created the Asociación de Mujeres Intelectuales in late January.[21] Along with several journalists and literary colleagues, Luz Valle formed a more politically focused group, the Guatemalan wing of the Unión de Mujeres Americanas, just a month later.[22] Although they self-identified as literary societies, the level of organization displayed by urban ladinas immediately following Ubico's resignation reveals the true intent of these clandestine organizations. Within hours, it was precisely this group of women that formed the national campaign for suffrage. Among the original members of these clandestine organizations, Elisa Hall de Asturias, Gloria Menéndez Mina de Padilla, and Angelina Acuña de Castañeda now formed the core of this new suffrage movement.[23]

As the first Guatemalan woman to graduate with a law degree, Graciela Quan Valenzuela assumed leadership of the organization and the campaign for suffrage.[24] She and her comrades faced several critical challenges in this inaugural suffrage movement. First, there had been no previous suffrage movements upon which Quan Valenzuela could extend her contemporary ideals due to the negligible democratic tradition in Guatemala's political history. In fact, there had been a profound lack of meaningful voting practices due to the political stranglehold enjoyed the by economic elite. To exacerbate this reality, a generalized and profound lack of education served to alienate the vast majority of Guatemalans from all manner of political and public life. Consequently, Guatemalans had had little opportunity to practice or even contemplate the meaning of political democracy. Despite these historical challenges, the new organization's immediate task was to reform the constitution that Ubico had rewritten in 1935 to explicitly exclude women from citizenship.

Their fight was ultimately successful because of Quan Valenzuela's keen understanding of her political context. Reminiscent of Luz Valle's nod to modernity in her arguments for greater sociopolitical access, Quan Valenzuela also drew upon deeply rooted Liberal notions of modernity and progress, presenting suffrage for women as a natural extension of these concepts. She argued that women's citizenship was simply an element of broader historical processes already occurring in the North Atlantic region, in countries that the Guatemalan political and economic elite wanted to emulate. Furthermore, disenfranchisement of women violated the historical value Liberalism placed upon an individual's liberty of conscience. Quan Valenzuela argued that women's suffrage was a simple matter of social justice, because the 1935 constitutional restriction of women had no evidentiary basis. Basing her conclusions on the Guatemalan constitution, she argued that literate ladinas fit the established parameters for citizenship, which included literacy along with civic and economic engagement.[25]

Given that literate ladinas fit the parameters for intellectual fitness demanded of citizens, Quan Valenzuela built her case on an effective strategic argument used by other Latin American feminists. Rather than using the rights-based argument employed by northern feminists, she employed the differences-based model that celebrated maternalism. Preempting her opponents, who would no doubt see feminism as an attack on the mutually reinforcing concepts of both motherhood and femininity, Quan Valenzuela emphasized that women's identity as mothers should not preclude their eligibility for citizenship. In fact, it might even support their eligibility. As Asunción Lavrin notes, this was not a novel approach, and those who opposed suffrage had used this argument effectively against suffragists across Latin America.[26] Remaining within the traditional bounds of maternal feminism, Quan Valenzuela connected women's individual rights as mothers to Liberal notions of citizenship. Her association between women as mothers and Liberal notions of individualism created the successful foundation for the suffrage campaign and solidified maternalism as a central element in Liberal ladina feminism for the remainder of the revolutionary decade.

As Guatemala's first formal suffrage organization, the Unión Cívica Guatemalteca faced two fundamental obstacles. First, few Guatemalans, women or men, understood their civil rights and obligations due to a generalized lack of democratic practice and access to education. Although they were fighting for the rights of women to vote, the simple reality was that few Guatemalans had historically participated in the electoral process. Manuel Galich summarized this generalized lack of political practice years later, declaring: "We were all political illiterates."[27] To address the uncertain implications of democracy in these early days, the Unión Cívica Guatemalteca circulated basic information regarding both the civil rights and the obligations that women possessed at that time, as well as those they would acquire with citizenship. Their second and far more profound barrier, however, lay in the historical absence of any cross-class organizing and the deep sociopolitical and psychological divide between urban and rural, ladina and indigenous women. Understanding the significance of these obstacles, the Unión Cívica Guatemalteca attempted to alter these patterns by extending a call of invitation and welcome to all women, regardless of political affiliation, religion, or social status. They also invited all political parties, patriotic associations, and women's organizations to send representatives to their meetings. Despite these efforts, the organization remained relatively small, dominated by literate ladinas of the middle and upper classes, a testament to the resilience of both class and ethnic divides as well as to the still limited numbers of literate Guatemalan women. That the association was able to attract as many women as it did so quickly following Ubico's resignation, however, demonstrates the veracity of the ideals nurtured by journalists Luz Valle and Gloria Menéndez Mina through *Nosotras* and *Azul* during the long years of the Ubico dictatorship.

Guatemalan women had been intellectually isolated due to Ubico's restrictions on travel, which had denied them the opportunity to attend meetings available to their Central American peers. The reforms now sweeping Guatemala and across the isthmus allowed these women to meet with other, like-minded reformers for the first time. The Unión Cívica Guatemalteca now reached out to other Central Americans who supported suffrage, sending delegates to the Fourth National Unionist Convention in El Salvador. There, they discovered like-minded women who were also organizing for the vote. Argentina Díaz Lozano, Adriana Saravia de Palarea, and Elisa de Barrios from Quetzaltenango represented the Unión Cívica Guatemalteca, and they received help in drafting their motion for suffrage to the National Assembly from conference delegates in El Salvador.[28] Following these discussions in Santa Ana, one Guatemalan delegate declared that "women are much more careful in who they vote for precisely because it is women who suffer the most under bad governments. While men might suffer physically, it is women who suffer both in their bodies and in their souls."[29] The use of this specific argument is significant. As Charity Coker Gonzalez notes, emphasizing the relationship between a lack of democracy and the oppression of women was a tactic employed by the Pan American Women's Union (predecessor to the Inter-American Commission of Women) and then implemented by the Colombian women's movement.[30] Here, the Unión Cívica Guatemalteca was now using this same argument, indicative of their new ability to network with other suffragists across the region following the overthrow of Jorge Ubico.

Following the delegates' return to Guatemala, the Unión Cívica Guatemalteca formally launched a campaign for suffrage on September 23, 1944, with departmental affiliations throughout the country.[31] "We request that our honorable ruling junta recognize our citizenship and establish the fundamental obligations and rights. We request that this decree be put into effect or law in order to break the boundaries that keep us from exercising our freedom in the upcoming election."[32] Gloria Menéndez Mina clarified their request in the September edition of *Azul*, declaring that Guatemala was ready to accept an "optional vote" for literate women.[33] The adoption of this request underscores the historical litmus test for citizenship in Guatemala that privileged literacy. Although calls for enfranchisement had included references to universal suffrage since the resignation of Jorge Ubico, with the formal campaign underway the suffragists established the parameters of the debate. Understanding just how difficult their campaign was going to be, the Unión Cívica Guatemalteca reinforced the historical binary established by the Liberal state between literate women and rural, illiterate men rather than fighting for universal suffrage. In so doing, they excluded the vast majority of urban and rural women (see table 4.1).

The interim triumvirate established by Ubico following his resignation, however, did not follow up with promised elections, and the capital city remained in political limbo. Interim president General Juan Federico Ponce Vaides capitalized on the political uncertainty by bringing thousands of indigenous men into the city to march in support of his candidacy and, by proxy, the Ubico regime. For almost a month, groups of indigenous supporters were paid to march through the streets of the capital shouting and waving machetes, a resounding reminder that at least some rural indigenous communities had supported Jorge Ubico.[34] This particular strategy reveals two historical realities. First, the interim president effectively capitalized on the deep, racialized fear of many urban residents over a possible uprising of the rural indigenous population. Second, by September, the rhetorical binary of the suffrage debate had been established between rural, illiterate, and indigenous men over literate ladinas. The suffragists understood the tactic, and Angelina Acuña de Castañeda was the first to publicly express their collective anxiety in the face of such a possibility. Her frustration and anger over the political perception of women is evident in her question: "What spirit of justice allowed for the absurd vote of illiterate men over the value and merit of literate women?"[35] As literate Guatemalans, they met the existing constitutional requirements for citizenship more closely than did any illiterate men. Stymied by the resistance and hostility of urban men and the indifference demonstrated by a majority of women, Acuña de Castañeda exposed her anguish driven by decades of marginalization as well as her class bias. Her question would be answered in a variety of ways over the next few months.

The success of the October revolution and the establishment of the temporary ruling junta reinvigorated the suffrage campaign with its promise of elections and democratic rhetoric. Within a month, on November 25, 1944, the Unión Cívica

Guatemalteca launched the first Congreso Femenino Pro-Ciudadanía de la Mujer at the Casa del Pueblo on Sixth Avenue.[36] The first national congress on suffrage was attended by more than six hundred women calling on the participation of all Guatemalan women to unite in the struggle for suffrage.[37] The one-day meeting drew women from across the country, including the departments of Jalapa, San Marcos, Quetzaltenango, Sololá, Huehuetenango, Puerto Barrios, Mixco, Salamá, and El Progreso.[38] Organized by the stalwarts of the urban women's movement, the primary activists included Graciela Quan Valenzuela, Rosa de Mora, Argentina Díaz Lozano, Celeste de Espada, Gloria Menéndez Mina, Amy Valladares de Bolaños, María del Pilar, Nena Morales de Lara, Adriana Saravia de Palarea, and Marta Escobar de Richardson. Female affiliates from both the Frente Popular Libertador and Renovación Nacional united within the Unión Cívica Guatemalteca.

The rapid and at times uneasy political transformation occurring in Guatemala became immediately evident among the congressional participants. Opening the congress, San Marcos delegates Rosa Barrios de Perusina and Marta Lílian Rodas, both teachers, declared that "until the war [the October revolution], we believed that civic characteristics and duties were incompatible with the female duties of the home."[39] However, they came to the congress believing that it was now necessary for women of conscience to speak out in order to resolve political problems and express their support for the fledgling democracy. No doubt articulating the sentiments of many attendees, these two delegates now declared citizenship to be of utmost importance. Not all congressional delegates, however, shared these newfound convictions. Representing a new civic association, the Unión de Mujeres Guatemaltecas, Elisa Hall de Asturias declared that Guatemalan women were capable of civil participation, aligning their organization in support of suffrage for women.[40] Employing Luz Valle's argument, Hall de Asturias centered her claim on the simple fact that women had always been social participants, because the home represented the center of Guatemalan society. She implored women to understand that their actions had always benefited the nation, and the possibility to vote merely represented a new aspect of their traditional roles. "Women have the right to participate in the civic construction of Guatemala in all aspects of its grand new architecture."[41] However, Hall de Asturias fell short of aligning their association with other political parties in attendance and cautioned the congressional audience of the continued fear many women felt over moving rapidly into this new political realm.

Although the extent of political ambiguity in the ladina community would not become evident until the 1947 First Inter-American Congress of Women, Hall de Asturias's remarks illustrate the schism between those women who believed in political equality and those who did not necessarily feel comfortable being politically active. This schism has been the cause of pervasive tension within women's movements across Latin America, which Nikki Craske argues continues to exist within contemporary movements, as many women continue to reject an overtly political identity despite the political impact of their collective action.[42] At this particular juncture, as Guatemala stood on the cusp of a new democratic era, some of these new activists clearly wanted to create a political organization, while others were hesitant and even unwilling to express their goals for equality in political terms. Although Hall de Asturias herself overcame this political hesitation, eventually joining the feminist Alianza Femenina Guatemalteca, her assessment in the revolution's early days would prove to be accurate.[43]

Although they would frequently find themselves in conflict with their male peers, during the campaign for suffrage, the political interests of urban ladinas coalesced with those of some of their male counterparts as they sought to transform the entrenched political landscape. In an effort to bolster fragile revolutionary political alliances, representatives from the leading pro-revolutionary political parties attended the suffrage congress to demonstrate their personal support for women's suffrage. José García Bauer, Juan José Orozco Posadas (who had publicly supported suffrage during the Ubico regime), and Oscar Nájera Farfán went on record to state that presidential candidate Juan José Arévalo supported suffrage and promised to raise the issue immediately in the National Assembly should he be elected to office.[44] Even as they publicly supported suffrage, these male allies exposed their gendered bias regarding women's political participation. They thanked the conference attendees for their support in the creation of the pro-revolutionary political parties, specifically naming the female affiliates of the PAR and FPL. In so doing, they reiterated the vast gulf of opinion over how women's political participation was to be defined. Despite the fact that some of the delegates had founded these political parties alongside these particular male colleagues, the perception that women had merely supported male efforts was already deeply entrenched.

It was in fact urban ladinas who initiated the suffrage debate on July 3, 1944, which in turn expanded to a broader discussion over the nature of political citizenship. The public conversation that appeared in the national newspapers and among urban intellectuals focused on the two historically disenfranchised groups: women, and indigenous and illiterate rural men. These groups were

FIGURE 4.1 "Window to the People" / "Do not think that are you deceiving me with promises and lies; I already know your deeds and you know why I sigh."

imagined as a dichotomous pair by intellectuals and politicians alike, and the discourse revealed existing social divides and prejudices. Despite the fact that citizenship for indigenous men had been debated since the beginning of the Liberal era, questions over their merits as political actors remained.[45] While intellectuals such as Antonio Goubard Carrera, David Vela, and Luz Valle had advocated for a more respectful relationship between ladinos and indigenous peoples, significant fears remained strong over a possible shift in the existing social racial hierarchy. In contrast, the political inclusion of women had rarely been discussed in the public square, and consequently there was even greater hesitation over their possible enfranchisement. For those who valued the traditional hierarchical structure, the participation of both women and indigenous men in the public sphere was a threatening prospect. A cartoon circulating around this time epitomizes the racialized and gendered fears raised by the deliberations over the possible citizenship of both women and indigenous men (fig. 4.1; the original has a penciled-in date of 1944). Pro-revolutionary parties are portrayed as a seductive mistress, a sexualized image of the revolution's political implications. Front and center in the image is the racialized fear of indigenous men as sexually threatening and provocative. The sexuality, emotionality, and questionable ethics encapsulated by this image are factors that suffragists had to repeatedly navigate throughout the suffrage campaign.[46] The latent sexualized fears exposed by any challenge to Guatemala's sociopolitical hierarchy were clear. Revolutionary political parties and, by association, pro-revolutionary women were not to be trusted. Indigenous women are completely absent from this rhetorical image, affirming their historical invisibility as political actors and contributors to the economy.

Although the suffragists faced significant political opposition, they enjoyed some powerful male allies who now moved to publicly support the campaign. Following the national congress, front-page analysis on the historical exclusion of women appeared in national newspapers, including *Nuestro Diario*, which outlined the constitutional debates and amendments for women's citizenship that had occurred since 1871. This summary detailed the progression of the debate on suffrage and the language utilized by the constitution's creators. The editor of *El Imparcial* made the audacious claim that a majority of male Guatemalans were comfortable with middle-class literate women voting. "Is there an argument against female suffrage?" he asked. No, he "did not believe so."[47] Federico Castañeda Godoy called the inability of women to vote a crime, although he noted that giving the same right to illiterate men was both an error and a danger to social harmony.[48] He was careful, however, to distinguish between women of various classes based on their education and ability to discern the political process. The editor of *Nuestro Diario*, however, openly supported unrestricted suffrage for women, declaring that an authentic democracy is a pure and complete democracy.[49]

Urban ladinas enjoyed a particular advantage over their illiterate male counterparts, which they now effectively employed in their suffrage campaign. Using the literary networks they had developed in Guatemala City over the prior two decades, they now defended their claim to citizenship personally. Leading educators and writers María Albertina Gálvez and Malin D'Echevers, who had attended the suffrage congress, issued passionate editorials the following week.[50] Indicative of their moderate Liberal political ideals, both women relied on traditional arguments effectively employed to support their case. Gálvez emphasized women's strength and heroism in dangerous situations in an attempt no doubt to evoke memories of the June teachers' march. Concluding her brief piece, Gálvez noted that only in Christianity had women enjoyed a legitimacy denied to them by the rest of society. D'Echevers attempted to assuage the fears of many Guatemalans by affirming that women would take great care in the sacred duty of citizenship and voting. Although it appears to have been a lost cause by November, D'Echevers also argued that illiterate women had the ability to practice citizenship with the same care and caution as literate women. Her experience in the education system again shone through in her support of suffrage for all Guatemalans, echoing the concerns she had recorded in *Nosotras* in 1933.

As the suffrage campaign escalated, socially influential ladinos hostile to the possibility entered the debate. Prominent physician Carlos Fletes Sáenz, whose condemnation of Luz Valle in 1937 had sparked such rhetorical ire in *El Imparcial*, resurfaced with equal vehemence. Representing ideas that were no doubt held by many Guatemalans, he likened the suffrage debate regarding women to that of two parents asking their male child what he would like to be when he grew up.[51] Repeatedly asking the child whether he would like to be a doctor, a lawyer, or a priest, the child eventually decides to become a doctor when he sees a doctor driving a beautiful car. According to Fletes Sáenz, the moral of the story is, if you repeat a question often enough and promise material riches, the person will say yes. Fletes Sáenz concluded that the struggle for women's suffrage was analogous to this story. In his opinion, suffrage was window dressing for the new revolutionary politicians, and therefore it had no substance. More insidiously, however, his story dramatized this critical legal campaign by comparing women to children, who were both apparently unprepared to make life-changing decisions such as choosing a profession or casting a vote. The point was, if you asked women enough times whether they wanted to vote, they would eventually say yes.

Public opposition to suffrage, however, came not only from ladinos but from other ladinas within the suffragists' own circles, whose arguments the suffragists found more difficult to combat. Campaign organizers had named several elite ladinas as honorary chairs including Rosa de Mora, Irene de Peyré, and María Herrera de Aschkel, all distinguished social reform leaders and educators. The Unión Cívica Guatemalteca also included one young woman from an elite family who had recently returned to Guatemala. Alaíde Foppa Falla's response to her appointment as honorary chair contained both surprise and resistance, and her series of articles that followed articulated two prevalent concerns over shifting gender roles.[52] At issue for Foppa Falla was the concern that women would lose their femininity and sexual desirability with political engagement. She hoped that her fellow Guatemalans would shift their focus to humanist concerns for the welfare of the country without embracing feminism, reminding them that intelligence must not be confused with feminism. Foppa Falla's caution exposed the central conundrum in which many Latin American women struggled, namely that of the relationship between feminism and femininity. Asunción Lavrin summarizes the ideas articulated by Foppa Falla as an example of "women who supported legal and economic reforms for women but nurtured a deep prejudice against the concept of feminism, taking it as an ideology that promoted the masculinization of women and competition with men."[53] Foppa Falla's antisuffragism presented a significant challenge for the ladina movement because it was doubtlessly shared by many in the capital city, a position that Susan Marshall refers to as the "gender class position" of elite women.[54] As her son Julio Solórzano recalled in 2013, at this point in her life Foppa Falla believed that women had gained the rights to education and many professions and therefore did not need the right of suffrage.

Her perspective shifted over the coming years, demonstrating the transition experienced by many Guatemalan women during the revolutionary decade. She eventually joined the prominent women's group Alianza Femenina Guatemalteca during the Árbenz presidency, in 1950, and worked for the IGSS actively supporting revolutionary institutional and educational reforms. Following the overthrow of Árbenz, Foppa Falla left Guatemala with her husband, Alfonso Solórzano, and their children, moving to Mexico, where she became a university professor, teaching literature at several universities.[55] As Foppa Falla matured, she became increasingly aware of the inequities experienced by Latin American women. This consciousness in turn radicalized her feminism, and she eventually founded Mexico's first feminist journal, *Fem*, influencing an entire generation of young women in Mexico and Central America, some of whom have assumed leadership roles in Guatemala's contemporary feminist movements.[56] While not many elite women followed Foppa Falla's intellectual transformation, her individual experience highlights the complex journey that women underwent as they wrestled with new feminist ideas and the opportunities offered by revolutionary politics. Like many Guatemalans who dared to publicly express their political ideals throughout the twentieth century, Alaíde Foppa Falla paid with her life when she was disappeared in 1980 by the military government under President Fernando Romeo Lucas García.

On December 5, 1944, just days before the presidential elections, the provisional governing junta granted women the theoretical right to citizenship. The Unión Femenina Guatemalteca received a telegram that Decree 17, "women's right to citizenship," had been passed by the governing revolutionary junta. In addition, the word "men" had been removed from the constitutional wording for citizenship, reverting back to the historical reference to "los guatemaltecos," which held the linguistic potential of inclusion for women. The official explanation for the constitutional change reflected the historical reality. "For so long, women have been denied their basic rights based only on the simple fact that they are born women."[57] The suffragists were exuberant and began making arrangements to participate in the December presidential elections. In the days leading up to the elections, hundreds of ladinas registered to vote. In preparation for their potential vote, *Nuestro Diario* noted that lists of registered women had been compiled.[58] While enfranchisement was not granted in time for the presidential elections, women from the Frente Popular Libertador participated in the electoral process by helping at the voting stations.

These preliminary overtures in support of the suffrage campaign in no way guaranteed women success. The constitutional reforms needed approval by the National Assembly, a political space largely unchanged by the revolution, still dominated by Ubico-era politicians. The October revolution introduced a diversity of politicians and a new president for the National Assembly. However, unlike other revolutionary movements that overthrow an existing political system, the bulk of the Ubico-era politicians remained as sitting deputies. Therefore, following the December presidential elections in which Juan José Arévalo was overwhelmingly elected to office, suffragists increased their activism, appearing before the National Assembly in late January to directly plead their case.[59] In early February, four hundred women of the Renovación Nacional held a large rally to garner public support for their cause. María Consuelo Pereira, Juan José Orozco Posadas, Ana Clemencia Aldana, Alicia González, and Julia Urrutia were among those who spoke publicly on behalf of their constitutional rights. Decades later, Urrutia recalled this activism with pride and excitement.[60]

As the most influential woman in Guatemala City, Gloria Menéndez Mina utilized her position as editor of *Azul* to advocate for suffrage.[61] Immediately following the November 20 congress on suffrage, Menéndez Mina traveled to Washington, DC, to meet with representatives of the defunct Inter-American Commission of Women, accompanied by Elisa de Barrios of Quetzaltenango. Her visit included a meeting with US first lady Eleanor Roosevelt, who congratulated Menéndez Mina and by extension all Guatemalans for the recent defeat of Jorge Ubico (an ironic statement, given the historical US support for the dictator). Buoyed by the international support, Menéndez Mina returned home and presented the suffrage case in a groundbreaking article on February 8, 1945, "We Are Already Citizens." Menéndez Mina employed a different strategy from those of Luz Valle and Graciela Quan Valenzuela. Rather than using constitutional arguments, she reminded her readers of the recent revolutionary activities, which, she argued, qualified Guatemalan women for citizenship. With few examples to draw upon as proof for her claims, she used the martyr model of the June march to argue the suffrage case. Highlighting the teachers' acts of heroism and courage under fire, she questioned whether the revolution would have been successful without the contributions and blood sacrifices of women. As noted scholar on power and the state Hannah Arendt reminds us, the demonstration of courage has been used as a political virtue par excellence, and "only those men who possessed it could be admitted to a fellowship that was political in content and purpose."[62] Now in Guatemala, Menéndez Mina used this concept to demonstrate that ladinas were fit for political participation. She could have chosen the imagery of Guatemalan women engaged in battle during the October revolution, as Luz Valle had effectively employed in her exposé on a new patria (see chapter 3). However, while courage in battle as proof of political acuity served women well in later prolonged revolutionary struggles such as in Cuba and Nicaragua, it was not as effective in 1945 Guatemala.[63] Understanding her sociopolitical context, Menéndez Mina relied almost exclusively on the June march. Given the deep ambivalence a majority of men and women felt over women's political inclusion, Menéndez Mina's strategic focus on the moral outrage of urban women in the line of military fire would prove to be the correct one.[64]

In anticipation of the classic argument against citizenship for women, Menéndez Mina reiterated that not all women were so influenced by Catholicism as to preclude civic responsibility. At the present time, she argued, the tiny Central American nation of Guatemala had an opportunity to make a disproportionately large impact across Latin America, and their inclusion in the new constitution would benefit not only women but the nation as a whole. "We ought to prepare ourselves, train ourselves; to create a new patriotism, oriented in the concepts of our newly acquired freedom."[65] Unlike Valle, who argued for cross-class inclusion, Menéndez Mina's new patriotism unequivocally included women's equality but within a less expansive model of feminism. She knew that this was the type of moderate political activism ambivalent ladinas might embrace, and one that uncertain ladinos could endorse.

The nature of the constitutional debate that surrounded women's suffrage in March 1945 reflected the deep sociopolitical ambivalence with which male politicians regarded any public or political role for women, confirming the veracity of Menéndez Mina's approach.[66] Questions surrounding the illiterate male vote centered on their ability to read and write, which proponents argued was not in direct correlation to civic consciousness. Similar arguments, however, were not applied to the question of female voting.[67] The debate surrounding women's political participation centered on their intellect and moral aptitude, because a majority of lawmakers did not believe women to be capable of either emotional or psychosocial rational thought.[68] According to Dr. Jorge Mario García Laguardia's own account of the debate, the restriction of full suffrage was based on a concern that religious belief was a powerful force for women, thereby eliminating any possibility of rational thought.[69] As politician Francisco Villagrán de León pointed out, legislators were concerned over the possible influence of the confessional on women. Along with Villagrán de León, the majority of the National Assembly believed that women presented a danger to Guatemala's national progress because of their conservatism, the centrality of Catholicism, and their love of traditional order.[70] The arguments that ultimately swayed the opinions of the National Assembly in the final minutes of the debate demonstrated the astuteness of Gloria Menéndez Mina's theoretical approach. Focusing on the June march rather than the October revolution, several politicians used personal examples of women's heroism. The daughters of congressman Sandoval had been injured in the October fighting, while the wife of José Rólz Bennett, Julieta Castro de Rólz Bennett, had been shot in the leg in the teachers' march of June 25, 1944 (fig. 3.1).[71] Although legislators Marroquín Rojas (he would vote against suffrage) and Manuel Galich recalled incidents of valor demonstrated by women across the country at key strategic sites, in the final hours of the debate women's participation in the June march convinced policy makers of their civic maturity and ability to participate in Guatemala's national political life. Supported by twenty congressional representatives, literate women were granted the right to a secret vote on March 9, 1945.[72] A final concession to the bill's opponents mandated that voting be made optional for literate women, rather than obligatory as it was for men.[73] The debate and final vote illustrates the tensions between the revolution's commitment to creating a new democratic political sphere and women's presumed conservatism. The result in Guatemala was the limited extension of suffrage, excluding the vast majority of women. It is a final irony that while politicians aligned with the revolutionary administration supported suffrage as a democratic ideal, they never actively sought the women's vote over the ensuing ten years. Revolutionary leaders consistently demonstrated their conviction that illiterate and indigenous men were more acceptable as political partners than women, suggesting that gender had indeed trumped race in Guatemalan revolutionary politics.

The time line of events between July 1944 and March 1945 makes it abundantly clear that without the continuous petitions by the suffragists, the idea would have quietly faded from the revolutionary agenda. Ladina activism ignited a citywide debate, exposing both allies and foes. Ladinas effectively mobilized hundreds if not thousands of women and men to a cause that likely would have been ignored by a National Assembly still dominated by the old political guard and landed elites steeped in a patriarchal and hierarchical sociopolitical milieu. The question of suffrage galvanized Guatemala's first formal feminist movement, and their success represented the most critical legal reform urban ladinas achieved during the revolutionary decade. Their dependence upon events in June served as proof of their political acuity, while legitimizing their claim to citizenship also essentially affirmed existing gender norms. As a political strategy, this approach drew a larger number of relatively conservative supporters. A more radical assertion of political rights would have likely ended in defeat, given the particular sociopolitical climate in 1944. It is also clear from their later affiliations that not all of these women supported a radical social revolution. Although this platform was embraced by the majority of these women, how they chose to employ their new political citizenship would quickly divide them. Consequently, the suffragists continued to promote civic registration among urban women, because a majority of these women remained apolitical.[74]

Incomplete suffrage exacerbated the gendered fault lines for the remainder of the revolutionary decade. The historically underfunded education system meant that literacy rates remained low despite an intensive literacy campaign, and national literacy rates reached only 23.9 percent for women five years into the revolutionary project (table 4.1).[75] With better access to education, literacy rates for urban ladinas rose to 68.9 percent. However, the literacy rate for indigenous women remained low throughout the decade, with only three out of every one hundred indigenous women theoretically able to access political citizenship.[76] This divide between women was solidified during the 1947 municipal elections, as ladina women eagerly stood in line to vote, some for the first time, while indigenous women remained on the political sidelines, selling snacks to the expectant voters.[77] The revolution, thus, created a vast gulf between women who could enjoy their first opportunity at political participation, and women who could not. While some were integrated into the political system (albeit imperfectly), many more women remained on the sidelines politically, economically, and educationally. Consequently, although suffrage was the most critical legal battle ladinas waged, it also solidified their politically privileged position, while the vast majority of women remained unaffected by it.

The enfranchisement of literate women came too late for the presidential elections, and so the first opportunity for political involvement came with the

TABLE 4.1 National Literacy Rates, 1950[1]

URBAN-RURAL / ETHNIC GROUPS	POPULATION	LITERACY RATES	MEN	WOMEN
Population	2,751,506	28.1%	32.1%	23.9%
Ladino	1,261,545	49.1%	52.7%	45.5%
Indigenous	1,489,961	9.7%	14.14%	4.8%
Urban	661,035	58.8%	65.3%	52.9%
Ladino	475,893	73.1%	78.9%	68.9%
Indigenous	185,142	20.6%	30.3%	11.1%
Rural	2,090,471	17.3%	21.4%	13.1%
Ladino	785,652	32.9%	36.7%	28.8%
Indigenous	1,304,819	8.4%	12.0%	4.0%

1. Dirección General de Estadística, *Censos de la República de Guatemala*, 1950.

TABLE 4.2 Eligible Women Voters in the Municipality of Guatemala, 1950[1]

Population	151,903[2]
Ladina	141,034
Indigenous	10,869
Urban	98,191[3]
Ladina	94,233
Indigenous	3,968
Rural	53,712[4]
Ladina	46,811
Indigenous	6,901

1. These statistics are taken from the 1950 census for women twenty years and older. This is as close as can be estimated for women over eighteen years of age.

2. Dirección General de Estadística, *Censos de la República de Guatemala*, 1950, 112–13.

3. Ibid., 114.

4. Ibid., 117–19.

municipal elections a year later. In spite of the pervasive ambivalence over the political acuity of women, the first women entered the political arena in the 1946 municipal elections. The well-known poet Magdalena Spínola Vda. de Aguilar and María de Irigoyen both ran for council seats. Highlighting their membership in the suffrage association, their campaign propaganda presented them as symbols of the wisdom and political capacity of the new female citizen.[78] Ironically, both women ran under the alcalde ticket of Clemente Marroquín Rojas (editor of the paper *La Hora*), who had voted against suffrage for women. However, as he would later clarify publicly in 1947, Marroquín Rojas had changed his mind in the ensuing months, and he embraced women not only as citizens but also as fellow political representatives (see chapter 5). Just a year later, another suffragist ran for deputy in the National Assembly during the January 24–26, 1947, election cycle, this time representing an even better-known revolutionary leader. Silverio Ortiz Rivas, a labor leader and artisan who had formed the Workers' League allying with the conservative pro-church Unionist Party in 1920, again emerged as an important revolutionary leader in 1944, heading the Partido Renovación Socialista.[79] With its long history of suffrage activism, the party now ran Angelina Acuña de Castañeda, the influential suffragist, poet, and teacher, on their ticket for the National Assembly.[80] The Partido Renovación Socialista had been openly advocating for the equal rights of both men and women for decades, but its influence during the revolutionary decade would be subsumed by more powerful revolutionary parties.[81]

During their initial forays into the political sphere, the ladina community supported all women entering politics across the ideological spectrum. In 1948, lawyer María del Carmen Vargas and Adriana Saravia de Palarea (who was part of the suffrage campaign) ran for the National Assembly.[82] They represented the two political poles present during the revolutionary era—the pro-revolutionary stance that some feared was affiliated with communism, and the ultraconservative pro-church party, the Partido de Unificación Anticomunista (PUA).[83] Although their electoral bids were unsuccessful, for the politically active ladinas, these two candidates represented a new hope for inclusion and increased social and political influence. Luz Valle articulated the perspective of many readers in her editorials as she encouraged everyone to participate in the upcoming municipal elections. "It would be something great for us, because we can begin to build strong support in regard to laws and institutions favorable to women."[84] Despite clear ideological differences between these two particular candidates, Valle reflected the dominant ideology among ladinas in the early years of the revolution. Quite simply, all women would benefit from having women in positions of political power regardless of their specific affiliations. Following the 1948 elections, the political stakes increased as local and national Guatemalan politics became increasingly intertwined with the broader Cold War conflict. This polarization found its way into the women's movement itself, and the shared experience of political repression gave way to a fragmentation that would continue to expand and define the urban ladina women's movement.

Recruiting the Political Ladina and the 1948 Municipal Elections

Although the struggle against Jorge Ubico had united the urban population, the ensuing practice of democracy now exposed deep political fault lines. These divisions emerged quickly, and the political terrain throughout the Arévalo era proved to be a messy business. As political novices, those in power struggled to address the gulf between democratic ideals and democratic practice. Yearning for power and still accustomed to the historical absence of democratic participation, political opponents refused to accept the electoral results of both the presidential and municipal campaigns despite a relatively free and fair democratic process.[85] The military remained suspicious and divided, and as a result Arévalo had to fend off close to thirty attempted coups d'etat, many of which were staged in collusion with conservative political parties unhappy with the election results.[86] Fierce competition existed not only between political parties of both pro- and antirevolutionary factions but within the parties themselves, and internal dynamics remained unstable as alliances shifted, coalesced, and failed almost as quickly as they were formed. The antirevolutionary movement in collusion with the church hierarchy maintained a steady campaign of anticommunist propaganda intended to further destabilize an already uncertain future for the Arévalo administration and its supporters. It made frequent and false claims that the government intended to expel the archbishop, Mariano Rossell y Arellano, energizing its constituents (see chapter 7 for more details). To maintain a modicum of social and political stability, the government repeatedly suspended constitutional guarantees, which served to confirm the opposition's speculations that the Arévalo administration was an authoritarian and even communist regime.

This intractable political landscape proved to be particularly challenging for civic-minded ladinas. Within a broader patriarchal context, those women involved in pro-revolutionary parties found few politicians interested in their vote. Focused on structural reforms, the revolutionary state had directed its attention to resolving or at least addressing elements of the existing economic disparity through wage increases, labor unions, and labor codes. Already largely disinclined to see women as potential allies in this battle, this approach brought revolutionary politicians into an alliance with working-class and rural men, an alliance that continued to solidify over the next decade. In presidential elections, the hundreds of urban ladinas who participated in female party affiliates and unions, and as heads of households, offered little electoral assistance against the backdrop of hundreds of thousands of rural and working-class male voters. This mathematical reality solidified the revolutionary state's political alliance with the rural male voter within an intensely competitive electoral landscape.

There is a caveat to this particular electoral map, however, and it lay with Guatemala City's municipal elections, which proved to be highly successful for these same parties due to the relatively large number of literate urban ladinas who voted. Out of several municipal elections held in 1948, 1950, and 1952, the 1948 campaign was a pivotal moment for ladina political activism and the antirevolutionary political movement. Here, the hundreds and thousands of urban ladina voters had the power to change the electoral map. In fact, the veracity of feminized political influence was fully revealed in the municipal sphere. Although politics was a masculine jurisdiction, the municipality signified a fusion of the political and domestic realms precisely because it encompassed issues primarily related to the local neighborhood. For women voters, municipal elections symbolized an extension of the female domestic sphere, and their meaning for women became immediately evident by women's overwhelming response in 1948.[87]

The conservative political parties and the Catholic Church were the first to identify the political potential of the ladina vote. The newly enfranchised bloc of rural and working-class men offered conservative parties little hope of gaining presidential power. Although conservative politicians had voted against women's suffrage during the suffrage debates, the class and ethnic composition of the electorate required them now to ally with the newly enfranchised literate women. As a result, the antirevolutionary movement effectively recruited thousands of urban women to its cause. While neither the conservative political parties nor the women involved with them publicly advocated for the return of Jorge Ubico, they worked diligently to maintain the gender and class hierarchies he had reinforced for the remainder of the revolutionary era. Dawn Teele has suggested that "the women that mobilize and the issues they fight for can inform expectations about the preferences of women that are the most likely to be politically active once suffrage is extended."[88] However, urban ladinas in Guatemala City contradict this notion. As novices in the political realm (as were many of their male counterparts), the vast majority of urban women were hesitant to engage with any particular ideology. The message of socioeconomic equality and unionism of the revolutionary parties found little resonance with urban middle-class ladinas, who seldom crossed the historical barrier that maintained the home and family as the only legitimate feminized space. The threat of communism, a message perpetuated by the antirevolutionaries, however, spoke directly to their deepest concerns, and in the face of the growing global threat of communism, women responded rapidly to register their political affiliation. For these women, the 1948 municipal elections offered an opportunity to vote on matters that directly affected their families' well-being. Despite the obvious contradiction with their conservative gender norms, the conservatives who endorsed women in the municipal elections were able to do so because of the dominant meaning of the municipality in Latin American politics.

Employing a familiar and valued maternalistic discourse, the antirevolutionary movement effectively fused accepted gender roles with Catholicism in their political opposition to both the Arévalo and then the Árbenz governments. Identifying the uncertainty and even anxiety created by the shifting gender and class hierarchies already evident in the first months of the revolutionary project, conservatives argued that only women had the ability to preserve the status quo or, in their words, to save the nation. In all scenarios, the revolution was portrayed as a danger for Guatemalan mothers and their families. Although what was really at stake here was the possible dismantling of the traditional socioeconomic structure designed to benefit Guatemala's elite, conservatives did not state such concerns overtly. Rather, they wove elite socioeconomic anxieties into the traditional gender structure and traditional notions of motherhood, a strategy that historian Sandra McGee Deutsch argues was particularly effective for the right-leaning and conservative politicians precisely because it simultaneously reinforced the existing class hierarchy.[89] As a result, they uniformly addressed female constituents as mothers, a role eagerly embraced by the vast majority of the urban population. Politicizing the cherished role of motherhood accomplished two simultaneous and contradictory political goals for the Guatemalan opposition. It honored the contributions of women, encouraging them to remain in the home, while also effectively drawing them into the political realm in order to protect the home. The large number of women drawn into this political milieu demonstrated a dramatic and contradictory transition, from an apolitical role as mother to a political role as actor capable of saving their nation. While poor and working-class women (both ladina and indigenous) may have held similar social precepts, they could not live out these traditional notions of femininity and gender construction due to the need for all household members to contribute to the household economy, a reality that held particular truth for single female heads of household. Therefore, urban middle- and upper-class ladinas who could sustain such gender constructions and vote became the intended target of these political messages.

The antirevolutionary opposition identified and utilized this potential political power from the first moments of the revolutionary era. As one of the most viable presidential candidates running against Juan José Arévalo, Adrián Recinos targeted ladinas directly despite their continued disenfranchisement, employing and projecting the influential sphere of the home onto the political stage. His party, the Frente Nacional Democrático, directed its 1944 presidential campaign toward those Guatemalan women who were uncomfortable with the changing attitudes toward women's roles initiated by the revolutionary candidates.[90] Recinos's "rights of women" campaign was reminiscent of Ubico's paternalistic language. Since the home was the primary locus of identity, he promised to put an end to unjustly abandoned wives, who were the victims of bad marriages and disrespected by youth. "Protection for the infant and the mother" became Recinos's electoral promise. He also emphasized religious liberty, and he eagerly campaigned for and incorporated women into his campaign. For his efforts, Recinos was rewarded with a strong contingent of women who worked diligently for his electoral victory.[91] Although Recinos lost by a wide margin to Arévalo, who won 85 percent of the literate male vote, his campaign rhetoric set the tone for other conservative parties that followed.

The political discourse shifted substantially over the next several years as internal and external opposition to the revolutionary project became increasingly hostile, employing the Cold War language of communist affiliation interwoven with Catholic theology to gain support for the conservative cause. During the 1930s, the Vatican had become increasingly concerned about the advance of communism and socialist principles. Events such as the Mexican revolution and the subsequent Cristero Rebellion had intensified the Catholic Church's fears about the incursion of communism into Latin America. In an effort to combat its growing popularity, Pope Pius XI issued an edict on communism and its detrimental effects on the family in 1937.

> Communism is particularly characterized by the rejection of any link that binds women to the family and the home, and her emancipation is proclaimed as a basic principle. She is withdrawn from the family and the care of her children, to be thrust instead into public life and collective production under the same conditions as man.[92]

Drawing upon Catholic anticommunist rhetoric and merging it with Guatemalan gender norms, Archbishop Rossell y Arellano initiated a powerful antirevolutionary campaign with an alliance of urban Guatemalan women at its core. His position was a defensive one, arguing that the church was in a position to protect women from the dual threat of changing gender norms in the wake of the recent revolution along with the emergence of communism. He called upon women to act on behalf of their "natural" roles as mothers and wives in order to preserve the traditional order and resist social change. The archbishop declared that it was the duty of all women to rise up against such danger before communism embedded itself in Guatemalan society. In order to incite an atmosphere of social instability and fear, the archbishop appealed to what he assumed were "universal" feminine concerns of faith and family. Astutely identifying these commonly held gender norms among the majority of urban women, Rossell y Arellano became the informal leader of an antirevolutionary movement comprising the political elite, conservative parties, and members of the urban ladina community.

The opposition to Jacobo Árbenz's presidential candidacy directed this rhetoric particularly at female voters during the 1950 elections, the only presidential election in which literate women had been eligible to participate up to this point. Árbenz won the election handily thanks to the rural and indigenous male vote supplemented by the support of the two most powerful revolutionary political parties and organized labor.[93] While he and his wife, María Vilanova de Árbenz, campaigned for the support of women (ironically working hard for the rural and indigenous vote, where the vast majority of women were illiterate and therefore disenfranchised), few overt messages were directed at the urban ladina voter. In contrast, however, the candidates who ultimately ran a distant second and third to Árbenz actively sought the urban ladina vote, acutely aware of their own precarious political position.

By the 1950 presidential elections, US foreign policy makers steeped in their bipolar Cold War worldview were convinced that the Guatemalan revolutionary project presented a significant threat to the Western Hemisphere. The United

Fruit Company had been particularly effective in convincing the State Department that Arévalo was unduly influenced by communism, an accusation that was far more about their own economic bottom line than it was about any specific political ideology.[94] They couched these economic interests in terms of the "communist threat," the political buzzword of the time. The rhetoric of the 1950 campaigns directed at literate women came to focus almost exclusively on the need to protect Catholicism, the home, the family, and the dignity of Guatemalan women against this potential threat.[95] Although they had been unified their efforts to overthrow Ubico, many in the urban ladina community now came to believe that the revolutionary state represented a danger.

Conservative political parties aligned with the church directed their campaigns at women in similar ways. In every case, they claimed that the revolutionary government was dangerous and aligned with communism. The party slogans fused notions of Catholicism initially with the removal of Arévalo and then Árbenz from government, and argued that only women had the ability to save the nation. Since only literate women could vote, this particular strategy had limited success, and only a few municipal elections were affected by this new voting block. Ironically, the church became far more successful at recruiting women to its cause than the revolution, a fact apparently lost on the government at the time but one that would have serious consequences.[96]

The Central Femenina del Partido Reconciliación Democrática Nacional and the Partido de Unificación Anticomunista were among the most successful parties to exploit this tactic.[97] Employing gendered fear tactics, these parties maintained a steady diatribe against Árbenz. They warned that the very fabric of the Guatemalan family would be destroyed should he be elected. Exiled for an attempted coup against the Arévalo administration, Miguel Ydígoras Fuentes returned to run for president against Árbenz.[98] Trusted by conservatives and former supporters of Jorge Ubico, he was supported by a right-wing civic coalition that included a significant number of urban ladinas. Understanding the power of this new voting block, Ydígoras Fuentes focused intensely on women by incorporating a female candidate for council, Graciela Hernández de Zirión.[99] As an educated ladina, Hernández de Zirión was someone with whom eligible urban female voters could identify. Arguing that the previous presidential election had revealed the strength of women voters (referring to the civic support women gave to Arévalo), she urged women to assume a politically active role in national politics. Hernández de Zirión promised that if she were elected, she would defend the rights of women and children, and of Guatemalans in general.[100]

However, unlike moderate candidates who referred back to the June 1944 march to confirm women's political acuity, conservative activists such as Hernández de Zirión turned to foreign examples. In a strategy that became common among those seeking the female vote, Hernández de Zirión demonstrated the political impact of women in industrialized countries such as the United States and Great Britain. Invoking the popular Latin American conservative feminist and Nobel laureate Gabriela Mistral, she urged women to unify as a Catholic voting bloc in order to save themselves from communism. Although Ydígoras Fuentes lost in 1950, he would later win his 1958 presidential bid following the assassination of Carlos Castillo Armas.

> Women of Guatemala, Alert
>
> To the Christian Catholic mother of any religious profession:
>
> Mothers, wives, sisters, friends, and girlfriends, all mothers must be religiously united against this enormous danger; together we can achieve the pious redemption of our people and our children, facing this effort for the spiritual improvement of humanity.
>
> Be assured, Guatemalan women, that the propaganda of other candidates who say that they are the defenders of our freedom of conscience and religion, is an absolute lie since their commitment to communism is well known and their plan to gain votes is based on lies and deception.
>
> —Miguel Ydígoras Fuentes, Presidential Candidate
>   Bloques Femeninos Ydigoristas, November 8, 1950[101]

Ultimately trailing a distant third to Árbenz and Ydígoras Fuentes, Jorge García Granados also utilized the powerful Catholic female voting bloc in his 1950 presidential bid. García Granados emphasized his civilian identity to his advantage, positioning himself between the right-wing candidacy of Ydígoras Fuentes and the revolutionary Árbenz, both of whom were affiliated with the military. The grandson of Liberal revolutionary hero Miguel García Granados, Jorge García Granados became involved in politics as a university student during the Unionista movement of 1920. Exiled by Jorge Ubico, he returned to Guatemala following Ubico's resignation in June and became the most important civilian leader involved in the October revolution. García Granados called on Guatemalans to avoid further suffering by voting for a president who would respect their Catholic faith, claiming that their devotion to the family must extend to the voting booth, where they could endorse their personal convictions. Basing his political campaign on a spiritual appeal to urban women, he attracted hundreds of ladinas to campaign on his behalf throughout the city.[102] García Granados thus discredited both the veracity of the extreme conservative opposition to suffrage and elevated the role of women to that of a religious ministry. It was a traditional message, but it drew hundreds of women into the national elections who otherwise might have abstained. Echoing the sentiments of other political moderates, he, too, reached back to the June 1944 march to demonstrate the civic consciousness of women.

> Catholic women of Guatemala
>
> We, the Catholic women of Guatemala—those of the civic exploits of 1944—appeal again to the conscience of Guatemalan women. . . .
>
> Mothers, wives, sisters, all Catholic women of this country, we suffered the disgrace of dictatorship, and therefore we have the obligation to struggle to prevent the suffering of future generations.
>
> JORGE GARCÍA GRANADOS.
>
> Whoever respects the ideas of others always respects the religion of any man or woman. For this reason, sisters in faith and in the religion of Christ, it is necessary to support the candidacy of the most civil man in Guatemala:
>
> JORGE GARCÍA GRANADOS.[103]

The presidential elections have been the primary focus of revolutionary history, but in actuality much of the real political power lay at the municipal level. As historian Jim Handy argues, municipal elections were critical for Guatemala's fledgling democracy and held particular meaning for both pro- and antirevolutionaries. Abolished by Jorge Ubico, municipal autonomy was reinstated in the 1945 constitution and then reinforced by Decree 226 in April 1946. Pro-Arévalo politicians maintained a particular attachment to local autonomy, which acted as a counterbalance to previous centralizing tendencies during the Ubico era. In order to consolidate their political position and to ensure that reform legislation was enacted, the government sought the cooperation of the local governments.[104] Deputies were elected according to departments, and one deputy was chosen for every fifty thousand or fraction over twenty-five thousand within a department.[105] Municipal elections were arranged so that half of the electoral body changed every two years in order to preserve legislative continuity. Since fully one half of the Congress was up for election, the stakes were high during the 1948 municipal elections.¹⁰⁶ Therefore, while the rural male voter dominated presidential elections, the critical voters in the municipal elections were the urban literate ladinas.

The gendered dynamics of the 1948 municipal elections were intensified by the growing Cold War rhetoric that was becoming increasingly effective against the pro-revolutionary political parties. Until 1948, the Catholic Church and the supporting antirevolutionary movement had directed voters to abstain from the vote in protest of the Arévalo government. The government's economic policies, particularly the 1947 Labor Code, elicited opposition from the powerful landowners' association, the Asociación General de Agricultores (AGA), who argued that recent labor shortages and work disruptions were the result of these new workers' rights.¹⁰⁷ These social and legal changes provided the perfect political fodder for Archbishop Rossell y Arellano's opposition and the first real opportunity for him to assert his political influence.¹⁰⁸ Calculated to influence the voting practices of women, the archbishop issued a series of pastoral letters.¹⁰⁹ The first letter, issued on June 8, 1948, was titled "Instrucción pastoral de Monseñor Mariano Rossell y Arellano al pueblo católico de Guatemala: Sobre el deber y condiciones del sufragio"; Guatemalans were urged to perform their civic responsibility by registering to vote. However, Rossell y Arellano advised caution in the choice of political candidate. "In no situation should a Catholic vote for a candidate whose politics or ideology obstructs the church or loosens the public morality and order."¹¹⁰ Guatemalans were living in dangerous times, according to Rossell y Arellano, in which oppressive totalitarian and communist governments abounded. Careful to avoid specific accusations against the Arévalo administration, the archbishop nevertheless attempted to cultivate fear through his dire predictions. Although the archbishop and his supporters claimed the intent of the letter to be purely apolitical, the implications of Rossell y Arellano's remarks appeared clear to everyone.¹¹¹ Clemente Marroquín Rojas, editor of the conservative newspaper *La Hora*, made a specific note of the archbishop's tactical shift, and the US State Department noted that the church and its affiliates had violated the rules of nonintervention between church and state according to Article 29 of the Guatemalan constitution.

In an apparent response to the archbishop's call, the antirevolutionary opposition formed an umbrella organization at the end of June 1948. Designed to encourage voter registration among the conservative Catholic sector, the Unión Nacional Electoral (UNE) encouraged the exercise of suffrage as the only legal method to overthrow the current administration.[112] Under the aegis of the UNE, a coalition of opposition groups emerged, including the Liga Democrática Guatemalteca Contra el Comunismo, the Alianza Guatemalteca Electoral, and the Partido de Trabajadores Republicano-Democrático (PTRD).[113] While those behind this organization claimed its intentions to be those of a nonpartisan civic organization, the UNE's affiliation to both old-guard politicians and the church was very clear. The UNE galvanized latent fears among a significant element of the urban population, and a female affiliate of the UNE was immediately formed, designed to campaign for the women's vote.[114] Representing the Liga Democrática Guatemalteca contra el Comunismo, Adriana Saravia de Palarea had been one of the founding members of the Asociación de Mujeres Intelectuales in January 1944.[115] She subsequently assumed a leadership role in the movement against the revolutionary government throughout the remainder of the 1940s and 1950s, which confirms the temporary quality of the unity created among the urban ladina community in order to overthrow Ubico. Utilizing the buzzwords of the period, the UNE claimed that Guatemalan sovereignty was in trouble and that communism was close at hand. Since women had closer ties to the church than did men, they would suffer the most severe consequences at the hands of an anticlerical communism. Consequently, women needed to act in this moment in order to avert the catastrophe of communism.

There was an immediate and remarkable rise in the number of women at the registration polls following the pastoral letter and the creation of the UNE. This political shift caught the attention of all the national newspapers, and they charted the course of female voter registration over the next several months, noting the steady rise in political participation.[116] *Nuestro Diario* reported that 203 women had registered by the end of June.[117] *Diario de Centro América* also followed the situation closely, noting that while 6 women were registered in April, 25 in May, and 87 by June, in July the number rose sharply to 740. By August, *El Imparcial* recorded the current number of registered female voters at 2,729 and triumphantly announced that, judging by the number of women who were daily registering, 10,000 women would vote in November and December.[118] *La Hora* noted in mid-July that between 25 and 50 women were registering daily in the capital city alone, with more than a thousand already registered for the national *diputados* and alcaldes.[119] The paper continued to chart the rising numbers, claiming that 2,829 had registered in August, 4,500 by the beginning of October, and finally 5,000 by the middle of November.[120] While the number of registered women varied among the sources, the indisputable fact was that women had responded to the archbishop's clarion call for political reform. The conservative parties were also caught unawares by this rapid rise in the number of politically active women, considering that they had previously believed that women were not interested in politics.[121] In the final tally, 3,000 women had registered with the UNE, while another 2,000 registered for other political parties.[122]

The archbishop's call was so effective that he followed up with a second treatise. In "Al pueblo católico sobre el deber de la caridad en la práctica del sufragio electoral," published on October 12, the archbishop reminded his readers that the only mission of the Guatemalan Catholic was the victory of God in the voting booth.[123] There was, however, another purpose behind this second letter. As successful as the recruitment of women had been, the numbers were clearly not going to be sufficient to defeat the revolutionary candidates. Consequently, in this second letter, the archbishop addressed the working class, stressing the high cost of living and the tremendous economic disparities between rich and poor.[124] In a blatant attempt to recruit a group he had consistently ignored, the

TABLE 4.3 Registered Voters, 1947–1953[1]

YEAR	LITERATE WOMEN	LITERATE MEN	ILLITERATE MEN
1947 (municipal)[2]	**3,769[3]	*134,263	*225,304
1948 (municipal)	**5,998	**42,853	**6,286[4]
1950 (presidential)	*26,000[5]		
1952 (municipal)[6]	*38,710 (6%)	*237,941 (37%)	*366,140 (57%)[7]
1953 (municipal)	Unavailable	Unavailable	Unavailable

* National statistics
** Municipality of Guatemala statistics

1. Women and men were not separated in the final electoral tabulations. But the national papers carefully recorded the number of each gender who registered. This table is based on these sources.
2. *Nuestro Diario*, July 8, 1947.
3. *Nuestro Diario*, July 8 and 9, 1947.
4. *Diario de Centro América*, November 25, 1948. The total number of actual voters was 42,179 literate males, 6,195 illiterate males, and 5,722 women. Accordingly, the total number of absent voters was 674 literate males, 91 illiterate males, and 276 women.
5. *El Imparcial*, November 1, 1950.
6. *El Imparcial*, October 31, 1952. At the end of September, of 568,826 who had registered, 339,250 were illiterate men, 205,036 were literate men, and 21,788 were women.
7. Silvert, *A Study in Government*, 59.

archbishop called for a new social justice.[125] Just days before the 1948 elections, on November 15, the archbishop published yet a third pastoral letter, entitled "Carta pastoral sobre la justicia social, fundamento del bienestar social." Again, he warned his parishioners against the dangers of communism.[126] "Every vote received casts two ballots, one for the official candidate and the other for the immense struggle against the government."[127] Having now violated constitutional law twice, Rossell y Arellano became increasingly brazen, referring to the revolutionary candidates as "lobos burgueses con piel de obreros" (bourgeois wolves in workers' clothing).[128] *Diario de Centro América* immediately denounced this statement as a perverse lie, accusing the archbishop of inflaming an already tense political situation. It appears, however, that escalating the political stakes is clearly what the archbishop intended to do.[129]

The growing urban polarization was reflected in the four national newspapers, *La Hora*, *El Imparcial*, *Diario de Centro América*, and *Nuestro Diario*. The first two were by and large sympathetic to antirevolutionary sentiment and political activities, while the last two carried more pro-government articles. *El Imparcial* attempted to create fear among rural male voters, suggesting that illiterate men might have their right to vote taken away, an unlikely event given their support of the revolutionary political parties.[130] It also spent time defending the archbishop and the meaning behind his actions.[131] The response from the pro-revolutionary perspective was scathing, as these newspapers repeatedly accused the archbishop of flagrant constitutional violations.[132] The Partido Acción Revolucionaria linked the Unión Nacional Electoral with the Catholic Church, while the Frente Popular Libertador accused them of Ubico-style politics.[133] Catholic papers were quick to defend their leader. The newspaper *El Verbum* refuted all accusations that the church had formed a political party.[134]

This helped generate an intense political milieu for the municipal elections, which were held during November 26–28. In the aftermath, observers concluded that voting turnout had been high.[135] Although the voting itself was uneventful, clashes between pro- and antirevolutionary supporters punctuated the days following the elections, prompting the suspension of constitutional guarantees on December 2, 1948.[136] Despite the unprecedented number of female political participants, in fact the number remained extremely small in comparison to the total number eligible to vote. Out of the total 94,233 ladina and 3,968 indigenous eligible voters in Guatemala City, only approximately 6,000 women registered to vote.

Increasingly suspicious of the Arévalo administration, the US State Department observed the 1948 municipal elections closely. They were quick to make the connection between the archbishop's pastoral letter and the rise of female electoral registrations, concluding that an average of seventy women registered daily in response to Rossell y Arellano's letter. They identified the political potential of women's committees who went door to door to encourage women to register to vote.[137] "The fact that several thousand women have registered in Guatemala City as a result of the archbishop's appeal is indisputable evidence of the effectiveness of church influence."[138] While the State Department would later work covertly with the archbishop to facilitate the overthrow of Jacobo Árbenz, at this juncture it was critical of the church's political interference. Despite their criticism, however, the power of gender utilized by the anticommunist rhetoric was quite clear to State Department observers.

One of the fundamental questions here is why the conservative and antirevolutionary campaigns were so effective among urban voters.[139] The revolutionary

TABLE 4.4 Population Growth and Voter Turnout in Elections, 1944–1958[1]

YEAR	POPULATION	REGISTERED VOTERS	% OF POPULATION REGISTERED	ACTUAL VOTE	% OF REGISTERED VOTERS
1944 (presidential)	2,408,889	310,000	12.9	302,456	97.6
1948	Unavailable	54,096[2]	Unavailable	36,165[3]	66.85
1950[4] (presidential)	2,845,551	583,300[5]	21.5	485,531	70.4
1954	3,211,158	689,985	21.5	485,531	70.4
1958 (presidential)	3,592,283	736,400	20.5	492,274	66.8

1. *Guatemala: Election Factbook*, 13.

2. Ibid. 42,179 were literate voters, 6,195 were illiterate voters, and 5,722 were women.

3. Ibid. Out of 17,000 voters, 7,000 were illiterate and 4,000 were women.

4. *Nuestro Diario*, November 14, 1951. The presidential results were as follows: Jacobo Árbenz, 242,901; Miguel Ydígoras Fuentes, 68,146; Jorge García Granados, 30,016; Victor Manuel Giordani, 16,181; Manuel Galich, 6,264; Clemente Marroquín Rojas, 5,479; and Arcadio Chévez Guillén, 3,137 votes.

5. *Nuestro Diario*, August 30, 1951. This national paper claimed 616,289 voters, which contradicted this result.

We Are Already Citizens 179

opposition relied on contemporary gender constructions and the generalized apolitical nature of the ladina community. Responding to the uncertainty of the Arévalo era, women aligned themselves with those political parties that promised to restore sociopolitical order and maintain the patriarchal hierarchy affirmed through traditional gender roles.[140] Much to the chagrin of the pro-revolutionary political parties, a majority of these women registered for the opposition. Rossell y Arellano demonstrated his awareness of the potential strength of the female vote against the revolutionary political candidates and utilized it effectively. While the archbishop used front groups to promote his political agenda, the extent of his affiliation with the conservative political parties is clear. The church repeatedly noted the social problems created by the advent of the "modern" woman that upset the traditional role of middle- and upper-class women. When it suited its purpose, however, the church called forth these women to temporarily transgress gender norms and participate in the political process.

Margaret Power's analysis of the role of gender in Chilean politics provides a valuable comparison with Guatemalan political events. Concerned over the possible victory of socialist candidate Salvador Allende over Eduardo Frei Montalva, the US State Department actively intervened in Chile's electoral process during the 1964 presidential campaign. Drawing on constructions of gender then prevalent in Chile, US officials designed a campaign that engendered anticommunism and fear, equating Allende with communism and communism with the destruction of the family. Known as the "Scare Campaign," such gendered appeals could effectively influence political choices and determine the outcome of elections, as US officials learned. Their contribution to Allende's defeat "encouraged U.S. officials to employ the Scare Campaign as a model for other anti-Communist projects in Latin America."[141] Power's examination of the 1964 Scare Campaign reveals that US government officials went beyond simply projecting gendered language and stereotypes onto other nations and peoples. They also incorporated ideas about gender into the construction of their foreign policy.[142] The State Department's close observation of Guatemalan politics in 1948 is suggestive that they employed lessons learned throughout the rest of Latin America in the following years. The power of gender evidenced so clearly in their opposition to the Guatemalan revolution become entrenched in Cold War rhetoric and was immediately transplanted to other Latin American regions perceived to be in danger of communist influence.

The antirevolutionary movement continued to reap the electoral rewards of US strategy. Just as in Chile, the Guatemalan moderates and those on the left were unable to challenge a powerful message that embodied gender, anticommunism, and the sanctity of the family. The element of terror elicited by this triad proved particularly difficult to counteract, as would become evident by the social destabilization achieved by the marches and demonstrations that occurred throughout the Árbenz era. Pro-revolutionary women advocated tirelessly on behalf of both the Arévalo and Árbenz governments, highlighting the social reforms benefiting so many thousands of women and children.[143] Despite their much smaller impact on elections in Guatemala, conservatives employed the same gendered images of communism and fear within the antirevolutionary movement. In 1949, engineer Martín Prado Vélez (Partido de Trabajadores Republicano-Democrático) won the municipal election with a decisive victory. Observers were quick to note that the five thousand votes with which he beat out his opponent corresponded roughly to the six thousand women who voted.[144] The winner of the mayoral race in Guatemala City just two years later, Juan Luis Lizarralde, also attributed his success to the large number of female voters.[145] His opponent, Humberto González Juárez, however, attributed his defeat to Lizarralde's superior campaign organization and the alleged propaganda of the Catholic Church. Further, González Juárez warned that the revolutionary parties should prepare for a new attack from reactionary forces in close alliance with large foreign companies. What he failed to acknowledge, however, was the decisive vote of female constituents.

The 1948 municipal elections represent a singular moment in revolutionary history. During no other electoral period did ladinas respond so rapidly and in such numbers to register their political affiliation. Despite clear evidence to the contrary, pro-revolutionary politicians appeared to be unwilling to entertain the possibility that women voters had influenced the outcome of the elections. This particular electoral defeat played a pivotal role in Guatemala City during the Árbenz presidency. The US State Department claimed that the political loss by González Juárez was a general defeat for the pro-revolutionary parties, who had united to endorse his candidacy. US officials also suggested that this loss was more important than Prado Vélez's earlier victory in 1949.[146] Despite this type of analysis and direct evidence, the pro-revolutionary parties did not shift their campaign strategies in the municipal contests to include the woman's vote following 1948 and 1949. In retrospect, while the decision to limit the political participation of illiterate women did not affect the electoral outcomes in the rural areas, it served to strengthen the antirevolutionary movement in the capital city. Not only were critical antirevolutionary politicians elected to office, but it

We Are Already Citizens 181

contributed to a growing and powerful perception in Guatemala City that the revolution itself was in jeopardy. The thousands of urban ladinas campaigning door to door and standing in lines at the polling stations were powerful visible evidence.

In the aftermath of the successful antirevolutionary movement in 1954, politicians had clear evidence of women's political acuity through countless demonstrations and several significant electoral results. Whether women developed long-term notions of citizenship through this action is debatable. However, as Kristina Boylan notes in her work on Catholic women in Mexico, "it is unfair to dismiss women who mobilized for the church as cultural dupes.... It undervalues women's contributions to their churches as well as the opportunities religious participation provides for education, decision making, and public activism."[147] These women seized the opportunity to act on their own definitions of civic duty, which they understood to be to vote against the revolutionary government. In so doing, the worst fears of pro-revolutionary politicians were realized. The resurgence of repeated military dictatorships following 1954 makes it difficult to assess the long-term results of suffrage in the Guatemalan democratic process, although there is some suggestion of a shift in the political consciousness of gendered voting norms. The power of the conservative ladina voter was consecrated by the election of Rosa de Mora as deputy to the National Assembly in 1956.[148] The founder of the Sociedad Protectora del Niño, Mora had participated in the suffrage movement and significant political events during the Arévalo presidency. However, she remained relatively conservative and eventually withdrew her support of the revolutionary project, as many of her peers ultimately did as well.

Conclusion

The intersection of gender, ethnicity, and the emerging Cold War played a critical role in the formation of revolutionary politics, a triad that simultaneously expanded and limited notions of the political Guatemalan. From its inception, the revolution did not succeed in shifting gender norms in the political sphere. The public perception of what constituted political action remained unchanged, and male privilege remained intact particularly within the sacrosanct political realm. Despite their unrefuted intellectual and social contributions to the formation of pro-revolutionary political parties, women remained on the margins. Revolutionary politicians remained unwilling to address gendered reforms, failing to tap into the energy of politically minded women. In turn, the generalized lack of civic participation solidified notions of Guatemalan women as defenders of the home, the traditional gender order, and the church. Those opposed to the revolution shifted their efforts to a far more effective strategy of social destabilization through public demonstrations. Effectively merging the threat of communism with the well-being of Guatemalan women, the opposition galvanized a largely apolitical segment of the urban population into a powerful social movement. Capitalizing on the perceived moral superiority of women, their innumerable demonstrations and protests lent an air of legitimacy to an antirevolutionary crusade designed to protect the economic elite.

It was the struggle for suffrage that initiated the revolution's first overtly feminist association. Gloria Menéndez Mina's proclamation in February 1945 that "we are already citizens" revealed the passion and political acuity present among a small and influential group of urban ladinas. For decades, these literary figures and educators had claimed their right to citizenship, weighing in on political and social issues as Guatemalans and not as women during years of Liberal dictatorships, which simultaneously narrowed the definitions of citizenship and eliminated any such possibility. Employing the June march as evidence of their civic identity and courage, Menéndez Mina successfully argued that women had demonstrated the necessary qualifications for citizenship. The enfranchisement excluded the vast majority of women, however, significantly weakening the sociopolitical power of the woman's vote. The paradox of the Guatemalan suffrage movement is that a majority of women who registered and voted were not the pro-revolutionary middle-class or working-class ladinas who had participated in the suffrage campaign but rather the conservative urban supporters of the Catholic Church and the antirevolutionary movement.

The ambiguity created by the dialectical relationship between gender norms and ladina activism was embodied in the 1948 municipal elections. Archbishop Mariano Rossell y Arellano successfully incorporated a large number of women into his opposition movement through the exploitation of two central aspects of Guatemalan identity: traditional notions of gender and the Catholic faith. His political strategy claimed that both Catholicism and the ideals of womanhood/motherhood cherished particularly by the middle and upper classes were in jeopardy under the revolutionary governments. Couching his arguments in the language of religious persecution, Rossell y Arellano stated that the revolution was merely a continuation of the historical Liberal anticlericalism of the prior seventy years. The result could only be communism, which threatened not only the Catholic faith but also the sanctity of the home, where women reigned as protectors of these ideals. Essentially, he melded commonly held notions of gender and religious faith into one powerful threat. The reassertion of traditional and strictly defined gender roles by the Catholic Church and those who supported the antirevolutionary movement served as another obstacle to potential changes. Since motherhood defined a majority of urban ladina identities, electoral campaigns that reminded them continuously of the threat to their families, homes, and way of life were particularly effective.

The antirevolutionary movement accurately identified and played on these fears in the capital city. The combination of the powerful indigenous vote, which vastly outnumbered the ladino vote, along with the new politically active ladina proved to be a powerful warning message for the conservative bloc. Despite deep misgivings over the fluidity (however slight) of gender roles, conservative and antirevolutionary political parties violated their own principles regarding gender to engage with a new political ally, namely urban ladinas. While many women eagerly moved from a culture dominated by domesticity to one where the home and national politics interacted, reforming a wide variety of social spaces, politicians and society alike remained uncertain of the outcome.

Five

EVEN A GRAIN OF SAND
URBAN LADINAS, THE COLD WAR, AND THE FIRST INTER-AMERICAN CONGRESS OF WOMEN, GUATEMALA CITY, 1947

Welcome to Guatemala, the land of free men and women.
—Elisa Martínez de Arévalo, 1947

Without doubt, the celebration of the First Inter-American Women's Congress has signaled a critical moment in the evolution of the political and social life of women in the three Americas.
—Malin D'Echevers, 1947

The purpose of the congress is to establish the position of women of this hemisphere in relation to international and inter-American problems vital to the maintenance of peace and democracy; to determine the most effective means of cooperation; and to strengthen the ties of friendship and understanding between the women of the Americas.
—Heloise Brainerd, 1947

The First Inter-American Congress of Women held in Guatemala City in 1947 occurred at a pivotal moment in both the urban ladina movement and the Guatemalan revolution. Just two years into the revolutionary project, these women had already achieved several sociopolitical accomplishments, including suffrage for literate women and the creation of the comedores infantiles and guarderías infantiles. However, they continued to be stymied by male colleagues unwilling to integrate them into any real political power within the revolutionary state structure. Eager to break out of their political isolation on both the national and the international stage, they therefore enthusiastically accepted the invitation to host the First Inter-American Congress of Women. Political inexperience had not prepared the ladinas, however, for the political opposition that emerged both within Guatemala and among the international community for their association with the congress. Under intense international scrutiny, the Guatemalan women's movement was required to define its feminist ideals and political ideology, as they struggled to successfully organize the event. Set within the embryonic spasms of the Cold War, the ideological drama that unfolded in the weeks preceding and following the congress permanently split the Guatemala City women's movement into two distinct political and ideological camps.

The democratic euphoria that followed the post–World War II era was all too brief as relations cooled between wartime allies the United States and the Soviet Union. In its place, a transition toward security in lieu of democracy and populist social reforms quickly took hold. As the political climate shifted across Latin America to align with the anticommunist posture of the United States, most of the populist openings had closed by 1948. Despite the United States' emphasis on security and renewed militarization, under Juan José Arévalo, Guatemala continued on its modest social and economic reform program. Therefore, when Elisa Martínez de Arévalo opened the 1947 congress with the words "Welcome to Guatemala, the land of free men and women," she was articulating a political reality. In 1947, Guatemala was one of the few locations where it was possible to hold such an audacious event as the Inter-American Congress of Women.

The congress was initiated by the US section of the Women's International League for Peace and Freedom (WILPF) and was specifically organized to create a counterdiscourse to the growing military escalation of the early Cold War era. It outlined resolutions designed to promote global democracy and peace, support associations in the struggle for basic human rights, and advance both political and civil rights for women. Its resolutions held up both the United Nations charter on disarmament as well as the 1945 Act of Chapultepec. In the face of growing East-West hostilities, the women of the First Inter-American Congress affirmed a faith in democratic movements as the path to eliminating political extremes on the rise from both the right and the left. The ideas presented at this conference, however, directly contradicted the ideology simultaneously developing at the Inter-American Treaty of Reciprocal Assistance in Rio de Janeiro in August 1947, also known as the Rio Pact.

The 1947 Inter-American Congress of Women positioned Guatemalan women against a complex interrelated web of international actors and states within the context of the emergent hostilities of the Cold War. The Guatemalan government's direct political opposition to the Rio Pact and the WILPF's message of demilitarization placed these political novices against the powerful militarization of US foreign policy. The volatile atmosphere surrounding the message of global peace had serious consequences for the ladinas organizing the congress in Guatemala City. As they struggled to identify their own political ideologies vis-à-vis those of their male contemporaries and other women across the Americas, these women discovered that this small congress had international repercussions. The subsequent opposition fostered by the United States toward the congress revealed the vulnerability of local groups and the extent to which matters internal to Guatemala could be determined by its large and powerful neighbor to the north. Consequently, an analysis of the 1947 congress and the ladinas who organized it uncovers the extent of the Cold War's influence in local geopolitical events.

Analysts of the Cold War in Guatemala have focused predominantly on the influence of US foreign policy on the national political trajectories of the Arévalo and Árbenz governments while paying less attention to local factors.[1] More recent scholarship has begun to uncover the extent to which localized struggles over land, labor, and natural resources rarely escaped the "powerful undertow" of the Cold War.[2] Without serious examination of local social and cultural identities and political agency, Greg Grandin argues, little can be understood about the Cold War's impact on local Guatemalan associations and networks.[3] However, within this complex nexus of international and local Cold War dynamics, even less attention has been paid to the experiences of women. Pioneering historian Francisca de Haan argues that prevailing notions of gender were deeply intertwined within the binary positions developed by Cold War rhetoric, all of which had particularly complex consequences on women's organizations deemed subversive by the United States.[4] Policy analyst Frank Costigliola argues that "to construct meaning by conceptualizing things in terms of pairs that require one thing to be not just dissimilar but the negation of the other. . . . These binary oppositions help shape meaning, both in discussions of foreign policy and in more general discourse."[5] Odd Arne Westad expands on this analysis to argue that the way in which gender was employed within the Cold War nexus extended to the use of language, the very core of conceptual power: "Not only were gender relations closer to the core of the conflict both in terms of representation and in language than we have previously thought, they were actively employed by policy makers."[6] Employing this analysis to examine the political context of the 1947 congress reveals the dichotomous perspective of Cold War policy makers and the disruptive nature of the women's congressional message. The escalation of hegemonic military security throughout the Americas

Even a Grain of Sand 187

was conceived as a masculine project based on national alliances across the hemisphere. The congressional conclusions that socioeconomic reforms and social justice represented a more productive path to hemispheric security directly contradicted the conclusions reached by the US State Department.

The trifecta of transnationalism, gender, and democratic idealism present at the 1947 congress directly threatened the ideals being presented simultaneously in Rio de Janeiro. As the United States organized for hemispheric hegemony and military security, organizations and events such as the WILPF and the 1947 congress were dismissed as communist fronts by US foreign policy analysts. The threat of communism essentially erased the intellectual contributions regarding democracy and sociopolitical reforms presented in Guatemala City in 1947. With the singular exception of Francesca Miller's discussion in her groundbreaking volume *Latin American Women and the Search for Social Justice*, the 1947 Inter-American Congress of Women has been removed from history.[7]

Guatemala and Transnational Organizing

Latin American women discovered early in their activism that transnational organizing was an effective tool to achieve their goals. Beginning with the Pan American Scientific Congresses of the 1890s, Latin American women used international congresses to debate concerns including hygiene, child care, nutrition, and maternal welfare, all issues that operated well within traditional feminine interests.[8] In 1910, South American women gathered in Buenos Aires in the first Congreso Femenino Internacional to debate topics ranging from international law to health care to the problems of married working women. By the mid-1940s, the effectiveness of transnational organizing had been proven. Although women frequently had difficulty getting their voices heard in their own countries, the support they needed existed from their sisters across the continent.

Guatemalan women, however, had limited opportunities to attend such meetings, hindered by dictatorial regimes from organizing and traveling outside the country, and were therefore political novices in both the local and transnational arena. Those Guatemalans who were able to attend several Pan American meetings, however, in fact played prominent roles. Guatemalan politician and writer Máximo Soto Hall first initiated a women's rights proposal at the Fifth International Conference of American States at Santiago, Chile, in 1923.[9] Leaving Guatemala in 1919 just before the overthrow of Manuel Estrada Cabrera, Soto Hall moved to Argentina but continued to represent Guatemala at the Pan American meetings. Considering Soto Hall's earlier treatise in 1913 advocating a very limited role for women outside the home (see chapter 1), he had clearly shifted his position when he moved to include women as government representatives at the Pan American meetings. As Ann Towns explains, although Soto Hall's proposal did not receive much overt support, Chilean women picked up on the proposal and lobbied for its passage.[10] The resolution was not adopted in 1923 but set the stage for the 1928 International Conference of American States in Havana, Cuba, directly leading to the successful creation of the Inter-American Commission of Women (CIM).

The CIM, which met for the first time in Havana in 1930, was charged with the task of carrying out the resolutions of the 1923 meetings, which included an investigation of the status of women from all twenty-one member countries.[11] Teacher and later president of the Asociación de Maestras Católicas de Guatemala Irene de Peyré represented Guatemala at this first official meeting. In 1933, Guatemalan delegate José González Campo chaired the committee on the civil and political rights of women, which resulted in the world's first diplomatic resolution for suffrage. Such opportunities were short lived however, and due to the travel restrictions imposed by Jorge Ubico during his thirteen-year dictatorship, no other ladinas attended an international meeting again until the 1944 revolution. These scant encounters were not supported by either state or local institutions and therefore had minimal benefits for the urban ladina community, who remained largely isolated from their continental peers. Therefore, when ladinas associated with educational, literary, and social reform circles were invited to host the First Inter-American Congress of Women, they eagerly seized the opportunity, unaware of the implications of international organizing on the eve of the Cold War.

The congress was initiated by the Women's International League for Peace and Freedom.[12] An organization with roots in World War I, the WILPF was founded at the International Congress of Women in The Hague on April 28, 1915, on two premises: namely, that global conflicts could be mediated through peaceful means and that political democracy was intrinsically linked with basic human rights, including women's legal equality and suffrage.[13] As director of the US section of the WILPF, Heloise Brainerd was particularly concerned with strengthening relationships with Latin American women in order to create a hemispheric peace movement. The organization developed relationships with Latin American women's groups during CIM meetings throughout the 1920s. While Latin American women focused a majority of their efforts on the equal status of women, these activists also took firm positions on international issues

Even a Grain of Sand 189

of peace and principles of nonintervention. Consequently, Brainerd invited thirteen Latin American women who shared the WILPF's antiwar perspectives to a celebratory meeting in Haverford, Pennsylvania, on May 25, 1945.[14] While they all expressed concern over the emerging conflict between the United States and the Soviet Union, its possible effects on Latin America dominated the agenda. As Brainerd recorded: "Those of us who are from Latin America consider that we are under the obligation of preventing our countries from being dragged into a conflict which they have not brought about, and in which they would be innocent victims solely because of circumstances beyond their control."[15] Therefore, although the inaugural organizational meeting was ostensibly held for the celebration of the WILPF's thirtieth anniversary, the gathering quickly assumed a far more serious purpose. In the weeks following the German surrender in May 1945, women in the WILPF determined that a larger hemispheric event was necessary to establish woman's position on peace and democracy. It was here that the seed for 1947 congress was created.[16]

Heloise Brainerd was perhaps the best-suited woman to create an interhemispheric coalition at this time.[17] As director of the US section of the WILPF, she had successfully cultivated connections for several decades, particularly concerned about developing positive relations between the United States and Latin America. Brainerd had long hoped to draw Latin American women into the peace movement, and she traveled widely throughout the Americas, bringing fresh energy and new perspective to the transnational organization. Her engagement with Latin American women marked a departure from previous transnational leaders such as Carrie Chapman Catt, who demonstrated a disdain for the emphasis on motherhood that Latin American feminists fostered in their movements. As Lynn Stoner notes, US feminists had historically acted out of their own cultural and political biases, and had not supported Latin American suffrage movements.[18] Therefore, Brainerd represented a new model for intercultural dialogue and was successful in creating positive relationships with Latin American women.[19]

Brainerd established a steering committee for a potential congress consisting of six Latin American women: Carmen Sánchez de Bustamante Calvo de Lozada (Bolivia), Ángela Acuña de Chacón (Costa Rica), Roselia Caballero de Schotland (Cuba), Olga Poblete de Espinosa (Chile), Mélida Luz Palacios de Wolter (El Salvador), and Paulina Gómez Vega (Colombia). Although these women were Latin American, they all resided in the United States as either students or spouses of diplomats or UN ambassadors. In other words, they represented the political and educational elite in their own nations and were therefore quite immune from the localized consequences of their political ideas and actions. An official invitation was sent out to associations across the hemisphere to inform them of the upcoming congress, calling for both donations and delegates to attend this groundbreaking call for world peace.[20]

The official WILPF reports indicate that Guatemala City was the delegates' first choice as a venue for the congress due to the enthusiasm with which women there received the idea. However, choosing a site for the congress was in fact more complex and directly related to the emerging global geopolitics during 1945–1947. Hope for peace quickly turned to skepticism once the United States used the atomic bomb against Japan, potentially normalizing nuclear weapons in future conflict. The delegates' concerns grew as relations cooled between wartime allies the United States and the Soviet Union. US foreign policy increasingly reflected this deepening polarization throughout the Americas, based on a militarized dogmatism that tolerated neither political nuances nor solutions focused on social issues apart from any state system fully aligned with US foreign policy. An international circular released in the spring of 1946 reveals the level of the WILPF's preoccupation with this threat.

> We have just lived through what is perhaps the greatest upheaval in history, and yet it seems to us that already people are beginning to forget the past. We note also that the possibility of a new conflict is accepted with a certain indifference or fatalism, an attitude which is the more shocking when one considers that at the same time there is a general belief that, should a new war break out, we would witness this time the end of a civilization—the end of four thousand years of struggle for survival against both nature and man.[21]

The United States would solidify this hemispheric alliance during the conference in Rio de Janeiro in August 1947.

Given this political context, Brainerd believed that WILPF's ideas on pacifism would clearly not be well received by many national governments (including the United States), and only Cuba, Nicaragua, Bolivia, Chile, Ecuador, Panama, and Venezuela had WILPF national sections. To draw participation from Latin America, the committee's original plan included holding the congress in a centralized site such as Havana, Cuba, or Caracas, Venezuela. By late 1946, the hemisphere had already begun the transition toward security-based politics, ending the majority once held by populist and democratic governments and leaving Guatemala as one of the few democratic administrations in Latin America.[22] Francesca Miller argues that Guatemala in fact provided a more open space for freedom of discussion than did the United States.²³ The Arévalo administration's support of democratic ideals, social reforms, the subordination of the military to civil authority, and freedom of expression made Guatemala City the ideal location, and the opposition mounted by the US State Department in the preceding weeks verifies Miller's contention.²⁴

In light of the decreasing possibilities for a venue, Brainerd contacted educator María Albertina Gálvez in Guatemala City (the well-known educator whom the ladina community had hoped would be named minister of education under the Arévalo administration).²⁵ So long denied the opportunity to engage with other women in the Americas, the urban ladina community eagerly agreed to host the Inter-American Congress of Women. In her correspondence with Brainerd, Albertina Gálvez noted that they were intensely interested in organizing and hosting the congress, happy to contribute "even a grain of sand" to their efforts.²⁶ The urban ladina community shared the WILPF's concerns about militarization and pacifism, an interest cultivated by Gloria Menéndez Mina through her journal *Azul* (see chapter 2), and now Gálvez and Menéndez Mina along with close associates formed a new WILPF section in Guatemala in November 1946.

The new Guatemalan section of the WILPF represented a cross section of ladinas active in education, social reform, journalism, and the arts, a social profile that characterized the early revolutionary ladina community. By April 1947, more than seventy Guatemalan women were directly involved in the challenge of planning and hosting the congress.²⁷ Guatemala's first female lawyer, Graciela Quan Valenzuela de Reina, became president of the organizing committee, while newly appointed director of the city's second women's normal school, the Escuela Normal para Señoritas "Centro América," Julia Meléndez de DeLeón, served as vice president. The remainder of the committee consisted of politically active women such as Angelina Acuña de Castañeda, Mélida Montenegro de Méndez (president of the Asociación de Damas Pro-Comedores Infantíles), Rosa de Mora (founder of the Sociedad Protectora de Niño), and journalist Luz Valle.²⁸ As the congressional organizing progressed, the organizers were offered unprecedented travel opportunities. Luz Valle and Sara Basterrechea Ramírez along with several others attended international meetings in the United States focused on Pan American affairs throughout the first half of 1947, while Concha Castillo, María Cristiana Beltraena, Olga Castillo, and María Luisa Gálvez attended meetings for the Pan American day in Connecticut in April.²⁹

While the Guatemalan women involved with the WILPF may have been political novices on the international stage, Heloise Brainerd and the Arévalo administration clearly understood the political implications of the congress. Strongly influenced by Roosevelt's "Good Neighbor" policy, Brainerd was keenly aware of her association with the Pan American Union and its close ties to imperialism in Latin America. In the months leading up to the event, Brainerd insisted that the congress was not to be "just another international meeting of women for mutual association and the interchange of ideas. It is to be a powerful effort, in the face of the peril of atomic and bacterial warfare, to enlist the organized, intelligent cooperation of women for peace."[30] To achieve this, Brainerd called for all women associated with the meeting to be independent of any state sponsorship, as formal state alliances had historically stymied progress on social, political, and peace issues. Therefore, the 1947 congress represents a marked departure from all previous transnational women's meetings. The Arévalo government also understood that their own political discourse of democracy in the post–World War II era, with their commitment to working-class participation in politics as well as social and economic improvements for the poor sectors of society, placed them on a collision course with the United States.[31] Eager to offset the growing misinformation campaign launched by the United States against the fledgling social democracy, President Arévalo personally approved both the Guatemalan section of the WILPF and the Inter-American Congress of Women itself. Both María Albertina Gálvez and Gloria Menéndez Mina enjoyed a personal relationship with Juan José Arévalo and his wife, Elisa Arévalo de Martínez (Menéndez Mina became the first lady's personal secretary following the Congress) and used their professional positions to gain their support for the proposed congress.[32]

While all the women in attendance agreed that action must follow their meeting, the implications of such an overtly political position would become very complex. The resolutions adopted at the 1947 congress reflected the sociopolitical concerns that emerged during the brief post–World War II period of openness including literacy, education, democracy, and race relations, along with universal disarmament, suffrage, and the eradication of fascism. In the weeks leading up to the event, however, it would become increasingly evident that such ideas would come into conflict with the emphasis on hemispheric security. Just how this impacted each of the women involved would depend upon the geopolitical power of their specific nation, a political inequity that would challenge the creation of a transnational women's movement.

Ladinas and the Cold War

By all accounts, preparations for the 1947 congress were enthusiastically undertaken in Guatemala City. Fund-raising activities were held throughout the first half of 1947, including a theater production and a soccer match at the national stadium. Now free to travel, Guatemalan women from the organizing committee traveled to meet with members of the WILPF in the United States. The stakes for Guatemala's first international and transnational women's meeting were high, and news about the upcoming event surfaced repeatedly in the capital city's newspapers. To fully prepare Guatemalans for the event, information about the Women's International League for Peace and Freedom and the First Inter-American Congress of Women was disseminated throughout the capital and the entire country in national papers.[33]

Abruptly, however, just three weeks before the arrival of the delegates, *El Imparcial* announced that the congress had been cancelled. Within days, three other national newspapers confirmed the August 2 story and verified the rumors that the Guatemalan section of the WILPF had been disbanded.[34] The WILPF's Washington office was also notified that the Guatemalan section of the WILPF now declined the invitation to host the congress and had been disbanded as an organization. All monies raised for the event would be given to charity. This announcement stunned the congress's high-profile organizers, including the director of the entire event, Heloise Brainerd, who apparently had been caught completely unawares by this news. Although all the factors related to this sudden turn of events would not be known for quite some time, the urban ladina community had just entered the global Cold War, a conflict that would influence their lives over the following decades.

As those involved struggled to understand this rather extraordinary turn of events, the precise details surrounding the decision began to surface. According to the women at the center of the controversy, the decision to cancel the congress was made during a meeting at the historical center of Guatemalan feminism and women's activism, the Instituto Normal de Señoritas, Belén. In a meeting described by one participant as "a tortuous event," the congressional organizers publicly announced to the larger committee that they had been accused of communist sympathies. While it was not immediately clear who had made these accusations, their responses to the allegations became a pivotal turning point in determining the outcome of the congress. Some believed that they should move forward with the congress despite the accusations. Malin D'Echevers urged her colleagues to resist such baseless slander, asking: "How can you be indifferent in the face of this shameful conflict, which will have sad continental consequences."[35] She expressed sadness that their anxiety and internal conflict had been exposed before the entire nation and worried about Guatemala's reputation among international women's associations.[36] However, another faction led by the influential suffrage leader Graciela Quan Valenzuela de Reina was in favor of canceling the congress. No doubt speaking for many other women, Quan Valenzuela believed that the ladinas' contributions to the recent overthrow of Jorge Ubico was the only evidence necessary to demonstrate their pro-democratic political stance. Quite bluntly, she declared these insinuations to be intolerable, frightening, and frankly incomprehensible.[37] Despite their confusion over the precise nature of the allegations, one thing became perfectly clear. Under the weight of these accusations, the unity that had characterized the ladina movement in the capital city since June 1944 now broke.

Although the initial explanations for the cancellation focused on the accusations of communism as well as some complicated logistical details typical of an international event, the reality of what had created the crisis was far from clear for those involved in the congress.[38] With the benefit of historical hindsight, however it is clear that, in fact, four separate yet interconnected events generated the situation, all of which reflected the frailty of the political autonomy of those countries that existed outside the centers of power during the Cold War.[39] The nature of the congress itself and its emphasis on peace was the first obstacle for the international organizers. Born in the spasms of World War I, the Women's International League for Peace and Freedom's primary mission had always been to advocate for global peace. Now faced with growing militarization, just a month before the congress was due to open, Heloise Brainerd appeared before the US House Foreign Affairs Committee on behalf of the WILPF to express the league's opposition to the Inter-American Military Cooperation Act, which would be formally ratified at the August Rio de Janeiro conference. On July 2, 1947, Brainerd urged the committee to reevaluate its spending priorities.

> We ... urge that instead of the huge sums which would be required to implement the Inter-American Military Cooperation Act, even a part of them be devoted to the upbuilding of our sister nations in meeting their basic human needs. With a rising standard of living and of culture down there ... the United States can enjoy real security in its own Hemisphere—a security which no amount of arms can bring.[40]

Even a Grain of Sand 195

Along with Brainerd's plea for an alternative to the escalation of arms, she divulged that the WILPF was hosting a congress in Guatemala City the following month.⁴¹ Brainerd questioned her government's motives for establishing military bases in the Pacific and encouraged House committee members to open a dialogue with the Soviet Union.⁴² In the post–World War II era, peace held multiple meanings, and it had become a political tool that the former Soviet ally was now wielding against the United States. As Jadwiga Pieper Mooney explains: "In well-publicized worldwide campaigns, the Soviets began to label the US a warmongering nation, in stark contrast to the supposed communist devotion to the cause of peace."⁴³ As the WILPF became increasingly vocal in its support of global peace, Brainerd's strong stance against her own government's military policies in the Americas placed the 1947 congress on the wrong side of the rapidly polarizing Cold War politics.

The WILPF's public position on the international trip taken by Argentine first lady Eva Perón only added to the rhetoric of communist affiliations. During Perón's now famous European tour, she received a grandiose reception by Spain's fascist leader, Francisco Franco. In response to her association with the Spanish dictator, several groups, including the Guatemalan labor union Confederación General de Trabajadores and the US section of the WILPF, sent petitions to France requesting that Perón be denied entry into that country. The French press responded by accusing both organizations of being communist sympathizers.⁴⁴ The Guatemalan section of the WILPF, after hearing the French accusation, directly questioned Brainerd about the WILPF's political position. D'Echevers reported that this particular turn of events had created a growing anxiety among Guatemalans over the feasibility of hosting the congress and the true political orientation of the WILPF.

The last two factors related to the nature of the revolutionary project and more specifically to the Arévalo administration. By the end of World War II, populist democracies were emerging throughout Latin America, and the Harry Truman administration in the United States had been generally sympathetic. However, by mid-1947, the geopolitical landscape had shifted significantly, and the United States was growing increasingly distrustful of Arévalo's internal economic and labor policies. Although the Labor Code of May 1, 1947, brought a modicum of social security to Guatemalans, whose salaries and safety policies had earlier been set at the discretion of wealthy landowners and the US-based United Fruit Company, the new law disrupted labor relations between Guatemalan workers and the US company. When the UFCo refused to comply with the new law, workers responded with work stoppages and labor strikes.[45] Subsequent US attempts to intervene with the Guatemalan government on behalf of the UFCo promoted a policy of conflict toward the Arévalo administration. Historian Jim Handy argues: "The national debate over communism affected Guatemalan relations with the United States and became intertwined with Guatemala's treatment of U.S. business interests. Arévalo shuffled cabinet ministers, abandoned legislation, and restricted labor to placate U.S. concerns."[46] Despite Arévalo's condemnation of communism and his firm belief in capitalism, his fundamental approach that Guatemala work as ally with the United States rather than as a proxy state placed him at odds with Washington.[47] The United States only endorsed those social reforms that respected its own economic interests. From this perspective, the many middle-class and urban ladinos and ladinas who demonstrated even modest support for social reforms and nationalistic sentiments were branded as extremists, including even the conservative Clemente Marroquín Rojas.[48] Despite assurances from the director general of the Pan American Union, Alberto Lleras Camargo, that the WILPF was not considered a leftist organization, Guatemala's warm reception of the congressional delegates and the WILPF only confirmed Washington's suspicions of communist infiltration in the country.[49] Therefore, the broad-based political and intellectual support of the 1947 congress established yet another affront to the continental hegemony the United States was forging in the Cold War gestational period.

While State Department officials were growing increasingly suspicious about the nature of the Arévalo administration, they were also tracking the activities of the president's wife, Elisa Martínez de Arévalo. By 1947, Guatemalan elite circles had lost their initial enthusiasm for the president and his wife due to the particular direction of social reforms initiated by the first lady. Her insistence that poor and working-class women be included in any social reform organizations had not been well received by elite social reformers, who subsequently withdrew their support (see chapter 3). They did, however, communicate their concerns to US State Department officials, who interpreted the first lady's refusal to retain the traditional class structure in her child care centers as yet another challenge to the social hierarchy perceived necessary to hemispheric security.[50]

It was finally Guatemala's political position at the impending inter-American conference in Rio de Janeiro that solidified US opinion about the Central American country. The Inter-American Treaty of Reciprocal Assistance depended upon the compliance of all nations in the Americas to stand together in self-defense. By July 1947, the State Department had begun a public campaign against the

Arévalo administration for its refusal to sign the Rio Pact. However, they failed to mention the reason why Guatemala was unwilling to ratify the treaty. Arévalo's government was willing to ratify the treaty but withheld formal ratification on the condition that the United States pressure Great Britain to acknowledge Guatemala's sovereignty over Belize.[51] Guatemala's stance in Rio attracted the opposition of the Americans as well as of the Mexicans, otherwise traditional allies of Guatemala. On at least two separate incidents, national Mexican newspapers accused Arévalo himself of being communist.[52] The conflict between Guatemala and the United States continued throughout August as the Guatemalan delegates in Rio de Janeiro refused to ratify the Rio Pact.[53]

The impact of these simultaneous factors is evident in a statement issued by the US State Department a few years later. Apart from the numerous errors in this short quotation, including the official name of the group organizing the congress, it is clear how these factors coalesced in 1947 to bolster the State Department's suspicions of communism in Guatemala.

> In the troubled year of 1947, a group called "congreso pacifista de mujeres americanas" was organized in Guatemala City. It was denounced several times as a "front" group organization but it succeeded, with the help of friendly authorities, in taking hold to the extent that Mrs. Elisa Martínez Arévalo was named honourary president. Hearing was given in this "feminine" event to exponents of American communism both from the north and the south. Among those "ambassadors" there appeared some North Americans who made out-of-session pro-communist declarations and encouraged the idea of forming a communist party in this country. Nela Martínez, cultural delegate from Ecuador and communist party member, openly participated in the congress, remaining in the country for a period of 20 days or more, and encouraged the fight of the communists to establish their "new party."[54]

The State Department's political position here is clear. However, the department's particular use of language also exposes the deeper gendered nature of the United States' imperialist approach that shaped their Cold War rhetoric. Historian Laura Briggs has established how important the role of sexuality and gender was in US imperialist discourses earlier in the twentieth century, which the Americans now transformed into an effective Cold War rhetorical weapon.[55] Within this context, then, the word "feminine" was not intended to identify the participants as female but rather to diminish the significance of the event and the organizations supporting it, minimizing its clear sociopolitical and intellectual contributions. Men who challenged US policies were frequently feminized in official US responses, according to Frank Costigliola, thereby trivializing and demasculinizing them. "U.S. officials often responded to an ally's resistance to American policy with emotive language that depoliticized and trivialized the difference of opinion. Such emotion-laden language read political disagreements as evidence that the ally was unreasonable or incapable."[56] However, when the State Department was faced with political opposition from women's organizations and was therefore unable to undermine their ideas utilizing a feminine critique, it intensified its attacks by labeling such organizations as communist "front" groups. This had the effect of trivializing and dismissing women's sociopolitical intellectual contributions and inverting their legitimate concerns and political positions into those of the "enemy."

The reactions of the Guatemalan section of the WILPF ended the original WILPF organization. But the ladina community received an unprecedented level of support from their male peers in the face of these accusations, and a majority of the national newspapers seized on the issue, adamantly refuting any affiliations with communism.[57] Political leaders who had been critical of women's political or public participation urged the organizers now to stand their ground against international scrutiny. Prominent newspaper editor of *La Hora* Clemente Marroquín Rojas, who had opposed suffrage for literate women in 1945, used his journalistic position to proclaim his strong support for the congress and its organizers. He publicly predicted that even if the WILPF might be sympathetic to communism, they were incapable of converting Guatemala into a communist republic, and he now urged them to reconsider their decision and take an overtly political stance. "Now, dear women, the struggle is clear: it is time to leave the house to fight, to freely struggle dialectically with communist ideology."[58] With Guatemala's international reputation at stake, those men who had obstructed ladina political efforts now moved to defend them, demonstrating the contradictions inherent in patriarchal Guatemala. The newspaper editor and legislator Marroquín Rojas admitted that he had voted against the political participation of women in the 1945 constitutional debate that granted suffrage to literate women in the belief that they were conservative and traditional, characteristics that many politicians feared would cause women to work against revolutionary ideals. The leadership women demonstrated in organizing the congress and their ability to withstand international pressure, however, caused Marroquín Rojas as well as many others to change their minds. Although women's actions and martyrdom during the revolution had not changed the perspective of many Guatemalan men, now, with

Even a Grain of Sand 199

the country's reputation at stake both in Rio de Janeiro and in Guatemala City, men such as Marroquín Rojas characterized Guatemalan women as politically energetic and audacious. In the midst of growing international tensions between Guatemala and the United States, these politicians understood the value of the First Inter-American Congress of Women and urged urban ladinas to stand defiantly against these accusations. While these gendered transformations and public support for the congress may have indeed been sincere, they also reflected the broader national concerns of the revolutionary leaders. In 1947, Guatemala was rapidly emerging as one of the first sites of the Cold War. Should Guatemalan women fail to resist international accusations of communism, the power of the US accusations would only be confirmed. The fickle nature of Cold War politics became only too clear in the years that followed. Politically conservative Marroquín Rojas, who became one of the most vocal critics of the Árbenz administration, was himself eventually labeled a communist in the aftermath of the 1954 overthrow of Jacobo Árbenz by the US government. He would resign from the National Assembly in 1955 over the retaliatory violence of the Carlos Castillo Armas government against the civilian population.[59]

The Unión de Mujeres Democráticas

In response to the crisis in early August, Heloise Brainerd rushed to Guatemala City to revive the defunct congress. During an emergency meeting again held at the Instituto Normal de Señoritas, Belén, Brainerd attempted to reassure her audience of ex-WILPF members and other interested persons that she did not represent a communist organization, insisting that many of the women in the US section of the WILPF were quite conservative.[60] Brainerd was only partially successful in counteracting the power of the international accusations of communism, and many women refused to continue any affiliation with the WILPF. However, a number of influential women were persuaded that the WILPF was not a front group for communism, and a new group formed out of the defunct Guatemala section of the organization. Composed of politically and socially active women, they named their new organization the Unión de Mujeres Democráticas (UMD), or the Union of Democratic Women, a name they believed accurately portrayed their intentions. Vocal supporter of Brainerd and the WILPF during the crisis, Malin D'Echevers now became the leader of the new organization, which included members of political parties, labor unions, and teaching associations. Several former WILPF women also joined the UMD including Argentina Díaz Lozano, Olimpia Vda. de Barrientos, and the editor of *Azul*, Gloria Menéndez Mina de Padilla. Other key members of the group included Marta Delfina Vásquez, María Isabel Foronda de Vargas, Elisa Hall de Asturias, Helena Leiva de Holst, Marta Zuleta, Magdalena Spínola, Clemencia Rubio de Herrarte, Mélida Luz de Walters, María Luisa Lainez, Angelina Acuña de Castañeda, María del Carmen Vargas, and Aída Doninelli Vda. de Véliz.[61] These women represented a variety of revolutionary political parties and had developed some political experience over the prior two years. Their immediate project was the formation of an emergency task force designed to complete plans for the upcoming congress.

The women of the newly formed Unión de Mujeres Democráticas faced a daunting political terrain. The polarizing rhetoric emerging from the developing tensions of the Cold War allowed for little if any political moderation. They had to either deny any association with communism and the WILPF, or actively engage with the accusations and refute the insinuations. Those who were once again involved with the congressional planning remained bitter about their colleagues' abandonment of the congress. Highly critical of her peers who refused to join the new organization, D'Echevers believed that those women involved in organizing the congress held clear political ideals and were therefore less susceptible to foreign influence.[62] For decades, these women had resisted dictatorships and intellectual repression, forging deep bonds within the urban ladina community. Now, those who moved forward with plans for the congress felt betrayed because a majority of the original organizers did not join the new organization, remaining skeptical of Brainerd's true ideology. The most outspoken opponent was the former president of the WILPF, Graciela Quan Valenzuela de Reina, who declined any further affiliation with the group. Two other nationally recognized women, Rosa de Mora (influential social reformer) and Luz Valle (editor of *Nosotras*) also remained adamantly opposed to the congress. Although Mora and Valle would continue to work for social reform and women's rights, they represented an emergent core of a new women's group. Deeply pro-democratic, antifascist, and nationalistic, they held strong feminist positions on the legal and civil equality of women. However, they were not willing to confront the institutional and political structures related to militarization, imperialism, and poverty. Remaining essentially Liberal in their political perspective, they were unwilling to challenge US hegemony in Latin America. While their critics believed that they lacked a political consciousness, the women who ended their affiliation with the congress may have understood only too well the national and international implications of their political affiliations. It would be this same group of women who remained silent in the waning days of the revolution, unwilling to defend the revolution they had risked their lives to create.

The women of the new UMD now assumed a leadership role in all facets of the week-long congress, enjoying an autonomous sociopolitical space free of male interference. First lady Elisa Martínez de Arévalo served as the honorary president, while Argentina Díaz Lozano acted as second vice president and Malin D'Echevers de González as secretary general. The organizers took advantage of the situation to pay homage to three Guatemalan educators and writers who had been particularly important to the women's movement, naming Carmen Zebadua Vda. de Méndez, Irene de Peyré (Guatemala's first representative to the 1930 Inter-American Commission of Women), and Laura Rubio Vda. de Robles as honorary members.[63] In an effort not to isolate themselves in the face of such intense international opposition, the women of the UMD issued an invitation to a wide spectrum of Guatemalan women's associations.[64] As a result of this particular strategy, the congress was attended by women representing associations from conservative Catholic groups and political parties to a variety of labor unions. In addition to the hundreds of Guatemalan women attending the two public sessions, sixty-eight official delegates attended from eighteen countries, the majority of whom came from the United States and Guatemala.[65]

The 1947 Inter-American Congress of Women was a pivotal moment in hemispheric women's movements drawing on decades of feminist activism. In marked contrast to previous Inter-American Commission of Women meetings, the women who attended the 1947 congress did not represent formal government associations. Although the formidable Panamanian Gumersinda Páez served as president of the entire proceedings, representing the defunct Inter-American Commission of Women, the others represented a variety of women's transnational associations and clubs.[66] Not constrained by an allegiance to a specific nation-state, the delegates advocated for principles that defied nationalistic concerns that aligned closely with the 1945 Inter-American Conference on Problems of War and Peace, or the Chapultepec Conference, in Mexico City.[67] The goals of the 1947 Inter-American Congress of Women were highly democratic, antiimperialistic, egalitarian, and transnational in scope—a fusion of the Chapultepec declarations with the ideals formulated by the defunct CIM and the WILPF, and reflecting decades of Popular Front Pan American feminism.[68] Their final resolutions included a commitment to social and economic justice, and to issues of imperialism, racism, and colonialism.[69] In short, the congress presented a fundamentally different imagined world where authoritarianism was best contained not by force but through the improvement of the living conditions of all people.[70] Hoping that these first seeds would find fertile ground, the women gathered in Guatemala City in August 1947 believed that this was only the first volley of hope in an increasingly complex sociopolitical arena.[71]

The women of the 1947 congress affirmed a faith in ties of friendship and understanding as vital elements for continental security, with two primary concerns dominating the congressional agenda.[72] The first called for an improvement in the quality of life for those Americans without access to basic human rights including education, adequate nutrition, and health care. Far reaching in their implications, the visionary ideas postulated by these women reflected the broad sense of ethics inherent in their work. Representing a continuation of the CIM's goals, one of the committees addressed concerns over the social inequities these women believed to be obstacles to democracy. One committee chaired by Ana Rosa Tornero de Bilbao la Vieja of Bolivia addressed the "struggle for human rights"—proposing a long list of reforms of which the most critical were the eradication of illiteracy, equal pay for equal work, the elimination of illegitimacy as a social indicator, and freedom of expression.[73]

The delegates also advocated for an increased political presence of women in all levels of government, a position that was a departure from all previous transnational meetings in its highly politicized conversation.[74] At this historical juncture, a significant number of delegates did not enjoy basic legal rights in their home countries, including citizenship, and the status of women dominated many of the resolutions. A resolution led by Lucila Rubio de Laverde of Colombia asserted that women must have civil, political, and legal rights for a true democracy to flourish.[75] The vice president of the defunct Inter-American Commission of Women, Amalia de Castillo Ledón from Mexico, called for the civil and political rights of women, an issue that had been left unresolved during the Eighth International Conference of American States on the Political and Civil Rights of Women, by the Inter-American Commission of Women in 1938.[76] Congressional resolutions urged American nations to enact the United Nations and Chapultepec initiatives that called for freedom in marriage and the abolition of laws permitting men to murder their wives in cases of adultery. They furthermore presented declarations for the financial support of children born outside of marriage. This final resolution represented a comprehensive, socially democratic package for the Americas.

The second concern reflected the primary agenda of the WILPF in issues of global warfare, and US foreign policy and militarization. These women fervently believed that, as women, they held solutions for the world unique to their sex. Disenfranchised both socially and politically, a majority of the delegates had not participated in the decision making that had created these deep inequities and social problems. In response, the resolutions adopted reflected not only a deep clarity regarding the needs of women living in Latin America but also an awareness of the global ramifications of violence. The final declarations presented a comprehensive and authoritative program that guaranteed the existence and success of democracy at its most fundamental level.

Many organizers and attendees shared a belief that women offered a moralizing influence to the political arena, and an aura of women's moral superiority pervaded the congressional dialogue on the demilitarization of the Americas. Historically, Latin American women had effectively used qualities perceived to be inherent to womanhood in order to gain access to the political or even the public arena. As Asunción Lavrin notes: "Their presumed 'higher sensitivity' to others' feelings and their higher sense of moral duty were the bases for their claim to a place in the sun."[77] Here, too, working from the premise that women "are accustomed to working for the love of a cause rather than for purely financial and personal rewards," the delegates approved of both control of militarization and disarmament of atomic weapons as the keys to future peace.[78] Chilean women encouraged nations to hold to the principles and peace initiatives proposed by the Chapultepec Conference and the United Nations, critical of the continental rearmament concurrently being proposed in Rio de Janeiro. The delegation argued that the money would be better spent on the "rehabilitation of the people" in the form of schools, public works, and research centers for peace. The participants of the congress in Guatemala should "firmly repudiate the plans for the military collaboration of American countries. They [were] contrary to peace and to the sovereignty of the American peoples, and totally ignore[d] the economic, social, and cultural reality that these countries now confront[ed]."[79] Directly criticizing the complete absence of female delegates at the Rio convention, the congress affirmed the appointment of women to important positions at the United Nations. The congress's twelve resolutions included raising the standard of living for all peoples, thereby incorporating them into democratic practices; fostering constitutional civil rights for women; and requesting immediate consideration of the proposals for universal disarmament presented in the General Assembly of the United Nations in December 1946.[80]

The comprehensive nature of the women's goals was evident in the series of cables they sent to world leaders.[81] They sent the first cable to General George Marshall of the United States, who was participating in the Rio conference, urging him and the other delegates there to halt the escalation of armaments in favor of continent-wide social programs and economic development. The second cable was directed to the president of the Rio conference, Raul Fernández, urging him to break ties with dictators Rafael Trujillo of the Dominican Republic and Anastasio Somoza García of Nicaragua, as well as Spanish dictator Francisco Franco. The third cable thanked the US first lady, Eleanor Roosevelt, for her work toward world peace. The fourth acknowledged the tireless efforts of Dr. Paulina Luisi of Uruguay, thanking her on behalf of Latin American women.

Guatemala and Belize

The ideological core of the 1947 congress rested upon notions of strength in transnational solidarity, directly contradicting the hypernationalism and hemispheric security discussions of the Rio Pact. Frequently at odds with their own governments, these women gathered to find common ground for their own legal and civil rights along with their call for disarmament. In addition to thematic topics, each of the delegations presented an issue of particular concern to their organization. Among the many diverse social issues raised, Bolivian indigenous women spoke out in support of Jewish people, while Brazilian women raised issues on peace and working women. Women from Colombia expressed concern for the poverty of European women and children left devastated by World War II. Ecuadoran women supported all six of the commission reports, including a comprehensive plan to educate, industrialize, demilitarize, and develop Latin America. Problems of inter-American relations were raised by women from El Salvador. Haitian women called for the constitutional equality of men and women. Mexicans raised awareness over housing problems for the poor. Living under the Somoza family regime, Nicaraguans highlighted the suffering of people living under political dictatorships. Peruvians highlighted the issue of antidemocratic systems and human rights, while Puerto Ricans called attention to matters of world peace. While each group focused specifically on either women-centered events or political repression that affected women, the Guatemalan delegation diverged from this trend.

The highly nationalist fervor raised by the accusations of communism against urban ladinas resurfaced during the women's congress. In direct contrast to the antinationalist topics raised by all the other women's organization, the Guatemalan women called for the formal international recognition of Guatemala's sovereignty over the neighboring British colony of Belize.[82] In one of the two public evening sessions, Malin D'Echevers presented Guatemala's legal claim to Belize. As the author of the document, she offered the congressional delegates a historical accounting of the controversy between Guatemala and the territory of Belize going back to the time of Elizabeth I (1558–1603). While it may have been a new topic for some in attendance, the boundary dispute between Guatemala and Britain had been a long-standing diplomatic quagmire, which D'Echevers now outlined.[83] The current boundaries in 1947 had been determined by a treaty in 1859, a document in which both parties agreed to develop a road to improve trade and general relations.[84] Failure to build this road led to the revival of the controversy in 1940 by Jorge Ubico, and Guatemala's new constitution in 1945 formalized its claim to Belize. While this claim remained unilateral, as Krista Wiegand notes, negotiations between the two sides would not resume again until the 1960s. Both of the revolutionary governments under Arévalo and Árbenz further invigorated nationalist sentiments regarding Guatemala's legal sovereignty over Belize, an ideal that permeated every facet of official policy, including educational textbooks.[85] In her conclusion, D'Echevers requested the solidarity of all those women present in Guatemala's quest for the repatriation of Belize, a struggle that was both "right and just."[86]

The decision to present this highly nationalistic claim before a congress otherwise dedicated to a transnational and antinationalist agenda can only be understood within Guatemala's particular political context in 1947. In fact, the question over Belize's sovereignty had historically been a successful tool for raising nationalist fervor when the country was undergoing a crisis. As his sociopolitical control declined, Jorge Ubico used the issue of Belize to garner internal unity. He adeptly drew the United States into Guatemala's conflict with Great Britain, capitalizing on Washington's increasingly adamant anticolonial position in an effort to gain this critical ally, although he was ultimately unsuccessful. As Kenneth Grieb notes: "The postwar world-power balance did provide Washington with the ability to impose a settlement on terms favorable to Guatemala if it had desired to do so."[87] By 1947, the United States had set its sights on hemispheric security in the broader Cold War scenario. If it had been unwilling to support its Guatemalan ally Jorge Ubico, the United States had even less reason to support the new Arévalo administration's claims to Belize. Arévalo's unwillingness to support the security pact in Rio de Janeiro along with his government's modest nationalistic economic reforms confirmed US suspicions about Guatemala's Cold War position.

The inclusion of Guatemala's claim to Belize in the congress's agenda was intended to bolster both the country's fragile democracy and its inter-American reputation. By 1947, Guatemala's internal political conflicts had become increasingly evident and its population polarized. Arévalo's government believed that its claim to Belize had the potential to unite an otherwise troublesome citizenry, even if only temporarily. Guatemala was also under increasing pressure from the inter-American community to sign off on the Rio Pact. Although Arévalo had agreed to sign the Treaty of Reciprocal Assistance (Guatemala actually was the second nation to sign it), he did so on the condition that Great Britain return Belize to Guatemalan sovereignty. While it is debatable whether the women had any positive effect on hemispheric support for Guatemala's claim, the UMD's provocative stance on Belize confirmed the United States' worst fears about Arévalo's government. Even when the rhetoric demanded hemispheric security at the expense of regional concerns, it was clear that Guatemala would not reconsider its position.

The choice to present such a nationalistic issue by the Guatemalan women's movement also reveals the tensions inherent in transnational movements for those from smaller and less powerful countries. Many of the ladinas involved in the 1947 congress had historically nurtured ideals regarding transnationalism and had been active in a Central American unity movement that had been in existence since the turn of the century. Working alongside women across the Americas had long been a dream for Guatemalan women isolated by dictatorial regimes. In the post–World War II era, however, this idealism conflicted directly with the very survival of Guatemalan democracy. The 1947 congress offered Guatemalan women the opportunity to present their national concerns on their own terms to an international audience. The question of Guatemala's sovereign claim to Belize also offered the ladina women's movement a critical opportunity to align themselves with their male colleagues, who were otherwise unwilling to incorporate them into any real political power.[88]

Living the Cold War

The challenge of inter-American organizing became immediately apparent in the aftermath of the congress. While a majority of the congressional delegates shared deeply held convictions on human rights, women's rights, and social justice, they were divided on how to achieve them. In defiance of the growing hemispheric domination by the United States, the congress's fourth committee directly addressed the political relationship between the United States and the rest of the Americas. Chaired by Matilde Elena López of El Salvador (she was already on the CIA's radar for her affiliation with the Communist Party of El Salvador), the committee's resolutions addressed the United States' unwillingness to adhere to the final draft of the Act of Chapultepec. The committee claimed that the act's peaceful, liberating, and progressive spirit had been misinterpreted. Consequently, the resolution of the fourth committee called for the US government to uphold democratic principles in all American republics by revoking the Taft-Hartley Act (which directly violated the Act of Chapultepec with regard to workers' rights); by respecting the right of self-determination for all nations and territories, including Puerto Rico; and by completely withdrawing from all strategic bases in Latin America.[89] The committee's resolution included the following declaration:

> The First Inter-American Congress of Women . . . in accordance with the Charter of the United Nations . . . will defend democratic principles and institutions by all available means, such as the press, the schools, and in all other legitimate ways. Furthermore, it declares that each and every one of the representatives of American nations attending the Congress will oppose, by peaceful means, any tendency or movement of an antidemocratic nature which would menace democracy and peace in America.[90]

The Ecuadoran delegate Nela Martínez reminded all delegates that true hemispheric security could only be achieved through the resolution of a broad range of social inequities.[91]

This challenge to the United States' growing hemispheric hegemony served as a lightning rod for another crisis. Following the congress, many women in attendance publicly expressed concerns over the anti-imperialistic political ideologies held by some of the delegates, reigniting the tensions of early August.[92] Accusations of leftist extremism surfaced from several congressional delegates, including Ana Rosa Chacón from Costa Rica, claiming that the intent of the congress conflicted with the reality of the discussions that took place.[93] She abstained from an August 23 vote on the second commission, which included resolutions designed to promote peace and democracy in the Americas. On August 26, Chacón sent a letter to *Nuestro Diario* publicly removing herself as an official delegate, joined by members of the Unión de Mujeres Democráticas. Both Gloria Menéndez Mina and Graciela Quan Valenzuela de Reina (who attended the congress despite her misgivings) raised their own doubts about some of the topics raised during the sessions, also abstaining from several votes on the final day.[94]

At the heart of the matter for all three of these women lay the congressional call to immediately disarm the Americas (in direct contradiction to the Rio Pact simultaneously being drafted in Rio de Janeiro) and to work for a better understanding with the Soviet Union in order to diffuse the burgeoning Cold War. For these women, the recent events of World War II suggested that disarmament was utopian and premature, especially in light of the current global situation. Menéndez Mina cautioned restraint over this proposal, as she believed that the human spirit remained violent and, for the sake of their children and grandchildren, that the congress should proceed cautiously with this resolution. Finally, Quan Valenzuela and Menéndez Mina believed that the congress did not sufficiently acknowledge issues of personal ethics and spirituality in the issues raised, and questioned the prevalent anti-US sentiments of the resolutions.[95]

Even those Guatemalan journalists who supported the Arévalo administration attacked the congress for its communist tendencies, surprising many of the delegates, who had assumed that Guatemala would provide a more open political space. In response, María Eloisa García Etchegoyen of Chile published an article in *Diario de Centro América* accusing the press of printing statements the women had never made. Congressional president Gumersinda Páez rose in defense of the congress, claiming that if it was communist, then so were the Atlantic Treaty, the United Nations, and the constitutions of Panama, Venezuela, and Brazil.[96] Other delegates also came to the defense of the congress. On August 28, María Odilia Castro Hidalgo (representing the Centro Femenino de Estudios Eugenio María de Hostos in Costa Rica) publicly supported the congressional delegates in *Diario de Centro América*. Castro Hidalgo claimed that Ana Rosa Chacón did not genuinely represent ideas held by Costa Rican women. Although she expressed discomfort over publicly criticizing her colleague, Castro Hidalgo believed that in the interest of justice, she was obligated to defend the overall intent of the congress.[97] She affirmed the openness of the congress to all ideas and believed that its resolutions for the Americas were visionary. Because Chacón did not vote in the final resolutions, Castro Hidalgo asserted that she had no right to accuse the other delegates of any ill intent. Castro Hidalgo claimed that her vision of a congress open to all ideas was not shared by everyone, including a delegate from Haiti, Alice Garoute. Garoute, in turn, denounced this statement in an article a few days later upon her return home, proclaiming her complete support of the congress.[98]

The emergence of these conflicts reflected several critical realities for Guatemalan women, and for Latin American women in general. First, the overt political opposition espoused by the US section of the WILPF toward their own government was not always possible for Latin American women, who frequently lived under repressive and violent dictatorships. Furthermore, the economic hegemony of the United States within the Americas made the ramifications of such political conflicts potentially dangerous for Latin Americans. The presence of the United Fruit Company in Guatemala and its growing conflicts with the Arévalo government complicated any challenges to US foreign policy for Guatemalan women. The US members of the WILPF did not have to live with the consequences of their political stance in the same way as their Latin American sisters. While their motives may have been ideologically well intentioned, women from the United States did not have the experience of living under US foreign policy and were unable to appreciate its implications at times. This is evidenced by Heloise Brainerd's comments just a few months after the congress:

> In spite of the many handicaps, especially the great distances between the countries of this hemisphere and the impossibility of visiting them often, we feel that satisfactory progress is being made in carrying out the purpose of this Committee: to bring Latin American women into the peace movement and help them solve their own political and social problems.[99]

Along with a slight air of condescension, Brainerd's statement revealed a fundamental reality and challenge in transnational organizing. Some women by virtue of their national identity had more power than others to set the agenda for international meetings, a tendency in the WILPF identified by Megan Threlkeld in her analysis of Pan American women's movements.[100] The idea for the 1947 congress had originated in the United States among women who by virtue of their nationality and class would not face the full brunt of US foreign policy conclusions. Downplaying the role the United States had historically played in exacerbating Latin America's social and political problems, Brainerd reflected a pressing problem present in US women's international activism. Helen Laville identifies the double bind inherent in transnational organizations in which US women attempted to fulfill both the imperatives of international sisterhood as well as national goals.[101] As the 1947 congress demonstrated, despite their best intentions, women representing groups such as the WILPF frequently interacted within an imperialistic framework.

For their part, Guatemalan women enjoyed neither the experience of political participation in a dictatorship-laden history nor the political leverage available to groups such as the WILPF's US section. The apolitical stance enforced upon them by decades of political repression created a movement that remained relatively conservative. While some women of the Unión de Mujeres Democráticas were emerging from this cocoon within the aura of political and intellectual freedom made available to Guatemalans during the revolutionary era, a majority continued to believe their political role as women to be as moral prophets against the waste and degradation of war. During this gestational period, they could not envision this role outside the sphere of religious faith and traditional Liberal ideology, nor within what they considered to be an anti-imperialistic stance.

The reemergence of the conflict in the days following the congress solidified the rift within the ladina community. Decades of dictatorship had suppressed ideological differences, and in the early, heady days of the revolution, ladinas enjoyed a temporary sense of commonality. In their mutual struggle for legal and civil equality, they formed associations and civic organizations in spite of these differences. However, the tension brought on by international accusations of communism revealed the ideological plurality within the movement. While accusations of communism were rebuffed by all women involved in the congress, their implications held more significance for some than for others. Many Guatemalan women could not afford the type of radicalism available to women in the United States. As would become very evident within a few years, the approval or disapproval of the United States could have dire consequences.

While the Unión de Mujeres Democráticas spoke out occasionally on Guatemala's claim to Belize in the following years, the group did not maintain a high public profile. It is not evident whether they encouraged civic participation during the highly contested elections of 1948 and 1950. The feminisms articulated in *Nosotras* and *Azul* that characterized the UMD movement did not take such public political risks again. While some women maintained a high public profile, such as Gloria Menéndez Mina in her role as Elisa Martínez de Arévalo's personal secretary, most of them did not, instead seeking alliances outside the public view. Despite the ideological divisions among the women, the congress provided ladinas with the first opportunity to establish transnational relationships. Following the congress, they repeatedly hosted travelers en route to other such conferences, maintaining contact with WILPF organizers.[102] For their part, WILPF members, particularly in the United States, actively advocated on behalf of Guatemala, sending letters to the US secretary of state with regard to labor disputes between the United Fruit Company and Guatemalan workers.

Even a Grain of Sand 211

Concerned by the political overthrow of Jacobo Árbenz in June 1954, they advocated directly to the US State Department and continued to publicly denounce their own government for its participation in the 1954 coup against Árbenz.[103]

The First Inter-American Congress of Women served the pro-revolutionary movement well, and the Guatemalan media covered the congress extensively.[104] The Congress of Women served as a symbol of international solidarity during a critical historical moment for the country as the Arévalo administration did not ratify the Treaty of Reciprocal Assistance.[105] Furthermore, the very existence of the congress defied the international opposition created by accusations of communism; Guatemalan women had defended national sovereignty. Delegates were invited on tours of the National Palace, the guarderías infantiles, and the comedores infantiles, providing a showcase for revolutionary social reforms.[106] The Arévalo government formally acknowledged the inter-American congressional delegates, inviting Gumersinda Páez to address the Guatemalan National Assembly on issues of women's rights. It was the first time a woman had ever addressed a legislative body in Guatemala, and her appearance was well received.[107] Páez remained in Guatemala after the congress, attending and leading a variety of functions. On August 30, she held a one-day conference to discuss communism and democracy. As might be expected, international scrutiny and controversy surrounded her continued presence in Guatemala, and the Guatemalan government defended her appearance to the international press on more than one occasion.[108]

Conclusion

The 1947 First Inter-American Congress of Women urgently believed that the way to hemispheric security lay in meeting the basic needs of people living throughout the Americas. It defined a new women's movement that defied nationalism and promoted a broad-based coalition of women around subjects of peace, democracy, and fundamental human rights for all within the Americas. The organizers withstood international pressure that sought to hinder the event. However, their message was subsumed by another hemispheric vision for security, one led by the United States that advocated for increased militarization and the marginalization of political diversity. Although the US State Department did much to bury the resolutions taken up in Guatemala City, the Congress of Women, flying in the face of growing hemispheric militarization, established the theoretical foundation for decades of female activism. Congressional organizers spoke eloquently and prophetically on global issues, accurately predicting the cost in human terms should the Cold War be allowed to escalate as it ultimately did, utilizing precious financial resources that might otherwise have been spent on education and health care. The congress's insistence on the commonality of the human experience was at odds with the extreme nationalism of the post–World War II era. The women who gathered in Guatemala City represented independent and democratic women's movements distinct from government agencies or existing international organizations such as the Pan American Union or the temporarily defunct Inter-American Commission of Women. The congress's politicized nature directly conflicted with the broader emergent Cold War ideology simultaneously being formulated at the Rio conference. Finally, the congress represented an ideal of sisterhood, of an imagined community of interest based on gender that transcended notions of nationhood.

The sisterhood so vividly demonstrated by this hemispheric congress ironically did not find the same expression in Guatemala's urban ladina community itself. The ladinas accepted political diversity amid their ranks, even welcoming it as a marker of true democracy, as Luz Valle indicated (see chapter 4). However, the insinuation of communist affiliations was a frightening threat for many of these women, as communism was perceived as an ideology far more sinister than merely an economic theory. The antirevolutionary movement would effectively position communism as tantamount to an attack on the family, the traditional role of women, and maternal ideals. While members of the urban ladina community adopted increasingly overt feminist ideals, they never rejected the supremacy of children and family in their own lives and those of other women. The very notion that they might be mistaken for communist sympathizers was a truly devastating threat and one that few were willing to challenge, however erroneous they knew these claims to be. Political novices in both the national and international arenas, these women felt too vulnerable to align themselves with radical ideology, whether it was communist or not. As noted by Greg Grandin, the Cold War terror did in fact silence some of these women.[109] Although it did not moderate their social idealism, it effectively split the fragile and critical unity that had been achieved by this small group of reformers, a unity they never recovered. Many of these women maintained political neutrality, creating an irreparable rift between them and their colleagues that would resurface occasionally throughout the revolutionary decade.

The 1947 congress exemplifies the complexity of gender during the revolutionary era. Men like Clemente Marroquín Rojas rose to defend the urban ladinas against accusations of communism, declaring that their actions had changed his mind about their political acumen. The female president of the 1947 congress spoke officially to the National Assembly, an unprecedented event in Guatemala. The state welcomed the congressional delegates, believing that the conversation at their congress supported the administration's own ideals, which were concurrently being challenged in Rio de Janeiro. In the months following the pivotal experience, however, there was little change in gender relations. Pro-revolutionary political parties continued to disregard the political power of women, and as a result few women responded to the critical municipal elections in 1948. The congress itself, however, remained a significant moment for those who had been involved in its organization. They created transnational connections whose significance cannot be underestimated in a history of isolation; Graciela Quan Valenzuela in fact became the head of the Inter-American Commission of Women in 1956. The connections were also important psychologically if not realistically in the isolating months leading up to Árbenz's overthrow in June 1954. The congress revealed the veracity of ladina claims with respect to their political abilities and goals. After decades of bargaining, these women were finally able to demonstrate their political ideas in a public forum that benefited the Arévalo administration and all revolutionary supporters. The congress contradicted the Rio Pact and supported Guatemala's singular protest among the increasingly unanimous international rhetoric of the Cold War. Men openly advocated for women to take a leadership role during an international forum, and they expressed pride in their actions. During this critical historical juncture, dominant gender norms were transcended as Guatemalan men's and women's interests coalesced over the congress.

The most critical outcome of the 1947 congress for urban ladinas was its exposure of the political diversity within their community. The tenacity and leadership capabilities of women were revealed on the international stage during a period of intense political opposition. This examination of events surrounding the 1947 congress in the Guatemalan context also reveals the nature of US opposition, and US willingness to interfere in the affairs of another sovereign nation. These two interrelated elements revealed the extent of the political diversity among urban ladinas, and their ultimate incompatibility. The conflict forced them to articulate their own political ideologies, and the freedom they enjoyed in Guatemala at that time allowed them to express a previously unknown diversity. As a result, this split gave rise to a second women's movement, the Alianza Femenina Guatemalteca, which was more overtly political in its orientation and activities.

Six

LIVING IN THE WORLD WE IMAGINED
THE ALIANZA FEMENINA GUATEMALTECA, SOCIALIST FEMINISM, AND THE COLD WAR, 1950–1954

For the economic, political, and cultural equality of women!
—*Alianza Femenina Guatemalteca, June 20, 1950*

Love for family should not be an obstacle in the struggle for one's country, or to banish the tyranny and abuse of all humanity. This should be the objective of all conscious women who have a clear understanding of what it is like to live fully.
—*Ester de Urrutia, July 1, 1953*

Women workers, peasant women, and any working woman will find in the Alianza Femenina Guatemalteca an organization like any of the union organizations, an ally to fight to improve their salaries, provide better living conditions for children and working women, and incorporate all sectors of society in our struggle for the progress and independence of our country and for the happiness and tranquility of the Guatemalan home.
—*Alianza Femenina Guatemalteca, June 20, 1950*

The 1947 First Inter-American Congress of Women was a pivotal moment for the urban ladina movement. While some of the delegates expressed deep concern over the congress's opposition to US-led militarization as the path to hemispheric security, a small group of women were electrified by the anti-imperialistic message and found the sociopolitical ideals expressed to be precisely the ideology for which they had been searching. Embracing the social and class critique expressed during the congress, this group integrated the historically significant maternalism exemplified by the Elisa Martínez de Arévalo social reform circles with an overt political agenda. Implementing motherhood as one of the critical motivators for their social and economic reforms, the women who formed the Alianza Femenina Guatemalteca expanded it to include a structural analysis of the revolution. Discontented with the results of their analysis, women of the Alianza crossed both class and ethnic divides to align themselves with the working poor and indigenous women. Moving effortlessly between radical political activism and traditional gendered ideals of mothering, they confronted the very foundations of Guatemala's economic and patriarchal structure that maintained women's inequitable position. As a result, the women of the Alianza Femenina Guatemalteca stood alone among their peers as they struggled to identify and rectify Guatemala's foundations that simultaneously privileged men and disenfranchised women.

As the second president of the revolutionary era, Jacobo Árbenz increased the pace of the social and economic reforms enacted during the Arévalo presidency to address some of Guatemala's worst economic disparities. Focusing on historical class and economic inequalities and the unequal distribution of land, the 1952 Agrarian Reform was one the most significant reform projects of the Árbenz administration, becoming the lightning rod around which both pro- and antirevolutionary forces revolved. When the women of the Alianza, however, added a gendered critique to this sociopolitical analysis, these same leaders were not ready or willing to engage. Rather, the Alianza's insistence that the revolution break out of its deeply rooted patriarchy and include women of all social classes was met with hostility and resistance. They were not deterred and engaged directly with revolutionary politics, crossing the sociopolitical divide outlined by *Diario de Centro América*'s editor in 1948. The women affiliated with formal political parties all faced intense discrimination and more often than not were disregarded for their contributions. The work of the organization as well as their newsletter *Mujeres: Boletín de Alianza Femenina Guatemalteca* were frequently absent from other pro-revolutionary journals and organizational listings of the time; evidence of this political amnesia can be found throughout the Árbenz years.

The Alianza Femenina Guatemalteca became involved in a wide variety of social and political organizations, although their work primarily focused on three central sites of inequality: maternal and child welfare reforms, working-class women, and Guatemala's socioeconomic structure. In a pattern similar to that of broader political processes from 1950 to 1954, the nature of the Alianza's work grew more comprehensive as the organization matured. Therefore, the three national conferences the Alianza helped to organize or initiate revealed an increasing depth of analysis and an escalation in their efforts to address structural inequalities. In keeping with their continued support of the children's homes and nutrition centers established by Elisa Martínez de Arévalo, the 1951 conference on children evaluated the status of children after six years of revolutionary reform. A second national conference held in August 1953 incorporated men and women from across the country to address the high cost of living, affecting the poor and working class. The third national conference held by the Alianza, in November 1953, was the first Guatemalan national women's conference, and it was during this meeting that they revealed a comprehensive indictment of patriarchal privilege and the desperate need for a shift in Guatemalan gender norms. The brevity of the Árbenz presidency affected the Alianza's ability to enact much of their agenda, and so the ideals and conferences outlined in this chapter largely remained embryonic.

The historical period during which the Alianza Femenina Guatemalteca was active does not have a well-developed historiography and has generally been disregarded as an insignificant era due to the persistence of the North Atlantic–based "wave" theory.[1] This traditional historiography based on US, Canadian, and European women's movements emphasizes the campaigns for suffrage in the early twentieth century and then leaps into the 1960s and the new civil and legal rights movements. Latin American researchers have altered this periodization slightly to identify two specific time periods critical for Latin American women's movements. The first period extends from the 1930s to the 1950s, emphasizing the movements that politically enfranchised some women. The second era then skips two decades to the mid-1970s and the 1975 United Nations Decade for Women World Conference held in Mexico City. Initiated by the Women's International Democratic Federation, the groundbreaking global gathering of women and its aftermath are generally understood to mark the beginning of a new era in feminist organizing. While both of these periods deserve more scholarly attention than they have received, this particular model neglects the critical existence of groups such as the Alianza Femenina Guatemalteca and presupposes that political citizenship remained the primary concern of women's movements. A recent work edited by Adriana Valobra and Mercedes Yusta addresses this glaring gap in our understanding of Latin American women's movements during this time period. *Queridas camaradas* (Dear Comrades) charts the work of socialist- and communist-affiliated women's organizations from the 1940s to the 1960s, shattering existing paradigms of women's activism. The Alianza belongs in this new historiographic space that tracks women's organizations across the political spectrum and categorizations. Therefore, both the 1947 Inter-American Congress of Women (which provided the platform for the 1975 UN conference in Mexico City) and groups such as the Alianza demonstrate the need to revise

Living in the World We Imagined 217

the traditional periodization because they provide the foundational ideologies for later Guatemalan (and Latin American) feminist movements that emerged during the 1980s and 1990s.

Cold War Gender Politics: Birth of the Alianza Femenina Guatemalteca

The origins of the Alianza are deeply rooted in the Guatemalan revolutionary sociopolitical context. It emerged out of the 1947 Inter-American Congress of Women in Guatemala City, where ideas regarding economic justice, global peace, and gender equality resonated with a small but pivotal number of women in the Unión de Mujeres Democráticas.[2] These women found the socioeconomic critiques expressed at the congress to be precisely the ideological concepts they had been struggling to articulate, amorphous ideals still unresolved during the first years of Guatemala's political democracy. First lady María Vilanova de Árbenz herself noted that it was during the congress that she first discovered the words that expressed her own political ideals. Consequently, in the weeks following the congress, some in the Unión de Mujeres Democráticas formed another organization, drawn together by a shared feminist and social-justice consciousness along with a willingness to engage in direct political activity.[3] The significance of the 1947 congress in the formation of this new organization is evidenced by the byline in their monthly newsletter, *Mujeres*, which identified the Alianza as members of Block 2 of the Federación de Mujeres de las Américas, an organization formed at the end of the 1947 congress (see chapter 5).[4]

Following the formal emergence of the Alianza in October 1947, the group cultivated a small but growing presence among women in the pro-revolutionary political parties. Their affiliations with high-ranking members of the Arévalo government and the Women's International League for Peace and Freedom (WILPF) gave them unusual access to international actors for such a young organization. Within a few months, they had hosted their first official meeting with a delegation from the United Nations, led by Carmen Bustamante de Lozada.[5] By 1948, the group had sent delegates to attend a conference in Bogotá, Colombia. The Alianza remained out of the national spotlight until the election of Jacobo Árbenz in 1950, when their affiliation with first lady María Vilanova de Árbenz moved them onto the national and international stage. They utilized their newsletter, *Mujeres*, to disseminate their ideas, and it ran from June 20, 1950, to the end of the revolutionary period, edited by Lily M. de Alvarado.[6]

The Alianza has been generally associated with the urban political elite, attracting professionals and intellectuals of the urban middle and upper classes. This reputation is generally accurate during the first years of its existence, as its small membership consisted of socially conscious urban ladinas as well as writers and educators from the pro-revolutionary political party affiliates. A majority of ladinas distanced themselves from the Alianza over its emphasis on class and gender analysis, which broke with traditional social and class barriers. Their insistence that the revolution could be claimed by women of all ethnicities and social classes was a position few urban ladinas felt comfortable embracing. Their monthly newsletter certainly indicates that a majority of their membership at this early stage were literate urban residents. Although few of the Alianza's papers have survived, according to existing documents, some its first members included María Vilanova de Árbenz, Helena Leiva de Holst, Haydée Godoy, Mélida Luz Palacios, María Isabel Foronda de Vargas, Angelina Acuña de Castañeda, María del Carmen Vargas, Aída Doninelli Vda. de Véliz, and Romelia Alarcón Folgar.[7] A 2011 publication by the Guatemalan feminist organization Asociación la Cuerda includes the names of women who became high-profile members of the Alianza during the 1950s such as Concepción Castro, María Saucedo, Dolores Montenegro, Leonor Paz y Paz, Irma Chávez de Alvarado, Ester de Urrutia, and Laura Pineda.[8]

The Alianza's multifaceted approach to its work attracted women from all the revolutionary political parties, its members having affiliations with the Partido Acción Revolucionaria, Partido de Integridad Nacional, and Partido de la Revolución Guatemalteca.[9] Women in executive positions frequently held official membership in multiple political parties. Ester de Urrutia, for example, belonged to several pro-revolutionary parties including the Renovación Nacional, the Partido Acción Revolucionaria, and the Partido de la Revolución Guatemalteca.[10] A representative of the labor union Sindicato de Trabajadoras del Beneficios de Café, Hortensia Hernández Rojás, was also the leader of the female affiliate of the Comité Político Nacional de los Trabajadores, while she and Matilde Elena López were both executive members of the Partido Revolucionario Obrero de Guatemala (PROG).[11] The leadership between the Partido de la Revolución Guatemalteca and the Alianza was virtually indistinguishable at times during the early 1950s.[12] Some women, like Angelina Acuña de Castañeda, who ran for office under the Partido Renovación Socialista ticket in 1948, came to the organization with political experience, while others such as Marta Enríquez, representing the Sindicato Central de Costureras, rose to national prominence through working-class lived experience and labor organizing. Although the Alianza never identified itself as a Communist Party affiliate and actively refuted such identification (Guatemala's official Communist Party was in fact illegal during the Arévalo administration), several members of the Alianza maintained formal affiliations, including Hortensia Hernández Rojás, Haydée Godoy, Irma Chávez de Alvarado, and Dora Franco y Franco.[13] They eagerly worked with other like-minded organizations across the sociopolitical spectrum, and while no official Guatemalan female political party formed as in other Latin American nations, the Alianza came the closest to fulfilling such a role.[14]

As the organization matured, however, the majority of the Alianza membership ultimately were poor, rural, working-class women, representing a radical departure from previous ladina movements. The seeds of class consciousness had been planted by writers such as Vicenta Laparra de la Cerda, Luz Valle, and Gloria Menéndez Mina, who had publicly concluded that the social reform movement was merely a small payment for a large debt, establishing a clear recognition of economic inequities among women's organizations in Guatemala City (see chapter 3). What distinguishes the Alianza from these previous declarations is how members responded to socioeconomic concerns. Consequently, as the Alianza matured, it actively recruited women from the urban and rural working class, who brought with them a wealth of working and union experience.

One of the best-known members of the Alianza came from the working class, and she no doubt influenced the organization's class consciousness. Known to many as simply the "doña of the revolution," Ester de Urrutia, along with her husband Manuel Urrutia, had been involved in union activism since the early 1920s, as Manuel was a member of the powerful typographers' union, the Sindicato de Tipografía, one of Guatemala's older labor unions.[15] Although the unions had been banned and largely repressed during the Ubico presidency, the union members of the 1920s reemerged following his overthrow in 1944. Ester and Manuel threw themselves into politics in the days following Ubico's overthrow and remained active for the rest of their lives, except for the years they spent in Argentina as political exiles. The Urrutia family had already been involved in the Renovación Nacional before the October revolution and, as one of the leaders of the new female affiliate, Ester de Urrutia spoke at the memorial service for murdered newspaper editor Alejandro Córdova.[16] Ester defied political allegiances, however, by working with an array of political parties during the revolution, assuming leadership roles in the Partido Acción Revolucionario, the Partido de la Revolución Guatemalteca, and the Partido Guatemalteco del

Trabajo between 1944 and 1954.[17] Ester also worked with civic organizations, including Elisa Martínez de Arévalo's guarderías infantíles, and directly with market women. In the Alianza, Ester found women of common revolutionary ideals for ethnic, gender, and class equality, and during the 1950s she gained national prominence for her work. Her activism led her to a leadership role in the Alianza despite the fact that she only had a sixth-grade education, and she went on to represent the organization at a wide variety of national and international conferences including the Second Inter-American Congress of Women in Mexico City in October 1951, and the 1953 Women's International Democratic Federation meeting in Copenhagen.[18] In the final year of the revolutionary project, Ester became secretary general of the Alianza. Although she could be considered exceptional in her leadership abilities and feminist consciousness, she nevertheless symbolizes all that was possible for working-class women during these critical ten years. While María Chinchilla Recinos has come to symbolize the sacrifice of urban ladinas at the beginning of the revolution, it was women such as Ester de Urrutia who nurtured and sustained its ideals. However, unlike Chinchilla Recinos, who emerged as a comfortable and sympathetic revolutionary symbol, Urrutia disrupted class, ethnic, and gender norms and as a result has largely been forgotten.

The Alianza's overt attempts to cross ethnic and class lines to create a broad-based female coalition indicated a dramatic shift from any other Guatemalan women's movements.[19] Ester de Urrutia's working-class background along with the influence of women affiliated with the Communist Party such as Hortensia Hernández Rojás, Graciela Amaya García, and Matilde Elena López, the latter two from El Salvador, brought a clear class consciousness to the Alianza. Although individual women and male allies had consistently called for the legal and social equality of women since the 1880s, a formal organization had never fused these ideas within a class and gender analysis. Only Elisa Martínez de Arévalo had created a successful collaboration with market women, and there is little evidence that a formal cross-class alliance was formed. For the Alianza, all Guatemalan women were to be included in the revolutionary project. "The working woman, the peasant woman, any working woman should find in the Alianza Femenina Guatemalteca a unified place to struggle alongside labor unions and rural organizations to improve salaries, to improve the living conditions of children and working women, and to work together with other social sectors for the progress and independence of Guatemala and for the peace and happiness of the Guatemalan home."[20] Although the leadership maintained

Living in the World We Imagined 221

formal roles, the overall composition of the Alianza was rather informal. Behind all of their efforts lay the fundamental goal of creating a national organization of women representing the concerns of all Guatemalan women.[21]

By late 1953, the Alianza's membership had increased by 600 percent from the preceding year, extending into twelve departments.[22] The Alianza encouraged rural women to form committees in order to identify their specific social and economic needs. Once a group reached ten people, the Alianza incorporated it as an official affiliate. The ideological structure underlying these committees was a grassroots approach based upon the belief that women were capable of identifying their own needs, which no doubt was attractive to many rural women whose concerns had been so long ignored, and they rapidly outnumbered the original urban members. By the time they held their first and only national congress in November 1953, at least 1,377 separate committees were represented, including 450 groups from the capital city, 677 from Escuintla, and 250 from Santa Rosa. Their records suggest that the Alianza's message resonated primarily in rural agricultural areas dominated by the United Fruit Company, with a strong union base. Although the exact number of involved women remains unclear, calculating these numbers suggests that there were at least 13,770 women associated with the Alianza, making this the largest women's organization of its kind in Guatemala. Although the Alianza existed as a national organization led by politically powerful women such as María Vilanova de Árbenz, it primarily comprised small, localized committees.

The nature of their organization and the Alianza's political and intellectual contributions have been largely distorted by the Cold War, effectively obscuring their accomplishments. The US State Department and the CIA played a critical role in shaping the historical narrative of the Alianza as they attempted to build a case against supposed communist infiltration into Guatemala. Historians have grappled extensively with these accusations and concluded that, while Árbenz had developed a working relationship with Guatemala's small Communist Party, his own party had not been manipulated by an international communist conspiracy.[23] Rather, his government applied a series of socioeconomic reforms to a national system designed historically to benefit only the rich and disenfranchise the vast majority of the population. While some of Árbenz's closest allies were members of the Guatemalan Communist Party, the reforms his government applied, such as the 1952 Agrarian Reform Law, intrinsically reflected Guatemala's deep, historical economic inequities.[24]

This same level of scrutiny has not been directed at the women of the Alianza, who remain frozen in time as "communist fronts" by unforgiving Cold War polemics. At the heart of this historical obscuring is the gendered nature of US imperialism, which characterized the country's Cold War battles. Based on a hypermasculinized worldview, the US State Department effectively used gendered rhetoric against opponents of the United States, feminizing individuals and shaming their political or intellectual positions. When these opponents were women, this gendered rhetoric reduced them to sexual objects devoid of ideological and political intent. The characterizations of the Guatemalan revolution and its participants by historians Ronald Schneider and Rollie Poppino epitomize just this type of marginalization. Basing their analysis on primary sources from the State Department and the US public relations industry, they described the Alianza as a communist "front" group for the Árbenz government, carrying out the "sinister intentions of the communist plot" as wives and lovers of the communists.[25] These statements trivialize their work as independent political and intellectual actors. Their historiographic conclusions were in fact based on the earlier work of Daniel James, who has come to exemplify the common historiographic assumptions regarding the Alianza in 1954.

> Its membership was never publicized but was presumably large, since it consisted mostly of the female relatives of Communists and their sympathizers.... The AFG was not, as its secretary pointed out to a *Daily Worker* correspondent, an "organization of bourgeois and middle-class women who crocheted things"; it was, she proudly emphasized, a militant participant in "workers"—that is, Communist—struggles.[26]

James's misinterpretation of the Alianza's self-definition and his presumption of their secrecy (a projection of the fear then pervading the United States) can in fact be linked to a deliberate attempt by elements in the United States to mischaracterize the Árbenz state. As J. T. Way points out, United Fruit Company executives contacted the US Congress and the mainstream press to convince them that Guatemala had fallen into the Soviet sphere.[27] The insistence by some Alianza members that theirs was not an organization of bourgeois women who "crocheted things" and the proud declaration of their alliance with working-class women was a statement not about their political affiliation but rather about their active participation in a cross-class feminist social organization that was a radical departure from any previous Guatemalan women's movement. Historian Jadwiga Pieper Mooney has identified this trend in the polarized climate of the 1950s, noting that any women's political organizations unwilling to align themselves with US foreign policy were labeled as "front groups" for communist groups, thereby trivializing and dismissing their intellectual and political contributions.[28] This scholarly trend has extended into Guatemala itself, and with little analysis of the association, their contributions to the revolutionary decade have been largely dismissed.

The Alianza's affiliation with a variety of transnational women's organizations further fueled State Department speculation over their suspected communist affiliations. The 1947 congress organized by the WILPF initially placed Guatemalan women on the State Department's Cold War radar. Their condemnation grew when the Alianza joined the Women's International Democratic Federation, and in fact historians inaccurately identified the origins of the Alianza to the WIDF's inaugural 1945 meeting in Paris.[29] Founded on November 29, 1945, at the International Congress of Women in Paris, the WIDF's interrelated conceptual emphasis on antifascism, global peace, women's rights, and better living conditions for children resonated deeply with the Alianza's ideals for their own sociopolitical context.[30] Rapidly becoming the largest women's organization in the world, the WIDF drew its membership from a wide variety of other women's organizations.[31] Despites its involvement with the United Nations, for the US State Department, the WIDF's large membership from countries in the Soviet sphere and the Global South placed it firmly on the wrong side in the Cold War.[32]

The Alianza's official position against militarization and their alliance with these two international organizations identified them as peace activists, a sociopolitical ideology that became a rhetorical pawn in the Cold War discourse.[33] Alianza leaders such as Ester de Urrutia believed strongly in pacifism and spoke out at great length on the dangers of war, particularly related to actions they believed to be imperialistic such as the Korean War. "We have clearly seen that we ought not to conform to what is happening in Korea, because this will oppose our human principles and will also betray the hopes of our brothers and sisters of the world. It would betray the people that suffer because of the actions of guerrillas and imperialism still creating pain and death in an unequal war stealing the lives of men, women, and children."[34] As the US reactions to the 1947 congress had already demonstrated to Guatemalan women, any discussion that privileged peace over militarization or social reform over national security would be met with resistance. For their campaigns against the war in Korea, the Alianza was repeatedly accused by opposition both in Guatemala and at the US State Department of communist affiliations. In what would become a reoccurring rebuttal to such accusations, Ester declared: "We have been told that our struggle

FIGURE 6.1 The Ester and Manuel Urrutia family. Courtesy of the author.

for peace is 'communist.' What ignorance! Peace has neither political affiliation nor ideology; peace is simply peace."[35] It was with unmitigated joy that Ester de Urrutia, the Alianza, and hundreds of other Guatemalans received the news of the armistice in Korea on July 27, 1953.

As one of the leading scholars on gender and the Cold War, historian Francisca de Haan argues that Cold War ideology and the fear of reprisal was highly effective in silencing the historical contributions of women involved in transnational organizations such as the WILPF and WIDF. The US-sponsored anticommunist hysteria fueled by the House Un-American Activities Committee played a critical role in obscuring the existence of international organizations such as the Alianza as well as the national affiliates of the WILPF and WIDF. As Jacqueline Castledine argues, women in the United States who "challenged Cold War doctrines by engaging in peace politics were unfeminine and a threat to democracy, while those who endorsed U.S. Cold War policy by working on the margins of the political system could strengthen America in its defense against communism."[36] The parallels in the experiences of politically independent women in the United States and in Guatemala are striking. The US branch of the WIDF, the Congress of American Women (CAW), was established in March 1946 and within a year claimed to have a membership of 250,000. However, by 1950, the CAW was forced to disband as a consequence of political persecution by the House Un-American Activities Committee and the US Justice Department.[37] As a member of the CAW, the formidable feminist Gerda Lerner attended the 1948 WIDF conference in Budapest.[38] When she came under scrutiny from the House Un-American Activities Committee, Lerner burned all of her notes and papers, an eerie parallel with women in the Alianza such as Ester de Urrutia, who in the terrifying days following the resignation of Jacobo Árbenz burned all of her personal papers.[39] This self-silencing through the destruction of personal documents completed the historical erasure of the Guatemalan women's efforts, a chilling example of the power and fear exerted by the US State Department and the CIA during the Cold War.[40] Although the Alianza provided the ideological foundations for a variety of contemporary feminist organizations, their groundbreaking efforts and indeed their very existence have been effectively erased from the public memory of Guatemalans and historians alike.[41] The Alianza is not alone in this fate; women's groups across the globe found that their political activism, social justice work, and gender equity efforts were vilified by the cacophony of Cold War fearmongering.

María Vilanova de Árbenz: An Unlikely Revolutionary Feminist

The sociopolitical background of the second revolutionary presidential wife and member of the Alianza, María Vilanova de Árbenz, could not have contrasted more with that of her predecessor, Elisa Martínez de Arévalo. As the daughter of an elite El Salvadoran coffee grower, Vilanova de Árbenz's familial origins made her future revolutionary activism unlikely. However, her marriage to Jacobo Árbenz and her experiences in the aftermath of Jorge Ubico's resignation awakened her class consciousness. These small stirrings found full fruition in the work of the Alianza Femenina Guatemalteca. While Vilanova de Árbenz shared Martínez de Arévalo's concerns for social reform and poverty, her approach reflected a more comprehensive political stance. In other words, while Elisa Martínez de Arévalo lovingly applied bandages to Guatemala's social wounds, Vilanova de Árbenz ripped them off to examine what had caused the wounds.

Born on April 17, 1915, María Vilanova de Árbenz grew up in El Salvador, although she was connected to Guatemala through her mother, María Dolores

Castro Arrechea, a member of an elite Guatemalan family.[42] Her mother's friendship with Guatemalan Isabel Asturias brought María Vilanova to the country in 1935, when she was only twenty years old.[43] When her mother returned to El Salvador following the visit, María remained behind to study. She was already well educated, having attended the College of Notre Dame in Belmont, California, but the depression had made education abroad difficult, even for families of the Vilanovas' wealth and status. In an ironic twist of fate, María met her husband and future revolutionary, Jacobo Árbenz, at a dance in honor of Jorge Ubico's birthday on November 11, 1938.[44] Although her parents disapproved of their relationship, the gregarious, intelligent, young Salvadoran woman and the serious and introverted young military man were married on March 14, 1939.[45] With the birth of their first daughter nine months later, María's parents forgave the young couple, and the family reconciled.

María Vilanova de Árbenz's political consciousness emerged slowly. It was her father José Antonio Vilanova Kreitz's participation in the 1932 massacre of some thirty-two thousand Salvadoran peasants that first disrupted her elite privileged position. As Vilanova de Árbenz recounted to historian Piero Gleijeses: "He spoke of it in such a matter of fact way.... We killed so many." According to her, while the event did not trouble her father, it disturbed her greatly, and Gleijeses concluded that she had begun to feel uncomfortable with her elite status from an early age. "Something was terribly wrong, even though she hardly knew what and why. These were just doubts, shadows of questions that a conventional marriage might well have stifled."[46] Instead, Vilanova de Árbenz met Jacobo Árbenz, with whom she enjoyed a strong intellectual relationship.

Her new husband was quiet, introverted, and brilliant, someone who matched her desire for social and political change in Guatemala. Born in 1913, his ancestry was Swiss German, and he grew up in a middle-class family in Quetzaltenango. Although Árbenz grew up comfortably, his father became addicted to morphine and lost his pharmacy business, ultimately killing himself, and Árbenz was forced to relinquish any hope of attending university. His only resort was to attend Guatemala's military academy, the Escuela Politécnica, on a scholarship. There, Árbenz proved to be an outstanding student, receiving the highest grades ever recorded. Consequently, in March 1937, Árbenz was posted to the Escuela Politécnica, where he taught military subjects, history, and physics. In 1943, he was promoted to captain. During his brief tenure in the regular corps prior to his military posting, Árbenz met Francisco Javier Arana. When he was fired from his post for his anti-Ubico sentiments, he fled to El Salvador, where he and

Arana organized a band of revolutionaries. Following Ubico's resignation at the end of June 1944, Árbenz also resigned from the army to protest the imposition of Juan Federico Ponce Vaides as interim president. He immediately began plotting a political overthrow with other members of the military.[47] Aware of these activities, Ponce Vaides created a secret list of Guatemalans deemed dangerous to his administration, which included Árbenz.[48] Consequently, María Vilanova de Árbenz and her children fled Guatemala in August 1944, remaining in El Salvador with her parents until the October revolution, returning to a liberated country on October 26, 1944. Árbenz was only thirty-seven years old when he became president six years later in 1950, the youngest president in Latin America. Following his 1954 overthrow, he lived in exile in Mexico City, where he died in 1971 at the age of fifty-seven. Árbenz's decision to end his own life is widely believed to be the result of long-term depression related to the overthrow of his government.

During the revolutionary era, Vilanova de Árbenz quickly adapted to her role as the spouse of a high-profile political leader. She, along with the other two wives of the ruling junta, Leonor de Toriello and Dora Amalia de Arana, visited those injured in the October 1944 fighting.[49] Her political transformation continued during the Arévalo presidency, shifting significantly following the 1947 First Inter-American Congress of Women. The gathering offered many ladinas, including Vilanova de Árbenz, the opportunity to explore a variety of sociopolitical solutions for the challenges facing the Americas. As Vilanova de Árbenz recounted to Piero Gleijeses, she was exposed to the philosophy of Karl Marx and socialist ideas for the first time during the 1947 congress.[50] She and Jacobo read Marx together and began discussing its implications for Guatemala. As Gleijeses concludes, "Jacobo and María were, in fact, partners in a process of radicalization that began slowly and became increasingly rapid. They shared the same evolution, the same beliefs and the same friends."[51] Despite this clear admission of a growing political and intellectual transformation, Vilanova de Árbenz has continued to downplay her own role during the revolutionary decade. In an autobiography of her life with Jacobo Árbenz, *Mi esposo, el presidente Árbenz* (2003), she focuses almost exclusively on her personal life with Jacobo, and their love for one another.[52] In fact, she describes all of her work with the Asociación de Comedores y Guarderías Infantíles and the Alianza Femenina Guatemalteca in a few rather vague sentences about working for social and cultural advancements for women: "During the period I lived in Guatemala, a social group began that wanted to get women involved in politics. This movement was determined to make an advance in political participation. We did not forget about the teacher María Chinchilla, who symbolized the popular, patriotic movement and who died heroically in the streets at the hands of the military."[53] While this directly contradicts the wealth of evidence that documents her contributions to the Alianza and Guatemala as first lady, it exemplifies the self-silencing that has continued to operate among the country's most significant revolutionary leaders and the Árbenz family. In the spotlight of the Cold War controversy that swirled around her husband and the 1954 overthrow of his government, her reticence to divulge her activism is understandable and confirms Patrick Iber's conclusions.[54]

Vilanova de Árbenz's prominent role in both Guatemalan society and politics earned her the vitriolic ire of revolutionary opponents as well as those politicians and advisers closest to her husband. The US House of Representatives even blamed Vilanova de Árbenz for her husband's affiliation with communist ideas. As J. T. Way argues, dependent upon the fertile rumor mill of the political opposition, it was essential that the US State Department discredit both Árbenz as a dupable fool (an image solidified by a photo of Árbenz stripped to his underwear following his resignation) and his wife as a dangerous conspirator. "Gender discourse quickly became an arrow in the quiver of propagandists and political apologists attempting to justify invading Guatemala and overthrowing a democratically elected government."[55] Even Árbenz's closest political associates went on record to vilify his wife, accusing her of extramarital affairs and political conspiracies that contributed to his eventual resignation.[56] While many of Árbenz's inner circle held progressive sociopolitical ideals regarding class, their social critique did not include gender. Given the Alianza's increasingly vocal rebukes over both public and private patriarchal misbehavior, their animosity against Vilanova de Árbenz is not surprising. Although little analysis exists on Latin American feminist organizations during the 1950s and 1960s, the few contemporary examples indicate that this type of hostility was not unusual. In his work on Peruvian feminist Magda Portal, Iñigo García-Bryce argues that although Portal was one of the key founders of the American Popular Revolutionary Alliance (APRA), her feminist analysis marginalized her from APRA's center of power.[57]

The bandages that Árbenz de Vilanova ripped off to identify Guatemala's social wounds essentially disrupted the country's gender norms, projecting a new kind of first lady and mother onto the national stage. Although Martínez de Arévalo received some opposition from the elite for her insistence that poor women be involved in the social reform movement, her work remained within the bounds of traditional maternal roles, which earned her admiration from the majority of Guatemalans as "mother" of all Guatemalan children. María Vilanova de Árbenz, on the other hand, not only assumed the directorship of the national orphanage and nutrition centers, as was expected of her social station, but also immediately entered the political realm, directly campaigning for and with her husband. She personally accompanied Jacobo as he campaigned during his 1950 presidential bid and urged women to join her in the political arena through her affiliation with the Alianza. In doing so, Vilanova de Árbenz assumed a profile as first lady that far surpassed that of her predecessor, whose own efforts with regard to social reform had set the standard for Guatemala and perhaps even Latin America. Vilanova de Árbenz's adoption of a decidedly political stance extended an image of motherhood and womanhood into the national political realm in Guatemala at the highest level. In so doing, she has few equals in Latin America during this period, including Eva Perón, whose efforts remained closely aligned with her husband's political ambitions rather than with Argentine women.

Feminism, Socialism, and the Alianza Femenina Guatemalteca

For decades, Guatemalan women who held any element of a feminist consciousness had been socially and politically marginalized to the point of inertia, relegated to imagining a world in which they wished to live. The revolutionary decade offered women their first sustained opportunity in which to act upon a wide variety of these covertly nurtured ideals, and women involved with the Alianza threw themselves into virtually every available social, political, and economic reform movement, maintaining an almost frenetic pace of activism. Therefore, while only remnants of this organization and what its members contributed survived the post-1954 archival destruction (see the introduction for issues related to primary sources), they cast a wide swath, and their activities in a myriad of associations expose their convictions. The feminism that emerged from their complex gender, class, and ethnic analysis defies the simplistic classifications established by Cold War rhetoric. Employing what Devaleena Das refers to as "the epistemological tool of experience," the Alianza embraced a wide variety of feminist and sociopolitical strategies to address the complex sociopolitical issues facing Guatemalan women.[58] Inspired by the ideas presented at the 1947 First Inter-American Congress of Women, their membership in the Women's International Democratic Federation, and the maternal feminism already well entrenched in Guatemalan women's circles, the Alianza incorporated socialist analysis, weaving together a feminism firmly grounded in the Guatemalan context of the mid-twentieth century. They embraced democratic principles and suffrage for all women, including indigenous women, calling for women's right to land ownership during the pivotal 1952 Agrarian Reform as well as increasing social safety nets for children. They insisted that class and ethnic analysis be integrated into state-sponsored social reforms. The result was an integrated feminism that sought to address the inequalities of their sociopolitical context, and they emerged as tireless advocates for a wide variety of working women, advocating for more reforms with each passing year.

Although the multifaceted socialist approach used by the Alianza was unsettling to many urban ladinas, it was not unusual for feminists in other parts of Latin America.[59] In fact, by 1950, socialist ideas had already had an extraordinary influence on the essence and goals of feminism throughout Latin America.[60] As Asunción Lavrin notes, feminists in the Southern Cone grappled with "their complex reality: its class and landownership structure, its economic and demographic problems, its ethnic diversity, and its cultural and intellectual traditions."[61] Faced with a set of complex socioeconomic challenges, Latin American women rarely identified a dichotomy between equal rights feminism and social feminism. They perceived no inherent conflict between demanding equal civil and political status and preserving their socially protected roles as wives and mothers.[62]

Despite this identified reality in Latin American feminist movements, there has been relatively little historical analysis on the contributions of socialist women's movements in Latin America, particularly during the early and mid-twentieth century. As Norma Stoltz Chinchilla explains:

> It took a while to rediscover and disseminate examples of socialist and working-class women's efforts to make women's equality a priority in early twentieth-century social movements such as the socialist women in the autonomous Movement for the Liberation of Chilean Women (MEMCH) in the 1930s and the more than 50,000 Mexican women representing some 800 organizations and a variety of social sectors and classes organized in the autonomous coalition Frente Unico Pro Derecho de la Mujer.[63]

The Alianza's clear alignment with socialist ideals, however, did not translate into an official political identification. There is no evidence to support the US State Department's hysterical charges against the Alianza as a communist "front" group for Soviet infiltration into the Americas. Although several women did officially join the Guatemalan Communist Party, such as Dora Franco y Franco

Living in the World We Imagined 231

and Irma Chávez de Alvarado, the organization itself remained politically independent and never used formal labels.⁶⁴ Marcela Ríos Tobar notes a similar tendency with Chilean women during the 1970s:

> Despite this clear connection with socialist ideals, feminists of the period very seldom used the label of socialist as part of their political identity. As long as the number of feminists remained small and their main preoccupation was differentiating themselves from other politically active women, feminists did not see a need to use labels to differentiate among each other.⁶⁵

The Alianza embraced socialist ideas and feminism in equal measure, providing the foundation for future Guatemalan feminist movements such as the Unión Nacional de Mujeres de Guatemala (UNAMG). However, as Ana María Cofiño Kepfer points out, the opposition the Alianza experienced within the Cold War context due to their identification with socialist and communist ideas caused them to downplay the radical implications of their structural analysis.⁶⁶

The Alianza's position on the array of sociopolitical structural critiques and their anti-imperialism stance confirms their status as socialist feminists. However, one of the central conundrums for socialist women was the overwhelming tendency in socialist movements to relegate gender issues as secondary to class, an analytical bias common during the 1940s and 1950s. "Women's issues became secondary to the more important goal of working-class revolution because [the] solution of the 'woman question' supposedly would accompany the revolutionary transformation of society."⁶⁷ In contrast to some other contemporary socialist women of the period, however, the Alianza refused to relinquish their gender analysis, a position they were likely able to maintain because of their independence from an official political party or male-dominated movement, a strategy more commonly managed by socialist feminists during the 1970s and 1980s.⁶⁸ Therefore, an analysis of the Alianza's activities and intellectual contributions to the Guatemalan revolutionary project is a critical contribution to the field of socialist women's movements in Latin America during the understudied period of the 1950s.

Although the organization offered a critical space for women to live out their social and political ideals, it also acted as a relatively stable political arena in an otherwise volatile political climate. The dynamics and political rhetoric during the Árbenz era were fraught with infighting as both pro- and antirevolutionary political parties grappled for power and influence against one another and with Árbenz himself. There were four pro-revolutionary parties when Árbenz took office: the Partido Acción Revolucionaria (PAR), Renovación Nacional (RN), Frente Popular Libertador (FPL), and Partido de Integridad Nacional (PIN). In July 1951, a split within the PAR gave birth to the Partido Socialista (PS). Within the year, the five parties merged and became the Partido Revolucionario Guatemalteco. However, this coalition fell into disarray within weeks, and most people returned to their original political affiliations.[69] The small Guatemalan Communist Party emerged in the early 1950s led by José Manuel Fortuny, Alfredo Guerra Borges, and Victor Manuel Gutiérrez.[70] The Communist Party had originally been formed in 1923 but was for all practical purposes destroyed by Jorge Ubico in 1932. The Arévalo administration was more tolerant, although Arévalo officially banned the party from Guatemala in an attempt to deflect the US State Department's increasing hostility. Under Jacobo Árbenz, the Communist Party was legalized in 1952 as the Partido Guatemalteco del Trabajo (PGT). The PGT eventually held four of the fifty-eight congressional seats, and some of its members were part of Árbenz's trusted inner circle, although the government itself did not formally identify with the party. The remainder of the political parties in existence at the time aligned themselves with either the Arévalo or Árbenz administrations, or as the opposition.

As an autonomous female organization, the Alianza replicated the sanctuary of the female space established by Elisa Martínez de Arévalo and her circle of social reformers. Although they enlarged the sociopolitical space for women, the Alianza remained a distinctly female association, and they were frequently critical of other Guatemalan women who remained apolitical or even worked against the revolution.[71] Their political independence from any political party or official state apparatus facilitated their ability to sustain their structural and gendered analysis, which increasingly set them against their male peers. Insisting that women had both the right and the obligation to participate fully in Guatemalan society, they essentially inverted the social gendered construction of parallel spheres identified by *Diario de Centro América*'s editor in 1948. At their 1953 congress, they declared that "women cannot abandon the problems of agrarian reform, industrialization, the peace movement, and national sovereignty to the realm of men, and society cannot be separated into two spheres."[72] While their autonomy allowed the Alianza to continue their advocacy, within Guatemala's hierarchical and patriarchal context, their gendered critiques and overt political activism made them frequent targets of rhetorical attacks by both the pro- and antirevolutionary sectors. They retained their intellectual integrity by insisting that their work was based upon the needs of Guatemalan women.

Living in the World We Imagined 233

The women in the Alianza assumed an ideological position distinct from the Martínez de Arévalo social reform movement, duplicating the increasingly class-based sociopolitical reforms trajectory of the Arévalo and Árbenz administrations. Now able to act as well as write about a Guatemala that included women, the Alianza turned their energies to identify social needs and to question the underlying reasons for them. The economic and political critiques articulated during the 1947 congress helped them develop new questions, and the answers they discovered around access to health care, the nutritional status of children, and school attendance were devastating. During the Arévalo era, urban ladinas had been instrumental in creating the first social welfare institutions, using the abysmally poor statistics on infant mortality, access to medical care, and school attendance to justify their efforts. The Alianza now extended this analysis into an even more integrated and sophisticated sociopolitical model. The maternalism that galvanized the work of the social reform movement under Martínez de Arévalo remained a critical component of the Alianza's feminism through which they now expanded into a structural analysis. Scholar Nikki Craske identifies this type of feminism as "learned motherhood," which includes characteristics of caring and nurturing that are culturally defined.[73] The Alianza embraced this "learned motherhood" approach assuming a systematic approach to these overwhelming challenges through a series of conferences focused on the welfare of children and women. They established the status of Guatemala's children, and of familial well-being, as fundamental measures of the revolution's success or failure. In so doing, the Alianza created a feminist ideology that fused maternalism with a high degree of class and gender consciousness, creating an image of the political mother.

Deeply imbued maternalism within a feminist framework is not a new concept in Latin American women's movements. As Asunción Lavrin points out, because motherhood had a social function, it also held political meaning.[74] While women across the hemisphere had been effectively using this idea, the Alianza became the first organization in Guatemala to formally merge maternalism with an overtly political feminist agenda. Ester de Urrutia, the 1953–1954 executive secretary of the Alianza and the mother of seven children, articulated the synergy between the concepts of motherhood and political activism for the Alianza: "Familial love should not be an obstacle to the revolutionary struggle but should be the primary purpose to combat tyranny and abuse of all humanity. This must be the objective of all conscious women who have a clear concept of what it means to live fully."[75] For Urrutia, familial love brought one into the political struggle in the most genuine and authentic manner possible.

As a sociopolitical tool, the emphasis on maternalism created a complex terrain for Guatemala's first feminist organization. While maternalism had been promoted and celebrated as the quintessential contribution of urban ladinas during the Arévalo presidency, it also continued to promote traditional gender roles, projecting a kind, gentle, and nurturing image of mother. Even this modest shift in the image of Guatemalan motherhood prompted strong reactions from the antirevolutionary movement. Seizing upon maternalism as an effective rhetorical weapon, the opposition political parties maintained that the revolution would destroy the country's traditional family structure, employing a popular notion used by anticommunists. Therefore, the use of motherhood became a potent attack against the Árbenz administration, supposedly aligned with the international Soviet sphere. Women like Ester de Urrutia challenged this antagonism, arguing that it was precisely her role as a mother that propelled her to act. She argued that fighting against political tyranny and human abuse in order to protect one's children was appropriate behavior for all mothers, and she frequently expressed frustration that a majority of urban ladinas were reticent to participate in the political sphere. "As women, their heart, their ideas, and their revolutionary idealism bound them to one another in a single spirit of struggle," she wrote, and they must continue to struggle for peace, agrarian reform, and the rightful place of women.[76] Although motherhood played an important role in the Alianza's ideological feminist framework, when they translated it into a systematic and institutional critique, it threatened Guatemala's entire sociopolitical hierarchical and patriarchal structure.

Evidence of the Alianza's integrated approach came quickly as the first lady, María Vilanova de Árbenz, was appointed to the directorship of the Asociación de Comedores and the Asociación de Guarderías Infantíles, replacing Elisa Martínez de Arévalo.[77] In this new position, she assumed a more involved role than her predecessor. Vilanova de Árbenz reorganized the association from two separate affiliations into one national organization, the Asociación de Comedores y Guarderías Infantíles.[78] She appointed Gloria Bruni de Shaw as vice president, a position that would be replaced every two years. The official reorganization occurred just days before the First National Conference on the Defense of Children, and it is striking for several reasons.[79] First, an entirely new group of women assumed leadership roles; whether this shift was a mutual decision or whether it

Living in the World We Imagined 235

represented an arbitrary decision by Vilanova de Árbenz is unclear. The goals of the new Asociación closely reflected those of the Árbenz administration, which placed an ever increasing emphasis on economic reform. While the 1944 "society of friends" had strongly affirmed that social reforms must be accompanied by significant economic reforms, a majority of these women had not envisioned a fundamental restructuring of Guatemala's economic and social hierarchy. Under Vilanova de Árbenz's leadership, the Asociación assumed a more political stance, and conflicts continued to emerge between women of the two presidencies. To improve labor rights and wages, Liliam Jiménez de Leiva established a union within the Asociación, increasing salaries by 60 percent.[80] Despite assurances that they were not required to join, the presence of a union created conflict between some of the workers and the administration. The secretary for one of the Asociación's centers reported to Vilanova de Árbenz that Jiménez de Leiva was being bothered by anti-unionists.[81] For some of the workers, a union in the daycare centers suggested a dangerous shift in political ideology, a radical position many were not willing to assume. Ironically, while Martínez de Arévalo came under criticism from elite women's associations for her insistence that poor women be included in any social reform movements, Vilanova de Árbenz was attacked for making changes to the children's organization. While the political elites had criticized Martínez de Arévalo for her apparent lack of self-esteem, Vilanova de Árbenz was critiqued for being too sure of herself and too politically minded.

A new association, the Comidés Pro-Nutrición Escolar, expanded its original mandate to include programs for school-age children, distributing milk to schools.[82] It also created four temporary homes for children of both sexes who for unusual circumstances needed a place to stay. These homes offered services similar to those of the guarderías infantiles, namely medical care, social services, education, and recreational services. The nutrition centers increased their service to include vaccinations from Dr. Oscar Batres and J. Antonio Muñoz. These centers also served preschool children aged between two and six years who were in good health.[83] The number of nutrition centers and homes continued to increase, and by November 1951, there were a total of twenty-nine children's nutrition centers and homes in Guatemala City, and in the departments of Quetzaltenango, Totonicapán, Chimaltenango, Cobán, El Progreso, Jalapa, Antigua, Salamá, Puerto Barrios, and Zacapa. In total, the Asociación served over fifteen thousand children.[84] By 1954, the organization had created two maternity hospitals with a bed capacity of over two hundred, a sanatorium for children with tuberculosis in Guatemala City, two children's hospitals in the capital and one in Puerto Barrios, and sixty-one free consultation clinics, fifty-six of which were state run while five were in private hands.[85] The Asociación petitioned the Ministry of Public Health and Social Assistance for use of a building on the farm of La Aurora, for the installation of a tuberculosis vaccination site.[86] The Alianza also funded specific projects like buying X-ray machines.[87]

Following this shift, the Asociación's former leader, Mélida Montenegro de Méndez, virtually disappeared from the public record, emblematic of the broader shift in leadership across the capital city. The complete silence during the early 1950s from the social reform circle of Martínez de Arévalo suggests a radical split within the Asociación's administration based on political ideology. The incoming leadership of the Asociación challenged the very basis of economic inequality and thereby alienated many of the social reformers of the Arévalo period who were unwilling or unable to implement the necessary radical changes, echoes of the crisis in the ladina community following the 1947 congress.

What is remarkable about the leadership transition of the Asociación is the complete silence that surrounded it. In an era defined by freedom of expression, conflicts were routinely worked out in the national press. However, not even the antirevolutionary press carried any news of a conflict or fundamental split in the urban ladina social reform community. The silence of the more moderate women throughout the Árbenz years is suggestive of a vast gulf in the urban ladina community first created during the 1947 congress and widened by events during the Árbenz presidency. In the political volatility of the revolutionary decade, political diversity demonstrated by the urban ladina movements reflected the variety of sociopolitical solutions posited by these women. While the precise nature of these relationships is not clear, the attitude toward the Árbenz government of the women involved during the Arévalo era is very evident. In the waning days of the Árbenz government, the politically moderate ladinas remained utterly silent, coming to the aid of neither the Alianza nor even the daycare and nutrition centers. In fact, when María de Castillo, wife of Carlos Castillo Armas (the leader of the antirevolutionary movement who overthrew Jacobo Árbenz), assumed leadership of the Asociación de Comedores y Guarderías Infantíles, Gloria Menéndez Mina's new women's journal *Mujer* lauded her efforts as if they were of her own creation.

The impact of political motherhood under the Alianza with the support of a state focus on structural inequities extended social reforms into the legal system. Influenced by their attendance at the Ninth Pan American Child Congress held in Caracas in 1949, the Árbenz administration assumed a more systematic approach

Living in the World We Imagined 237

to social reforms.⁸⁸ This politicization of childhood coalesced with the goals of other institutions, and evidence of a more systematic approach came through the organization of a national conference. One year into the Árbenz presidency, the Asociación organized Guatemala's first Conference on the Defense of Children, held during December 14–21, 1951, to systematically address the persistent social problems that plagued the country.⁸⁹ More than sixty-five organizations and over 350 delegates attended from across the political spectrum.⁹⁰ The Alianza sent María Isabel Foronda de Vargas Romero, Irma Chávez de Alvarado, Haydée Godoy Arellano, Matilde Elena López, and Hortensia Hernández Rojás as delegates.⁹¹ The Alianza representatives brought four resolutions to the conference, including a broad-based program to support nutritional needs, provide bathing facilities for children of both sexes who otherwise lacked such facilities, increase maternity leave for nursing mothers to six months, and improve sanitary conditions. The president of the conference was Guatemala's director of public education, Carlos González Orellana, while Dr. Guillermo Balz, Rosa de Mora (of the Sociedad Protectora del Niño), Dr. Carlos Lara, and Alfonso Solórzano (Alaíde Foppa Falla's spouse) served as vice presidents.⁹²

The week-long conference on the condition of Guatemala's children reached one unavoidable conclusion, which set the sociopolitical agenda for the following three years as the delegates forged into new areas of reform. Quite simply, Guatemala's deep, historical socioeconomic inequities lay at the root of the festering social wounds, and without a fundamental and systematic restructuring, the problems of malnutrition and access to education for the vast majority of children would not be resolved. Although this conclusion had many possible implications, the conference organizers held three to be of utmost importance. Their first goal was to strengthen the family economically so that children could develop in a healthy manner. To achieve this, Guatemala needed to strengthen social assistance for children and mothers and to control alcoholism, perceived to be a concern among the working class. The second goal was to create legislation designed to protect children, which included recommendations for a civil code for minors, to address the issue of truant children who worked rather than attended school.⁹³ The issue of education for all Guatemalan children was a well-intentioned proposal but demonstrates the continued class bias, which did not address the reasons for truancy. The truth was that the education system was not a welcoming space for indigenous communities, and most children did not attend school because they were needed to financially support their families. The second commission at the end of the conference would acknowledge these serious historical structural inequities. The third goal was global in nature and aimed at discussing conflicts and the repercussions of war on children, a concern directed at the growing imperialist presence of the Cold War.[94]

The conference was closed by the creation of four commissions, led by Dr. Gilberto Burke, Manuel A. Santos, Haydée Godoy Arellano, and José Solis Rojas, respectively, designed to address four primary areas of concern: economics, education, socioeconomic problems, and legal reform.[95] For the delegates, poverty represented the root cause of all the challenges facing Guatemalan children. This included low salaries for working parents as a result of lack of enforcement of labor laws, which stipulated minimum salaries in both city and country. A second commission addressed education, exposing the historical neglect of this institution. Guatemala still lacked school buildings and teachers, especially indigenous teachers, and possessed a rural education system in which, out of 381,075 children, only 40,939 were in school due to a lack of resources. There was also a lack of vocational schools and teachers for special needs. The third commission focused on socioeconomic problems. The conference's fourth commission advised a revision of laws with respect to women and children, protection laws for children, and six months of maternity leave following birth.[96] Although these recommendations were considered radical, the desperate social conditions experienced by more than 80 percent of all Guatemalans render these conclusions somewhat modest (see chapter 3). The conference highlighted the severe challenges faced by Guatemala's children and those concerned with their well-being. Its comprehensive exploration of these factors was reflected in its equally bold conclusions. Of its many conclusions, the most significant perhaps lay in the development of the Consejo Nacional de la Infancia, an umbrella organization designed to coordinate all social reforms related to children.[97] As part of the conference, delegates visited existing children's centers, including the Jardín de Niños and Ciudad de los Niños in Guatemala City and El Manchén in Antigua.[98] They also met with Juan José Orozco Posadas of the National Assembly, presumably to promote permanent legislative action.[99] As María Vilanova de Árbenz stated in her final speech, without a complete economic transition, these problems would persist in the country. Those attending the conference agreed to support the economic reforms of the Jacobo Árbenz government, particularly those designed to address the historical inequities in land ownership.[100] The conclusions reached by the conference delegates reinforced one central conviction. Quite simply, without agrarian reform, Guatemala's semifeudal conditions would persist.[101]

The inclusive and visionary nature of the Alianza's maternal socialist approach was most evident in the last two years of the revolution. Following the conference on children, the Alianza shifted their attention to one of their core goals; namely, to incorporate rural and indigenous women. Their examination of working-class women revealed the extent to which they contributed to the national economy and were simultaneously ignored by the revolutionary masculine realm. The Alianza's assertions that the revolution was incomplete without the inclusion of domestic workers; poor, rural, and working-class ladinas; and indigenous women were nothing less than radical in the context of class and ethnic relations in Guatemala. The alliances created among the women of the Alianza Femenina Guatemalteca were very young in June 1954, and how successful the Alianza might have been in the long term will never be known.

The Alianza's cross-class tactic is evident in the type of analysis they developed, creating a two-pronged approach in their evaluation of the revolution's impact on working-class women. First, they identified the various roles women played in both the formal and the informal labor market. To that end, they identified four primary groups of working women in these two economies, including those who worked in factories, domestic workers, market women, and rural agricultural women. One of the most visible groups of working women included those connected with formal small industries, some of whom were members of the newly formed revolutionary labor unions. Despite the labor reforms that highlighted salary discrepancies and poor working conditions, such as the 1947 Labor Code, women continued to be ignored. The Alianza identified two subgroups within this particular group, women who worked in textile factories and women who took their sewing work home. Despite new salary minimums, women working in factories (the majority of whom worked in the textile industry) continued to be discriminated against, often not receiving the mandated Q1.25 daily wage. The Alianza acknowledged an exception to the rule in the Federación de Trabajadores Textiles, whose female members were receiving the minimum wage.

The Alianza's advocacy for unionized women attracted criticism from some labor leaders, particularly those in the urban industries. During the Árbenz administration, the labor unions were in a defensive mode and did not want to create further labor disruptions by demanding higher wages for women. Reflecting the dominant view that women's incomes were secondary to household welfare, union leaders expressed unwillingness to advocate for higher wages for women. While the exact number of female heads of household is not available, the possibility of civil disruption provided a convenient excuse not to advocate for their female colleagues. Patriarchal perception privileged male labor over that of women, and the Alianza's interference in union matters did not endear them to male unionists.[102] While they were concerned over the lower salaries they received in comparison with their male counterparts, urban working women were also primarily concerned about the safety of their children. According to Alianza statistics, for every fifteen working women, eleven had children. In Guatemala City, the Sociedad Protectora del Niño operated four houses for children with a total capacity for 960 children, with seven guarderías infantiles of equal capacity. The Alianza stated the rather obvious problem: quite simply, these services were insufficient for the number of children in need, particularly as these centers served only children over the age of two.[103]

Their inquiries into the experiences of working-class women brought the Alianza into alignment with the most invisible social sector in Guatemala City. Ubiquitous to the urban middle-class and upper-class household, domestic workers made up the majority of working-class women in the capital city. Dominated by rural and indigenous women, domestics worked without adequate job or personal security. Although the exact number of domestic workers is difficult to determine, according to 1950 national census data, 38,189 women worked in the capital.[104] This number, however, contradicts earlier data from 1940 that placed the number of domestics at over 84,000.[105] It is not likely that the total number of workers dropped by more than half within ten years. Despite the statistical discrepancies, the undeniable fact is that domestic workers represented the majority of working women in Guatemala City. Nevertheless, this segment of urban society remained invisible to revolutionary reformers. The disconnection between domestic workers and the revolutionary project remained so profound that when interviewed years later, one domestic worker revealed that she was not aware that a revolution had ever occurred in Guatemala City.[106]

The Alianza set out to identify the needs of domestic workers, whom they recognized as doubly exploited, first by their occupation and second by their invisibility, acknowledging the paucity of safeguards these women had. They experienced medical and physical neglect, poor wages, and sexual exploitation by male members of their household. Frequently alone and kinless, domestic workers and their children frequently worked fourteen-hour days, with no minimum guaranteed wage. Many young girls came to the capital with no family support, dependent upon the goodwill of their employers. In many cases, the streets were safer than these homes, as employers perceived domestics to be sexually available to all household males.[107] In addition, many domestic workers were from other parts of Central America, further isolating these women from one another

Living in the World We Imagined 241

linguistically and culturally. Despite the advancement of labor laws during the revolution, domestic workers were not incorporated into any meaningful labor legislation, further contributing to their invisibility. As Cindy Forster succinctly concludes, when the 1947 Labor Code overtly excluded domestic workers from any sort of labor protection or law, the revolution "enshrined the subordination of domestics."[108]

The unprecedented conclusions regarding working women were showcased in the Alianza's 1953 national congress. First, they acknowledged the valuable social service performed by domestic workers; many Alianza members no doubt were beneficiaries of just such service in their own homes, and they now vowed to provide protections for these women and children. Second, they publicly identified the abuse domestic workers suffered at the hands of their employers. In particular, they raised the issue of sexual abuse, laying the responsibility on the men of the family. They noted that if a domestic worker became pregnant, either the child was abandoned to the street or the worker herself was dismissed, because such pregnancies carried the obvious signs of patriarchal misbehavior. The Alianza publicly deplored these actions and called on all employers to change their behavior.[109]

The Alianza's public acknowledgment of sexual misbehavior in a public forum was historically unprecedented in Guatemala. Aside from Luz Valle's hint at the issue of abuse of domestic workers in 1936, ladinas had never addressed this very personal issue in such a public manner. Furthermore, the Alianza acknowledged the issue of sexual abuse of women during a period when this subject was not widely discussed in the upper echelons of Guatemalan society. Challenging men to modify their private behavior in the context of a national conference was an action whose significance cannot be underestimated. The men to whom the Alianza addressed their concerns were their own colleagues, peers, and perhaps in some cases their own spouses. In so doing, the Alianza's analysis and conclusions stand alone.

Unwilling to wait for broader structural changes, the Alianza developed their own strategy to assist working women. First, they pledged to create new organizations, mostly through labor unions, to increase salaries and improve working conditions for women. They also vowed to work for equal wages between men and women, and to achieve a minimum wage in both the urban and rural areas of Q1.25 and Q.80, respectively. Fourth, they agreed to work for an eight-hour workday, and finally, to create more centers for children of these workers, working alongside the government to protect both mothers and children. The Alianza pledged support to domestic workers, whom they urged to create organizations specifically designed to defend their own human and worker rights.[110] There is also some suggestion that the Alianza attempted to form a labor union for domestic workers and advocated for improved wages. The Alianza was a singular voice for this ignored and frankly invisible segment of Guatemalan society.[111]

Despite these unprecedented conclusions, the work of the Alianza must be examined in its particular context. According to their own analysis, Alianza members believed that domestic workers' inequitable social position came from two sources, their exploitative bosses and their backward culture, a singular comment that is not further explained.[112] Whether this referred to women's subservient attitude or their need to work outside of their own communities is unknown. This perspective, however, conveyed a common idea in the ladino community that melded a lifestyle born of intense poverty with indigenous cultural practices. Guatemalans outside of indigenous communities could not easily differentiate between the two aspects, and this comment reveals the complexity of social reform across the spectrum of class and culture in revolutionary Guatemala. Although Alianza members were among the very few in the ladino community to address such issues, they did so in the context of a society deeply polarized by ethnicity. While this does not detract from their efforts, it perhaps sheds some light on their own perceptions of and ambiguous attitudes toward Guatemala's indigenous communities. Equally important, however, is that in every other reference to women who likely would have been indigenous, the Alianza consistently used phrases related to their economic status or their social role of motherhood, an emphasis born out of their class consciousness.

In order to achieve these ambitious goals for working-class women, the Alianza took leadership roles in a variety of national labor congresses such as the Second Congreso Sindical Nacional in 1954, advocating directly to union leaders about the needs of working-class women. They invited labor representatives to their national congress in November 1953.[113] The Alianza's activism for working women found a positive reception from rural and campesino organizations. They became deeply involved in rural issues and were invited to participate in the third annual conference of the Confederación Nacional Campesina de Guatemala, held during February 19–21, 1954.[114] The outcome of their involvement is difficult to assess given that Árbenz was overthrown within four months of that conference.

The Alianza's ideological alignment with rural and working-class women exposed the gendered significance of the country's informal economic sector. For a majority of Guatemalan women, the informal economy *was* the economy, to

Living in the World We Imagined 243

paraphrase J. T. Way.[115] Making up the largest number of women in Guatemala, rural women lived and worked under the most onerous conditions imaginable. Despite the simple fact that they were integral to the economic foundation of Guatemala, they had been historically marginalized by the state, including the revolutionary project. By all accounts of the era, these women worked the longest hours at the most thankless tasks and were arguably subject to the most extreme degradation.[116] Women of the Alianza were so shocked by their findings that they were forced to conclude that rural women lived in feudal conditions.[117] They pointed out that few people in the capital city had any idea about the type of work rural women were required to do and the horrible living conditions under which they survived.[118] Along with the daily chores of caring for children, grinding corn, fetching water, and weaving, rural women were required to work alongside their male family members in the agricultural industry.[119] To bolster their argument that rural women were deserving of reforms, the Alianza highlighted their economic contributions during their 1953 national congress. Ninety percent of Guatemala's coffee was picked by women working twelve-, fourteen-, and sixteen-hour days. Since farm managers only paid male family members, this agricultural labor went unpaid. In addition, few rural families had sufficient nutrition, eating only beans, tortillas and chiles, or even just tortillas and salt. It is small wonder that the Alianza concluded that rural women were victims of incredible exploitation due to horrific working conditions and the patriarchal views of men who saw them only as instruments or beasts of burden.[120]

These findings galvanized the Alianza to expand their organization into the rural areas, believing that the revolution would remain incomplete without the inclusion of rural and indigenous women. The Alianza chose Dora Franco y Franco, Ester de Urrutia, and Daisy Alfaro to initiate this relationship with rural women. The three women visited farm communities on a weekly basis (every Sunday, the only day rural women had some time off from work) throughout the Árbenz era to understand the challenges of rural women as well as to recruit them into the organization.[121] They had two primary goals during these visits. First, the Alianza fervently believed that only after the development of a self-consciousness about their rights as women and workers could these women change their lives.[122] Within this consciousness building, the Alianza now began to advocate for the enfranchisement of illiterate women.[123] Illiterate women had been excluded in the 1945 optional enfranchisement, and the Alianza understood their potential power as voters.

The second goal was the recruitment of these women into their organization.

They focused their energies on the two closest rural departments, Escuintla and Santa Rosa, which both had strong labor associations. Records indicate that Alianza members visited the regions of Mauricio, Los Cerritos, El Salto, and Camantulul. By 1953, the Alianza had 677 committees in Escuintla and 250 in Santa Rosa. In doing so, the Alianza cemented their distinction as one of the only organizations that consistently worked to support and enhance the lives of working women.[124]

The Alianza's alliance with rural women brought them into direct conflict with one of Jacobo Árbenz's most popular and controversial social reforms, Decree 900, and the Agrarian Reform. The Agrarian Reform Law of 1952 mandated the first redistribution of land since the Spanish conquest and became the pinnacle reform of the Árbenz presidency. By the revolutionary era, the United Fruit Company held 566,000 acres of land and employed more than fifteen thousand workers, and thus agrarian reform struck at the heart of Guatemala's historically entrenched, inequitable social and economic structure.[125] Scholars such as Piero Gleijeses have argued that since only uncultivated land could be expropriated for redistribution, Decree 900 was in effect a moderate law cast in a capitalist mold.[126] Already suspicious of Guatemala's revolutionary project, the US State Department perceived this to be an attack on a US business and saw it as further evidence of Árbenz's communist affiliations. For landless Guatemalans, however, the 1952 law continues to stand as a shining moment among centuries of impoverishment. While the precise figure is unknown, it is generally believed that roughly one hundred thousand heads of families received land (some place the number slightly higher or lower). Along with land, the reform also provided credit to help families pay for the land.[127] By 1953, the benefits of the reform were apparent. Campesino families had more food, clothes, and access to education.

The Alianza strongly supported the land reform law because it directly benefited rural women, but it immediately became apparent that the law was not being applied equally to both male and female heads of households.[128] The Alianza assigned María Jérez Rivera de Fortuny as the director for land distribution to women.[129] Few records of the land reform law survived the 1954 overthrow and even less regarding its application to women. However, these few sources detail just how entrenched the bias against rural women had become, and how clear this was to the Alianza. Rural women came to their contacts in the Alianza, who then directly petitioned the National Agrarian Reform Commission. One such letter of protest was written by Ester de Urrutia, who described how a single mother whose request for land as head of her household was denied solely on the basis that she was a woman.[130] Applying the same gendered analysis they had used in other situations, the Alianza again challenged the patriarchal system, which had remained intact even after radical reforms. "In countries that have maintained backward feudalism, they have also preserved habits and mentality including a false morality that authorizes men to reduce women to objects without property, supreme servitude, and obedience."[131] Their confrontations with the male hierarchy made their way onto the front pages of national papers. Printing both his picture and his name, the Alianza challenged one local Agrarian Reform Committee member in Alotenango to change his mind.[132] His response was simply, "I refuse to give land to women." In the face of this intransigence, the Alianza resolved to integrate women into the national agrarian reform program through equal access to credit, fair prices for their crops, and improved available agricultural technology.[133] In order to mobilize women to defend their right to land ownership, the Alianza vowed to increase their contacts with rural communities and associations.[134]

The experiences of rural and indigenous women with the agrarian reform process echo the experiences of other working-class women with labor unions and political enfranchisement. While the revolutionary rhetoric of full democratic participation clearly included women of all social classes, the reality proved to be far more complex. In a historical context of political repression and economic deprivation, it was inconceivable to a majority of Guatemalan men that they must now share in the revolutionary bounty. The patriarchal model upon which Guatemala's socioeconomic structures were founded had not been fundamentally shifted by the few years of democratic practice. The idealized family model that privileged male paid labor and female household duties as wife and mother remained firmly intact. Therefore, women's demands for fair wages in the labor unions and for land as head of household appeared to be unnecessary, as they were seen as "secondary" contributors to individual households. Their requests also directly competed with those of men for limited resources, a reality that most men of all social classes were not willing to address.

Although the Alianza has been associated with rural working-class women, they also created an alliance with market women in several markets in Guatemala City. Together, they established a commission to investigate working conditions at Market no. 2.[135] Their conclusions were disturbing to say the least. Many of the market women did not have a stand for their produce, selling food directly on the ground, while their children spent long periods of time in the market because the local comedores infantiles did not remain open long enough. In response, the Alianza's commission petitioned the municipal representative to establish a safe working environment for the women and their children.[136] Furthermore, they decided that the market needed its own daycare center, another guardería. On January 21, 1954, a fire destroyed many of the stalls and goods at another market. Members of the Alianza helped to establish an emergency committee, the Comité de Locatarias (Market Women's Committee), which included María S. de Galich, Ester de Urrutia, Victoria Chajón Chúa, Julia Zapata de Frike, and Julia de Cruz. They worked with representatives of the Partido de la Revolución Guatemalteca and market women Josefina Rodríguez and Anita de Mejía to distribute clothing, food, and money.[137]

The Alianza's cross-class alliance with the market women also facilitated a growing awareness of the economic vulnerability of women in the informal economy during the revolutionary era. Although scholars have not explored the state of the economy during the revolutionary decade, through the lens of class and gender, it was a significant factor for the growing internal opposition. Guatemala moved into the revolutionary period with a robust economy (thanks in part to Jorge Ubico's austerity measures and his intolerance for corruption), and it remained strong under both governments despite market fluctuations and inflation. Even the archbishop, who usually found little to praise about the revolutionary governments, touted Guatemala's economic bonanza in a 1948 pastoral letter.[138] This strong economic growth was mitigated by the country's continued dependence upon coffee and fruit, making Guatemala vulnerable to the ebbs and flows of the international market. The absence of a large and sustained domestic market also reduced the benefits of strong coffee prices in the post–World War II economic boom. Consequently, the cost of basic goods rose substantially throughout the Arévalo regime due in part to his attempts to placate opposition from the Guatemalan elite as well as growing criticism from the US State Department.

By 1947, the United Fruit Company had become vocal against the Arévalo government, which responded by modifying some of the revolution's reforms. During this pivotal year, Arévalo eased the Labor Code by placing restrictions on workers' ability to strike for substantial pay increases. On September 1, 1947, the government also removed all controls on the production, distribution, and sale of basic goods such as sugar. The price of bread was frozen, and minimum prices were set on corn, cotton, wheat, and meat.[139] In a final blow, the president terminated the Guatemalan Office of Price Stabilization in early November 1947, ending all rationing and distribution controls, with few exceptions.[140] As a result, inflation on daily staples continued at a steady pace throughout the late 1940s and early 1950s, peaking during 1949 (see table 6.1). The Arévalo government attempted to ease the impact of inflation through a series of initiatives including credit to rural farmers, modest land redistribution, and an extensive social security network, but these had only limited results. In 1948, the Instituto de Fomento de Producción (Institute for Production Promotion) was created to encourage the production of domestic food items through the expansion of loans and agricultural cooperatives. Arévalo, however, was unsuccessful in curbing a growing government deficit and instituted an income tax. Although the strength of the labor unions resulted in a generalized increase of wages in the formal economy during this same era, these gains were reduced by the inflation rate.

By the 1950s, these economic fluctuations were becoming truly onerous for the poor and working class. Sugar and corn had doubled in price since 1944, while other basic food staples such as rice and beans more than tripled. In contrast, families working in the formal economy earned as little as sixty to eighty quetzals monthly.[141] As Jim Handy notes, although wages increased dramatically, "the booming inflation rate ate up most of the real gains in income."[142] While those of the middle class were largely insulated from these fluctuations, those dependent upon the informal economy felt its impact most keenly. The rise of sugar prices in particular caused an outcry from those women who earned a living making sweets. For poor women whose livelihood depended upon sugar, every fluctuation reduced their daily profits. According to a report issued by the Alianza in 1953, 85 percent of Guatemalan families did not receive enough income to meet their nutritional needs, a statistic that continues to echo eerily into the present.[143] Women such as Ester de Urrutia had been working with poor and market women in Guatemala City since 1944, and in the face of this growing economic strain, they convinced the Alianza to adopt a strategy to address the high cost of living early in their organization.[144] It became one of their most important issues, and they included the phrase "Luchemos contra la carestía de la vida" (We are struggling against the high cost of living) as a catchphrase at the bottom of every issue of their monthly bulletin *Mujeres*, campaigning for a reduction in sugar prices.[145]

The growing inflation had become an effective battle cry for the revolutionary opposition by August 1953, prompting the creation of a national conference on the high cost of living. The Alianza joined forces with the female sections of all the pro-revolutionary political parties to participate (three women from each party attended).[146] Initiated by the Confederación General de Trabajadores de

Guatemala (CGTG) labor union, the organizing committee included a wide variety of unions, political parties, and civil organizations.[147] All those involved in the project believed that the participation of market women was of critical importance, and they were invited to join the dialogue.[148] The final committee included economic lawyers Guillermo Noriega Morales and Justo Rufíno Cabrera, Elsa de Guerra Borges of the Alianza, María del Pilar Arroyo of the Liga de Locatarias, Bernardo Lemus of the Alianza de la Juventud Democrática de Guatemala, José Luis Caceros and Juan Cuéllar Lorenzana of the CGTG, and Clodoveo Torres Mozz and Otilio Marroquín of the Confederación Nacional Campesina de Guatemala.[149]

The three-day conference, held during August 26–28, 1953, examined and highlighted the root causes of Guatemala's international economic vulnerability and its internal economic disparity. More than 350 people attended the conference, and its resolutions demonstrated a wide range of concerns, both urban and rural.[150] The delegates analyzed several issues believed to be key factors affecting the poorest Guatemalans, including the high cost of transportation, rent and housing, food, medicine, clothing, and low wages. Among the many root causes identified, the elite stranglehold on the economy remained the primary contributing factor to the current problem, and the committee laid the responsibility for at least some of their country's economic woes on this small privileged sector. A lack of industrialization and technological improvements in the agricultural sector were also believed to be contributing factors. The delegates' analysis of the situation led to the creation of a twelve-page document, which outlined a comprehensive plan for controlling the inflation rate. First, the committee assured the nation that economic factors were under the control of the government. Second, they pointed out that inflation had begun in the years prior to the revolution, thereby absolving the revolutionary governments of complete responsibility. Third, they highlighted Guatemala's dependence on its mono-agricultural economy and the foreign monopoly on transportation and land.[151] One of the most significant resolutions acknowledged that women workers were particularly discriminated against due to the inequity of their wages.[152] The delegates created a permanent commission to monitor the inflation rate and to advocate for changes as they saw fit.[153] Among those appointed to this permanent national committee were Ester de Urrutia and Dora Franco y Franco of the Alianza, economist Carmen Vargas de Amézquita, and Maximina Valdés representing the market women. A national campaign was initiated at the end of the conference with a call to increase minimum daily wages, even asking for donations to help the country's poorest families. Within ten months, however, the revolution ended, and so did their work.

The Overthrow of Jacobo Árbenz and the End of the Alianza Femenina Guatemalteca

After ten years of sociopolitical reform, Guatemala's revolutionary democratic experiment came to an abrupt end in June 1954. The ramifications of this reality came swiftly, as one by one, reformers, politicians and organizers, teachers and campesinos vanished or went into hiding. The embassies of Mexico and Argentina became the temporary home to hundreds of Guatemalans identified as "communists" by the US State Department and the new government headed by General Carlos Castillo Armas, appointed leader of the invasion force. Schoolchildren were brought to the National Palace to view enlarged images of tortured bodies, savage acts supposedly committed by the Árbenz government.[154] The physical impact of the antirevolutionary violence had an inordinate impact on the rural population, however. While those in the urban areas sought refuge or left the country, the majority of the direct violence landed on rural workers and farms, particularly on those who had been union leaders or had received land during the Agrarian Reform. The exact death toll throughout the country remains unknown, but testimonies of those who survived the period speak of seeing bodies floating by in the rivers for days and of mass graves. Fear returned to the country in the summer of 1954, a simmering and pervasive anxiety that has filtered down through the decades to the present day.[155]

Just how the revolutionary project came to such a sudden end has been the focus of much of the historiography surrounding the Guatemalan revolution. While the initial analysis focused extensively on the well-known collusion between the Central Intelligence Agency, the US State Department, and the United Fruit Company, more recent scholarship includes factors internal to Guatemala itself. Here, a general consensus has been reached by historians. Although the Guatemalan revolution affected the country's entire population, it primarily originated from, and benefited, the urban ladino and ladina middle class. It has become increasingly evident that the key to the revolution's eventual demise also lies in this same social sector. Jim Handy, one of the first historians to suggest this, argues that despite the presence of the US administration, the threat of an invasion force, and diplomatic isolation from the rest of Latin America, internal sociopolitical dynamics proved to be the ultimate testing ground for

TABLE 6.1 Prices on Primary Commodities, 1940–1952[1]

		1940	1941	1942	1943	1944	1945	1946	1947	1948	1949	1950	1951	1952
corn	/lb	1.5	1.5	0.0	2.2	2.5	3.1	3.1	3.0	4.3	6.0	5.0	5.0	3.4
beans	/lb	3.0	2.2	0.0	4.3	4.7	6.9	6.5	4.5	8.0	12.7	8.7	6.0	11.0
rice	/lb	3.5	3.5	0.0	5.4	5.1	8.6	9.6	7.9	9.9	12.5	9.6	14.5	11.5
sugar	/lb	4.0	4.0	0.0	4.0	4.4	5.0	5.8	6.3	8.4	8.4	7.1	8.0	8.0
flour[2]	/lb	6.4	6.0	0.0	7.0	8.0	8.2	9.5	11.3	13.1	13.6	12.2	13.0	13.6
flour	/lb	5.3	5.1	0.0	6.2	.6.9	7.1	8.5	9.8	11.8	13.2	11.3	11.0	11.9
coffee	/lb	10.0	10.0	0.0	15.9	18.0	20.3	26.9	33.06	35.7	44.9	54.3	60.0	60.0
lard	/lb	12.8	11.1	0.0	25.8	31.0	36.2	42.8	38.7	42.2	46.9	31.9	39.0	32.3
eggs	/lb	16.1	14.8	0.0	21.6	25.4	35.2	39.3	41.7	47.5	69.2	58.2	58.0	59.3
meat	/lb	6.0	6.0	0.0	6.0	8.2	11.2	12.0	12.8	14.2	21.2	19.2	15.0	16.0
coal	Q							1.05	1.30	1.31	1.34	1.37	1.37	1.38
wood	Q							1.00	1.12	1.13	.99	1.20	1.15	1.18

1. GD, Container 6, "Informe de Alianza Femenina Guatemalteca a la Comisión de Defensa y Protección de la infancia del Primer Congreso Nacional," November 26, 2.

2. Two categories of flour were listed; the first is foreign import, and the second is domestic.

the Guatemalan revolutionaries.[156] Susanne Jonas concurs, concluding that a sizeable portion of the urban petty bourgeoisie, who were initial supporters of the revolution, eventually went along with its destruction: "Many of them were primarily interested in their own advancement; they were ambivalent about giving workers and peasants an independent power base."[157] The increasing activism of the rural and working class following the 1952 Agrarian Reform also amplified urban middle-class concerns despite the rhetorical class consciousness of the revolutionary leaders.

Historians have also concluded that the role of the Guatemalan military was another significant factor in the overthrow of Jacobo Árbenz. Although he was highly respected within the military ranks (a factor that historians believe minimized the number of coup attempts against his administration), both Handy and Jonas contend that the decentralized and democratic nature of the military contributed to its ambivalence and lack of response to Castillo Armas. The activism of the rural population threatened the military, who vocally declared their resolve to defend Árbenz and Guatemala from any foreign invaders.[158] Therefore, the military's apathetic support of the Árbenz administration can be understood in light of their concern about the growing rural unrest, which the military did not want to get out of hand.[159] Greg Grandin summarizes this new direction:

> Would the revolution have endured if the United States had not interfered or would internal contradictions have forced its demise? Although the answer cannot be known, the question shifts the focus to include the role Guatemalans played in the making of their own history. It is important to make this shift not just out of political sympathy but also to understand how larger structures of power articulate with local interests and tensions: if capitalism and imperialism think globally, they need to act locally if they are to succeed.[160]

The Alianza's experiences during the months leading up to Árbenz's overthrow exemplify these conclusions.

The fear of an invasion was palpable in early 1954 as rumors spread throughout the pro-revolutionary sectors. As the United States effectively isolated the country, it signed defense treaties with both Honduras and Nicaragua in 1954.[161] Cut off from previous allies, Árbenz imported arms from Czechoslovakia, and delegates from the United States used this event to justify their stance against Guatemala at the Tenth Inter-American Conference of the Organization of American States in Caracas in March 1954. The State Department seized upon the arms deliveries as confirmation of communist infiltration into the American hemisphere. Guatemala's hopes were dashed when they were left to stand alone against the United States during the conference, despite informal assurances from a majority of Latin American nations that they would not support an antirevolutionary position. When the final vote was tallied on an anticommunist resolution proposed by the United States, all but Guatemala had voted against the besieged nation, with Mexico and Argentina choosing to abstain, a result that all but sanctioned a foreign invasion.

The most fervent Árbenz supporters now prepared for an armed struggle.[162] Even though the Alianza had participated in the global peace movement, they now shifted their organization into a military one.[163] The executive committee of the Alianza sent out a notice to members, instructing them to organize brigades against an invasion force. Members were told to report to prearranged headquarters should the need arise so that Guatemalan women could defend their independence, progress, and national honor.[164] The Alianza also assured the government and the army of their support to defend national sovereignty against the bands of traitors in the pay of the United Fruit Company, naming their all-female brigade in honor of María Chinchilla Recinos.[165] In the growing crisis, they reorganized their association, renaming themselves the Alianza Femenina Guatemalteca y Compania, Sociedad en Comandita. Commercially, the association would be known as the Granjas Femeninas de Capacitación.[166] To date, there has been little analysis on the preparation of the revolutionaries against the possibility of invasion, in an erroneous conclusion perhaps that it did not exist. Some sources, however, suggest that a significant underground movement awaited word from Árbenz to actively resist the forces of Castillo Armas. That call never came.

The Alianza also reached out to their international colleagues for support, namely from two of the largest transnational women's organizations, the WILPF and the WIDF. By March 1954, they had called on everyone who supported the enfranchisement of illiterate women, the alleviation of the high cost of living, social security, the establishment of child-care centers, a minimum wage, and more schools; they outlined the sociopolitical democratic progress Guatemala had made following decades of dictatorship. Once again, the Alianza reiterated that Guatemala was not a satellite of international communism. They accused the United Fruit Company of conspiring with the United States to maintain their economic monopoly in Guatemala, as they had done in both Nicaragua and the Dominican Republic.[167] Understanding that the United States would not leave the Árbenz administration in power, the WILPF and the WIDF now responded

Living in the World We Imagined 253

to this crisis. Declaring the threatened invasion to be imperialistic and illegal in the international courts, leadership from both groups used what influence they had with the United States and the international community. Heloise Brainerd wrote a personal letter to the US State Department to advocate directly on behalf of Guatemala. In the following months, she and others continued to inform all within their circle of the injustice their Guatemalan peers were experiencing.[168]

The women of the Alianza became increasingly isolated in the waning months of the revolution, clearly revealing that they had been abandoned by all but the most ardent revolutionaries. Their insistence that the law be applied equally to both men and women with regard to land reform, union wages, and civil protection for domestic workers placed them at odds with the majority of their middle- and upper-class peers. In Guatemala City, most ladinas had been unwilling to support their critique of Guatemala's social, economic, and gendered structure. Two weeks before the end, the Alianza issued their final declaration:

> The enemies of freedom and progress want to prevent the democratic development of Guatemala and violently overthrow the patriotic regime of Colonel Jacobo Árbenz, under which the people have been able to fight with full guarantees in defense of their interests, for more bread for our homes and for our children. The enemies of our freedom and our independence want to sow terror and death and give the country back to the plundering of foreign monopolies.
>
> The Guatemala Women's Alliance calls upon people of all political ideologies and religious creeds to occupy a first-rank place in the struggle waged today by our people. Women must fight shoulder to shoulder against those who organize foreign intervention, against those who want to turn back the wheel of history and plunge our people into dictatorship.[169]

No one answered this plea.

Almost ten years to the day after María Chinchilla Recinos was killed in the presence of hundreds of middle-class ladinas, the revolution's second democratically elected president, Jacobo Árbenz, resigned from his position and sought exile in the Mexican embassy. Árbenz turned the government over to Carlos Díaz, who outlawed the Communist Party but endorsed the continuation of Árbenz's social reforms. The counterrevolutionary invasion under Castillo Armas continued, however, and on June 29, 1954, he replaced Díaz with Elfego Monzón, essentially ending the revolution. The US State Department concluded their intervention successfully, considering that the operation had cost fewer than one hundred lives.[170] The real death toll, however, emerged in the weeks and months that followed, with the persecution and murder of thousands of Guatemalans, particularly in the rural areas. This repression was so brutal that within a year those who were implementing the new policies were forced to acknowledge the terrible cost of their actions on Guatemalans.

The Alianza was permanently ruptured by the abrupt conclusion of the Árbenz presidency. While Guatemalans were accustomed to regime changes and dictatorial military coups d'etat, the end of the Árbenz government was a different sort of political transition. Its political leadership went into exile, and its accumulated knowledge was now scattered across Latin America. The silence and terror that emerged put an end to Guatemala's integrated feminist movement, which would not emerge again until the 1980s and 1990s, when, during genocidal levels of violence, groups of Mayan indigenous women and ladinas once again organized into feminist groups with ideals reminiscent of those of the Alianza Femenina Guatemalteca.[171]

The Urrutia family became a target in the weeks following the overthrow of Jacobo Árbenz, and their experience mirrored that of thousands of other Guatemalans who were forced to go into exile. Ester's position as secretary general of the Alianza marked her as an enemy of the new Guatemalan regime, and both Ester and Manuel sought refuge in the Argentine embassy, where they remained for three months.[172] Typical of her personality, while in the embassy Ester spoke with and comforted other Guatemalans seeking refuge there whose lives had been so radically interrupted. Among the many refugees, Ester developed a friendship with a young man who shared her asthma condition. The two spent hours discussing the Guatemalan revolution and its many sociopolitical ideals. Ester de Urrutia's contribution to the growing revolutionary mentality of Ernesto Guevara, or "Che" as he later became known to the world, would become apparent in a few years' time. Along with hundreds of other Guatemalan women, her daughter, Julia, pleaded for an audience with the new President Castillo Armas to defend their family members who had sought shelter in ten embassies around the capital city. Julia Urrutia waited outside the National Palace for days and was ultimately the only petitioner to be received by Castillo Armas. She discussed her mother's situation and was given permission to bring her daily food and comfort. At the end of July 1954, Ester and Manuel Urrutia, along with members of their family and several hundred other Guatemalans, were allowed to leave for exile in Argentina.[173] The couple returned in 1956 and immediately resumed their work. Ester herself continued to work with groups of market women and remained politically engaged until her death in 1964.[174]

Conclusion

The revolutionary decade stands alone as a singular point in Guatemalan history during which the idealism of politically active women could be realistically achieved. Following the emergence of the cross-class alliance of women who helped bring about the Guatemalan revolution in June and October 1944, some urban ladinas discovered that their struggle had only begun. Consequently, they initiated a second revolution, one in which historically disenfranchised women were sought out as public social actors. The first six years of feminist activism pioneered a broader vision that included the transformation of Guatemala's foundational structures. Influenced by the needs of working-class, rural, and indigenous women, a new political and maternal feminism emerged from within the social reform movement embodied by the Alianza Femenina Guatemalteca. The simple freedom to act autonomously was a critical factor in the rise of the type of feminism embraced by these women. Their gender analysis regarding socioeconomic conditions drew them to new and startling conclusions regarding the historical barriers of ethnicity and class that separated Guatemalan women from one another. Unlike many of their middle-class counterparts, who feared a radical revolutionary transformation among the rural poor, the Alianza actively sought out poor and working-class women to fulfill their revolutionary goals. They aligned themselves with those who needed the revolution the most and yet who often seemed to be the most invisible to those in power. While poor and rural women were the rhetorical targets of reform, the patriarchal structure shielded them from becoming direct recipients of reform, subsumed within broader class analysis and a traditional family structure. Without the complete integration of all Guatemalans women and men, the Alianza believed the revolution to be incomplete. Incorporating this idea in all of their projects, they successfully created a world they had so long only been able to imagine. This transformation held up for only a very brief moment in time, but it did happen.

No longer willing to stay within the gendered parameters of female activism, the Alianza extended their reforms to examine the structural obstacles restricting and oppressing Guatemalan women. The particulars of Guatemala's entrenched economic inequities facilitated by deep racism required the Alianza to carry out the type of analysis few others were doing in 1950s Guatemala. The economic and social structural analysis they integrated into their legal and social reforms distinguishes the Alianza from all previous women's organizations in Guatemala. Maintaining an autonomous space, they insisted that gender be integrated into the state's policies. They drew their authority from the firsthand experiences of Guatemalan women of all social classes and ethnicities, and argued that women's concerns must be considered alongside other revolutionary concerns. While the Alianza actively engaged with socialist structural analysis, they also insisted that gender be included in the broader class and structural evaluations. Their work with nutrition and daycare centers brought them into direct contact with the most marginalized in Guatemala City, and in society in general. The awareness they developed through their examination of class and gender drew their attention to groups of traditionally marginalized and invisible women including factory workers, domestics, market women, and women working in the rural agricultural sector.

Analysis of the Alianza's activities also reveals the limitations of the Guatemalan revolution. Their ideals broke through the historical barriers between urban and rural, ladina and indigenous women. They undertook the struggle for women's equality across race and class in all aspects of life, including economic, civil, political, and social. While revolutionary laws began to address the deep, gendered disparity, the Alianza directly challenged the very heart of patriarchy and racism by incorporating the concerns of rural and poor working-class women. They broke new ground in both class and race relations, initiating national conferences on the defense of children and the high cost of living and advocating for agrarian reform on behalf of rural women. Their insistence that rural and indigenous women be included in the revolutionary project threatened the very basis of the racial and class privileges that sustained the urban ladino and ladina middle class. Uncomfortable with the radicalism of their ideas, the majority of politically active ladinas during the Arévalo period did not join. What the effects of their organization might have been joins the many questions left unanswered by the revolution's abrupt end. For the most politically outspoken women, the overthrow of Árbenz marked an end to their work. The leadership of the Alianza along with many educators and social reformers left Guatemala, some never to return.

Seven

GOD DOESN'T LIKE THE REVOLUTION
THE ARCHBISHOP, THE MARKET WOMEN, AND THE GENDER OF ECONOMY, 1944–1954

Fellow Catholics: our freedom of conscience is in danger, and our Church and its representatives are seriously threatened.
—*Concha Estéves, October 1953*

Let us campaign against communism in the name of God and with God, but never guided by petty political interests. . . . Every Catholic must fight against communism because of their identity as a Catholic.
—*Mariano Rossell y Arellano, April 4, 1954*

On the afternoon of July 11, 1951, a labor dispute between the director of a state-run orphanage and its employees erupted into a violent standoff. Hundreds of women from the nearby central market rushed to the scene to protest the dismissal of several employees. The conflict, which eventually involved several thousand people, persisted for two full days and resulted in at least four deaths with injuries to more than seventy others, many of whom had been innocent bystanders. In response to the civilian clash around the orphanage, the Centro Educativo Asistencial, all constitutional guarantees were suspended for the next thirty days in order to restore social order in the capital city. As instigators of the event, the women working in the market around the cathedral in the central plaza were catapulted onto the national stage as the new symbols of an antirevolutionary movement rapidly growing in the face of the Jacobo Árbenz administration's increasingly comprehensive socioeconomic reforms. Mobilized by a perceived threat to their social, religious, and economic interests, the market women emerged as unlikely allies of those anxious to preserve the economic monopoly of the elite landowners, a strong patriarchal society, and the strength of conservative political parties.

The July uprising marked a new phase in the growing internal opposition to the revolutionary project spearheaded by the Catholic Church hierarchy and its archbishop, Mariano Rossell y Arellano, who is generally regarded as the informal leader of the antirevolutionary movement. Historians have focused extensively on his covert collusion with both the US Central Intelligence Agency and the State Department, contributing to the historiographic trend with respect to the external factors related to the revolution's downfall.[1] The political alliances the archbishop developed with internal opposition movements, however, have received far less attention despite highly publicized events such as the July riot, and fundamental questions regarding the internal antirevolutionary alliance between the archbishop and urban women remain unanswered.[2]

Urban women of all social classes in fact became a critical element in the Catholic Church hierarchy's strategy against the revolutionary government, and the archbishop sought out women to support the antirevolutionary campaign in two fundamental ways. Although initially reluctant to acknowledge female suffrage granted to literate women in 1945, once he understood its potential, Rossell y Arellano wrote frequent pastoral letters urging Guatemalan women to vote against the revolution and its threat to faith and national security. Following the 1948 municipal elections and a general recognition that the opposition could not win in the electoral arena due to the overwhelming numbers of rural male voters, the antirevolutionary movement shifted its strategy to an arguably far more effective approach. Drawing upon the social power of public demonstrations by hundreds (and frequently thousands) of middle- and upper-class ladinas, the antirevolutionary movement effectively mobilized urban residents against the revolution and its purported threat to family, home, and faith. While the traditional sociopolitical structure was momentarily disrupted by the overthrow of Jorge Ubico, only a small number of women joined politically active groups such as the Alianza Femenina Guatemalteca, and a majority of women were unwilling to engage in a complete transformation of the social order. As the antirevolutionary movement gained strength, the very women who had helped to initiate the revolution now moved to a sociopolitical position that included a strong anticommunist and antirevolutionary stance. The veracity of this transition became evident in the countless demonstrations dominated by urban women during the final years of the revolution. Consequently, this chapter reveals that just as the revolutionary project has been fundamentally imagined as a masculine endeavor, so too has its demise.

The church and its allies also created an alliance with the city's market women, who had captured the public's attention and galvanized the revolutionary opposition. While the 1944 revolution claimed María Chinchilla Recinos as its symbol against Jorge Ubico, the antirevolutionary movement also gained an iconic image for those who wished to overthrow it. Charismatic and illiterate, Concha Estéves led the market women in Guatemala City, emerging as one of the most enduring and curious images of this multifaceted antirevolutionary social movement. Sought out by the powerful university student antirevolutionary organization, the Comité de Estudiantes Universitarios Anticomunistas (CEUA), and political parties for their emphatic anticommunism, Estéves and the market women initiated and participated in countless street protests following the July incident at the orphanage. They became indelibly linked with the mounting political opposition against Jacobo Árbenz and his working relationship with the small Guatemalan Communist Party. Like so many others in Guatemala City, the market women held a variety of opinions regarding the revolution. While some of them worked directly with Elisa Martínez de Arévalo and the Asociación de Comedores, and then with María Vilanova de Árbenz and the Asociación de Comedores y Guarderías Infantiles, other market women protested against any revolutionary reforms vigorously. Despite their multifaceted affiliations and activism distinct from the religious and political agenda of Guatemala's elite, the market women's reputation remains closely linked with that of the Guatemalan Catholic Church and its archbishop, Mariano Rossell y Arellano.

The women who worked in the market occupied a unique sociopolitical space in Guatemala City, a site in which traditional gender roles held less authority than elsewhere. Understanding the market women's antirevolutionary activism reveals a complex world where gender, the economy, class, and public opinion interacted. As the cost of living rose steadily throughout the revolutionary decade, its economic impact was particularly onerous on market women. Working in the informal economy, market women were particularly vulnerable to price fluctuations. Their activism against the country's inflation therefore was not incongruous with their social position but was a logical response to an increasingly difficult economic situation. The struggle brought the market women into the public sphere, aligning them with the political ideology of Guatemala's economically privileged and politically powerful. In so doing, the market women offered legitimacy to an antirevolutionary movement whose self-interest in overthrowing the

Árbenz government was blatantly apparent. The revolutionary era's economy and the subsequent high cost of living has received little historical attention, and an examination of it provides another key to the intricacies of Guatemala's internal political opposition to the revolution during this highly studied ten years.

Consideration of the relationship between urban women of all social classes and the church-sponsored opposition augments the small but growing body of literature that explores the internal dynamics of the Guatemalan revolutionary period. Francesca Miller was the first to question the role of the anticommunist women's movement, through church affiliations or private charitable institutions, suggesting that they may have served to create and sustain antirevolutionary sentiment against Árbenz.[3] More recently, scholars have argued definitively that it is no longer possible to see the overthrow of Jacobo Árbenz as merely a product of US intervention, crediting groups such as the market women as significant in the outcome of June 1954.[4] The multifaceted and coordinated efforts by women of all social classes including the market women disallow the possibility that they acted as mere pawns in the dangerous international game of foreign intervention initiated by the archbishop. Rather, these women acted very much on their own terms, working pragmatically with the people who most suited their needs and ideologies.

The Catholic Church, Gender, and the Guatemalan Revolution

On the eve of the revolution, the Guatemalan Catholic Church hierarchy appeared an unlikely leader of an antirevolutionary movement. Following the desamortización, the church became so weakened that by 1944 there were a mere 130 priests in the country for a population of over 3 million.[5] More than a quarter of this number (40 priests) resided in Guatemala City for its 170,000 inhabitants.[6] As Bruce Calder concludes, the church had become "small, poor, disorganized and uninfluential in national life. There were few priests and Catholic institutions outside of the churches—formal Catholicism was weak while popular and syncretistic Catholicism prospered."[7] In response, church authorities centralized the institution's power in the capital, drawing significant moral authority from its traditional construction of patriarchy and family. Although religious leaders such as Rossell y Arellano attempted to portray the church as a champion of the poor and the working class, they held to traditional paternalistic notions of divine providence that allowed for human inequalities in order for the rich to govern the poor. Historian Douglass Sullivan-González argues that, rather than focusing on

Pope Leo XIII's *Rerum Novarum* and its emphasis on the worker and laborers, Guatemalan clerics elected to use race or ethnic identity as a defining principle to establish a coherent religious vision.[8] In this pre–Vatican II era, the Catholic hierarchy maintained that the poverty and misery pervading Guatemalan society was not due to class conflict or the profound inequities in the social system, but rather a national rejection of Catholic moral precepts that the church believed provided meaning and dignity to Guatemalans.

Several critical shifts in church-state relations and personnel in the years leading up to the 1944 revolution fundamentally altered ecclesiastical fortunes. Although liberalism had been a traditional adversary of the church, an alliance emerged between the Ubico state and the church with the installation of Archbishop Rossell y Arellano in 1939 (1939–1964). The two were drawn together over their shared conservative political and social ideologies, and Rossell y Arellano's appointment is rumored to have been approved by Ubico himself.[9] Both Rossell y Arellano and Ubico hated communism and held to ideals of an authoritarian government, social stability, and respect for a hierarchical society. Although Ubico's government maintained the traditional Liberal anticlerical stance, his was a mellowed position that permitted the return of previously abolished religious orders. In 1937 he allowed the Jesuits to teach in the archdiocesan seminary, while the Maryknollers, who had been forced out of China, arrived in 1943. Ubico's admiration of Spain's fascist leader, Francisco Franco, earned him the support of Spanish priests, who strongly supported the Franco regime. In turn, Ubico benefited from Falangist propaganda that buttressed his arbitrary rule. These factors helped to solidify the church hierarchy as a conservative and reactionary institution, deeply suspicious of all social reform, whose political and social models rested on totalitarian and hierarchical structures.[10]

Professionally, Archbishop Rossell y Arellano came of age during the last years of Manuel Estrada Cabrera's long dictatorship, and he drew effectively upon these experiences in his own struggle against both the Arévalo and Árbenz administrations. Born in Esquipulas on June 18, 1894, Mariano Rossell y Arellano was ordained to the priesthood in 1918 on the cusp of the 1920 revolution. The Catholic Church was at the forefront of this loosely affiliated movement, as members of the clergy and particularly Bishop José Piñol y Batres emerged as outspoken leaders against the dictator, helping to create a citywide opposition movement. Ultimately, the bishop was imprisoned for his political activities and then released for exile to Rome in 1919.[11] During these turbulent years, Rossell y Arellano rose rapidly within the Catholic hierarchy and was subsequently exiled in 1922 for his own antigovernment statements while serving as the private secretary to Archbishop Luis Javier Muñoz y Capurón. Constructing parallels between the anticlerical liberalism of Estrada Cabrera and the Arévalo and Árbenz revolutionary governments during the 1940s and 1950s, Rossell y Arellano assumed the leadership of a broad political coalition comprising conservative political parties, the upper class, and the landed elite. Piero Gleijeses argues that the "scions of the upper class were not willing to invest energy or money in electoral politics, a distasteful and bothersome distraction from social and economic pursuits."[12] Consequently, they were more than willing to let the church act as their political front and Rossell y Arellano to serve as the traditional caudillo moving firmly into alignment with elite landholders and entrepreneurs.[13]

The particularities of the Guatemalan revolution made it difficult for the church to position itself within the new sociopolitical milieu. Unlike in the Mexican revolution, Guatemalan leaders did not reject Catholicism but used it as a transformative tool in the state's expansion of its social welfare activities on a national scale.[14] Rather than setting itself apart from religion, the revolution understood itself to be acting out Christian tenets of social reform such as the protection and care of children, the reform of the economy, and the integration of neglected sectors of society, albeit in only a limited way at times. Although the constitution formally separated the church and state institutionally, the Guatemalan revolution utilized a unique rhetoric of socialism, Christianity, social welfare, and democracy. Juan José Arévalo's "spiritual socialism," as it became known, directly challenged the traditional programs supported by the church and made it difficult for the Catholic hierarchy to claim an oppositional space against it. The nutrition centers, daycare centers, and medical clinics established under the guidance of the Arévalo and Árbenz administrations directly challenged the church's claim as the protector of the family, particularly the sacred relationship between mother and child. Additionally, the Arévalo government directly criticized the paucity of social programs in existence at the outset of the revolution in a message to the National Assembly on March 1, 1945.[15] This public criticism of the Catholic Church along with the rapidly forming social welfare movement severely limited the effectiveness of any antirevolutionary rhetoric.

Tensions between the Catholic hierarchy and the government emerged immediately following the installation of President Arévalo and the adoption of the new constitution on March 15, 1945. The conflict grew out of constitutional Article 25, which maintained the historical separation of church and state. Arévalo believed that the separation of church and state was mutually beneficial, wanting neither a revival of the old religious controversies nor a church-sponsored political party.[16] When this traditional Liberal stance was reconfirmed, despite an overtly democratic administration, the Catholic hierarchy initiated its assault on the government. Equating the Liberal dictatorship of Estrada Cabrera with the democratically elected Arévalo administration, the archbishop now claimed that Article 25 was an instrument of religious persecution.[17] However, given the distinctiveness of the revolutionary state from all previous administrations, the church's historical polemic against Liberalism was not an effective strategy.

While the archbishop claimed that the church was under assault in the new revolutionary era, the church in fact benefited from the political and social freedoms offered by Arévalo's government, and there was little evidence of a strain in church-state relations in the early days.[18] In the weeks that followed the October revolution, Rossell y Arellano urged his priests to maintain political neutrality and to focus on edifying the spiritual realm.[19] Denied the opportunity to publish under the Ubico administration, the church now began publication of the newspaper *Acción Social Cristiana* in January 1945. In the weeks leading up to the new constitution in March, Rossell y Arellano, along with four bishops, sent a letter of congratulations to the Guatemalan National Assembly for its promise of religious freedom as decreed in the revolutionary junta's agenda.[20] These freedoms, argues Sullivan-González, may have in fact worked very much in favor of the opposition movement: "Rossell y Arellano took full advantage of the nearly unimpeded propagation of his anti-Communist crusade."[21] Rather than exiling their political opponents as their predecessors had done, both the Arévalo and Árbenz administrations remained committed to freedom of speech and democracy.

Consequently, Rossell y Arellano was required to create a new rhetoric in his battle against a popular revolutionary government precisely because the ethos of the Guatemalan revolution directly confronted the hierarchical ideology of the church and previous Liberal dictatorships. Revolutionary leaders hoped to bring the country into the modern capitalist world within a democratic and nationalistic milieu. The 1945 constitution introduced under President Arévalo granted a new framework for political and social life, guaranteeing such basic rights as limited weekly work hours and maternity benefits, not to mention enfranchisement for literate women and all men. A series of health and social reforms addressed such primary necessities as potable water, sewage systems, basic health-care clinics, social security benefits, and an expansive literacy campaign aimed at educating both urban and rural peasants.[22] Although Arévalo's policies remained somewhat amorphous and more intellectual than practical, his presidency set the stage for the more comprehensive economic reforms that included the 1952 Agrarian Reform under his successor, Jacobo Árbenz.[23]

The larger Catholic Church was a complex socioreligious institution, and clergy and lay leaders held a variety of opinions about the new administrations. Sullivan-González argues that to focus exclusively on the archbishop "obscures the dynamic heterogeneity of Catholic responses toward the revolutionary government."[24] While Gleijeses maintains that the lower hierarchy and clergy fell lockstep in line with Archbishop Rossell y Arellano, both Blake Pattridge and Sullivan-González argue that the Catholic body politic was in fact divided in its reactions to the revolutionary government. Rossell y Arellano found himself isolated even among his fellow clergy, the head of a "house divided," a divergence of opinions that extended to the highest levels of the Catholic hierarchy.[25] The clergy, lay leaders, and confraternities (brotherhoods) embedded in rural parishes understood the impact of the Arévalo and Árbenz reform policies on the lives of Guatemala's rural, poor, and indigenous communities and generally supported the administrations' efforts.[26] Even the Vatican assumed a moderate position, and its representative, the papal nuncio Gennaro Verolino, worked openly with the Árbenz government.

In an attempt to gain a foothold in this sociopolitical milieu, the archbishop now turned his attention to those social groups who were direct beneficiaries of revolutionary reforms, namely the working class and women. Returning to the church's late-nineteenth-century emphasis on workers and labor rights, the church hierarchy attempted to improve its relationship with existing Catholic labor unions, inviting the Liga Obrera to a reading of the nineteenth-century *Rerum Novarum* in May 1945.[27] In a clear attempt to co-opt the rapidly growing national labor movement, the Catholic Action Program was initiated on March 12, 1946. Although the church tried to belittle the benefits of government reforms by associating them with communism, its hysterical rhetoric held little sway in the face of the moderate economic reforms of the Arévalo administration. Electoral results revealed that opposition to the revolution found limited support from male workers and rural men (see chapter 4). Using public instruments such as the Catholic newspaper *Acción Social Cristiana*, the church intensified its efforts and by 1946 began to link Article 25 with the first signs of communism in Guatemala.[28] Pro-revolutionary newspapers quickly challenged this assertion with accusations of fascism, but were ultimately unsuccessful in undermining its disruptive message.[29] When *Acción Social Cristiana* openly accused the Arévalo administration of communist sympathies in October 1945, the government suspended the paper's publication for two months, further inflaming the situation.[30] Less than two months later, the church issued a pastoral letter defending the existing inequitable class structure as divinely ordained. Ultimately, Rossell y Arellano was unable to co-opt large numbers of the working class, who were no longer docile and accepting of their servile status in the Catholic workers' movement.

The archbishop and his conservative allies had done everything possible during the electoral process of the late 1940s and the national election of 1950 to undermine the candidacies of pro-revolutionary candidates. The overwhelming majority with which Árbenz won the presidential election in 1950 made it clear that the revolution could not be defeated by democratic means. Increasing its opposition, the Catholic hierarchy became more successful in its cultivation of antirevolutionary sentiment among middle- and upper-class women in Guatemala City, drawing on their strong historical sociopolitical ties. Following the desamortización of the nineteenth century, elite and middle-class women moved into the gaps left vacant by religious personnel. Stripped of its extensive financial foundation, the church became dependent upon its wealthy patrons to assist in its hospitals and social welfare programs, such as the Hospicio Nacional Centro Educativo (renamed the Centro Educativo Asistencial in 1951), the national orphanage at the center of the 1951 violence.[31] These groups raised money for social welfare programs sponsored by the church without which the institution's few social projects might not have survived. Urban women had also played a significant role during the March 11, 1920, public demonstrations against Manuel Estrada Cabrera.[32] Now the archbishop adopted a similar strategy, extending into the public sphere the traditional Catholic mantra that women were protectors of the home who worked tirelessly during the revolution to maintain the traditional gender structure in alignment with the church's hierarchical and patriarchal view of society.

The first hints of this new strategy emerged quickly as Rossell y Arellano escalated the anticommunist gendered rhetoric, which proved to be highly effective in the mobilization of urban women of all social classes. While the rhetoric rarely contained specific accusations, the veiled threat against Guatemalan society and families galvanized many women. Asserting that mothers had the most to lose with the advent of communism, the archbishop effectively united dominant notions of womanhood with fear of social change. As Margaret Power aptly notes in her work on Chile's antirevolutionary women's movement during the 1970s, when "societies... conflate womanhood with motherhood, women respond decisively to what they perceive to be a threat to their children and their families."[33] Although integrating women into national political life countermanded Rossell y Arellano's gendered social order, he temporarily suspended his own norms to incorporate them into the antirevolutionary movement to suit the church's needs. In order to maintain Guatemala's gendered hierarchy, these women abandoned traditional notions of gender at least temporarily.

Taking their fight to the streets, these women staged countless marches, protests, and demonstrations to express their political dissatisfaction with the Arévalo and Árbenz administrations.[34] The street protests rapidly assumed a familiar pattern, one that had immediate and at times disruptive effects on urban society.[35] A rumor about the possible exile of the archbishop or, more commonly, about a specific act committed by the government would trigger a protest. The ensuing protest frequently sparked localized violence, resulting in injuries and sometimes even the death of a participant or bystander. Invariably, the demonstration invoked a response from the police, and the demonstrators and church hierarchy would, in turn, claim persecution of religious freedom. The government frequently counterresponded with the suspension of constitutional guarantees for a brief period of time in order to restore social order. During his political tenure, Arévalo survived close to thirty attempted coups d'etat, which Jim Handy notes were the result of intrigues by conservative political parties that failed to do well in the polls. Consequently, in combination with the church-sponsored demonstrations, Guatemala City was the site of political chaos, social unrest, and even fear.[36]

The first significant public demonstration occurred just a few months into Arévalo's presidency as the church began its campaign against the new government. Just a year after urban women had played a significant role in the overthrow of Jorge Ubico, women entered public life again. Calling themselves the Comité de Defensa Católica, this group of women staged the first large demonstration against the government on August 25, 1945. Claiming the authority to act on behalf of the suffering people of Guatemala, the women demonstrated with the express purpose of reclaiming Catholicism from those who were using it for unscrupulous purposes.[37] While this first demonstration was designed to register dissatisfaction with the continued constitutional separation of church and state, they demonstrated again a year later on August 25, 1946, with a gathering of more than four thousand people to mark the anniversary.[38] This second demonstration was met, however, by pro-revolutionaries, and on September 8,

1946, by a massive outpouring of support for the Arévalo government. Invoking the memory of María Chinchilla Recinos's sacrifice, this counterdemonstration urged women to rise from their complacency and pay attention to the reality of the new democracy. Sponsored by the female affiliates of pro-revolutionary parties, they were also joined by delegates from the Asociación Cívica Femenina, which had formed in the days following Ubico's overthrow and participated in the suffrage congress, and the Comité Femenino Pro-Manifestación Popular. Here, too, they utilized the same religious language, arguing that the wealthy elite could not be using religion for good purposes. Since God stood on the side of the poor and humble, they would not be the ones to use religion for political advantage. Declaring that women were no longer an unconscious mass, pro-revolutionaries urged all women to wake up politically, inviting everyone to join the nascent democracy emerging in Guatemala.[39] The rhetorical debate between pro- and antirevolutionary forces employed competing feminine moralities, rhetorical positions that would intensify as the decade proceeded. Both sides used Catholicism and religious belief in general to defend their political position, arguing that they were acting on behalf of God.

In the context of limited enfranchisement, these public protests imbued female demonstrators with political legitimacy, elevating women to the status of genuine political actors. The 1945 constitution limited enfranchisement to only literate women, excluding the vast majority of Guatemalan women from political participation, specifically 70 percent of ladinas and 96 percent of indigenous women. The available statistics on female voting during the 1940s indicate that even among eligible women voters, few took advantage of this hard-won legal reform. In this gendered political landscape, public demonstrations were one of the few viable political options for women. In her analysis of the effects of limited suffrage on the revolutionary leadership, historian Cindy Forster concludes that marginalizing women politically had direct benefits for the opposition: "Thousands of housewives, market sellers, and petty bourgeois women swelled the ranks of the anti-Arbenz forces, and tens of thousands of campesinas remained objects rather than subjects of their own history."[40] Alleviating this exclusion by expanding the private sphere of home and motherhood into the public square, urban women created a cross-class movement, couched within the familiar gendered framework of wife and mother. Perceived to be acting within accepted gender roles—protecting their families and the Catholic faith—these demonstrators created the impression of a strong antirevolutionary movement in the capital city. Temma Kaplan argues that "women's public protests, even when framed in entirely traditional notions of femininity, convey important political messages about the strength of women."[41] The organizations formed by these groups of women influenced a broad political sphere and created a viable and credible social space legitimating the antirevolutionary movement. Manuel Castells argues that "space is an expression of society," and so the occupation of public space by antirevolutionary demonstrators suggested that all was not well with the Guatemalan revolution.[42] In turn, these seemingly informal and spontaneous demonstrations, as many of the protests were purposely misrepresented to be, created critical connections between the civil associations and the governing class.[43]

These urban associations helped to shape a clear social identity capable of interacting with the nation-state.[44] Their occupation of this public political space was further validated because they acted upon traditional gender norms. Protecting the home and family was not a political act per se, and women were entitled to occupy such space with regard to defense of home, family, and faith. As Michelle Chase argues in her work on urban Cuban women during the 1950s, when women, the implicit defenders of home, family, and morality, stood up to authorities, their actions had particular resonance.[45] The demonstrations by urban women were therefore imbued with gendered validity. Therefore, not only did the anticommunist demonstrations invigorate an antirevolutionary movement designed to maintain elite socioeconomic power, but the women involved in the movement reempowered an ailing and arguably weakened religious institution through the reinforcement of its deep sociopolitical gender ideals.

The public split in the urban ladina movement in August 1947 exemplified the growing divide in the capital city and intensified the antirevolutionary organizations and public anticommunist rhetoric among Guatemala City's women. The antirevolutionary movement claimed that the 1947 labor laws, the introduction of social security, the 1947 Congress of Women, and the administration's resistance to the Rio Pact all proved that the Arévalo government was moving firmly into alignment with communism despite the fact that it had outlawed the Guatemalan Communist Party. The women who were concerned about the government's direction now formed a new organization with an overtly anticommunist identity, the Partido Unificación Anticomunista-Cristianidad Femenina de Guatemala. The party was active by 1949, staging a large demonstration against communism on April 28, 1949. The unexplained death of revolutionary hero Francisco Javier Arana in July 1949 only escalated the developing anticommunist movement among urban ladinas. Arana enjoyed significant public popularity and was considered a serious presidential candidate for the 1950 elections. His death outside of Guatemala City on the night of July 18 sparked outrage across Guatemala City and incited a mass public protest.[46] Rumors abounded over possible suspects, and the antirevolutionary groups now solidified the connection between their opposition to the government and the global influence of communism.

With the election of Jacobo Árbenz in 1950, the antirevolutionary movement gained momentum, and no issue captured their attention more than the 1952 Agrarian Reform Law. Designed to address Guatemala's deep, historical economic inequities, the reform redistributed unused portions of land purchased from the United Fruit Company. The centerpiece of the Árbenz presidency, the law redistributed nearly one million acres to more than one hundred thousand peasants.[47] The modest land expropriations (for which the United Fruit Company was paid) earned the joint opposition of Guatemala's landed elite, the United Fruit Company (whose CEO was the brother of the head of the US Central Intelligence Agency), and the hierarchy of the Roman Catholic Church.[48] In response to the land redistributions, demonstrations erupted as countless organizations were created and re-formed, the opposition fluidly moving from one protest to another. The Comité Femenino Anticomunista organized multiple demonstrations from March through June following the enactment of the 1952 Agrarian Reform Law. One of the more successful women's organizations to respond to the law was the Comité Nacional Central Femenino Anticomunista. Protesting under the mantra of "peace, bread, and independence" from fascist conspirators (conflating Árbenz as both communist and fascist), they staged one of the largest demonstrations of the decade on March 23, 1952. Believing that Catholicism contained the perfect democratic ideals, the women in these organizations repeatedly called for the inclusion of basic Catholic tenets in the Guatemalan constitution under the banner of "God, Patriotism, and Liberty." This organization continued its activities until the overthrow of Jacobo Árbenz in June 1954, maintaining its belief that his government was a communist plague on their nation.

Although the benefits to his antirevolutionary position were clear, the archbishop carefully distanced himself from his supporters' activities, particularly as the demonstrations became increasingly violent. The US State Department carefully tracked the mobilization of urban women and the way in which the archbishop appeared to incite their public protests, even expressing concern over his violation of constitutional law, which prohibited any political action by the church.[49] During one antigovernmental protest in 1946, the State Department recorded that "during the course of the manifestation in front of the National

Palace, the archbishop appeared in one of the windows of the archbishop's palace but apparently refrained from blessing the people who surrounded his window, giving a rather restrained greeting and a wave of his hand."[50] In defense of his actions, the archbishop clarified his position regarding the political activities of his supporters:

> Catholics may belong to those political parties whose ideology is not in conflict with the doctrine of the church and as a consequence, participate in discussions and manifestations of the same provided that they are free, peaceful, and dignified; but it is not desirable to intermix religious aspirations in matters of political order. In consequence, their participation in such manifestations will be in the exclusive character as citizens. . . . It is understood that the manifestation is supported by political parties and therefore, the invitation to participate is not made to the Catholic populace as such. . . . The present communication does not intend to favor or impede any manifestation but only to establish the position that the name of Catholics be taken always in its just and Christian sense, removed from any political interest.[51]

Rossell y Arellano continued to maintain his claim that antigovernment support was motivated by purely apolitical purposes intended only for the benefit of the Guatemalan people and the Catholic faith. However, his alliance with the informal public demonstrations was clear to even his strongest ally. This particular element confirms Margaret Power's suggestion that the United States used gender to foment anticommunist sentiment among women in Latin America during the 1960s. Women in Guatemala's antirevolutionary movement consequently represent the first volley in the highly gendered Cold War spearheaded by the United States.[52]

In direct contrast, women in the pro-revolutionary political parties and the Alianza Femenina Guatemalteca responded immediately to these accusations with their own protests and public denouncements. In the first years of the Arévalo presidency, the Asociación Cívica Femenina was particularly active in defending the revolutionary project, something that would change during the Árbenz era. In broadsides distributed throughout the city, women of the Asociación and other pro-revolutionary groups reminded residents that the revolution had been democratically elected and had followed the constitution, insisting that they were defending the popular will as well as their religious faith. The coalition urged the revolutionary opposition not to abuse the sociopolitical freedom available under the new government.[53] The Alianza was extremely vocal in their rejection of such labels, voicing both frustration and even anger over these accusations. They insisted that they, too, were faithful Catholics and had no interest in taking religious freedom away from anyone: "The Alianza is not a communist organization. Rather, it is a growing organization that accepts women without prejudice of their political or religious affiliation. The only condition for acceptance to the Alianza is to accept their struggle for Peace, for Democracy, and for the rights of women and children."[54] While they frequently used the same rhetoric in their defense, it appears to have not held the same authority for capital city residents. The antirevolutionary movement's accusations of a communist conspiracy simply did not fit with the reality of the revolution. Despite the fact that those in support of the revolution were also middle-class reformers, Catholic, anticommunist, and antifascist, their defensive rhetoric was drowned out.

While their actions may appear to be contradictory and fundamentally in tension with the rationale used to overthrow the dictator Jorge Ubico, the ideological shift among urban ladinas was indicative of a broader transition occurring across Latin America during the late 1940s and 1950s. A majority of the women in the *Nosotras* and *Azul* networks held fundamentally liberal political views, democratic ideals that valued a stable state with traditional governing institutions.[55] While there is no direct evidence to link the social reformers of the Juan José Arévalo era with these antirevolutionary protests, the absolute silence of high-profile women such as Gloria Menéndez Mina in the face of this political drama is noteworthy. What is clear is that while journalists such as Menéndez Mina and Luz Valle, who held considerable sway among their urban readership, continued to advocate relentlessly for the legal and social rights of all Guatemalan women, they remained silent on the political administrations of both Arévalo and Árbenz. While they may not have held extreme views against either administration, as the global rhetoric regarding communism increased, so too did their fears about the nature of the Guatemalan revolutionary project. Although they supported nationalism, democracy, and even in some cases anti-imperialism, many in this circle now moved to an intransigent position of anticommunism in the belief that they were defending the values of motherhood and family. Although their ideological position appears to contradict their core values, as Patrick Iber points out, "Latin America's Cold War was unusual because, with the United States as the imperial power, liberation and anti-Communism were often in tension, if not total conflict."[56] Despite their tremendous efforts to reform women's legal and social position, they maintained a fundamentally moderate political perspective given the powerful threat of communism.

The ever increasing number of public demonstrations verified this shift among all women in Guatemala City, and particularly among middle- and upper-class ladinas. Some of the very women who had recently taken to the streets to protest and overthrow dictator Jorge Ubico now returned to these same streets to protest the new democratic government, an irony that cannot have been lost on observers. For Guatemalan women, the potency behind the threat of communism was not just related to a perceived threat to their Catholic faith but to something equally critical to their core identity. In 1937, Pope Pius XI had issued an edict on communism linking it to the destruction of home and family, warning women of its threat to the very heart of their gendered identities.[57] Not only did this strike at the core of Guatemala's traditional gender construct, where women were elevated as protector and sustainer of the family, it resonated across class and ethnic divides.

The Market Women and the Antirevolutionary Movement

By 1950, urban women in Guatemala City had developed a sustained political presence for the first time. Representing a cross section of class and political ideologies, the hundreds and thousands of women demonstrating through the streets served as a powerful antidote to the revolutionary reforms. Overtly calling for the return of traditional gendered social hierarchies and acting in defense of the Catholic Church, their efforts posed a serious threat to both the Arévalo and the Árbenz governments. Using their identity as mothers to call for political change, their efforts were perceived to be within the appropriate gender and class boundaries, and these ladinas were understood to be acting on behalf of their own self-interest. The 1951 incident at the orphanage discussed above, however, introduced a fundamentally new element into the antirevolutionary movement. The market women joined the opposition representing a new social sector, and their antirevolutionary activism engaged the city's imagination. Socially and economically disenfranchised, the market women had been identified as potential recipients of social reforms. Their opposition to the revolutionary government, however, inverted their traditional sociopolitical standing, and they emerged as a potent political force. Unlike the middle- and upper-class women, whose demonstrations represented the moral superiority of motherhood, the market women's actions were interpreted differently. Middle- and upper-class observers did not bestow a higher moral plane on the market women due to their marginalized social status, and the power of their activities was understood for its disruptive influence. Consequently, the demonstrations and social disruptions organized by the market women held a particularly significant symbolism; they embodied the very social sector the revolution had come to save.

As a public economic sphere, the urban markets represented a complex arena, at once perceived to be necessary as well as dirty and dangerous. With hundreds of vendors and shoppers present at any one time, the marketplace was, and is, a cacophony of smells and sounds. Fruits, vegetables, meats, and woven textiles along with hundreds of other sundry items are contained within a single space. The work itself is physically demanding, with vendors working twelve- to sixteen-hour days, often with children and extended family members. Many of the markets are outdoors, with little protection from the sun and rain. By the twentieth century, some of the markets had been enclosed and protected from the elements, but many vendors continued to sell their products in the open, often displaying edible and nonedible products together on the ground. Few markets had any facilities, with no running water or electricity, and small children spent the day exposed to the elements, in hygienic conditions the Alianza referred to as catastrophic.[58] The health surveys taken during the early 1940s indicate that the majority of the vendors' children did not receive adequate nutrition. As a result, the markets and the women themselves were frequently the targets of the state's modernization reforms, in the Liberal political quest to replicate European cities and clean up what government officials perceived to be dirty, unhygienic places of food consumption.[59] However, in their attempts to modernize the marketplaces, local and state authorities frequently came into conflict with the market women, who held a healthy skepticism of the state. These conflicts could become intense and even violent when authorities attempted to intervene by imposing cleanliness standards or increasing taxes. The most unlikely allies of the powerful elite, most market women lived outside the capital, traveling daily into the center to work, literally and figuratively occupying a marginalized space in the city and in the hearts and minds of the city's residents.

The marketplaces were also dynamic, economically transgressive public spaces dominated by women where traditional gender roles held less power than elsewhere.[60] As poor, single mothers and market vendors, they were free of husbands and male oversight.[61] Many of the women were indigenous, although not all of them wore the traditional indigenous clothing known as *traje*.[62] Women often inherited their market stalls from their mothers, and they in turn passed them down to their own daughters. Required to work outside the home to feed their children, market women by the very nature of their work violated deeply held notions of women's traditional roles. The antithesis of the private, hallowed domain of home, the marketplace was what Guatemalan society dictated as public space, outside the bounds of gender norms, where, David Carey argues, gender and ethnic identity became more ambivalent.[63] Although they frequently verbalized notions of faith and motherhood like their middle- and upper-class neighbors, market women, and the markets themselves, were frequently associated with immorality.[64] The commonly used slang term for market woman in Guatemala City is *locataria*, indicative of their complex social role. Although the term literally translates as someone who is local or has a local stall in the market, it also carried negative connotations suggestive of poverty and ignorance. When abbreviated to *loca* or crazy, the implications of the identity are clear. Although market women were the most economically vulnerable, they were also potentially the most liberated of all Guatemalan women, existing outside the patriarchal norms of both family and the formal economy, frequently and consistently acting upon their own set of sociopolitical ideas.

Guatemala City's Central Market, encircling the National Cathedral, lies just a few blocks from the site of the 1951 orphanage riot; it was the core of a network of markets that operated during the 1940s and 1950s. Seven other markets were spread out across Guatemala City: South Market no. 1, South Market no. 2, Colón Market, Guarda Viejo Market, La Palmita Market, Villa Guadalupe Market, and Cervantes Market. The national census did not include market women as an economic category until 1950, at which time it recorded a total of four thousand market women nationally, although given the tenuous nature of the informal economy, the true number of women working in the markets is likely much higher.[65]

The market women who emerged during the 1951 incident were the antithesis of all stereotypes, and no one more than their leader, Concha Estéves. Remembered for her bold and strong-willed opposition, she challenged public perceptions of the marginalized market woman. Her charismatic leadership galvanized women across the city, and she became a champion for the Catholic Church and an outspoken opponent of the Árbenz government and communism. Following their incorporation into the national anticommunist movement, the Comité Anticomunista de Locatarias, led by Estéves, participated in countless public protests and demonstrations alongside the Comité de Estudiantes Universitarios Anticomunistas and others. Due to her illiteracy, Estéves seldom appears in written records and rarely assumed formal leadership of any organization. She has, however, become emblazoned in the Guatemalan collective memory for her strength of conviction and daring actions.⁶⁶ In part, this is due to her continued activism following the overthrow of Jacobo Árbenz. Although she is forever remembered for her antirevolutionary work, she maintained an independence from any specific political ideology, as evidenced by her persistent advocacy for her fellow market women during the post-Árbenz era. Frequently in conflict with local officials, she continued to petition authorities in Guatemala City for material improvements to the markets throughout the 1950s. When the Central Market was substantially renovated during the early 1980s, Estéves once again led the younger market women on a daylong protest against the insufficient size of the new stalls as well as the higher rental prices.⁶⁷ Despite the political repression of all civilians during the eighteen-month presidency of Efraín Ríos Montt (1982–1983), Estéves continued her lifetime of advocacy in the midst of seemingly impossible odds.⁶⁸ Having found her political voice during the revolutionary era, Estéves maintained a public profile for the remainder of her life.

For many of the market women, the only stable institutional presence in their working lives was the Catholic clergy and the Hospicio Nacional Centro Educativo. In a world devoid of health care or educational and financial resources, institutions such as the Hospicio, the orphanage at the heart of the 1951 conflict, provided the sole safety net for these women and their children in times of extreme poverty or death in their family. With deep sociospiritual roots in the capital city, the Hospicio served as a home and educational center for orphans, the disabled, the elderly, and impoverished mothers.⁶⁹ Established in 1857 through private initiatives, the Hospicio was staffed by the Sisters of Charity, who received dispensation from exile during the Liberal reforms due to their social significance. They had served at the Hospicio for almost a century providing education, spiritual guidance, and general physical care for the children. Damaged in the 1917 and 1918 earthquakes, the building had been repaired, and by the mid-twentieth century again served as a home to hundreds of children ranging in age from infancy to young adulthood. It was their allegiance to this historic center of safety that mobilized the market women to act in its defense in 1951.

The conflict that erupted in early July had actually begun several months earlier with the appointment of a new director at the Hospicio, Gabriel Alvarado, a Spaniard in exile from the Franco regime.⁷⁰ Ideologically aligned with the Árbenz administration, Alvarado changed the institution's name to the Centro Educativo Asistencial (Center for Educational Assistance), a name he believed to be more indicative of its new social and secular mission.⁷¹ Under his management, the staff were encouraged to join the influential national teachers' union, the Sindicato de Trabajadores de la Educación de Guatemala (STEG).[72] Seven women from the Sisters of Charity refused to join, along with a significant number of other unaffiliated workers. In response to the escalating dispute, Alvarado transferred three of the sisters to another institution in the provincial city of Mazatenango on June 30.[73] Others who were unwilling to join the teachers' union were summarily dismissed.

The remaining staff immediately reached out to broader Catholic institutions and alumni of the Hospicio for support against this perceived injustice, and the ensuing public debate assumed the familiar polemic of pro- and anticommunist accusations. Alumni petitioned directly to President Árbenz for the return of the sisters to their positions, emphasizing the physical and spiritual care they as children had received under the sisters' care.[74] Organizations including the Asociación de Madres Cristianas (Association of Christian Mothers) and the Asociación de Maestras Católicas (Catholic Teachers' Association) argued that the religious women should not be removed because they were the only source of maternal love for many of the orphaned children.[75] Within a few days, several more Catholic educational institutions demonstrated in support of the Sisters of Charity including the female institutions Colegio de Santa Rosa, Colegio de Santa Teresita, the English American School, Colegio de Cultural Femenina, and Colegio del Belga-Guatemalteco y el Carmen; and the men's school, the Colegio de Juventud.[76] For their part, members of the teachers' union working at the orphanage emphatically claimed that the conflict was not about religion but rather about the quality of education provided to the children. The workers repeatedly stated that they themselves were Catholic and were therefore not in opposition to either the moral or spiritual tenets of the church (reminiscent of similar statements by the Alianza Femenina Guatemalteca). Rather, they claimed that the sisters had incited an atmosphere of hostility in the name of anticommunism, and the union teachers demanded a public retraction of such anticlerical and emotionally laden accusations.[77] Following days of negotiations, an official petition was presented to Jacobo Árbenz on July 9, 1951, with more than a thousand signatures, the majority of which came from market women. Their demands included the removal of Gabriel Alvarado, the reinstatement of fifty-eight dismissed employees, improvement in the school's nutrition program, and the return of the three sisters reassigned to Mazatenango.

Following more than a week of escalating tensions, those workers opposed to the director and the union declared a strike on July 11, 1951. They then rang a bell to attract women from the nearby market.[78] Hundreds of other women and men joined the gathering crowd, and by most estimates, approximately 1,500 people were soon gathered in front of the Centro Educativo Asistencial. The crowd remained for hours, shouting "Down with communism and up with religion," demanding to speak with the municipal representative. At 8:15 p.m., Archbishop Mariano Rossell y Arellano arrived to investigate the situation. When he attempted to enter the building, however, he was prevented from doing so by the police. He left the scene after several hours, "exhorting the crowd to be peaceful." Although Rossell y Arellano stated that they had a right to defend the children, he cautioned the demonstrators to be prudent in their actions, indicative of good Catholics. The assistant minister of education, Carlos González Orellana, arrived to mediate, but to no avail. While this event was taking place, another group of women and men simultaneously attacked the Escuela Jacobo Sánchez, the publishing center for the Communist Party paper, *Octubre*. Although the people inside escaped, the editor was seriously injured.[79]

The violence intensified the next morning when hundreds of market women gathered again in front of the children's home. They set fire to a car in the vicinity and then moved directly to the National Palace, where they tried to physically force their way into the building. A government representative agreed to meet with a delegation of women from the Central Market, led by Carlotta de Castellanos, Oliva Dolores Solares Vda. de Montes, Teresa Alegría Ramírez, Jacoba A. de Madrid, and Albertina de López. During the meeting, Ernesto Cofiño was appointed the new director of the children's home, and he immediately reinstated the religious sisters and other discharged workers. Apparently satisfied, Castellanos asked the crowd to disperse, claiming no further responsibility should they continue their demonstration. However, when a politician emerged from his office, the crowd surged toward him, shouting, "He is a communist!" Although the politician, Miguel Enrique Viteri Batres, escaped, his car was burned and destroyed. When members of the fire department and the military moved to put out the flames, they, too, were attacked. This action led to gunfire, which killed at least four people (René Rodríguez, Roberto Pérez, and two unidentified people) and injured more than seventy others. July 12 ended with the suspension of all constitutional guarantees in an attempt to restore social order. The constitution was reinstituted thirty days later.[80]

Although by 1951 the capital city newspapers had aligned themselves into pro- and antirevolutionary camps, the events surrounding the Hospicio and the market women were reported with remarkable consistency. Perhaps even more significant is that, despite the intrigue depicted by various newspapers, the depth and complexity of the relationships between the market women, the workers at the orphanage, and the Catholic clergy were made apparent by how the events played out. The immediate response by the market women to the ringing bell indicates a prearranged signal. The arrival of the archbishop at the site of an apparently minor labor dispute confirms the collusion between the archbishop and the women, despite the archbishop's denial. Although Rossell y Arellano pleaded for calm, his own attempts to gain entrance to the facility validated and enforced the market women's protests, thereby escalating the stakes of the protest itself. Of all the available sources, the US State Department's account establishes the most direct collusion between the archbishop and the market women, consistently suggesting a much closer relationship between the market women and the archbishop than did either pro- or antirevolutionary sources in Guatemala.

In the ensuing uproar over the incident, a public debate over the actions of the market women took center stage. The apparent collusion between the archbishop and the market women was perplexing to Guatemalan observers. For many pro-revolutionaries, the market women's protests were acts of irrationality. The revolution was, after all, intended precisely to benefit social groups such as the market women, at least rhetorically if not always in reality. For many, the market women's bold public protests against the revolutionary government of Jacobo Árbenz appeared to be self-destructive, since powerful socioeconomic institutions such as the Catholic Church had rarely if ever fought for the interests of poor and marginalized women. Some revolutionary supporters feared that these women were being exploited by people with unscrupulous motives (no doubt a reference to the archbishop).[81] Pro-revolutionary women who frequently expressed frustration and anger over the political apathy or opposition demonstrated by their social peers now questioned who really had created the situation. In fact, the Alianza Femenina Guatemalteca openly accused the church of recruiting these women to promote an antirevolutionary agenda under the false pretense that the Catholic faith was being persecuted.[82]

As further proof of this alliance, critics pointed to a previous incident in 1948 in which a large crowd of market women lay across the front steps of the archbishop's residence in response to a rumor about his possible expulsion from Guatemala. They dispersed only after the chief of the armed forces, Colonel Francisco Javier Arana, appeared personally with assurances that the archbishop would not be expelled.[83] Although there is no direct evidence connecting Rossell y Arellano with the initiation of such rumors, he and the antirevolutionary groups clearly benefited from the ensuing social unrest. Furthermore, he did nothing to clarify such erroneous perceptions. The public perception among some observers that the market women served as mere dupes in a larger and more dangerous game between Rossell y Arellano and the outside influence of the United States remained a dominant sentiment. No one, it appears, believed that the market women were capable of acting upon their own motivations, concluding that they were either naïve or corruptible. Within the context of Guatemalan race relations, the fact that many market women were also indigenous furthered these negative perceptions. In the imaginations of many urban residents, the market women became complicit with the moral vacuum of the antirevolutionary movement through ignorance, gullibility, or even duplicity.

While the events at the orphanage in July captivated urban residents of all political stripes, the praise and critique that followed focused on the actions of the market women rather than on their motivations. In fact, there appears to have been little interest in exploring their motivations. Unlike with political demonstrations initiated by middle- and upper-class women, observers could not assign specific political or economic motivations to this particular social sector. So pervasive was this perception that even those who benefited from and supported their actions believed the market women to be acting at the behest of the archbishop rather than their own ideals. In her study of popular movements, Temma Kaplan pays particular attention to the role of women, and her conclusions find resonance with the reactions of observers within Guatemala City. Kaplan notes that women of the popular classes seldom leave evidence in their own words about the reasons for their actions: "This paucity of evidence has caused many who study crowd behavior to focus on acts rather than thoughts. It has led others to associate irrationality and spontaneity with collective action."[84] Given the high illiteracy rates among the market women, few left written records. Kaplan's analysis here mirrors the responses of many observers in Guatemala City following the July 1951 events, given the deep racial and class divides in the capital.

Although a generalized bias against the market women disavowed them as political actors in the growing polarization of the revolution, an examination of their activities in fact reveals a clear trail of actions and written words that indicate their specific motives throughout the revolutionary decade. While the market women acted on behalf of and perhaps even at the behest of the archbishop at times, the ideas they expressed directly contradict the conclusions reached by both pro- and antirevolutionary observers. In the hours following the public demonstration at the orphanage, journalists reported clear factors that motivated the women's actions. As several of the women recounted, they believed that the children living at the institution were being starved and mistreated. There were even rumors that suggested the girls were being sexual abused by male staff members.[85] Their first efforts had been to hand food in to the children through the windows of the building. Journalists from *El Imparcial* interviewed women at the scene, one of whom declared that "as mothers, which many of us are, we cannot look with indifference at the struggle of these children, orphans of the people."[86] Couching her response within the traditional parameters of acceptable public activism, at least this market woman clearly valued traditional notions of motherhood and morality in much the same way as women of the middle and upper classes. In addition to the question of safety, some women also hoped that the religious sisters would be allowed to remain in order to give the children a moral education, something that was "foundational for all people of good moral character."[87] Claiming their identity as dignified mothers, the market women beseeched President Árbenz to remedy this grave error and restore the sisters to their positions.[88] Although unable to reproduce ideal domestic structures and traditional gender roles in their own lives, the market women nevertheless held to these ideals and incorporated dominant gender norms. However, despite their insistence that they acted upon their conviction as mothers, market women were not granted the same gendered value as mothers of the middle and upper classes. While the market women articulated the concerns of a wide variety of urban citizens, the rhetoric in response to their actions indicates the way in which their motives were dismissed.

The public perception of the market women as incapable of rational political thought belies a deeper and far more complex socioeconomic context. Spurred by economic hardships brought on by the increasing cost of living throughout the revolutionary decade, the antirevolutionary activities of the market women must be placed within the broader context of the economic instability and vulnerability that affected all poor, working-class women. In the days following the October revolution, women from the market immediately formed committees to create better working conditions and benefits for their children, and they continued to work closely with all levels of the government, including with the wife of President Arévalo, Elisa Martínez de Arévalo.[89] It is critical to note that they formed local social reform committees in their markets immediately following the October revolution prior to the arrival of the first lady in their market places. The result of this collaboration was the establishment of nutrition centers in the marketplaces where the children of the market women enjoyed breakfast and lunch, along with a safe place to play and nap. The market women also called for better personal working conditions, successfully gaining new market stalls and sanitary facilities in the markets.[90] Furthermore, market women across the capital city and in rural towns staged a variety of protests against any local politicians, both conservative and revolutionary, when they were unfairly taxed. In direct contrast to the public bewilderment over their activities, examining the market women's actions in fact reveals a broad array of sociopolitical motivations. While their religious affiliation and long-standing relationship with the orphanage located near the Central Market were significant factors in their antigovernment demonstrations, an examination of the specific activities in which they were engaged throughout the revolution reveals the complexity of their behavior toward and against the government, making it difficult to reduce their motivation to a single religious element.

When analyzed within their particular socioeconomic position, it is overwhelmingly evident that the Guatemalan market women took advantage of every opportunity to advocate for their own needs. The market women were pragmatists, working with whoever was willing to help them.[91] This is in fact corroborated by a wide variety of evidence from throughout the revolutionary decade that links the activism of the market women with concerns over the high cost of living, an issue they raised just days after the resignation of Jorge Ubico. In fact, while market women from around the country frequently imbued their rhetoric with religious motivation, economic concerns lay at the heart of almost all their advocacy. Inflation plagued the Arévalo years; the cost of living had risen 300 percent since 1946.[92] The government responded by raising real wages for urban workers, particularly members of influential unions. Therefore, groups such as teachers and railway workers fared the best, and these groups were the strongest revolutionary supporters.[93] Inflation affected the poor and economically vulnerable most directly, and no group was more vulnerable to the ebbs and flows of prices than the market women. Numerous newspaper articles noted the difficulties they experienced throughout the early 1950s. Women from the Mixco Market who made and sold chocolates insisted that even a tiny fluctuation in sugar prices made the difference between just breaking even and earning a small profit, and they implored the government to subsidize the sugar industry.[94] The Alianza actively supported them and campaigned for a reduction in sugar prices.[95]

As every price fluctuation affected market women exponentially, they played an active role in this national issue, working with the Alianza Femenina Guatemalteca, who frequently advocated on their behalf. In conjunction with the

Alianza, Maximina Valdés from the Liga de Locatarias (League of Market Women) served on a committee created to investigate and alleviate the high cost of living. A national conference was held in August 1953 to address the high inflation rate, in which the market women played an integral role.[96] Although they are generally believed to have aligned themselves with the Catholic Church and its antirevolutionary platform, many market women also worked closely with labor unions, both the Arévalo and Árbenz governments, and the Alianza Femenina Guatemalteca. Some market women joined the Alianza, and they actively participated in several labor unions and political parties, including the Partido de la Revolución Guatemalteca.

The opposition was quick to identify the political benefit of this economic strain and used it effectively in their antirevolutionary efforts. An active debate emerged between *El Imparcial* (the paper became increasingly critical of the government) and *Nuestro Diario* (pro-revolutionary) throughout the latter half of 1951. *Nuestro Diario* tried to dispel rumors of the devaluation of the quetzal, accusing others of creating false rumors to stir up the public.[97] In turn, *El Imparcial* accused *Nuestro Diario*'s editors of being organs of government propaganda.[98] The political environment rapidly became so polarized that by November 1951, the editors of *Nuestro Diario* claimed that there were only two political camps, the revolution and those who opposed it.[99] While it is likely that the opposition ran exaggerated stories in order to create social fear, the fact remained that inflation was a serious challenge to the Árbenz government. By early August 1953, the female sections of all pro-revolutionary political parties joined forces with the Alianza Femenina Guatemalteca to organize and participate in the conference against inflation.[100] All those involved in the project believed that the participation of the market women was of critical importance. Under the auspices of the Liga de Locatarias, the market women were invited to join the dialogue (see chapter 6 for more details).[101]

The significance of the economic crisis for the market women is demonstrated by a meeting they had with Jacobo Árbenz on April 6, 1953. In a seven-point address, the women outlined their needs to the president, all of which were economic or political in nature.[102] In fact, their written petition specifically emphasized the socioeconomic nature of their problems. Of primary importance to the market committee was the need for improved ventilation in their particular market, increased market space, and improved relations with the Guatemalan municipal representative, concerns that were immediate and local. Indeed, since 1951, the market women had been voicing their concern over increased municipal taxation.[103] Their accusation of unfair taxation was not without precedent. In August 1951, for example, the market women of Antigua (the former capital city of Guatemala), aroused by an increase in municipal tax on market vendors, staged a protest that ultimately forced the mayor to resign. The city council reinstated a former conservative mayor, and the council itself resigned. Public demonstrations ensued, and the government sent in reinforcements when the conservative mayor was arrested.[104] Completely absent from the women's petition was any reference to government policies related to the church or allegations of communist sympathies.

Although the historical lives of market women in Latin America have been largely ignored, several works of scholarship support the conclusions reached here. In her work on Peruvian market women, Linda Seligmann uncovered similar economic motivations for political action undertaken by the women. Resilient in transcending the daily abuses created by their marginal position, women in Cuzco, as Seligmann notes, mobilized for political reasons when their economic livelihood was threatened.[105] While the women's motives for political activism frequently coalesced with those of other sectors of society, Seligmann cautions that "it would be wrong to assume that collective solidarity necessitates homogeneity."[106] Rather, she argues that it is critical to examine the context for the mobilization and its meaning for each particular group.[107] Luz Marina Torres uncovered similar factors in her work on market women in Managua during the Sandinista era (1979–1990).[108]

As other scholars have pointed out, the high profile market women achieved during their antirevolutionary activism in Guatemala City is not unprecedented.[109] Several of these scholars have noted that market women have traditionally occupied a separate sphere of influence. The power and prestige they hold within their own economic circles have the capacity to extend into other realms, such as religious bodies or politics. Anthropologist Ashley Kistler has studied Q'eqchi' market women in San Juan Chamelco, contending that "they reinforce their high status through their participation in other prestigious social realms."[110] The potentially disruptive social meaning behind their activities was quickly understood by the antirevolutionary movement, and the July 1951 protest became a watershed event, solidifying the significance of the market women in that movement. Although the market women had been involved in a wide range of political activities, their social power and political potential was not fully appreciated by the opposition until the protest at the orphanage. Already highly critical of the government, university students formed an anticommunist committee within days of the July events.[111] They formally announced the establishment of the Comité de Estudiantes Universitarios Anticomunistas (CEUA) in early September. In the following weeks, groups antagonistic to the revolutionary government formed an umbrella organization called the Partido Unificación Anticomunista (PUA). Some of the market women joined this organization and formed their own subcommittee, the Comité Anticomunista de Locatarias.[112] This group immediately recruited both market women and other women to the greater antirevolutionary cause.[113] Following the July 1951 protest, the CEUA invited them to join the official antirevolutionary movement, and some of the market women formed the Locatarias Anticomunista soon afterward. In mid-September, the archbishop erected a statue to honor the recent efforts of the market women, which was funded by some elite women in gratitude for the demonstration at the orphanage. The market women in turn promised to protect the country.[114] On September 1, 1951, the Árbenz government announced that the rural minimum wage would be increased to 80 centavos.[115] In the weeks that followed, this new coalition ramped up their antirevolutionary efforts, culminating in a very large demonstration in October 1951 initiated by the CEUA.[116]

The overthrow of Jacobo Árbenz solidified the contributions of the market women within the antirevolutionary movement. Hailed as heroines by some journalists, leaders of the market women including Concha Estéves were invited to a breakfast with two prominent politicians, H. Abraham Cabrera Cruz and Mario Antonio Montenegro, in early September 1954.[117] With the assistance of benefactors, they began publication of a newspaper, *La Voz de la Locataria*, the first issue appearing on September 4, 1954. First lady Odilia de Castillo Armas paid an official visit to South Market at the end of July, and *Diario de Centro América* ran photos of the joyous meeting as the market women celebrated around the president's wife.[118] Just six months earlier, the South Market women had asked María Vilanova de Árbenz to be the *madrina* of their market.[119] In keeping with their new national stature and their contributions to the antirevolutionary movement, Concha Estéves and a small delegation of market women met with US Ambassador John Peurifoy on October 7, 1954, to acknowledge their work in the overthrow of Árbenz.[120]

Despite this beneficial political alliance, the market women did not embrace the military government of Castillo Armas uncritically. Having found their voice, they employed their newfound social influence to advocate for material improvements in their markets. The fact that the market women continued their activism regarding economic issues following the overthrow of Jacobo Árbenz in

June 1954 further supports the premise for the importance of economic motivators. A decade later, these women were again singled out and invited to a Mass commemorating the tenth anniversary of the July 1951 incident at the orphanage, the Centro Educativo Asistencial.[121]

Indicative of their deeply rooted marginalized position, the negative public perception of the market women did not change following the success of the antirevolutionary movement. Even while describing their pivotal social role in the overthrow of Jacobo Árbenz in 1954, the editor of *El Imparcial* painted the market women in derogatory terms. Referring to them as faithful and spiritual Guatemalans, he nevertheless described them as ignorant, simple, and oblivious to the full impact of their diligent protection of the archbishop.[122] Norma Stoltz Chinchilla notes this same attitude from the elite in her analysis of political mobilization in Chile in the early 1970s, during a critical stage of the opposition to revolutionary president Salvador Allende. Chinchilla argues that right-wing strategists mobilized women purely to embarrass and harass government officials and not out of concern for their needs.[123] In her work on the antirevolutionary women's movement in Chile during the early 1970s, Margaret Power argues that "women provided the opposition with a symbol of resistance that appeared to be apolitical—and therefore highly legitimate," and the Guatemalan market women would certainly have been considered apolitical by the clerical and economic elite.[124] Furthermore, not only were they acting on behalf of the Catholic Church and faith, their continued protests provided an effective foil to the revolutionary ideology purporting that the reforms were designed to benefit the poor and the working class.

Despite the unmitigated success of the market women, many in Guatemala refused to believe that they possessed genuine nationalist spirit or political savvy, or even the ability to understand the consequences of their actions. Even while they contributed incontrovertibly to the social instability created by the antirevolutionary forces that provided internal impetus for the overthrow of Árbenz, the market women's actions could not bridge the deeply entrenched class divisions in Guatemala. Despite the fact that the market women were well organized before the creation of groups such as the CEUA, the students' movement claimed responsibility for the work of the women. Ultimately, the activism of the market women mirrors the actions and experiences of pro-revolutionary women's movements. Just as the revolutionary project usurped the energies and activism of ladina organizations, effectively marginalizing their contributions to this pivotal decade, so too did the antirevolutionary opposition with respect to women's groups that came to their aid. While Archbishop Rossell y Arellano continues to dominate the narrative of those in opposition, the full impact of the market women's efforts that led to the overthrow of Jacobo Árbenz has been diminished by the sharp divisions of class, ethnicity, and gender.

Conclusion

During the antirevolutionary movement, Archbishop Mariano Rossell y Arellano successfully garnered the support of women by manipulating two central aspects of Guatemalan identity in his antirevolutionary campaign: traditional notions of gender and the Catholic faith. His political strategy claimed that both Catholicism and the ideals of womanhood and motherhood, cherished particularly by the middle and upper classes, were in jeopardy under the Arévalo and Árbenz governments. Rossell y Arellano couched his opposition in the language of religious persecution, stating that the new governments were merely a continuation of the historical liberal anticlericalism of the prior seventy years. The result of such anticlericalism, he argued, could only be communism, which threatened not only the Catholic faith but also the sanctity of the home, where women reigned as protectors of family and faith. Essentially, he melded commonly held notions of gender and religious faith into one powerful threat.

The presence of the market women in the antirevolutionary movement assisted the archbishop's struggle in several significant ways. They represented precisely the social sector from which the revolution claimed its legitimacy: namely, the poor and disenfranchised. Antirevolutionary market women posed a powerful counterpoint to the political legitimization of the rural man. Furthermore, these poor women claimed the same spiritual authority as did elite and middle-class women, verifying the church's claim that communism would threaten the centrality of faith without the formation of Guatemalan gender roles. While they do not fit into established social parameters, their perspective on communism echoed the sentiments of their middle- and upper-class counterparts.

The women's movements in support of the church and the antirevolutionary coalition were a powerful public symbol against the revolutionary government. The strongest alliance built by the archbishop, however, came not from the middle- and upper-class ladina population but rather from a sector of poor, working-class women who rallied around his ideological rhetoric. The market women became the perfect symbols for the archbishop's struggle against the Árbenz government, and their passionate support of the archbishop and fervent opposition to anything labeled "communist" led them on countless marches and public demonstrations during the Árbenz administration. Although the public perceived their activism to be motivated simply by religious concerns, the market women held a socioeconomic rationale as well. Spurred by economic hardships, their protest activities must be placed within the broader context of their economic instability and vulnerability as poor, working-class women. It is indeed ironic that one of the most powerful men in Guatemala received protection from some of the most vulnerable and impoverished of his parishioners. While the market women may have benefited more directly from reforms brought about by the revolution, they became the face of those Guatemalans who most opposed its existence and helped to bring it down.

The market women occupied the most complex of sociopolitical positions during the revolutionary decade, defying simple categorization. While some of the market women eagerly worked with Elisa Martínez de Arévalo's social reform movement and the Alianza's economic initiatives, others aligned themselves with the antirevolutionary elite through the archbishop and the Catholic Church. In spite of their vulnerable economic position and social marginalization, they engaged with the burgeoning Cold War political rhetoric that linked the revolutionary government with communism and actively worked for its overthrow. Analysis of their activities expands the established conclusions regarding resistance to the revolution. As poor, working-class women who were frequently also heads of their households, they interpreted the revolution's success or failure through the lens of the economy. They occupied an oppositional space to the revolution legitimized by the Catholic Church and the antirevolutionary movement, to voice economic concerns that otherwise might have been ignored, exposing the gender of the economy by their protests.

Epilogue

THE RETURN TO SILENCE

After more than seventy years of struggle, punctuated by politically repressive dictatorships, a profound new silence descended upon Guatemala once again following Jacobo Árbenz's resignation from the presidency on June 26, 1954. All those directly involved in the revolutionary government or pro-revolutionary projects went into hiding, many initially to the Mexican or Argentine embassies in Guatemala City. Leaders such as Ester de Urrutia destroyed all written evidence of their work. Only music could be heard over the radio, and Guatemala City was transformed once again into a dangerous and hostile landscape. As an eyewitness to these events, scholar Jean Franco's most vivid memory of these anxious days is that of Alaíde Foppa Falla reading her poems over the radio during the curfew. As Franco notes, literature became the sole avenue to voice this drama of loss and dislocation, "not only because it articulated the utopian but also because it is implicated in its demise."[1] Many of these writing women had not supported the Árbenz government, as they deemed its goals too radical. Reminiscent of their earlier strategies in the face of political repression, women returned to the literary world to express their sociopolitical ideas, as all else appeared to be too dangerous.

After a brief respite from publication, the national papers returned, printing long lists of Guatemalans now determined to be enemies of the state. Many of the ladinas involved with children's centers and education were among those whose names appeared in the lists. Guatemalans loyal to the new regime of Carlos Castillo Armas were encouraged to round up these "communists," and many teachers and school directors lost their positions. Some were arrested, and in one case the female director of a normal school outside the capital city was severely beaten. Harrowing tales of heroism by those who had fought alongside Castillo Armas appeared in the newspapers, along with unsubstantiated accounts of torture endured by Guatemalans under the Árbenz presidency. Countless revolutionary-era policies were reversed in the days and weeks that followed. The June 25 teachers' march was now co-opted by the victors, who claimed that the 1944 struggle had been finally concluded ten years later with an end to oppressive rule and the return to democracy without a caudillo.[2] There were immediate calls to reverse the enfranchisement of illiterate voters, threatening thousands of rural male voters.[3] By early 1955, voting for illiterate men had become optional rather than obligatory and the right to vote rescinded for anyone who publicly opposed the government.[4] The assets of those who had worked for the government under Jacobo Árbenz were frozen, as in the case of Alaíde Foppa Falla and her family.[5]

Following the abrupt end of the revolutionary project, the rupture in the urban ladina movement became more clearly defined. The women of the Arévalo era did not answer the pleas of the Alianza Femenina Guatemalteca to come to the aid of the revolution, and the writers and readers aligned with *Nosotras* and *Azul* remained utterly silent. The women's army formed in the heady days of the post-Ubico era had dismantled, and its reformist soldiers reconfigured their ideals by honoring the new first lady, Odilia de Castillo Armas, who assumed the presidency of the child-care centers. Her efforts in the area of child protection and education were now lauded as groundbreaking by those who had maintained the social reform dreams during the prerevolutionary years of dictatorship.[6] Gloria Menéndez Mina returned to the national stage the following year, founding another journal for women entitled *Mujer*. Here, the literary voices of the 1920s, 1930s, and 1940s emerged again, filling the pages with poetry and literature alongside photos of beautiful European-looking women. It ran for two years, published jointly by Menéndez Mina and Angelina Acuña de Castañeda. The contributors to *Mujer* included familiar names such as Luz Valle, Laura Rubio de Robles, Rosa de Mora, María del Pilar, Alaíde Foppa Falla, Martha Josefina Herrera, and María Albertina Gálvez. Whatever their misgivings about the series of military dictatorships that emerged in the post-1954 era, many of the Arévalo-era feminists reverted to their traditional literary strategy to cope with a hostile and dangerous political terrain.

The reconstitution of a conservative, maternal Guatemalan feminism was symbolized in the Christmas message of Odilia de Castillo Armas on December 24, 1956. Echoing the gender norms of the Ubico era, she praised Guatemalan women for their work as mothers and teachers. In essence, this message resurrected the maternal aspects of revolutionary feminism and assured women that they were welcome within these precise parameters of the new regime.[7] Odilia de Castillo Armas reimagined the Guatemalan woman as a maternally oriented social reformer, permanently alienating those women who had fused structural critique in their maternal feminism. Symbolically replacing the likes of women such as Ester de Urrutia and María Vilanova de Árbenz, the socially acceptable women of the Ubico era were elevated into leadership roles, representing Guatemalan women on the international stage. Educator Irene de Peyré became the Guatemalan representative to the Inter-American Commission of Women, and suffragist lawyer Graciela Quan Valenzuela attended several of the meetings.[8] In 1955, Quan Valenzuela became the counselor on social work for the president's Department of Social Affairs, representative of the Ministry of Foreign Affairs to the National UNESCO Committee in Guatemala, and vice chair of the organizing committee of the Council of Social Welfare for Guatemala. Rosa de Mora, founder of the Sociedad Protectora del Niño, was elected to the National Assembly as a *diputado* and assumed office on March 15, 1956, to become the first woman elected to public office in Guatemala. Mayoral candidate Juan Luis Lizarralde, who attributed his victory to the female constituency, now moved to thank the market women for their antirevolutionary efforts with the construction of two new markets in early 1955.[9] The most conservative of the Arévalo social reformers had reemerged, ensuring that traditional gender norms would not be disturbed, and in the following years María Chinchilla Recinos's name continued to be invoked and celebrated annually on June 25.

It is clear that the Guatemalan revolution had not disrupted the deeply rooted gender constructions. While urban ladinas benefited from the sociopolitical freedoms the revolution afforded, its limitations were palpable. The revolutionary rhetoric drew them into the public sphere and into direct political participation. The revolutionary project, however, appears to have acted against the interests of those women who transgressed traditional gender norms. As long as women remained within their maternal parameters, their efforts were applauded and raised up as part of the revolutionary banner. However, within this acceptance, there remained a tacit discomfort with their presence.

Ironically, the very revolution that facilitated the emergence of a full-blown social reform movement as well as a socialist feminist organization also contributed to the erasure of this feminist story. The resignation of Jacobo Árbenz in the face of military invasion ruptured a continuum of ladina activism that had existed since the 1880s. The destruction and dispersal of pivotal primary documents of the era solidified the silence created in June 1954. The violence perpetuated by a series of military governments since 1954 has affirmed this historical amnesia through the removal of any Guatemalans who attempt to recover these stories.

Female intellectuals and activists continue to be disappeared and murdered. Even when the threat of violence is not imminent, the lack of archival sources in Guatemala itself make any comprehensive study virtually impossible and contribute to the historical silencing of urban ladinas.

One of the primary purposes of this work has been to restore at least a segment of women in Guatemala City to the historical record, as they have been so effectively erased from the national memory and historical consciousness. What this story reveals is a complex, significant, and palpable feminist movement that emerged and survived under the most difficult political circumstances, a feminist consciousness that emerged slowly and sporadically, as women struggled to critique and identify Guatemala's gendered structures in a context of repressive dictatorial political regimes and entrenched patriarchy. Education was the foundation for this early feminist activism, and in turn this vanguard of female teachers worked to preserve a modicum of intellectualism in a nation devoid of such opportunities. Although the Liberal governments maintained a steady rhetoric about the significance of education, such policies were rarely implemented, since an educated populace was not in the best interest of dictatorial regimes. Although what educators were able to accomplish was limited by lack of funding and material support, the teachers themselves became the conduit for change as they nurtured a feminist consciousness during decades of repression.

As such, the rise and trajectory of Guatemalan feminism defies generally held patterns across Latin America. Despite the fact that a discernable feminist movement can be identified as early as the 1880s, the women involved in the urban movements achieved few legal or civic successes. The 1920s saw the introduction of suffrage and new accessibility to education, but this progress stopped short of real reform. In fact, during the Jorge Ubico regime, laws reinforced women's subservient social and political role. This pattern of repression and reprieve continued during the seventy years under examination here. Urban middle-class women would struggle for access to education, civil and political equality, and public acceptance of women as intelligent and capable of political engagement. Each of these movements surfaced briefly before being submerged by another wave of repression. The teacher training center, the Instituto Normal de Señoritas, Belén, nurtured and sustained these movements, a female-centered space of intellectual safety for urban ladinas. While the most visible leaders of these movements occupied a middle-class social position, some of the most important feminist figures rose to prominence from very humble beginnings, including first lady Elisa Martínez de Arévalo, Vicenta and Jesús Laparra, and Ester de Urrutia.

These women created a symbolic bridge across the rural and urban divide that attracted many to their movement, an attribute particularly prevalent with the Alianza Femenina Guatemalteca.

Following the formal October revolution, the urban ladinas of Guatemala City fought for and achieved two additional revolutions between 1944 and 1954. First, women from every social sector literally risked their lives for the birth of a new revolutionary government in the events of June and October 1944. As the revolution emerged and transformed society, however, it became increasingly evident to these women that they needed to undertake another type of revolution, quite simply, one that included women. Two interconnected but distinct agendas were formulated. One spoke of economic reform, dignity, and intellectual and civil freedom for the nation. The second addressed needs specific to women. Here, urban ladinas fought for and won the right of suffrage, the establishment of daycare and nutrition centers for poor and working-class women and their children, the right to participate in national politics, increased access to education, a literacy campaign, and even the right to own their own land and act as heads of household.

After the highly visible and successful campaign for limited suffrage, only the Alianza Femenina Guatemalteca made any attempt to address the reality that a majority of women had not been enfranchised and therefore remained politically marginalized. Most urban ladinas shifted their energies to focus on the desperate social conditions in which a majority of Guatemalan children lived. The feminist movements of the Arévalo period were the direct descendants of the visions nurtured under the earlier dictatorships, and they were poised and ready to act once the opportunity presented itself. Although the early movements primarily included Guatemala's educated elite—women such as Rosa de Mora, Gloria Menéndez Mina, Luz Valle, Mélida Montenegro de Méndez, and Angelina Acuña de Castañeda—they worked diligently to achieve civil and political equality for all Guatemalan women. Unified in their struggle to defeat Ubico and gain political equality, these urban ladinas presented a united front against poverty, homelessness, and illiteracy despite their politically diverse perspectives. The primary characteristic of this first wave of revolutionary feminist activity was its focus on maternal concerns, addressing the overwhelming health-care and educational needs of Guatemala's children and poor families. The comedores infantíles and guarderías infantíles improved the lives of Guatemala City's poorest residents through education, hygiene, health care, and child-care programs, transforming the daily lives of thousands of working mothers and their children.

While men actively worked out the politics of the day, women of various political ideologies took on the most neglected aspects of the Guatemalan nation—its forgotten people, its health services, its education—and tried to remove the worst of the social ills afflicting their nation.

The 1947 First Inter-American Congress of Women revealed the political diversity among the urban ladinas of the early revolutionary period. Challenged by global Cold War dynamics, a new group of women emerged, willing to openly engage in politics. These women possessed a political consciousness distinct from that of their suffragist counterparts that sought not only to address the suffering of Guatemala's impoverished but to question the very economic, social, and political structures that maintained this inequity. Embracing the maternalism of the Arévalo feminists, the women of the Alianza Femenina Guatemalteca expanded beyond the maternalistic boundaries of women's political activity. They engaged in their own gender analysis of the revolution, were discontented with its results, and subsequently crossed both race and class lines to align themselves with poor and indigenous women. The women of the Alianza stand alone in their analysis, which revealed how the foundations of Guatemalan society simultaneously privileged men and disenfranchised women.

Despite the indisputable contributions of Elisa Martínez de Arévalo and María Vilanova de Árbenz to urban ladina movements, little if any attention has been paid to them. Under their leadership, unprecedented social reforms occurred, creating a distinctly new sense of nationalism as the poor and oppressed were directly brought into the national revolutionary project. Drawing like-minded women to their causes, these two women helped create distinct types of women's movements and notions of feminism. Through their very presence, Guatemalan women gained access to the political process at the highest levels. When the national political process did not accommodate their altruistic ideals, both Martínez de Arévalo and Vilanova de Árbenz sought broad-based civil support for their activities, essentially working outside the bounds of the political process. During the 1950s, under the leadership of Vilanova de Árbenz, the Alianza directly confronted the gender-biased reform policies of her husband's government. In short, Martínez de Arévalo and Vilanova de Árbenz provided a new model of a politically committed Latin American woman.

The paradox of the Guatemalan revolutionary period is that the most politically active women of the revolution were neither of the pro-revolutionary middle class nor of the poor working class, for whom many of its social reforms were designed, but were rather the conservative, urban supporters of the Catholic Church. One of the central ironies of the revolution is that the church itself then succeeded in building a strong alliance with a sector of poor, working-class women for its antirevolutionary agenda, who rallied around the ideological rhetoric of anticommunism, Catholicism, and the increasingly high cost of living. The market women drew national attention to their antirevolutionary cause, effectively destabilizing Guatemalan society through their numerous demonstrations. The informal leader of the market women, Concha Estéves, remains nationally recognizable and is even spoken of in admiration by ardent revolutionaries.

A study of Guatemalan women contributes to a more nuanced understanding of the eventual overthrow of the revolution. While there is no one simple answer, this work highlights the failure of the revolution to take the citizenship of women and their potential political power seriously.[10] The continuation of patriarchal mores was a significant obstacle to their integration into national life. Although the revolutionary rhetoric called for equality, it failed to put this equality into practice. Without a fundamental reevaluation of gender roles, Guatemalan women were faced with continuous opposition in all aspects of their work, except that which was deemed appropriate to their gender. This study illustrates one aspect of how larger structures of power, in this case masculine power, interacted with and frequently obstructed the social reforms and revolutionary work initiated by women. While its complexity defies a single explanation, the exclusion of urban ladina women of all social classes from full revolutionary participation must now be integrated into the explanation of its demise.

The analysis undertaken here also suggests that the support of both female voters and poor market women for the antirevolutionary movement was a critical element in the ultimate demise of the revolution. The revolution's failure to integrate Guatemalan women themselves and needs specific to gender had dire consequences. Although the rhetoric of reform permeated the revolutionary period, including the equality of all Guatemalans, the practice of equality for women was severely limited. The Catholic Church successfully integrated a large number of antirevolutionary women into its ranks through the manipulation of two central aspects of Guatemalan identity: traditional notions of gender and the Catholic faith. Archbishop Mariano Rossell y Arellano melded commonly held notions of gender and religious faith into one powerful threat.

Although literate Guatemalan women were granted the vote, the revolutionary politicians paid little attention to them following their integration in March 1945. Ironically, these pro-revolutionary politicians were most concerned about women voting for conservative candidates based on their allegiance to the Catholic Church. However, the pro-revolutionary politicians did not follow up on these concerns, implying that they continued to discount the potential significance of the female voter. The archbishop, however, understood their power in municipal elections and actively recruited them to vote for pro-Catholic or pro-conservative political parties. These antirevolutionary women were an indication of the revolution's failure to include women in its social and political agenda. Fundamentally, the politicians were unable or unwilling to speak to the needs of women in Guatemala City and failed to incorporate their energy into the national project. The Catholic Church successfully manipulated gender norms in order to gain support from both literate women, who demonstrated their political opposition at the voting stations, as well as illiterate women, whose innumerable demonstrations and political protests created social instability and the perception of a demoralized revolutionary government.

The revolution's failure to integrate the new female voting block into its agenda had unexpected results. The female vote became a critical element in the successful antirevolutionary campaign against both the Arévalo and Árbenz governments. Based on analysis of the voting practices and political activities of women, few literate women took advantage of the opportunity. This lack of civic participation solidified notions of Guatemalan women as defenders of the home, the traditional order, and the church, characteristics that had initially created distrust of suffrage. Analysis of suffrage during the revolution suggests that policy makers made a critical miscalculation. The women most likely to support the revolution, the rural and the poor, were precluded from participation by the enfranchisement of only literate women. The maintenance of patriarchal values among those otherwise believed to be radical and moderate revolutionaries thwarted efforts by feminist organizations to advance the revolution's reforms to enact significant social changes. Along with the latent contradictions over the incorporation of peasants and workers, analysis must now include women and gender as a critical factor.

An examination of the motivating factors for the market women reveals several new aspects integral to understanding the success of the antirevolutionary movement. Commonly understood to be instigated primarily by the US State Department and the Central Intelligence Agency, the antirevolutionary movement is here explored using a distinctly internal approach, and this book's conclusions expand currently held understandings of this political opposition. Significant inflation created economic difficulties for Guatemala's poorest, including the market women. Analyses of these women suggest that the high cost of living played a critical role in their antirevolutionary leanings.

For the majority of the period covered by this study, women held social and political influence only through literary and journalistic endeavors. Through the Herculean efforts of women such as Vicenta and Jesús Laparra, Rosa Rodríguez López, Luz Valle, and Gloria Menéndez Mina, a few Guatemalan women published in their own voice. The informal social networks established through their journals and writings created a cohesive identity for urban ladinas outside of mainstream politics and society at large. Their ability to retain a separate feminist vision of themselves made it possible for these women to survive decades of patriarchy and dictatorial regimes. In essence, through their literary legacy, they wrote women back into Guatemalan history.

Urban ladinas continue to imagine a place for themselves in contemporary Guatemala. While the 1954 overthrow of Jacobo Árbenz marks a definitive break in the legacy of activism that began in the 1880s, the ideals postulated by women in the Alianza Femenina Guatemalteca continued on among individuals flung across the hemisphere. Some of these social and political ideals found new voice among young women who joined resistance movements during the 1960s. Feminist movements reemerged during the 1970s and 1980s despite intense state-sanctioned violence and terror. These movements resurrected many of the social and political ideals urban ladinas struggled for during the Guatemalan revolution, with a notable shift. These new movements embraced women across the rural and urban, and class and ethnic divides to form diverse associations that the women of the Alianza had dreamed of and struggled for forty years earlier. Along with all the social and political concerns of an earlier era, new voices calling for sexual equality, antihomophobia laws, and measures against sexualized and family violence joined the chorus. In the summer of 2015, as Guatemala City was once again rocked by mass demonstrations, now against the presidency of Otto Pérez Molina, signs appeared from among the crowds reading: "The children of Árbenz have awoken." Despite the deep repression Guatemalan women have struggled against, their ideals and hopes remain, and urban ladinas are still imagining a place for themselves.

Appendix A

NAMING THE NAMELESS

A Work in Progress: Naming the Nameless

One of the goals of this study has been to identify as many Guatemalan women as possible, to simply name those who have been nameless for decades and centuries. A majority of the women identified in this work represent the urban, the ladina, and the educated. The names are arranged in chronological order under each chapter as they appear in the primary sources.

Introduction

Julia Urrutia. She was an educator and was very active during the revolutionary years. She marched in the June 25, 1944, demonstration. She spoke at several important rallies during the campaign for suffrage. Eventually, she moved to the experimental community of Poptún to work as a teacher. In her eighties in 2004, she has continued to promote the rights of women, particularly in the areas of education and birth control.

Chapter One

Vicenta Laparra de la Cerda. She was born in 1831 and died on January 29, 1905. There is more detail on her life in chapter 1.

Jesús Laparra. Older sister to Vicenta Laparra de la Cerda, she edited and published the first book for Guatemalan women, *Ensayos poéticos*, in 1854. In 1884, the year before the appearance of the journal *La Voz de la Mujer*, Jesús published her second book, *Ensueños de la mente*. Jesús died in January 1887. There is more detail on her life in chapter 1.

Desideria Reyes de Laparra. She was married to Nicolás Laparra and was the mother of Vicenta and Jesús Laparra. She died in 1836.

Josefa Laparra. She was the sister of Vicenta and Jesús Laparra.

Rafaela del Águila. She was a teacher and contributor to the journal *El Ideal*. On June 28, 1888, Águila become the director of the Escuela Normal de Señoritas, the renamed Primera Normal de Señoritas, which became a leader center for the promotion of women's education. Águila, along with *El Ideal* colleague Adelaida Chavéz, played a central role in the modernization of Guatemala's school curriculum in the first pedagogical congress held in 1881.

J. Adelaida Chávez. She was on the editorial board of *El Ideal*. She played a central role in the modernization of Guatemala's school curriculum in the first pedagogical congress held in 1881.

Isabel M. de Castellanos. She was on the editorial board of *El Ideal*.

Carmen P. de Silva. She was on the editorial board of *El Ideal*.

Celinda D. Darmes. She was a freelance contributor to *El Ideal*.

Sara María G. S. de Morena. She was a freelance contributor to *El Ideal*.

Doña Encarnación Robles de Barillas. She was president of the Catholic charity La Sociedad de Caridád and in that role became the benefactor of *El Ideal*. She was also the wife of Guatemalan president Manuel Lisandro Barillas.

Dolores Mesa. She participated in the first pedagogical congress held in Guatemala City in 1881.

Dolores Nájera. She participated in the first pedagogical congress held in Guatemala City in 1881.

Concepción Santa Cruz. She participated in the first pedagogical congress held in Guatemala City in 1881.

WOMEN INJURED DURING THE 1920 REVOLUTION

María Luisa Gabriel, aged 19, from Rabinal
Francisca Tovar, aged 12, from Guatemala City
María Iriarte, aged 32, from Guatemala City
Micaela Barrientos, aged 35, from Amatitlán
Magdalena Flores, aged 23, from Guatemala City
Mercedes Montenegro, aged 55, from Guatemala City
Martina Medina, aged 36, from Guatemala City
Dolores Sánchez, aged 35, from Guatemala City
Asunción García de Gómez, aged 30, from San Raymundo

Sara Flores, aged 5, from Guatemala City
Manuela Villavicencio, aged 32, from Guatemala City
María Arévalo, aged 19, from Guatemala City
Albertina Orellana, aged 16, from Guatemala City
Julia Reyes, aged 21, from Guatemala City
Mercedes U. del Valle, Joaquina Flores, Julia Martínez, Margarita Jaimes,
 Juana Paniagua, and Magdalena Aguilar, all aged 50
Concepción Morales and Celestina López, both aged 35
Francesca Mendoza, María Chacón, Beatriz Ortega Castro, Isabel Ortega
 Castro, Cayetana Vda. de Paniagua, and Encarnación Méndez,
 all aged 24
Fidela Rivera, aged 17
Aurelia Castellanos, aged 28
Argelia Gómez (young girl)
Clara Catoj (young girl)
Dolores Morelos, aged 26
and four unidentified women

Encarnación Nufio Duarte. In 1943, Encarnación celebrated fifty years of teaching. She acknowledged the role of both Rafaela del Águila and the Instituto Normal de Señoritas, Belén, as significant influences on her career.

Luz Castillo Díaz Ordaz. From Quetzaltenango, she was the first woman from Central America to receive a law degree.

Rosa de Mora. One of the three founders of the Sociedad Protectora del Niño, she was a consistent presence among social reformers from the 1920s to the 1950s. She worked diligently to promote health-care reform in Guatemala City for poor women and children, and she wrote a book on puericultura. She played an active role throughout the Juan José Arévalo administration and was eventually elected to the National Assembly in 1956 as the body's first female *diputado*. Rosa was married to the physician Federico Mora.

María Herrera de Aschkel. She was one of the three founders of the Sociedad Protectora del Niño.

Marta Escobar de Richardson. She was one of the three founders of the Sociedad Protectora del Niño.

Anita R. Espinoza. She is noted for her academic accomplishments early in her life.[1] She later became director of the Instituto Nacional Central de Señoritas and served as president of the women's auxiliary of the Red Cross in the 1920s.

Isaura de Menéndez Mina. Her literary contributions appeared in several journals throughout the 1910s and 1920s including *El Grito del Pueblo, Vida,* and *Revista del Trabajo.* She appears to have held a high profile in the literary community and was the mother of journalist Gloria Menéndez Mina.

Several women were noted as influential in the establishment of the Escuela Normal Superior, including Amalia Samayoa Aguilar, Aída Martínez R., Martina Cordero de León, María Josefa Estrada, Dorotea T. de Barrera, and Hortensia Aguilar.

Amalia Samayoa Aguilar. She was the director of the Escuela Normal Central de Preceptoras. She also ran the Escuela de Artes y Oficios Femeniles. A school was eventually named in her honor in 1953.

Alicia Aguilar Castro. She was one of three teachers chosen to study overseas to improve their methodology. Aguilar Castro went to Belgium.

María Teresa Llardén de Molina. She founded a preparatory school, the Escuela Preparatoria, in 1918. She was the first educator in Guatemala to promote a bachelor's degree program, believing that education was a principle necessity of life. She wrote a column for several months in *El Imparcial* promoting the secularization of education. Her two daughters, Elisa Molina Llardén de Farner and Clara Molina Llardén, each served as director of the school after her death in 1924.

Marta Julia Castañeda G. She was the leader of one of the female affiliates of the Partido Unionista.

The first female labor strike was held in November 1925. The leaders of the organizing committee were Berta Reyes, Ernestina Sierra, Elisa Murga, and Amelia Villagrán.

Rosa Rodríguez López. She was president of the Sociedad Gabriela Mistral. She grew up surrounded by wealth and privilege in her native Guatemala. Her mother, Alicia López Sarana, who was originally from Colombia, was a prominent socialite married to Ernesto Rodríguez Robles, a powerful coffee grower. With the help of a coterie of servants and tutors, Alicia and Ernesto reared four children, one son and three daughters, on their sprawling estate. Rosa received an education appropriate to her station and gender, spoke Spanish and French, and showed an early aptitude for poetry.

Graciela Rodríguez López. She was Rosa's sister and worked with her in the Sociedad Gabriela Mistral. She remained in Guatemala, and her name changed to Graciela de Mata Amado once married. Graciela worked with Gloria Menéndez Mina as a reporter for *Azul*.

Matilda Rivera Cabeza. She served as the vice president for the Sociedad Gabriela Mistral.

Elisa Mencos R. She served as the secretary for the Sociedad Gabriela Mistral.

Magda Mabarak. She was one of the original founders of the Sociedad Gabriela Mistral.

Martha Josefina Herrera. She was a well-known writer and was married to Guatemala's ambassador to Chile. He was apparently sent to Chile in 1938 pursuant to Jorge Ubico's policy of exiling his political opponents to diplomatic posts overseas.

The Sociedad Gabriela Mistral also worked with other high-profile writers in Guatemala City, including Clara Rubio de Escalar and María de Michel.

Dolores Ramírez Fontecha. She ran the library established by the Sociedad Gabriela Mistral.

Dolores Monroy. She was the director of the Escuela de Artes y Oficios Femeniles.

Josefina Saravia E. She contributed articles to the journal *Vida* for the Sociedad Gabriela Mistral, and to the labor journal *Revista del Trabajo*.

Laura Rubio de Robles. She was involved in the Sociedad Gabriela Mistral. Her name appears throughout the 1920s, 1930s, 1940, and 1950s in both elite social reform organizations and literary associations.

Alicia G. Martínez. She was the first woman to graduate from the Escuela Nacional de Telegrafos on September 14, 1922.

Irene de Peyré. She attended the Seventh International Conference of American States in Montevideo in 1933. She was also very involved in the campaign for suffrage in 1944–1945. It is possible that she is related to María Peyré, the president of the Asociación de Maestras Católicas de Guatemala.

Chapter Two

Luz Valle. She was the editor of *Nosotras*, a journal published for women from 1932 to 1941. She was born on October 18, 1896. There is more detail on her life in chapter 4.

Gloria Menéndez Mina (de Padilla). She was the editor of *Azul*, a journal published for women from 1939 until 1949. There is more detail on her life in chapter 4.

Amália Valle. The sister of Luz Valle, she worked at *Nosotras* as the staff administrator.

The regional representatives for the journal *Nosotras* included María de Trocoli in Antigua, Elvira de Ramírez in Amatitlán, Elódia de Rodríguez in Quetzaltenango, Olga Waldheim in Zacapa, María Luis de Figueroa in Santa Lucía, Matilde Ovalle in Suchitepéquez, María Teresa Quintana in Sololá, and Elena Galindo in Huehuetenango.

Aurea Hernández de León. She worked as the codirector of *Azul* and was the daughter of Ubico supporter and newspaper editor Federico Hernández de León.

Julia Meléndez de DeLeón. She was an educator and defended Luz Valle in a series of articles published in *El Imparcial* in 1937. She became a leader in the struggle for suffrage and was appointed director of the new Escuela Normal para Señoritas "Centro América," established in Guatemala City on April 11, 1946.

In 1947, a Central American peace group was organized representing many of the women from within both Luz Valle's and Gloria Menéndez Mina's social circles.[2] The members of the Sociedad por Paz de Centro América included Estebana C. Vda. de Barrientos (she was a member of the Bahá'ís and the theosophical society), Anita Z. Vda. de España, Rosa A. Vda. de Saravia E., Manuela Vda. de Mathew, María del Pilar, Olivia de Wyld, Narcisa Villa Nueva, Isaura de Menéndez Mina, Luz Valle, Albertina de Samayoa, Josefina Saravia E., Amalia Samayoa Aguilar, María L. Rodríguez, Ana Gilma Mendoza, María Carrascosa, Graciela de León, and Sara Cerna Zepeda.

Graciela Quan Valenzuela. She was from Antigua and graduated from the Instituto Normal de Señoritas, Belén, in June 1931. She received her law degree in December 1943, becoming Guatemala's second female lawyer. Quan Valenzuela was involved in the campaign for suffrage, acting as its first president.

Luz Méndez de la Vega. She wrote a women's page in the newspaper *El Liberal Progresista* during the early 1940s.

Malin D'Echevers. She married into the elite Wyld Ospina family and was very much involved with writing and supporting Luz Valle and Gloria Menéndez Mina. From all available information, it appears that she changed her birth name, Amalia Castillo, to Malin D'Echevers; she was a prominent writer who had been affiliated with the Sociedad Gabriela Mistral during the 1920s. Malin was an influential member of the Unión de Mujeres Democráticas and assisted in the 1947 First Inter-American Congress of Women.

In March 1933, in *Nosotras*, Luz Valle featured teachers from across the country. She included a list of schools and their directors: the Escuela de Artes y Oficios Femeniles (the director was Amalia Samayoa Aguilar, and the teachers were Delfina Murga, María Luisa Rodríguez, María Luisa Vda. de Escobar, Cóncha de Berdúo, Rosa de Zelaya, and Carmen de Loessener); the Instituto Nacional Central de Señoritas (the director was Anita R. Espinoza, and the teachers were Marieta de González, Josefina Ruiz, Margarita Aragón, Blanca Palma, Toti Morosso, Elvira García Aguilar, Virginia Cruz, Edelmira Pérez, Manuela Monzón, Aída Martínez, Rosario Putzus, Berta Ramírez, Coesa de León, Emma de López, María Cóbar de Rubio, Octavia de Jáuregui, María Vda. de Panagos, María Luis Rodríguez, and Carmen de Bocanegra); the Escuela Delfino Sánchez (the director was Rosalina Peña); the Colegio Europeo (director was María Cristina B. de Rólz); el Colegio de Santa Teresita (the director was Rosita Molina Midence); the Colegio el Sagrado Corazón (the director was Susana I. de Palomo); the Escuela Nacional de Niñas Republica Argentina (the director was Tula Ortega); the Escuela Normal de Maestras para Párvulos; and the Escuela Gabriela Mistral (the director was Natalia Górriz de Morales; she is also listed as director of the Escuela Normal de Maestras para Párvulos, and Yolanda de Argueta is listed as one of the teachers).

Although no teachers from the Instituto Nacional Central de Señoritas are listed, *Nosotras* names the women who graduated with a teaching degree, including Alicia García Salas, Alicia Sánchez, Berta Cintora Funes, Ester Deleón, Bertha Nájera, Concha Azmitia, Alicia J. Castellóu, Adriana Muñoz, Adela Jiménez, Alicia Herrera, Mercedes Sánchez, Mirthala Rodríguez, Luz Mayorga, Francisca Fernández, Martha Sardá, Berta Mazariegos, Lidia Aldana, Laura Sarti, Estele Colón, Cristina Rodríguez, Dora Balcárcel, Carmen Corzo, Martha de León, Elena Perdomo, Concha Ruíz, Concha Berganza, Francisca Toledo, Berta Recinos, Olga Cintora Funes, Concha Fernández, Catalina Herrera, Blanca Mélida Hurtado, Raquel Gordillo, Rosalía Guzmán, Zoila Luz Ruano, Raquel Divas,

Mélida Lanza, Mercedes Román, Olivia Peña, Flora Chavarría, Carmen Lima, Francisca Carranza, Olivia Sanchinel, Elvira Escobar, Graciela Cisneros, and Guadalupe Alvarado. The following women graduated with bachelor's degrees: Francisca Fernández Hall, Mélida Lanza, Elena Perdomo, Berta Recinos, Zoila Luz Ruano, Marta Bouscayrol, Berta Cintora Funes, Olga Cintora Funes, Alicia García Salas, Concha Fernández, and Carmen Valdés. Women who graduated with teaching diplomas from the Instituto Normal de Señoritas de Quetzaltenango included María Piedad Jiménez, Alicia Herrera, Sara Orteiz, María Linda Diaz, Concha Lagrange, Hena Bocnegra, Carmen Galicia, Isabel Burgess, Leonor Molina, Magdalena Reyes, and Caridad Barrientos. Women who graduated with teaching diplomas from the Instituto Normal de Señoritas de Chiquimula included Julia Orozco, Jovita Aldana, Domitilia Rodríguez, Zoila Ramírez, Margarita Porta, Rosa Retana, Encarnación Palma, Isabel España, Corina Ayala, Margarita Siguí, Cristina Marroquín, Olimpia Porta, Luisa Lemus y Lemus, Elena Guzmán, María Antonia Casasola, M. Cristina Portillo, Jovita Swanson, Marta Ayala, María Chew, Guillermina Godoy, and Bernarda Cordón. Women who graduated with diplomas in practical arts from the Escuela de Artes Femeniles de Quetzaltenango included Emelda de León, Emma Díaz, Josefina Cabrera, Marta Saldaña, Isabel Rellano, Francisca R. Sánchez, Ofelia González, Albertina G. Ruíz, Amelia Lafuente, Angelina Funes, Julia Barrios, and Amanda Santizo. Women who graduated with teaching diplomas from the Escuela Normal de Señoritas de Antigua included Julia Sandoval, Isabel Figueredo, Evelia Calderón, Victoria Moralos, Marta Palomo, Marta García, Julia Berta Sánchez, Clemencia Salazar, Rosa Marta Aceituno, Olga Alicia Vides, Clemencia Molina, Matilde Gaitán, M. Antonia Acevedo, Luz Medina, Marta Samayoa, Celia Marroquín, and Julia García V. Finally, Susana Montealegre and Marí Ester Montealegre are listed as teachers at the Colegio María Auxiliadora.

Magdalena Spínola de Aguilar Fuentes. She was a well-known poet and played an important role in the campaign for suffrage. Her father, Rafael Spínola, was also a well-known Guatemalan writer. Magdalena's husband was killed by Jorge Ubico during the 1930s. She ran as a council member as a political affiliate of Clemente Marroquín Rojas in the 1946 municipal elections.

María del Pilar. She contributed poetry to Luz Valle's *Nosotras*. She continued writing throughout the 1940s and 1950s, and her work reappeared in Gloria Menéndez Mina's journal *Mujer* in 1955.

Natalia Górriz Vda. de Morales. She was born on July 21, 1869. Her father was

Colonel Manuel Górriz and her mother, Mercedes Porras de Górriz. The family moved to Guatemala City in 1876, where she attended the Escuela Normal Central and the Instituto de Señoritas. She got a teaching license in November 1884, and she graduated in science and letters the following year. On May 8, 1885, she was named director of the Escuela Complementaria de Niños. In 1887, she became the secretary of public instruction. In the 1930s, she was the director of the Escuela Normal de Maestras para Párvulos and the Escuela Gabriela Mistral.

Chapter Three

María Chinchilla Recinos. She was a young teacher who was killed by Jorge Ubico's forces on June 25, 1944. She became the symbol of the Guatemalan revolution.

Aída Sándoval, Hilda Balaños, and *Esperanza Barrientos.* They were injured in the June 25, 1944, event.

Julieta Castro de Rólz Bennett. She was injured in the June 25, 1944, attack on protesting teachers. Her injury played a significant role during the congressional debate on women's suffrage.

Many people were injured or killed during the events of June 25, 1944. During the morning events, the following names appeared in *El Imparcial*: Enrique Muñoz Meany, Carlos Illescas, Otto Raúl González, Micaela Arias de Alvarado, Jesús Alvarado, René Berger, Celso Cerezo, Carlos Navarrete, Gregorio Flores, Tomás Leal, Julio y Rogelio Ramírez Contreras, Edgar Lenhoff, Carlos Vela D., Carlos García Manzo, Marta López, Tito Oliva, Teófilo Meléndez (fourteen years old), Francisco Aguilar P., Abelardo López, and Jesús Polanco.

The following names appeared in the afternoon list: María Chinchilla (Recinos), Dolores Gallardo, Soledad Samayoa, Afrain Jiménez Archila, Celso de León Rabanales, Miguel García Valle, Urbano Posadas, Antonio Rivas, Esperanza Barrientos Fuentes, Alicia de la Cruz, Francisco Us, Aída Sándoval, and Francisca Arango.[3]

The following people were treated for their wounds in their own homes, indicating their high social status: Ella Alfaro de Castillo and Sally Rawson (both from Costa Rica), Julieta Castro de Rólz Bennett, Cristina Paniagua, and Beatriz Irigoyen Arzú.

The October revolution also had female martyrs. Among the hundreds of names listed, here are the women who were killed: Augusta Arriaga, Candelaria Reyes (age 17), Amalia Figueroa (26), Berta Luz Figueroa Méndez (26), Blanca de Saavedra (23), Margarita Orellana de Ruíz (27), Basilia Arias (33), Josefa Pérez (26), Graciela Cruz Grijalva (33), Thelma Yolanda, María España Vda. de Méndez, Graciela López (82), Berta Rubin, Argelia G. de Panjagua (18), Francesca Gómez, Blanca Rosa Castillo (18), Isabel Montesino (16), Julia H. de Galino (18), María de García (36), Lidia Quiroz (48), Carmen Monterroso (15, operating room), María Rafaela Monterroso (24), Nieves Escobar (23), Anita Granacos (35, operating room), Enriqueta Monzón (17, operating room), Juana González (33), Virginia Estrada (18, operating room), Dolores Pérez Méndez (13, operating room), Concepción Escobar (22, operating room), Carmen Goshon (34, operating room), María Luisa Morales (22, operating room), Concepción Rosales, Señora Keller (23), Rosalia Pérez (44), María Antonia Ramírez, Catalina Marroquín (19), Raquel Paniagua (35), Arcadia Gramajo (24), Zoila Saravia (37), and Rosa Castañeda (18).

Three others were killed on October 20, when a bomb fell on their house: Margarita Lorenzana Zepeda de Rubí, her daughter María Albertina Rubí Lorenzana, and her nephew.

Berta de Figueroa. She played a prominent role in the October uprising. Her role was featured in the newspaper *Nuestro Diario.*
Angelina Acuña de Castañeda. She was a poet from El Salvador. Acuña de Castañeda had a radio program for women during the Ubico regime. She was an educator and played an active role in Guatemalan politics during the revolutionary years. She ran for the National Assembly in 1947 and participated in the suffrage campaign.

A school of social work was established in 1949. The leaders of the new institution included a significant number of women: Rosa de Mora (one of the founders of the Sociedad Protectora del Niño); Carmen Rodríguez Beteta (Asociación Nacional de Muchachas Guías); Dr. María Isabel Escobar, Graciela Quan Valenzuela de Reina (lawyer), and Miss Wisks of the Club Altrusas; Marina Tinoco and Luz de León (representing Acción Católica); Marta Escobar de Richardson (representative of the Casa del Niño); doña Mélida Montenegro de Méndez (representative of the Asociación de Comedores); doña Herda de Engel (representative of the Boy Scouts); and Lily de Pullín (of the Sociedad Protectora del Niño).[4] While the Instituto Guatemalteco de Seguridad Social represented a critical step forward in social reform, its efforts were concentrated on the formal labor market, which was dominated by men.[5]

María Albertina Gálvez. She was the director of the National Library for sixteen years (1929–1945). Gloria Menéndez Mina tried to have Gálvez named to the position of minister of public education in 1945.

The committee designated to design and initiate the national literacy campaign in 1944 included Elisa Hall de Asturias, Angelina Acuña de Castañeda, Lily de Jongh Osborne, María Ortega de Newbill, and Alaíde Foppa Falla.

Chapter Four

The Asociación de Mujeres Intelectuales was created in January 1944. Its membership included Malin D'Echevers de González, Magdalena Spínola de Aguilar Fuentes, Stella Márquez, María del Pilar Vásquez de García, Margarita Leal, Angelina Acuña de Castañeda, Josefina Saravia de Alfaro, Adriana Saravia de Palarea, and Romelia Alarcón Folgar.

The Unión de Mujeres Americanas was created in February 1944. Its membership included Clemencia Rubio de Herrarte, Luz Valle, Carmen Ydígoras, Magdalena Spínola de Aguilar Fuentes, María Luisa Samayoa, Margarita Leal, Josefina Bosque, María Hortensia Pinto, Ana Josefina Pellecer L., Esperanza Rodríguez Ojeda, Marta Grace Rosales C., and Matilde Chinchilla.

Enriqueta López y López de Gómez. She was the initial leader of the female affiliate of the Renovación Nacional. Other significant leaders included Josefina Bosque, María Hortensia Pinto, Ana Josefina Pellecer L., Esperanza Rodríguez Ojeda, Marta Grace Rosales C., and Matilde Chinchilla.

Women organized their own affiliate group of the Frente Popular Libertador. Mélida Montenegro de Méndez (mother of future politicians Julio and Mario Méndez Montenegro, and president of the Asociación de Comedores) was named president, with Concha González Solis as vice president.

Leaders of the suffrage committee, the Comité Pro-Ciudadanía, included Gloria Menéndez Mina, Graciela Quan Valenzuela, Magdalena Spínola, and Clemencia Rubio de Herrarte.

The members of the Unión Cívica Guatemalteca were Graciela Quan Valenzu-

Naming the Nameless 309

ela, Elisa Hall de Asturias, Gloria Menéndez Mina, Angelina Acuña de Castañeda, María del Pilar Vásquez de García, Zoila Putzeys Vda. de Utrera, Magdalena Spínola, Romelia Alarcón Folgar, Clemencia Rubio de Herrarte, Laura Zachrisson de Bendfeldt, Adriana Saravia de Palarea, Julia Paíz, María Albertina Gálvez, Irene de Peyré, Rosa de Mora, María Herrera de Aschkel, Alaíde Foppa Falla, Elisa de Barrios, and Dominga de Álvarez.

Angelina Acuña de Castañeda. She was a teacher, poet, and political activist, active in a wide variety of women's associations throughout the 1930s and 1940s. She ran as a candidate for the Partido Renovación Socialista in 1947. She played an active role in the campaign for suffrage.

Four hundred women of the Renovación Nacional held a large rally to garner public support for their cause. Among those who pleaded with the National Assembly for civic inclusion were María Consuelo Pereira, Juan José Orozco Posadas, Ana Clemencia Aldana, Alicia González, and Julia Urrutia

The women who signed the initial declaration for suffrage in 1944, as listed in *El Imparcial* (the editors indicate that many more women signed but are not listed), are the following: Graciela Quan Valenzuela, Elisa Hall de Asturias, Gloria Menéndez Mina de Padilla, Romelia Alarcón Folgar, Elsa Rudeke de Asturias, Luz Molina de Rólz Bennett, María Albertina Gálvez, Luz Cobos Batres, Julia Cobos Batres, María de Irigoyen, Carmen de Arzú, Sara A. de Irigoyen, Isaura de Menéndez Mina, Angelina Acuña de Castañeda, Adela Corieto, María Mercedes Castillo de Toriella, Clemencia Gómez, Adelina Pullín de Moreno, Marta Vlaminck de Castillo, Irene de Peyré, Julieta Castro de Rólz Bennett, Mimi Asturias de Aycinena, Matilde P. de Durán, Carmen Durán de Del Cid, Lilia Pivvaral de Midence, Angela B. Paz, Elvira S. de Rodríguez Cerna, Alicia Cemborain, María Consuelo Arango, Laura de Arroyo, Estela Bolaños, Ofelia O. de Balcárcel, Rosa Margarita Barrios, María A. Castro, Sara C. de León, Amparo Franco Cordón, Aída Castillo, Mercedes Ceballos, Mirtala Castro, Rebeca Colombari Guillermina Coronado, Elsie Dalchow, Julia M. de León, Estela Drago, Sara Escobar, Emma Rosa González, E. Molina Gudiel, E. Izaguirre, Ester Lee, Consuelo López Q., María Hortenisa Lima, Mélida Montenegro de Méndez, Clemencia Muralles, Elsie E. Montenegro, Aída Martínez, Sofía G. Martínez, Algeria Morales, Otilia de Medrano, Isabel Yauragui de Núñez, María Teresa Orellana, Clara Andreu de Petrilli, Berta Alicia Pinillos, Graciela Palomo Keller, Ernestina Porras, Adriana Saravia de Palarea, Julia Paíz, Alicia Edelmira Pérez, Consuela Rodríguez,

Blanca E. de Reliquate, Lucy Sello, Julia de Schlesinger, Elvira E. Villacorta, Estela Villaseñor, Ana María B. Valle, Carmen Ydígoras Fuentes, Obdulia de Argueta, Elsa R. de Asturias, Clemencia Beteta, Concha Bautista, Amparo Barrios, Lucila Bonilla, Carlota Cifuentes, Clara Escobar, Telma Carrera, Alejandra Cifuentes, Margarita Cemborain, Marta de Castillo, Julia Mejía, María Teresa Mirón, Marisabel Pérez, Berta de Putzeys, Carmen A. de Putzeys, Mirtala Rodríguez, María Luisa de Ruiz, Dora René de Ruiz, Margot Bonilla, Rosa Delía Tábora, and Victoria Díaz Valdés.

The Congreso Femenino Pro-Ciudadanía de la Mujer was held on November 25, 1944. The representatives from regional departments included: for Quetzaltenango, Piedad de Mora, Florinda de Wedojlije, and Lucila Rodas; for San Marcos, Julieta Enríquez and Julia de Arreaga; for the Unión Femenina Guatemalteca in San Marcos, Marta Lilia Rodas and Rosa Barrios de Perusina; for Sololá, Marta Letona de Rivera, Rosa Amelia Ramírez, and Zoila Marina López; for Huehuetenango, María Leonor Sosa and Leonor Sosa (who claimed that the revolution had not yet come to their region), and Olga Vides; for Retalhuleu, Carmen Cabrera, María Octavia Enríquez, and Virginia Rodríguez; for Cobán, Tancho Linares and Carmen S. de Muñoz; for Salamá, Aracely Cojulún and Rosalía Valdés; for Jutiapa, Amparo Mencos and Alicia Machorro; for Jalapa, Isabel de Sandoval, Estela Palma, Tania Palma, Berta Elvira Godoy, and Elodía de Rodríguez; for Cuilapa, Olga Castillo M.; for Puerto Barrios, María Reresa de Reyes, Concha Coba de Gutiérrez, and María Mercedes Ceballos; for Mixco, Roselia Solórzano; for Antigua, Consuelo Rojas de Rojas, Victoria Godoy Cofiño, and Marina Schwartz; for El Progreso, Cándida Rosa Orellana; and for Santa Rosa, Olga Castillo. Victoria Chajón Chúa represented the Renovación Nacional.

Graciela Hernández de Zirión. She ran as a political candidate under the Miguel Ydígoras Fuentes presidential ticket in 1950.
María de Irigoyen. She ran as a council member under the Clemente Marroquín Rojas ticket in 1946.
Adriana Saravia de Palarea. She ran as a political candidate during the 1948 *diputado* elections for the conservative Partido Unificación Anticomunista. She ran again for the National Assembly in 1950.
María del Carmen Vargas. She held a degree in economics and ran for a pro-revolutionary party as a candidate for the National Assembly in 1948. In 1949, she participated in a United Nations conference as a Guatemalan representative.

Chapter Five

THE GUATEMALAN SECTION OF THE WOMEN'S INTERNATIONAL
LEAGUE FOR PEACE AND FREEDOM

The president was Graciela Quan Valenzuela de Reina; the vice president was Julia Meléndez de DeLeón; the secretaries were Angelina Acuña de Castañeda, G. Consuelo Rodríguez, and María Albertina Gálvez; the treasurer was María del Carmen Vargas; and the subtreasurer was Zoila Putzeys. General committee members included Mélida Luz Palacios de Wolter, Lucila Vda. de Aguirre Velásquez, Magdalena Spínola Vda. de Aguilar Fuentes, Romelia Alarcón Folgar, Olimpia Vda. de Barrientos, and Aurelia Sandoval Coronado. Also noted as general consultants were Natalia Morales de Lara, Mélida Montenegro de Méndez, María de Sellares, Luz Valle, and Rosa de Mora.

By early 1947, the Guatemalan section of the WILPF included: Estebana C. Vda. de Barrientos, Anita Z. Vda. de España, Rosa A. Vda. de Saravia E., Manuela Vda. de Mathew, María del Pilar, Olivia de Wyld, Narcisa Villa Nueva, Isaura de Menéndez Mina, Luz Valle, Albertina de Samayoa, Josefina Saravia E., Amalia Samayoa Aguilar, María L. Rodriguez, Ana Gilma Mendoza, María Carrascosa, Graciela de León, and Sara Cerna Zepeda.

The Unión de Mujeres Democráticas membership included Argentina Díaz Lozano, Olimpia Vda. de Barrientos, Gloria Menéndez Mina de Padilla, Malin D'Echevers, Marta Delfina Vásquez, María Isabel Foronda de Vargas, Elisa Hall de Asturias, Helena Leiva de Holst, Marta Zuleta, Magdalena Spínola, Clemencia Rubio de Herrarte, Mélida Luz de Walters, María Luisa Lainez, Angelina Acuña de Castañeda, María del Carmen Vargas, and Aída Doninelli Vda. de Véliz.

The Guatemalan women who attended the Second Inter-American Congress of Women in Mexico City in 1951 included Ester de Urrutia, Otilia Oségueda de García, Josefina de Vitola, Chita Ordóñez de Balcárcel, María Isabel Foronda de Vargas, Carmen Morán, Victoria Moraga Martínez, Haydée Godoy, Clemencia H. de Soto, and Hortensia Hernández Rojás.

Chapter Six

The membership list of the Alianza Femenina Guatemalteca in April 1950 includes Lucila Vda. de Aguirre, Elisa Hall de Asturias, María Cristiana Vilanova de Árbenz, Mimí Comte, Romelia Alarcón Folgar, Haydée Godoy Arellano,

María Isabel Foronda de Vargas Romero, Dora Franco y Franco, Alicia González, Elsa C. de Guerra, Hortensia Hernández Rojás, María Luisa Silva, Ester de Urrutia, María del Carmen Vargas, Berta de Oségueda, Otilia Oségueda de García, Enriqueta Vda. de Gómez Flores, Clemencia Rubio Vda. de Herrarte, Helena Leiva de Holst, María del Pilar, Victoria Martínez, Matilde Elena López, Marta Delfina Vásquez Castañeda, Argentina Díaz Lozano, Mélida Luz Palacios, Aída María Rodríguez, Angelina Acuña de Castañeda, Violeta de Montero, and Ana Clemencia Aldana.

An updated list from 1951 or 1952 includes Victoria Ballugo, María Luisa Bolaños, Susana de Rojás, Eugenia Asturias, Elia de Mejía, Zoila Victoria Rui, Argelia Hernández, Graciela de Pinto Usaga, María Elena Pinto, María Castillo, Josefina Vda. de Vitola, Angelina de Ortiz, Matilda de Cuenca, Anita Vda. de Gutiérrez, Carmen Contreras, Argentina Hurtado, Pilar Vda. de Pivaral, Aurelia Sandoval, María Carlota Vda. de Falk, Ana María Falk, Olivia Chang, Otilia de Balcárcel, Cristina de León Castillo, Ester Sandoval de Castañeda, Paulina González, Zoila Estrada Marian, Celia de Castillo, Marta E. Mena Estrada, Lidia Ordoñea, Yolanda Ordoñea, Amanda de Martínez, Lidida Angela Vásquez, Catalina Flores, Concha Flores, Marta Ramírez, Carmen Marroquín, América García, Delfina Estévez, Ester Estévez, Aurora Vda. de Orozco, Elvira Avendaño, Luvia Mencizabal, Laura Monteroso, Raquel Vda. de Farrán, Emilia Fernández, Josefina Godoy, Tina Vda. de López, Blanca Agreda, Elvira Velázquez, Elena Velásquez, Susana Folgar, Carmen Díaz, María Luisa Estrada, Laura Marroquín, Victoria Escalante, Emilia Piedrasante, Isabel González, Cristiana Paíz, Juana Saravia, Edelmira Saravia, Josefina de Vásquez, and Cristina de Carranza.

Appendix B

Guatemalan Female Jobs Profile, 1920–1950

PROFESSION	1920	1940	1950
Civil engineers/architects	–	–	1
Electrical engineers	–	–	1
Agronomists	–	–	2
Clothing designers and draftswoman	–	–	5
Technicians	–	–	2
Chemists	–	–	3
Pharmacists	5	29	40
Medical/dental lab technicians	–	–	85
Laboratory technicians	–	–	87
University professors	–	–	26
Schoolteachers	1,134	3,083	5,524
Scientists	–	–	8
Lawyers	–	6 (includes notaries)	4
Doctors	–	8	10
Dentists	–	3	2
Medical assistants	–	–	3
Nurses	–	260	276

PROFESSION	1920	1940	1950
Other medical professionals	–	–	106
Massage therapists	–	–	9
Writers/journalists	–	–	13
Musicians/music teachers	1	27	69
Artists	–	–	12
Actors	–	–	63
Professional dancers	–	–	9
Priests/ministers	277	–	3
Social workers	–	–	52
Religious workers/nuns	43	108	137
Singers	–	–	53
Librarians	–	–	2
Photographers	–	14	29
Public servants/national	–	–	43
Public servants/municipal	–	–	1
Diplomats/consuls	–	–	15

Appendix C

School Attendance, 1950

	FEMALE PERCENTAGES	MALE PERCENTAGES	TOTAL PERCENTAGES
National	12.1	16.1	14.1
Dept. of Guatemala	27.3	35.3	31.2
Sacatepéquez	20.1	26.3	23.2
Petén	18.5	18.5	18.5
Quetzaltenango	15.2	21.5	18.4
Izabal	15.6	17.6	16.6
El Progreso	14.9	17.3	16.1
Escuintla	13.9	15.9	15.0
Zacapa	13.1	16.0	14.5
Retalhuleu	12.2	15.7	14.0
Suchitepéquez	12.0	15.5	13.8
San Marcos	9.5	14.8	12.2
Chimaltenango	8.6	13.6	11.2
Santa Rosa	10.7	11.7	11.2
Jalapa	9.7	11.7	10.7
Chiquimula	10.2	11.0	10.6
Jutiapa	10.3	10.2	10.2
Totonicapán	3.7	11.0	7.3
Huehuetenango	5.5	8.8	7.1
Baja Verapaz	5.4	8.2	6.6
Sololá	4.9	8.1	6.5
Alta Verapaz	3.6	7.3	5.4
Quiché	3.3	5.8	4.6

Appendix D

Number of Teachers, 1950

	WOMEN	MEN	TOTAL
National[1]	5,524	2,675	8,199
Dept. of Guatemala[2]	1,972	904	2,876
El Progreso	123	44	167
Sacatepéquez	190	100	290
Chimaltenango	138	124	312
Escuintla	206	89	295
Santa Rosa	180	78	238
Sololá	86	68	154
Totonicapán	77	51	128
Quetzaltenango	467	227	694
Suchitepéquez	246	113	359
Retalhuleu	122	61	183
San Marcos	409	185	594
Huehuetenango	232	136	368
Quiché	99	96	195
Baja Verapaz	65	43	108
Alta Verapaz	142	145	287
Petén	45	44	87
Izabal	90	29	119
Zacapa	123	43	166
Chiquimula	197	86	283
Jalapa	129	55	184
Jutiapa	193	70	263

1. The national numbers are broken down specifically to highlight university professors, secondary and primary teachers, and scientists.

2. The department statistics are not broken down as specifically as the national numbers; the statistics highlighted in this table include professors, teachers, and scientists. Teachers, however, make up the majority of these numbers, specifically with regard to women.

INTRODUCTION

1. Sixth Avenue, or La Sexta, has a prominent place in Guatemala City history.

2. *El Imparcial*, August 1, 1944. An excerpt taken from *Azul*, June 1944; and Contreras Vélez, *Génesis y ocaso*, 17. Contreras Vélez witnessed the attack on the teachers from his apartment balcony and estimated that there were between two and three hundred women present at the march.

3. Galich, *Del pánico al ataque*, 345; and *El Imparcial*, March 8, 1945. Esperanza Barrientos played a key role in the female affiliate of the Frente Popular Libertador.

4. *Azul*, June 1944. The Asociación de Maestras Católicas was formed on October 13, 1942. Its leader, Irene de Peyré, took up a collection for María Chinchilla's mother and grandmother.

5. AGCA, Hojas Sueltas, July 1, 1944. The three leaders handpicked by Jorge Ubico to fill in for him were Juan Federico Ponce Vaides, Buenaventura Pineda, and Eduardo Villagrán Ariza. Newspapers stopped printing during this tumultuous period, and when they opened again in the first days of July, they were filled with detailed accounts of recent events.

6. Saxon, *To Save Her Life*, xvii.

7. Ibid., xvi.

8. Departamento de Publicidad de la Presidencia de la República, *Primera colonia agrícola de Poptún*. Arévalo established the community of Poptún in the department of Petén during his presidency as an experimental intentional agricultural community.

9. See Herrera and Jacob, "Testimonies of Guatemalan Women," 160–68; Ciencia y Tecnología en Guatemala, *Situación de la mujer en Guatemala*; Anderson, *Granddaughters of Corn*; Zur, *Violent Memories*; Colom, *Mujeres en la alborada*; Green, *Fear as a Way of Life*; Stern, *Naming Security, Constructing Identity*; Christensen and Castillo Rodas, *Voces de 4 mujeres*; Aguilar and Méndez de la Vega, *Rompiendo el silencio*; Berger, *Guatemaltecas*; Soriano Hernández, *Mujeres y guerra*; Solórzano, *Aliadas en resistencia o resistencia a las alianzas?*; and McAllister, "Rural Markets, Revolutionary Souls, and Rebellious Women."
Other efforts have focused on the role of women in the revolutionary struggle, such as González and Kampwirth, *Radical Women in Latin America*; Luciak, *After the Revolution*; and Forster, *La revolución indígena y campesina*.

10. Smith, *Guatemalan Indians and the State*, 3.

11. Taracena Arriola, *Etnicidad, estado y nación en Guatemala*, 416.

12. Menjívar, *Enduring Violence*, 15.

13. Hale, *Más que un Indio*.

14. See Smith, *Guatemalan Indians and the State*; and Nelson, *A Finger in the Wound*.

15. The Spanish conquest of regional groups in 1524 initiated five hundred years of economic, legal, and social inequality between indigenous communities and Spanish-speaking peoples.

Currently, Guatemala is composed of several groups of peoples who are linguistically, culturally, and historically distinct from one another: the Pueblo Maya, speaking at least twenty languages; the ladino and ladina; the Garífuna (descendants of Caribbean slaves, and Carib and Arawak peoples); peoples of African descent; and the Xinka (a non-Mayan indigenous group).

16. Nelson, *A Finger in the Wound*, 102.

17. Dary Fuentes, *Entre el hogar y la vega*, 55–56.

18. Menjívar, *Enduring Violence*, 14–16.

19. Guzmán Bockler, *Colonialismo y revolución*.

20. Nelson, *A Finger in the Wound*, 35.

21. Gloria Menéndez Mina identified a family in her journal *Azul* as indigenous, Rosa Rodríguez López used a derogatory word to describe a maid, and the Alianza Femenina Guatemalteca discussed the "backward culture" of domestic workers.

22. The fact that indigenous women are not explicitly identified in ladina writings can also be explained by racism or a lack of interest.

23. Deutsch, *Crossing Borders*, 4.

24. Jaquette, *The Women's Movement in Latin America*, 13.

25. Scott, "Gender: A Useful Category," 171–72.

26. See Lavrin, *Women, Feminism, and Social Change*; Shepherd, Brereton, and Bailey, *Engendering History*; Besse, *Restructuring Patriarchy*; Caulfield, *In Defense of Honor*; Dore and Molyneux, *Hidden Histories of Gender and the State*; Hutchison, "Add Gender and Stir?," 267–87; Ehrick, *The Shield of the Weak*; and Macpherson, *From Colony to Nation*.

27. See González-Rivera, *Before the Revolution*.

28. Casaús Arzú, "La voz de las mujeres guatemaltecas"; and Casaús Arzú, "Las redes teosóficas de mujeres en Guatemala."

29. Monzón, "Entre líneas."

30. McCreery, "This Life of Misery and Shame"; Chinchilla, "Industrialization, Monopoly Capitalism, and Women's Work"; and Carrillo Padilla, *Luchas de las guatemaltecas*.

31. Carrillo and Chinchilla, "From Urban Elite to Peasant Organizing," 141.

32. Carrillo and Chinchilla, "From Urban Elite to Peasant Organizing"; and Menjívar, *Enduring Violence*.

33. Ruiz, "Luisa Moreno and Latina Labor Activism," 177.

34. Ehrick, *The Shield of the Weak*, 9.

35. Ibid.

36. Mohammed, "Writing Gender into History," 22.

37. Kaplan, "Female Consciousness and Collective Action," 545.

38. Enloe, *Bananas, Beaches and Bases*, 44.

39. Kandiyoti, "Bargaining with Patriarchy," 275.

40. Mooney, *The Politics of Motherhood*, 9. Jadwiga E. Pieper Mooney notes that "gender-based hierarchies in patriarchal societies have continuously assigned a disproportionate amount of political power to men and have set limits to women's rights as citizens. Simultaneously, women have contested, challenged and expanded the boundaries of patriarchal restrictions."

41. McClintock, "Family Feuds," 63. Feminist scholar Anne McClintock has outlined the necessary elements for a feminist critique of a nation, and ladinas here measure up to her requirements.

McClintock argues that a "feminist theory of nationalism must be strategically fourfold: investigating the gendered formation of sanctioned male theories; bringing into historical visibility women's active cultural and political participation in national formations; bringing nationalist institutions into critical relation with other social structures and institutions, while at the same time paying scrupulous attention to the structures of racial, ethnic and class power that continue to bedevil privileged forms of feminism."

42. There are several iterations of this organization throughout the decade. The nutrition centers were referred to as the Asociación de Comedores e Infantíles, while the daycare centers were called the Asociación de Guarderías Infantíles. Over the decade, these two organizations were cited as the Asociación de Damas Pro-Comedores Infantíles and the Asociación Pro-Comedores Infantíles. During the Árbenz presidency, the two organizations were formally joined into one.

43. Ronald Schneider's 1958 communist indictment of the Arévalo and Árbenz governments in *Communism in Guatemala, 1944 to 1954*, was the first with this particular emphasis; see also Schneider's *Case Study in Insurgency and Revolutionary Warfare: Guatemala, 1944–1954*. Later and more sophisticated analyses are found in Richard Immerman's *The CIA in Guatemala*, Walter LaFeber's *Inevitable Revolutions*, Nick Cullather's *Secret History*, and Stephen Schlesinger and Stephen Kinzer's *Bitter Fruit*, all of which focus on the destructive effect of US intervention on Guatemalan efforts to establish a stable and democratic nation.

44. See Handy, *Gift of the Devil*; Handy, *Revolution in the Countryside*; Jonas, *The Battle for Guatemala*; Grandin, *The Blood of Guatemala*; and Forster, *The Time of Freedom*.

45. Scholarship dedicated to the less dominant Liberal periods of the nineteenth and twentieth centuries focuses almost exclusively on Guatemala's political structure or on personalities. An exception to this is David McCreery's *Rural Guatemala, 1760–1940*.

46. Forster, *The Time of Freedom*, 5.

47. Ibid., 2.

48. Ibid., 7. Forster maintains that patriarchy was largely unaffected by the revolution, a position that this study supports.

49. See also Deutsch, *Counterrevolution in Argentina*.

50. The Inter-American Treaty of Reciprocal Assistance was a hemispheric mutual security agreement signed in 1947 and implemented in 1948. Its central principle contained in its articles is that an attack against one signatory country is to be considered an attack against them all.

51. Spenser, "Standing Conventional Cold War History on Its Head," 381. Spenser is herself referencing Odd Arne Westad (*The Global Cold War*, 396).

52. Dirección General de Estadística, *Censo General de la República de Guatemala levantado en 26 de Febrero de 1893*, 195. In 1893, the national census recorded that out of a total population of 1,364,678, only 99,553 people could read and write. A decade earlier, in the 1880s, only 25,033 Guatemalans could read, the vast majority of whom would have been male.

53. Levenson, "Living Guatemala City," 34. Deborah Levenson notes that industrialization did not occur until the 1970s.

54. McCreery, "This Life of Misery and Shame," 337.

55. See Handy, *Revolution in the Countryside*, 1–22, for further information on population relocations prior to 1944; and Dirección General de Estadística, *Analisis del censo urbano de la capital levantado el 22 de Febrero de 1938*, 7. Until the mid-1920s, few indigenous people lived in Guatemala

City. The 1938 census for Guatemala City notes that 92.95 percent of the city's population was ladino/ladina in 1921, and 93.21 percent in 1938.

56. Komisaruk, *Labor and Love in Guatemala*, 9; and Dirección General de Estadística, *Censo General de la República de Guatemala levantado el año de 1880*, 20. Guatemala City had a population in 1880 of 57,928, of whom 34,322 were female. Women remained the majority of the city's population throughout the period under study.

57. *Bulletin of the Pan American Union* (August 1923) and *El Imparcial* (September 15, 1924; October 12, 1924) carry photos of new factories where all the workers employed are women, including a cardboard factory where thirty women were hired. *El Imparcial* noted small two factories manufacturing cigarettes and chocolates.

58. Komisaruk, *Labor and Love in Guatemala*, 246.

59. See Levenson-Estrada, *Trade Unionists against Terror*; Offit, *Conquistadores de la Calle*; O'Neill, *City of God*; O'Neill and Thomas, *Securing the City*; Smith and Adams, *After the Coup*; Way, *The Mayan in the Mall*; and Levenson, *Adiós Niños*.

60. See Forster, *The Time of Freedom*; and Jonas, *The Battle for Guatemala*.

61. The broadsides collection is a unique primary source. It contains individual papers designed to disseminate information on the street.

62. Immerman, *The CIA in Guatemala*, 41.

CHAPTER ONE

1. Hugo Cruz Rivas, "Mujeres que entran y salen de la historia," 86.
2. Palmer, "A Liberal Discipline," 4–8.
3. Dunkerley, *Power in the Isthmus*, 63.
4. Burns, *The Poverty of Progress*; Handy, *Gift of the Devil*; Dunkerley, *Power in the Isthmus*; Woodward, *Central America: Historical Perspectives*; Palmer, "Central American Union or Guatemalan Republic?"; Torres Rivas, *History and Society in Central America*; McCreery, *Rural Guatemala*; Dosal, *Power in Transition*; and Lujan Muñoz, *Las revoluciones de 1897*.
5. A few works have begun to create a picture of urban life during the late nineteenth and early twentieth centuries in Guatemala City. See Witzel de Ciudad, *Más de 100 años del movimiento obrero urbano*; Casaús Arzú, "La voz de las mujeres guatemaltecas"; Casaús Arzú, "Las redes teosóficas de mujeres en Guatemala"; Casaús Arzú and García Giráldez, *Las redes intelectuales centroamericanas*; Way, *The Mayan in the Mall*; and Kirkpatrick, "Optics and the Culture of Modernity."
6. McCreery, *Rural Guatemala*, 173–74.
7. Craske, *Women and Politics in Latin America*, 163.
8. Kit, "The Fall of Guatemalan Dictator, Manuel Estrada Cabrera," 105–28.
9. Código Civil de la República de Guatemala, 1877, 33.
10. Carey, "Runaway Mothers and Daughters," 189.
11. Soto Hall, *Instrucción moral y cívica*, 8.
12. Palmer, "A Liberal Discipline,"110; and Miller, "Catholic Leaders and Spiritual Socialism," 80.
13. Although the church assigned women a secondary role in religion and society, the Vatican reached out to the working class through a papal bull, the *Rerum Novarum*, in 1891 (Pope Leo XIII, 1878–1903). By 1920, forty separate societies and associations had been formed. A further ninety-six unions and associations were created during the 1920s. Women took advantage of the church's

interest and played an active role in the creation of both associations and unions. The first Catholic female labor association formed in 1921, the Sindicato Católico de Señoras y Señoritas Empleadas de Comercio y Talleres. The church's actions, however, did little to alleviate the severe poverty of Guatemala's working class.

14. Komisaruk, *Labor and Love in Guatemala*, 246.

15. Carey, "Forced and Forbidden Sex," 357–89; and Carey, "Runaway Mothers and Daughters," 189.

16. The group of deputies included Manuel Ramírez, Domingo Estrada, Antonio Lazo Arriaga, José Salazar, Javier Ruíz Aqueche, José Farfán, Vicente Sáenz, Francisco Angulano, Miguel Carrillo, Mariano F. Padilla, Salvador Barrútia, Felipe Cruz, Valerio Irangaray, Próspero Morales, Felipe Neri Prado, Antonio Girón, and Joaquín Yela.

17. For further information, see Carrillo Samayoa and Torres Urízar, *Nosotras, las de la historia*, 42–45.

18. Rivas, *Capacidad jurídical de la mujer y derechos*, 11.

19. Ibid., 56.

20. Palmer, "A Liberal Discipline," 8. Palmer suggests that the Liberal state's contradictory rhetoric of nationalism and modernization offered some hope for inclusion.

21. Power, *Right-Wing Women in Chile*, 47. Power notes that in Chile, the constitutional wording also did not directly deny women the right to vote, and in the early 1880s several Chilean women registered to vote.

22. The rural-to-urban migration for young professional teachers has been well established by historians across Latin America. See Palmer and Rojas Chaves, "Educating Señorita," 45–82.

23. For a full history of Quetzaltenango, see Grandin, *The Blood of Guatemala*, 56. During the 1830s, Quetzaltenango had a population of 7,442, with 3,298 ladinos/ladinas and 4,149 K'iche' Maya.

24. *El Imparcial*, August 1, 1945, editorial; and *El Liberal Progresista*, September 3, 1941, editorial.

25. *El Imparcial*, August 1, 1945, editorial.

26. Figueroa Marroquín and Acuña de Castañeda, *Poesía femenina guatemalense*, 397–98. According to Figueroa Marroquín and Acuña de Castañeda, the Laparra family returned to Quetzaltenango in 1854, while other sources claim that the date was 1850.

27. *El Imparcial*, August 3, 1945, editorial. According to the editorial, by Magdalena Spínola, Vicenta gave birth to their first child, María Josefina, on August 7, 1854. The couple had four additional children: Luz, Cayetano, Angela, and Salvador.

28. It would not have been difficult to have ideological differences with one's colleagues or superiors within the political milieu of Carrera's conservative government during the 1850s. There is no other information on the couples' moves.

29. *El Imparcial*, August 3, 1945, editorial. Magdalena Spínola, author of the editorial, notes the date of Salvador's birth as 1886. This is likely wrong, as it would have made Vicenta fifty-five years old when she gave birth. Furthermore, Vicenta began publication of her second journal in 1887, and it is unlikely that she could have done this while paralyzed. It is far more likely that Salvador was born in 1866, when Vicenta was thirty-five years old.

30. Jesús Laparra, "A mi hermana Vicenta, en su dias," in Laparra, *Ensueños de la mente*, 9.

31. *El Ideal*, January 14, 1888.

32. *El Imparcial*, August 3, 1945, editorial.

33. In her work on Nicaraguan women during the nineteenth century, *Before the Revolution: Women's Rights and Right-Wing Politics in Nicaragua, 1821–1979*, Victoria González-Rivera uncovers a few women writing to express their political views. See also Botting and Matthews, "Overthrowing the Floresta-Wollstonecraft Myth," 64–83.

34. Finzer, "Poetisa Chic," 30–31.

35. Lavrin, "La literatura testimonial en Latinoamérica," 89. Lavrin argues that the testimonio as a historical and subjective narrative has existed since the conquest in the sixteenth century.

36. *El Ideal*, March 24, 1888.

37. See also Burns, *The Poverty of Progress*; Handy, *Gift of the Devil*; McCreery, *Rural Guatemala*; Grandin, *The Blood of Guatemala*; Forster, *The Time of Freedom*; and Kirkpatrick, "Optics and the Culture of Modernity."

38. Kirkpatrick, "Optics and the Culture of Modernity," 50–51.

39. *El Ideal*, December 17, 1887.

40. Miller, *Latin American Women*, 80.

41. *La Voz de la Mujer*, August 22, 1885.

42. *El Imparcial*, August 2, 1945, editorial; and *El Ideal*, December 17, 1887, 4.

43. *La Voz de la Mujer*, September 12, 1885.

44. *El Ideal*, December 10, 1887; and Wagner, *The History of Coffee in Guatemala*, 65. The journalists who wrote for *El Ideal* were part of a Catholic women's community and benevolent society.

45. *El Ideal*, March 24, 1888. It is evident in the journal's articles that the writers had close ties with other journalists across Central America and even South America, but no specific names of non-Guatemalan writers were ever given.

46. *El Ideal*, March 24, 1888.

47. *La Voz de la Mujer*, August 22, 1885, 2.

48. Dirección General de Estadística, *Censo General de la República de Guatemala levantado en 26 de Febrero de 1893*, 13. The attitudes of the ruling elites are evident in the 1893 census.

49. *La Voz de la Mujer*, November 14, 1885.

50. Ibid.

51. Carey, *I Ask for Justice*, 83.

52. Ibid.

53. *La Voz de la Mujer*, August 31, 1885.

54. *La Voz de la Mujer*, September 12, 1885.

55. Ibid.

56. Miller, *Latin American Women*, 74.

57. Lavrin, *Women, Feminism, and Social Change*, 358.

58. Mooney, *The Politics of Motherhood*. Mooney explores the transformation from motherhood as a political tool for socially engaged women in chapter 5 of her book.

59. *La Voz de la Mujer*, August 22, 1885.

60. *La Semana Católica*, March 26, 1894. Vicenta and Jesús Laparra were part of a broader Catholic women's community that frequently challenged the government's policies.

61. *La Voz de la Mujer*, November 14, 1885.

62. Ibid.

63. Evidence of their activism can be seen in the Catholic journal *La Semana Católica*.

64. *La Voz de la Mujer*, August 22, 1885.

65. Asamblea Nacional Constituyente, *Diario de las sesiones de la Asamblea Constituyente de 1879*, 14.

66. *El Ideal*, December 10, 1887.

67. Sabato, "On Political Citizenship," 1310–13.

68. Ibid., 1313.

69. The papal pronouncement of 1891, the *Rerum Novarum*, institutionalized the outreach societies created by these elite Catholic women.

70. Dore, *Myths of Modernity*, 3. Dore explores the economic transition of the Nicaraguan Liberal government and suggests another theory: "There the rise of private property and forced labor was part of a great transformation, but not to capitalism. In the era from 1870 to 1930, class relations between coffee planters and debt peons were regulated directly through the exercise of patriarchal forms of coercion and consent, not indirectly by market mechanisms. . . . In Diriomo, the coffee revolution accomplished none of these. It gave birth to individual peasant proprietorship; it institutionalized forced labor and fortified, rather than undermined, nonmarket patriarchal relations. Taken together, these impeded more than promoted capitalist development."

71. McCreery, "This Life of Misery and Shame," 337.

72. To date, nineteenth-century Liberal economic policy in Guatemala has received little scholarly attention. See Chinchilla, "Industrialization, Monopoly Capitalism, and Women's Work"; McCreery, *Rural Guatemala*; and Grandin, *The Blood of Guatemala*.

73. *La Voz de la Mujer*, August 31, 1885, 1–2.

74. *El Imparcial*, August 2, 1945, editorial.

75. The sociopolitical impact of the migration of rural Latin American women to urban centers has been explored in a few articles but for the most part remains a vastly understudied phenomenon. For an example, see Palmer and Rojas Chaves, "Educating Señorita."

76. *La Voz de la Mujer*, September 5, 1885.

77. Woodward, *Rafael Carrera and the Emergence of the Republic of Guatemala*, 438; and González Orellana, *Historia de la educación en Guatemala*, 280. By 1865, there were thirty-one schools in the Department of Guatemala, teaching 1,435 boys and 902 girls out of a population of close to 70,000. The 133 teachers responsible for this task were all clergy. Nationwide, out of a total population of close to a million people, 203 primary schools for boys and 45 for girls provided education to 8,074 children. Until the late nineteenth century, Guatemala had no teacher training centers and was dependent solely on the availability of Catholic priests and nuns.

78. *El Ideal*, January 21 1888.

79. *El Ideal*, February 4 and March 24, 1888. The journal reprinted an article written by Señora doña Concepción Gimeno de Flaquer.

80. González Orellana, *Historia de la educación en Guatemala*, 281–83. This law was reformed on April 7, 1877, to unify legislation for primary, secondary, and university education.

81. Ibid., 282–85. The amendments of October 13, 1879, April 1882, and November 23, 1882, made primary education mandatory for children up to fourteen years of age; included education in cultural topics (such as music), morality, and physical education; and implemented a general reorganization of the national administration of education.

82. The 1880 census does not list teaching as an occupation.

83. González Orellana, *Historia de la educación en Guatemala*, 280, 285.

84. McCreery, *Rural Guatemala*, 345.

85. González Orellana, *Historia de la educación en Guatemala*, 294–301.

86. Woodward, *Rafael Carrera and the Emergence of the Republic of Guatemala*, 442. A few religious orders attempted to rectify educational access for young women during the nineteenth century. The Bethlemite nuns opened the Colegio de Belén for girls in 1860. While it had difficulties in its early years, by 1864, Woodward notes, thirty-five students lived at the school while forty more young women attended while living at home. During a time when education was rarely available to nonelite children, it is significant to note that thirty students attended on partial tuition waivers and more than two hundred girls did not pay any tuition at all. Thus, amid a paucity of educational opportunities for Guatemalan women, it appears that there was at least this one school, which provided services not only to those from middle- and upper-class families able to afford tuition but also apparently to those from the lower classes as well.

87. Ibid., 302–3. The Instituto Normal de Señoritas, Belen, remained the only normal school for women well into the twentieth century, and a majority of the teachers highlighted in national newspapers during the 1920s, 1930s, and 1940s were all graduates of its program.

88. Dirección General de Estadística, *Censo General de la República de Guatemala levantado en 26 de Febrero de 1893*, 199. The census listed 1,177 teachers of public instruction, although it did not distinguish between men and women.

89. *La Voz de la Mujer*, November 14, 1885. The article "La mujer estudiosa" claimed that men were actually afraid of educated women and did not really want the possible social changes that educated women would usher in.

90. *La Voz de la Mujer*, November 14, 1885.

91. *El Ideal*, January 21, 1888.

92. Miller, *Latin American Women*, 36.

93. González Orellana, *Historia de la educación en Guatemala*, 316. The goal of the congress was to explore new educational methodologies and open up dialogue among teachers. Following this congress, the Ministry of Public Education established the Academía de Maestros in order to create a network of support for teachers in Guatemala City. This institution allowed teachers to keep in touch with one another and provided them with up-to-date educational materials. Three other women also participated in the first pedagogical conference: Concepción Santa Cruz, Dolores Nájera, and Dolores Mesa. The Escuela Normal de Señoritas continues to function. This institution educated generations of young women and remained the capital city's only normal school for women until the revolution in 1944.

94. Miller, *Latin American Women*, 35; and Palmer and Rojas Chaves, "Educating Señorita."

95. Handy, *Gift of the Devil*, 80.

96. Carey, *I Ask for Justice*, 41.

97. See for example, García Granados, *Cuaderno de memorias*; and Miguel Ángel Asturias, *El Señor Presidente*, originally published in 1946.

98. Witzel de Ciudad, *Más de 100 años del movimiento obrero urbano*, 40.

99. Some believe that Estrada Cabrera was born out of wedlock, and perhaps it is this personal history that prompted his creation of a maternity center for poor and vulnerable women.

100. The records of the Asilo de Maternidad Joaquina provide a snapshot of the working-class

population. Not only had every single woman migrated from a rural area outside of the capital, but with the exception of three, all reported employment in an array of jobs specified by David McCreery in the table below (McCreery, "This Life of Misery and Shame"). The women ranged in age from fifteen to forty-two, with the majority between seventeen and twenty-six.

Seamstress	6	Housewife	3	Cook	3
Laundress	10	Cashier	1	Tortilla Maker/Seller	3
Shopkeeper	6	Miller	4	Cigarette Roller	1
Servant/Domestic	23	Cigarette Maker	3	No occupation	1

101. González Orellana, *Historia de la educación en Guatemala*, 331–39.

102. Chinchilla, "Industrialization, Monopoly Capitalism, and Women's Work," 39.

103. Górriz de Morales was a distinguished educator in Guatemala City and wrote several short histories on Guatemala and colonial women.

104. The entire collection can be found at the Archivo General de Centro América.

105. AGCA, Hojas Sueltas.

106. Levenson-Estrada, *Trade Unionists against Terror*, 16; and *El Unionista*, February 10, 1920. The venue for these new voices was *El Unionista*, a journal first published on January 15, 1920, that advocated the overthrow of the president.

107. Witzel de Ciudad, *Más de 100 años del movimiento obrero urbano*, 73.

108. *Diario de Centro América*, April 15–17, 1920. At least thirty-six women were injured or killed in the street protests against Estrada Cabrera in an event that became known as the 1920 revolution. See appendix A for a complete list of names.

109. See Wade Kit ("The Fall of Guatemalan Dictator, Manuel Estrada Cabrera" and "The Unionist Experiment in Guatemala") for detailed accounts of the revolution and the presidency of Carlos Herrera.

110. The journal *Vida* ran from the fall of 1925 until the spring of 1927.

111. Kit, "The Unionist Experiment in Guatemala," 33.

112. Scott, foreword to *Everyday Forms of State Formation*, ix.

113. *El Unionista*, March 26 and May 14, 1920. Female affiliations of the Partido Unionista existed throughout the country, including the Señoras de Chiquimula, the Señoras de Barberena, the Comité de Señoras Joaquina, and the Club Unionista Femenina Bandera Federal de Masagua.

114. Kit, "The Fall of Guatemalan Dictator, Manuel Estrada Cabrera," 117; and García Granados, *Cuaderno de memorias*, 217.

115. *El Unionista*, May 25, 1920.

116. Ibid.

117. *El Unionista*, March 19, 1921.

118. Asamblea Nacional Constituyente, *Diario de las sesiones de la Asamblea Constituyente de 1879*, 14; and Jones, *Guatemala Past and Present*, 105.

119. By 1920, only New Zealand (1893), Australia (1902), Finland (1906), Canada (1918), and the United States (1920) had enfranchised at least some women.

120. Asamblea Nacional Constituyente, *Dictamen de la Comisión Extraordinaria de reformas a la constitución*, 4–5, 27.

121. *Studium*, June 1921, 9.

122. *Studium*, March–April 1921, 15–17; and *Studium*, July 1921, 8–11.

123. For further details on suffrage in Costa Rica, see Rodríguez Sáenz, *Un siglo de luchas femeninas*.

124. *El Unionista*, April 26, 1920; and Asamblea Nacional Constituyente, *Dictamen de la Comisión Extraordinaria de reformas a la constitución*, 4–5, 27.

125. That is my current conclusion, given the lack of evidence. It is clear, however, that many of these workers had a clear consciousness about the inequities of women. The creation of a formal association may have also been hampered by widespread illiteracy.

126. *El Unionista*, September 1926. An earlier labor law had been established in April 1921.

127. *El Imparcial*, November 9 and 20, 1926.

128. See Carrillo Padilla, "Sufridas hijas del pueblo," 157–73.

129. Casaús Arzú, "La voz de las mujeres guatemaltecas," 201–3.

130. *Studium*, August–September 1923, 57.

131. Horan and Meyer, *This America of Ours*, 319. Mistral traveled to Mexico for a six-month period of study and stayed for two years at the behest of the Mexican government. A Chilean educator and poet, Mistral (1889–1957) rose to national prominence by winning a literary contest on December 12, 1914. By 1922, her work in Chile's education system caught the attention of Mexican writer and politician José Vasconcelos, who invited Mistral to organize his country's libraries and education system, under the auspices of the Mexican Ministry of Education.

132. *Bulletin of the Pan American Union*, June 1927; and *Vida*, March 20, 1926. Rosa Rodríguez López reviewed *Lecturas para mujeres* for her readers; twenty thousand copies were published in the first edition. In "A New Organization of Labor," Mistral argues that the brutality of the factory now extends to women:

> They have been caught in the quagmire of professions of no spiritual significance whatever, of unadulterated and hideous greed—woman herself is to blame. . . . We demand that human labor be so organized that all work will fall into three groups: Group A, trades or professions reserved for men; Group B, trades or professions reserved for women because of the physical ease or their direct relation to the child; Group C, professions or trades open to both. . . . Her new organization of labor is based upon the principle that women should seek their trades within the mission marked out for them by nature. Women's natural place is never far from the child or the suffering of children. . . . Her natural professions are those of teacher, physician, nurse, social welfare worker, defender of juvenile delinquents, writer of literature for children . . . [and] in the fields of medicine, arts, trades. . . . Women should direct primary education . . . and this return of woman to her own is beginning to be urgent.

133. Ruiz, "Luisa Moreno and Latina Labor Activism," 175–76. Rodríguez López was born Blanca Rosa Rodríguez López on August 30, 1907. As Vicki Ruiz, who is currently working on a biography of Rosa Rodríguez López, explains: Rodríguez López grew up surrounded by wealth and privilege in her native Guatemala. Her mother, Alicia López Sarana, who was originally from Colombia, was a prominent socialite married to Ernesto Rodríguez Robles, a powerful coffee grower. With the help of a coterie of servants and tutors, Alicia and Ernesto reared four children, one son and three daughters, on their sprawling estate. Rodríguez López received an education appropriate to her station and gender, spoke Spanish and French, and showed an early aptitude for poetry.

134. Vicki Ruiz writes:

> Enrolling as a student at the Universidad Nacional Autónoma de México (UNAM) and working as a journalist for a Guatemalan daily, [Rosa Rodríguez López] participated in a burgeoning cultural renaissance taking place in the aftermath of the Mexican Revolution, enjoying the heady avant-garde atmosphere and consorting with the likes of Diego Rivera and Frida Kahlo. In 1927 she published a poetry collection, *El vendedor de cocuyos* (Seller of Fireflies), and married Miguel Ángel de León, an artist sixteen years her senior. The next year would find the artistic couple in New York City, searching for their own version of the American dream. It was not a particularly propitious time for such a move, given the looming economic calamity. When their daughter Mytyl arrived in 1929, their fortunes had declined to the extent that they were living in a crowded tenement in Spanish Harlem, where Rosa found employment as a seamstress. (Ruiz, "Class Acts")

135. *El Imparcial*, November 4, 1925; and *Azul*, September–October 1949, 26–27.

136. García Granados, *Cuaderno de memorias*, 176. Theosophical ideas appear to have been influential among many elite and educated Guatemalan women. Jorge García Granados notes in his book that his mother-in-law had read widely on Helena Blavatsky, the founder of theosophy.

137. *Vida*, November 25, 1925.

138. *El Ideal*, March 10, 1888.

139. Rosa Rodríguez López, "La necesidad del feminismo en el orientaciones para la mujer," *Vida*, November 25, 1925.

140. *El Imparcial*, November 21, 1925.

141. Ibid., 176.

142. Herrera, "Civilicemonos."

143. *El Imparcial*, November 21, 1925.

144. See Ruiz, "Class Acts," for further information on the progression of Rodríguez López's evolving ideologies.

145. *El Imparcial*, January 16, 1926; and José Epaminondas Quintana, in *Vida*, January 23, 1926.

146. *Vida*, December 12, 1925.

147. *El Imparcial*, April 12, 1926. The newspaper reported that both Rosa Rodríguez López and Martha Josefina Herrera visited the newspaper office to request space for the school.

148. *Azul*, September–October 1949, 26–27; and *El Imparcial*, February 14, 1927. In 1927, a delegation from the Sociedad Gabriela Mistral went to Mexico City to celebrate a literary event. Martha Josefina Herrera represented Guatemala and, according to the newspaper articles, visited Rosa Rodríguez López. The last reference to Rodríguez López in any of the national newspapers occurs on April 12, 1926, in *El Imparcial*. The SGM had opened the Escuela de Artes y Oficios Femeniles, and both Rodríguez López and Herrera are mentioned in the article.

149. *El Imparcial*, December, 2, 1926, editorial.

150. *El Imparcial*, November 27, 1926.

151. *El Imparcial*, December 25, 1926.

152. González Orellana, *Historia de la educación en Guatemala*, 340; Jones, *Guatemala Past and Present*, 334; and Dirección General de Estadística, *Censo de la República de Guatemala, 1921*, 287, 516. Out of the 1,134 teachers, 167 were under the age of twenty-one.

153. Dirección General de Estadística, *Censo de la República de Guatemala, 1921*, 67–71.

154. *Bulletin of the Pan American Union*, June 1920, 686–87. There were also five practical schools for women and eighteen manual training schools for men. *Nuestro Diario*, June 27, 1928. Rural illiteracy was also believed by some to be the primary cause of crime and poverty and therefore needed to be addressed.

155. The educators who gathered in Guatemala City drew up a plan for sweeping reforms, with ten primary goals. They included:

1. Kindergartens. A system to be adopted under the best organization.
2. Rudimentary and rural schools. Part of the campaign against illiteracy and the basis of the organization.
3. Illiteracy in adults. Methods of initial operation, and curriculum of night and Sunday schools; proper trends for education catering to the interests and needs of students.
4. Reform and unification of instruction.
   A. Primary: Preparation of students to earn a living considered suitable for their environment.
   B. Normal: Preparation of primary teachers.
   C. Secondary: Basis of professional studies and medium of general culture.
5. Adaptation of textbooks for primary schools.
6. Manual training in primary schools: fundamentals, purpose, and choice of a proper system.
7. Physical training: chief purpose.
8. Moral and civic education: fundamentals and aims.
9. Education of Indians: most practical methods.
10. Faculty.
    A. Uniform plan of promotion and rewards.
    B. Foreign study for teachers, and employment of teachers from other countries.
    C. Leave of absence and benefit pay for the sick and disabled.
    D. Vacation colonies and sanatoriums.
    E. Pensions for invalids.

156. *Bulletin of the Pan American Union*, July 1923 and March 1924; and González Orellana, *Historia de la educación en Guatemala*, 360. González Orellana notes that the Universidad Popular was closed in 1932 under the dictatorship of Jorge Ubico and reopened in October 1944.

157. González Orellana, *História de la educación en Guatemala*, 343.

158. *Bulletin of the Pan American Union*, September 1927, 935.

PRIMARY SCHOOL	ENROLLMENT	ATTENDANCE
1922	82,997	64,725
1923	89,484	80,566
1924	92,911	80,819
1925	105,314	77,838
1926	103,899	80,997

159. Ibid.

TEACHER TRAINING	ENROLLMENT	ACTUAL ATTENDANCE
Normal Schools	850	757
Secondary Schools	745	616
Special Schools	1,463	1,097
Colleges	588	588

160. *Bulletin of the Pan American Union*, May 1928, 530. When the university was closed and why is not clear.

161. González Orellana, *História de la educación en Guatemala*, 340–41, 348–49. Two congresses were held during the 1920s to address the educational crisis in Guatemala. The first was held in 1923, and the primary resolutions included a reform of primary education; the creation of a new normal school; an increase in the duration of normal school study from three to four years; the creation of a normal school (Escuela Normal Superior) specializing in subjects such as pedagogy, mathematics, language, geography, and history; and the granting of bachelor's degrees to teachers so that they could enter the National University. The second congress took place in 1929, during which a revision of educational pedagogy and an analysis of the most urgent problems took place. Several women were among those most influential in the establishment of the Escuela Normal Superior, including Amalia Samayoa Aguilar, Aída Martínez R., Martina Cordero de León, María Josefa Estrada, Dorotea T. de Barrera, and Hortensia Aguilar (González Orellana, *História de la educación en Guatemala*, 358).

162. *Nuestro Diario*, January 7, 1930. The editorial piece was titled "Los nuevos rumbos en la educación de las mujeres."

163. *El Imparcial*, December 18 and May 15, 1926. In an article titled "La mujer de hoy," the author argued that women needed to have access to the same education as men, as the lack of education was not good for women, their families, or their country.

164. The column first appeared on August 22, 1922, and ran until at least October 7, 1922.

165. *El Imparcial*, September 9, 1922.

166. *El Imparcial*, August 12, 1922.

167. *El Imparcial*, August 19, September 9, and October 7, 1922.

168. *Nuestra Diario*, July 9, 1952; and *La Hora*, July 9, 1952. Llardén de Molina founded the school in 1917, but it was damaged in the earthquake of 1918. She reopened it on June 3, 1918. When she died in 1924, María Aguirre became the new director of the school. In 1926, Llardén de Molina's daughter, Elisa Molina Llardén de Farner, took over the directorship. The school had more than five thousand students who eventually became priests, military people, university teachers, workers, and later communists and anticommunists. Clara Molina Llardén became the director in July 1927.

169. *La Hora*, July 9, 1952.

170. *Nuestra Diario*, July 9, 1952; and *La Hora*, July 9, 1952.

171. J. F. Juárez Muñoz, "Por la moralidad de nuestras hijas," *El Imparcial*, August 11, 1922.

172. *El Imparcial*, September 19, 1924. An editorial, "La instrucción sin educación," reminded readers that, despite the current influence of positivism on education, morality and religiosity were still strong. Dr. Carlos Fletes Sáenz authored a strong rebuttal to Juárez Muñoz's article on August 26, 1922.

173. *El Imparcial*, January 15, 1927. The article, "Miedos ridículos," was written by an anonymous author.

174. Shattuck, *A Medical Survey of the Republic of Guatemala*, 237; and *Bulletin of the Pan American Union*, February 1926. A medical survey was done by a team of US doctors during the 1920s and early 1930s. *Bulletin of the Pan American Union*, September 1925; and *Bulletin of the Pan American Union*, January 1923. The infant mortality rate was 22.4 per 1,000 live births in 1922 and 92.7 per 1,000 live births in 1934 (Shattuck, *A Medical Survey of the Republic of Guatemala*, 24). Children born to unmarried mothers also increased in number from 935 per 1,000 in 1922 to 1,776 per 1,000 in 1934. These statistics are not a reflection of a decline in health care but rather inaccuracy in data collection. The 1922 data reflects an absence in record keeping, and the increased number of stillbirths in 1934 merely reveals more accurate data. However, since these infant mortality rates represent conditions far below those of wealthier Latin American countries, one must conclude that they, too, did not accurately record the full extent of the lack of health care in Guatemala. See Lavrin, *Women, Feminism, and Social Change*, 100–101. Lavrin notes infant mortality rates of 102 per 1,000 between 1913 and 1915 for Argentina, and 147 per 1,000 in 1915 and 100 per 1,000 in 1921 for Montevideo, Uruguay, for an average of 110 per 1,000.

175. *Studium*, January, February, and March 1922.

176. Casaús Arzú and García Giráldez, *Las redes intelectuales centroamericanas*, 207.

177. Guy, "The Politics of Pan-American Cooperation," 456.

178. *Nosotras*, September 1934.

179. *El Imparcial*, October 31, 1945. The SPN opened on October 31, 1920. Between 1920 and 1945, Emilia Vda. de Escamilla, Irene Oliveros de Peyré, Luisa C. Vda. de León, Carmen de Lazo, Cayetana G. de Castañeda, María Herrera de Aschkel, and Rosa de Mora acted as president of the center. Of the directors of the three individual centers, Haas and León Cofiño were single, while García was married. Four physicians provided free medical services to the children—Dr. Perdomo, Dr. Aschkel, Dr. Rivera Iriarte, and Dr. Mora.

180. Guy, *Women Build the Welfare State*, 6.

181. The Rockefeller Foundation was formed in 1913. Its mission is to promote the well-being of humanity, and it has focused on the root causes of serious global problems. The foundation's work has been influential in the professionalization of public health and the development of vaccines for yellow fever. For further information on the Rockefeller Foundation and health, see Farley, *To Cast Out Disease*; Schneider, *Rockefeller Philanthropy and Modern Biomedicine*; and Palmer, *Launching Global Health*.

182. *El Imparcial*, June 11, 1924. The SPN held a conference on puericultura with Dr. Mora with the support of neighboring women's groups.

183. *Bulletin of the Pan American Union*, August 1921, 171–72. The congress was split into two parts, the first several days (September 11–14) concentrating on educational issues and the end of the week (September 15–20) focusing on health needs.

The campaign against childhood diseases included: sanitary inspection of milk; free medical consultation for children under two years of age; the foundation of an open-air school for children; the opening of a ward in the sanatorium for tubercular children; vacation colonies for schoolchildren; a special children's hospital; the collection and study of statistics related to the causes of infant mortality; and the foundation of a society for the protection of children.

The campaign for housing sanitation included: houses for workers, and a competition modeling worker houses in both urban and rural settings; prizes for poor children who, with little or no expenditure, beautified their homes and rendered them more sanitary; prizes for the best large gardens and home gardens planted by children; the improvement of conditions in the schools; and a "clean-up" campaign encouraging the inculcation of the habit of cleanliness.

The campaign for dietetics included: the frequent publication, for free national distribution, of pamphlets containing lists of expensive foods, their values, and their nutritive content, with rules for food preparation and advice on hygiene.

The campaign for general child culture included: the teaching of child culture in the schools; the opening of a children's reading room at the National Library; the elimination of street begging by children; a consideration of games and exercises suitable for developing the physique of children; the establishment of a juvenile court to handle all children's cases; the foundation of a house of correction for wayward children; the addition of manual training workshops at every school in which those not going to study a profession might learn a trade; the development of persistence and the desire to succeed by effort; and propaganda in the schools against the manufacture and use of alcohol.

184. Lavrin, *Women, Feminism, and Social Change*, 103. Puericultura was a new subject being introduced in women's education. As Lavrin notes: "Training women to provide better care would save children's lives and give mothers a sense of responsibility and pride about their role. The scientific care of children was a logical corollary to the pedagogical reform of the late nineteenth century, when the science of preserving health was directed toward those 'called to undertake the high and sacred duties of maternity.'"

185. *Bulletin of the Pan American Union*, July 1928, 736.

186. Carey, *Engendering Mayan History*, 31–44. The Guatemalan Ministry of Health initiated licensing requirements for midwives in 1935, but few felt compelled to comply despite the threat that any midwife who failed to attend a training course when requested to do so was prohibited from practicing her profession. David Carey looks at one indigenous woman who was renowned as a midwife and resisted the state's efforts to acculturate the medical information. Although these measures were ostensibly implemented to improve medical care, the historical racial divide between the ladino and indigenous communities made the indigenous community suspicious of medical interference. As Carey notes: "The state's attempt to control midwives and further imbue their communities with Western ideologies was, in part, predicated on a social structure that privileged ladinos and denigrated Maya." In a country where a majority of the people lived in rural and isolated areas and did not speak Spanish, and where roughly 90 percent of rural women were illiterate, the women who lived outside of the capital city and who practiced midwifery resisted such state efforts, depending instead upon the instruction offered by female community elders.

187. *Studium*, January, February, and March 1922.

188. Guy, "The Politics of Pan-American Cooperation," 457.

189. Ibid., 452.

190. *Bulletin of the Pan American Union*, February 1924. On November 1, 1923, the twenty women graduated, including a mother and daughter. A small note to the article in the *Bulletin of the Pan American Union* indicated that other mothers were suspicious of their daughters attending the course.

191. *Bulletin of the Pan American Union*, July 1923, 82–83.

192. *Bulletin of the Pan American Union*, October 1923. Espinoza was likely also from an elite

social class. Her educational accomplishments were listed in the national paper the *Diario de Centro América* on October 26, 1887, while she was still very young.

193. *Bulletin of the Pan American Union*, August 1923; May 1926; and June 1923, 615–16. Under Decree 813 issued on February 13, 1923, all charitable organizations fell under the authority of the government, particularly those having to do with women and children. See also *Bulletin of the Pan American Union*, March 1, 1924.

194. *El Imparcial*, October 21, 1943.

195. *El Ideal*, April 28, 1888; and *El Imparcial*, July 28, 1945.

CHAPTER TWO

1. Drinot and Knight, *The Great Depression in Latin America*, 8.
2. Ríos Tobar, "Feminism Is Socialism, Liberty and Much More," 130.
3. Finzer, "Poetisa Chic," 77.
4. There are three primary trends within the current historiography on the Ubico dictatorship. Historians such as Joseph A. Pitti, "Jorge Ubico and Guatemalan Politics in the 1920s," and Kenneth Grieb, *Guatemalan Caudillo: The Regime of Jorge Ubico, Guatemala, 1931–1944*, explore the Ubico regime through the man himself, analyzing his rise to power and the impact of his policies on Guatemala. The second trend, exemplified by Guatemalan historians, explores the period as it related to Ubico's overthrow and the following decade of revolution. Works by Carlos Samayoa Chinchilla, *El dictador y yo*, and Rafael Arévalo Martínez, *Ubico*, examine how the social policies on health care, education, and political ideology of the 1920s remained dormant but not dead during the 1930s. They explore the reemergence of these ideas in the months immediately following Ubico's overthrow in 1944. A third historiographic trend examines the Ubico regime within regional rural studies, such as Cindy Forster's article "Violent and Violated Women: Justice and Gender in Rural Guatemala, 1936–1956," and her book *The Time of Freedom*; Greg Grandin's *The Blood of Guatemala*; and David Carey's *I Ask for Justice: Maya Women, Dictators, and Crime in Guatemala, 1898–1944* and *Engendering Mayan History*. The latter represents the first full-length monograph focused on one particular group of Guatemalan indigenous women.
5. See Dosal and Peláez Almengor, *Jorge Ubico*; Samayoa Chinchilla, *El dictador y yo*; and Arévalo Martínez, *Ubico*.
6. See Grieb, *Guatemalan Caudillo*; and Pitti, "Jorge Ubico and Guatemalan Politics."
7. Way, *The Mayan in the Mall*; and Kirkpatrick, "Optics and the Culture of Modernity."
8. See also Forster, "Violent and Violated Women"; and Carey, *I Ask for Justice*.
9. See Gibbings, "In the Shadow of Slavery"; Gibbings, "Mestizaje in the Age of Fascism"; and Gibbings, "Another Race More Worthy of the Present."
10. Kandiyoti, "Bargaining with Patriarchy," 275.
11. *Azul*, January 1, 1941.
12. See Carey, "Forced and Forbidden Sex"; Carey, "Runaway Mothers and Daughters"; and Carey, *I Ask for Justice*.
13. Dosal, *Power in Transition*, 64.
14. Handy, *Gift of the Devil*, 88.
15. Drinot and Knight, *The Great Depression in Latin America*, 188.
16. Ibid., 190.

17. There appear to be some exceptions to the abolishment of labor unions. Documents in the AGCA contain references to women's labor unions throughout the 1930s.

18. Forster, *The Time of Freedom*, 27.

19. Randolph, "The Diplomatic History of Guatemala," 68. On September 17, a dozen men faced the firing squad, and one week later another five men were executed.

20. Ibid., 75.

21. The AGCA contains references to the arrest and imprisonment of women by Ubico's forces. Ana Cofiño Kepfer's recent chapter "Las primeras comunistas en Guatemala" notes that around twenty-five women were arrested for political organizing. She derived this information from Arturo Taracena Arriola and Omar Lucas Monteflores's work, *Diccionario biográfio del movimiento obrero urbano de Guatemala, 1877–1944*.

22. See Carey, *I Ask for Justice*; and Way, *The Mayan in the Mall*. This sentiment has been shared by many Guatemala City residents I have gotten to know while researching this project.

23. Grieb, *Guatemalan Caudillo*, 34.

24. An example of this type of writing can be found in Hernández de León, *Viajes presidenciales*.

25. See Cindy Forster, *The Time of Freedom*; Carey, *I Ask for Justice*; and Gibbings, "Another Race More Worthy of the Present."

26. Way, *The Mayan in the Mall*, 38.

27. Dirección General de Estadística, *Quinto censo general de población, levantado el 7 de Abril de 1940*. Nationally, 3,083 female teachers made up 60.9 percent of all teachers.

28. Ramírez Rodríguez, *Profesora María Chinchilla Recinos*.

29. González-Rivera, *Before the Revolution*, 49. González-Rivera notes that the Nicaraguan constitution was also changed in 1939 to explicitly exclude women. Asamblea Constituyente Guatemala, *Reforma constitucional de 1935*, 451.

30. Lavrin, *Women, Feminism, and Social Change*, 167. As Lavrin points out, other Latin American countries had already legalized this type of practice. Here, Ubico duplicates the practice, justifying it with nationalistic and patriotic language.

31. *El Liberal Progresista*, March 29, 1940.

32. *El Liberal Progresista*, February 11, 1941.

33. Carey, *I Ask for Justice*.

34. Forster, *The Time of Freedom*, 27.

35. Power, *Right-Wing Women in Chile*; and Deutsch, *Las Derechas*.

36. Besse, *Restructuring Patriarchy*, 5.

37. Ríos Tobar, "Feminism Is Socialism, Liberty and Much More," 130.

38. Finzer, "Poetisa Chic," 11. This influence can be best seen by those active among the Generación del 20 writers.

39. Isaura de Menéndez Mina appeared throughout the 1910s and 1920s in such diverse publications as *El Grito*, *Revista del Trabajo*, and *Vida*. She also appeared on the editorial page in the 1944 edition of *Azul* celebrating the overthrow of Jorge Ubico. This is the only time that Gloria Menéndez Mina did not write the editorial page, granting this privilege to her mother. She was born on November 2, 1912, and in 1946 she gave birth to a six-and-a-half-pound baby boy named Lionel Padilla Menéndez Mina.

40. *Studium*, April and May 1923; and *Diario de Centro América*, September 13, 1920.

41. *El Imparcial*, June 1924.

42. She continued to contribute to *El Imparcial* extensively throughout the 1940s and 1950s in the editorial columns *Los Ojos de Mujer* (A Woman's Eyes), *El Mundo Feminine* (The Feminine World), and *El Mirador Feminine* (The Feminine Perspective).

43. Casaús Arzú and García Giráldez, *Las redes intelectuales centroamericanas*, 226. The Vitalist Movement was created following a visit to Guatemala by its Salvadoran founder, Alberto Masferrer. Casaús Arzú notes that Josefina Saravia E. also joined the group along with members of the Generación del 20.

44. Racine, "Alberto Masferrer and the Vital Minimum," 209, 237. Karen Racine argues that Masferrer's ideas were important to many Central American reformers and revolutionists, including Juan José Arévalo.

45. Casaús Arzú and García Giráldez, *Las redes intelectuales centroamericanas*, 226.

46. Finzer, "Poetisa Chic," 77–78.

47. *Azul*, January 1, 1945.

48. *Azul*, February–March, 1949, 32.

49. The journal *Nosotras* ran from 1932 until 1939; not all of the editions have survived.

50. Racine, "Alberto Masferrer and the Vital Minimum," 209.

51. *El Liberal Progresista*, March 5, 1941. Federico Hernández de León's other daughter, Alida, worked with him at *Nuestro Diario*. Hernández de León also emerged out of the Generación del 20.

52. *Azul*, April 30, 1943.

53. Forster, *The Time of Freedom*, 27; and Arévalo Martínez, *Ubico*, 65.

54. Magdalena Spínola (1886–1975) herself was a significant literary figure in the capital city, and events in her life inspired her to become part of the revolutionary movement to overthrow Jorge Ubico. Her husband was personally murdered by President Ubico and, as a result, she and her family were ostracized during the 1930s. Ultimately, she reemerged as an important literary figure during the 1940s and remained prominent for the rest of her life.

55. Lavrin, *Women, Feminism, and Social Change*, 35.

56. *Azul*, September 15, 1940.

57. *El Liberal Progresista*, August 9, 1941.

58. *Nosotras*, July 1932, editorial.

59. Finzer, "Poetisa Chic," 8–10.

60. Jones, *Guatemala Past and Present*, 337.

61. Dirección General de Estadística, *Censo General de la República de Guatemala levantado el año de 1880*, 20; Dirección General de Estadística, *Analisis del censo urbano de la capital levantado el 22 de Febrero de 1938*, 19; and Dirección General de Estadística, *Quinto censo general de población, levantado el 7 de Abril de 1940*, 867–69. Valle and Menéndez Mina were two of three total female journalists in the capital, with one female lawyer (until Graciela Quan Valenzuela's law degree in 1943 made two), eight doctors, three dentists, and twenty-nine female pharmacists.

62. *Nosotras* had staff in eight departments, including María de Trocoli in Antigua, Elvira de Ramírez in Amatitlán, Elódia de Rodríguez in Quetzaltenango, Olga Waldheim in Zacapa, María Luis de Figueroa in Santa Lucía, Matilde Ovalle in Suchitepéquez, María Teresa Quintana in Sololá, and Elena Galindo in Huehuetenango.

63. *El Imparcial*, June 19, 1943. An article in *Azul*, no. 77, entitled "Azul y Revista de la Cruz Roja"

noted the temporary merger of the women's journal *Azul* and the Red Cross. Gloria Menéndez Mina, Martha Josefina Herrera, Romelia Alarcón Folgar, Lucía Alzamora, Marina Spross de Baca, and Luís Pastori are all listed as important writers and contributors to the Red Cross.

64. It also appears that other urban women from across Guatemala aligned themselves with these two feminist ideals, as both Valle and Menéndez Mina reference women from across the country. However, a thorough investigation of these trails is beyond the purview of this study.

65. *Vida*, December 12, 1925, 1–2; and February 13, 1926, 7–9.

66. Casaús Arzú and García Giráldez, *La redes intelectuales centroamericanas*. Casaús Arzú traces Valle's intellectual development to an intellectual circle influenced by J. Fernando Juárez Muñoz, a member the Generación del 1898.

67. Adams, "Antonio Goubaud Carrera," 26.

68. Valle continued to write throughout the 1944–1954 era, and her editorials consistently raised concerns over indigenous women and children.

69. *Nosotras*, May 1932. This article featured the marriage of an indigenous couple, highlighting the ceremony and related cultural practices. It included two photos of the couple.

70. *El Imparcial*, February 6 and February 13, 1937.

71. Adams, "Antonio Goubaud Carrera," 25; and Figueroa Ibarra, "The Culture of Terror," 196.

72. Handy, *Revolution in the Countryside*, 50. The work done at the Instituto Indigenista Nacional in Guatemala helped pave the way for the Agrarian Reform Law in 1952.

73. Adams, "Antonio Goubaud Carrera," 19, 28.

74. For a full exploration of this debate and the work of Antonio Goubard Carrera, see Adams, "Antonio Goubaud Carrera."

75. *Nosotras*, March 1932.

76. Witzel de Ciudad, *Más de 100 años del movimiento obrero urbano*, 332. The presence of a lone Catholic labor union, the Unión de Señoras, during a period when all labor unions were illegal further supports the idea that Ubico allowed conservative female associations to exist. A sole edition of *La Mujer Obrera* (1936) was found in the AGCA in Guatemala City in 2002. This one issue suggests that the union was a Catholic women's union, and the dating on the journal itself indicates that it began publication in 1931. It may have been the Sindicato Católico de Señoras y Señoritas Empleadas de Comercio y Talleres, begun in 1921, or another, unknown union.

77. Lavrin, "Female, Feminine and Feminist," 1.

78. Lavrin, *Women, Feminism, and Social Change*, 33.

79. Lavrin, "Female, Feminine and Feminist."

80. *Azul*, October, 15, 1942.

81. *Azul*, September 15, 1942.

82. *Azul*, November 1, 1940, 93.

83. *Azul*, October 15, 1942.

84. *Azul*, September 15, 1942.

85. *Nosotras*, November 1932, editorial.

86. *Nosotras*, July 1932, editorial.

87. *El Imparcial*, March 24 and April 3, 1937.

88. *El Imparcial*, May 5, 1937.

89. See Lavrin, *Women, Feminism, and Social Change*, chapter 1.

90. *El Imparcial*, June 2, 1937.

91. *El Imparcial*, June 4 and June 9, 1937.

92. *El Imparcial*, June 17, 1937.

93. Kaplan, "Final Reflections," 262–63.

94. *El Imparcial*, June 28, 1937.

95. In a less sensational debate, Valle also takes on a Mariano Valverde, who attacks the issue of women and modernity in *El Imparcial* in June 1938.

96. *El Imparcial*, August 12, September 18, and October 16, 1937.

97. *Nosotras*, May 1934.

98. *Azul*, February 1, 1941.

99. *Azul*, February 15, 1941.

100. *Azul*, February 1, 1940.

101. Lavrin, *Women, Feminism, and Social Change*, 35.

102. See Miller, *Latin American Women*; and Lavrin, *Women, Feminism, and Social Change*.

103. Lavrin, *Women, Feminism, and Social Change*, 133.

104. See McCreery, "This Life of Misery and Shame." The topic of prostitution was addressed sporadically in national newspapers throughout the period covered by this book.

105. *El Liberal Progresista*, April 24, 1941.

106. Levenson-Estrada, *Trade Unionists against Terror*, 111.

107. Ibid., 67; Gleijeses, *Shattered Hope*, 17; and *El Liberal Progresista*, May 15, 1941.

108. Elisa Muralles Soto, personal interview, July 2004.

109. Grieb, *Guatemalan Caudillo*, 267–68.

110. *El Liberal Progresista*, May 16, 1941.

111. The date was April 27 and the decree number was 1264.

112. *Nosotras*, March 1932. Malin D'Echevers married into the elite family of Wyld Ospina; she was very much involved in the literary community and supported Valle and Menéndez Mina. Born Amalia Castillo, she changed her name to Malin D'Echevers and worked as a writer affiliated with the Sociedad Gabriela Mistral during the 1920s.

113. *Nosotras*, May 1932; *Bulletin of the Pan American Union*, July 1923, 82–83; and González Orellana, *Historia de la educación en Guatemala*, 343. The Popular University, managed by the Federation of University Students in Guatemala City, had opened in April 1923. It was specifically created for the working class, and courses were offered at night and on the weekends. Its creators designed the school to combat illiteracy, diffuse scientific principles, improve social education and arouse an interest in education generally, and teach the principles of sanitation, hygiene, and personal health necessary to keep men (and women) strong and healthy.

114. González Orellana, *História de la educación en Guatemala*, 267.

115. GD, "Informe de Alianza Femenina Guatemalteca a la Comisión de Defensa y Protección de la infancia del Primer Congreso Nacional," November 26, 1953, 5.

116. Barascout, *Le edad de los escolares y su valor*, 7.

117. González Orellana, *História de la educación en Guatemala*, 401–2.

118. Carey, *Engendering Mayan History*.

119. Whetten, *Guatemala: The Land and the People*, 199. Whetten notes that in 1955, despite ten years of revolutionary reforms, 84 percent of rural teachers had not studied beyond the sixth grade.

120. Benedict Anderson, *Imagined Communities* (London: Verso, 2006).
121. Vaughan, *Cultural Politics in Revolution*, 7.
122. Ibid., 5.
123. *Nosotras*, February and March 1932.
124. *Nosotras*, August 1934.
125. Ibid., 267.
126. González Orellana, *Historia de la educación en Guatemala*, 360.
127. *Nosotras*, March 1933.
128. *Azul*, May 1, 1943.
129. *Nosotras*, July 1932.
130. *Vida*, April 10, 1926, 15.
131. *Vida*, April 17, 1926, 9–10, 14.
132. Ibid., 8; and Vásquez, *La mujer en el hogar*. Vásquez also published an article in *Vida*, "La educación de la mujer" (April 17, 1926), which summarized his ideas later published in *La mujer en el hogar*.
133. Jones, *Guatemala Past and Present*, 105.
134. *El Imparcial*, March 13, 1937, and January 9, 1937.
135. *Azul*, June 15, 1941.
136. *Azul*, July–August 1945. A meeting took place at the home of Magdalena Spínola, who, along with Graciela Quan Valenzuela, was making a legal case for Gálvez's appointment to the Ministry of Public Education.

CHAPTER THREE

1. Forster, *The Time of Freedom*, 23.
2. Sabato, "On Political Citizenship."
3. Drinot and Knight, *The Great Depression in Latin America*, 8.
4. For a partial list, see the following works: Lavrin, *Women, Feminism, and Social Change*; Shepherd, Brereton, and Bailey, *Engendering History*; Besse, *Restructuring Patriarchy*; Caulfield, *In Defense of Honor*; Dore and Molyneux, *Hidden Histories of Gender and the State*; Bayard de Volo, *Mothers of Heroes and Martyrs*; Hutchison, "Add Gender and Stir?"; Ehrick, *The Shield of the Weak*; Macpherson, *From Colony to Nation*; Mooney, *The Politics of Motherhood*; and Guy, *Women Build the Welfare State*.
5. Porter, "Women, Family Formation, and the Welfare State," 212–20.
6. Guy, *Women Build the Welfare State*.
7. Jaquette, *The Women's Movement in Latin America*, 13.
8. For further details on the role of university students in the overthrow of Jorge Ubico, see Vrana, *This City Belongs to You*.
9. A few copies of these notes have survived and are housed in the AGCA.
10. Chase, "Women's Organisations and the Politics of Gender," 545.
11. *El Imparcial*, July 2, 1944. In the morning, Enrique Muñoz Meany, Carlos Illescas, Otto Raúl González, Micaela Arias de Alvarado, Jesús Alvarado, René Berger, Celso Cerezo, Carlos Navarrete, Gregorio Flores, Tomás Leal, Julio and Rogelio Ramírez Contreras, Edgar Lenhoff, Carlos Vela D., Carlos García Manzo, and Marta López are among those listed as injured, burned, or killed. Tito

Oliva, Teofilo Meléndez (fourteen years old), Francisco Aguilar P., Abelardo López, and Jesús Polanco were all taken to the hospital. During the afternoon, Dolores Gallardo, Soledad Samaoa, Efrain Jimenez Archila, Celso de León Rabanales, Miguel García Valle, Urbano Posadas, Antonio Rivas, Esperanza Barrientos Fuentes, Alicia de la Cruz, Francisco Us, Aída Sándoval, Francisca Arango, and many more too numerous to mention were taken to the hospital. Among those taken to their own homes by the secretary of the Mexican embassy were Ella Alfaro de Castillo, Sally Rawson (both Costa Rican), Julieta Castro de Rólz Bennett, and Cristiana Paniagua. Also listed as injured is Beatríz Irigoyen Arzú.

12. *El Imparcial*, July 4, 1944.

13. Forster, *The Time of Freedom*, 85.

14. *El Imparcial*, July 10, 1944.

15. *El Imparcial*, February 10, 1945. Their credibility was enhanced by the signature of one of María Chinchilla's aunts.

16. Cupples, "Between Maternalism and Feminism." As Cupples notes, "Sandinista discourses of gender and nationalism constructed women as either heroic warriors or self-sacrificial mothers," and Orlando Valenzuela's 1984 photo, *Miliciana de Waswalito*, embodied both ideals.

17. Kampwirth, *Feminism and the Legacy of Revolution*, 19. "Originally a photograph, the image of the nursing guerrilla was reproduced in many forms, including public murals, postcards, and the official poster that commemorated the tenth anniversary of the revolution."

18. For a partial list see Molyneux, "Mobilization without Emancipation?"; Randall, *Gathering Rage*; Smith and Padula, *Sex and Revolution*; Bayard de Volo, *Mothers of Heroes and Martyrs*; González and Kampwirth, *Radical Women in Latin America*; Isbester, *Still Fighting*; Luciak, *After the Revolution*; Kampwirth, *Feminism and the Legacy of Revolution*; Shayne, *The Revolution Question*; and Bayard de Volo, "A Revolution in the Binary?"

19. The short length of Guatemala's 1944 revolution is exceptional in comparison with the later revolutions in Cuba (triumphant in 1959), Nicaragua (triumphant in 1979), El Salvador (1970s–1992), and the civil war in Guatemala (1960–1996).

20. Some scholars such as J. T. Way have suggested recently that the revolution itself remained primarily a military project and does not represent a significant deviation from the historical militarization of Guatemalan politics.

21. My conclusion here contradicts Lorraine Bayard de Volo's argument for "violence and war as key factors that sustained masculinity's privilege. In sum, gender difference lends meaning to revolutionary war, and war reinforces gender inequality—a feedback loop suggesting contradictions within militarized revolutions that aim to enhance equality." See Bayard de Volo, "A Revolution in the Binary?," 414.

22. Moghadam, "Gender and Revolutionary Transformation."

23. Molyneux, "Mobilization without Emancipation?"

24. Ibid., 232–33.

25. Scholarship on Guatemala City during the 1970s suggests a similar social milieu. For example, see Levenson-Estrada, *Trade Unionists against Terror*.

26. *El Imparcial*, July 6, 1944.

27. A partial list of books on the revolution includes Forster, *The Time of Freedom*; Gleijeses, *Shattered Hope*; Grandin, *The Blood of Guatemala*; Grandin, *The Last Colonial Massacre*; Handy,

Revolution in the Countryside; Immerman, *The CIA in Guatemala*; James, *Red Design for the Americas*; LaFeber, *Inevitable Revolutions*; León Aragón, *Caída de un régimen*; Schlesinger and Kinzer, *Bitter Fruit*; Schneider, *Communism in Guatemala*; and Schneider, *Case Study in Insurgency*.

28. *Nuestro Diario*, October 21 and October 26, 1944; and *El Imparcial*, November 17, 1944. Three people were killed on October 20, when a bomb fell on their house.

29. The labor leader Silverio Ortiz became a pivotal civilian in the revolution's victory.

30. Forster, *The Time of Freedom*, 86–87.

31. *El Imparcial*, December 11, 1944.

32. *Nuestro Diario*, November 15, 1944, 5.

33. *Nuestro Diario*, October 28, 1944. In the following weeks, a few noticed the absence of women from the daily lists of revolutionary heroes appearing in the national newspapers, and the editor of *Nuestro Diario* moved quickly to rectify this error.

34. Shayne, *The Revolution Question*, 128.

35. *El Imparcial*, December 9, 1944.

36. Ibid.

37. *El Imparcial*, December 14, 1944, editorial.

38. *El Imparcial*, August 1, 1944; reprinted from *Azul*, June 1944.

39. Isaura de Menendez Mina, "Épica gloriosa," *Azul*, October 1944, 3.

40. *El Imparcial*, December 8, 1944.

41. *El Imparcial*, December 12, 13, and 14, 1944.

42. *El Imparcial*, December 15 and 22, 1944.

43. *El Imparcial*, December 7, 1944.

44. Forster, *The Time of Freedom*, 98.

45. Chavarría Flores, *Analfabetismo en Guatemala*, 10, 51–52; and González Orellana, *Historia de la educación en Guatemala*, 368.

46. Barascout, *La edad de los escolares y su valor*, 5.

47. Carey, *Engendering Mayan History*, 181.

48. Barascout, *La edad de los escolares y su valor*, 21, 29.

49. González Orellana, *Historia de la educación en Guatemala*, 483. González Orellana played an integral role in educational and related reforms. He also represented Guatemala at the Tenth Inter-American Conference of the Organization of American States (the Caracas Conference) in 1954.

50. Dirección General de Estadística, *Censos de la República de Guatemala, 1950*.

51. González Orellano, *Historia de la educación en Guatemala*, 401–2.

52. Suslow, "Social Security in Guatemala," 30.

53. Ministerio de Educación Pública, *Indice: Editorial del pueblo*, 38; and *Nuestro Diario*, April 23, 1946.

54. Dirección General de Estadística, *Censos de la República de Guatemala, 1950*, 219, 223–30.

55. An undated pamphlet describes the role of teachers in identifying illness among their students. AGCA, Hojas Sueltas.

56. Forster, *The Time of Freedom*, 98.

57. *Azul*, July–August 1945.

58. The important teachers' union, the Sindicato de Trabajadores de la Educación de Guatemala, will not be discussed here.

59. *El Imparcial*, August 21 and 23, 1944, editorial.

60. Porter, "Women, Family Formation, and the Welfare State," 212.

61. Juárez y Aragón, *Natalidad y mortalidad infantil en la Ciudad de Guatemala*, 62, 24, 57. The study took place from January to June 1943. Juárez y Aragón believed that the data was so incomplete that he was reluctant to draw definite conclusions.

62. Guatemalan Documents (GD), Container 6, "Informe de Alianza Femenina Guatemalteca a la Comisión de Defensa y Protección de la infancia del Primer Congreso Nacional," November 16, 17, 18, 1953, 1.

63. For a complete history of public health legislation from independence to the revolution, see Salazar, "Resumen de las leyes y disposiciones," 26–39.

64. Suslow, "Social Security in Guatemala," 32, 65. The predominant direct causes of infant mortality were diarrhea, enteritis, intestinal parasites, and malaria, the latter accounting for 20 percent of all deaths. In 1946, 62,115 deaths altogether were recorded nationwide, but only 5,764 of those who died had received medical attention; and in 1947, of all births recorded, only 3.77 percent occurred in hospitals.

65. *Nuestro Diario*, July 3 and 5, 1947.

66. Juárez y Aragón, *Natalidad y mortalidad infantil en la Ciudad de Guatemala*, 63.

67. Ibid., 34; and *Nuestro Diario*, July 3, 1947.

68. Ortega Ávila, *Mortalidad materna y mortinatalidad*, 12, 29, 45.

69. *Diario de Centro América*, November 4, 1949.

70. Ortega Ávila, *Mortalidad materna y mortinatalidad*, 46.

71. AGCA, Jefatura Política de Guatemala, 1945–1946.

72. Ortega Ávila, *Mortalidad materna y mortinatalidad*, 39.

73. Rosemblatt, "Charity, Rights, and Entitlement," 557.

74. There is little information available on the life and work of Martínez de Arévalo.

75. *Mujeres: Boletín de Alianza Femenina Guatemalteca*, June 20, 1952, 4.

76. Fraser and Navarro, *Evita: The Real Life of Eva Perón*; Navarro, "Wonder Woman Was Argentine"; and Guy, *Women Build the Welfare State*.

77. Cabrera Cruz, "Análisis y propuesta de diseño"; and Méndez Pérez and García, "Situation Faced by Institutionalized Children."

78. "Mrs. Arevalo quickly discouraged and destroyed all possibility of a joint effort and she, personally, chose to work with teachers, market women and people who were ready to cater to her and in whom she was sure to find complete subservience." "Comedores y Guarderías Infantíles," PBSUCCESS Report, Central Intelligence Agency, March 29, 1954, 1.

79. Vilanova de Árbenz, *Mi esposo, el president Árbenz*, 71.

80. GD, Container 3, March 11, 1952. There is a note from María Árbenz to Ismael González Arévalo and wife (ambassadors to Argentina) to thank Eva Perón for her financial contributions. Perón died on July 26, 1952.

81. Guy, *Women Build the Welfare State*, 81.

82. For a broader discussion on how social reform programs were implemented and engineered by the state in the post-Árbenz era, see Way, *The Mayan in the Mall*, chapters 2, 3.

83. Social reform programs created by middle- and upper-class philanthropists directed at working-

class women have a long history in Latin America. For a partial list, see Lavrin, *Women, Feminism, and Social Change*; Porter, *Working Women in Mexico City*; Guy, *Women Build the Welfare State*; and Ehrick, *The Shield of the Weak*.

84. See Guy, *Women Build the Welfare State*; and Sanders, *Gender and Welfare in Mexico*.

85. For a full accounting of these child congresses, see Guy, *Women Build the Welfare State*; Sanders, *Gender and Welfare in Mexico*; Guy, "The Pan American Child Congress"; and Guy, "The Politics of Pan-American Cooperation."

86. Final Act of the Ninth Pan American Child Congress, Caracas, Venezuela, January 5–10, 1948.

87. *Nuestro Diario*, October 27, 1944. Women of Colón Market had already organized on their own behalf, María González Roldan, Soledad C. de Orantes, Trinidad M. de Jiménez, Angelina Peralta, Carmen P. de Martínez, María del Cid, Olivia de Pérez, Rosario Pachco, Felipa Medine, and Delfina Porres having leadership positions.

88. The most critical meetings occurred on February 20, March 10, and April 5, 1945.

89. *Guarderías nacionales y comedores infantiles: Origen, organización, propósitos.*

90. Ibid., 11.

91. Sanders, *Gender and Welfare in Mexico*, 60.

92. *El Imparcial*, October 10, 1946.

93. González Orellana, *Historia de la educación en Guatemala*, 486.

94. *Nuestro Diario*, March 1, 1946. The sanatorium was renamed the Sanatorio Elisa Martínez de Arévalo, established on the Nacional La Aurora farm.

95. *La Hora*, August 26, 1948.

96. *Nuestro Diario*, January 23, 1946. While Elisa Martínez de Arévalo acted as honorary chairwoman and worked diligently, other women formed the executive committee. The director/president was Mélida Montenegro de Méndez, and the treasurer was Rodolfo Castillo Azmitia.

97. Despite the significance of this work, there is little evidence of it remaining. One of the best sources of information can be found among the papers of the Alianza Femenina Guatemalteca, who prepared a history of the Comedores Infantiles for their first national congress in 1953.

98. *Nuestro Diario*, August 3, 1946.

99. GD, Container 26, "Breve resumen historico de la asociación," 2; and Monzón Lemus, *Camino de adolescente*.

100. *El Imparcial*, October 10, 1946, and September 23, 1947. According to one report in 1945, the centers raised Q11,245.87, while only spending Q5,129.34. Suslow, "Social Security in Guatemala," 37.

101. *El Imparcial*, August 21, 1944, editorial.

102. GD, Container 26, "Breve resumen historico de la asociación," September 15, 1950, 8; and *Nuestro Diario*, October 24, 1950. The hospital in Puerto Barrios also had X-ray equipment.

103. *El Imparcial*, December 18, 1948. A wide variety of social organizations sent representatives for this meeting including Guillermo Mata Amado (Rosa Rodríguez López's brother in law) from the Club de Leones; Carlos H. de León of the Cámara Junior; Carlos Federico Mora of the Rotary Club and National League against Tuberculosis; Luis Valladares y Aycinena and Eloy Amado Herrera, both representing the Popular University; Roberto Nocedo and Carmen Rodríguez Beteta of the Girl Guides; María Isabel Escobar, Graciela Quan Valenzuela de Reina, and Miss Wisks, all representing the Club Altrusas; Marina Tinoco, Luz de León, and Julio Urruela representing Acción

Católica; Marta Escobar de Richardson from the Sociedad Protectora del Niño; Mélida Montenegro de Méndez of the comedores infantiles; Adolfo Amado P. and Herda de Engel from the Boy Scouts; Eduardo Mayor of the Antituberculosis League and the Boy Scouts; Antonio Goubard Carrera from the Instituto Indigenista Nacional; Walter Pettit from the United Nations; Ricard Ponce of the Red Cross; Rosa de Mora and David Vela of the National Guatemala Journalists; and Carlos María Campos of the Institute of Social Security.

104. Suslow, "Social Security in Guatemala," 65–72. The IGSS was established via Decree 295 on October 30, 1946. Among its many goals, the IGSS provided protection against industrial accidents, invalidity, and general illness; insurance for maternity, old age, and death; and assistance for widows and orphans. It sought to train social workers who would work throughout the country, focusing particularly on the needs of indigenous communities, "whose habits, customs, and beliefs . . . encourage the witch rather than the doctor."

105. *El Imparcial*, December 18, 1948.

106. *Azul*, February–March 1949, 43–45.

107. Ibid. The instructors included Manuel Antonio Girón, Antonio Goubaud Carrera (director of the Instituto Indigenista Nacional), Jorge Brenes, and Manuel Luís Escamilla from the University of San Carlos.

108. Guy, "The Politics of Pan-American Cooperation," 450–56.

109. Ehrick, *The Shield of the Weak*.

110. *Nuestro Diario*, August 27, 1947. The delegates from the First Inter-American Congress of Women visited the homes and nutrition centers by special invitation of Mélida Montenegro de Méndez. Again, on July 18, 1951, Montenegro de Méndez invited the ambassador from El Salvador to visit the centers.

111. *Diario de Centro América*, September 29 and 30, 1949; and Santamaría Ambriz, "La Unión de Universidades de América Latina." Included among the attendees were Elisa Martínez de Arévalo, Elvira L. de Aldana, Teresa del Alcázar de Orozco, Gloria de Shaw, and Luz V. de Castejón from the guarderías nacionales and comedores infantiles, along with Lily de Pullín, Marta Escobar de Richardson, and Señoras de Meillon and de Peralta.

112. Adams, *Crucifixion by Power*, 281.

113. Carey, *Engendering Mayan History*, 133.

114. *La Hora*, July 7, 1948.

115. Maxine Molyneux, "Mobilization without Emancipation?," 232.

CHAPTER FOUR

1. The presidential election occurred during December 17–19, 1944. The elections for congressional delegates or *diputados* took place during December 28–30, 1944.

2. This chapter will not explore the complexities of the municipal elections. For further information, see Grandin, *The Blood of Guatemala*; and Handy, *Revolution in the Countryside*.

3. The initial dates were November 12–14, 1948, then changed to November 26–28, and then were finally set for December 10–12, 1948.

4. Ehrick, *The Shield of the Weak*; García-Bryce, "Transnational Activist: Magda Portal"; Guy, *Women Build the Welfare State*; Hahner, *Emancipating the Female Sex*; Lavrin, *Women, Feminism, and Social Change*; Macpherson, *From Colony to Nation*; Pernet, "Chilean Feminists"; Power, *Right-*

Wing Women in Chile; Rodríguez Sáenz, *Un siglo de luchas femeninas*; Stoner, *From the House to the Streets*; and Towns, "The Inter-American Commission of Women."

5. This particular insight was offered by Donna Guy at the Rocky Mountain Council on Latin American Studies in April 2013 during a panel discussion. The contemporary political practices of women have received some scholarly attention of late, particular surrounding political transitions such as in Chile following the reemergence of democracy in the post-Pinochet era, in Argentina in the postmilitary era, and in Nicaragua during and following the Sandinista revolutionary era.

6. Contreras Vélez, *Génesis y ocaso*; Galich, *Del pánico al ataque*; García Bauer, *Nuestra revolución legislativa*; García Laguardia, *La revolución del 20 de Octubre de 1944*; León Aragón, *Caída de un régimen*; Nájera Farfán, *Los estafadores de la democracia*; Pellecer, *Asalta-caminos en la historia de la revolución*; and Peláez Almengor, *Guatemala 1944–1954*.

7. Nájera Farfán, *Los estafadores de la democracia*, 39–40.

8. Gleijeses, *Shattered Hope*, 33–35. Piero Gleijeses notes that the Renovación Nacional was formed by a group of eight friends who met at the home of Mario Efraín Nájera Farfán. He makes no mention of the others who signed the formal document, in particular a number of women present whose names are also among those listed. No record of these meetings has surfaced to date.

9. Taracena Flores Collection, "Revolution and Counterrevolution in Guatemala, 1944–1963," July 2, 1944. The thirteen women included Bertha F. de Arriago, María A. Silva, Luz C. de Estrada Ricci, María Fernández, Manuela Rodríguez, Enriqueta Flores, S. Carlota Herrera, Anibal Medina G., Delia E. López, Trinidad López A., M. Luz de Morgan, and Blanca Luz Mejia J.

10. *El Imparcial*, July 7, 1944.

11. An analysis of the Guatemalan revolutionary political parties has yet to be done. Consequently, there is a general lack of understanding regarding the internal dynamics of these political parties.

12. *El Imparcial*, August 18 and 19, 1944. The leadership committee included the secretary, Ana Josefina Pellecer L., as well as Esperanza Rodríguez Ojeda and Marta Grace Rosales C. Some of the young women working on this campaign included Josefina Bosque, María Hortensia Pinto, and Matilde Chinchilla.

13. *El Imparcial*, August 23, 1944. Speakers at this meeting included María Consuelo Pereira and Laura Cruz. Others on the leadership committee included the secretary, Zoila Luz Méndez; vice secretary, María Luisa Silva; treasurer, Olitia Nuñez; and members at large Julia Meléndez de DeLeón (the author of the 1937 debate over gender in *El Imparcial*), Ofelia Ninfa Cabrera (a teacher), Aída Chávez, Laura Samayoa, and María Isabel Foronda de Vargas (who became an active member of the Alianza Femenina Guatemalteca and attended the Second Inter-American Congress of Women). Mélida Montenegro de Méndez (mother of future mayor of Guatemala City Mario Méndez Montenegro and president of the Asociación de Damas Pro-Comedores Infantíles) served as president, with Concha González Solis as vice president.

14. Miller, *Latin American Women*, 112. In a year when relatively few women participated in politics, women represented from 10 to 15 percent of the membership of political parties in Brazil, Uruguay, and Argentina. Although the total experience of Latin American women in politics is far from complete, such diffusing of political power was repeated, as the formidable Magda Portal of the Alianza Popular Revolucionaria Americana (Peru) reveals. See García-Bryce, "Transnational Activist: Magda Portal."

15. AGCA, Hojas Sueltas, August 1944.

16. During his presidential campaigns, Ubico's national newspaper *El Liberal Progresista* listed

hundreds if not thousands of women's names from across the country who claimed to support his candidacy. Many of these names were indigenous in origin.

17. Bayard de Volo, *Mothers of Heroes and Martyrs*, 33.

18. There are very few sources available on the activities of these women in the existing archives in Guatemala or the Library of Congress.

19. As Piero Gleijeses notes in *Shattered Hope*, despite the historical attention paid to the Guatemalan revolution, there has been no analysis of the revolutionary political parties.

20. *El Imparcial*, November 30, 1944; and Taracena Flores Collection, July 10, 1944, no. 330. The group originally named itself Políticos y Asociaciones Cívicas Independientes Pro: Candidatura del Arévalo. The group's name was later changed to the Comité Pro-Ciudadanía.

21. *El Imparcial*, January 31 and May 18, 1944. The poet Magdalena Spínola Vda. de Aguilar Fuentes served as vice president, and Stella Márquez acted as secretary. The group's secretaries included María del Pilar Vásquez de García and Margarita Leal, while Angelina Acuña de Castañeda, Josefina Saravia de Alfaro, Adriana Saravia de Palarea, and Romelia Alarcón Folgar served as general committee members. Among the others named as active members were Rosa Vda. de Saravia, Clemencia Morales Tinoco, Carlota Villatoro, and Amanda Castilla.

22. *El Imparcial*, February 17, 1944. Carmen Ydígoras and Magdalena Spínola Vda. de Aguilar Fuentes served as vice secretaries, and María Luisa Samayoa and Margarita Leal as treasurers. General committee members included María del Pilar Vásquez de García, Lena H. de Gueydan, María Albertina Gálvez, Elisa Hall de Asturias, and Angelina Acuña de Castañeda. Other members listed are Josefina Bosque, María Hortensia Pinto, Ana Josefina Pellecer L., Esperanza Rodríguez Ojeda, Marta Grace Rosales C., and Matilde Chinchilla.

23. The treasurer was María del Pilar Vásquez de García, and the vice treasurer was Zoila Putzeys Vda. de Utrera. General committee members included Magdalena Spínola Vda. de Aguilar Fuentes, Romelia Alarcón Folgar, Clemencia Rubio Vda. de Herrarte, Laura Zachrisson de Bendfeldt, Adriana Saravia de Palarea, Julia Paíz, María Albertina Gálvez, Irene de Peyré, Rosa de Mora, María Herrera de Aschkel, María Alaíde Foppa, Elisa de Barrios, and Dominga de Álvarez.

24. Some sources list Quan Valenzuela as the second female *lawyer* in Guatemala, but it appears that she was the first woman in the country to obtain a law degree.

25. Quan Valenzuela, "Ciudadanía opcional para la mujer Guatemalteca," 23.

26. Lavrin, *Women, Feminism, and Social Change*, 37.

27. Gleijeses, *Shattered Hope*, 17.

28. *Labores de la Cuarta Convención Nacional Unionista Reunida en Santa Ana, El Salvador, Centro América el 15 de Septiembre de 1944*, 29. Delegates from across Central America met to discuss the possible union of their five countries.

29. Graciela González, *Azul*, October 1944.

30. Coker Gonzalez, "Agitating for Their Rights," 699.

31. *El Imparcial*, November 24, 1944; and AGCA, Hojas Sueltas, "Mujeres retaltecas," n.d. Affiliations of the national suffrage campaign existed across the country including in Livingston with president Juana R. de Dedet (general members were Evangelina Marroquín, Natalia G. de Estrada, Adelina Marroquín, and secretary teacher Lucila Morales); in Puerto Barrios with president Marí Teresa de Reyes and vice president Marí de Jesús Delgado (general members were María Rodríguez Zoila Girón, Rosa Margarita Sandoval, Luz Fajardo, Rosa Zamora, and secretary Juana Elizondo); as

well as smaller affiliates in Ciulapa, Sololá, Momostenango, Quetzaltenango, Ostuncalco, Tamahú, Escuintla, and Amatitlán.

32. *El Imparcial*, September 23, 1944. The Unión Cívica Guatemalteca included a motion in their initial communication that they intended to introduce to the Guatemalan National Assembly, which they had drafted with the support of other Central American women during the recent meeting in Santa Ana, El Salvador. At the Santa Ana meeting, a motion was presented to include women in all their nations' basic definitions of citizenship and suffrage.

33. *Azul*, September 1944, 19.

34. Gleijeses, *Shattered Hope*, 27–28.

35. *El Imparcial*, November 25, 1944; and *Labores de la Cuarta Convención Nacional Unionista Reunida en Santa Ana, El Salvador, Centro América el 15 de Septiembre de 1944*.

36. To date, no records of the event itself have been found. One reference, an advertisement, exists in the Hojas Sueltas collection at the AGCA. The advertisement states that the central directors of the Frente Popular Libertador and Renovación Nacional invite all Guatemalan women to the first women's suffrage congress to be held on November 25, 1944.

37. *Bulletin of the Pan American Union* 79 (January–December 1945): 29–30; Taracena Flores Collection, November 23, 1944, no. 87; and Monzón, "Entre líneas," 101. Graciela Quan Valenzuela, Gloria Menéndez Mina, Magdalena Spínola, Romelia Alarcón Folgar, Clemencia Rubio de Herrarte, Laura Zachrisson de Bendfeldt, Adriana Saravia de Palarea, and María Albertina Gálvez were the main leaders of this civic movement.

38. *Nuestro Diario*, August 26, 1944; and *Nuestro Diario*, November 23, 24, and 25, 1944. *Nuestro Diario* also recorded Elisa Hall de Asturias and Angelina Acuña de Castañeda among the congressional leadership. *Nuestro Diario*, November 27, 1944, 16. The congress was opened by Mélida Montenegro de Méndez. Julia Meléndez de DeLeón followed with words reflecting the intense emotions present among those in attendance. (Her actual words are not recorded.)

39. *Nuestro Diario*, November 27, 1944.

40. Hall de Asturias was related to Máximo Soto Hall, the writer and initiator of women's suffrage at the Fifth International Conference of American States at Santiago, Chile, in 1923.

41. *El Imparcial*, November 24, 1944.

42. Craske, *Women and Politics in Latin America*, 199.

43. Hall de Asturias appears in the Alianza's membership list for the first time in April 1950.

44. *Nuestro Diario*, November 27, 1944. Orozco Posadas could legitimately claim his support for women's suffrage. He had publicly supported this cause during the Ubico regime in an article titled "Las mujeres son más buenas que los hombre" in *El Imparcial*, January 3, 1938. Future politicians Carlos Manuel Pellecer and Manuel María Avila Ayala also attended the congress. Oscar is likely the brother of Mario Efraín Nájera Farfán.

45. See Casaús Arzú, "La voz de las mujeres guatemaltecas"; Casaús Arzú, "Las redes teosóficas de mujeres en Guatemala"; Casaús Arzú and Peláez Almengor, *Historia intelectual de Guatemala*; and Casaús Arzú and García Giráldez, *Las redes intelectuales centroamericanas*.

46. *Azul*, September 1944, 18.

47. *El Imparcial*, November 29, 1944, editorial.

48. *El Imparcial*, February 10, 1945.

49. *Nuestro Diario*, February 7 and 8, 1945.

50. *El Imparcial*, November 30, 1944. The editorial page was full of articles on women and suffrage, including those by Gálvez and D'Echevers.

51. *El Imparcial*, November 29, 1944. Editorial. His writings first appeared in the early 1920s. He wrote a medical column on puericultura in El Imparcial.

52. *El Imparcial*, November 4, 22, and 24, 1944, editorials.

53. Lavrin, *Women, Feminism, and Social Change*, 35.

54. Teele, *Forging the Franchise*, 39.

55. *El Imparcial*, July 21, 1954. In a rather ironic twist of fate, Alaíde found herself on another list in July 1954 as the government of Carlos Castillo Armas attempted to punish those who had either worked with the revolutionary government or been supportive of it. The pro-revolutionary employees had their wages frozen by the new government.

56. Julio Solórzano, personal interview, Winnipeg, Manitoba, June 20, 2013.

57. *El Imparcial*, December 6, 1944.

58. *Nuestro Diario*, December 18, 1944.

59. *El Imparcial*, January 30 and February 5, 1945. *El Imparcial* noted that a female lawyer brought the suffragists' case before the National Assembly. Although no name is mentioned, it is likely that the lawyer was either Graciela Quan Valenzuela or Amalia Castillo.

60. *El Imparcial*, February 6, 1945; and *Nuestro Diario*, February 5, 1945.

61. *Nuestro Diario*, November 15, 1944; and *Nuestro Diario*, December 1, 1944, 9. Menéndez Mina ran articles in *Azul* in support of suffrage, written by pro-suffragists such as Guatemala's ambassador to Costa Rica, Alfonso Carrillo, who questioned why women were equal to men in all areas except in the area of the vote.

62. Arendt, *The Human Condition*, 36.

63. Isbester, *Still Fighting*, 49.

64. It is important to note that Menéndez Mina used the June uprisings to validate women's citizenship, while Luz Valle employed the actions of both June and October. Menéndez Mina was far more conservative than some of her fellow suffragists, and while she was a tireless advocate for women's civil and legal rights, her own political position and social status made her less comfortable with the overt military role played by women in October.

65. *Nuestro Diario*, February 8, 1945, editorial.

66. Handy, *Revolution in the Countryside*, 24. Handy notes that suffrage for illiterate men and for women led to the most heated of debates.

67. *El Imparcial*, February 1, 1945. The fifteen-member commission that created the preliminary constitution included suffrage as optional and secret for all literate women, but the measure needed to be passed by the entire assembly.

68. *Nuestro Diario*, January 25, 1945.

69. García Laguardia, *La revolución del 20 de Octubre de 1944*, 23, 31.

70. Ibid., 23; and *La Hora*, August 6, 1947.

71. Marroquín Rojas, *Cronicas de la constituyente del 45*, 164.

72. Ibid., 163; *Nuestro Diario*, March 9, 1945; and *El Imparcial*, March 9, 1945. The politicians who voted for suffrage included David Guerra Guzmán, Humberto Sosa, Luis Díaz Gómez, Carlos Manuel Pellecer, Saúl Calderón, Ernesto Marroquín Wyss, Rubén Loarca Duarte, Juan de Dios

Díaz O., Adolfo López Valdés, Julio Bonilla González, Julio Godoy, José Torón España, Manuel Galich, A. Pereira Echeverría, Eduardo Arreola, Dantón Jiménez de León, José Luis Bocaletti, J. M. Mazariegos, José R. Lemus, González Lanforth, Francisco Mota, Julio César Ordóñez, Ovidio Rodas Corzo, José Manuel Fortuny, G. Morales, and A. J. Sotomayor.

73. *El Imparcial*, June 1, 1945. The struggle was not over for the Unión Femenina Guatemalteca, as they continued to petition for voter registration sites for all the new citizens included in the 1945 constitution.

74. Ministerio de Gobernación, Trabajo y Previsión Social, *Constitución de la República de Guatemala decretada por la Asamblea Nacional constituyente en 11 de Marzo de 1945*, 8.

75. Only 360,695 Guatemalan females over the age of seven were considered literate out of a total of 1,268,681, for a literacy rate of 28 percent. This discrepancy can be explained by the inaccuracies of the 1940 census as compared with that of 1950.

76. Forster, "Violent and Violated Women," 56; and Forster, *The Time of Freedom*, 102.

77. *Diario de Centro América*, December 8, 1947.

78. Taracena Flores Collection, December 7, 1945, no. 499. Among those who worked for their campaigns were Concha Asturias, Clara Graciela Villacorta L., and Rebeca Asturias.

79. Levenson-Estrada, *Trade Unionists against Terror*, 16; and Forster, *The Time of Freedom*, 91. Following the overthrow of the Carlos Herrera government in 1921, Ortiz Rivas and his colleagues initiated the Guatemalan section of the Central American Communist Party, which was disbanded in 1931 by Jorge Ubico. Ortiz Rivas played an integral role in the October revolution when he sent runners to the barrios to recruit more workers at a critical point in the battle between Ubico's military and those loyal to the revolution.

80. Taracena Flores Collection, January 1947, nos. 827–30, 833; Taracena Flores Collection, nos. 827–29; and *Nuestro Diario*, December 14, 1946. Acuña de Castañeda wrote a book of poems called *La gavilla de Ruth*. She also joined the Unión de Mujeres Democráticas, who organized the 1947 First Inter-American Congress of Women (see chapter 5).

81. The other party to openly advocate for the inclusion of all Guatemalans was the Renovación Nacional.

82. *Diario de Centro América*, July 9, 1949. Carmen Vargas participated in a conference in Lake Success, New York, as an economic representative of Guatemala. She was also the Guatemalan representative to the United Nations.

83. *Nuestro Diario*, November 12, 1948.

84. *El Imparcial*, November 22, 1948. The editorial on Carmen Vargas and Saravia de Palarea was written by Luz Valle.

85. All historians of this era affirm the fundamental openness and fair democratic process of the revolutionary elections.

86. Handy, *Revolution in the Countryside*, 33. Handy notes that the numerous coup attempts were the result of intrigues by conservative political parties that failed to do well in the polls.

87. Power, *Right-Wing Women in Chile*, 51. Margaret Power bases her argument on the work of Julieta Kirkwood (*Ser política en Chile*, 119–20) and Elsa Chaney (*Supermadre*, 21–24).

88. Teele, *Forging the Franchise*, 31.

89. Deutsch, "Spreading Right-Wing Patriotism," 235–36.

90. Handy, *Revolution in the Countryside*, 32. President of the National Assembly, Recinos refused to accept the results of the presidential election and Arévalo's presidency following his own defeat in November 1944.

91. AGCA, Hojas Sueltas, 1944; *Nuestro Diario*, October 12, 1944; and Taracena Flores Collection, nos. 84, 182, 1, 109.

92. Pope Pius XI, "Atheistic Communism," in Treacy, *Five Great Encyclicals*, 181.

93. Silvert, *A Study in Government*. Árbenz received 258,987 votes out of 404,739 ballots cast, while Miguel Ydígoras Fuentes came in second with 72,796 votes.

94. For further information, see Gleijeses, *Shattered Hope*, chapter 5.

95. Taracena Flores Collection, n.d., nos. 1130, 1133.

96. The urban population was vastly outnumbered by the rural segment and by illiterate rural men, who overwhelmingly supported both Arévalo and Árbenz.

97. Taracena Flores Collection, n.d., nos. 1130, 1133.

98. For a full accounting of Ydígoras Fuentes's presidential run against Árbenz, see Gleijeses, *Shattered Hope*, chapter 4, "The Election of Jacobo Arbenz." Once a general under Jorge Ubico, Ydígoras Fuentes competed with Carlos Castillo Armas for the presidency of Guatemala following Árbenz's overthrow in June 1954. He later successfully ran for president in 1958 following the assassination of Castillo Armas and held the position until 1963, when another coup d'etat brought Colonel Enrique Peralta Azurdia into power.

99. *El Imparcial*, December 15, 1950. Hernández de Zirión later wrote a book on Ydígoras Fuentes, *Datos biográficos del general e ingeniero Miguel Ydígoras Fuentes* (1961).

100. Taracena Flores Collection, March 27, 1950, no. 1156; and AGCA, Hojas Sueltas, May 1950.

101. *El Imparcial*, November 8, 1950.

102. One of his political campaign advertisements was signed by more than 340 women, and there may have been others with similar female endorsement (García Granados, *Cuaderno de memorias*, 21). As García Granados himself relates:

> In 1934, he [Ubico] uncovered a conspiracy against him. . . . Seventeen men were seized, given a farcical trial in which they were not even permitted defense attorneys, and sentenced to be shot. Although I [Jorge García Granados] had no part in this conspiracy, I wrote Ubico a strong letter charging that the trial was a mockery of the law, and urging him to pardon the condemned. Ubico replied by sending a squad of police to arrest me in my home, take me to the place of execution, and force me to be an eyewitness to the shooting of the seventeen. Then I was thrown in prison and held in solitary confinement for months, not even permitted to receive news of my family. In late 1934 I went into exile to Mexico. (García Granados, *Cuaderno de memorias*)

The grandson of the Liberal revolutionary hero of 1871, Miguel García Granados, Jorge first became involved in politics as a university student during the Unionista movement of 1920. After becoming a lawyer, he continued his political interest, serving as a deputy during the Chacón administration and into the early period of Ubico. . . . Upon Ubico's fall, he immediately returned to Guatemala and was the most important civilian leader involved in the October revolution. He has subsequently served not only as president of the Constituent Assembly but also as president of the first revolutionary Congress, ambassador to Washington and the United Nations, and as a member of the United Nations Palestine Commission. (Silvert, *A Study in Government*, 15)

103. *El Imparcial*, November 6, 1950.
104. Jim Handy writes:

Municipal government in Guatemala was incredibly complex and varied from region to region, from municipio to municipio, and even from cantón to cantón within the same municipality. The definition of "community" varied from place to place. In some locales, the municipal government truly reflected a cohesive entity, and the system of a dual hierarchy of religious and secular offices controlled by a board of governors embodied in the *principales* was energetic and responsive. In others, the term "community" more closely corresponded to an aldea some distance from the municipio capital or a separate cantón within but distinct from the capital itself. (Handy, *Revolution in the Countryside*, 57)

For further information on the issue of municipal autonomy, see García Bauer, *Nuestra revolución legislativa*.

105. If a department had a low population, it had the right to a minimum of one deputy. In 1954, the Congress was composed of fifty-six deputies, and all were elected for a period of four years.

106. Silvert, *A Study in Government*, 41.

107. Handy, *Revolution in the Countryside*, 33. On May 1, 1947, Guatemalan politicians passed the first comprehensive labor code, which affirmed the right to unionize, afforded protection from unfair dismissals, guaranteed the right to strike within a conciliation mechanism, stipulated a forty-eight-hour workweek, regulated the employment of women and adolescents, and established basic standards of health and safety in the workplace. The greatest opponent of this bill was the United Fruit Company, whose refusal to comply with the new laws caused work stoppages and strikes. US attempts to intervene with the Guatemalan government on behalf of the UFCo generated conflict in the Arévalo administration. As Jim Handy notes: "The national debate over communism affected Guatemalan relations with the United States and became intertwined with Guatemala's treatment of U.S. business interests. Arévalo shuffled cabinet ministers, abandoned legislation, and restricted labor to placate U.S. concerns" (Handy, *Revolution in the Countryside*, 35). For their efforts to appease the United States, the Arévalo administration was rewarded with increased violent opposition.

108. *La Hora*, June 14, 1948. The 1948 municipal elections were closely followed by the alcalde elections in January 1949 in Guatemala City. The campaign rhetoric was designed to influence both of these races.

109. The first one was issued on June 8, the second on October 16, and the third on November 16, 1948.

110. Mariano Rossell y Arellano, "Instrucción pastoral de Monseñor Mariano Rossell y Arellano al pueblo católico de Guatemala: Sobre el deber y condiciones del sufragio," 4.

111. "Civismo apolítico," *El Imparcial*, August 7, 1948; Mariano Rossell y Arellano, "UNE es civismo: No política," *El Imparcial*, August 20, 1948; and Records of the US Department of State Relating to Internal Affairs of Guatemala, June 18, 1948.

112. Records of the US Department of State Relating to Internal Affairs of Guatemala, June 29, 1948; and *Nuestro Diario*, June 26, 1948.

113. Records of the US Department of State Relating to Internal Affairs of Guatemala, August 11 and October 5, 1948.

114. *El Imparcial*, June 26, July 17, and July 21, 1948.

115. *Nuestro Diario*, June 19, 1948; and AGCA, Hojas Sueltas, June 19, 1948. "Liga Democratica Guatemalteca Contra el Comunismo," *Boletín*, no. 1. The other woman's name on this bulletin was Margarita Azmitia de Luna. Other members included Dr. Joquin Barnoya, Lic. Jesús Unda Murillo, Ing. Carlos Enrique Azurdia, Rogelio Ramila, Francisco Urrejola, and Aturo Castillo B.

116. *Diario de Centro América*, July 27, 1948.

117. *Nuestro Diario*, June 28, 1948.

118. *El Imparcial*, August 12, 1948.

119. *La Hora*, July 2 and July 26, 1948.

120. *La Hora*, August 28, 1948. In light of all the registrations, Hernán Hurtado Aguilar, writing in *La Hora*, declared that the government had quadrupled the number of voting stations.

121. *La Hora*, March 10, 1947. The leader of the Partido de Trabajadores Republicano-Democrático, Manuel María Herrera, noted that women represented approximately half of the four hundred thousand eligible voters in the capital city.

122. *La Hora*, November 16, 1948.

123. Mariano Rossell y Arellano, "Exhortación de Monseñor Mariano Rossell y Arellano arzobispo de Guatemala al pueblo católica sobre el deber de la caridad en la práctica del sufragio electoral," October 12, 1948.

124. *El Imparcial*, November 19, 1948, editorial.

125. Mariano Rossell y Arellano, "Carta pastoral sobre la justicia social, fundamento del bienestar social," November 15, 1948, 4.

126. Also published in *El Verbum*, November 15, 1948.

127. *El Verbum*, June 13, 1948, 5. "Cada votante recibio dos boletos, una con los candidatos oficiales (la unica ecogencia), otra con una cruz inmensa que significaba oposición al gobierno."

128. Rossell y Arellano, "Carta pastoral sobre la justicia social," 7.

129. *Diario de Centro América*, November 16, 17, and 22, 1948.

130. *El Imparcial*, June 26 and July 17, 1948.

131. *El Imparcial*, August 7, 1948. The paper argued that the archbishop was not telling Guatemalans who to vote for but rather was warning them against communist institutions.

132. *Diario de Centro América*, July 27, 1948; and *Nuestro Diario*, June 25, 1948.

133. *Nuestro Diario*, July 3, 1948.

134. *El Verbum*, June 27, 1948.

135. *Diario de Centro América*, November 29 and December 8, 1948.

136. *Diario de Centro América*, November 30 and December 2, 1948. The suspensions of Articles 25, 31, 33, 34, 35, 36, 37, 43, and 48 were particularly enforced.

137. Records of the US Department of State Relating to Internal Affairs of Guatemala, July 1, 1948.

138. Records of the US Department of State Relating to Internal Affairs of Guatemala, June 23, June 25, July 1, and July 23, 1948; and *Nuestro Diario*, June 18, 1948. Of the 41,000 citizens who had registered to vote by the beginning of July, 1,598 were women.

139. Margaret Power asks a similar question of the women's movement in Chile: "Although my questions can only be speculative, I wonder what would have happened if FRAP [Frente de Acción

Popular] had adopted the positions advanced by some of its female members who questioned aspects of male domination. Would this challenge to patriarchal control have generated support among women, or would it have only served to alienate the Left's male base while not winning over the critical number of women?" Power, "The Engendering of Anticommunism," 942.

140. Power, "Defending Dictatorship," 302.

141. Power, "The Engendering of Anticommunism," 942, 953. Allende went on to win the presidency in 1970.

142. William Robinson points out that the US State Department continued to manipulate gender norms in the more recent 1990 Nicaraguan presidential elections. Robinson, *A Faustian Bargain*.

143. AGCA, Hojas Sueltas. Hundreds of broadsides, pamphlets, and other electoral propaganda pieces were created that outlined the social reforms and urged women to embrace these changes. They consistently used similar rhetoric promoting Catholicism, faith, and anticommunism in response to accusations, but they were not effective.

144. *La Hora*, February 12, 1949; and *El Imparcial*, December 3, 1948.

145. *El Imparcial*, November 30, 1951.

146. Records of the US Department of State Relating to Internal Affairs of Guatemala, 1950–1954, December 1, 1951.

147. Boylan, "The Feminine 'Apostolate in Society,'" 171.

148. It is exceedingly difficult to track the political activities of conservative women following the overthrow of Árbenz due to the frequency of military coups and dictatorial governments that flourished in the following decades.

CHAPTER FIVE

1. Grandin, *The Last Colonial Massacre*; Joseph and Spenser, *In From the Cold*; Rock, *Latin America in the 1940s*; and Joseph, LeGrand, and Salvatore, *Close Encounters of Empire*.

2. Joseph and Spenser, *In from the Cold*, 4–5.

3. Grandin, *The Last Colonial Massacre*, 189.

4. Haan, "Continuing Cold War Paradigms," 548.

5. Costigliola, "The Nuclear Family," 168–69.

6. Westad, *Reviewing the Cold War*, 10.

7. Miller, *Latin American Women*, 132.

8. Miller, "Latin American Feminism and the Transnational Arena," 12; and Miller, "Feminism and Transnationalism," 571. Pan American Scientific Congresses were held in Buenos Aires in 1898, Montevideo in 1901, Rio de Janeiro in 1905, and Santiago in 1908, with most delegates being Argentinian, Chilean, Uruguayan, and Brazilian women. For further study on Latin American women's congresses, see Miller, *Latin American Women*; Lavrin, *Women, Feminism, and Social Change*; and Stoner, *From the House to the Streets*.

9. Seventh International Conference of American States, Third Committee: Civil and Political Rights of Women, Minutes and Antecedents, Montevideo, 1933, 34.

10. Towns, "The Inter-American Commission of Women," 790.

11. Miller, "Latin American Feminism and the Transnational Arena," 16, 21.

12. Catherine Foster, *Women for All Seasons*, vii.

13. WILPF members believed that, as women, they added a sense of ethics to conversations sorely

lacking in such. In short, the WILPF advocated for changes in economic and social conditions that promoted peace and democratic progress rather than war. The organization became an international vehicle through which women worked for peace in a manner men had proven themselves incapable of. For more complete histories of the WILPF, see Catherine Foster, *Women for all Seasons*; and Carrie Foster, *The Women and the Warriors*.

14. Heloise Brainerd lived from 1881 to 1969. After she graduated from Smith College in Northampton, Massachusetts, Brainerd spent three years in Mexico. She became connected with the Pan American Union in Washington, DC, eventually becoming chief of the Division of Education, which expanded into the Division of Intellectual Cooperation. She was an active member of the Jane Addams Peace Association. In 1935, Brainerd resigned from the Pan American Union and became the chair of the Committee on the Americas and chair of the Division of Inter-American Work, for the WILPF. She resigned from the WILPF in 1953.

15. Swarthmore College Peace Collection (SCPC), Heloise Brainerd, "To Women's Organizations in the Americas," Reel 130.24, May 25, 1945. Latin Americans understood only too well the implications of US foreign policy. The United States had been invading Latin American countries since the nineteenth century to institute political and economic policies favorable to US business and political interests.

16. SCPC, International Circular Letter no. 7, Reel 28, September 1947, 16.

17. Threlkeld, *Pan American Women*, 177

18. Stoner, *From the House to the Streets*, 113.

19. Threlkeld, *Pan American Women*, 177.

20. SCPC, WILPF, International Executive Committee, Geneva, July 1948, "Interim Report to the International Executive Committee of the WILPF," Heloise Brainerd, n.p.; SCPC, International Circular Letter no. 3, "To the WILPF National Sections, International Members, and Subscribers to Pax," Reel 28, November 1946, 32; and SCPC, "To Women's Organizations in the Americas," Reel 130.24, May 25, 1945. Other Latin American women who attended the inter-American conference at Haverford included Stella Dolores S. Monteiro from Brazil, Marian Forero from Colombia, Lilia Ramos from Costa Rica, Leticia Guerrero from Ecuador, Luce Duvivier from Haiti, Ana María Berlanga from Mexico, Ana María Morínigo from Paraguay, Sara Frias from Peru, and Elisa Gusiffe Osborne from Uruguay.

21. SCPC, International Circular Letter no. 2, "To the WILPF National Sections, International Members, and Subscribers to Pax," Reel 28, May 1946, 11.

22. SCPC, Heloise Brainerd, chair of the US Section, "Interim Report to the International Executive Committee of the WILPF," Reel 12, May 1946, 11.

23. Miller, *Latin American Women*, 127.

24. AGCA, Programa del Primer Congreso Interamericano de Mujeres, August 20–27, 1947, 11–12.

25. The records do not indicate why Brainerd chose to contact Gálvez. From existing material, it appears that the two women had a common friend.

26. SCPC, María Albertina Gálvez, "Excerpts from a Few of the Replies Made by Women's Associations and Prominent Women," Reel 130.24.

27. *Diario de Centro América*, April 8, 1947. Along with its president, Graciela Quan Valenzuela de Reina, the committee included Luz Valle (the former editor of *Nosotras*), Mélida Montenegro de Méndez (the mother of a future conservative alcalde in Guatemala City), Elena de Oliva, Dr. María

Isabel Escobar (Guatemala's first woman doctor and the woman heralded by *Azul* as the exemplar of a strong and intellectual Guatemalan woman), poet Angelina Acuña de Castañeda, Esther de Pérez, Consuelo Rodríguez (listed as a chess player), writers Celeste de Espada and Isaura de Menéndez Mina (the latter a nationally renowned writer from the 1920s), Gloria Menéndez Mina (editor of *Azul*), Olimpia Vda. de Barrientos, Rosa de Mora (one of the founders of the Sociedad Protectora del Niño in 1921), lawyer Sara Basterrechea Ramírez, symphony director Judith Bravo, teachers Alicia Muñoz and Natalia Morales de Lara, and artists Aracely Palarea Saravia, Consuelo Flamenco, and Esther Álvarez Vda. de López Barrios, along with Matilde Balcárcel, Romelia Alarcón Folgar (future executive of the Alianza Femenina Guatemalteca), and Sara de Bergara. Honduran writer and poet in exile Argentina Díaz Lozano also played a significant role in the final days of preparation.

28. G. Consuelo Rodríguez and María Albertina Gálvez acted as secretaries, and María del Carmen Vargas and Zoila Putzeys as treasurers. General committee members included Mélida Luz Palacios de Wolter, Lucila Vda. de Aguirre Velásquez, Magdalena Spínola Vda. de Aguilar Fuentes, Romelia Alarcón Folgar, Olimpia Vda. de Barrientos, and Aurelia Sandoval Coronado. Natalia Morales de Lara, Mélida Montenegro de Méndez, María de Sellares, Luz Valle, and Rosa de Mora supported the organizers as congressional consultants. The organizers included some familiar writers from the 1920s and 1930s such as Josefina Saravia E., Amalia Samayoa Aguilar, Luz Valle, María del Pilar, and Isaura de Menéndez Mina.

29. *El Imparcial*, April 18, May 8, and May 9, 1947. Lawyer Sara Basterrechea Ramírez went to a Pan American meeting on the civil and social status of women.

30. SCPC, Heloise Brainerd, Inter-American Congress of Women, Organizing Committee Letter, Reel 130.24, February 11, 1947.

31. Bethell and Roxborough, *Latin America between the Second World War and the Cold War*, 327–28.

32. SCPC, Heloise Brainerd, Inter-American Congress of Women, Organizing Committee Letter, Reel 130.24, February 11, 1947.

33. *Nuestro Diario* noted several benefits for the upcoming congress. On March 11, 1947, a benefit for the Guatemalan section of the WILPF was held. Aracely Palarea Saravia directed a play that acted as a fund-raiser for the congress on March 17. On July 18, a soccer match was held in the national stadium to raise money for the upcoming congress. *Nuestro Diario* also ran informational articles about the WILPF and the congress. *El Imparcial* ran stories on the upcoming congress on February 11, 15, and 26, March 3, April 18, and May 9, 1947, while *Diario de Centro América* ran stories on April 8 and July 2.

34. *Diario de Centro América*; *La Hora*; *El Imparcial*; and *Nuestro Diario*, August 4, 1947.

35. *La Hora*, August 4, 1947.

36. Fellow congressional organizer Argentina Díaz Lozano also published an article in support of D'Echever's position further revealing the depth of the conflict within the Guatemalan section of the WILPF.

37. *El Imparcial*, August 4, 1947; and *La Hora*, August 4, 1947.

38. *Diario de Centro América*, August 4, 1947; and *Nuestro Diario*, August 5, 1947. According to Guatemala section president Quan Valenzuela and secretary Celeste de Espada, the group had been promised $25,000 from the United States but to date had received no money to assist with congress

plans. Furthermore, they had not received a single reservation for the congress, nor had they been able to obtain a list of delegates presumably registered according to the US section of the WILPF. These problems were inexplicable to the Guatemalans until they became more aware of the extreme political tendencies of the WILPF. The following day, on August 5, Quan Valenzuela and Espada announced that the money earmarked for the congress was to be donated to the Liga Nacional contra la Tuberculosis (National League against Tuberculosis).

39. When precisely the Cold War emerged in Latin America is a matter of some debate. Scholars such as Iñigo García-Bryce argue that the early manifestations of the Cold War can actually be traced back to the 1920s and 1930s, while Patrick Iber argues that the cultural Cold War began with the rise of the peace movement in Latin America during the late 1940s. My use of the term "early Cold War" during the post–World War II era is not meant to necessarily support either of these positions but rather to position Guatemalan women within the global processes playing out between the United States and the Soviet Union as their alliance dissolved during the late 1940s. See García-Bryce, "Transnational Activist: Magda Portal"; and Iber, *Neither Peace nor Freedom*.

40. SCPC, Heloise Brainerd, "Statement on H.R. 3836 before House Foreign Affairs Committee," July 2, 1947, 1–4.

41. SCPC, Heloise Brainerd, "The Inter-American Military Cooperation Act," June 1947.

42. *La Hora*, August 4, 1947.

43. Mooney, "Fighting Fascism," 55.

44. *La Hora*, August 4, 1947. The cable was published in *Diario de Centro América* as issued by the Associated Press from Paris.

45. Handy, *Revolution in the Countryside*, 29. "The company [UFCo] viewed the provisions for union organization only in large agricultural enterprises as discrimination, arguing (erroneously) that it was the only such firm in the country."

46. Ibid., 35.

47. Gleijeses, *Shattered Hope*, 117.

48. Ibid., 102.

49. SCPC, Alberto Lleras Camargo, "The Director General of the Pan American Union Sends His Best Wishes to the Congress of Women," n.d.; and *La Hora*, August 12, 1947.

50. "Mrs. Arevalo quickly discouraged and destroyed all possibility of a joint effort and she, personally, chose to work with teachers, market women and people who were ready to cater to her and in whom she was sure to find complete subservience." "Comedores y Guarderías Infantiles," PBSUCCESS Report, Central Intelligence Agency, March 29, 1954, 1.

51. Immerman, *The CIA in Guatemala*, 93–94.

52. Taracena Flores Collection, no. 721, "El comunista presidente de Guatemala sabotea la conferencia de Río de Janeiro," July 12, 1947; and no. 722, "Carta abierta de acusación."

53. *Diario de Centro América*, August 21 and 22, 1947.

54. Records of the US Department of State Relating to Internal Affairs of Guatemala, enclosure to Dispatch no. 538 dated November 27, 1950, from the American Embassy, Guatemala.

55. Briggs, *Reproducing Empire*.

56. Costigliola, "The Nuclear Family," 165, 168–69.

57. *Nuestro Diario*, August 9, 1947.

58. Clemente Marroquín Rojas, *La Hora*, August 6, 1947, editorial.

59. *El Imparcial*, March 5, 1955. Marroquín Rojas resigned as representative of the department of Jalapa on January 22, 1955, and his resignation was accepted on March 5, 1955.

60. *El Imparcial*, August 5, 1947.

61. *Diario de Centro América*, August 7, 1947; and *Nuestro Diario*, August 12, 13, and 14, 1947.

62. AGCA, Memoria del Primer Congreso Interamericano de Mujeres, celebrado en la capital de Guatemala, August 21–27, 1947, 18.

63. AGCA, Proyecto de reglamento del Congreso Interamericano de Mujeres, August 21–27, 1947. María Eloisa García Etchegoyen was second secretary and Carmen Sánchez de Bustamante Calvo de Lozada acted as technical assistant. Mildred Burgess acted as first vice president, and Heloise Brainerd served as first secretary. This committee set the daily program and the number and dates of the plenary sessions, made all final resolutions, and established plans to study six designated topics.

64. *Diario de Centro América*, August 7, 1947. The groups they invited included the Sindicato de Trabajadores de la Educación de Guatemala, Sindicato de Trabajadoras Intelectuales y Artistas Revolucionarios, Asociación de Maestras Católicas de Guatemala, Asociación de Damas Ropero Auxiliar de Santiago, Asociación de Estudiantes de Humanidades, Asociación de Madres Católicas, Federación Regional Central de Trabajadoras, Confederación General de Trabajadores de Guatemala, Federación Sindical de Guatemala, Cadetes de Cristo, Partido Acción Revolucionaria, Renovación Nacional, and Frente Popular Libertador.

65. AGCA, Memoria del Primer Congreso Interamericano de Mujeres, 5, 13–14. The number of countries represented by delegates ranges from sixteen to nineteen, depending on the source. The congress program lists representatives from eighteen nations. Two nights were set aside for public participation, August 22 and 25. The North American associations represented included the Women's International League for Peace and Freedom, US section; the Zonta International; the Pan American League (Miami); the National Federation of Business and Professional Business Women's Clubs; the Pilots Club International; the National Council of Negro Women; and the National Association of Altrusa Clubs. Along with the women from the Unión de Mujeres Democráticas, the Guatemalans who responded to the invitation to participate included the Sindicato de Trabajadores de la Educación de Guatemala; the Asociación de Damas Pro-Comedores Infantíles; the female sections of the political parties Partido Acción Revolucionaria and Renovación Nacional; the Sindicato Central de Costureras; el Sindicato de Trabajadoras del Beneficios de Café, Escuintla; and the Guatemalan section of a group called the Unión de Mujeres Americanas.

66. Argentine María Teresa Ferrari de Gaudino represented the Federación de Mujeres Universitarias and the Asociación de Mujeres Tituladas del Uruguay. Ana Rosa Tornero de Bilbao la Vieja represented Ateneo Femenino from Bolivia. Three Canadians, Beatrice Brigden, Helen Drury, and Mildred Fahrni, came as delegates of the Women's International League for Peace and Freedom, Local Council of Women, National Council of Women of Canada, and Association of Canadian Clubs. Colombians Lucila Rubio de Laverde and Soledad Peña represented the Alianza Femenina Colombiana and Unión Femenina de Colombia, respectively. The Costa Rican Centro Femenino de Estudios Eugenio María de Hostos sent María Odilia Castro Hidalgo and Corina Rodríguez López. Four Chilean female organizations sent María Mercedes Rivera Urquieta to represent their interests: the Asociación Cristianas Femeninas, Consejo Nacional de Mujeres, Sección Femenina del Circulo Pro Paz y Cooperación Américana, and Federación Chilena de Instituciones Femenina. Guatemalan Malin D'Echevers de González also represented the Cuban La Cruz Blanca de la Paz. Gumersinda

Páez, president of the 1947 congress, was a lawyer, a member of the Panamanian legislature, and president of the Inter-American Commission of Women.

67. Longley, *In the Eagle's Shadow*, 187; and Immerman, *The CIA in Guatemala*, 94. Held a month before Arévalo's inauguration in March 1945, the Chapultepec Conference was held to strengthen wartime cooperation against possible military threats. Its resolutions emphasized that all activities be consistent with the principals of the emerging United Nations. The Guatemalan delegation at Chapultepec recommended the condemnation of intervention by a state in the internal or external affairs of another state. Guatemala also recommended that all American republics abstain from recognizing and maintaining relations with antidemocratic regimes, especially those that had come to power through a coup against a democratically elected government. The Declaration on Reciprocal Assistance and American Solidarity of March 3, 1945, was devoted to principles of international law and the union and solidarity of American peoples for the defense of their rights and the maintenance of international peace.

68. Wamsley, "A Hemisphere of Women," 244; and Marino, *Feminism for the Americas*, 226.

69. Miller, *Latin American Women*, 116.

70. AGCA, Memoria del Primer Congreso Interamericano de Mujeres, 27.

71. AGCA, Memoria del Primer Congreso Interamericano de Mujeres, Malin D'Echevers, "Introduction," 18.

72. AGCA, Proyecto de reglamente del Congreso Interamericano de Mujeres, 3; and SCPC, "Resolutions of the First Inter-American Congress of Women, Guatemala City," Reel 130.24, August 21–27, 1947.

73. AGCA, Proyecto de reglamente del Congreso Interamericano de Mujeres, 3–6.

74. Miller, *Latin American Women*, 130.

75. AGCA, Memoria del Primer Congreso Interamericano de Mujeres, 45.

76. Pernet, "Chilean Feminists," 682. Corinne Pernet notes that the Roosevelt administration, including Eleanor Roosevelt, opposed the equal rights treaty that a majority of Latin American women wanted on the conference agenda, as the Americans believed that it would hurt protective legislation for women in the United States.

77. Lavrin, *Women, Feminism, and Social Change*, 48.

78. AGCA, Proyecto de reglamente del Congreso Interamericano de Mujeres, 1–2.

79. Antezana-Pernet, "Peace in the World and Democracy at Home," 179. "In the Chilean press, however, the congress in Guatemala was largely ignored. *El Mercurio*, for instance, commented only on the declared opposition of the congress to atomic weapons. It then published a 'letter of resignation' from the Costa Rican delegate, who complained the congress was 'pro-Soviet' and ignored the threat that communism posed to the world."

80. AGCA, Proyecto de reglamente del Congreso Interamericano de Mujeres, 3.

81. Ibid., 135–37.

82. Macpherson, *From Colony to Nation*.

83. See Grieb, "Jorge Ubico and the Belice Boundary Dispute"; Young and Young, "The Impact of the Anglo-Guatemalan Dispute"; and Wiegand, "Nationalist Discourse and Domestic Incentives."

84. Wiegand, "Nationalist Discourse and Domestic Incentives," 352.

85. Many intellectuals and politicians weighed in on the matter of Belize during the revolutionary decade. For examples, see Ministerio de Relaciones Exteriores, *La controversia sobre Belice*; Barreda

de Evián, *Arreglo pacífico de controversia internacionales*; Carrillo, *Algunos aspectos jurídicos*; Carrillo, *El caso de Belice*; Alvarado, *La cuestión de Belice*; Leyton Rodríguez, *Belice es tierra de Guatemala*; and Alvarado, *Lo que ha pasado con Belice*.

86. AGCA, Malin D'Echevers, "Belice es tierra de Guatemala," Memoria del Primer Congreso Interamericano de Mujeres, 111.

87. Grieb, *Guatemalan Caudillo*, 232.

88. It is unclear whether the women were aware that their country's claim to Belize was just another form of colonialism. It is likely, however, that they would have persisted in their claim given the challenges facing the nascent democratic government and its supporters in 1947.

89. AGCA, Proyecto de reglamente del Congreso Interamericano de Mujeres, 6–7.

90. Ibid., 8.

91. Records of the US Department of State Relating to Internal Affairs of Guatemala, enclosure to Dispatch no. 538 dated November 27, 1950, from the American Embassy, Guatemala. Nela Martínez was labeled a communist by the US State Department for her work with the 1947 congress, and for her signature on the Act of Chapultepec.

92. *Nuestro Diario*, August 30, 1947; and *El Imparcial*, August 26, 1947.

93. *Nuestro Diario*, August 26, 1947. Chacón's letter was reprinted and dated August 24.

94. *Nuestro Diario*, August 26, 27, and 30, 1947, editorial. Although Quan Valenzuela did not participate in the formation of the UMD in early August, she attended the congress.

95. *Nuestro Diario*, August 27, 1947; and *El Imparcial*, August 27 and 28, 1947.

96. *Diario de Centro América*, August 27, 1947.

97. *Diario de Centro América*, August 28, 1947. A teacher and a nurse, Castro Hidalgo had been instrumental in the First Inter-American Congress on Education in Havana, Cuba, in 1939.

98. *Diario de Centro América*, August 30, 1947.

99. SCPC, Letter from Heloise Brainerd, WILPF, US section, Reel 130.30, DG43, November 1, 1947.

100. Threlkeld, *Pan American Women*, chapter 2.

101. Laville, "A New Era in International Women's Rights?," 50.

102. Over the next several years, *Nuestro Diario* covered a series of high-profile visits between women of the Unión de Mujeres Democráticas and former delegates of the 1947 congress. In 1948, *Nuestro Diario* noted visits with international delegates on February 26, March 18, and March 22 (Clemencia Rubio de Herrarte, Malin D'Echevers, Elisa Hall de Asturias, Argentina Díaz Lozano, Helena Leiva de Holst, María del Pilar, Olimpia Vda. de Barrientos, Mélida Luz Palacios de Wolter, María del Carmen Vargas, Manuel Orellana, and Salvador Ley met with the visiting delegations). On June 7, 1950, Gumersinda Páez visited the home of Malin D'Echevers, along with Angelina Acuña de Castañeda, Stella Márquez, Romelia Alarcón Folgar, Lucila Vda. de Aguirre Velásquez, Olimpia Vda. de Barrientos, Griselda R. Pérez, Dalila Wyld Ospina, and María del Pilar. Páez participated in a small conference in Guatemala on June 12, 1950, meeting with Lucila Vda. de Aguirre Velásquez, Malin D'Echevers, Lily Vda. de Soto Hall, Romelia Alarcón Folgar, Magdalena Spínola, María del Pilar, Griselda R. Pérez, Stella Márquez, Olimpia Vda. de Barrientos, and Angelina Acuña de Castañeda.

103. SCPC, Letter from Carolyn B. Threlkeld, Chairman of the Latin American Committee, on the issue of the 1954 overthrow of Árbenz, Women's International League for Peace and Freedom, US section, Reel 130.30, DG43, November 1954.

104. *El Imparcial*, August 7, 12, 14, 16, 18, 21, 22, and 25, 1947; *Diario de Centro América*, August 18, 20, 21, 22, and 23, 1947; and *Nuestro Diario*, August 18, 20, 21, 22, 23, and 26, 1947.

105. *El Imparcial*, July 3 and September 19, 1950. On July 3, 1950, the Guatemalan Congress voted to join the Rio Pact, thereby giving in to international pressure. By 1950, a well-organized group of women from the capital city had begun to organize in support of the Rio Pact. Three hundred women formed a group to convince their own government to sign the agreement.

106. *Diario de Centro América*, August 27, 1947.

107. *Diario de Centro América*, August 23 and 24, 1947; *El Imparcial*, August 23, 1947; and *Nuestro Diario*, August 23 and 26, 1947.

108. *Nuestro Diario*, August 28, 1947.

109. Grandin, *The Last Colonial Massacre*, 189.

CHAPTER SIX

1. The wave paradigm devised for North America feminist movements has been largely discredited as a useful model for Latin America and has been increasingly critiqued by North American feminists themselves. See Laughlin et al., "Is It Time to Jump Ship?"

2. *Diario de Centro América*, September 1, 1949. *Diario de Centro América* claims that the Alianza helped to plan the First Inter-American Congress of Women. It is likely that the women who joined the Alianza after the congress were part of the Unión de Mujeres Democráticas.

3. The first public reference to the Alianza Femenina Guatemalteca appears in October 1947.

4. *El Imparcial*, January 5, 1951. The Federación de Mujeres de las Américas was an umbrella organization designed to assist all other women's associations. Created in the sixth commission of the congress led by Lucila Rubio de Laverde, a notable Colombian feminist, the Federación de Mujeres was organized to work together for democracy in the Americas and world peace. Those behind its formation believed that unless women from across the Americas had a permanent and independent organization in which to interact, their efforts of August 1947 would be fruitless. The federation functioned for the next five years, facilitating communication and alliances across North, South, and Central America. For women from small nations such as Guatemala, the federation served as an important network of support during times of inter-American crisis.

5. *Nuestro Diario*, November 13, 1947.

6. The majority of the organization's papers have been lost or destroyed with just a few copies in the Library of Congress and the national archives in Guatemala City. To date, I have uncovered three separate copies of *Mujeres*, dated October 1951, June 1952, and February 1953.

7. There are several lists of Alianza members during its early years. *Nuestro Diario*, May 7, 1948, and *Diario de Centro América*, September 1, 1949, provide the first full listing of the Alianza executive. María Isabel Foronda de Vargas is named as secretary general, Hortensia Hernández Rojás as secretary, Romelia Alarcón Folgar as legal secretary, Dora Franco y Franco as treasurer, Violeta de Montero as actos, Matilde Elena López as secretary of advertising, Victoria Moraga as secretary of culture, and Otilia Oségueda de García as children's liaison. A 1950 list found in the Hojas Sueltas collection of the AGCA names the executive of the Alianza Femenina Guatemalteca as the following: María Isabel Foronda de Vargas was the secretary general; Hortensia Hernández Rojás was the legal secretary; Helena Leiva de Holst was the secretary of the minutes; Violeta de Montero was the secretary of advertising; Josefina V. de Vitola was the secretary of organization; Matilde Elena

López was the secretary of culture; and Victoria Moraga and Romelia Alarcón Folgar served as the financial secretaries.

8. Carrillo Samayoa and Torres Urízar, *Nosotras, las de la historia*, 154. The authors do not provide any sources for the inclusion of these women, and it is likely that they are mentioned as high-profile members due to their contributions to the organization.

9. GD, Container 15, April 13, 1950. The Alianza Femenina Guatemalteca was a member of the Comité Nacional de Unidad Sindical (CNUS).

10. GD, Container 9.

11. GD, Container 15, October 31, 1946; GD, Container 9, June 1951, "Publicaciones del comte central del Partido Revolucionario Obrero de Guatemala (PROG)," Bosquejo Histórico Universal, Guatemala, June 1951, por Matilde Elena López.

12. GD, Container 8, August, 8, 1953. The leader of the female affiliate of the Partido de la Revolución Guatemalteca was Carmen Vargas de Amézquita.

13. The Guatemalan Communist Party records confiscated by the US State Department and currently held in the Library of Congress only contain these four women's names.

14. Lavrin, *Women, Feminism, and Social Change*, 45. Two women's associations were founded in Buenos Aires in 1920, the Partido Humanista and the Partido Feminista Nacional, in the hope they would be accepted as political parties.

15. There is trace evidence of Manuel Urrutia's activism in this particular union during the early 1920s. However, there is not sufficient information to make any definitive conclusions.

16. *El Imparcial*, October 6, 1944.

17. GD, Container 66, Correspondence and Official Papers, Partido de la Revolución Guatemalteca, 1950–1952. Ester de Urrutia's participation is obvious in tens of letters and internal memos.

18. *Octubre*, no. 119, February 19, 1953, 5; and *Diario de Centro América*, August 22, 1953. We have few direct words from Ester due primarily to the destruction of a majority of revolutionary documents in the months following Árbenz's overthrow. Most information regarding Ester and Manuel comes through their children and grandchildren, along with a few surviving documents discovered at the Library of Congress.

19. AGCA, Hojas Sueltas, 1950.

20. GD, Container 9, July 1, 1953, 7.

21. GD, Container 6, "Instructivo para la organización de comites de Alianza Femenina Guatemalteca," n.d.

22. GD, Container 6, "Informe de la secretaria general de A.F.G.," November 1953, 4.

23. See the following works: Gleijeses, *Shattered Hope*; Grandin, *The Blood of Guatemala*; Grandin, *The Last Colonial Massacre*; Handy, *Revolution in the Countryside*; Immerman, *The CIA in Guatemala*; Joseph and Spenser, *In From the Cold*; and Schlesinger and Kinzer, *Bitter Fruit*.

24. For a thorough analysis of Árbenz's relationship with Guatemala's Communist Party (the Partido Comunista de Guatemala, renamed the Partido Guatemalteco del Trabajo in 1952), see Gleijeses, *Shattered Hope*, chapter 7.

25. The most notable of such examples are found in Schneider's and Poppino's early works. James, *Red Design for the Americas*. The role of the Alianza during this time was not examined.

26. James, *Red Design for the Americas*, 17–18.

27. Way, *The Mayan in the Mall*, 77.

28. Mooney, "Fighting Fascism."

29. Cullather, *Secret History*; Miller, *Latin American Women*; Schneider, *Communism in Guatemala*; Schneider, *Case Study in Insurgency*; James, *Red Design for the Americas*; and Poppino, *International Communism in Latin America*.

30. Haan, "Continuing Cold War Paradigms," 550.

31. Ibid. Like the International Council of Women and International Alliance of Women, the WIDF was actively involved in the United Nations, although its contribution was interrupted from 1954 to 1967 when its consultative status in Category B was withdrawn, a direct consequence of Cold War politics at the UN. The WIDF initiated the famous 1975 UN Decade for Women, the starting point of large-scale UN activities directed at improving women's status worldwide.

32. The organization had 41 member organizations in 1945; 135 (from 117 countries) in 1985, when it celebrated its fortieth anniversary; and 142 (from 124 countries) in 1990. See Schneider, *Communism in Guatemala*; and Poppino, *International Communism in Latin America*.

33. The Soviet Union accused the United States of being a warmonger.

34. GD, Container 6, "Informe de A.F.G.," n.p.; words of Ester de Urrutia.

35. Ibid.

36. Castledine, *Cold War Progressives*, 28–29.

37. Haan, "Continuing Cold War Paradigms," 548.

38. Mooney, "Fighting Fascism," 55.

39. Julia Urrutia, personal interview, July 2004.

40. Iber, *Neither Peace nor Freedom*. As Patrick Iber notes in his work on the cultural Cold War, the impact of bodies with international reach such as the CIA and the US State Department was so powerful that individuals actually incorporated this silencing into their own actions and ideas.

41. In 2010, Ana Lorena Carrillo and Norma Stoltz Chinchilla published an article focused on cross-class and cross-ethnic feminist movements that emerged in Guatemala during the 1960s and 1970s. "From Urban Elite to Peasant Organizing" traced the activism of urban ladinas, highlighting the activities of a small group of activists and intellectuals who tried to contextualize international feminist ideas in Guatemala. This process helped transform their feminist visions to cross both rural and ethnic boundaries, which culminated in the emergence of inclusive feminist groups during the 1980s. However, the authors suggest that Guatemalan feminism was a relatively new concept. While this is a significant article for its emphasis on the role of women and gender during a period of terrible violence in Guatemala, it also highlights the historical disconnect with the contributions of the Alianza, which pioneered a similar ideological activism.

42. Vilanova de Árbenz, *Mi esposo, el presidente Árbenz*, 3.

43. Ibid., 5.

44. Immerman, *The CIA in Guatemala*, 41; and Gleijeses, *Shattered Hope*, 122–36.

45. Immerman, *The CIA in Guatemala*, 16, 135.

46. Gleijeses, *Shattered Hope*, 135–36.

47. Ibid., 139–40.

48. Ibid., 23.

49. *Nuestro Diario*, October 30, 1944.

50. Gleijeses, *Shattered Hope*, 141. "The first Marxist work came by chance into Jacobo's and María's hands. It was the *Communist Manifesto*, which María received at a women's congress, read, and

placed on Jacobo's bedside table before leaving for a brief vacation. . . . [María recalled,] 'It seemed to us that it explained what we had been feeling.'"

51. Ibid., 134.

52. Vilanova de Árbenz has kept tight control over papers and information regarding the political and personal life of her husband. Her autobiography carefully refutes many of the criticisms directed at his decisions and controversial events during the revolutionary period.

53. Vilanova de Árbenz, *Mi esposo, el presidente Árbenz*, 38.

54. Iber, *Neither Peace nor Freedom*.

55. Way, *The Mayan in the Mall*, 78.

56. Andreas Hoessli, dir., *Devils Don't Dream!* (Icarus Films, 1995).

57. García-Bryce, "Transnational Activist: Magda Portal," 680. Women in both the Cuban and Nicaraguan revolutionary movements during the 1960s, 1970s, and 1980s who maintained close affiliations with male political leadership found their autonomy and gender analysis significantly weakened, which confirms the benefits of the Alianza's autonomous approach.

58. Das, "Transnational Feminism Beyond Westoxification."

59. For groups similar to the Alianza, see Valobra and Yusta, *Queridas camaradas*.

60. Lavrin, "Female, Feminine and Feminist," 6.

61. Lavrin, "Unfolding Feminism," 249.

62. Threlkeld, *Pan American Women*, 150; and Lavrin, "Female, Feminine and Feminist," 14.

63. Chinchilla, "Marxist, Feminism, and the Struggle for Democracy," 295.

64. For further information on the socialist women's movements in Guatemala, see Chinchilla, "Marxist, Feminism, and the Struggle for Democracy." In her work on socialist women's movements, Norma Stoltz Chinchilla notes that just as important, because of its link to contemporary feminism, was the discovery by some male leftists of the importance of the invisible activities that make up daily life (*lo cotidiano*). This discovery, made because survival itself was threatened by the harsh conditions of military dictatorship, was interjected by some into theoretical discussions of the relationship between democracy and socialism.

65. Ríos Tobar, "Feminism Is Socialism, Liberty and Much More," 132.

66. Cofiño Kepfer, "Las primeras comunistas en Guatemala," 191.

67. García-Bryce, "Transnational Activist: Magda Portal," 685.

68. Ríos Tobar, "Feminism Is Socialism, Liberty and Much More," 131. See works on European and Latin American socialist women, including Engel, *Women in Russia*; Boxer and Quataert, *Socialist Women*; and Slaughter and Kern, *European Women on the Left*.

69. Gleijeses, *Shattered Hope*, 172.

70. Ibid., 139–45.

71. GD, "Informe de labores de la secretaria de asuntos femeninos," March 23, 1954; and AGCA, Hojas Sueltas, "Llamamiento de las mujeres de Guatemala," by the Alianza Femenina Guatemalteca, 1950.

72. "Congreso de la mujer guatemalteca," *Diario del Pueblo*, November 25, 1953, editorial.

73. Craske, *Women and Politics in Latin America*, 198.

74. Lavrin, "Female, Feminine and Feminist," 5.

75. GD, Container 9, July 1, 1953.

76. Ibid.

77. *Nuestro Diario*, December 5, 1951.

78. GD, Container 26, "Breve resumen historico de la asociación," 3. The new leaders of the Asociación de Comedores y Guarderías Infantíles were president, María Vilanova de Árbenz; vice president, Gloria Bruni de Shaw; secretary of minutes, Blanca Aris de Capuano; treasurer, Marco Antonio Asturias; medical adviser, Dr. J. Augusto González R.; general board members, Elvira L. de Aldana, Olga F. de Gracias, and Fausta de González Arévalo; coordinator, Rudolfo Figueroa Guillén; financial secretary, Atilio Bonilla Isaac; and legal adviser, Constantino Duarte Villela. GD, Container 26, Letter from María Vilanova de Árbenz, March 1, 1952. In May 1951, the Department of Social Services hired Lilly Zachrisson to work in the guarderías infantíles and *hogares* to investigate difficult family situations.

79. *Nuestro Diario*, December 3, 1951. Among the many who supported the joint efforts included Elena Fonseca Corleto, Gana de Silva Peña, Aída Godoy, Elsa de Sánchez, Mélida Palacios de Lado, Lilly Zachrisson, Julieta Hernández, Martha Asturias, Aída de García Gálvez, Aída María Rodríguez, Violeta de González Juárez, Dora de Díaz, Elsa Larios, Dr. Elena de Cartens, Sandra de Pinto, Carmen Velazco, Jorge Micheo, Donald Shaw Bruni, Dr. Gilberto Burke, Enrique Lima, Carlos González Orellana, Antonio Barrutía, Afraín Castillo, José Luján, and José Estrada Barrientos.

80. GD, Container 26, "Memorandum to María Vilanova de Árbenz from Liliam Jiménez de Leiva," January 6, 1953; and GD, Container 26, "Breve resumen historico de la asociación," 5.

81. GD, Container 26, "Letter to María Vilanova de Árbenz from Ester Hernández Rodas," February 10, 1953. According to Hernández Rodas, the secretary of the Asociación, Jiménez de Leiva was being bothered by anti-sindicalistas (anti-unionists). It is not clear who these people were. The Partido Guatemalteco del Trabajo agreed to support Jiménez de Leiva.

82. GD, Container 26, "Letter from María Vilanova de Árbenz to Dora Franco y Franco," January 7, 1954.

83. Ibid.

84. *Nuestro Diario*, November 30, 1951, editorial.

85. For further information on the Puerto Barrios hospital, see Cabrera Cruz, "Análisis y propuesta de diseño."

86. GD, Container 26, "Breve resumen historico de la asociación," 4.

87. *Nuestro Diario*, July 2, 1952.

88. Sanders, *Gender and Welfare in Mexico*, 96.

89. *Nuestro Diario*, December 11, 1951. In the weeks prior to the conference, a national debate emerged in the newspapers exploring the social conditions of children. Author N. Viera Altamirano wrote a series of articles on the rights of children.

90. *Nuestro Diario*, December 13 and 15, 1951. The first speaker of the conference was a teacher, Ester Rubio de Melgar, president of the organizing committee. Irma Chávez de Alvarado was listed as the coordinator of conference events.

91. GD, Container 26, December 12, 1951; and GD, Container 26, December 15, 1951. Conference president Carlos González Orellana outlined some of the essential problems facing Guatemala's children.

92. *Mujeres: Boletín de Alianza Femenina Guatemalteca*, October 1951. Many others took on leadership roles, including Olga F. de Gracias (treasurer); Carmen Vargas de Amézquita (economist); and Mélida Luz Palacios (social worker). Mélida Luz Palacios, from El Salvador, was María

Vilanova de Árbenz's personal secretary. Vilanova de Árbenz, *Mi esposo, el presidente Árbenz*, 72. Others included Matilde de Cuenca (nurse); Carmen Bartlett S. (teacher); Carmen Mirón (teacher and librarian); Blanca Rosa Echeverría (special teacher in education of the blind); María de Sellares (teacher); Marilena López (drama teacher); Olimpia Vda. de Barrientos (teacher); Helena Leiva de Holst (teacher); Otilia de Balcárcel (director of the Escuela Normal de Maestras para Párvulos); and Ofelia Ninfa Cabrera (director of the Escuela de Artes y Oficios Femeniles). Delegates from the Asociación de Comedores y Guarderías Infantíles included Dr. Valenzuela, Dr. Guillermo Balz, Monzón Malice, and Constantino Duarte Villela.

93. No specific details were given as to the exact legislative changes the delegates wanted to put into place. There are few sources on this conference.

94. *Nuestro Diario*, November 17, 1951, 7.

95. *Nuestro Diario*, November 21, 1951. Although the specific conclusions of the December conference are not recorded in greater detail, later papers written by the Alianza Femenina Guatemalteca on the defense of children were no doubt taken from this historic conference.

96. DG, Container 6, "Informe de Alianza Femenina Guatemalteca a la Comisión de Defensa y Protección de la Infancia," 2–4.

97. *Nuestro Diario*, December 14, 1951.

98. Ibid.

99. Orozco Posadas was the National Assembly representative who had attended the women's suffrage conference in 1944.

100. *Nuestro Diario*, November 21, 1951.

101. *Acción Campesina: Vocero de la Confederación Nacional Campesina de Guatemala*, April 15, 1951. A national conference was held on February 2–4, 1951, to discuss economic reform, particularly agrarian reform.

102. *Nuestro Diario*, July 26, 1952.

103. GD, Container 6, "Informe de la comisión de AFG, situación de las mujeres que trabajan," 3.

104. Dirección General de Estadística, *Censos de la República de Guatemala, 1950*, 219.

105. Dirección General de Estadística, *Quinto censo general de población, levantado el 7 de Abril de 1940*, 867–69.

106. Forster, *The Time of Freedom*, 103. Forster notes that domestic labor remains among the most thinly documented of occupations. "The sheer number of servants tilts the sex ratio toward women in most of Guatemala's urban areas yet domestics appear in the written record like ghosts, usually through the eyes of their employers."

107. See Levenson, "Living Guatemala City," 28–32, for the story of María Cruz and her experience as a domestic beginning in 1938; and Menchú, *I, Rigoberta Menchú*.

108. Forster, *The Time of Freedom*, 102.

109. GD, Container 6, "Informe de la comisión de AFG, situación de las mujeres que trabajan," 3.

110. GD, Container 9, "Letter to the Señor Secretario de la Juventud Perregista, Carlos García Manzo," April 14, 1954.

111. Ibid., 5.

112. GD, Container 6, "Informe de la comisión de AFG, situación de las mujeres que trabajan," 3. "Las trabajadoras domésticas, muchas veces influídas políticamente por su atraso cultural y el contacto permanente con sus expotadores."

113. GD, November 4, 1953. Angela García, Hortensia Hernández Rojás, and Elsa de Guerra Borges represented the Partido Guatemalteco del Trabajo as delegates to the Alianza's first national congress.

114. GD, Container 11, February 19, 1954.

115. Way, *The Mayan in the Mall*, 75.

116. Forster, *The Time of Freedom*, 102.

117. GD, Container 6, "Informe de la comisión de AFG, situación de las mujeres que trabajan," November, 1953, 4.

118. Ibid., 1.

119. Carey, *Engendering Mayan History*, 92. The oral testimonies of Kaqchikel women as found in Carey's work support the conclusions postulated by the Alianza.

120. GD, Container 6, "Informe de AFG a la comisión la mujer y la reforma agraria," November 1953, 4.

121. *Mujeres: Boletín de Alianza Femenina Guatemalteca*, February 1953, 5.

122. GD, Container 6, "Informe de la comisión de AFG, situación de las mujeres que trabajan."

123. *El Imparcial*, August 6, 1951.

124. *Tierra Nuestra*, May 1954, 7.

125. Gleijeses, *Shattered Hope*, 90.

126. Ibid., 152.

127. For more details on the 1952 Agrarian Reform Law, see Gleijeses, *Shattered Hope*; Grandin, *The Blood of Guatemala*; and Handy, *Revolution in the Countryside*.

128. *Mujeres: Boletín de Alianza Femenina Guatemalteca*, June 20, 1952; and February 1953, 2.

129. Similar to María Vilanova de Árbenz, Jeréz Rivera de Fortuny has said very little about her involvement in land reform. During a personal conversation, Cindy Forster noted that Jeréz Rivera de Fortuny said almost nothing about her work, although she was the head of the women's division for land reform. The few surviving documents suggest that this was a difficult position, fighting both the logistics common in bureaucratic institutions and patriarchal structures.

130. GD, Container 10, n.d. This letter protested the Confederación Nacional Campesina de Guatemala's local official, who would not distribute land to women.

131. *Diario del Pueblo*, November 25, 1953, editorial.

132. *Diario de Centro América*, February 8, 1954.

133. Jim Handy, in *Revolution in the Countryside*, notes that there is evidence that the Alianza Femenina Guatemalteca established a rural credit union only for women. The available documents do not confirm plans for or the existence of such an institution.

134. Handy, *Revolution in the Countryside*, 3.

135. *Mujeres: Boletín de Alianza Femenina Guatemalteca*, June 20, 1952.

136. Ibid.

137. GD, Container 6, Partido de la Revolución Guatemalteca, "Informe de labores de la secretaria de asuntos femeninos," March 23, 1954, 2–3. Carmen Vargas de Amézquita was secretary of the female wing of the Partido de la Revolución Guatemalteca.

138. Mariano Rossell y Arellano, "Carta pastoral sobre la justicia social, fundamento del bienestar social," November 15, 1948, 5.

139. *Bulletin of the Pan American Union*, July 1948, 408.

140. Handy, *Revolution in the Countryside*, 56.
141. *Nuestro Diario*, July 21, 1947.
142. Handy, *Revolution in the Countryside*, 29–30.
143. GD, Container 6, "Llamamiento a la conferencia contra el alto costo de la vida," July 27, 1953, 9.
144. *Diario de Centro América*, November 8, 1948.
145. *Mujeres: Boletín de Alianza Femenina Guatemalteca*, October 1951; and GD, Container 6, "Energica protesta de AFG por el acaparamiento de azucar," n.d.
146. *Diario de Centro América*, July 12, July 24, and August 6, 1953.
147. *Diario de Centro América*, August 7, 1953, editorial.
148. *Diario de Centro América*, August 26, 1953.
149. GD, Container 6, "Comité preparatorio de la Conferencia contra el Alto Costo de la Vida," July 21, 1953; and *Diario de Centro América*, August 21, 1953.
150. *Diario de Centro América*, August 29 and 31, 1953. The resolutions were printed in the conference's own publications as well as in national newspapers.
151. GD, Container 6, "Llamamiento a la Conferencia contra el Alto Costo de la Vida," July 27, 1953, 1–3.
152. GD, Container 6, "Resoluciones de la Conferencia contra el Alto Costo de la Vida," August 29, 1953.
153. The permanent committee included José Guillén, economist; Roberto Fanjul, minister of the economy; Enrique Santa Cruz, of the Instituto de Fomento de Producción; Manuel Noriega Morales, president of the Bank of Guatemala; Antonio Iglesias, industrialist; Francisco Fajardo, farmer; Javier Ramos M., pharmacist; Víctor Manuel Gutiérrez and Mario Morales Vielman, of the Confederación General de Trabajadores de Guatemala; José Alberto Cardoza, of the Federación Gráfica; José Luis Caceros, of the Sindicato de Acción y Mejoramiento Ferrocarrilero; Leonardo Castillo Flores, of the Confederación Nacional Campesina de Guatemala; Ciriaco Hernández, of the Liga de Inquilinos; Ester de Urrutia and Dora Franco y Franco, of the Alianza Femenina Guatemalteca; Bernardo Lemus, of the Alianza de la Juventud Democrática de Guatemala; Carmen Vargas de Amézquita, economist; Edgard Tuna, of the Town Council; Maximina Valdés, representing market women; Ricardo Ramírez, of the Frente Universitario Democrático; Francisco Silva Falla, of the Partido de la Revolución Guatemalteca; Julio Estrada de la Hoz; and Consuelo Pereira de Vásquez, of the Renovación Nacional.
154. Mario Higuerros was ten years old in 1954 and vividly remembers his shock at being forced to look at horrifying images of tortured people. As Higuerros related to me in a conversation, the children were told that this was the result of a communist government, which was why it had been overthrown by Castillo Armas.
155. See Forster, *The Time of Freedom*; Grandin, *The Blood of Guatemala*; Grandin, *The Last Colonial Massacre*; and Carey, *Engendering Mayan History*.
156. Handy, *Revolution in the Countryside*, 169.
157. Jonas, *The Battle for Guatemala*, 35.
158. Handy, *Revolution in the Countryside*, 204.
159. Jonas, *The Battle for Guatemala*, 35.
160. Grandin, *The Blood of Guatemala*, 202.

161. Handy, *Revolution in the Countryside*, 178–79; and Immerman, *The CIA in Guatemala*, 149.

162. *Diario de Centro América*, June 9, 1954. Pro-revolutionary organizations also indicated their support for the beleaguered Árbenz administration. The permanent committee on the high cost of living sent Árbenz a letter committing their organization to the government's support. Their final act declared that the "criminal aggression against Guatemala is the cause of inflation."

163. *Diario de Centro América*, June 9, 1954.

164. *Diario del Pueblo*, June 14, 1954; and *El Imparcial*, June 15, 1954.

165. GD, Container 6, n.d.

166. GD, Container 6, n.d. "Formed by María Vilanova de Árbenz and the Alianza Femenina Guatemalteca for the purpose of: forming agricultural schools for Guatemalan women; arranging better use of land; distributing technical information about agriculture, dietetics, etc.; purchasing and selling agricultural products and implements; and performing all kinds of negotiations and operations in connection with agriculture and education."

167. *Diario del Pueblo*, March 17, 1954.

168. SCPC, "Letter from Carolyn B. Threlkeld, Chairman of the Latin American Committee, on the Issue of the 1954 Overthrow of Árbenz," Women's International League for Peace and Freedom, US Section, Reel 130.30, DG43, November 1954.

169. *Diario del Pueblo*, June 14, 1954.

170. Immerman, *The CIA in Guatemala*, 42.

171. See Carrillo and Chinchilla, "From Urban Elite to Peasant Organizing"; Berger, *Guatemaltecas*; and the journal *La Cuerda* to understand the nature of these contemporary feminist movements.

172. *Diario de Centro América*, August 17, 19, and 20, 1953; and *El Imparcial*, July 31, 1954.

173. *El Imparcial*, July 31, 1954.

174. See Dan Saxon's *To Save Her Life* for more details on the Urrutia family.

CHAPTER SEVEN

1. See Immerman, *The CIA in Guatemala*; Cullather, *Secret History*; Schlesinger and Kinzer, *Bitter Fruit*; and Grandin, *The Last Colonial Massacre*.

2. A concerted effort was also made to collect evidence in order to indict the revolutionary supporters as communist sympathizers. The US State Department and the CIA, who assisted the Guatemalan military in their overthrow of Árbenz, gathered these materials, and they are currently held in the Library of Congress as the Guatemalan Documents collection. In addition, following the overthrow of Árbenz in June 1954, countless documents were destroyed by Guatemalans themselves in an attempt to protect themselves from retribution by the new military government. Catholic Church sources are also unavailable; the archives of the Guatemalan Catholic Church (Archivo Histórico Arquidiocesano Francisco de Paula García Peláez) were opened for a brief period during the late 1980s and early 1990s, but were then closed again. Consequently, the history of Rossell y Arellano's early years is currently unavailable from direct ecclesiastical sources. The market women left few primary sources. There are a handful of broadsides (in the Taracena Flores Collection) related to their activities, and seven editions of *La Voz de la Locataria*, a newspaper they published in 1954, the year following the overthrow of Jacobo Árbenz.

3. Miller, *Latin American Women*, 124–34.

4. Jonas, *The Battle for Guatemala*, 35–36; and Grandin, *The Blood of Guatemala*.

5. Using data by Bendana Perdomo, Douglass Sullivan-González argues that in 1924 Guatemala had only eighty-five priests for 116 parishes. When Rossell y Arellano assumed the office of archbishop, he made it his top priority to improve the quality and quantity of priests. Sullivan-González, *The Black Christ of Esquipulas*, 130.

6. Palmer, "A Liberal Discipline," 110; and Miller, "Catholic Leaders and Spiritual Socialism," 80.

7. Calder, "The Catholic Church in the Context of Guatemalan Politics," 4.

8. Sullivan-González, *The Black Christ of Esquipulas*, 130.

9. Miller, "Catholic Leaders and Spiritual Socialism," 86.

10. Ibid., 86, 99; Grandin, *The Last Colonial Massacre*, 78; and Gleijeses, *Shattered Hope*, 49.

11. Kit, "The Fall of Guatemalan Dictator, Manual Estrada Cabrera," 112–14. On May 12, 1919, Bishop Piñol y Batres preached the first of nine sermons alluding to the evils of tyranny.

12. Gleijeses, *Shattered Hope*, 49.

13. Miller, "Catholic Leaders and Spiritual Socialism," 95.

14. Grandin, *The Last Colonial Massacre*, 167.

15. Miller, "Catholic Leaders and Spiritual Socialism."

16. Ibid., 89.

17. *Acción Social Cristiana*, March 15 and April 12, 1945.

18. Miller, "Catholic Leaders and Spiritual Socialism," 89.

19. Rossell y Arellano, "Carta circulo del excelentisimo señor arzobispo de Guatemala a sus sacerdotes y declaración de principios acerca de la presente situación," November 8, 1944.

20. *El Verbum*, February 12, 1945.

21. Sullivan-González, *The Black Christ of Esquipulas*, 143.

22. Handy, *Gift of the Devil*, 107–8.

23. LaFeber, *Inevitable Revolutions*, 112.

24. Sullivan-González, *The Black Christ of Esquipulas*, 139.

25. Pattridge, "The Catholic Church in Revolutionary Guatemala."

26. Ibid. Sullivan-González supports Pattridge's take on the political positions of the Catholics and lower clergy during the revolution.

27. Taracena Flores Collection, no. 479, n.d.

28. *Acción Social Cristiana*, February 28, 1946.

29. Miller, "Catholic Leaders and Spiritual Socialism," 93; and *Nuestro Diario*, January 1945. The first sign of change in the apparently cordial relationship came in January 1945, when the pro-government paper *Nuestro Diario* accused the church of becoming involved in politics and spreading Falangism.

30. *Acción Social Cristiana*, December 6, 1945; and Records of the US Department of State Relating to Internal Affairs of Guatemala, June 18, 1945.

31. Cardenal, "The Church in Central America," 254. Cardenal argues that the Sisters of Charity were granted dispensation from exile due to their indispensable work in the San Vicente de Paul Hospital.

32. The conservative Catholic women's newspaper *La Verdad* (The Truth) was published for several years, defending the faith and denouncing liberalism. It is clear that these women held strong antiliberal political views and expressed solid support for a national resurgence of the Catholic Church. These activities maintained a critical Catholic identity among wealthier urban ladinas in the

prerevolutionary decades. Urban women of the upper social circles who were aligned with Catholic organizations, consisting predominantly of members of the Partida Unionista, also rapidly moved to support the efforts of the new government. The women of *La Verdad* did not advocate for gender reform, and their vocal pro-clerical support reflected the conservative nature of those in the Partido Unionista.

33. Power, *Right-Wing Women in Chile*, 90.

34. There were a large number of political demonstrations against the Arévalo and Árbenz presidencies. Here is a partial list of dates on which they occurred, compiled from newspapers, US State Department records, and the Taracena Flores Collection: March 17, 1947; March 22, 1947; July 20, 1948; July 29, 1948; July 18–19, 1949; July 26, 1949; March 24, 1949; April 28, 1949; March 20, 1952; March 23, 1952; and December 12, 1952.

35. I am treating the street protests and the activities of market women separately, although many of the market women participated in these street demonstrations. The leaders of these protests appear to have been middle-class ladinas and not poor working women, although this is purely speculative.

36. Handy, *Revolution in the Countryside*, 33.

37. AGCA, Hojas Sueltas, August 1945.

38. AGCA, Hojas Sueltas, September 12, 1946.

39. AGCA, Hojas Sueltas, September 1946.

40. Forster, *The Time of Freedom*, 215.

41. Kaplan, "Female Consciousness and Collective Action," 545.

42. Castells, *The Power of Identity*.

43. Sabato, "On Political Citizenship."

44. I am indebted to Hilda Sabato's work on these kinds of informal associations and how they interact with governing powers.

45. Chase, "Women's Organisations and the Politics of Gender," 448. See also Chase, *Revolution within the Revolution*.

46. The circumstances surrounding Francisco Arana's death have never been fully revealed. A full accounting of this event is beyond the scope of this book. See Piero Gleijeses, *Shattered Hope*, chapter 3, for further details about this pivotal moment.

47. Handy, *Gift of the Devil*, 128–29. The UFCo controlled over 550 million acres and cultivated less than 15 percent of it. The National Agrarian Reform Commission expropriated a total of 372,000 acres of fallow land.

48. Schlesinger and Kinzer, *Bitter Fruit*, 227–33. Guatemala's era of democracy ended following an air assault on June 18, 1954, when Árbenz resigned from his presidency. General Carlos Castillo Armas assumed the presidency and within eighteen months had driven all but one half of one percent of the peasants who had received land off of that land. Guatemala's "democratic spring" was followed by such a backlash of military dictatorships and genocidal violence against the country's citizens that even the most ardent Árbenz opponents concluded that the events of June 1954 had been nothing short of a disaster.

49. Records of the US Department of State Relating to Internal Affairs of Guatemala, "Subject: Political Comments of *Acción Social Cristiana*," June 18, 1945. The brief mentions that the periodical does not honor Article 29, which states that religious societies and groups may not take part in politics nor in questions related to labor organization.

50. The State Department acknowledged this as early as August 26, 1946.

51. Records of the US Department of State Relating to Internal Affairs of Guatemala, August 24, 1946, 2; translation by the State Department.

52. Power, *Right-Wing Women in Chile*, 85.

53. AGCA, Hojas Sueltas, September 8, 1946.

54. *Diario del Pueblo*, March 27, 1952.

55. Deutsch, "Argentine Women against Fascism," 233.

56. Iber, *Neither Peace nor Freedom*, 13.

57. Pope Pius XI, "Atheistic Communism," in Treacy, *Five Great Encyclicals*, 181.

58. GD, Container 6, "Informe de la comisión de AFG, situación de las mujeres que trabajan," 4.

59. *El Imparcial*, April 5, 1934; and *Diario de Centro América*, October 27 and 28, 1920.

60. For work on market women elsewhere, see Porter, *Working Women in Mexico City*; Seligmann, *Peruvian Street Lives*; and Carey, "Hard Working, Orderly Little Women."

61. Way, *The Mayan in the Mall*, 75. A survey taken during 1972 found that 80 percent of informal street vendors were female heads of household.

62. Taracena Flores Collection, no. 3327. Many photos in the national newspapers show market women wearing traje.

63. Carey, "Hard Working, Orderly Little Women," 580.

64. Porter, *Working Women in Mexico City*, 149.

65. Dirección General de Estadística, *Censos de la República de Guatemala, 1950*, 239. Although an accurate number is not available, there were certainly hundreds of market women working in the city in the 1940s and early 1950s. It is in the 1950 census that market women were acknowledged as economic contributors.

66. Concha Estéves is remembered by all Guatemalans with whom I have spoken, both those who opposed and those who supported the revolution.

67. *Prensa Libre*, December 3, 1982.

68. Ibid.

69. For more information on this institution, see Fuentes Girón, *Del Hospicio Nacional Centro Educativo*; and González Orellana, *Historia de la educación en Guatemala*, 488–91.

70. Schneider, *Communism in Guatemala*, 304. The national newspaper *La Hora* does not give an exact date for Alvarado's appointment but on July 2, 1951, states that he had begun his tenure as director three months earlier.

71. González Orellana, *Historia de la educación en Guatemala*, 490. González Orellana notes that the shift in the institution's mission reflected the Árbenz government's emphasis on social assistance as a temporary rather than a permanent condition. These changes factored in the eventual adoption of the orphaned or abandoned children.

72. *El Imparcial*, July 6, 1951. The members of union were listed as Jesús Zapata G., J. A. Saravia, Alberto Ramírez, Julio Sandoval B., Alfonso Trujillo, and Saturnina Morales M.

73. *El Imparcial*, July 2, 1951.

74. *El Imparcial*, July 4, 1951.

75. *El Imparcial*, July 6, 1951.

76. *El Imparcial*, July 7, 1951.

77. *El Imparcial*, July 5 and 6, 1951.

78. Records of the US Department of State Relating to Internal Affairs of Guatemala, July 13, 1951, 2.

79. *El Imparcial*, July 12, 1951; Records of the US Department of State Relating to Internal Affairs of Guatemala, July 13, 1951, 2–3; and *Diario de Centro América*, July 12, 1951. *La Hora* states that the archbishop left at 10:30 p.m.; *Diario de Centro América*, July 12, 1951.

80. *El Imparcial*, July 9, 1951; and *Nuestro Diario*, July 13, 1951. The exact number of dead and injured is unclear.

81. During the early 1950s, such suggestions were frequent in pro-revolutionary newspapers such as *Nuestro Diario*, *Diario de Centro América*, and *Octubre*.

82. *Nuestro Diario*, July 24, 1951.

83. *El Imparcial*, July 21, 1948.

84. Kaplan, "Female Consciousness and Collective Action," 548.

85. *Diario de Centro América* and *Nuestro Diario*, July 12, 1951.

86. *El Imparcial*, July 11, 1951.

87. Ibid.

88. Ibid.

89. *Nuestro Diario*, October 27, 1944. The women of Colón Market organized a committee with María González Roldan, Soledad C. de Orantes, Trinidad M. de Jiménez, Angelina Peralta, Carmen P. de Martínez, Marla del Cid, Olivia de Pérez, Rosario Pachco, Felipa Medine, and Delfina Porres in leadership positions.

90. *Nuestro Diario*, December 19, 1946; and *Octubre*, March 19, 1953.

91. I am indebted to several people for the particular direction of this argument. Just how varied the market women's motivations were became clear during a conversation I had with the daughter of a woman who worked in the Central Market during the 1950s. When I questioned the daughter about her mother's experiences during the revolution, her response was unequivocal. Her mother had hated the revolution and hated the conditions in the country at that time. When I inquired further as to why, again her answer was clear. Her mother had told her that everything became so expensive that it had been almost impossible to feed her family.

In personal conversations, Dr. Karla Koll also raised the comparison with market women in Managua, Nicaragua, during the 1980s revolutionary period. Although there is little documentation, market women in Managua staged similar types of protests against the Sandinista government as inflation rose to an astounding 36,000 percent in mid-1988. Consequently, no one kept money in the bank or even saved, but rather spent each day's earnings immediately before it further devalued. Market women continued their protests well into the Violeta Chamorro presidency during the 1990s. They, too, framed their protests in religious terms during the Sandinista era, although their grievances were clearly linked to economic issues.

92. *Diario de Centro América*, August 9, 1951.

93. Gleijeses, *Shattered Hope*, 42–43.

94. *Nuestro Diario*, September 25, 1951. Thirty to thirty-five women from Mixco petitioned the government.

95. GD, Container 6, "Energica protesta de AFG por el acaparamiento de azucar," n.d.

96. *Diario de Centro América*, August 26, 1953.

97. *Nuestro Diario*, September 14 and 21, 1951.

98. *Nuestro Diario*, October 4, 1951.
99. *Nuestro Diario*, November 10, 1951.
100. *Diario de Centro América*, July 12 and August 6, 1953.
101. *Diario de Centro América*, August 26, 1953.
102. *Diario de Centro América*, April 8, 1953.
103. *Octubre*, April 3, 1952, 3.
104. Records of the US Department of State Relating to Internal Affairs of Guatemala, August 30, 1951.
105. Seligmann, *Peruvian Street Lives*, 198–99.
106. Ibid., 201.
107. Ibid., 21.
108. Torres, "Women in Nicaragua."
109. See Kistler, *Maya Market Women*, specifically chapter 4 for further discussion on the influence of market women outside the marketplace.
110. Ibid., 81.
111. Grandin, *The Last Colonial Massacre*, 83.
112. Taracena Flores Collection, no. 1517, October 3, 1951. The Comité Anticomunista de Locatarias invited all market women to join the PUA and attend its meetings. Women on the committee included Carlota Medina, Concha Estéves, Gloria Castillo, Jacoba de Madrid, Angela Valenzuela, Natividad L. de Contreras, Matilde Hernández, Marcelina Zamora, Perfecta Vásquez, Micaela de Molina, Socorro Vásquez, María Monzón, Placida Rosales, Cruz Díaz Sutter, María Alvarez, Clementa Mejia D., Tomasa Sosa de Tejada, Paula García, Mercedes Ruano, Jesús Madrid, Mercedes de Barrientos, Cristina Rivera, Albertina Chávez, Juana Rivera, Felisa García, María García, Amelia Ramírez, Guadalupe de la Cruz, Marcela Franco de Madrid, Angela Rodríguez, Irene de Mejicanos, Juana Aguilar, Jesús Coronado Torres, Elisa de Arriola, and Marcela Aragon.
113. Taracena Flores Collection, no. 2279.
114. *El Imparcial*, September 17, 1951.
115. *El Imparcial*, September 1, 1951.
116. *El Imparcial*, August 26, 1951, and October 1951.
117. Taracena Flores Collection, no. 3329.
118. *Diario de Centro América*, July 29, 1954.
119. *Diario de Centro América*, February 9, 1954.
120. *La Voz de la Locataria*, September 4, 1954.
121. Taracena Flores Collection, no. 2384.
122. *El Imparcial*, July 16, 1954, editorial.
123. Chinchilla, "Mobilizing Women," 88.
124. Power, *Right-Wing Women in Chile*, 192.

EPILOGUE

1. Franco, *The Decline and Fall of the Lettered City*, 1.
2. *El Imparcial*, June 25 and 27, 1955.
3. *El Imparcial*, July 6, 1954.
4. *El Imparcial*, February 22 and March 7, 1955.

5. *El Imparcial*, July 21, 1954.

6. *El Imparcial*, July 30, 1954.

7. Odilia de Castillo Armas, "Mensaje a la mujer guatemalteca," *Mujer*, December 24, 1956.

8. *Mujer*, no. 1, May 1955.

9. *El Imparcial*, February 28, 1955.

10. Carlson, ¡*Feminismo! The Woman's Movement in Argentina*, 186.

APPENDIX A

1. *Diario de Centro América*, October 26, 1887.

2. *El Imparcial*, October 18, 1937.

3. *El Imparcial*, July 2, 1944.

4. *El Imparcial*, December 18, 1948.

5. Suslow, "Social Security in Guatemala," 77. By March 31, 1951, there were 3,171 registered employers in Guatemala with a total coverage of more than 170,000 workers, a majority of whom were rural. Women, however, experienced deep discrimination in the rural agricultural sector and were usually not counted as official employees.

Bibliography

Archival Sources

GUATEMALA CITY

Archivo General de Centro América (AGCA)
Hermeroteca. Collection of political flyers and pamphlets, 1944–1954, called the Hojas Sueltas. Includes miscellaneous journals, labor newspapers, bulletins, and magazines. The national daily newspapers *El Imparcial, Diario de Centro América, La Hora,* and *Nuestro Diario* are also housed here.

GOVERNMENT DOCUMENTS, GUATEMALA

Adams, Richard N. *Un análisis de las creencias y prácticas médicas en un pueblo indígena de Guatemala.* Guatemala: Ministerio de Educación Pública, 1952.

Alianza Cívica de Asociaciones Femeninas. *Cartilla cívica popular: Para capacitación de los ciudadanos.* Guatemala: n.p., n.d.

Arévalo, Juan José. *Escritos complementarios.* Guatemala: Ministerio de Educación, 1988.

———. "Informe presidencial sobre la situación política del país." Guatemala, 1947.

———. *Qué significan las escuelas "federación": Solución guatemalteca en un conflicto universal entre la arquitectura y la pedagogía.* Guatemala: Ministerio de Educación Pública, 1949.

Asamblea Constituyente Guatemala. *Reforma constitucional de 1935: Antecedentes texto taquigráfico de los debates sostenidos en la comisión de la constituyente que abrió dictamen sobre la materia.* Guatemala: Tipografía Nacional, 1936.

Asamblea Nacional Constituyente. *Diario de las sesiones de la Asamblea Constituyente de 1879: Reimpreso por acuerdo de la Comisión de Régimen Interior de la Asamblea Constituyente de 1927 en observancia de disposición de la Asamblea Legislativa de 1925.* Guatemala: Tipografía Nacional, 1927.

———. *Dictamen de la Comisión Extraordinaria de reformas a la constitución.* Guatemala: Tipografía Sánchez y de Guise, 1921.

Barascout, Jorge E. *La edad de los escolares y su valor como determinante en el fenómeno educativo: Un índice de su evolución.* Guatemala: Ministerio de Educación Pública, May 1946.

Chavarría Flores, Manuel. *Analfabetismo en Guatemala.* Guatemala: Comité Nacional de Alfabetización, 1950.

Código Civil de la República de Guatemala, 1877. Guatemala: Imprenta de El Progreso, 1877.

Comité Nacional de Alfabetización. *Campaña nacional de alfabetización: Instructivo general.* Guatemala: Comité Nacional de Alfabetización, June 1948.

Departamento de Publicidad de la Presidencia de la República. *Primera colonia agrícola de Poptún.* Guatemala: Departamento de Publicidad de la Presidencia de la República, 1950.

Dirección General de Estadística. *Censo General de la República de Guatemala levantado el año de 1880*. Guatemala: Establecimiento Tipográfico de El Progreso, 1882.

———. *Censo General de la República de Guatemala levantado en 26 de Febrero de 1893 por la Dirección General de Estadística*. Guatemala: Tipografía y Encuadernación Nacional, 1894.

———. *Censo de la República de Guatemala, 1921*. Guatemala: Talleres Gutenberg, 1924.

———. *Analisis del censo urbano de la capital levantado el 22 de Febrero de 1938 considerado en sus cifras globales*. Guatemala: Dirección General de Estadística, 1939.

———. *Quinto censo general de población, levantado el 7 de Abril de 1940*. Guatemala: Tipografía Nacional, 1942.

———. *Censos de la República de Guatemala, 1950*. Guatemala: Talleres Gutenberg, 1951.

Guarderías nacionales y comedores infantíles: Origen, organización, propósitos. Guatemala: n.p., 1948.

Ministerio de Educación Pública. *Alfabeto para los cuatro idiomas indígenas mayoritarios de Guatemala: Quiché, Cakchiquel, Mam y Kekchí*. Guatemala: Instituto Indigenista Nacional, Ministerio de Educación Pública, 1946.

———. *Bases, organización y programas de la campaña regional de alfabetización y extension cultural en el Departamento de Jalapa*. Publicación no. 5. Guatemala: Comité Nacional de Alfabetización, October 1948.

———. "Circular número 1, a directores y maestras de sección de escuelas parvularias oficiales y particulares de la república, Marzo de 1954." Guatemala: Ministerio de Educación Pública, 1954.

———. "Circular número 1, Orientaciones generales para el periodo de organización del trabajo escolar primario, Diciembre de 1952." Guatemala: Ministerio de Educación Pública, 1952.

———. *Cuatro estudios estadístico-educativos de la escuela guatemalteca*. Guatemala: Ministerio de Educación Pública, July 1946.

———. *Indice: Editorial del pueblo*. Año 1, no. 1, agosto de 1946. Guatemala: Ministerio de Educación Pública, Dirección de Educación Extraescolar, 1946.

Ministerio de Gobernación, Trabajo y Previsión Social. *Constitución de la República de Guatemala decretada por la Asamblea Nacional constituyente en 11 de Marzo de 1945*. Guatemala: Tipografía Nacional, 1945.

Ministerio de la Defensa Nacional. *Reglamento de alfabetización para el ejercito nacional de la revolución*. Guatemala: Ministerio de la Defensa Nacional, 1946.

Ministerio de Relaciones Exteriores. *La controversia sobre Belice durante el año de 1945*. Guatemala: Publicaciones del Ministerio de Relaciones Exteriores, 1946.

Salazar, Francisco. "Resumen de las leyes y disposiciones dictadas sobre sanidad publica en Guatemala." *Boletín Sanitario de Guatemala* 15, no. 53 (1945): 26–39.

Soto Hall, Máximo. *Instrucción moral y cívica: Minervalias de 1913*. Guatemala City: Marroquín Hermanos, 1917.

Vargas R., Gonzalo. *En Buen Camino*. Guatemala: Ministerio de Educación Pública, Campaña Nacional de Alfabetización, n.d.

———. *Nuevo Día!* Guatemala: Ministerio de Educación Pública, Campaña Nacional de Alfabetización, n.d.

UNITED STATES, GENERAL COLLECTIONS

Guatemalan Documents (GD). Manuscript Division, Library of Congress, Washington, DC.
Nettie Lee Benson Latin American Collection, University of Texas at Austin.
Records of the US Department of State Relating to Internal Affairs of Guatemala. Washington, DC: National Archives, National Archives and Records Administration, 1988.
Taracena Flores Collection, "Revolution and Counterrevolution in Guatemala, 1944–1963," University of Texas at Austin.
Women's International League for Peace and Freedom Papers, 1915–1978, Swarthmore College Peace Collection (SCPC).

UNITED STATES, GOVERNMENT DOCUMENTS

Bulletin of the Pan American Union. Washington, DC: Government Printing Office, 1910–1948.
Case Study in Insurgency and Revolutionary Warfare: Guatemala, 1944–1954. Washington, DC: Special Operations Research Office, 1964.
Final Act of the Ninth Pan American Child Congress, Caracas, Venezuela, January 5–10, 1948. Washington, DC: Organization of American States, 1948.
Final Act of the Special Assembly of the Inter-American Commission of Women, Buenos Aires, Argentina, August 8–24, 1949. Washington, DC: Pan American Union, 1949.
Holly, Susan, ed. *Foreign Relations of the United States, 1952–1954, Guatemala.* Washington, DC: Government Printing Office, 2003.
Organization of American States. *Inter-American Commission of Women, 1928–1973.* Washington, DC: General Secretariat, Organization of American States, 1974.
Records of the US Department of State Relating to Internal Affairs of Guatemala, 1950–1954. Wilmington, DE: Scholarly Resources, 2001.
Seventh International Conference of American States, Third Committee: Civil and Political Rights of Women, Minutes and Antecedents, Montevideo, 1933.

NEWSPAPERS AND PERIODICALS

Acción Campesina: Vocero de la Confederación Nacional Campesina de Guatemala
Acción Social Cristiana
Azul
Boletín Indigenista: Organo trimestral del Instituto Indigenista Interamericano
La Cuerda
Diario de Centro América
Diario del Pueblo: Organo del Partido de la Revolución Guatemalteca
El Heraldo Católico
La Hora
El Ideal
El Imparcial
El Liberal Progresista
La Mujer Obrera
Mujer

Mujeres: Boletín de Alianza de Femenina Guatemalteca
Nosotras
Nuestra Guatemala
Nuestro Diario
Octubre
Prensa Libre
Revista del Maestro
Revista del Trabajo
La Revolución
La Semana Católica
Studium
Tierra Nuestra
El Unionista
El Verbum
La Verdad
Vida
La Voz de la Locataria
La Voz de la Mujer

UNPUBLISHED DOCUMENTS

Aden, Robert Clark. "Teacher Training in Guatemala." PhD diss., George Peabody College for Teachers, 1955.

Cabrera Cruz, Héctor Alberto. "Análisis y propuesta de diseño del hospital nacional infantil Elisa Martínez en Puerto Barrios, Izabal." PhD diss., Universidad de San Carlos de Guatemala, 2005.

Calder, Bruce J. "The Catholic Church in the Context of Guatemalan Politics, Society and Culture from 1940 to the Present." Paper presented at the Seventeenth International Congress of the Latin American Studies Association, Los Angeles, September 24, 1992.

Carrillo, Alfonso. "La mujer guatemalteca y su situación jurídica." Unpublished document, San José, Costa Rica, 1940.

Das, Devaleena. "Transnational Feminism Beyond Westoxification: Theory and Praxis." Paper presented at the Workshop in Transnational Feminism/Atelier sur le Féminisme Transnational, McMaster University, Hamilton, Ontario, May 2018.

Finzer, Erin S. "Poetisa Chic: Fashioning the Modern Female Poet in Central America, 1929–1944." PhD diss., University of Kansas, 2008.

Gibbings, Julie. "Another Race More Worthy of the Present: Race, History, and Nation in Alta Verapaz, Guatemala, c. 1860–1940s." PhD diss., University of Wisconsin–Madison, 2012.

Kirkpatrick, Michael D. "Optics and the Culture of Modernity in Guatemala City since the Liberal Reforms." PhD diss., University of Saskatchewan, September 2013.

Komisaruk, Catherine Helen. "Women and Men in Guatemala, 1765–1835: Gender, Ethnicity, and Social Relations in the Central American Capital." PhD diss., University of California, Los Angeles, 2000.

Labores de la Cuarta Convención Nacional Unionista reunida en Santa Ana, El Salvador, Centro América el 15 de Septiembre de 1944.

Maynard, Eileen Anne. "The Women of Palin: A Comparative Study of Indian and Ladino Women in a Guatemalan Village." PhD diss., Cornell University, 1963.
Palmer, Steven Paul. "A Liberal Discipline: Inventing Nations in Guatemala and Costa Rica, 1870–1900." PhD diss., Columbia University, 1990.
Palomo de Castillo Armas, Odilia. "Mensaje a la mujer guatemalteca." Unpublished document, December 24, 1954.
Pitti, Joseph A. "Jorge Ubico and Guatemalan Politics in the 1920s." PhD diss., University of New Mexico, 1975.
Quan Valenzuela, Graciela. "Ciudadanía opcional para la mujer Guatemalteca." Thesis, Universidad Nacional, Facultad de Ciencias Jurídicas y Sociales, December 1943.
Randolph, David Eugene. "The Diplomatic History of Guatemala during the Administration of President Jorge Ubico: 1931–1944." Master's thesis, Arizona State University, 1980.
Ruiz, Vicki L. "Class Acts: Latina Feminist Traditions, 1900–1930." Presidential address delivered at the annual meeting of the American Historical Association, Atlanta, January 8, 2016.
Suslow, Leo Arthur. "Social Security in Guatemala: A Case Study in Bureaucracy and Social Welfare Planning." PhD diss., University of Connecticut, 1954.
Wamsley, Esther Sue. "A Hemisphere of Women: Latin American and U.S. Feminists in the IACW, 1915–1939." PhD diss., Ohio State University, 1998.

Secondary Sources

Acosta-Belén, Edna, and Christine E. Bose, eds. *Researching Women in Latin America and the Caribbean*. Boulder, CO: Westview Press, 1993.
Adams, Abigail E. "Antonio Goubaud Carrera: Between the Contradictions of the Generación de 1920 and U.S. Anthropology." In *After the Coup: An Ethnographic Reframing of Guatemala 1954*, edited by Timothy J. Smith and Abigail E. Adams, 17–48. Urbana: University of Illinois Press, 2011.
Adams, Richard Newbold. *Crucifixion by Power: Essays on Guatemalan National Social Structure, 1944–1966*. Austin: University of Texas Press, 1970.
Aguilar, Yolanda, and Luz Méndez de la Vega, eds. *Rompiendo el silencio: Justicia para las mujeres víctimas de violencia sexual durante el conflicto armado en Guatemala*. Guatemala City: Instituto de Estudios Comparados en Ciencias Penales de Guatemala, 2006.
Alba, Victor. *Politics and the Labor Movement in Latin America*. Stanford, CA: Stanford University Press, 1968.
Alexander, Robert. *Organized Labor in Latin America*. New York: Free Press, 1965.
Alvarado, Rafael. *La cuestión de Belice*. Quito: Editorial Colón, 1949.
Alvarado, Ricardo E. *Lo que ha pasado con Belice*. Guatemala City: Escuela Normal Rural Pedro Molina, 1959.
Alvarez, Sonia E. *Engendering Democracy in Brazil: Women's Movements in Transition Politics*. Princeton, NJ: Princeton University Press, 1990.
Anderson, Benedict. *Imagined Communities: Reflections on the Origin and Spread of Nationalism*. London: Verso, 2006.
Anderson, Marilyn. *Granddaughters of Corn: Portraits of Guatemalan Women*. Willimantic, CT: Curbstone Press, 1988.

Antezana-Pernet, Corinne A. "Peace in the World and Democracy at Home: The Chilean Women's Movement in the 1940s." In *Latin America in the 1940s: War and Postwar Transitions*, edited by David Rock, 166–86. Berkeley: University of California Press, 1994.

Arendt, Hannah. *The Human Condition*. Chicago: University of Chicago Press, 1958.

Arévalo, Juan José. *Guatemala, la democracia y el imperio*. Guatemala City: Ediciones Nueva Era, 1955.

Arévalo Martínez, Rafael. *Ubico*. Guatemala City: Tipografía Nacional, 1984.

Armitage, Susan H., with Patricia Hart and Karen Weathermon, eds. *Women's Oral History: The Frontiers Reader*. Lincoln: University of Nebraska Press, 2002.

Asturias, Miguel Ángel. *El Señor Presidente*. Mexico City: B. Costa-Amic, 1946.

Bacchetta, Paola, and Margaret Power, eds. *Right-Wing Women: From Conservatives to Extremists around the World*. New York: Routledge, 2002.

Barnes, John. *Evita, First Lady: A Biography of Eva Perón*. New York: Grove Press, 1978.

Barreda de Evián, Daniel. *Arreglo pacífico de controversia internacionales y la cuestión de Belice*. Guatemala City: Imprenta Iberia, 1947.

Bauer Paiz, Alfonso. *Antología de ensayos*. Guatemala City: Consejo de Instituciones de Desarrollo de Guatemala, 1995.

Bayard de Volo, Lorraine. *Mothers of Heroes and Martyrs: Gender Identity Politics in Nicaragua, 1979–1999*. Baltimore: Johns Hopkins University Press, 2001.

———. "A Revolution in the Binary? Gender and the Oxymoron of Revolutionary War in Cuba and Nicaragua." *Signs: Journal of Women in Culture and Society* 37, no. 2 (Winter 2012): 413–38.

Berger, Susan A. *Guatemaltecas: The Women's Movement, 1986–2003*. Austin: University of Texas Press, 2006.

Besse, Susan K. *Restructuring Patriarchy: The Modernization of Gender Inequality in Brazil, 1914–1940*. Chapel Hill: University of North Carolina Press, 1996.

Bethell, Leslie, and Ian Roxborough, eds. *Latin America between the Second World War and the Cold War, 1944–1948*. Cambridge: Cambridge University Press, 1992.

Black, George, with Milton Jamail and Norma Stoltz Chinchilla. *Garrison Guatemala*. London: Zed Books, 1984.

Botting, Eileen Hunt, and Charlotte Hammond Matthews. "Overthrowing the Floresta-Wollstonecraft Myth for Latin American Feminism." *Gender and History* 26, no. 1 (April 2014): 64–83.

Boxer, Marilyn J., and Jean H. Quataert, eds. *Socialist Women: European Socialist Feminism in the Nineteenth and Early Twentieth Centuries*. New York: Elsevier North-Holland, 1978.

Boylan, Kristina. "The Feminine 'Apostolate in Society' versus the Secular State: The Unión Femenina Católica Mexicana, 1929–1940." In *Right-Wing Women: From Conservatives to Extremists around the World*, edited by Paola Bacchetta and Margaret Power, 169–82. New York: Routledge, 2002.

Briggs, Laura. *Reproducing Empire: Race, Sex, Science, and U.S. Imperialism in Puerto Rico*. Berkeley: University of California Press, 2002.

Burns, E. Bradford. *Eadweard Muybridge in Guatemala, 1875: The Photographer as Social Recorder*. Berkeley: University of California Press, 1986.

———. *The Poverty of Progress: Latin America in the Nineteenth Century*. Berkeley: University of California Press, 1980.

Calder, Bruce Johnson. *Crecimiento y cambio de la Iglesia Católica guatemalteca, 1944–1966*. Guatemala City: Editorial José de Pineda Ibarra, 1970.

Calvert, Peter. *Guatemala: A Nation in Turmoil.* Boulder, CO: Westview Press, 1985.

Cardenal, Rodolfo. "The Church in Central America." In *The Church in Latin America, 1492–1992,* edited by Enrique Dussel, 243–70. New York: Orbis Books, 1992.

Carey, David, Jr. *Engendering Mayan History: Kaqchikel Women as Agents and Conduits of the Past, 1875–1970.* New York: Routledge, 2006.

———. "Forced and Forbidden Sex: Rape and Sexual Freedom in Dictatorial Guatemala." *The Americas* 69, no. 3 (January 2013): 357–89.

———. "'Hard Working, Orderly Little Women': Mayan Vendors and Marketplace Struggles in Early-Twentieth-Century Guatemala." *Ethnohistory* 55, no. 4 (Fall 2008): 579–607.

———. *I Ask for Justice: Maya Women, Dictators, and Crime in Guatemala, 1898–1944.* Austin: University of Texas Press, 2013.

———. *Our Elders Teach Us: Maya-Kaqchikel Historical Perspectives.* Tuscaloosa: University of Alabama Press, 2001.

———. "Runaway Mothers and Daughters: Crimes of Abandonment in Twentieth-Century Guatemala." *Journal of Family History* 38, no. 2 (April 2013): 188–222.

Carlson, Marifran. *¡Feminismo! The Woman's Movement in Argentina from Its Beginnings to Eva Perón.* Chicago: Academy Chicago Publishers, 1988.

Carrillo, Alfonso. *Algunos aspectos jurídicos de la controversia angloguatemalteca sobre Belice.* Guatemala City: Universidad de San Carlos, Asociación de Abogados de Guatemala, 1948.

———. *El caso de Belice ante la conciencia de América.* Guatemala City: Tipografía Nacional, 1948.

Carrillo, Ana Lorena, and Norma Stoltz Chinchilla. "From Urban Elite to Peasant Organizing: Agendas, Accomplishments, and Challenges of Thirty-Plus Years of Guatemalan Feminism, 1975–2007." In *Women's Activism in Latin America and the Caribbean: Engendering Social Justice, Democratizing Citizenship,* edited by Elizabeth Maier and Nathalie Lebon. New Brunswick, NJ: Rutgers University Press, 2010.

Carrillo Padilla, Lorena. *Luchas de las guatemaltecas del siglo XX: Mirada al trabajo y la participación política de las mujeres.* Antigua, Guatemala: Ediciones del Pensativo, 2004.

———. "Sufridas hijas del pueblo: La huelga de las escogedoras de café de 1925 en Guatemala." *Mesoamérica* 15, no. 27 (June 1994): 157–73.

Carrillo Ramírez, Alfredo. *Evolución histórica de la educación secundaria en Guatemala, desde el año 1831 hasta el año 1969: 138 años de historia.* 2 vols. Guatemala City: Editorial José de Pineda Ibarra, 1971–1972.

Carrillo Samayoa, Andrea, and Jacqueline Torres Urízar, eds. *Nosotras, las de la historia: Mujeres en Guatemala (siglos XIX–XXI).* Guatemala City: Asociación la Cuerda; Secretaría Presidencial de la Mujer, 2011.

Casaús Arzú, Marta Elena. "Las redes teosóficas de mujeres en Guatemala: La Sociedad Gabriela Mistral, 1920–1940." *Revista Complutense de Historia de América,* no. 27 (2001): 219–55.

———. "La voz de las mujeres guatemaltecas en la década de 1920." *Cuadernos Americanos,* no. 89 (2001): 198–229.

Casaús Arzú, Marta Elena, and Teresa García Giráldez. *Las redes intelectuales centroamericanas: Un siglo de imaginarios nacionales (1820–1920).* Guatemala City: F&G Editores, 2005.

Casaús Arzú, Marta Elena, and Óscar Guillermo Peláez Almengor, eds. *Historia intelectual de Guatemala.* Guatemala City: F&G Editores, 2001.

Castells, Manuel. *The Power of Identity*. Malden, MA: Blackwell, 1997.

Castledine, Jacqueline. *Cold War Progressives: Women's Interracial Organizing for Peace and Freedom*. Urbana: University of Illinois Press, 2012.

Caulfield, Sueann. "The History of Gender in the Historiography of Latin America." *Hispanic American Historical Review* 81, nos. 3–4 (February 2001): 449–90.

———. *In Defense of Honor: Sexual Morality, Modernity, and Nation in Early-Twentieth-Century Brazil*. Durham, NC: Duke University Press, 2000.

Centro de Investigaciones Regionales de Mesoamérica. *La revolución guatemalteca*. Colección "Para que Todo el Pueblo Lea," Campaña de Fomento de la Lectura, no. 16. Guatemala City: Editorial Oscar de León Palacios, 1994.

Chaney, Elsa M. *Supermadre: Women in Politics in Latin America*. Austin: University of Texas Press, 1979.

Chase, Michelle. *Revolution within the Revolution: Women and Gender Politics in Cuba, 1952–1962*. Chapel Hill: University of North Carolina Press, 2015.

———. "Women's Organisations and the Politics of Gender in Cuba's Urban Insurrection (1952–1958)." *Bulletin of Latin American Research* 29, no. 4 (October 2010): 440–58.

Chinchilla, Norma Stoltz. "Industrialization, Monopoly Capitalism, and Women's Work in Guatemala." *Signs: Journal of Women in Culture and Society* 3, no. 1 (February 1977): 38–56.

———. "Marxism, Feminism, and the Struggle for Democracy in Latin America." *Gender and Society* 5, no. 3 (September 1991): 291–310.

———. "Mobilizing Women: Revolution in the Revolution." *Latin American Perspectives* 4, no. 4 (Autumn 1977): 83–102.

———. *Nuestras utopías: Mujeres guatemaltecas del siglo XX*. Guatemala City: Agrupación de Mujeres Tierra Viva, 1998.

Christensen, Kirza, and Marleny Castillo Rodas, eds. *Voces de 4 mujeres: Ventanas a la milpa*. Quetzaltenango, Guatemala City: Proyecto Linguistico Quetzalteco, 2005.

Ciencia y Tecnología en Guatemala. *Situación de la mujer en Guatemala*. Mexico City: Ciencia y Tecnología en Guatemala, 1987.

Cleary, Edward L., and Hannah Stewart-Gambino, eds. *Conflict and Competition: The Latin American Church in a Changing Environment*. Boulder, CO: Lynne Rienner, 1992.

Clune, Lori. *Executing the Rosenbergs: Death and Diplomacy in a Cold War World*. Oxford: Oxford University Press, 2016.

Cofiño Kepfer, Ana María. "Las primeras comunistas en Guatemala." In *Queridas camaradas: Historias iberoamericanas de mujeres comunistas*, edited by Adriana Valobra and Mercedes Yusta. Buenos Aires: Miño y Dávila Editores, 2017.

Coker Gonzalez, Charity. "Agitating for Their Rights: The Colombian Women's Movement, 1930–1957." *Pacific Historical Review* 69, no. 4 (November 2000): 689–706.

Colom, Yolanda. *Mujeres en la alborada: Guerrillas y participación femenina en Guatemala, 1973–1998*. Guatemala City: Artemis and Edinter, 1998.

Contreras Vélez, Alvaro. *Génesis y ocaso de la revolución de octubre del 44*. Guatemala City: Academia de Geografía e Historia de Guatemala, 1994.

Costigliola, Frank. "The Nuclear Family: Tropes of Gender and Pathology in the Western Alliance." *Diplomatic History* 21, no. 2 (Spring 1997): 163–83.

Craske, Nikki. *Women and Politics in Latin America*. New Brunswick, NJ: Rutgers University Press, 1999.

Craske, Nikki, and Maxine Molyneux, eds. *Gender and the Politics of Rights and Democracy in Latin America*. Basingstoke, Hampshire, England: Palgrave, 2002.

Cruz Rivas, Hugo. "Mujeres que entran y salen de la historia." In *Mujeres, género e historia en América Central durante los siglos XVIII, XIX y XX*, edited by Eugenia Rodríguez Sáenz. San José: UNIFEM/Plumsock Mesoamerican Studies, 2002.

Cullather, Nick. *Secret History: The CIA's Classified Account of Its Operations in Guatemala, 1952–1954*. Stanford, CA: Stanford University Press, 1999.

Cupples, Julie. "Between Maternalism and Feminism: Women in Nicaragua's Counter-Revolutionary Forces." *Bulletin of Latin American Research* 25, no. 1 (January 2006): 83–103.

Daley, Caroline, and Melanie Nolan, eds. *Suffrage and Beyond: International Feminist Perspectives*. New York: New York University Press, 1994.

Dary Fuentes, Claudia. *Entre el hogar y la vega: Estudio sobre la participación femenina en la agricultura de El Progreso*. Guatemala City: Facultad Latinoamericana de Ciencias Sociales, 1994.

Deutsch, Sandra McGee. "Argentine Women against Fascism: The Junta de la Victoria, 1941–1947." *Politics, Religion and Ideology* 13, no. 2 (June 2012): 221–36.

———. *Counterrevolution in Argentina, 1900–1932: The Argentine Patriotic League*. Lincoln: University of Nebraska Press, 1986.

———. *Crossing Borders, Claiming a Nation: A History of Argentine Jewish Women, 1880–1955*. Durham, NC: Duke University Press, 2010.

———. *Las Derechas: The Extreme Right in Argentina, Brazil, and Chile, 1890–1939*. Stanford, CA: Stanford University Press, 1999.

———. "Spreading Right-Wing Patriotism, Femininity, and Morality: Women in Argentina, Brazil, and Chile, 1900–1940." In *Radical Women in Latin America: Left and Right*, edited by Victoria González and Karen Kampwirth, 223–48. University Park: Pennsylvania State University Press, 2001.

Díaz, Arlene J. *Female Citizens, Patriarchs, and the Law in Venezuela, 1786–1904*. Lincoln: University of Nebraska Press, 2004.

Dore, Elizabeth, ed. *Gender Politics in Latin America: Debates in Theory and Practice*. New York: Monthly Review Press, 1997.

———. *Myths of Modernity: Peonage and Patriarchy in Nicaragua*. Durham, NC: Duke University Press, 2006.

Dore, Elizabeth, and Maxine Molyneux, eds. *Hidden Histories of Gender and the State in Latin America*. Durham, NC: Duke University Press, 2000.

Dosal, Paul J. *Power in Transition: The Rise of Guatemala's Industrial Oligarchy, 1871–1994*. Westport, CT: Praeger, 1995.

Dosal, Paul J., and Óscar Guillermo Peláez Almengor. *Jorge Ubico (1931–1944): Dictadura, economía y "La tacita de plata."* Guatemala City: Centro de Estudios Urbanos y Regionales, Universidad de San Carlos de Guatemala, 1996.

Drinot, Paulo, and Alan Knight, eds. *The Great Depression in Latin America*. Durham, NC: Duke University Press, 2014.

Dunkerley, James. *Power in the Isthmus: A Political History of Modern Central America*. London: Verso, 1988.

Dussel, Enrique, ed. *The Church in Latin America, 1492–1992*. New York: Orbis Books, 1992.
Ehrick, Christine. *The Shield of the Weak: Feminism and the State in Uruguay, 1903–1933*. Albuquerque: University of New Mexico Press, 2005.
Engel, Barbara Alpern. *Women in Russia, 1700–2000*. Cambridge: Cambridge University Press, 2004.
Enloe, Cynthia. *Bananas, Beaches and Bases: Making Feminist Sense of International Politics*. Berkeley: University of California Press, 1989.
Farley, John. *To Cast Out Disease: A History of the International Health Division of the Rockefeller Foundation (1913–1951)*. New York: Oxford University Press, 2004.
Farnsworth-Alvear, Ann. *Dulcinea in the Factory: Myths, Morals, Men, and Women in Colombia's Industrial Experiment, 1905–1960*. Durham, NC: Duke University Press, 2000.
Ferro, Cora, and Ana María Quirós. *Mujer, realidad religiosa y comunicación*. San José: Editorial Universitaria Centroamericana, 1988.
Few, Martha. *Women Who Live Evil Lives: Gender, Religion, and the Politics of Power in Colonial Guatemala*. Austin: University of Texas Press, 2002.
Figueroa Ibarra, Carlos. "The Culture of Terror and the Cold War in Guatemala." *Journal of Genocide Research* 8, no. 2 (June 2006): 191–208.
Figueroa Marroquín, Horacio, and Angelina Acuña de Castañeda. *Poesía femenina guatemalense*. Vol. 1. Guatemala City: Editorial Universitaria, 1977.
Fiol-Matta, Licia. *A Queer Mother for the Nation: The State and Gabriela Mistral*. Minneapolis: University of Minnesota Press, 2002.
Flores, Marco Antonio. *Fortuny: Un comunista guatemalteco*. Guatemala City: Facultad Latinoamericana de Ciencias Sociales, 1994.
Forster, Cindy. *La revolución indígena y campesina en Guatemala: 1970 a 2000*. Guatemala City: Universidad de San Carlos de Guatemala, 2012.
———. *The Time of Freedom: Campesino Workers in Guatemala's October Revolution*. Pittsburgh: University of Pittsburgh Press, 2001.
———. "Violent and Violated Women: Justice and Gender in Rural Guatemala, 1936–1956." *Journal of Women's History* 11, no. 3 (Autumn 1999): 55–75.
Foster, Carrie A. *The Women and the Warriors: The U.S. Section of the Women's International League for Peace and Freedom, 1915–1946*. Syracuse, NY: Syracuse University Press, 1995.
Foster, Catherine. *Women for All Seasons: The Story of the Women's International League for Peace and Freedom*. Athens: University of Georgia Press, 1989.
Franco, Jean. *The Decline and Fall of the Lettered City: Latin America in the Cold War*. Cambridge, MA: Harvard University Press, 2002.
Fraser, Nicholas, and Marysa Navarro. *Evita: The Real Life of Eva Perón*. New York: W. W. Norton, 1996.
French, John D., and Daniel James, eds. *The Gendered Worlds of Latin American Women Workers: From Household and Factory to the Union Hall and Ballot Box*. Durham, NC: Duke University Press, 1997.
Fried, Jonathan L., Marvin E. Gettleman, Deborah T. Levenson, and Nancy Peckenham, eds. *Guatemala in Rebellion: Unfinished History*. New York: Grove Press, 1983.
Friedman, Elisabeth J. *Unfinished Transitions: Women and the Gendered Development of Democracy in Venezuela, 1936–1996*. University Park: Pennsylvania State University Press, 2000.

Fuentes Girón, Manuel. *Del Hospicio Nacional Centro Educativo del siglo XIX y principios del siglo XX*. Guatemala City: Librerías Artemis Edinter, 1999.

Galich, Manuel. *Del pánico al ataque*. Guatemala City: Editorial Universitaria, 1977.

Gamio de Alba, Margarita. *La mujer indígena de Centro América*. Mexico City: Instituto Indigenista Interamericano, 1957.

García Bauer, José Francisco. *Nuestra revolución legislativa*. Guatemala City: Tipografía Nacional, 1948.

García-Bryce, Iñigo. "Transnational Activist: Magda Portal and the American Popular Revolutionary Alliance (APRA), 1926–1950." *The Americas* 70, no. 4 (April 2014): 677–706.

García Granados, Jorge. *Cuarderno de memorias, 1900–1922*. Guatemala City: Librerías Artemis Edinter, 2000.

García Laguardia, Jorge Mario. *La reforma liberal en Guatemala: Vida política y orden constitucional*. Guatemala City: Editorial Universitaria, 1972.

———. *La revolución del 20 de Octubre de 1944*. Guatemala City: Institución del Procurador de los Derechos Humanos, 1994.

Garrard-Burnett, Virginia, "Indians Are Drunks and Drunks Are Indians: Alcohol and *Indigenismo* in Guatemala, 1890–1940." *Bulletin of Latin American Research* 19, no. 3 (July 2000): 341–56.

———, ed. *On Earth as It Is in Heaven: Religion in Modern Latin America*. Wilmington, DE: Scholarly Resources, 2000.

Gaviola Artigas, Edda, and Lissette González Martínez, eds. *Feminismos en América Latina*. Guatemala City: Facultad Latinoamericana de Ciencias Sociales, 2001.

Gibbings, Julie. "In the Shadow of Slavery: Historical Time, Labor, and Citizenship in Nineteenth-Century Alta Verapaz, Guatemala." *Hispanic American Historical Review* 96, no. 1 (February 2016): 73–107.

———. "*Mestizaje* in the Age of Fascism: German and Q'eqchi' Maya Interracial Unions in Alta Verapaz, Guatemala." *German History* 34, no. 2 (June 2016): 214–36.

Gleijeses, Piero. *Shattered Hope: The Guatemalan Revolution and the United States, 1944–1954*. Princeton, NJ: Princeton University Press, 1991.

González, Victoria, and Karen Kampwirth, eds. *Radical Women in Latin America: Left and Right*. University Park: Pennsylvania State University Press, 2001.

González Orellana, Carlos. *Los educadores y la escuela paralela en Guatemala y Costa Rica*. Guatemala City: Editorial Universitaria, 1985.

———. *Historia de la educación en Guatemala*. Guatemala City: Editorial Universitaria, 1980.

González-Rivera, Victoria. *Before the Revolution: Women's Rights and Right-Wing Politics in Nicaragua, 1821–1979*. University Park: Pennsylvania State University Press, 2011.

Gorlier, Juan Carlos, and Keith Guzik. *La política de género en América Latina: Debates, teorías, metodologías y estudios de caso*. La Plata, Argentina: Ediciones Al Margen, 2002.

Gramsci, Antonio. *A Gramsci Reader: Selected Writings, 1916–1935*. Edited by David Forgacs. London: Lawrence and Wishart, 1999.

Grandin, Greg. *The Blood of Guatemala: A History of Race and Nation*. Durham, NC: Duke University Press, 2000.

———. *The Last Colonial Massacre: Latin America in the Cold War*. Chicago: University of Chicago Press, 2004.

Green, Linda. *Fear as a Way of Life: Mayan Widows in Rural Guatemala.* New York: Columbia University Press, 1999.

Grieb, Kenneth J. *Guatemalan Caudillo: The Regime of Jorge Ubico, Guatemala, 1931–1944.* Athens: Ohio University Press, 1979.

———. "Jorge Ubico and the Belice Boundary Dispute." *The Americas* 30, no. 4 (April 1974): 448–74.

Guatemala: Election Factbook. Washington, DC: Institute for the Comparative Study of Political Systems, 1966.

Guy, Donna. "The Pan American Child Congress, 1916 to 1942: Pan Americanism, Child Reform, and the Welfare State in Latin America." *Journal of Family History* 23, no. 3 (July 1998): 272–91.

——— "The Politics of Pan-American Cooperation: Maternalist Feminism and the Child Rights Movement, 1913–1960." *Gender and History* 10, no. 3 (November 1998): 449–69.

———. *Women Build the Welfare State: Performing Charity and Creating Rights in Argentina, 1880–1955.* Durham, NC: Duke University Press, 2009.

Guzmán Bockler, Carlos. *Colonialismo y revolución.* Mexico City: Siglo XXI, 1975.

Haan, Francisca de. "Continuing Cold War Paradigms." *Women's History Review* 19, no. 4 (September 2010): 547–73.

Hahner, June. *Emancipating the Female Sex: The Struggle for Women's Rights in Brazil, 1850–1940.* Durham, NC: Duke University Press, 1990.

Hale, Charles. *Más que un Indio/More Than an Indian: Racial Ambivalence and Neoliberal Multiculturalism in Guatemala.* Santa Fe: School of American Research Press, 2006.

Handy, Jim. *Gift of the Devil: A History of Guatemala.* Boston: South End Press, 1984.

———. "National Policy, Agrarian Reform, and the Corporate Community during the Guatemalan Revolution, 1944–1954." *Comparative Studies in Society and History* 30, no. 4 (October 1988): 698–724.

———. *Revolution in the Countryside: Rural Conflict and Agrarian Reform in Guatemala, 1944–1954.* Chapel Hill: University of North Carolina Press, 1994.

Hartness, Ann. *Revolution and Counterrevolution in Guatemala, 1944–1963: An Annotated Bibliography of Materials in the Benson Latin American Collection.* Austin: General Libraries, University of Texas at Austin, 1984.

———. *Revolution and Counterrevolution in Guatemala, 1944–1963: An Annotated Guide to Street Literature in the Benson Latin American Collection.* Austin: General Libraries, University of Texas at Austin, 1995.

Hernández de León, Federico. *Viajes presidenciales: Breves relatos de algunas expediciones administrativas del General D. Jorge Ubico, presidente de la república.* Guatemala City: Tipografía Nacional, 1940.

Hernández de Zirión, Graciela. *Datos biográficos del general e ingeniero Miguel Ydígoras Fuentes.* Guatemala City: Editorial José de Pineda Ibarra, 1961.

Herrera, Luz Alicia, and Maria Alice Jacob. "Testimonies of Guatemalan Women." *Latin American Perspectives* 7, nos. 2–3 (Late Spring–Summer 1980): 160–68.

Herrera, Martha Josefina. "Civilicemonos." *Vida,* December 19, 1925.

Holleran, Mary. *Church and State in Guatemala.* New York: Columbia University Press, 1949.

Horan, Elizabeth. *Gabriela Mistral: An Artist and Her People.* Washington, DC: Organization of American States, 1994.

Horan, Elizabeth, and Doris Meyer, eds. *This America of Ours: The Letters of Gabriela Mistral and Victoria Ocampo*. Austin: University of Texas Press, 2003.
Hutchison, Elizabeth Quay. "Add Gender and Stir? Cooking Up Gendered Histories of Modern Latin America." *Latin American Research Review* 38, no. 1 (2003): 267–87.
———. *Labors Appropriate to Their Sex: Gender, Labor, and Politics in Urban Chile, 1900–1930*. Durham, NC: Duke University Press, 2001.
Iber, Patrick. *Neither Peace nor Freedom: The Cultural Cold War in Latin America*. Cambridge, MA: Harvard University Press, 2015.
Immerman, Richard H. *The CIA in Guatemala: The Foreign Policy of Intervention*. Austin: University of Texas Press, 1982.
Isbester, Katherine. *Still Fighting: The Nicaraguan Women's Movement, 1977–2000*. Pittsburgh: University of Pittsburgh Press, 2001.
ISIS Women's Journal. *Growing Together: Women, Feminism, and Population Education*. Santiago: ISIS International, 1988.
———. *The Latin American Women's Movement: Reflections and Actions*. Santiago: ISIS International, 1986.
James, Daniel. *Red Design for the Americas: Guatemalan Prelude*. New York: John Day, 1954.
Jaquette, Jane S., ed. *The Women's Movement in Latin America: Feminism and the Transition to Democracy*. Boston: Unwin Hyman, 1989.
Jensen, Kimberly, and Erika Kuhlman. *Women's Transnational Activism in Historical Perspective*. Dordrecht, Netherlands: Republic of Letters, 2009.
Jonas, Susanne. *The Battle for Guatemala: Rebels, Death Squads, and U.S. Power*. Boulder, CO: Westview Press, 1991.
Jones, Chester Lloyd. *Guatemala Past and Present*. Minneapolis: University of Minnesota Press, 1940.
Joseph, Gilbert M., Catherine C. LeGrand, and Ricardo D. Salvatore, eds. *Close Encounters of Empire: Writing the Cultural History of U.S.-Latin American Relations*. Durham, NC: Duke University Press, 1998.
Joseph, Gilbert M., and Daniela Spenser, eds. *In from the Cold: Latin America's New Encounter with the Cold War*. Durham, NC: Duke University Press, 2008.
Juárez y Aragón, Oscar. *Natalidad y mortalidad infantil en la Ciudad de Guatemala durante un período de seis meses*. Guatemala City: Universidad Nacional, 1944.
Kampwirth, Karen. *Feminism and the Legacy of Revolution: Nicaragua, El Salvador, Chiapas*. Athens: Ohio University Press, 2004.
———. *Women and Guerrilla Movements: Nicaragua, El Salvador, Chiapas, and Cuba*. University Park: Pennsylvania State University Press, 2002.
Kandiyoti, Deniz. "Bargaining with Patriarchy." *Gender and Society* 2, no. 3 (September 1988): 274–90.
Kaplan, Temma. "Female Consciousness and Collective Action: The Case of Barcelona, 1910–1918." *Signs: Journal of Women in Culture and Society* 7, no. 3 (Winter 1982): 545–66.
———. "Final Reflections: Gender, Chaos, and Authority in Revolutionary Times." In *Sex in Revolution: Gender, Politics, and Power in Modern Mexico*, edited by Jocelyn Olcott, Mary Kay Vaughan, and Gabriela Cano, 261–76. Durham, NC: Duke University Press, 2006.
Kirkwood, Julieta. *Ser política en Chile: Los nudos de la sabiduría feminist*. Santiago: Editorial Cuarto Propio, 1990.

Kistler, S. Ashley. *Maya Market Women: Power and Tradition in San Juan Chamelco, Guatemala.* Urbana: University of Illinois Press, 2014.

Kit, Wade. "The Fall of Guatemalan Dictator, Manual Estrada Cabrera: U.S. Pressure or National Opposition?" *Canadian Journal of Latin American and Caribbean Studies* 15, no. 29 (1990): 105–27.

———. "The Unionist Experiment in Guatemala, 1920–1921: Conciliation, Disintegration, and the Liberal Junta." *The Americas* 50, no. 1 (July 1993): 31–64.

Kobrak, Paul. *Organizing and Repression in the University of San Carlos, Guatemala, 1944 to 1996.* Washington, DC: American Association for the Advancement of Science, 1999.

Komisaruk, Catherine. *Labor and Love in Guatemala: The Eve of Independence.* Stanford, CA: Stanford University Press, 2013.

LaFeber, Walter. *Inevitable Revolutions: The United States in Central America.* New York: W. W. Norton, 1984.

Laparra, Jesús de. *Ensueños de la mente: Dedicados a la juventud centro-americana.* Guatemala City: n.p., 1884.

Laughlin, Kathleen A., Julie Gallagher, Dorothy Sue Cobble, Eileen Boris, Premilla Nadasen, Stephanie Gilmore, and Leandra Zarnow. "Is It Time to Jump Ship? Historians Rethink the Waves Metaphor." *Feminist Formations* 22, no. 1 (Spring 2010): 76–135.

Laville, Helen. "A New Era in International Women's Rights? American Women's Associations and the Establishment of the UN Commission on the Status of Women." *Journal of Women's History* 20, no. 4 (Winter 2008): 34–56.

Lavrin, Asunción. "Female, Feminine and Feminist: Key Concepts in Understanding Women's History in Twentieth Century Latin America." Occasional Lecture Series, no. 4. Department of Hispanic, Portuguese, and Latin American Studies, University of Bristol, November 1988.

———. "La literatura testimonial en Latinoamérica como experiencia de mujeres." In *Actas del 51 Congreso Internacional de Americanistas*, edited by Jorge Hidalgo L., 89–104. Santiago: Universidad de Chile, 2003.

———. "Unfolding Feminism: Spanish-American Women's Writings, 1970–1990." In *Feminisms in the Academy*, edited by Domna C. Stanton and Abigail J. Stewart, 248–73. Ann Arbor: University of Michigan Press, 1995.

———. *Women, Feminism, and Social Change in Argentina, Chile, and Uruguay, 1890–1940.* Lincoln: University of Nebraska Press, 1995.

León, Magdalena, ed. *Mujeres y participación política: Avances y desafíos en América Latina.* Bogotá: Tercer Mundo Editores, 1994.

León Aragón, Oscar de. *Caída de un régimen: Jorge Ubico—Federico Ponce, 20 de Octubre 1944.* Guatemala City: Facultad Latinoamericana de Ciencias Sociales, 1995.

Levenson, Deborah T. *Adiós Niños: The Gangs of Guatemala City and the Politics of Death.* Durham, NC: Duke University Press, 2013.

———. "Living Guatemala City, 1930s–2000s." In *Securing the City: Neoliberalism, Space, and Insecurity in Postwar Guatemala*, edited by Kevin Lewis O'Neill and Kedron Thomas, 25–48. Durham, NC: Duke University Press, 2011.

Levenson-Estrada, Deborah. *Trade Unionists against Terror: Guatemala City, 1954–1985.* Chapel Hill: University of North Carolina Press, 1994.

Leyton Rodríguez, Rubén. *Belice es tierra de Guatemala.* Mexico City: Ediciones R. Leyton Prado, 1953.

Longley, Kyle. *In the Eagle's Shadow: The United States and Latin America*. Wheeling, IL: Harlan Davidson, 2002.

López Beltrán, Carlos Gregorio. "Alberto Masferrer, Augusto César Sandino: Antiimperialismo, espiritualismo y utopía en la década de 1920." *Revista Complutense de Historia de América* 35 (2009): 87–108.

López Bruni, Ricky, ed. *Ciudad de Guatemala ayer y hoy*. Cali, Colombia: Imprelibros, 2005.

Luciak, Ilja A. *After the Revolution: Gender and Democracy in El Salvador, Nicaragua, and Guatemala*. Baltimore: Johns Hopkins University Press, 2001.

Luján Muñoz, Jorge. *Las revoluciones de 1897, la muerte de J. M. Reina Barrios y la elección de M. Estrada Cabrera*. Guatemala City: Librerías Artemis Edinter, 2003.

Macías, Anna. *Against All Odds: The Feminist Movement in Mexico to 1940*. Westport, CT: Greenwood Press, 1982.

Macpherson, Anne S. *From Colony to Nation: Women Activists and the Gendering of Politics in Belize, 1912–1982*. Lincoln: University of Nebraska Press, 2007.

Maier, Elizabeth, and Nathalie Lebon, eds. *Women's Activism in Latin America and the Caribbean: Engendering Social Justice, Democratizing Citizenship*. New Brunswick, NJ: Rutgers University Press, 2010.

Mariñas Otero, Luis. *Las constituciones de Guatemala*. Madrid: Instituto de Estudios Políticos, 1958.

Marino, Katherine M. *Feminism for the Americas: The Making of an International Human Rights Movement*. Chapel Hill: University of North Carolina Press, 2019.

Marroquín Rojas, Clemente. *Cronicas de la constituyente del 45*. Guatemala City: Tipografía Nacional, 1970.

Martini Orozco, Margarita. *Hacía la escuela activa en la educación Guatemalteca*. Guatemala City: Universidad de San Carlos de Guatemala, 1951.

McAllister, Carlota. "Rural Markets, Revolutionary Souls, and Rebellious Women in Cold War Guatemala." In *In from the Cold: Latin America's New Encounter with the Cold War*, edited by Gilbert M. Joseph and Daniela Spenser, 350–80. Durham, NC: Duke University Press, 2008.

McClintock, Anne. "Family Feuds: Gender, Nationalism and the Family." *Feminist Review*, no. 44 (Summer 1993): 61–80.

McCreery, David. *Rural Guatemala, 1760–1940*. Stanford, CA: Stanford University Press, 1994.

———. "'This Life of Misery and Shame': Female Prostitution in Guatemala City, 1880–1920." *Journal of Latin American Studies* 18, no. 2 (November 1986): 333–53.

Menchú, Rigoberto. *I, Rigoberta Menchú: An Indian Woman in Guatemala*. Translated by Ann Wright. London: Verso, 1984.

Méndez Pérez, Lucrecia, and Ligia de García. "Situation Faced by Institutionalized Children and Adolescents in Shelters in Guatemala." Guatemala City: President's Office for Social Welfare, n.d.

Menjívar, Cecilia. *Enduring Violence: Ladina Women's Lives in Guatemala*. Berkeley: University of California Press, 2011.

Miller, Francesca, "Feminism and Transnationalism." *Gender and History* 10, no. 3 (November 1998): 569–80.

———. "Latin American Feminism and the Transnational Area." In *Women, Culture, and Politics in Latin America: Seminar on Feminism and Culture in Latin America*, edited by Emilie Bergmann et al., 10–26. Berkeley: University of California Press, 1990.

———. *Latin American Women and the Search for Social Justice*. Hanover, NH: University Press of New England, 1991.

Miller, Hubert J. "Catholic Leaders and Spiritual Socialism during the Arévalo Administration in Guatemala, 1945–1951." In *Central America: Historical Perspectives on the Contemporary Crises*, edited by Ralph Lee Woodward Jr., 85–105. New York: Greenwood Press, 1988.

Mistral, Gabriela. *Lecturas para mujeres*. Mexico City: Secretaría de Educación, 1923.

Moghadam, Valentine. "Gender and Revolutionary Transformation: Iran 1979 and East Central Europe 1989." *Gender and Society* 9, no. 3 (June 1995): 328–58.

Mohammed, Patricia. "Writing Gender into History: The Negotiation of Gender Relations among Indian Men and Women in Post-Indenture Trinidad Society, 1917–47." In *Engendering History: Caribbean Women in Historical Perspective*, edited by Verene Shepherd, Bridget Brereton, and Barbara Bailey, 20–47. New York: St. Martin's Press, 1995.

Molyneux, Maxine. "Mobilization without Emancipation? Women's Interests, the State, and Revolution in Nicaragua." *Feminist Studies* 11 no. 2 (Summer 1985): 227–54.

Monzón, Ana Silvia. "Entre líneas: Participación política de las mujeres en Guatemala (1944–1954)." In *Mujeres, género e historia en América Central durante los siglos XVIII, XIX y XX*, edited by Eugenia Rodríguez Sáenz. San José: UNIFEM/Plumsock Mesoamerican Studies, 2002.

———. *Rasgos históricos de la exclusión de las mujeres en Guatemala*. Guatemala City: Sistema de Naciones Unidas, 2001.

Monzón García, Samuel Alfredo. *Estado y políticas educativas en Guatemala: Aproximación al problema de las políticas educativas en Guatemala, 1944–1980*. Guatemala City: Editorial Universitaria, 1993.

Monzón Lemus, Cristóbal. *Camino de adolescente: La vida de Ramón en el barrio "El Gallito."* Guatemala City: Delgado Impresos, 1990.

Mooney, Jadwiga E. Pieper. "Fighting Fascism and Forging New Political Activism: The Women's International Democratic Federation (WIDF) in the Cold War." In *De-Centering Cold War History: Local and Global Change*, edited by Jadwiga E. Pieper Mooney and Fabio Lanza, 52–73. London: Routledge, 2013.

———. *The Politics of Motherhood: Maternity and Women's Rights in Twentieth-Century Chile*. Pittsburgh: University of Pittsburgh Press, 2009.

Mooney, Jadwiga E. Pieper, and Jean Campbell. *Feminist Activism and Women's Rights Mobilization in the Chilean "Círculo de Estudios de la Mujer": Beyond Maternalist Mobilization*. Ann Arbor: Center for the Education of Women, University of Michigan, 2009.

Mooney, Jadwiga E. Pieper, and Fabio Lanza, eds. *De-Centering Cold War History: Local and Global Change*. London: Routledge, 2013.

Nájera Farfán, Mario Efraín. *Los estafadores de la democracia: Hombres y hechos en Guatemala*. Buenos Aires: Santiago del Estero, 1956.

Navarro, Marysa. "Wonder Woman Was Argentine and Her Real Name Was Evita." *Canadian Journal of Latin American and Caribbean Studies* 24, no. 48 (1999): 133–52.

Navarro, Marysa, and Virginia Sánchez Korrol, eds. *Women in Latin America and the Caribbean: Restoring Women to History*. Bloomington: Indiana University Press, 1999.

Nelson, Diane M. *A Finger in the Wound: Body Politics in Quincentennial Guatemala*. Berkeley: University of California Press, 1999.

Offit, Thomas A. *Conquistadores de la Calle: Child Street Labor in Guatemala City*. Austin: University of Texas Press, 2010.

Olcott, Jocelyn, Mary Kay Vaughan, and Gabriela Cano, eds. *Sex in Revolution: Gender, Politics, and Power in Modern Mexico*. Durham, NC: Duke University Press, 2006.

O'Neill, Kevin Lewis. *City of God: Christian Citizenship in Postwar Guatemala*. Berkeley: University of California Press, 2010.

O'Neill, Kevin Lewis, and Kedron Thomas, eds. *Securing the City: Neoliberalism, Space, and Insecurity in Postwar Guatemala*. Durham, NC: Duke University Press, 2011.

Ortega Ávila, Moisés. *Mortalidad materna y mortinatalidad en la Ciudad de Guatemala*. Guatemala City: Universidad de San Carlos de Guatemala, 1948.

Palmer, Steven. "Central American Union or Guatemalan Republic? The National Question in Liberal Guatemala, 1871–1885." *The Americas* 49, no. 4 (April 1993): 513–30.

———. *Launching Global Health: The Caribbean Odyssey of the Rockefeller Foundation*. Ann Arbor: University of Michigan Press, 2010.

Palmer, Steven, and Gladys Rojas Chaves. "Educating Señorita: Teacher Training, Social Mobility, and the Birth of Costa Rican Feminism, 1885–1925." *Hispanic American Historical Review* 78, no. 1 (February 1998): 45–82.

Pattridge, Blake. "The Catholic Church in Revolutionary Guatemala, 1944–1954: A House Divided." *Journal of Church and State* 36, no. 3 (Summer 1994): 527–40.

Peláez Almengor, Óscar Guillermo, ed. *Guatemala 1944–1954: Los rostros de un país*. Guatemala City: Centro de Estudios Urbanos y Regionales, 1999.

Pellecer, Carlos Manuel. *Asalta-caminos en la historia de la revolución de Octubre 1944*. Guatemala City: Artemis and Edinter, 1994.

Pernet, Corinne A. "Chilean Feminists, the International Women's Movement, and Suffrage, 1915–1950." *Pacific Historical Review* 69, no. 4 (November 2000): 663–88.

Poppino, Rollie E. *International Communism in Latin America: A History of the Movement, 1917–1963*. New York: Free Press of Glencoe, 1964.

Porter, Susie S. "Women, Family Formation, and the Welfare State in Latin America." *Journal of Women's History* 25, no. 3 (Fall 2013): 212–20.

———. *Working Women in Mexico City: Public Discourses and Material Conditions, 1879–1931*. Tucson: University of Arizona Press, 2003.

Power, Margaret. "Defending Dictatorship: Conservative Women in Pinochet's Chile and the 1988 Plebiscite." In *Radical Women in Latin America: Left and Right*, edited by Victoria González and Karen Kampwirth, 299–324. University Park: Pennsylvania State University Press, 2001.

———. "The Engendering of Anticommunism and Fear in Chile's 1964 Presidential Election." *Diplomatic History* 32, no. 5 (November 2008): 931–53.

———. *Right-Wing Women in Chile: Feminine Power and the Struggle against Allende, 1964–1973*. University Park: Pennsylvania State University Press, 2002.

Racine, Karen. "Alberto Masferrer and the Vital Minimum: The Life and Thought of a Salvadoran Journalist, 1868–1932." *The Americas* 54, no. 2 (October 1997): 209–37.

Ramírez Rodríguez, Oscar Enrique. *Profesora María Chinchilla Recinos: Centenario de su nacimiento (2 de septiembre de 1909 2 de septiembre de 2009)*. Guatemala City: US Agency for International Development, 2009.

Randall, Margaret. *Gathering Rage: The Failure of Twentieth-Century Revolutions to Develop a Feminist Agenda*. New York: Monthly Review Pess, 1992.

Rendón, Catherine. *Minerva y la palma: El enigma de Don Manuel*. Guatemala City: Librerías Artemis Edinter, 2000.

Rey, Julio Adolfo. "Revolution and Liberation: A Review of Recent Literature on the Guatemalan Situation." *Hispanic American Historical Review* 38, no. 2 (May 1958): 239–55.

Ríos Tobar, Marcela. "'Feminism Is Socialism, Liberty and Much More': Second-Wave Chilean Feminism and Its Contentious Relationship with Socialism." *Journal of Women's History* 15, no. 3 (2003): 129–34.

Rivas, Rodolfo G. *Capacidad jurídical de la mujer y derechos que le reconoce la legislación civil de Guatemala*. Guatemala: Tipografía Sánchez y de Guise, 1896.

Robinson, William I. *A Faustian Bargain: U.S. Intervention in the Nicaraguan Elections and American Foreign Policy in the Post–Cold War Era*. Boulder, CO: Westview Press, 1992.

Rock, David, ed. *Latin America in the 1940s: War and Postwar Transitions*. Berkeley: University of California Press, 1994.

Rodríguez Sáenz, Eugenia, ed. *Mujeres, género e historia en América Central durante los siglos XVIII, XIX y XX*. San José: UNIFEM/Plumsock Mesoamerican Studies, 2002.

———, ed. *Un siglo de luchas femeninas en América Latina*. San José: Editorial de la Universidad de Costa Rica, 2002.

Rosemblatt, Karin. "Charity, Rights, and Entitlement: Gender, Labor, and Welfare in Early-Twentieth-Century Chile." *Hispanic American Historical Review* 81, no. 3 (February 2001): 555–85.

Ruiz, Vicki L. "Luisa Moreno and Latina Labor Activism." In *Latina Legacies: Identity, Biography, and Community*, edited by Vicki L. Ruiz and Virginia Sánchez Korrol, 175–92. New York: Oxford University Press, 2005.

———. "Of Poetics and Politics: The Border Journeys of Luisa Moreno." In *Women's Labor in the Global Economy: Speaking in Multiple Voices*, edited by Sharon Harley, 28–45. New Brunswick, NJ: Rutgers University Press, 2008.

Ruiz, Vicki L., and Virginia Sánchez Korrol, eds. *Latina Legacies: Identity, Biography, and Community*. New York: Oxford University Press, 2005.

Sabato, Hilda. "On Political Citizenship in Nineteenth-Century Latin America." *American Historical Review* 106, no. 4 (October 2001): 1290–315.

Sabino, Carlos. *Guatemala, la historia silenciada (1944–1989)*. 2 vols. Guatemala City: Fondo de Cultura Económica, 2008.

Samayoa Chinchilla, Carlos. *El dictador y yo*. Guatemala City: Editorial José de Pineda Ibarra, 1967.

Sanborn, Helen J. *A Winter in Central America and Mexico*. Boston: Lee and Shepard, 1886.

Sanders, Nichole. *Gender and Welfare in Mexico: The Consolidation of a Postrevolutionary State*. University Park: Pennsylvania State University Press, 2011.

Santamaría Ambriz, Rocío. "La Unión de Universidades de América Latina: 51 años en la historia de la educación superior latinoamericana." *Universidades* 51, no. 21 (January–June 2001): 29–35.

Saxon, Dan. *To Save Her Life: Disappearance, Deliverance, and the United States in Guatemala*. Berkeley: University of California Press, 2007.

Schlesinger, Stephen, and Stephen Kinzer. *Bitter Fruit: The Story of the American Coup in Guatemala*. 2nd ed. Cambridge, MA: Harvard University Press, 1999.

Schneider, Ronald M. *Case Study in Insurgency and Revolutionary Warfare: Guatemala, 1944–1954*. Washington, DC: Special Operations Research Office, 1964.

———. *Communism in Guatemala, 1944 to 1954*. Foreign Policy Research Institute, University of Pennsylvania. New York: Frederick A. Praeger, 1958.

Schneider, William H., ed. *Rockefeller Philanthropy and Modern Biomedicine: International Initiatives from World War I to the Cold War*. Bloomington: Indiana University Press, 2002.

Scott, James C. Foreword to *Everyday Forms of State Formation: Revolution and the Negotiation of Rule in Modern Mexico*, edited by Gilbert M. Joseph and Daniel Nugent, vii–xii. Durham, NC: Duke University Press, 1994.

Scott, Joan Wallach, ed. *Feminism and History*. Oxford: Oxford University Press, 1996.

———. "Gender: A Useful Category of Historical Analysis." In *Feminism and History*, edited by Joan Wallach Scott. Oxford: Oxford University Press, 1996.

Seligmann, Linda J. *Peruvian Street Lives: Culture, Power, and Economy among Market Women of Cuzco*. Urbana: University of Illinois Press, 2004.

Shattuck, George Cheever. *A Medical Survey of the Republic of Guatemala*. Washington, DC: Carnegie Institution, 1938.

Shayne, Julie D. *The Revolution Question: Feminisms in El Salvador, Chile, and Cuba*. New Brunswick, NJ: Rutgers University Press, 2004.

Shepherd, Verene, Bridget Brereton, and Barbara Bailey, eds. *Engendering History: Caribbean Women in Historical Perspective*. New York: St. Martin's Press, 1995.

Sieder, Rachel. "'Paz, progreso, justicia y honradez': Law and Citizenship in Alta Verapaz during the Regime of Jorge Ubico." *Bulletin of Latin American Research* 19, no. 3 (July 2000): 283–302.

Silva Girón, César Augusto, ed. *Vivencias de la revolución del 20 de Octubre de 1944*. Guatemala City: Serviprensa Centroamericana, 1994.

Silvert, K. H. *A Study in Government: Guatemala*. Part 1, *National and Local Government since 1944*. New Orleans: Middle American Research Institute, Tulane University, 1954.

Skinner-Klee, Jorge, ed. *Legislación indigenista de Guatemala*. Mexico City: Instituto Indigenista Interamericano, 1954.

———. *Revolución y derecho: Una investigación sobre el problema de la revolución en el derecho guatemalteco*. Guatemala City: Editorial José de Pineda Ibarra, 1971.

Slaughter, Jane, and Robert Kern. *European Women on the Left: Socialism, Feminism, and the Problems Faced by Political Women, 1880 to the Present*. Westport, CT: Greenwood Press, 1981.

Smith, Carol A., ed. *Guatemalan Indians and the State, 1540 to 1988*. Austin: University of Texas Press, 1990.

Smith, Lois M., and Alfred Padula. *Sex and Revolution: Women in Socialist Cuba*. Oxford: Oxford University Press, 1996.

Smith, Timothy J., and Abigail E. Adams, eds. *After the Coup: An Ethnographic Reframing of Guatemala 1954*. Urbana: University of Illinois Press, 2011.

Solórzano, Ivonne. *Aliadas en resistencia o resistencia a las alianzas? Un acercamiento al movimiento de mujeres en Guatemala*. Guatemala City: Facultad Latinoamericana de Ciencias Sociales, 2006.

Soriano Hernández, Silvia. *Mujeres y guerra en Guatemala y Chiapas*. Mexico City: Universidad Nacional Autónoma de México, 2006.

Spenser, Daniela. "Standing Conventional Cold War History on Its Head." In *In from the Cold: Latin*

America's New Encounter with the Cold War, edited by Gilbert M. Joseph and Daniela Spenser, 381–95. Durham, NC: Duke University Press, 2008.

Stanton, Domna C., and Abigail J. Stewart, eds. *Feminisms in the Academy*. Ann Arbor: University of Michigan Press, 1995.

Stephen, Lynn. *Women and Social Movements in Latin America: Power from Below*. Austin: University of Texas Press, 1997.

Stern, Maria. *Naming Security, Constructing Identity: "Mayan Women" in Guatemala on the Eve of "Peace."* Manchester: Manchester University Press, 2005.

Stoner, K. Lynn. *From the House to the Streets: The Cuban Woman's Movement for Legal Reform, 1898–1940*. Durham, NC: Duke University Press, 1991.

———. *Latinas of the Americas: A Source Book*. New York: Garland, 1989.

Streeter, Stephen M. *Managing the Counterrevolution: The United States and Guatemala, 1954–1961*. Athens: Ohio University Center for International Studies, 2000.

Suárez Findlay, Eileen J. *Imposing Decency: The Politics of Sexuality and Race in Puerto Rico, 1870–1920*. Durham, NC: Duke University Press, 1999.

Sullivan-González, Douglass. *The Black Christ of Esquipulas: Religion and Identity in Guatemala*. Lincoln: University of Nebraska Press, 2016.

Taracena Arriola, Arturo. *Etnicidad, estado y nación en Guatemala, 1808–1944*. Vol. 1. Guatemala City: Centro de Investigaciones Regionales de Mesoamérica, 2003.

Taracena Arriola, Arturo, and Omar Lucas Monteflores. *Diccionario biográfico del movimiento obrero urbano de Guatemala, 1877–1944*. Guatemala City: Editorial de Ciencias Sociales, 2014.

Teele, Dawn Langan. *Forging the Franchise: The Political Origins of the Women's Vote*. Princeton, NJ: Princeton University Press, 2018.

Thillet de Solórzano, Braulia. *Mujeres y percepciones políticas*. Guatemala City: Facultad Latinoamericana de Ciencias Sociales, 2001.

Threlkeld, Megan. *Pan American Women: U.S. Internationalists and Revolutionary Mexico*. Philadelphia: University of Pennsylvania Press, 2014.

Tinsman, Heidi. "A Paradigm of Our Own: Joan Scott in Latin American History." *American Historical Review* 113, no. 5 (December 2008): 1357–74.

Toriello Garrido, Guillermo. *A Popular History of Two Revolutions: Guatemala and Nicaragua*. San Francisco: Synthesis Publications, 1985.

Torres, Luz Marina. "Women in Nicaragua: The Revolution on Hold." *Envio*, no. 119 (June 1991).

Torres Rivas, Edelberto. *History and Society in Central America*. Translated by Douglass Sullivan-González. Austin: University of Texas Press, 1993.

Towns, Ann. "The Inter-American Commission of Women and Women's Suffrage, 1920–1945." *Journal of Latin American Studies* 42, no. 4 (November 2010): 779–807.

Treacy, Gerald C. *Five Great Encyclicals*. New York: Paulist Press, 1939.

Urruela Villacorta de Quezada, Ana María, ed. *La nueva Guatemala de la Asunción: 230 años de historia*. Guatemala City: Grupo Financiero de Occidente, 2006.

Valobra, Adriana, and Mercedes Yusta, eds. *Queridas camaradas: Historias iberoamericanas de mujeres comunistas*. Buenos Aires: Miño y Dávila Editores, 2017.

Vásquez, José V. *La mujer en el hogar*. Guatemala: Tipografía Nacional, 1929.

Vaughan, Mary Kay. *Cultural Politics in Revolution: Teachers, Peasants, and Schools in Mexico, 1930–1940*. Tucson: University of Arizona Press, 1997.

Vilanova de Árbenz, María. *Mi esposo, el presidente Árbenz*. Guatemala City: Editorial Universitaria, 2003.

Villacorta, J. Antonio. *Monografía del Departmento de Guatemala*. Guatemala: Tipografía Nacional, 1926.

Villamar Contreras, Marco Antonio. *Significado de la década 1944–1954 conocida como la revolución guatemalteca de Octubre*. Guatemala: n.p., 1993.

Vrana, Heather. *This City Belongs to You: A History of Student Activism in Guatemala, 1944–1996*. Oakland: University of California Press, 2017.

Wagner, Regina. *The History of Coffee in Guatemala*. Guatemala City: Villegas Editores, 2001.

Wasserstrom, Robert. "Revolution in Guatemala: Peasants and Politics under the Arbenz Government." *Comparative Studies in Society and History* 17, no. 4 (October 1975): 443–78.

Way, J. T. *The Mayan in the Mall: Globalization, Development, and the Making of Modern Guatemala*. Durham, NC: Duke University Press, 2012.

Westad, Odd Arne. *The Global Cold War: Third World Interventions and the Making of Our Times*. New York: Cambridge University Press, 2005.

———. *Reviewing the Cold War: Approaches, Interpretations, Theory*. Abingdon, Oxon, England: Frank Cass, 2000.

Whetten, David. *Guatemala: The Land and the People*. New Haven, CT: Yale University Press, 1961.

Wiegand, Krista E. "Nationalist Discourse and Domestic Incentives to Prevent Settlement of the Territorial Dispute between Guatemala and Belize." *Nationalism and Ethnic Politics* 11, no. 3 (2005): 349–83.

Witzel de Ciudad, Renate, ed. *Más de 100 años del movimiento obrero urbano en Guatemala*. Vol. 1, *Artesanos y obreros en el período liberal (1877–1944)*. Guatemala City: Asociación de Investigación y Estudios Sociales, 1991.

Woodward, Ralph Lee, Jr. *Central America: A Nation Divided*. New York: Oxford University Press, 1976.

———, ed. *Central America: Historical Perspectives on the Contemporary Crises*. New York: Greenwood Press, 1988.

———. *Rafael Carrera and the Emergence of the Republic of Guatemala, 1821–1871*. Athens: University of Georgia Press, 1993.

Yeager, Gertrude M., ed. *Confronting Change, Challenging Tradition: Women in Latin American History*. Wilmington, DE: Scholarly Resources, 1994.

Young, Alma H., and Dennis H. Young. "The Impact of the Anglo-Guatemalan Dispute on the Internal Politics of Belize." *Latin American Perspectives* 15, no. 2 (Spring 1988): 6–30.

Zur, Judith N. *Violent Memories: Mayan War Widows in Guatemala*. Boulder, CO: Westview Press, 1998.

Index

Page numbers in *italic* text indicate illustrations.

Acción Social Cristiana, 264, 265–66
Act of Chapultepec, 208
Acuña de Castañeda, Angelina, 190, 290, 308, 310; Alianza and, 219; Partido Renovación Socialista and, 166; suffrage and, 151, 154; UMD and, 201; WILPF and, 192
AGA. *See* Asociación General de Agricultores
Agrarian Reform law (1952), 216, 222, 250, 265; antirevolutionary movement and, 270; Rossell y Arellano and, 270–71; UFCo and, 245, 270
Águila, Rafaela del, 31, 33, 68, 300; home and, 40–41; Instituto Normal de Señoritas, Belén and, 43
Aguilar, Amalia Samayoa, 302
Aguilar Castro, Alicia, 302
Alfaro, Daisy, 244
Alianza Femenina Guatemalteca (Alianza), 4, 13, 37, 62, 214, 215, 233; Acuña de Castañeda and, 219; Centro Educativo Asistencial and, 279; Chinchilla Recinos, M., and, 112–13; class and, 220, 221, 223, 240, 247, 257, 294; communism and, 220, 222–24, 231–32; conferences of, 216–17; cost of living and, 248–49; education and, 99; ethnicity and, 221, 294; First Inter-American Congress of Women and, 218, 230; FPL and, 147–48; gender analysis of, 20–21, 256–57, 294; Hall de Asturias and, 156; indigenous people and, 231; labor and, 240–44, 246–47, 257; land reform law and, 245–46; literacy and, 244; market workers and, 246–47; members of, 219–20, 222, 312–13, 360n7; motherhood and, 215–16, 234–35, 237–38; *Mujeres* and, 218–19, 248; overthrow of Árbenz and, 253, 254; pacifism and, 224–25; religion and, 271–72; sexual abuse and, 242; sexuality and, 96; socialism and, 230–31, 239–40; UFCo and, 253; Urrutia, E., and, 3, 219, 220, 224–25, 244; US and, 222; Vilanova de Árbenz and, 82, 133, 218, 222, 228–29, 294. *See also* Asociación de Comedores y Guarderías Infantíles
Allende, Salvador, 180, 286
Alvarado, Gabriel, 276–77
American Popular Revolutionary Alliance (APRA), 229
Anderson, Benedict, 99
Antigua, 15
antirevolutionary movement, 13, 18–19, 21, 168; Agrarian Reform and, 270; Catholic Church and, 140, 167, 169, 295; communism and, 213, 272–73; Estéves and, 260, 275–76; gender norms and, 268–69; Hospicio Nacional Centro Educativo and, 126–27, 276; *El Imparcial* and, 283; Javier Arana and, 269–70; market workers and, 260–61, 273, 286–87, 295, 296; media and, 178; protests and, 266–67; Rossell y Arellano and, 21, 171, 259, 295; urban voters and, 179–80; US and, 180–81, 259, 271–72; violence and, 250; women voters and, 144, 183, 184, 295–97
aperturas (openings), 8, 23, 48
Árbenz, Jacobo, 2, 117, 145, 172; Agrarian Reform (1952) and, 216, 222, 245, 250, 265, 270–71; background of, 227; Catholic Church and, 263, 264; Communist Party and, 220, 222, 233, 260; Decree 900 and, 245; election of, 20, 266; Guatemalan Documents and, 4–5; land ownership and, 239; land reform law and, 245–46; market workers and, 261, 283–84, 285, 286, 287;

Árbenz, Jacobo (*continued*)
  military and, 252; motherhood and, 235; resignation of, 13, 254, 289, 291, 370n48; revolution (1944) and, 115; US and, 179, 212, 245, 250, 252–55; votes for, 144, 171. *See also* overthrow, of Árbenz
Archivo General de Centro América, 18
Arévalo, Juan José, 117, 144–45, 264; Catholic Church and, 263, 265–66; communism and, 171–72, 269; coups d'etat and, 267; educational reform and, 2, 57, 121; election of, 161; First Inter-American Congress of Women and, 193; inflation and, 247–48, 249, *251*, 282; labor reforms of, 127; pro-revolutionary movement and, 131; Rio Pact and, 197–98, 207, 212; suffrage and, 156; UFCo and, 210, 247–48; US and, 178–79, 196, 197, 206
Arévalo Martínez, Rafael, 71
Argentina, 57, 109, 132, 139, 188–89, 253, 345n14; exile in, 3, 230, 250, 255
Arriola, Arturo Taracena, 5
Arriola, Jorge Luis, 93–94
Asilo de Maternidad Joaquina, 136
Asociación Cívica Femenina, 268, 271
Asociación de Comedores y Guarderías Infantíles: Castillo, M., and, 237; Conference on the Defense of Children and, 235, 238–39; Jiménez de Leiva and, 236; Vilanova de Árbenz and, 235–36
Asociación de Damas Pro-Comedores Infantíles, 136
Asociación de Maestras Católicas de Guatemala (Catholic Teacher's Association), 1, 112, 189
Asociación de Mujeres Intelectuales, 309
Asociación General de Agricultores (AGA), 175
Asociación Pro-Comedores Infantíles, 136
Association of University Students, 49
Asturias Rosales, Miguel Ángel, 72, 85; Generación del 20 and, 51; *El Señor Presidente*, 24
Azul (journal), 153, 272; anticommunism and, 90; distribution of, 86; education and, 70, 87; Escobar in, 103; femininity and, 91; feminist consciousness and, 70, 87–88, 104; founding of, 82–83; Menéndez Mina, G., and, 46, 69, 70–71, 80, 81, 83, 96, 104, 106, 161; revolution (1944) and, 100; suffrage in, 153–54; teachers, 102; topics of, 83

Balaños, Hilda, *111*
Barillas, Manuel Lisandro, 33, 34–35
Barrios, Justo Rufino, 4, 27, 35; education and, 41; Ubico and, 73
Barrios M., Augusto Nero, 49–50
Basterrechea Ramírez, Sara, 192
Bayard de Volo, Lorraine, 149
Belize: D'Echevers on, 206; First Inter-American Congress of Women (1947) and, 205–6, 359n88; Ubico and, 206; UMD and, 211
Bennett, Julieta Castro de Rólz, *111*
Berger, Susan, 10
Bermúdez Maldonado, Herminia, 143
Besse, Susan, 79
Beteta, Carmen Rodríguez, 138
Bianchi, Matilde R. de, 136
Boylan, Kristina, 182
Brainerd, Heloise, 185, 210, 345n14; Gálvez and, 192; Inter-American Military Cooperation Act and, 195–96; overthrow of Árbenz and, 254; WILPF and, 189, 190, 191, 192–93, 194, 195–96, 200
Briggs, Laura, 198
Burgos-Debray, Elisabeth, 4

Cabeza, Matilda Rivera, 53, 303
Carey, David, 27, 35, 44, 78; *I Ask for Justice*, 10; Kaqchikel people and, 72–73, 99, 140
Carmen Vargas, María del, 166, 311
Carrillo Padilla, Ana Lorena, 5, 9–10
Casaús Arzú, Marta Elena, 5, 9
Castañeda G, Marta Julia, 302
Castañeda Godoy, Federico, 158
Castellanos, Isabel M. de, 33, 300
Castillo, María de, 237
Castillo Armas, Carlos, 200, 255, 285, 289–90
Castillo Armas, Odilia de, 290–91
Castro Hidalgo, María Odilia, 209
Catholic Action Program, 265
Catholic Church, 21, 322n13; *Acción Social Cristiana* and, 264, 265–66; antirevolutionary movement and, 140, 167, 169, 295; Árbenz and, 263, 264; Arévalo and, 263,

398 *Index*

265–66; comedores infantiles and guarderías infantiles and, 139–40; communism and, 167, 170–71, 273; *desamortización* and, 27, 60; divorce and, 27–28; education and, 59, 326n86; Estéves and, 275; gender norms and, 120, 180, 183–84; labor unions and, 337n76; market workers and, 260, 276, 288; *Rerum Novarum* and, 45; social welfare movement and, 263; *La Verdad* and, 369n32; *La Voz de la Mujer* and, 37; women voters and, 172–74, 180, 295–96. See also church and state, separation of
Catholic Teacher's Association (Asociación de Maestras Católicas de Guatemala), 1, 112, 189
Catt, Carrie Chapman, 190
CAW. *See* Congress of American Women
census (1950), 123
Central American Child's Welfare Congress, 63
Central American Institute of Pedagogy, 45
Central Femenina del Partido Reconciliación Democrática Nacional, 172
Centro Educativo Asistencial: Alianza and, 279; Alvarado and, 276–77; market workers and, 258–59, 266, 273, 275, 276–81, 284, 286; media and, 278–79, 281; Sisters of Charity and, 276, 277, 281; violence at, 258–59, 278
Cerda Medinacelli, César de la, 30
Cerna, Vicente, 25
CEUA. *See* Comité de Estudiantes Universitarios Anticomunistas
CGTG. *See* Confederación General de Trabajadores de Guatemala
Chacón, Ana Rosa, 208, 209
Chacón González, Lázaro, 23, 63
Chajón Chúa, Victoria, 136
Chapultepec Conference, 202, 203, 358n67; Act of Chapultepec and, 208
Chaves, Gladys Rojas, 43
Chavéz, J. Adelaida, 33, 300
child care, 141; education in, 55, 64; guarderías infantiles, 135–36; social reform movement and, 24, 62, 107; SPN and, 24, 61–62. *See also* comedores infantiles and guarderías infantiles
child protection movement, 60–61; Child Congress and, 133; comedores infantiles and guarderías infantiles and, 132; Comidés Pro-Nutrición Escolar and, 236; Consejo Nacional de la Infancia and, 239; Pan American Child Congress and, 132, 133, 239
Chile, 96, 189, 191, 232, 303, 353n139; Allende and, 180, 286; antirevolutionary women's movement in, 266–67; Chapultepec Conference and, 204; gender and politics in, 180–81; Mistral and, 328n131; Movement for the Liberation of Chilean Women, 231; Pinochet in, 79, 345n5; US intervention in, 180; women voters in, 323n21
Chinchilla, Carlos Samayoa, 71
Chinchilla, Norma Stoltz, 9, 45, 231, 286, 363n64
Chinchilla Recinos, María, *113*, 114, 221, 291, 307; Alianza and, 112–13; murder of, 1, 2, 76, 77, 111, 112, 149; Teachers' Day and, 113
church and state, separation of, 112, 175, 263–64; Comité de Defensa Católica and, 267
Church of San Francisco, 111
CIM. *See* Inter-American Commission of Women
citizenship, 49–50, 77, 88, 157, 183; Menéndez Mina, G., and, 183, 348n64; suffrage and, 119, 156, 160–61, 182
civil war, 4, 340n19
class, 5, 7–8, 26–27, 66, 108; Alianza and, 220, 221, 223, 240, 247, 257, 294; education and, 16–17, 45–46, 54, 238; feminism and, 362n41; health care and, 16–17; Martínez de Arévalo and, 130, 134–35, 141–42, 197, 236, 292; motherhood and, 273; revolution (1920) and, 47–48; revolution (1944) and, 116; SGM and, 53; social reform movement and, 109–10, 141, 229–30, 236; Ubico and, 73, 75; Valle, L., and, 85, 88
coffee, 325n70; female coffee pickers, 50–51; Liberal Party and, 25; *mandamiento* and, 5, 25; modernization and, 22–23; prices, 74, 76, 247
Cofiño, Ana, 5
Cofiño, Luz de León, 61
Coker Gonzalez, Charity, 153
Cold War, 14–15, 167, 171, 212–13, 292; gender and, 187; in Latin America, 356n39; self-censorship in, 225–26; WILPF and, 191

Index 399

Colegio Santiago, 140
Colón Market, 133–34
comedores infantíles and guarderías infantíles, 107, 125–26, 135, 141, 212, 293; Catholic Church and, 139–40; child protection movement and, 132; locations of, 136–37. *See also* Asociación de Comedores y Guarderías Infantíles
Comidés Pro-Nutrición Escolar, 236
Comité Anticomunista de Locatarias, 275
Comité de Defensa Católica, 267
Comité de Estudiantes Universitarios Anticomunistas (CEUA), 260, 285, 286
Comité Pro-Ciudadanía (Pro-Suffrage Committee), 81, 309
communism: Alianza and, 220, 222–24, 231–32; antirevolutionary movement and, 213, 272–73; Arévalo and, 171–72, 269; Catholic Church and, 167, 170–71, 273; First Inter-American Congress of Women and, 205–6; Marroquín Rojas and, 200, 213–14; pro-revolutionary movement and, 166; Rossell y Arellano and, 178, 183–84, 266; Ubico and, 82, 96, 102; US and, 196–98; Vilanova de Árbenz and, 229; WILPF and, 194–95, 200
Communist Party, 220, 222, 233, 260, 349n79
Confederación General de Trabajadores de Guatemala (CGTG), 196, 248–49, 367n153
Confederación Nacional Campesina de Guatemala, 243
Conference on the Defense of Children, 235, 238–39
Congreso Femenino Internacional, 188
Congreso Femenino Pro-Ciudadanía de la Mujer, 154–55, 311
Congress of American Women (CAW), 225–26
Consejo Nacional de la Infancia, 239
constitution (1879), 25–26, 38, 49, 112, 263–64, 268
Contreras, Leopoldo Sierra, 143
Córdova, Alejandro, 2, 95, 115, 220
Coronado Lira, Luis, 147
Costigliola, Frank, 187, 199
Craske, Nikki, 25, 156, 234
Cuba, 111, 113, 162, 269, 363n57
cultura de esperar, 17

Darmes, Celinda D., 33, 300
D'Echevers, Malin, 98, 100, 147, 185, 304–5, 338n112; Asociación de Mujeres Intelectuales and, 151; Belize and, 206; First Inter-American Congress of Women and, 194–95; UMD and, 200, 201
Las Derechas (Deutsch), 14
desamortización, 27, 60
Deutsch, Sandra McGee, 7, 14, 169
Diana, 119
Diario de Centro América, 106, 107, 178, 209, 216
Díaz Ordaz, Luz Castillo, 301
divorce, 27–28, 78
domestic workers, 16, 54, 242–43
Duarte, Encarnación Nufio, 68, 301
Durán, Ramón Aceña, 89–90

earthquakes, 15, 47
Eduardo Rodríguez, Manuel, 147
education, 27, 107, 141, 325n77, 325n81, 330n155, 331n161; activism and, 43, 293; Alianza and, 99; Arévalo and, 2, 57, 121; attendance, 316, 330n158; *Azul* and, 70, 87; Catholic Church and, 59, 326n86; Central American Institute of Pedagogy, 45; Central American Teachers' Conference, 57; child care and, 55, 64; class and, 16–17, 45–46, 54, 238; Estrada Cabrera and, 44–45, 56, 97; Generación del 20 and, 56; indigenous children and, 99, 100, 122, 140; Laparra de la Cerda and, 31, 41, 42–43, 68; literacy and, 59, 164; Llardén de Molina and, 58–59, 331n168; malnutrition and, 100–101; Menéndez Mina, G., and, 101, 103–4; midwifery and, 54; Minerva monuments and, 45; motherhood and, 42, 55, 64; *Nosotras* and, 70, 87, 101; poverty and, 100–101; school for social work, 109, 138, 139, 308–9; sex, 97; SGM and, 53, 55, 56, 59; student-teacher ratios, 98–99; Ubico and, 58, 77–78, 90, 97–99, 102–3; women's movement and, 40, 102. *See also* teachers, female
EGP. *See* Guerrilla Army of the Poor
Ehrick, Christine, 11, 139
El ángel caído (Laparra de la Cerda), 31
El Grito (journal), 46, 47, 80

400 *Index*

El Ideal (journal), 19, 24, 28, 38, 40; editorial board of, 33; education and, 42, 43; Laparra de la Cerda, Laparra and, 19, 24, 53; sales of, 32

El Imparcial (newspaper), 2, 47, 68, 178, 281; antirevolutionary movement and, 283; Bermúdez Maldonado and, 143; female coffee picker strike and, 51; López, R., Prado and, 22; on market workers, 286; suffrage and, 158, 310–11; Valle, L., and, 53, 55, 69, 80, 82, 95, 106, 116

El Liberal Progresista (newspaper), 78, 91

El Maestro (Guillén), 101

El Salvador, 30, 82, 96, 153, 226, 308, 347n32; Alianza and, 205, 208, 221; popular revolt in, 74–75; Vilanova de Árbenz in, 226–28

El Señor Presidente (Asturias), 24

El Verbum (newspaper), 178

Enduring Violence (Menjívar), 10

Enloe, Cynthia, 11

Ensueños de la mente (Laparra, Jesús), 30

Epaminondas Quintana, José, 55, 63, 64–65, 103

Escobar, María Isabel, 103, 138

Escobar de Richardson, Marta, 61, 67, 138, 155, 301

Escuela Normal de Señoritas, 42, 326n93

Escuela Normal para Señoritas, 122–23, 192

Escuela Normal Superior, 302

Escuela Preparatoria, 58

Espín, Vilma, 113

Espinoza, Anita R., 66, 301–2

Estela Lima, Carmen, 147

Estéves, Concha, 258; antirevolutionary movement and, 260, 275–76; market workers and, 275, 285, 295

Estrada Cabrera, Manuel, 4, 15, 46, 136, 326n99; education and, 44–45, 56, 97; Ley Protectora de Obreros and, 44; overthrow of, 23, 24, 44, 47; Partido Unionista and, 24, 44; protests against, 47, 67, 266; violence and, 43–44, 47

ethnicity, 5, 7, 108; Alianza and, 221, 294; gender and, 26–27. *See also* indigenous people; ladinos

Federación de Mujeres de las Américas, 218, 360n4

Federation of University Students, 57, 64

Fem (journal), 160

femininity, 91–92, 96

feminism, 8, 11, 36, 39, 109, 231, 320n41; class and, 362n41; education and, 58; idealism and, 62; Laparra de la Cerda and, 34; maternal, 7, 62, 119, 152, 234, 290–91, 294; Meléndez de DeLeón and, 95; Menéndez Mina, G., and, 92; patriotism and, 84; proto-feminism, 19; of SGM, 53, 54–55; Valle, L., and, 93, 94, 118, 119, 120, 201

feminist consciousness, 11, 70, 87–88, 104, 119

Ferrer, Pablo Rabasso, 48

Figueroa, Berta de, 116, 308

Finzer, Erin, 31, 70, 81, 82, 85

First Inter-American Congress of Women (1947), 15, 20, 155–56, 344n110, 355n27; agenda of, 203; Alianza and, 218, 230; Arévalo and, 193; Belize and, 205–6, 359n88; cables from, 204–5; cancellation of, 194–95; communism and, 205–6; D'Echevers and, 194–95; fourth committee of, 207–9; location for, 191–92; Menéndez Mina, G., and, 209; organizing committee for, 192, 354nn27–28; Páez and, 202, 209, 212; political diversity and, 214, 294; political opposition to, 185–86; Quan Valenzuela and, 195, 208–9; sisterhood and, 213; steering committee for, 190; US and, 186–87, 188, 215; WILPF and, 186, 189, 191

Fletes Sáenz, Carlos, 95, 159

Fontecha, Dolores Ramírez, 55, 303

Foppa Falla, Alaíde, 159, 160, 289

Forster, Cindy, 14, 20, 71–72, 120, 242, 268

Fortuny, María Jeréz Rivera de, 245, 366n129

FPL. *See* Frente Popular Libertador

Franco, Francisco, 196, 262

Franco y Franco, Dora, 220, 231–32, 244

Frente Nacional Democrático, 170

Frente Popular Libertador (FPL), 97, 134, 232–33, 309; Alianza and, 147–48; Montenegro de Méndez and, 136

Fuentes, Claudia Dary, 6

Galich, Manuel, 122, 148, 163

Gálvez, María Albertina, 104, 123, 193, 309; Brainerd and, 192; suffrage and, 158

Index 401

García Etchegoyen, María Eloisa, 209, 357n63
García Granados, Jorge, 173–74, 350n21
gender norms, 24, 141, 291, 295; antirevolutionary movement and, 268–69; Catholic Church and, 120, 180, 183–84; market workers and, 274–75; revolution (1944) and, 113–14, 143; US and, 353n142; voting and, 144
Generación del 20, 51, 52, 56, 60, 88, 101
Generación del 1898, 88
Gerlach, Federico, 50–51
Gibbings, Julie, 72
Gleijeses, Piero, 227, 228, 263, 265, 345n8
González, Haydée, 46, 47
González, Victoria, 14
González Campo, José, 189
González Solis, Concha, 147
Górriz Vda. de Morales, Natalia, 306–7
Goubard Carrera, Antonio, 89–90, 157
Granados, Miguel García, 25
Grandin, Greg, 14, 71–72, 187, 213, 252
Great Britain, 23, 173, 198, 205–6, 207
Grieb, Kenneth, 71, 97–98, 206
Guatemala City, capital inauguration, 15
Guatemalan Documents, 4–5, 368n2
Guatemalan National Bank, 27
Guatemaltecas (Berger), 10
Guerrilla Army of the Poor (EGP), 3
Guevara, Ernesto "Che," 255
Guillén, Flavio, 101
Guy, Donna, 35n5, 61, 62, 130, 139

Haan, Francisca de, 187, 225
Hall de Asturias, Elisa, 147; Alianza and, 156; suffrage and, 151, 155
Handy, Jim, 14, 174, 197, 248, 250–51, 351n104
health: children and, 125, 136, 332n183; infant mortality, 124–25, *128*, 332n174, 342n64; influenza epidemic (1918), 47; malnutrition and, 100–101
health care, 66, 141, 292; class and, 16–17; Epaminondas Quintana and, 64–65; maternal, 45, 137; physicians and, 97, 125; pregnancy and, 60, 63–65, 126
Hernández de León, Aurea, 83, 304
Hernández de León, Federico, 75, 83
Hernández de Zirión, Graciela, 172–73, 311

Herrera, Carlos, 47, 60, 67; labor and, 73; overthrow of, 50; revolution (1920) and, 48
Herrera, Martha Josefina, 53–54, 303
Herrera de Aschkel, María, 61, 67, 301
Higuerros, Mario, 367n154
"El hogar y la vida" (Valle), 96
Hojas Sueltas, 20
home, 40–41; gendered socioeconomic policies and, 69–70; patriarchy and, 38, 93–94; Valle, L., and, 125
Hospicio Nacional Centro Educativo, 258–59, 266, 273, 275; antirevolutionary movement and, 126–27, 276. *See also* Centro Educativo Asistencial
House Un-American Activities Committee, 225–26

I, Rigoberta Menchú (Burgos-Debray and Menchú), 4
I Ask for Justice (Carey), 10
IGSS. *See* Instituto Guatemalteco de Seguridad Social
indigenismo, 90
indigenous labor: market workers and, 274; vagrancy laws and, 75–76, 100
indigenous people, 2–3, 108, 319n15; Alianza and, 231; citizenship and indigenous men, 157; as domestic workers, 54; education and, 99, 100, 122, 140; female coffee pickers strike and, 51; Kaqchikel women, 10, 72–73, 99, 140; ladinos and, 5–6, 24; literacy and, 164; *mandamiento* and, 5, 25; Ponce Vaides and, 154; pro-revolutionary movement and, 157–58; revolution (1944) and, 116; *traje* and, 6, 274; Ubico and, 76–77; Valle, L., and, 84, 88–90, 101, 157; vote for indigenous men, 163, 171, 184
industrialization, 9–10, 15–16, 24, 25, 45, 249
"Industrialization, Monopoly Capitalism, and Women's Work in Guatemala" (Chinchilla), 9
infant mortality, 124–25, *128*, 332n174, 342n64
inflation: Arévalo and, 247–48, 249, *251*, 282; market workers and, 282–83
Instituto Guatemalteco de Seguridad Social (IGSS), 125, 138, 344n104
Instituto Interamericano del Niño, 132–34

Instituto Normal de Señoritas, Belén, 41–43, 86, 122, 194, 292
Inter-American Commission of Women (CIM), 82, 161, 189, 202, 213, 214, 291
Inter-American Military Cooperation Act, 195–96
Inter-American Treaty of Reciprocal Assistance (Rio Pact), 15, 20, 186, 197, 321n50; Arévalo and, 197–98, 207, 212; Rio conference and, 204–5
Irigoyen, María de, 166, 311

Jaquette, Jane, 8, 110
Javier Arana, Francisco, 115, 227–28, 269–70, 370n46
Jefatura Política, 18, 126
Jiménez de Leiva, Liliam, 236
Jonas, Susanne, 20, 252
José Orozco, Juan, 100, 132–34
Juárez Muñoz, J. Fernando, 59, 88
Juárez y Aragón, Oscar, 124

Kampwirth, Karen, 14
Kandiyoti, Deniz, 12, 72
Kaplan, Temma, 11–12, 94, 280
Kaqchikel women, 10, 72–73, 99, 140
Kirkpatrick, Michael, 17, 32, 71
Kit, Wade, 26, 47
Komisaruk, Catherine, 16, 27
Korean War, 224–25

labor, 16, 27, 65, 351n107, 374n5; Alianza and, 240–44, 246–47, 257; Arévalo and, 127; divorce and, 28; first female strike for, 302; Herrera and, 73; indigenous, 75–76, 100, 274; *mandamiento*, 5, 25; rural women and, 243–44; strike of female coffee pickers, 50–51; volunteerism and, 62; women's professional profile, *132*, *133*, *314–15*, 326n100. *See also* domestic workers
Labor Code (1947), 127, 175, 196, 269; domestic workers and, 242; UFCo and, 196–97
labor unions, 220, 240, 242, 246, 276–77; Catholic, 337n76; CGTG as, 248–49
ladinas. *See specific topics*
ladinos, 5–6, 24
La Escuela Normal (journal), 31
La Hora (newspaper), 148, 166, 175, 178

"La luz en el desierto" (A light in the desert) (Laparra, Jesús), 36
La Moderna coffee plantation, 50–51
La mujer en el hogar (Vásquez), 102
Laparra, Jesús, 66, 299; death of, 31; early life of, 29–30, 292; education and, 42–43; *Ensueños de la mente*, 30; *El Ideal* and, 19, 24, 53; "La luz en el desierto," 36; poetry of, 30–31; *La Voz de la Mujer* and, 19, 24
Laparra, Josefa, 300
Laparra, Nicolás, 29, 30
Laparra de la Cerda, Vicenta, 38, 66, 299, 323n29; *El ángel caído*, 31; double workday syndrome and, 39; early life of, 29–30, 292; education and, 31, 41, 42–43, 68; *Ensayos poéticos* and, 30; *El Ideal* and, 19, 24, 53; on motherhood, 35–36, 118; *La Semana Católica* and, 46; *La Voz de la Mujer* and, 19, 22, 24, 34–35
La Reforma, 24
La Semana Católica (journal), 46
Latin American Women and the Search for Social Justice (Miller), 188
La Verdad (newspaper), 369n32
La Voz de la Mujer (journal), 19, 28, 38, 39; Barillas and, 33, 34–35; Catholic Church and, 37; education and, 42, 43; Laparra, Jesús and, 19, 24; Laparra de la Cerda and, 19, 22, 24, 34–35; "La luz en el desierto" in, 36
Lavrin, Asunción, 84, 91, 96, 152, 231; Foppa Falla and, 159–60
Leo XIII (pope), 261–62
Levenson, Deborah, 97
Ley Orgánica de Instrucción Pública Primaria (1875), 41
Ley Protectora de Obreros, 44
Liberalism, 3–4, 40, 66; feminism and, 11; patriarchy and, 22; suffrage and, 151–52
Liga Nacional, 56
"A light in the desert " (La luz en el desierto) (Laparra, Jesús), 36
literacy, 59, 64, 294, 309; Alianza and, 244; constitution on, 25–26, 268; illiterate male vote, 144, 154, 162, 290; indigenous people and, 164; rates, *57*, 85, *86*, *165*, 321n52, 349n75; suffrage and, 12, 20, 158, 295–96; Valle, L., and, 119–20

Index 403

Llardén, Clara Molina, 58, 59
Llardén de Molina, María Teresa, 58–59, 302, 331n168
López, Graciela Rodríguez, 52, 303
López, Matilde Elena, 208
López, Rosa Rodríguez, 22, 54, *54*, 55, 84, 88, 302; early life of, 328n133; *Vida* and, 52, 53
López y López de Gómez, Enriqueta, 147, 309
Lorenzana, Raúl, 100–101
Lucas García, Fernando Romeo, 160
Luchas de las guatemaltecas del siglo XX (Carrillo Padilla), 9–10
Luis Lizarralde, Juan, 291

Mabarak, Magda, 53, 303
Maldonado Cifuentes, Josefina, 140–41
Mario García, Jorge, 163
market workers, 343n87, 370n35, 371n65, 372n91; Alianza and, 246–47; antirevolutionary movement and, 260–61, 273, 286–87, 295, 296; Árbenz and, 261, 283–84, 285, 286, 287; Catholic Church and, 260, 276, 288; Centro Educativo Asistencial and, 258–59, 266, 273, 275, 276–81, 284, 286; Estéves and, 275, 285, 295; gender norms and, 274–75; guarderías infantíles and, 135–36; inflation and, 282–83; Martínez de Arévalo and, 134–35, 221, 281–82, 288; Maximina Valdés and, 283–84; Rossell y Arellano and, 279–80, 285, 287–88
marriage: divorce and, 27–28, 78; female teachers and, 76–77, 78; Valle, L., and, 92–93
Marroquín Rojas, Clemente, 163, 197; communism and, 200, 213–14; *La Hora* and, 148, 166; WILPF and, 199
Marshall, Susan, 160
Martínez, Alicia G., 303
Martínez, Nela, 208
Martínez de Arévalo, Elisa, 20, 126, 128, 185, 215, 235, 294; background of, 129, 130, 292; class and, 130, 134–35, 141–42, 197, 236, 292; market workers and, 134–35, 221, 281–82, 288; maternal health care and, 137; Menéndez Mina, G., and, 82, 193, 211; social reform movement and, 107, 108, 129, 131, 134–35, 139–40, 229–30, 234, 236, 288; "society of friends" and, 130–31; UMD, 202
Martínez Durán, Carlos, 93, 94

Marxism, 11, 228, 362n50; *Rerum Novarum* and, 45
Masferrer, Alberto, 80, 88–89, 100
Mata Amado, Graciela de, 83
maternal feminism, 7, 62, 119, 141, 234, 294; Castillo Armas, O., and, 290–91; suffrage and, 152; Valle, L., and, 118
The Mayan in the Mall (Way), 17
McCreery, David, 16
media, 2, 33, 47; antirevolutionary movement and, 178; Centro Educativo Asistencial and, 278–79, 281; revolution (1944) and, 115, 116; Ubico and, 19, 71. *See also specific topics*
Meléndez de DeLeón, Julia, 95, 304; Escuela Normal para Señoritas and, 122–23, 192
Menchú, Rigoberta, 4
Mencos R., Elisa, 53, 303
Méndez de la Vega, Luz, 304
Menéndez Mina, Gloria: Asociación de Damas Pro-Comedores Infantíles and, 136; *Azul* and, 46, 69, 70–71, 80, 81, 83, 96, 104, 106, 161; citizenship and, 183, 348n64; education and, 101, 103–4; femininity and, 91–92; First Inter-American Congress of Women and, 209; Martínez de Arévalo and, 82, 193, 211; motherhood and, 92, 96; *Mujer* and, 237, 290; *Nosotras* and, 19; *Nuestro Diario* and, 143; patriotism and, 84; political position of, 272; revolution (1944) and, 118; suffrage and, 105, 151, 153–54, 155, 161–62; Ubico and, 83; UMD and, 200
Menéndez Mina, Isaura de, 46, 80, 88, 118, 302, 335n39
Menéndez Mina, Rubén, 83
Menjívar, Cecilia, 5, 6, 10
Mesa, Dolores, 300
midwifery, 54, 63–64, 333n185
Miller, Francesca, 42, 145, 149, 191–92; anticommunist women's movement and, 261; *Latin American Women and the Search for Social Justice*, 188
Minerva monuments, 45, 119
Ministry of Government and Justice, 60
Mistral, Gabriela, 173, 328n132; Chile and, 328n131; teosofía and, 52
modernization, 32, 37; coffee and, 22–23; education and, 40; Liberal, 17, 66; Valle, L., and, 151

Moghadam, Valentine, 114
Mohammed, Patricia, 11, 12
Molyneux, Maxine, 114, 115, 141
Monroy, Dolores, 303
Montenegro de Méndez, Mélida, 136, 138
Monzón, Ana Silvia, 3, 5, 9
Mora, Federico, 62, 63
Mora, Rosa de, 67, 138, 301; in Guatemalan Congress, 61–62; National Assembly and, 182, 291; SPN and, 108; suffrage and, 155, 182; UMD and, 201
Morena, Sara María G. S. de, 33, 300
Moreno, Adolfo, 49
motherhood, 41, 54, 91, 190, 273; Alianza and, 215–16, 234–35, 237–38; education and, 42, 55, 64; Laparra de la Cerda on, 35–36, 118; Meléndez de DeLeón on, 95; Menéndez Mina, G., and, 92, 96; Rossell y Arellano on, 183–84; Vilanova de Árbenz and, 229–30; women voters and, 168–69
Mujer (journal), 237, 290
Mujeres (newspaper), 218–19, 248
municipal elections: autonomy and, 174; 1948, 145, 181, 183, 259; 1946, 166; women voters in, 144, 168, 181
municipal government, 351n104
Muralles Soto, Elisa, 76–77, 97, 111, 147
Muralles Soto, Mélida, 76–77, 111
Muralles Soto, Morelia, 76–77, 111

nacionalidad, 88
Nájera, Dolores, 300
naming the nameless, 299–313
National Assembly, 73, 149, 161, 200, 214, 239, 263; Mora, R., and, 182, 291, 301; Páez addressing, 212; Partido Unionista and, 48; suffrage and, 153, 156, 161, 163, 164, 348n59; women running for, 166, 182, 308, 311
Nelson, Diane, 6
Nicaragua, 82, 113, 149, 162, 205, 325n70; revolutionary period in, 363n57, 372n91; US and, 252, 253
Nosotras, 54, 87, 89, 153, 272, 304, 336n62; distribution of, 86; education and, 70, 87, 101; feminist consciousness and, 70, 87–88, 104; *El Liberal Progresista* and, 91; revolution (1944) and, 110; teachers and, 101, 305–6; topics of, 83; Valle, L., and, 19, 69, 70–71, 81, 82, 101, 102, 104
Nuestro Diario (newspaper), 47, 125, 143, 178; pro-revolutionary movement and, 283; suffrage and, 158, 161
nutrition and daycare centers. *See* comedores infantiles and guarderías infantiles

October revolution. *See* revolution (1944)
openings. *See aperturas*
Ordóñez de Balcárcel, Chita, 150
Orellana, José María, 23, 47; education and, 121; violence and, 73
Orozco Posadas, Juan José, 72, 156, 161, 239, 310, 347n44
orphanage riot. *See* Centro Educativo Asistencial
Ortega Ávila, Moisés, 126, 136
Ortiz Rivas, Silverio, 47, 166
overthrow, of Árbenz, 3, 4, 179, 251–52, 297; Alianza and, 253, 254; market workers and, 261, 285, 286, 287; resignation and, 13, 254, 289, 291, 370n48; US and, 250, 253–55; violence and, 255

Padilla, Gregorio, 147
Páez, Gumersinda, 202, 209, 212
Pan American Child Congress, 132, 133, 239
Pan American Scientific Congresses, 188
Pan American society, 81
Pan American Women's Union, 153
Partido Acción Revolucionaria (PAR), 147, 149–50, 219, 232–33
Partido de Integridad Nacional (PIN), 232–33
Partido de Unificación Anticomunista (PUA), 166, 172, 285, 373n112
Partido Guatemalteco del Trabajo (PGT), 233
Partido Liberal Progresista, 149
Partido Nacional Revolucionario (PNR), 99
Partido Renovación Socialista, 166, 219
Partido Revolucionario Institucional (PRI), 99
Partido Socialista (PS), 233
Partido Unionista, 33; Estrada Cabrera overthrow and, 24, 44; Herrera and, 47, 67; Ortiz Rivas and, 47; suffrage and, 24, 48–49, 50; working-class and, 47

Index 405

patria: maternal feminism and, 119; new, 107, 119, 146, 162
Patria Potestad, 26
patriarchy, 22, 37, 67, 140, 297, 320n40; comedores infantiles and guarderías infantiles and, 139; education and, 42, 102–3; home and, 38, 93–94; Ubico and, 95
peace accords (1996), 17
Perón, Eva, 129, 130, 196
Pettit, Walter, 138
Peyré, Irene de, 189, 291, 303
PGT. See Partido Guatemalteco del Trabajo
Pilar, María del, 155, 306
PIN. See Partido de Integridad Nacional
Pinochet, Augusto, 79, 345n5
Piñol y Batres, José, 47, 262
Pius XI (pope), 170–71, 273
PNR. See Partido Nacional Revolucionario
Ponce Vaides, Juan Federico, 154, 228
Popular University, 57, 64, 98, 338n113
population, of Guatemala City, 85
Porter, Susie, 124
Power, Margaret, 14, 180, 266–67, 271, 286, 353n139
Prado, José de, 22, 56
Prado Vélez, Martín, 181
pregnancy, 78–79, 136; health care and, 60, 63–65, 126; midwifery, 54, 63–64, 333n185
PRI. See Partido Revolucionario Institucional
pro-revolutionary movement, 148, 167–68, 175, 178, 180; Arévalo and, 131; Asociación Cívica Femenina and, 268, 271; communism and, 166; counterdemonstration by, 268; indigenous people and, 157–58; *Nuestro Diario* and, 283; PAR and, 147, 156; political parties of, 232–33; US and, 181. See also revolution (1944)
prostitution, 96–97
Pro-Suffrage Committee. See Comité Pro-Ciudadanía
PS. See Partido Socialista
PUA. See Partido de Unificación Anticomunista
Public Charity Department, 66
puericultura, 97, 109; child welfare and, 60–61; Epaminondas Quintana and, 64, 65; Ubico and, 77
Pullín, Lily de, 138

Quan Valenzuela, Graciela, 55, 138, 201, 291, 304, 312; CIM and, 214; First Inter-American Congress of Women and, 195, 208–9; suffrage and, 103, 151–52, 155; WILPF and, 192
Quetzaltenango, 29–30

Radical Women in Latin America (González, V., and Kampwirth), 14
Recinos, Adrián, 170
Red Cross, 48, 66
Renovación Nacional (RN), 2, 134, 220, 232–33, 310, 345n8; Muralles Soto, E., and, 147; Urrutia, J., and, 161
reproductive rights, 24, 96
Rerum Novarum (papal encyclical), 45
revolution (1920), 8, 10, 19, 24, 45, 49, 327n108; cross-class collaboration and, 47–48; Herrera and, 48; suffrage and, 46; violence and, 300–301
revolution (1944), 4, 12–14, 20, 117, 293; *Azul* and, 100; Chinchilla Recinos and, 1, 2, 76, 77, 111, 112–13, 114, 149; class and, 116; Córdova and, 95, 115; gender norms and, 113–14, 143; Menéndez Mina, G., and, 118; teachers and, 111, 123, 143, 319n2; Ubico resignation and, 2, 69–70, 106–7, 110, 112, 114, 116, 146, 153, 334n4; Urrutia, E., and, 2–3; violence and death in, 1, 2, 76, 77, 111, 112, 113–14, 115, 163, 307–8
Reyes de Laparra, Desideria, 29, 30, 300
Rio conference, 204–5
Rio Pact. See Inter-American Treaty of Reciprocal Assistance
Ríos Montt, Efraín, 276
Ríos Tobar, Marcela, 79, 232
Rivas, Rodolfo G., 28, 49
RN. See Renovación Nacional
Robles de Barillas, Encarnación, 33, 300
Rockefeller Foundation, 63, 332n181
Roosevelt, Eleanor, 161
Rosemblatt, Karin, 127–28
Rossell y Arellano, Mariano (Archbishop), 140, 167, 175, 258, 261; Agrarian Reform law protests and, 270–71; antirevolutionary movement and, 21, 171, 259, 295; communism and, 178, 183–84, 266; elections and,

265–66; exile of, 262–63; market workers and, 279–80, 285, 287–88; on motherhood, 183–84; revolution (1944) and, 111–12; women voters and, 180, 266–67
Rubio de Herrarte, Clemencia, 136, 201
Rubio de Robles, Laura, 303
Ruiz, Vicki, 11

Sabato, Hilda, 38–39, 107
Sanders, Nichole, 135
Sándoval, Aída, *111*
Santa Cruz, Concepción, 300
Saravia de Palarea, Adriana, 155, 166, 311
Saravia E., Josefina, 303
Saxon, Dan, 3
Scare Campaign, 180
school for social work, 109, 138, 139, 308–9
School of Medicine and Surgery of the University of San Carlos, 64
Scott, James, 48
Second Inter-American Congress of Women, 221, 312
self-censorship, 44, 46; in Cold War, 225–26; of Urrutia, E., 289
Seligmann, Linda, 284
sex education, 97
sexual abuse, 78, 242, 297
sexuality, 297; Alianza and, 96; indigenous people and, 157–58; US and, 198–99, 223
SGM. *See* Sociedad Gabriela Mistral
Silva, Carmen P. de, 33, 40–41, 300
Silva, Felipe, 33
Sindicato de Trabajadores de la Educación de Guatemala (STEG), 276–77
Smith, Carol A., 5
socialism: Alianza and, 230–31, 239–40; gender and, 232
social reform movement, 23, 60, 67, 90–91, 128, 142, 220, 291; child care, 24, 62, 107; class and, 109–10, 141, 229–30, 236; institutionalization of, 108, 138, 139; Martínez de Arévalo and, 107, 108, 129, 131, 134–35, 139–40, 229–30, 234, 236, 288; revolution (1944) and, 120. *See also specific topics*
Social Security Act (1948), 127
Sociedad de San Vicente de Paul, 90–91, 108–9
Sociedad Gabriela Mistral (SGM), 9, 52, 64,
67, 80, 88, 303; education and, 53, 55, 56, 59; feminism of, 53, 54–55; formation of, 19; Ubico and, 67–68
Sociedad por Paz de Centro América, 304
Sociedad Protectora del Niño (SPN), 24, 55, 62, 64, 90–91; founding of, 61, 67, 182; health care and, 63, 66; Mora, R., and, 108
Sociedad Vitalista de Guatemala, 80
"society of friends," 124, 130–31, 141
Soto Hall, Máximo, 188–89
Spínola de Aguilar Fuentes, Magdalena, 75, 166, 306, 336n54
SPN. *See* Sociedad Protectora del Niño
STEG. *See* Sindicato de Trabajadores de la Educación de Guatemala
Stoner, Lynn, 190
Studium (journal), 47, 60, 63
suffrage, 10, 13, 145, *165*, 292, 293, 348n72; Acuña de Castañeda and, 151, 154; in *Azul*, 153–54; citizenship and, 119, 156, 160–61, 182; Congreso Femenino Pro-Ciudadanía de la Mujer and, 154–55; Fletes Sáenz and, 95, 159; Foppa Falla and, 159–60; Hall de Asturias and, 151, 155; *El Imparcial* and, 158, 310–11; incomplete, 163–64; indigenous people and, 100; labor movement and, 50; Liberalism and, 151–52; Liga Nacional and, 56; literacy and, 12, 20, 158, 295–96; male allies and, 156, 158; maternal feminism and, 152; Menéndez Mina, G., and, 105, 151, 153–54, 155, 161–62; Mora and, 155, 182; National Assembly and, 153, 156, 161, 163, 164, 348n59; *Nuestro Diario* and, 158, 161; Partido Unionista and, 24, 48–49, 50; Quan Valenzuela and, 103, 151–52, 155; revolution (1920) and, 46; SGM and, 53; Unión Cívica Guatemalteca and, 150, 152–55, 159; Unión Femenina Guatemalteca and, 119
Sullivan-González, Douglass, 261–62, 264, 265
Suslow, Leo, 125

Taft-Hartley Act, 208
teachers, female, 98, 103, 112, 239, 292, *317*; *Azul* and, 102; marriage and, 76–77, 78; *Nosotras* and, 101, 305–6; revolution (1944) and, 111, 123, 143, 319n2; travel and, 97, 153, 189; Ubico and, 77, 150

Index 407

teachers, male, 317
Teachers' Day, 113
Teele, Dawn, 168–69
teosofía, 51, 56–57, 109; education and, 58; Mistral and, 52; SGM and, 53
tertulias, 44, 81
testimonio, 31–32
To Save Her Life (Saxon), 3
traje (indigenous clothing), 6, 274
transnationalism, 188, 207, 209
Truman, Harry, 196

Ubico, Jorge, 1, 4, 72, 101, 104, 174, 292, 319n5; asylum for, 115; Belize and, 206; class and, 73, 75; coffee prices and, 74; communism and, 82, 96, 102; economy and, 74, 76, 97, 100; education and, 58, 77–78, 90, 97–99, 102–3; female teachers and, 77, 150; García Granados and, 350n21; gendered socioeconomic policies of, 69–70, 77–79, 90, 128; media and, 19, 71; Menéndez Mina, G., and, 83; Partido Liberal Progresista and, 149; patriarchy and, 95; publishing and, 19, 71; resignation of, 2, 69–70, 106–7, 110, 112, 114, 116, 146, 153, 334n4; Rossell y Arellano and, 262; SGM and, 67–68; social inequality and, 100; travel restrictions of, 97, 153, 189; vagrancy laws and, 75–76, 100; violence and, 73, 74–75, 76
UFCo. *See* United Fruit Company
UMD. *See* Unión de Mujeres Democráticas
UNE. *See* Unión Nacional Electoral
Unión Cívica Guatemalteca, 150, 152–53, 159, 309–10, 347n32; Congreso Femenino Pro-Ciudadanía de la Mujer and, 154–55
Unión de Mujeres Americanas, 151, 309
Unión de Mujeres Democráticas (UMD): Belize and, 211; D'Echevers and, 200, 201; members of, 200–201, 202
Unión Femenina Guatemalteca, 119
Unión Nacional Electoral (UNE), 175–77
United Fruit Company (UFCo), 171–72, 222, 223; Agrarian Reform and, 245, 270; Alianza and, 253; Arévalo and, 210, 247–48; Estrada Cabrera and, 44; Labor Code (1947) and, 196–97; overthrow of Árbenz and, 250

United Nations Decade for Women World Conference (1975), 217–18
United States (US), 45, 171–72, 250; Act of Chapultepec and, 208; Alianza and, 222; antirevolutionary movement and, 180–81, 259, 271–72; Árbenz and, 179, 212, 245, 250, 252–55; Arévalo and, 178–79, 196, 197, 206; communism in Guatemala and, 196–98; First Inter-American Congress of Women and, 186–87, 188, 215; foreign policy, 13, 180, 186–87; gender norms and, 353n142; Guatemalan Documents and, 4–5, 368n2; House Un-American Activities Committee and, 225–26; Nicaragua and, 252, 253; pro-revolutionary movement and, 181; Rossell y Arellano and, 259; sexuality and, 198–99, 223; WILPF and, 197, 210–12; Women's International League for Peace and Freedom and, 197. *See also* United Fruit Company
Universidad de San Carlos de Guatemala, 55, 57, 98
Universidad Femenina de México Adela Formosa de Obregón, 139
Urrutia, Ester de, 2, 111, 215, 225, 226, 292, 299; Alianza and, 3, 219, 220, 224–25, 244; in exile, 3, 4, 255–56; Guevara and, 255; self-censorship of, 289; work of, 220–21
Urrutia, Julia, 2, 3, 7, 111, 161, 255
Urrutia, Manuel, 220, 225, 255–56
Urrutia, Maritza, 3
Urrutia family, 225; in exile, 3, 4, 255–56; overthrow of Árbenz and, 255
US. *See* United States

vagrancy laws, 75–76, 100
Valdés, Maximina, 283–84
Valenzuela, Javier, 33
Valladares de Bolaños, Amy, 155
Valle, Amália, 304
Valle, Luz, 9, 13, 46–47, 83, 117, 141, 303; class and, 85, 88; education and, 101, 102–3; feminism and, 93, 94, 118, 119, 120, 201; "El hogar y la vida," 96; home and, 125; *El Imparcial* and, 53, 55, 69, 80, 82, 95, 106, 116; indigenous people and, 84, 88–90, 101, 157; literacy and, 119–20; marriage and, 92–93;

Martínez Durán and, 94; Masferrer and, 88–89; modernity and, 151; motherhood and, 91; new patria and, 146, 162; *Nosotras* and, 19, 69, 70–71, 81, 82, 101, 102, 104; political position of, 272; revolution (1944) and, 116; suffrage and, 105; UMD and, 201; Unión de Mujeres Americanas and, 151; WILPF and, 192; on women in politics, 166–67
Vasconcelos, José, 56–57
Vásquez, José, 102
Vaughan, Mary Kay, 99
Vela, David, 90, 157
Vicenta Laparra de la Cerda School, 68
Vida (journal), 47; health reform and, 63; López, R., and, 52, 53
Vilanova de Árbenz, María, 129, 133, 136, 363n52; Alianza and, 82, 133, 218, 222, 228–29, 294; Asociación de Comedores y Guarderías Infantiles and, 235–36; family of, 226–27; First Inter-American Congress of Women and, 218; motherhood and, 229–30
Villacorta, J. Antonio, 78
Villagrán de León, Francisco, 163
violence, 4, 289–90; antirevolutionary movement and, 250; assassinations, 82; Centro Educativo Asistencial and, 258–59, 278; Chinchilla Recinos and, 1, 2, 76, 77, 111, 112, 149; disappearance as, 292; domestic and sexual, 78, 242, 297; Estrada Cabrera and, 43–44, 47; Orellana and, 73; overthrow of Árbenz and, 255; revolution (1920) and, 300–301; revolution (1944) and, 1, 2, 76, 77, 111, 112, 113–14, 115, 163, 307–8; Ubico and, 73, 74–75, 76; women's movements and, 10
Vitalist Movement, 80–81, 88
vote, 170; antirevolutionary movement and urban, 179–80; for Árbenz, 144, 171; illiterate male, 144, 154, 162, 290; indigenous men and, 163, 171, 184; registered voters, *177*; turnout, *179*. See also women voters

Way, J. T., 17, 71, 76, 223, 229
WIDF. *See* Women's International Democratic Federation
WILPF. *See* Women's International League for Peace and Freedom
women in politics, 166; Mora, R., as, 61–62, 182, 291; National Assembly and, 166, 182, 291, 301, 308, 311; Valle, L., on, 166–67
Women's International Democratic Federation (WIDF), 224, 230–31, 253
Women's International League for Peace and Freedom (WILPF), 186, 253, 355n33, 355n38, 362n31; Brainerd and, 189, 190, 191, 192–93, 194, 195–96, 200; Cold War and, 191; communism and, 194–95, 200; First Inter-American Congress of Women and, 186, 189, 191; Guatemalan section of, 192–94, 199, 312; US and, 197, 210–12
women's movement. *See specific topics*
women's rights, 26, 39, 49–50, 84; biology and, 93–95; divorce and, 27–28, 78; public sphere and, 108; reproductive rights, 24, 96. *See also* suffrage
women voters, 145–46; antirevolutionary movement and, 144, 183, 184, 295–97; Catholic Church and, 172–74, 180, 295–96; in Chile, 323n21; motherhood and, 168–69; municipal elections and, 144, 168, 181; pro-revolutionary movement and, 181; registration of, 176–77, *177*, 178; Rossell y Arellano and, 180, 266–67; UNE and, 175–77
World War II, 92, 148

Ydígoras Fuentes, Miguel, 172, 173, 350n98

Index 409

www.ingramcontent.com/pod-product-compliance
Lightning Source LLC
Chambersburg PA
CBHW051204300426
44116CB00006B/426